T0234629

Lecture Notes in Computer Science 10346

Commenced Publication in 1973
Founding and Former Series Editors:
Gerhard Goos, Juris Hartmanis, and Jan van Leeuwen

More information about this series at http://www.springer.com/series/7410

Tanja Lange · Tsuyoshi Takagi (Eds.)

Post-Quantum Cryptography

8th International Workshop, PQCrypto 2017
Utrecht, The Netherlands, June 26–28, 2017
Proceedings

 Springer

Editors
Tanja Lange
Department of Mathematics and Computer
    Science
Technische Universiteit Eindhoven
Eindhoven
The Netherlands

Tsuyoshi Takagi
Institute of Mathematics for Industry
Kyushu University
Fukuoka
Japan

and

Graduate School of Information Science and
    Technology
University of Tokyo
Tokyo
Japan

ISSN 0302-9743   ISSN 1611-3349   (electronic)
Lecture Notes in Computer Science
ISBN 978-3-319-59878-9   ISBN 978-3-319-59879-6   (eBook)
DOI 10.1007/978-3-319-59879-6

Library of Congress Control Number: 2017942996

LNCS Sublibrary: SL4 – Security and Cryptology

Printed on acid-free paper

This Springer imprint is published by Springer Nature
The registered company is Springer International Publishing AG
The registered company address is: Gewerbestrasse 11, 6330 Cham, Switzerland

Preface

PQCrypto 2017, the 8th International Workshop on Post-Quantum Cryptography was held in Utrecht, The Netherlands, during June 26–28, 2017.

The aim of the PQCrypto conference series is to serve as a forum for researchers to present results and exchange ideas on the topic of cryptography in an era with large-scale quantum computers.

PQCrypto 2017 used a two-stage submission process in which authors registered their paper a week before the final submission deadline. The conference received 67 submissions from 24 countries all over the world. After a private review process and an intensive discussion phase with close to 400 discussion comments, the Program Committee selected 23 papers for publication in the proceedings. The accepted papers deal with code-based cryptography, isogeny-based cryptography, lattice-based cryptography, multivariate cryptography, quantum algorithms, and security models.

Along with the 23 contributed presentations, the program featured three excellent invited talks given by Jaya Baloo (KPN), Vadim Lyubashevsky (IBM Research), and Lieven Vandersypen (Technische Universiteit Delft), as well as a hot topic session and a question-and-answer session with the National Institute of Standards and Technology (NIST) about standardization of post-quantum cryptography.

Many people contributed to the success of PQCrypto 2017. We are very grateful to all of the Program Committee members, as well as the external reviewers for their fruitful comments and discussions on their areas of expertise. Special thanks go to Anita Klooster from the Technische Universiteit Eindhoven for taking care of the local arrangements.

June 2017

Tanja Lange
Tsuyoshi Takagi

PQCrypto 2017

The 8th International Conference on Post-Quantum Cryptography

Utrecht, The Netherlands
June 26–28, 2017

Program Chairs

Tanja Lange	Technische Universiteit Eindhoven, The Netherlands
Tsuyoshi Takagi	Kyushu University and University of Tokyo, Japan

Steering Committee

Daniel J. Bernstein	University of Illinois at Chicago, USA and Technische Universiteit Eindhoven, The Netherlands
Johannes Buchmann	Technische Universität Darmstadt, Germany
Claude Crépeau	McGill University, Canada
Jintai Ding	University of Cincinnati, USA
Philippe Gaborit	University of Limoges, France
Tanja Lange	Technische Universiteit Eindhoven, The Netherlands
Daniele Micciancio	University of California at San Diego, USA
Michele Mosca	University of Waterloo, Canada
Nicolas Sendrier	Inria, France
Tsuyoshi Takagi	Kyushu University and University of Tokyo, Japan
Shigeo Tsujii	Chuo University, Japan
Bo-Yin Yang	Academia Sinica, Taiwan

Program Committee

Martin Albrecht	Royal Holloway, University London, UK
Daniel J. Bernstein	University of Illinois at Chicago, USA and Technische Universiteit Eindhoven, The Netherlands
Joppe Bos	NXP Semiconductors, Belgium
Johannes Buchmann	Technische Universität Darmstadt, Germany
Wouter Castryck	KU Leuven, Belgium
Chen-Mou Cheng	Osaka University, Japan
Pierre-Louis Cayrel	Jean Monnet Université, France
Claude Crépeau	McGill University, Canada
Jintai Ding	University of Cincinnati, USA

Philippe Gaborit	Université Limoges, France
Steven Galbraith	Auckland University, New Zealand
Tim Güneysu	University of Bremen and DFKI, Germany
Sean Hallgren	Pennsylvania State University, USA
Yasufumi Hashimoto	University of the Ryukyus, Japan
Andreas Hülsing	Technische Universiteit Eindhoven, The Netherlands
David Jao	University of Waterloo, Canada
Stacey Jeffery	CWI, The Netherlands
Thomas Johansson	Lund University, Sweden
Tancrède Lepoint	SRI International, USA
Yi-Kai Liu	NIST, USA
Frédéric Magniez	CNRS, France
Michele Mosca	University of Waterloo and Perimeter Inst., Canada
Michael Naehrig	Microsoft Research, USA
María Naya-Plasencia	Inria, France
Ruben Niederhagen	Fraunhofer SIT, Germany
Christian Rechberger	University of Graz, Austria
Martin Rötteler	Microsoft Research, USA
Simona Samardjiska	Ss. Cyril and Methodius University, Macedonia and Radboud Universiteit, The Netherlands
Peter Schwabe	Radboud Universiteit, The Netherlands
Nicolas Sendrier	Inria, France
Daniel Smith-Tone	University of Louisville and NIST, USA
Fang Song	Portland State University, USA
Damien Stehlé	ENS Lyon, France
Rainer Steinwandt	Florida Atlantic University, USA
Krysta Svore	Microsoft Research, USA
Jean-Pierre Tillich	Inria, France
Ronald de Wolf	CWI and University of Amsterdam, The Netherlands
Keita Xagawa	NTT, Japan
Bo-Yin Yang	Academia Sinica, Taiwan

External Reviewers

Masayuki Abe	Eric Crockett	Louis Goubin
Saed Alsayigh	Luca De Feo	Leon Groot Bruinderink
Reza Azarderakhsh	Jean Paul Degabriele	Frédéric Grosshans
Lejla Batina	Jean-Christophe	Lei Hu
Jean-François Biasse	Deneuville	Marc Kaplan
Ryann Cartor	Amit Deo	Jean Belo Klamti
André Chailloux	David Derler	Fiona Knoll
Nai-Hui Chia	Leo Ducas	Stefan Kölbl
Craig Costello	Rachid El Bansarkhani	Lisa Kohl
Nicolas Courtois	Serge Fehr	Po-Chun Kuo
Alain Couvreur	Marc Fischlin	Thijs Laarhoven

Eunou Lee
Jason LeGrow
Chris Leonardi
Zhe Liu
Aaron Lye
Brice Minaud
Mohamed Saied Emam
  Mohamed
Fabrice Mouhartem
Xuyun Nie
Tobias Oder
Ray Perlner

Albrecht Petzoldt
Rachel Player
Thomas Pöppelmann
Ananth Raghunathan
Saraswathy
  Ramanathapuram
  Vancheeswaran
Joost Renes
Luis Ruiz-Lopez
Markku-Juhani
  O. Saarinen
Daniel Slamanig

Alan Szepieniec
Dave Touchette
Jeremy Vates
Dhinakaran
  Vinayagamurthy
Christine van Vredendaal
Weiqiang Wen
Bas Westerbaan
Thomas Wunderer

Contents

Multivariate Cryptography

Quantum Algorithms

Security Models

Code-Based Cryptography

A New Rank Metric Codes Based Encryption Scheme

Pierre Loidreau[✉]

DGA MI and Université de Rennes 1, Rennes, France
pierre.loidreau@m4x.org

Abstract. We design a new McEliece-like rank metric based encryption scheme from Gabidulin codes. We explain why it is not affected by the invariant subspace attacks also known as Overbeck's attacks. The idea of the design mixes two existing approaches designing rank metric based encryption schemes. For a given security our public-keys are more compact than for the same security in the Hamming metric based settings.

1 Introduction

The security of the main *post-quantum* (PQ) primitives relies on the difficulty of solving decoding problems in some metrics (Hamming metric for codes, Euclidean metric for lattices). The security of the encryption schemes is generally evaluated relatively to the best existing algorithms solving the considered problems.

At the beginning of the 90's another type of code-based cryptography emerged whose security was based on an alternative metric, the so-called rank metric [GPT91]. The difference with McEliece cryptosystem consists in the choice of the family of codes and in the choice of the metric. Originally, there was only one family of codes with an efficient algebraic polynomial-time decoding algorithm up to some bound, the family of Gabidulin codes [Gab85]. The initial proposals were attacked by Gibson who was able to recover a decoder from the public-key in polynomial time, [Gib95, Gib96]. Then, there was a succession of reparations and attacks, the latter being usually devastating. Overbeck in 2005 proposed a framework which could be adapted to all variants of Gabidulin codes based encryption schemes, [Ove05]. The structural weakness of the scheme came from the fact that Gabidulin codes contain a huge vector space invariant under the Frobenius automorphism. Exploiting this weakness lead to the complete cryptanalysis of all the previous Gabidulin codes based cryptosystems. From this date on, evolutions were proposed claiming to be secure against the existing attacks, [Gab08, GRH09, RGH10]. However, it was recently shown in [OKN16], that all existing variants could be reformulated as instances of the original problem, thus breakable in polynomial-time. Until now the common idea was that although rank metric would be a good candidate for designing code-based primitives with compact keys, a cryptosystem could not be designed from Gabidulin codes.

© Springer International Publishing AG 2017
T. Lange and T. Takagi (Eds.): PQCrypto 2017, LNCS 10346, pp. 3–17, 2017.
DOI: 10.1007/978-3-319-59879-6_1

In the paper we argue against this idea. We show that Gabidulin codes can be used to design effective and secure code-based cryptosystems, moreover with compact keys. By *secure* we mean that the complexity of an attack consisting in recovering a polynomial-time decoder for the public code is exponential. The point is to scramble sufficiently the structure of Gabidulin codes to avoid existing attacks. Concerning Goppa codes that are subfield subcodes of Generalized Reed-Solomon codes (GRS) on scrambles the structure by keeping the subcode formed with the binary vectors of the parent GRS code. Though GRS codes are unsuitable for use in cryptosystems, Goppa codes are widely admitted as being suitable and even the best choice for the design of secure code-based primitives and even PQ primitives, [AB315]. Unfortunately, this idea does not work for Gabidulin codes since subfield subcodes of Gabidulin codes are isomorphic to the direct product of Gabidulin codes over smaller fields, [GL08]. We propose a new approach mixing original ideas such as the structure of the encryption scheme and more recent ideas who led to the design of *Low Rank Parity-check Codes* (LRPC) based encryption schemes. This idea can also be considered as an adaptation to rank metric of an idea in Hamming metric whose interesting instances were broken, [BBC+16, COTG15]. For a given security of 128 and 256 bits, and a PQ security of 128 Mcbits, we propose a public-key size 20 times smaller than the proposition for *long term post-quantum systems*, in [AB315] relying on Goppa codes. The parameters being versatile, a designer can tune the parameters according to its needs (smaller key and larger ciphertext expansion or larger key and smaller ciphertext expansion for instance).

The structure of the paper is the following: First we define rank metric, the related decoding problems and we emphasize the fact that the complexity of generic decoding in rank metric is exponentially more difficult than in Hamming metric for the same settings. We evaluate the consequence of Grover algorithm on the generic decoding complexity in a PQ world. In a second part, we present how rank metric is commonly used in the design of encryption schemes. We also briefly detail the reason why Gabidulin codes based encryption schemes were broken. Finally, we show how to hide the structure of Gabidulin codes in a very simple manner, avoiding thus the main weaknesses of Gabidulin codes based cryptosystems. We also analyze the security of the encryption scheme against various attacks and propose sets of parameters.

2 Rank Metric Decoding Problems

In this section, we show that for the same settings, rank metric decoding problems are exponentially more difficult to solve than their counterparts in Hamming metric.

2.1 Rank Metric

As an ambient space we consider vectors of length n over a finite field $GF(2^m)$. Given basis $\mathfrak{B} = \{\beta_1, \ldots, \beta_m\}$ of $GF(2^m)$ regarded as a $GF(2)$–vector space, and a vector $\mathbf{x} = (x_1, \ldots, x_n) \in GF(2^m)^n$, we consider the transformation:

$$\mathbf{x} \mapsto \mathbf{X} = \begin{pmatrix} x_{11} & \cdots & x_{1n} \\ \vdots & \ddots & \vdots \\ x_{m1} & \cdots & x_{mn} \end{pmatrix}$$

where $(x_{11}, \ldots, x_{m1})^T$ is the binary expansion vector of x_i in the basis $\mathfrak{B}$, *i.e.*

$$x_i = \sum_{j=1}^{m} x_{ji} \beta_j.$$

The rank weight Rk($\mathbf{x}$) of vector $\mathbf{x}$ is: Rk($\mathbf{x}$) $\overset{def}{=}$ Rk($\mathbf{X}$), where Rk is the usual rank of a binary matrix. Rank metric is independent of the chosen basis and in the following of the paper, we will consider that a binary basis is fixed.

2.2   Decoding Problems

A rank code $\mathcal{C} \subset GF(2^m)^n$ is a set of vectors of $GF(2^m)^n$, together with the distance induced by rank metric.

In applications, it is usual to consider $\mathcal{C}$ as being an additive code. In that case, the minimum rank distance of $\mathcal{C}$ is the minimum rank weight of any non-zero codeword:

$$d_r(\mathcal{C}) \overset{def}{=} \min_{\mathbf{x} \in \mathcal{C} \setminus \{0\}} \mathrm{Rk}(\mathbf{x}).$$

If the code is $GF(2^m)$-linear of dimension k, it is called a $[n, k, d_r]$-code over $GF(2^m)$.

Problem 1 (Bounded distance binary rank decoding ($BDR_2(\mathcal{C}, t, \mathbf{y})$)).

– Instance:
  • *A 2^m-ary code $\mathcal{C} = <\mathbf{g}_1, \ldots, \mathbf{g}_K>_{GF(2)}$,*
  • *An integer t*
  • $\mathbf{y} \in GF(2^m)^n$
– Problem: *Find if it exists $\lambda_1, \ldots, \lambda_K \in GF(2)^K$ and $\mathbf{e} \in GF(2^m)^n$ of rank weight t, such that*

$$\mathbf{y} = \sum_{i=1}^{K} \lambda_i \mathbf{g}_i + \mathbf{e}$$

Solving $BDR_2(\mathcal{C}, t, \mathbf{y})$ is *NP*-hard. If one considers the matricial form of the problem by expanding every element of $GF(2^m)$ into a m-dimensional vector over $GF(2)$, then the associated decisional problem is an evolution of the *NP*-complete *MinRank* problem, [Cou01].

Though the complexity of this problem gives some arguments about the difficulty of decoding additive codes in rank metric, a designer will more probably consider linear codes over an extension field $GF(2^m)$. Therefore, it is more adequate to study the following decoding problem, for $GF(2^m)$-linear codes.

Problem 2 (Bounded distance 2^m-ary rank decoding ($BDR(\mathcal{C}, t, \mathbf{y})$)).

- Instance:
  - A 2^m-ary code $\mathcal{C} = <\mathbf{g}_1, \ldots, \mathbf{g}_k>_{GF(2^m)}$,
  - An integer t
  - $\mathbf{y} \in GF(2^m)^n$
- Problem: *Find if it exists* $\mu_1, \ldots, \mu_k \in GF(2^m)^k$ *and* $\mathbf{e} \in GF(2^m)^n$ *of rank weight* t, *such that*

$$\mathbf{y} = \sum_{i=1}^{k} \mu_i \mathbf{g}_i + \mathbf{e}$$

It is not known if the decisional version of this latter problem is *NP*-complete. However when one considers the dual problem called *Rank Syndrome Decoding problem* (*RSD*) a nice result from [GZ14] establishes that if *RSD* is in *ZPP* then this would imply that *ZPP* = *NP*. The *ZPP* class is the class of decisional problems solvable by a Turing machine such that:

- The machine runs in polynomial-time of the size of the input
- Answers YES, NO or ?;
- The answer YES or NO is the correct answer;
- It answers ? with probability at most $1/2$.

This statement backs up the feeling that decoding in rank metric is a hard problem.

2.3 Hamming Metric vs Rank Metric

In the design of encryption schemes whose security relies on a *difficult* problem, it is worthwhile to have precise estimation of the best effective complexity of the algorithms solving the problem for randomly and uniformly chosen parameters in a given space.

Decoding in Hamming Metric. The complexity of decoding up to some bound a *random code* in Hamming metric is an old problem, [Pra62]. Since the seminal work by Prange a lot of work was done to improve the asymptotic complexity or the effective complexity. The most efficient algorithms are smart refinements of the so-called *Information Set Decoding* (ISD).

The basics of ISD are: Suppose one wants to decode δn errors in a k dimensional code of length n over $GF(2^m)$, where δ is less than *Varshamov-Gilbert* (GV) bound to ensure the uniqueness of the solution. Then one chooses k columns of the generator matrix of the code. If these positions are error-free, and if the $k \times k$ matrix has full rank, then decoding consists in making some linear algebra computations and check if the obtained vector has Hamming weight $\leq \delta n$. If this fails then one chooses randomly another set of k positions and proceeds as before, until it works. If any k columns of the generator matrix form a non-singular matrix (MDS code), then after

$$\frac{\binom{n}{k}}{\binom{n-\delta n}{k}}$$

attempts, the probability of success is greater than 1/2. The average complexity of ISD is

$$n^3 \frac{\binom{n}{k}}{\binom{n-\delta n}{k}} \text{ operations in } GF(2^m).$$

For constant rate codes, *i.e.* $k = Rn$, provided that $0 < R < 1/2$, approximations of the Newton binomial gives a running time of: $\approx n^3 2^{n[H(R)-H(R-\delta)]}$ binary operations, where $H(R) = -R \log_2 R - (1 - R) \log_2(1 - R)$ is the binary entropy function. There has been many refinements of ISD. Still, the best decoding algorithms derive from ISD and have a complexity of

$$2^{c_{algo}(n+o(1))} \text{ ops. in the code alphabet,}$$

where c_{algo} is depends on the chosen algorithm, [BLP11,BJMM12,CTS16, MO15].

Decoding in Rank Metric. The first paper giving a precise estimation of the complexity of solving $BDR(\mathcal{C}, t, \mathbf{y})$ was published in the, 90's, [CS96] and was later improved in [OJ02]. Recently a survey unifying different approaches was published [GRS16].

Provided t is less than rank metric GV bound (ensuring uniqueness of the decoding), there exists an algorithm solving $BDR(\mathcal{C}, t, \mathbf{y})$ with probability $> 1/2$ running in:

$$m^3 2^{(t-1)\lfloor (k \min(m,n))/n \rfloor} \text{ binary ops.}$$

This implies in particular that if $m \geq n$ the running time is lower bounded by

$$m^3 2^{\delta R n^2} \text{ binary ops.}$$

Compared to the $n^3 2^{n[H(R)-H(R-\delta)]}$ complexity of generic ISD for Hamming metric, for the same set of parameters, decoding in rank metric is exponentially more difficult than in Hamming metric.

In Table 1, we fix some decoding complexity. In the second column and third column, we give parameters for codes whose average decoding complexity is approximately equal to the corresponding decoding complexity, in Hamming

Table 1. Comparisons of the decoding complexity of codes on GV bound for Hamming metric and for rank metric $[n, k, w]_q$ correspond to a q-linear code of length n, dimension k, correcting w errors in the considered metric

Dec. Complex.	Ham. Met. Gen. Mat.	Rank Met. Gen. Mat.
2^{128}	$[2400, 2006, 58]_2 \approx 100$ KB	$[48, 39, 4]_{2^{48}} \approx 2.2$ KB
2^{256}	$[4150, 3307, 132]_2 \approx 350$ KB	$[70, 50, 5]_{2^{70}} \approx 8.7$ KB

metric (2nd column) and rank metric (3rd column). The subscripts correspond to the size of the field alphabet, *i.e.* 2^m, if the considered field is $GF(2^m)$. Near the parameters we write the minimum size in bytes of the necessary information sufficient to characterize the corresponding code.

The complexity evaluations in Hamming metric are for binary codes and borrowed from [CTS16]. The chosen Hamming weight is close to the GV bound. This implies that these are the best possible codes, meaning that any other code satisfying the decoding complexity and rate requirements is necessarily longer than the proposed codes. Concerning rank metric, since for $m = n$, GV bound corresponds to $n(1 - \sqrt{k/n})$ [Loi14] we chose parameters relatively close to this bound to express the decoding complexity.

Remark 1. The comparison between rank metric and Hamming metric is not fair when one considers binary codes. Namely, if one fixes the alphabet of the field, the rate of the code in Hamming metric can be kept constant when the length goes to infinity. In the rank metric case however this has no sense to do this. The alphabet of the code has to grow to infinity. Therefore the comparison has a sense only when the alphabet size grows.

2.4 Post-quantum Security

A study of the PQ security of solving $BDR(\mathcal{C}, t, \mathbf{y})$ was already investigated in [GHT16]. Since the results are straightforward, we recall how to evaluate this PQ security.

In [Ber10] it is shown that the use of Grover's algorithm implies that the exponential term in the decoding complexity of ISD should be *square-rooted*. On our previous estimation of the decoding complexity this gives:

$$\approx n^3 2^{\frac{n}{2}[H(R) - H(R - \delta)]}$$

The most efficient algorithm solving $BDR(\mathcal{C}, t, \mathbf{y})$ solves the equivalent dual problem RSD, [GRSZ14]: Given a parity-check matrix $\mathbf{H}$ of an $[n, k, d]_r$ code $\mathcal{C}$ over $GF(2^m)$, find $\mathbf{e} \in GF(2^m)^n$ of rank weight t such that

$$\mathbf{y}\mathbf{H}^T = \mathbf{e}\mathbf{H}^T. \tag{1}$$

To stress how Grover's algorithm can be employed to improve the decoding complexity we need to recall the principles of the algorithm

- $\mathbf{e} = (e_1, \ldots, e_n)$ has rank weight $t \Rightarrow$ for all i, $e_i \in \mathcal{E}$, a t-dimensional binary subspace of $GF(2^m)$;
- Let $\mathfrak{B} = (\beta_1, \ldots, \beta_{t'})$, a basis of some $\mathcal{E}'$ such that $\mathcal{E} \subset \mathcal{E}'$;
- System (1) becomes: $\mathbf{y}\mathbf{H}^T = \mathfrak{B}\mathbf{T}\mathbf{H}^T$, where $\mathbf{T}$ and $\mathcal{E}'$ are unknown;
- W.l.o.g we can suppose $\beta_1 = 1$. Thus solving (1) consists in enumerating $t' - 1$ dimensional binary vector subspaces of $GF(2^m)$ and trying to solve the linear system of $(n - k)m$ equations and $t'n$ unknowns.

An assumption is that if the system is overdefined ($t'n \leq m(n-k)$) then the solution is unique. Therefore the average number of tries to find a suitable vector space is $2^{(t-1)\lfloor (k \min (m,n))/n \rfloor}$. Remaining linear algebra can be implemented with circuits in $O(n^3)$ size. We can apply Grover's algorithm. A lower bound estimation of the PQ complexity of solving $BDR(\mathcal{C}, t, \mathbf{y})$ is thus

$$m^3 2^{(t-1)\lfloor (k \min (m,n))/(2n) \rfloor} \text{ ops.}$$

3   Rank Metric Based Cryptography

In code-based cryptography, the security is estimated by the decoding complexity of random codes in the considered metric. This estimation requires that the public-key must look like *a random code*. This implies that the family of codes used as private-key space cannot be distinguished from a family of *randomly constructed codes*. Given a family $\mathcal{F}$ of $[n, k, d]$ codes over a finite field $GF(2^m)$ with known decoding algorithm up to errors of rank weight t, the original and general procedure to design the pair public/private key pair for a McEliece type cryptosystem is:

1. Select *randomly* a code in $\mathcal{F}$. The code is given by generator or parity-check matrix $\mathbf{G}$ under a form enabling an efficient decoding.
2. Publish a scrambled structure of $\mathbf{G} \to \mathbf{G}_{pub}$ such that $\mathbf{G}_{pub}$ looks like random. The scrambling procedure has to be a linear isometry of the metric.

Two types of decoding algorithms are considered:

- Algebraic decoding: It is used for Goppa codes in Hamming metric [McE78]. This family is recommended for *long-term* PQ security under well chosen parameters. In rank metric, only Gabidulin codes are of this kind.
- Probabilistic decoding: MDPC or QC-MDPC in Hamming metric [MTSB12], or LRPC in rank metric, [GMRZ13].

Since our interest concerns rank metric, we present how Gabidulin codes and LRPC are used in the design of code-based encryption schemes. We explain the reason why, until now, Gabidulin codes cannot be used in the design of secure encryption schemes. We also present the idea sustaining the design of the family of LRPC since this seminal idea is a natural path which leads us to propose a new families of codes with algebraic decoding to be used in the design of rank metric codes based cryptosystems.

3.1   Algebraic Decoding Based Cryptosystems

Gabidulin Codes. Let $n \leq m$ and let $\mathbf{g} = (g_1, \ldots, g_n) \in GF(2^m)$, where the $g_i's$ are linearly independent over $GF(2)$. Let $[i] = 2^i$ such that $x \mapsto x^{[i]}$ is the ith power of the Frobenius automorphism $x \mapsto x^2$. The code $Gab_k(\mathbf{g})$, is the linear code with generator matrix

$$\mathbf{G} = \begin{pmatrix} g_1 & \cdots & g_n \\ g_1^{[1]} & \cdots & g_n^{[1]} \\ \vdots & \ddots & \vdots \\ g_1^{[k-1]} & \cdots & g_n^{[k-1]} \end{pmatrix}, \tag{2}$$

i.e.

$$Gab_k(\mathbf{g}) = \{\mathbf{x}\mathbf{G} \mid \mathbf{x} \in GF(2^m)^k\}.$$

These codes can be decoded in polynomial-time for errors of rank weight up to $\lfloor (n-k)/2 \rfloor$, see [Gab85].

Invariant Subspace Attack. From the origins, see [GPT91], numerous designs of Gabidulin codes based encryption schemes were proposed relying on the model of McEliece cryptosystem. However, all these proposals were broken by derivations of the so-called *invariant subspace attack*. The reason is the inherent structure of the family of Gabidulin codes. A detailed analysis can be found in [Ksh07, OKN16].

We present the principle of the attacks. This is essential to understand where lies the weakness and how to get rid of it. In every proposed Gabidulin codes based encryption scheme, the public-key $\mathbf{G}_{pub}$ can be rewritten under the form

$$\mathbf{G}_{pub} = \mathbf{S}(\mathbf{X} \mid \mathbf{G})\mathbf{P}, \tag{3}$$

where $\mathbf{P}$ is a binary $(n+t) \times (n+t)$ invertible matrix, $\mathbf{G}$ is a matrix generating an $[n, k, d_r]$ Gabidulin code under the form (2), and $\mathbf{S}$ is an $u \times k$-matrix with entries in $GF(2^m)$, where $u \le k$. Now consider the action of $x \to x^{2^i} \stackrel{def}{=} x^{[i]}$ on the entries of $\mathbf{G}_{pub}$ denoted by $\mathbf{G}_{pub}^{[i]}$. We have

$$\mathbf{G}_{pub}^{[i]} = \mathbf{S}^{[i]}(\mathbf{X}^{[i]} \mid \mathbf{G}^{[i]})\mathbf{P}^{[i]}.$$

Since $\mathbf{P}$ is binary this implies

$$\mathbf{G}_{pub}^{[i]} = \mathbf{S}^{[i]}(\mathbf{X}^{[i]} \mid \mathbf{G}^{[i]})\mathbf{P}.$$

Let $\mathcal{C}_{pub}$ be the code generated by $\mathbf{G}_{pub}$ and let $\mathcal{C}_{pub}^{[i]}$ be the code obtained by raising the codewords of $\mathcal{C}_{pub}$ (resp. $\mathcal{C}$) to the ith power of the Frobenius automorphism. From the structure of the public code, we have

$$\dim\left(\mathcal{C}_{pub} + \cdots + \mathcal{C}_{pub}^{[i]}\right) \le \min(n, k+i+t). \tag{4}$$

If $\mathcal{C}_{pub}$ were a random u-dimensional code one would expect the dimension of $\mathcal{C}_{pub} + \cdots + \mathcal{C}_{pub}^{[i]}$ to be equal to $\min(n, (i+1)u)$ with a high probability. Hence the previous property provides a distinguisher of the public code. Moreover, if $k+i+t = n-1$, and if the dimension is exactly equal to 1 then a polynomial-time decoder for the public code can be recovered by simple elementary linear algebra.

3.2   Probabilistic Decoding Based Cryptosystems

Low Rank Parity-Check Codes. The principle consists in

- selecting randomly a λ-dimensional vector space $\mathcal{V} \subset GF(2^m)$.
- constructing an $(n - k) \times n$ matrix $\mathbf{H} = (h_{ij})$, where $h_{ij} \in \mathcal{V}$ are randomly selected.

The private-key consists of the knowledge of $\mathbf{H}$ and the public key is $\mathbf{G}_{pub}$, the generator matrix of the code with parity-check matrix $\mathbf{H}$ under systematic form. The key idea behind the decoding procedure is: Suppose one receives a ciphertext $\mathbf{y} = \mathbf{x}\mathbf{G}_{pub} + \mathbf{e}$, where $\mathbf{G}_{pub}\mathbf{H}_{pub}^T = 0$. Then

$$\mathbf{y}\mathbf{H}^T = \underbrace{\mathbf{x}\mathbf{G}_{pub}\mathbf{H}^T}_{0} + \mathbf{e}\mathbf{H}^T.$$

Since $\mathbf{e}$ has rank t its entries belong to a binary vector space $\mathcal{E}$ of dimension t. This implies that the entries of $\mathbf{y}\mathbf{H}^T$ belong to the binary vector space

$$\mathcal{E} * \mathcal{V} = \{ev \mid e \in \mathcal{E}, \; v \in \mathcal{V}\}.$$

The dimension of $\mathcal{E} * \mathcal{V}$ is upper bounded by $t\lambda$. If $\dim(\mathcal{E} * \mathcal{V}) = t\lambda$ a basis for $\mathcal{E}$ can be recovered with an estimated error probability of $2^{-(n-k+1-t\lambda)}$, [GRSZ14].

- The main strength of this scheme is that the private key is randomly selected with entries in a secret λ-dimensional vector space. Thus it prevents all types of attacks attempting to use some algebraic properties to break the scheme.
- Concerning the weaknesses of the scheme, the first one is that the estimated residual error decoding probability is non-negligible for small parameters. The second main weakness comes from the fact that the decoding is probabilistic. This could induce attacks on the model of [GSJ16] consisting in guessing the secret vector space by observing the behavior of a decoder.

4   The New Cryptosystem

In the case of Gabidulin codes, the strategy, which works for GRS codes, consisting of scrambling their structure by considering a subfield subcode is a dead-end. The reason is that a subfield subcode of a Gabidulin code is essentially isomorphic to the direct sum of Gabidulin codes over the subfield, [GL08].

Our approach consists in scrambling the codes via the choice of a randomly selected vector space of $GF(2^m)$ of fixed dimension. The essential idea comes from the rank multiplication property used to show that the LRPC decoding procedure works. This could also be interpreted as a rank metric equivalent of the idea in [BBC+16] which, for short, replaces the permutation matrix in McEliece cryptosystem by a matrix multiplying the Hamming weight of the vectors.

Proposition 1 (Rank multiplication). *Let* $\mathbf{P} \in M_n(\mathcal{V})$ *be an invertible matrix with entries in a binary λ-dimensional vector space $\mathcal{V} \subset GF(2^m)$. For all $\mathbf{x} \in GF(2^m)^n$, $Rk(\mathbf{xP}) \leq \lambda Rk(\mathbf{x})$.*

Proof. Consider $\mathbf{x} = (x_1, \ldots, x_n) \in GF(q^m)$ of rank weight r. Let $\mathcal{X} = <x_1, \ldots, x_n>$ be generated by $<y_1, \ldots, y_t>$. Suppose moreover that $\mathcal{V} = <\alpha_1, \ldots, \alpha_\lambda>$, then the entries of $\mathbf{xP}$, belong to the vector space $<y_i\alpha_j>_{i,j}$ which has dimension $\leq \lambda t$.

4.1   Design of the Encryption Scheme

The key generation procedure is the following:

– Private key:
  - A Gabidulin code of length n over $GF(2^m)$, dimension k with generator matrix $\mathbf{G}$ under the form (2);
  - A non-singular $k \times k$- matrix $\mathbf{S}$ with entries in $GF(2^m)$;
  - A λ-dimensional subspace of $GF(2^m)$, denoted by $\mathcal{V}$;
  - A non-singular matrix $\mathbf{P}$ with entries in $\mathcal{V}$, *i.e.* $\mathbf{P} \in M_n(\mathcal{V})$.
– Public key: $\mathbf{G}_{pub} = \mathbf{SGP}^{-1}$. The public code $\mathcal{C}_{pub}$ is generated by $\mathbf{G}_{pub}$.

The encryption and decryption procedures are:

– Encryption of $\mathbf{x} \in GF(2^m)^k$:
  - Choose a random vector $\mathbf{e} \in GF(2^m)^n$ of rank weight $\lfloor(n-k)/(2\lambda)\rfloor$;
  - Compute $\mathbf{y} = \mathbf{xG}_{pub} + \mathbf{e}$;
  - Send the encrypted message $\mathbf{y}$ to the receiver.
– Decryption of $\mathbf{y}$:
  - Compute $\mathbf{yP} = \mathbf{xSG} + \mathbf{eP}$;
  - Since $\mathbf{P}$ has entries in $\mathcal{V}$ and from Proposition 1 $\mathbf{eP}$ has rank weight $\leq \lambda\lfloor(n-k)/(2\lambda)\rfloor \leq \lfloor(n-k)/2\rfloor$, and can be decoded with $\mathbf{G}$;
  - Recover $\mathbf{xS}$ and $\mathbf{eP}$ by decoding and recover $\mathbf{x}$ by multiplying with $\mathbf{S}^{-1}$.

The public-key is a randomly chosen generator matrix of the code

$$\mathcal{C}_{pub} \overset{def}{=} \mathcal{C}\mathbf{P}^{-1} = \{\mathbf{cP}^{-1} \mid \mathbf{c} \in \mathcal{C}\}.$$

A corollary of Proposition 1 gives:

Corollary 1. *Let $\mathcal{C}$ be a $[n, k, d]_r$ code over $GF(q^m)$. Let $\mathcal{V}$ be a λ-dimensional subspace of $GF(q^m)$ seen as a $GF(q)$-vector space. And let $\mathbf{P} \in M_n(\mathcal{V})$. Then*

$$\mathcal{C}\mathbf{P}^{-1} \overset{def}{=} \{\mathbf{cP}^{-1} \mid \mathbf{c} \in \mathcal{C}\}$$

has dimension k and minimum rank distance $d' \geq \lfloor d/\lambda \rfloor$.

Proof. Since $\mathbf{P}$ is invertible $\mathcal{C}$ and $\mathcal{C}\mathbf{P}^{-1}$ have the same dimension. Concerning the minimum distance, suppose that $d' < d/\lambda$. Then let $\mathbf{c} \in \mathcal{C}\mathbf{P}^{-1} \neq \mathbf{0}$ with rank weight d'. By construction $\mathbf{cP} \in \mathcal{C}$. From Proposition 1, $Rk(\mathbf{cP}) \leq d'\lambda < d$, which implies that $\mathbf{cP} = \mathbf{0}$. Thus $\mathbf{c} = \mathbf{0}$, which contradicts the hypothesis.

4.2 Security Arguments

We analyze the security of the scheme.

1. The first type of attacks consists in decoding the ciphertext in the public code. We suppose that the public code cannot be distinguished from a *random* code. Therefore the complexity of recovering a plaintext from a ciphertext corresponds to the complexity of solving $BDR(\mathcal{C}_{pub}, \lambda \mathrm{Rk}(\mathbf{e}), \mathbf{y})$. From Sects. 2.3 and 2.4, we have:
   - Decoding complexity: $m^3 2^{(\lambda r - 1) \lfloor (k \min(m,n))/n \rfloor}$ binary operations.
   - PQ-security: $m^3 2^{\frac{1}{2}(\lambda r - 1) \lfloor (k \min(m,n))/n \rfloor}$ operations.
2. The question of the distinguishability of the public-code from a random code is raised. The arguments presented in Sect. 3.1 do not work. Namely, raising the public-key to the ith power of the Frobenius gives:

$$\mathbf{G}_{pub}^{[i]} = \mathbf{S}^{[i]} \mathbf{G}^{[i]} (\mathbf{P}^{-1})^{[i]}.$$

Matrix $\mathbf{P}$ has entries in $\mathcal{V}$, but the entries of $\mathbf{P}^{-1}$ have no reason to belong to some strict subspace of $GF(2^m)$. Therefore (4) is not satisfied and the usual distinguisher for a Gabidulin code does not work.

An attacker could try to recover a decoder for the public code by solving

$$\mathbf{H}_{pub} = \mathbf{HP}, \tag{5}$$

where $\mathbf{H}_{pub}$ is a $(n-k) \times n$ parity-check matrix of the public code $\mathcal{C}_{pub}$ under systematic form, $\mathbf{H} = (h_j^{[i]})$ is a parity-check matrix of a Gabidulin code, and $\mathbf{P}$ has entries in a λ-dimensional vector space.

W.l.o.g, we suppose that $\mathbf{H}$ is known. This hypothesis might seem very strong but if we consider the case $m = n$ this does not remove security. In that let $<h'_1, \ldots, h'_n>_2$ be a basis of $GF(2^m)$ regarded as a $GF(2)$–vector space, and let a matrix $\mathbf{H}' = ((h'_j)^{[i]})$ under the form (2). There exists a binary invertible matrix $\mathbf{M}$ such that

$$\mathbf{H} = \mathbf{H}'\mathbf{M}.$$

System (5) becomes $\mathbf{H}_{pub} = \mathbf{H}' \underbrace{\mathbf{MP}}_{\mathbf{P'}}$. Since $\mathbf{M}$ is binary, $\mathbf{P}'$ has entries in $\mathcal{V}$.

Under this setting, we investigate two ways of solving (5), which gives us a lower bound on the estimation of the complexity of recovering a decoder from the public-key.
   - System (5) is an underdefined affine system with $n \times n$ unknowns (the entries of $\mathbf{P}$) and $n(n-k)$ equations. Given a solution $\mathbf{P}_0$ of the system, an attacker has to search for a matrix in the coset $\mathbf{P}_0 + \mathcal{P}$ whose entries belong to a λ-dimensional vector space. A solution is to enumerate the coset of size $2^{m(n^2 - n(n-k))}$ and if the matrices belong to a common λ-dimensional vector space.
   - Another approach consists in decomposing the entries of $\mathbf{P} = (p_{ij})$ under the form $p_{ij} = \sum_{u=1}^{\lambda} \mu_{ij}^{(u)} \alpha_u$, where $\alpha_1, \ldots, \alpha_\lambda$ are candidates to be the

basis of $\mathcal{V}$, and the $\mu_{ij}^{(u)}$ are binary elements. Once the equations are projected on the binary field, we obtain a system with $mn(n-k)$ equations and $m\lambda + \lambda n^2$ unknowns. If $\alpha_1, \ldots, \alpha_\lambda$ is fixed then the system is linear and overdefined ($\lambda < n \leq m$) and can thus be solved in polynomial time. For the previous reasons, we estimate that a lower bound on the complexity of recovering a decoder corresponds to the enumeration of $\lambda - 1$-dimensional $GF(2)$-subspaces of $GF(2^m)$. The choice of $\lambda - 1$ rather than λ is justified since if $\lambda = 1$, *i.e.* $\mathcal{V} = <\alpha>$, then for some element $\alpha \in GF(2^m)$, it is obvious that an attack can be achieved in polynomial time. Namely, $\mathbf{P} = (1/\alpha)\mathbf{P}'$ with $\mathbf{P}'$ has entries in $GF(2)$. Therefore, we suppose that $1 \in \mathcal{V}$. The lower bound on the complexity is thus $2^{(\lambda-1)m-(\lambda-1)^2}$.

4.3   Choice of Parameters

Table 2 proposes some parameters for an expected security, and with a ciphertext expansion between 1.6 and 1.8. Since the parameters on can consider to decrease the key-size by increasing the expansion factor, but the designer has to note that case other types of decoding attacks can occur and should be taken into account, [GRSZ14].

Table 2. Proposition of parameters for the family of codes used in the cryptosystem

Param.	Dec. Sec.	PQ Dec. Sec.	K. Rec. Sec.	Key size
$m = n = 50,\ k = 32,\ \lambda = 3, t = 3$	$\approx 2^{81}$	$\approx 2^{49}$	$\approx 2^{96}$	3.6 KB
$m = 96,\ n = 64,\ k = 40,\ \lambda = 3, t = 4$	$\approx 2^{139}$	$\approx 2^{80}$	$\approx 2^{188}$	11.5 KB
$m = 128,\ n = 120,\ k = 80,\ \lambda = 5, t = 4$	$\approx 2^{261}$	$\approx 2^{141}$	$\approx 2^{496}$	51 KB

For a 2^{128} bits security the key-size proposed in [AB315] for a McEliece encryption scheme using Goppa codes is approximately of 1 MB. For an equivalent rate our proposal gives a public-key 20 times smaller.

5   Conclusion

We proposed a new code-based public-key cryptosystem based on the derivation of Gabidulin codes. We did not consider security reductions but presented detailed arguments why we think that our proposal makes it possible to design secure code-based encryption schemes in rank metric. Security conversion exist that take as input One-way encryption schemes and convert it into a *IND − CCA2* in the random oracle model, [KI01, BL04]. Our proposal is versatile and can be declined for finite fields of any characteristic since Gabidulin codes have the same structure over any finite field. To evaluate the security we need to replace 2 by the cardinality of the considered base field, say q if we consider Gabidulin codes over $GF(q^m)$.

Acknowledgments. The author expresses deep thanks to Alain Couvreur who pointed out the existence of a straightforward distinguisher if the parameters are not carefully chosen. The proposed parameters avoid the problem.

The author also wishes to thank the reviewers who made constructive comments to improve the quality of the paper and pointed out mistakes and misses in the original submission.

References

[AB315] Initial recommendations of long-term secure post-quantum systems, Technical report (2015). http://pqcrypto.eu.org/docs/initial-recommendations.pdf

[BBC+16] Baldi, M., Bianchi, M., Chiaraluce, F., Rosenthal, J., Schipani, D.: Enhanced public key security for the mceliece cryptosystem. J. Cryptol. **29**(1), 1–27 (2016)

[Ber10] Bernstein, D.J.: Grover vs. McEliece. In: Sendrier, N. (ed.) PQCrypto 2010. LNCS, vol. 6061, pp. 73–80. Springer, Heidelberg (2010). doi:10.1007/978-3-642-12929-2_6

[BJMM12] Becker, A., Joux, A., May, A., Meurer, A.: Decoding random binary linear codes in $2^{n/20}$: how $1 + 1 = 0$ improves information set decoding. In: Pointcheval, D., Johansson, T. (eds.) EUROCRYPT 2012. LNCS, vol. 7237, pp. 520–536. Springer, Heidelberg (2012). doi:10.1007/978-3-642-29011-4_31

[BL04]   Berger, T., Loidreau, P.: Designing an efficient and secure public-key cryptosystem based on reducible rank codes. In: Canteaut, A., Viswanathan, K. (eds.) INDOCRYPT 2004. LNCS, vol. 3348, pp. 218–229. Springer, Heidelberg (2004). doi:10.1007/978-3-540-30556-9_18

[BLP11] Bernstein, D.J., Lange, T., Peters, C.: Smaller decoding exponents: ball-collision decoding. In: Rogaway, P. (ed.) CRYPTO 2011. LNCS, vol. 6841, pp. 743–760. Springer, Heidelberg (2011). doi:10.1007/978-3-642-22792-9_42

[COTG15] Couvreur, A., Otmani, A., Tillich, J.-P., Gauthier–Umaña, V.: A polynomial-time attack on the BBCRS scheme. In: Katz, J. (ed.) PKC 2015. LNCS, vol. 9020, pp. 175–193. Springer, Heidelberg (2015). doi:10.1007/978-3-662-46447-2_8

[Cou01] Courtois, N.T.: Efficient zero-knowledge authentication based on a linear algebra problem MinRank. In: Boyd, C. (ed.) ASIACRYPT 2001. LNCS, vol. 2248, pp. 402–421. Springer, Heidelberg (2001). doi:10.1007/3-540-45682-1_24

[CS96]   Chabaud, F., Stern, J.: The cryptographic security of the syndrome decoding problem for rank distance codes. In: Kim, K., Matsumoto, T. (eds.) ASIACRYPT 1996. LNCS, vol. 1163, pp. 368–381. Springer, Heidelberg (1996). doi:10.1007/BFb0034862

[CTS16] Canto Torres, R., Sendrier, N.: Analysis of information set decoding for a sub-linear error weight. In: Takagi, T. (ed.) PQCrypto 2016. LNCS, vol. 9606, pp. 144–161. Springer, Cham (2016). doi:10.1007/978-3-319-29360-8_10

[Gab85] Gabidulin, E.M.: Theory of codes with maximum rank distance. Probl. Inf. Transm. **21**(1), 3–16 (1985)

[Gab08] Gabidulin, E.M.: Attacks and counter-attacks on the GPT public key cryptosystem. Des. Codes Cryptogr. **48**(2), 171–177 (2008)

[GHT16] Gaborit, P., Hauteville, A., Tillich, J.-P.: RankSynd a PRNG based on rank metric. In: Takagi, T. (ed.) PQCrypto 2016. LNCS, vol. 9606, pp. 18–28. Springer, Cham (2016). doi:10.1007/978-3-319-29360-8_2

[Gib95] Gibson, K.: Severely denting the Gabidulin version of the McEliece public key cryptosystem. Des. Codes Cryptogr. **6**(1), 37–45 (1995)

[Gib96] Gibson, K.: The security of the Gabidulin public key cryptosystem. In: Maurer, U. (ed.) EUROCRYPT 1996. LNCS, vol. 1070, pp. 212–223. Springer, Heidelberg (1996). doi:10.1007/3-540-68339-9_19

[GL08] Gabidulin, E.M., Loidreau, P.: Properties of subspace subcodes of Gabidulin codes. Adv. Math. Commun. **2**(2), 147–157 (2008)

[GMRZ13] Gaborit, P., Murat, G., Ruatta, O., Zémor, G.: Low rank parity check codes and their application to cryptography. In: Proceedings of the Workshop on Coding and Cryptography, WCC 2013, Bergen, Norway (2013). www.selmer.uib.no/WCC2013/pdfs/Gaborit.pdf

[GPT91] Gabidulin, E.M., Paramonov, A.V., Tretjakov, O.V.: Ideals over a non-commutative ring and their application in cryptology. In: Davies, D.W. (ed.) EUROCRYPT 1991. LNCS, vol. 547, pp. 482–489. Springer, Heidelberg (1991). doi:10.1007/3-540-46416-6_41

[GRH09] Gabidulin, E., Rashwan, H., Honary, B.: On improving security of GPT cryptosystems. In: Proceedings of IEEE International Symposium on Information Theory - ISIT 2009, pp. 1110–1114 (2009)

[GRS16] Gaborit, P., Ruatta, O., Schrek, J.: On the complexity of the rank syndrome decoding problem. IEEE Trans. Inf. Theory **62**(2), 1006–1019 (2016)

[GRSZ14] Gaborit, P., Ruatta, O., Schrek, J., Zémor, G.: New results for rank-based cryptography. In: Pointcheval, D., Vergnaud, D. (eds.) AFRICACRYPT 2014. LNCS, vol. 8469, pp. 1–12. Springer, Cham (2014). doi:10.1007/978-3-319-06734-6_1

[GSJ16] Guo, Q., Johansson, T., Stankovski, P.: A key recovery attack on MDPC with CCA security using decoding errors. In: Cheon, J.H., Takagi, T. (eds.) ASIACRYPT 2016. LNCS, vol. 10031, pp. 789–815. Springer, Heidelberg (2016). doi:10.1007/978-3-662-53887-6_29

[GZ14] Gaborit, P., Zémor, G.: On the hardness of the decoding and the minimum distance problems for rank codes, CoRR abs/1404.3482 (2014)

[KI01] Kobara, K., Imai, H.: Semantically secure McEliece public-key cryptosystems-conversions for McEliece PKC. In: Kim, K. (ed.) PKC 2001. LNCS, vol. 1992, pp. 19–35. Springer, Heidelberg (2001). doi:10.1007/3-540-44586-2_2

[Ksh07] Kshevetskiy, A.: Security of GPT-like public-key cryptosystems based on linear rank codes. In: 3rd International Workshop on Signal Design and Its Applications in Communications, IWSDA 2007 (2007)

[Loi14] Loidreau, P.: Asymptotic behaviour of codes in rank metric over finite fields. Des. Codes Cryptogr. **71**(1), 105–118 (2014)

[McE78] McEliece, R.J.: A public-key system based on algebraic coding theory, pp. 114–116, Jet Propulsion Lab, DSN Progress Report 44 (1978)

[MO15] May, A., Ozerov, I.: On computing nearest neighbors with applications to decoding of binary linear codes. In: Oswald, E., Fischlin, M. (eds.) EUROCRYPT 2015. LNCS, vol. 9056, pp. 203–228. Springer, Heidelberg (2015). doi:10.1007/978-3-662-46800-5_9

[MTSB12] Misoczki, R., Tillich, J.-P., Sendrier, N., Barreto, P.S.L.M.: MDPC-McEliece: new McEliece variants from moderate density parity-check codes, IACR Cryptology ePrint Archive, Report 2012/409 (2012)

[OJ02] Ourivski, A.V., Johansson, T.: New technique for decoding codes in the rank metric and its cryptography applications. Probl. Inf. Transm. **38**(3), 237–246 (2002). (English)

[OKN16] Otmani, A., Kalashi, H.T., Ndjeya, S.: Improved cryptanalysis of rank metric schemes based on Gabidulin codes (2016). http://arxiv.org/abs/1602.08549v1

[Ove05] Overbeck, R.: A new structural attack for GPT and variants. In: Dawson, E., Vaudenay, S. (eds.) Mycrypt 2005. LNCS, vol. 3715, pp. 50–63. Springer, Heidelberg (2005). doi:10.1007/11554868_5

[Pra62] Prange, E.: The use of information sets in decoding cyclic codes. IRE Trans. Inf. Theory **8**(5), 5–9 (1962)

[RGH10] Rashwan, H., Gabidulin, E.M., Honary, B.: A smart approach for GPT cryptosystem based on rank codes. In: Proceedings of IEEE International Symposium on Information Theory - ISIT 2010, pp. 2463–2467 (2010)

Ouroboros: A Simple, Secure and Efficient Key Exchange Protocol Based on Coding Theory

Jean-Christophe Deneuville[1]([✉]), Philippe Gaborit[1], and Gilles Zémor[2]

[1] University of Limoges, Limoges, France
jean-christophe.deneuville@unilim.fr
[2] University of Bordeaux, Bordeaux, France

Abstract. We introduce Ouroboros (The Ouroboros symbol is an ancient symbol which represents the notion of cyclicity in many civilizations), a new Key Exchange protocol based on coding theory. The protocol gathers the best properties of the recent MDPC-McEliece and HQC protocols for the Hamming metric: simplicity of decoding and security reduction, based on a double cyclic structure. This yields a simple, secure and efficient approach for key exchange. We obtain the same type of parameters (and almost the same simple decoding) as for MDPC-McEliece, but with a security reduction to decoding random quasi-cyclic codes in the Random Oracle Model.

Keywords: Post-quantum cryptography · Coding theory · Key exchange

1 Introduction

Code-based cryptography was introduced with the well-known McEliece cryptosystem in 1978: it is in the spirit of the Merkle-Hellman cryptosystem, where the main idea consists in masking an easy instance of a hard problem, hoping that the masking is hard to recover. The McEliece system based on its original family of codes – namely the binary Goppa codes – is still considered unbroken today, but many variants based on alternative families of codes have been proposed over the years and have turned out to be flawed, notably the variants based on the overly structured Reed-Solomon codes. The McEliece system has two main drawbacks: a very large key size and a security reduction to an ad-hoc problem, the difficulty of recovering the hidden structure of a decodable code from the public matrix.

© Springer International Publishing AG 2017
T. Lange and T. Takagi (Eds.): PQCrypto 2017, LNCS 10346, pp. 18–34, 2017.
DOI: 10.1007/978-3-319-59879-6_2

Over the years, researchers have tried to propose alternative schemes to overcome these issues. The first line of improvements consists in adding structure to the public matrix (like cyclicity for instance) in order to decrease the size of the public key. Several approaches were proposed from 2005 [12], and resulted in the McEliece variant based on the MDPC family of error-correcting codes [15], a very efficient family with a very weak structure, compared to classical decodable families. MDPC-McEliece is in the spirit of the NTRU cryptosystem but relies on the Hamming distance rather than on the Euclidean distance. In practice the system has a rather reasonable key-size, but a rather long message-size (comparable to the key-length), it also benefits from a very simple decoding algorithm (the BitFlip algorithm inherited from LDPC codes). Overall, its two main drawbacks are the lack of a security reduction to a classical decoding problem and the fact that the decoding algorithm is only probabilistic, making it hard to obtain precise probabilities of decryption failure for very low probabilities.

A new approach to code-based public-key encryption that broke completely with the McEliece paradigm was proposed by Alekhnovich in 2003 [2]. The focus of this approach is to derive a system with a security reduction to the problem of decoding random linear codes. This approach was very innovative but lead to large parameters, exceeding those of McEliece. An Alekhnovich-inspired approach that features cyclicity was recently proposed in [1]. The new scheme combines the advantages of a security reduction with small public-key sizes resulting from cyclicity and are based on the HQC and RQC (Hamming metric and rank metric quasi-cyclic) families. In practice for the Hamming metric and HQC codes, the obtained parameters are a little larger than for MDPC-McEliece, but the decryption failure is easier to evaluate for very low decryption failure probabilities, and decoding is less simple but still more efficient than for MDPC (decoding a small BCH code against using the BitFlip algorithm for large lengths).

High Level Overview of Our Contribution. The previous discussion was mainly focused on encryption algorithms. It is also possible to consider a Key Exchange protocol derived from an encryption algorithm, simply by considering that the public key is ephemeral and changed for each use of the protocol. (This is generally achieved through a Key Encapsulation Mechanism (KEM for short), this point is discussed in more details in Sect. 4.) In that case it is possible to accept low but fixed decryption failures (say) 10^{-5} rather than require proven decryption failures of $2^{-\lambda}$ for a security parameter λ. In that context the very simple BitFlip algorithm for MDPC decoding has renewed appeal since the difficulty of estimating the decoding failure probability is not a serious issue anymore.

Our approach borrows from both MDPC-McEliece and the Alekhnovich approach. In the McEliece paradigm, errors are purposefully added to a codeword, which the receiver can correct because he has a secret version of the code which comes with a decoding algorithm. In contrast, the Alekhnovich strategy consists of creating from a random public code a secret vector that is common to sender and receiver, except that the sender and the receiver's versions of this vector differ by some noise. The natural follow-up is then to resort to an auxiliary code in order to remove this noise. In the present work we use the Alekhnovich approach, except that there is no auxiliary code: the public-key is a random quasi-cyclic code with no extra structure (contrary to McEliece variants) but the noise that needs to be removed is decoded through the secret key that happens to generate an MDPC code.

A Structured Error for HQC Codes. The approach developed in [1] requires recovering a codeword of the form $\mathbf{mG}$, where $\mathbf{G}$ generates some public code of length n, from a quantity of the form $\mathbf{mG} + \mathbf{xr}_2 - \mathbf{yr}_1 + \epsilon$ where $\mathbf{xr}_2 - \mathbf{yr}_1 + \epsilon$ is of weight $\mathcal{O}(n)$, $\mathbf{xr}_2$ and $\mathbf{yr}_1$ are the cyclic products of small weight vectors, and ϵ is an independent small weight vector. The code generated by $\mathbf{G}$ is therefore chosen to be highly decodable, and in the context of HQC is only required to decode very large errors without taking into account the particular structure of the error. In fact, the errors induced by the HQC approach are very special, indeed looking closely at $\mathbf{xr}_2 - \mathbf{yr}_1 + \epsilon$, and considering the fact that the decoder knows $\mathbf{x}$ and $\mathbf{y}$, it is easy to see that the error has essentially a cyclic structure induced by $\mathbf{x}$ and $\mathbf{y}$, where $\mathbf{r}_1, \mathbf{r}_2$ and ϵ are the unknowns. Seeing this and taking into account the particular error structure, it is easy to reformulate the decoding problem for HQC code into a decoding problem of a quasi-cyclic MDPC code generated by $\mathbf{x}$ and $\mathbf{y}$ (known by the decoder). The only difference being the additional decoding of ϵ, but our experiments show that the BitFlip algorithm can be slightly modified in order to keep handling the case where the syndrome has a small additional error ϵ.

In practice this new approach based on the cyclic structure of the error, enables one to keep the security reduction present in HQC-based encryption and to include the simplicity of the BitFlip decoding algorithm used for MDPC codes (mildly tweaked). In some sense this new approach enables one to avoid the use of an external code as in HQC encryption. (The decoding problem is formally stated in Definition 9.) It comes with a price since it makes the evaluation of decryption failure probabilities more difficult, but the algorithm is especially well suited to Key Exchange for which failures are tolerated. In this paper we show that in practice our parameters are almost the same as those of MDPC-McEliece but with a security reduction to decoding quasi-cyclic random binary codes.

We prove that our protocol satisfies the passively secure requirement for KEMs – namely INDistinguishability under Chosen Plaintext Attacks (IND-CPA) – in the Random Oracle Model, with a reduction to a decisional form of the decoding problem for random QC-codes.

Our Contributions. To sum up: by considering the special structure of the error vector in the HQC approach our contributions show the following:

- it is possible to obtain a scheme based on the simple BitFlip decoder, with the IND-CPA property and with a security reduction to a decisional version of the decoding problem for random quasi-cyclic codes, whereas MDPC-McEliece has similar parameters but no such reduction,

- our approach improves on HQC-based encryption since in our new construction, the weight of the error vector that needs to be decoded has weight $\mathcal{O}(\sqrt{n})$ whereas the error weight is structurally in $\mathcal{O}(n)$ for HQC,
- the BitFlip decoder is still usable and decodes efficiently when there is an additional small error on the given syndrome, and
- by considering the use of ephemeral keys, an efficient key exchange protocol is obtained with a reasonable probability of failure.

Organization of the Paper. Section 2 gives background, Sect. 3 describes the new decoding problem, the modified BitFlip algorithm as well as the proposed Ouroboros protocol, Sect. 4 presents a security proof of this protocol with respect to the standard model for KEM, and finally Sect. 5 gives examples of parameters.

2   Background

2.1   Coding Theory and Syndrome Decoding Problems

Notation. Throughout this paper, $\mathbb{Z}$ denotes the ring of integers and $\mathbb{F}_q$ (for a prime $q \in \mathbb{Z}$) a finite field, typically $\mathbb{F}_2$ for Hamming codes. Additionally, we denote by $\omega(\cdot)$ the Hamming weight of a vector *i.e.* the number of its non-zero coordinates, and by $\mathcal{S}_w^n(\mathbb{F}_2)$ the set of words in $\mathbb{F}_2^n$ of weight w. Formally:

$$\mathcal{S}_w^n(\mathbb{F}_2) = \{\mathbf{x} \in \mathbb{F}_2^n, \text{ such that } \omega(\mathbf{x}) = w\}.$$

$\mathcal{V}$ denotes a vector space of dimension n over $\mathbb{F}_2$ for some positive $n \in \mathbb{Z}$. Elements of $\mathcal{V}$ can be interchangeably considered as row vectors or polynomials in $\mathcal{R} = \mathbb{F}_2[X]/(X^n - 1)$. Vectors/Polynomials (resp. matrices) will be represented by lower-case (resp. upper-case) bold letters. A prime integer n is said to be primitive if the polynomial $(X^n - 1)/(X - 1)$ is irreducible in $\mathcal{R}$.

For $\mathbf{x}, \mathbf{y} \in \mathcal{V}$, we define their product similarly as in $\mathcal{R}$, *i.e.* $\mathbf{xy} = \mathbf{c} \in \mathcal{V}$ with

$$c_k = \sum_{i+j \equiv k \mod n} x_i y_j, \text{ for } k \in \{0, 1, \ldots, n-1\}.$$

Our new protocol uses cyclic (or circulant) matrices. In the same fashion as in [1], $\mathbf{rot}(\mathbf{h})$ for $\mathbf{h} \in \mathcal{V}$ denotes the circulant matrix whose i^{th} column is the vector corresponding to $\mathbf{h}X^i \mod X^n - 1$.

Background on Coding Theory. We now provide some reminders on coding theory, the SD problem and its quasi-cyclic versions as defined in [1].

Definition 1 (Quasi-Cyclic Codes [15]). *For positive integers s, n and k, a linear code $[sn, k]$ code is said to be* Quasi-Cyclic *(QC) of order s if $\forall \mathbf{c} = (\mathbf{c}_1, \ldots, \mathbf{c}_s) \in \mathcal{C}$ it holds that that $(\mathbf{c}_1 X, \ldots, \mathbf{c}_s X) \in \mathcal{C}$ (i.e. the code is stable by a block circular shift of length n).*

In our case, we will only consider rate $1/s$ *systematic* quasi-cyclic codes. The parity-check matrix of such codes have the convenient shape below.

Definition 2 (Systematic Quasi-Cyclic Codes of rate $1/s$). *A QC $[sn, n]$ code of order s is said to be* systematic *if it admits a parity-check matrix of the form*

$$\mathbf{H} = \begin{bmatrix} \mathbf{I}_n & 0 & \cdots & 0 & \mathbf{A}_1 \\ 0 & \mathbf{I}_n & & & \mathbf{A}_2 \\ & & \ddots & & \vdots \\ 0 & & \cdots & \mathbf{I}_n & \mathbf{A}_{s-1} \end{bmatrix}$$

with $\mathbf{A}_1, \ldots, \mathbf{A}_{s-1}$ *circulant* $n \times n$ *matrices.*

Problems in Coding Theory. Most code-based primitives rely on the Syndrome Decoding (SD) problem, which has been proved NP-hard [5]. Even if there is no such complexity result for Quasi-Cyclic (QC) codes, the general belief is that the SD remains hard for such matrices. We use the same notations and definitions as [1] for this problem, namely Quasi-Cyclic Syndrome Decoding (QCSD). The following problems are defined for binary codes in the Hamming metric, but easily extend to codes over $\mathbb{F}_q$ and even to other metrics such as the rank metric.

Definition 3 (SD Distribution). *Let* $n, k, w \in \mathbb{N}^*$, *the SD (n, k, w) Distribution chooses* $\mathbf{H} \xleftarrow{\$} \mathbb{F}^{(n-k) \times n}$ *and* $\mathbf{x} \xleftarrow{\$} S_w^n(\mathbb{F}_2)$, *and outputs* $(\mathbf{H}, \sigma(\mathbf{x}) = \mathbf{H}\mathbf{x}^\top)$.

The SD distribution having been defined, we can now define the fundamental problem for code-based cryptography.

Definition 4 (Search SD Problem). *On input* $(\mathbf{H}, \mathbf{y}^\top) \in \mathbb{F}_2^{(n-k) \times n} \times \mathbb{F}_2^{(n-k)}$ *from the SD distribution, the* Syndrome Decoding Problem SD(n, k, w) *asks to find* $\mathbf{x} \in S_w^n(\mathbb{F}_2)$ *such that* $\mathbf{H}\mathbf{x}^\top = \mathbf{y}^\top$.

The SD problem has a decisional form, which asks to decide whether the given sample came from the SD distribution or the uniform distribution:

Definition 5 (Decisional SD Problem). *Given* $(\mathbf{H}, \mathbf{y}^\top) \xleftarrow{\$} \mathbb{F}_2^{(n-k) \times n} \times \mathbb{F}_2^{(n-k)}$, *the* Decisional SD Problem DSD (n, k, w) *asks to decide with non-negligible advantage whether* $(\mathbf{H}, \mathbf{y}^\top)$ *came from the SD(n, k, w) distribution or the uniform distribution over* $\mathbb{F}_2^{(n-k) \times n} \times \mathbb{F}_2^{(n-k)}$.

In order to propose reasonable key sizes, we base our proposition on QC codes. We adapt the previous problems to this configuration.

Definition 6 (s-QCSD Distribution). *Let* $n, k, w, s \in \mathbb{N}^*$, *the s-QCSD (n, k, w, s) Distribution samples* $\mathbf{H} \xleftarrow{\$} \mathbb{F}_2^{(sn-k) \times sn}$, *the parity-check matrix of a QC-code of order s and* $\mathbf{x} = (\mathbf{x}_1, \ldots, \mathbf{x}_s) \xleftarrow{\$} \mathbb{F}_2^{sn}$ *such that* $\omega(\mathbf{x}_i) = w$, *and outputs* $(\mathbf{H}, \mathbf{H}\mathbf{x}^\top)$.

Definition 7 ((Search) s-QCSD Problem). *For positive integers n, k, w, s, a random parity check matrix $\mathbf{H}$ of a systematic QC code $\mathcal{C}$ and* $\mathbf{y} \xleftarrow{\$} \mathbb{F}_2^{sn-k}$, *the* Search s-Quasi-Cyclic SD Problem s-QCSD (n, k, w) *asks to find* $\mathbf{x} = (\mathbf{x}_1, \ldots, \mathbf{x}_s) \in \mathbb{F}_2^{sn}$ *such that* $\omega(\mathbf{x}_i) = w$, $i = 1..s$, *and* $\mathbf{y} = \mathbf{x}\mathbf{H}^\top$.

Assumption 1. The Search s-QCSD problem is hard on average.

Although there is no general complexity result for quasi-cyclic codes, decoding these codes is considered hard by the community. There exist general attacks which use the cyclic structure of the code [13,19] but these attacks have only a very limited impact on the practical complexity of the problem. The conclusion is that in practice, the best attacks are the same as those for non-circulant codes up to a small factor.

Remark. Since systematic quasi-cyclic codes make up a large proportion of the whole ensemble of quasi-cyclic codes, restricting the s-QCSD Problem to systematic codes is not a significant specialisation.

Definition 8 (Decisional s-QCSD Problem). *For positive integers n, k, w, s, a random parity check matrix $\mathbf{H}$ of a systematic QC code $\mathcal{C}$ and $\mathbf{y} \xleftarrow{\$} \mathbb{F}_2^{sn}$, the* Decisional s-Quasi-Cyclic SD Problem s-DQCSD (n, k, w) *asks to decide with non-negligible advantage whether $(\mathbf{H}, \mathbf{y}^\top)$ came from the s-QCSD(n, k, w) distribution or the uniform distribution over $\mathbb{F}_2^{(sn-k) \times sn} \times \mathbb{F}_2^{sn-k}$.*

As for the ring Learning Parity from Noise problem, there is no known reduction from the search version of s-QCSD problem to its decisional version. The proof of [4] cannot be directly adapted in the quasi-cyclic case, however the best known attacks on the decisional version of the problem s-QCSD remain the direct attacks on the search version of the problem s-QCSD.

2.2 HQC Scheme

We now recall the Hamming Quasi-Cyclic (HQC) Scheme from [1], which shares some similarities with the proposed protocol. This scheme in turn is inspired by Alekhnovich's proposal based on random matrices [2], but is much more efficient due to the use of the cyclic structure. The main differences between HQC, Alekhnovich's scheme, and our proposal Ouroboros will be discussed in Sect. 3.3.

HQC uses two types of codes, a decodable $[n, k]$ code which can correct δ errors and a random double-circulant $[2n, n]$ code. Using the same notation as before, consider a linear code $\mathcal{C}$ over $\mathbb{F}_2$ of dimension k and length n (generated by $\mathbf{G} \in \mathbb{F}_2^{k \times n}$), that can correct up to δ errors via an efficient algorithm $\mathcal{C}.\mathsf{Decode}(\cdot)$. The scheme consists of the following four polynomial-time algorithms:

- Setup(1^λ): generates the global parameters $n = n(1^\lambda), k = k(1^\lambda), \delta = \delta(1^\lambda)$, and $w = w(1^\lambda)$. The plaintext space is $\mathbb{F}_2^k$. Outputs param $= (n, k, \delta, w)$.
- KeyGen(param): generates $\mathbf{q}_r \xleftarrow{\$} \mathcal{V}$, matrix $\mathbf{Q} = (\mathbf{I}_n \mid \mathbf{rot}(\mathbf{q}_r))$, the generator matrix $\mathbf{G} \in \mathbb{F}_2^{k \times n}$ of $\mathcal{C}$, sk $= (\mathbf{x}, \mathbf{y}) \xleftarrow{\$} \mathcal{V}^2$ such that $\omega(\mathbf{x}) = \omega(\mathbf{y}) = w$, sets pk $= (\mathbf{G}, \mathbf{Q}, \mathbf{s} = \mathsf{sk} \cdot \mathbf{Q}^\top)$, and returns (pk, sk).
- Encrypt(pk $= (\mathbf{G}, \mathbf{Q}, \mathbf{s}), \mu, \theta$): uses randomness θ to generate $\epsilon \xleftarrow{\$} \mathcal{V}$, $\mathbf{r} = (\mathbf{r}_1, \mathbf{r}_2) \xleftarrow{\$} \mathcal{V}^2$ such that $\omega(\epsilon), \omega(\mathbf{r}_1), \omega(\mathbf{r}_2) \leq w$, sets $\mathbf{v}^\top = \mathbf{Q}\mathbf{r}^\top$ and $\rho = \mu\mathbf{G} + \mathbf{s} \cdot \mathbf{r}_2 + \epsilon$. It finally returns $\mathbf{c} = (\mathbf{v}, \rho)$, an encryption of μ under pk.
- Decrypt(sk $= (\mathbf{x}, \mathbf{y}), \mathbf{c} = (\mathbf{v}, \rho)$): returns $\mathcal{C}.\mathsf{Decode}(\rho - \mathbf{v} \cdot \mathbf{y})$.

A key feature of HQC is that the generator matrix $\mathbf{G}$ of the code $\mathcal{C}$ is publicly known. In this way, the security of the scheme and the ability to decrypt only rely on the knowledge of the secret key to remove sufficiently many errors, so that the code $\mathcal{C}$ being used can decode correctly.

3   The Ouroboros Protocol

We begin this Section by restating formally the decoding problem obtained by providing a noisy input to the classical BitFlip Algorithm. We then describe an efficient modified BitFlip algorithm which actually solves the stated problem. Finally we describe our new key exchange protocol: Ouroboros.

3.1   Decoding Cyclic Errors

Our new key exchange protocol requires to decode cyclic errors. We therefore introduce a new problem that we call the Cyclic Error Decoding (CED) problem. Essentially, this problem asks to recover information hidden with some noise, where the noise has a cyclic structure. The problem is defined as follows:

Definition 9 (Cyclic Error Decoding (CED) Problem). *Let* $\mathbf{x}, \mathbf{y}, \mathbf{r}_1$ *and* $\mathbf{r}_2$ *be random vectors of length* n *and weight* $w = \mathcal{O}(\sqrt{n})$, *and let* $\mathbf{e}$ *be a random error vector of weight* $w_{\mathbf{e}} = cw$ *for some non-negative constant* c. *Considering the cyclic products of vectors modulo* $X^n - 1$, *the problem is defined as follows: given* $(\mathbf{x}, \mathbf{y}) \in (\mathcal{S}_w^n(\mathbb{F}_2))^2$ *and* $\mathbf{e_c} \leftarrow \mathbf{x}\mathbf{r}_2 - \mathbf{y}\mathbf{r}_1 + \mathbf{e}$ *such that* $\omega(\mathbf{r}_1) = \omega(\mathbf{r}_2) = w$, *the* Cyclic Error Decoding *problem asks to recover* $(\mathbf{r}_1, \mathbf{r}_2)$.

One can immediately notice that this problem essentially corresponds to an instance of the SD problem on matrix $\mathbf{H} = (\mathbf{rot}(\mathbf{x})^{\top}, \mathbf{rot}(\mathbf{y}^{\top}))$, with the particularity that the syndrome itself is faulty. Alternatively, it can also be thought of as a correct instance of the same problem, but on the longer matrix $\mathbf{H} = (\mathbf{rot}(\mathbf{x})^{\top}, \mathbf{rot}(\mathbf{y})^{\top}, \mathbf{I}_n)$.

A Modified BitFlip Algorithm. In the case when $w_e = 0$, the problem is exactly the MDPC problem [15]: now when $w_e \neq 0$ but remains small, the BitFlip decoder used for MDPC codes can be directly adapted to this case. The only difference is that the STOP condition is not that the weight of the recurring syndrome obtained at each step becomes 0 at some point but rather that its weight is lower than w_e (for $w_e \neq 0$).

We present in Algorithm 1 a slightly modified BitFlip algorithm following [9,15]. Our experiments showed that this Hamming-QC-Decoder algorithm can correctly perform decoding even when the input of the traditional BitFlip algorithm is a moderately noisy syndrome.

There exist different ways to tune the BitFlip algorithm, the reader is referred to [9] to see more details. In our version we consider the simple case wherea

---

Algorithm 1: Hamming-QC-Decoder$(\mathbf{x}, \mathbf{y}, \mathbf{e_c}, t, w, w_e)$

Input: $\mathbf{x}, \mathbf{y}$, and $\mathbf{e_c} = \mathbf{x}\mathbf{r}_2 - \mathbf{y}\mathbf{r}_1 + \mathbf{e}$, threshold value t required to flip a bit, weight w (resp. w_e) of $\mathbf{r}_1$ and $\mathbf{r}_2$ (resp. $\mathbf{e}$).

Output: $(\mathbf{r}_1, \mathbf{r}_2)$ if the algorithm succeeds, $\perp$ otherwise.

1 $(\mathbf{u}, \mathbf{v}) \leftarrow (\mathbf{0}, \mathbf{0}) \in (\mathbb{F}_2^n)^2$, $\mathbf{H} \leftarrow \left(\mathrm{rot}(-\mathbf{y})^\top, \mathrm{rot}(\mathbf{x})^\top\right) \in \mathbb{F}_2^{n \times 2n}$, syndrome $\leftarrow \mathbf{e_c}$;

2 **while** $[\omega(\mathbf{u}) \neq w$ **or** $\omega(\mathbf{v}) \neq w]$ **and** $\omega(\mathrm{syndrome}) > w_e$ **do**

3   sum $\leftarrow$ syndrome$\times \mathbf{H}$; /**   */

4   [f]No modular reduction

5   flipped_positions $\leftarrow \mathbf{0} \in \mathbb{F}_2^{2n}$;

6   **for** $i \in [\![0, 2n-1]\!]$ **do**

7   **if** sum$[i] \geq t$ **then**

8   flipped_positions$[i]$ = flipped_positions$[i] \oplus 1$;

9      $(\mathbf{u}, \mathbf{v}) = (\mathbf{u}, \mathbf{v}) \oplus$ flipped_positions;

10   syndrome = syndrome $-\mathbf{H} \times$ flipped_positions$^\top$;

11 **if** $\omega\left(\mathbf{e_c} - \mathbf{H} \times (\mathbf{u}, \mathbf{v})^\top\right) > w_e$ **then**

12   **return** $\perp$;

13 **else**

14   **return** $(\mathbf{u}, \mathbf{v})$;

---

threshold t is used at each step to make a decision on the bit to flip or not. We run many experiments for different sizes of parameters, in practice the results obtained show that for the parameters considered the w_e impacts decoding only marginally. The main impact is a slightly lower decoding probability.

3.2 Description of the Ouroboros Protocol

Our protocol requires a function f which constructs fixed weight vectors of given weight w from an entry r. In general for code-based protocols one requires an invertible function f (see [18]), but in our case since we only consider key exchange, f is not required to be invertible and a simple repetition of a hash function from the entry r, giving the positions of the '1' is enough to obtain random vectors of fixed weight. We denote such a function by f_w.

Description of the Protocol. Our protocol is described in a generic fashion in Fig. 1. It uses a hash function Hash $: \{0,1\}^* \longrightarrow S_w^n(\mathbb{F}_2)$. For $\mathbf{h}$ a random vector, Alice constructs a random syndrome $\mathbf{s}$ from its secret $\mathbf{x}, \mathbf{y}$. Upon reception of the syndrome $\mathbf{s} = \mathbf{x} + \mathbf{h}\mathbf{y}$ from Alice, Bob constructs its own random syndrome $\mathbf{s} = \mathbf{r}_1 + \mathbf{h}\mathbf{r}_2$ from random $\mathbf{r}_1$ and $\mathbf{r}_2$ of weight w, and also constructs a second syndrome $\mathbf{s}_\epsilon$ associated with $\mathbf{r}_2$ on one side and on the other side to a small weight vector $\mathbf{e}$ composed of two error vectors: the vector ϵ which will be the shared secret and the error $\mathbf{e}_r$ obtained from the secret $\mathbf{r}_1, \mathbf{r}_2$. Upon receiving $\mathbf{s}_r$ and $\mathbf{s}_\epsilon$, Alice computes $\mathbf{e_c} = \mathbf{s}_\epsilon - \mathbf{y}\mathbf{s}_r = \mathbf{x}\mathbf{r}_2 - \mathbf{y}\mathbf{r}_1 + \mathbf{e}_r + \epsilon$, which corresponds to the cyclic-error decoding problem with $\mathbf{e} = \mathbf{e}_r + \epsilon$. The value w_e is taken as $\omega(\epsilon) + \omega(\mathbf{e})$, in practice it can be a little smaller, but it does not change the decoding.

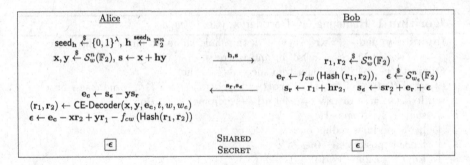

Fig. 1. Description of our new key exchange protocol. **h** and **s** constitute the public key. **h** can be recovered by publishing only the λ bits of the seed (instead of the n coordinates of **h**).

Having this double error is essential for the security proof. Upon reception of the two syndromes s_r and s_ϵ, Alice constructs an instance of the CED problem. The result of the CED decoder is then used to recover $e_r + \epsilon$ and the e_r part of the error is removed through the knowledge of (r_1, r_2).

3.3   Comparison with **HQC** and Alekhnovich

The Ouroboros approach differs fundamentally from the HQC approach concerning the decoding algorithm used. For HQC [1] (and Aleknovich's approach) the decoding code $\mathcal{C}$ does not depend on the error, the code is fixed and is only required to decode an error of the form $\mathbf{xr}_2 + \mathbf{yr}_1 + \epsilon$. Since $\mathbf{x}, \mathbf{y}, \mathbf{r}_1$ and $\mathbf{r}_2$ have weight in $\mathcal{O}(\sqrt{n})$, the code $\mathcal{C}$ has to decode $\mathcal{O}(n)$ errors. For Ouroboros we use the special cyclic structure of the error vector so that the code that is being decoded is necessarily a MDPC type code and the error that one needs to decode has weight $\mathcal{O}(\sqrt{n})$ rather than $\mathcal{O}(n)$. Having to decode a smaller weight error yields better parameters with the Ouroboros approach than with the HQC approach. However there is a price to pay, the BitFlip decoding algorithm leads to a probabilistic decoding where the decoding probability is obtained by simulation and is hard to estimate theoretically, whereas the HQC approach gives the freedom to choose an auxiliary code for decoding with a decoding failure probability easier to estimate.

4   Security of the Protocol

In this section we prove the security of our key exchange protocol. Following Alekhnovich's construction, HQC benefits from a security reduction against passive adversaries. This represents a strong advance compared to the MDPC-McEliece scheme. We note that the security proof from [1] carries over to our key exchange protocol.

Security Model. While encryption schemes and long-term key exchange protocols require strong semantic security against active adversaries, protocols meant to exchange purely ephemeral session keys (such as Key Encapsulation Mechanisms *aka* KEMs) are considered secure whenever they provide security against merely passive adversaries (*aka* INDistinguishability under Chosen Plaintext Attacks, or IND-CPA for short). This approach has been followed by several lattice-based key exchange protocols such as [7,10,11,17], or more recently the so-called NEWHOPE protocol [3]. Exchanging ephemeral keys through passively secure KEMS exploits the fact that a (say) 256 bits randomness string chosen by one party can be sent encrypted using the other party's (long term) public key so that both parties end up with shared secret randomness from which they can derive a secret symmetric key. Passively secure KEMs viewed as key exchanged protocols are covered by the IND-CPA security model [14]. (It turns out that this security model has been chosen with a minimal security requirement by NIST in its post-quantum call for proposal [16].) Therefore, we prove our key exchange protocol (viewed as a KEM) to be (passively) secure in this IND-CPA model.

IND-CPA. IND-CPA is generally proved through the following game: the adversary $\mathcal{A}$ chooses two plaintexts μ_0 and μ_1 and sends them to the challenger who flips a coin $b \in \{0,1\}$, encrypts μ_b into ciphertext c and returns c to $\mathcal{A}$. The encryption scheme is said to be IND-CPA secure if $\mathcal{A}$ has a negligible advantage in deciding which plaintext c encrypts. This game is formally described on the right (Fig. 2).

$$
\begin{array}{|l|}
\hline
\mathbf{Exp}^{ind-b}_{\mathcal{E},\mathcal{A}}(\lambda) \\
1.\ \mathsf{param} \leftarrow \mathsf{Setup}(1^\lambda) \\
2.\ (\mathsf{pk},\mathsf{sk}) \leftarrow \mathsf{KeyGen}(\mathsf{param}) \\
3.\ (\mu_0,\mu_1) \leftarrow \mathcal{A}(\mathrm{FIND}:\mathsf{pk}) \\
4.\ \mathbf{c}^* \leftarrow \mathsf{Encrypt}(\mathsf{pk},\mu_b,\theta) \\
5.\ b' \leftarrow \mathcal{A}(\mathrm{GUESS}:\mathbf{c}^*) \\
6.\ \mathrm{RETURN}\ b' \\
\hline
\end{array}
$$

Fig. 2. Experiment against the IND-CPA security

The global advantage for polynomial time adversaries (running in time less than t) is:

$$
\mathsf{Adv}^{ind}_{\mathcal{E}}(\lambda, t) = \max_{\mathcal{A} \leq t} \mathsf{Adv}^{ind}_{\mathcal{E},\mathcal{A}}(\lambda),
$$

where $\mathsf{Adv}^{ind}_{\mathcal{E},\mathcal{A}}(\lambda)$ is the advantage the adversary $\mathcal{A}$ has in winning game $\mathbf{Exp}^{ind-b}_{\mathcal{E},\mathcal{A}}(\lambda)$:

$$
\mathsf{Adv}^{ind}_{\mathcal{E},\mathcal{A}}(\lambda) = \left| \Pr[\mathbf{Exp}^{ind-1}_{\mathcal{E},\mathcal{A}}(\lambda) = 1] - \Pr[\mathbf{Exp}^{ind-0}_{\mathcal{E},\mathcal{A}}(\lambda) = 1] \right|.
$$

Hybrid Argument. Alternatively (and equivalently by the hybrid argument), it is possible to construct a sequence of games from a valid encryption of a first message μ_0 to a valid encryption of another message μ_1 and show that these games are two-by-two indistinguishable. We follow this latter approach and prove the security of our protocol (viewed as a KEM) similarly to [1]. Our proof can be thought as similar to [1], without their public code $\mathcal{C}$, and with ϵ playing the role of the message being encrypted.

Theorem 1. *The protocol presented in Fig. 1 is* IND-CPA *under the 2-DQCSD and 3-DQCSD assumptions.*

The proof is inspired from [1, Proof of Theorem 1], with some slight differences and adjustments. As mentioned at the beginning of this Section, the standard security model for a key exchange protocol such as Ouroboros (or NEWHOPE) is the same as passively secure KEMs [14]. In a KEM spirit, our key exchange protocol can be seen as an ephemeral key encryption protocol where the (long-term) public key is the syndrome s sent by Alice, and the plaintext (or shared secret randomness is the value ϵ encrypted in the ciphertext formed by s_r and s_ϵ.

Proof. Instead of directly proving that an PPT adversary only has a negligible advantage of distinguishing between two encrypted plaintexts, we construct a sequence of game transitioning from a valid encryption of a plaintext to a valid encryption of another plaintext. By showing these games to be two-by-two indistinguishable, the Hybrid argument allows us to obtain the claimed result. The sequence of games starts with a valid encryption of a message $\epsilon^{(0)}$ and ends with a valid encryption of message $\epsilon^{(1)}$. The aim is to prove that an adversary distinguishing one game from another can be exploited to break either the 2-DQCSD or the 3-DQCSD assumption (respectively on $[2n, n]$ or $[3n, n]$ codes) in polynomial time. Let $\mathcal{A}$ be a probabilistic polynomial time adversary against the IND-CPA of our scheme and consider the following games ($\mathcal{A}$ gets the output ciphertext at the end of each game).

Game G_1: This game corresponds to an honest run of the protocol. In particular, the challenger encrypts $\epsilon^{(0)}$ with x, y, r_1 and r_2 of small (*i.e.* correct) weight w.

Game G_2: This game is also an honest run of the protocol, still with the same plaintext $\epsilon^{(0)}$ but the challenger uses a random $e_r{}' \xleftarrow{\$} \mathcal{S}_{cw}^n(\mathbb{F}_2)$ instead of $f_{cw}(\mathsf{Hash}(r_1, r_2))$.

Game G_3: This game differs from G_2 in the fact that the challenger uses a random (*i.e.* fake) secret x and y random (resulting in a random s). He proceeds to the rest of the protocol honestly to encrypt $\epsilon^{(0)}$.

Game G_4: Similar to G_3. Additionally, the challenger samples $e_r{}'$, r_1 and r_2 at random (resulting in fake s_r and s_ϵ) to encrypt $\epsilon^{(0)}$.

Game G_5: In this game, the challenger creates a fake encryption of another plaintext $\epsilon^{(1)}$ (presumably but not necessarily different from $\epsilon^{(0)}$). He chooses $r_1', r_2', e_r{}^* \xleftarrow{\$} \mathbb{F}_2^n$ uniformly at random and runs the protocol.

Game G_6: Similar to G_5, but the challenger encrypts $\epsilon^{(1)}$ using valid, *i.e.* correctly weighted, randomness: r_1' and r_2' are sampled with the correct weight w, and $e_r{}^* \xleftarrow{\$} \mathcal{S}_{cw}^n(\mathbb{F}_2)$.

Game G_7: In this game, the challenger uses a correctly weighted secret key $\mathbf{x}$, $\mathbf{y}$ to encrypt $\epsilon^{(1)}$.

Game G_8: In this last game, the challenger uses the hash function to encrypt $\epsilon^{(1)}$, with $\mathbf{e_r}^* \leftarrow f_{cw}\left(\mathsf{Hash}\left(\mathbf{r}_1, \mathbf{r}_2\right)\right)$.

First, games G_1 and G_2 are indistinguishable under the Random Oracle assumption.

Secondly, games G_2 and G_3 are indistinguishable under the 2-DQCSD assumption. Indeed, assume we are given access to an oracle distinguishing these games. Any 2-DQCSD instance $\left(\left(\mathbf{I}_n, \mathbf{rot}(\mathbf{h})\right), \mathbf{s}\right)$ can be viewed as a public key. By providing this public key to the distinguishing oracle, we will be told whether it is valid, which is the configuration of game G_2, or not (game G_3). But this very key comes from the QCSD distribution in the former case and from the uniform distribution in the latter, which yields a 2-DQCSD oracle.

Then, games G_3 and G_4 both involve the encryption of the plaintext $\epsilon^{(0)}$, which is known to $\mathcal{A}$, who can hence compute:

$$\begin{pmatrix} \mathbf{s_r} \\ \mathbf{s_\epsilon} - \epsilon^{(0)} \end{pmatrix} = \begin{pmatrix} \mathbf{I}_n & \mathbf{0} & \mathbf{rot}(\mathbf{h}) \\ \mathbf{0} & \mathbf{I}_n & \mathbf{rot}(\mathbf{s}) \end{pmatrix} (\mathbf{r}_1, \mathbf{e_r}', \mathbf{r}_2)^\top$$

The syndrome $\left(\mathbf{s_r}, \mathbf{s_\epsilon} - \epsilon^{(0)}\right)$ follows the QCSD distribution in game G_3 and the uniform distribution over $\left(\mathbb{F}_2^n\right)^2$ in G_4. Assume an adversary is able to distinguish games G_3 and G_4, then it suffices to provide him with the syndrome and matrix described above to straightforwardly break the 3-DQCSD assumption.

Next, the outputs from games G_4 and G_5 follow the exact same distribution: they are uniformly random (hence making these games indistinguishable from an information theoretic point of view). Now that the messages being (falsely) encrypted have been permuted, the rest of the proof consists in proving the indistinguishability with a game involving a valid encryption of this second message.

We can start reintroducing correct values in the ciphertext. Games G_5 and G_6 are indistinguishable using the same argument as between G_3 and G_4: $\left(\mathbf{s_r}, \mathbf{s_\epsilon} - \epsilon^{(1)}\right)$ follows a uniform distribution for G_5 versus a QCSD distribution in G_6. Therefore an adversary distinguishing these games breaks the 3-DQCSD assumption.

Then, by reintroducing a $(\mathbf{x}, \mathbf{y})$ with correct weight, the argument from the second step also applies and an adversary distinguishing G_6 and G_7 can identify valid keys from invalid ones, hence breaking the 2-DQCSD assumption.

Finally, games G_7 and G_8 are again indistinguishable in the Random Oracle Model.

By the hybrid argument, an adversary against the IND-CPA experiment has an advantage (in the Random Oracle Model) bounded by:

$$\mathsf{Adv}^{\mathsf{ind}}_{\mathcal{E}, \mathcal{A}}(\lambda) \leq 2\left(\mathsf{Adv}^{2-\mathsf{DQCSD}}(\lambda) + \mathsf{Adv}^{3-\mathsf{DQCSD}}(\lambda)\right). \qquad \square$$

5   Parameter Sets

In this Section, since our Key Exchange protocol is based on an ephemeral encryption algorithm, we keep the same terminology: the public key corresponds to the data that Alice sends to Bob, and the message corresponds to the data sent by Bob to Alice upon receiving Alice's data. In the following we only give parameters for classical attacks, quantum safe parameters are derived by taking the square root of the complexity since the best attacks for our type of parameters $w \ll n$, it was proven in [8] that all known attacks lead to the exact same asymptotical complexity: the complexity of the classical Information Set Decoding (ISD), for which it is possible to apply directly Grover algorithm [6], and hence to divide the bit security level by 2.

5.1   Parameters

The threshold value t is the most sensitive parameter of both the original BitFlip algorithm and the modified one depicted in Algorithm 1. A little bit too big and the algorithm misses correct positions, a little bit too low and it includes wrong positions. Chaulet and Sendrier recently conduct a study on the worst-case behaviour of QC-MDPC codes, and gave some hints on how to choose this threshold value to maximize the error correcting capacity [9]. Based upon their results, we explored several values for t for our context where there is an additional error to consider and chose the lowest t (in order to optimize efficiency) giving a reasonable Decryption Failure Rate (DFR).[1]

The parameters we obtain are given in Table 1. For our parameters we chose the weight $w_{\mathbf{e}}$ in Table 1 of the additional error ϵ and the weight of $\mathbf{e_r}$ to be w, so that $w_{\mathbf{e}} = 2w$ in order to fit with the security reduction.

The security of our system is reduced to either decoding a word of weight $2w$ for a $[2n, n]$ or decoding an error of weight $3w$ for a $[3n, n]$ code. For a $[2n, n]$ code the attacker knows the weight of the error is (w, w) on each block of the matrix, a precise analysis is done in [9] and leads to an asymptotic complexity in 2^{2w}. For the case $[3n, n]$ the asymptotic complexity is better since the attacker chooses $\frac{2n}{3}$ columns among $2n$ columns, since the error distribution is (w, w, w) it leads to a complexity in $(\frac{3}{2})^{3w} = 2^{3 \log_2(3/2)w} \simeq 2^{1.75w}$, hence a little better than the attack on the $[2n, n]$ code. Notice also that for the MDPC matrix, the weight w has to be taken greater than what we consider in our case since in the case of the MDPC matrix, the attacker can search for all the cyclic permutations of the small weight vector and profit by a factor n for its attack, when in our case the factor is only $\sqrt{n}$ (see [19]). Finally, for our parameters, in order to avoid potential attacks based on the polynomial decomposition of $X^n - 1$, we chose n a primitive prime for $\mathbb{F}_2$. Overall Table 1 presents our results, the DFR is obtained by simulations on random instances with given parameters. The results show that our parameters are very close to parameters proposed by MDPC but profit by an IND-CPA security reduction to decoding random quasi-cyclic matrices.

---

[1] This terminology is borrowed from [15]. DFR is the fraction of decoding failures in a given number of decoding tests.

Table 1. Parameter sets for Ouroboros

Instance	n	w	$w_{\mathbf{e}}$	Threshold	Security	DFR
				Ouroboros parameters		
Low-I	5,851	47	94	30	80	$0.92 \cdot 10^{-5}$
Low-II	5,923	47	94	30	80	$2.3 \cdot 10^{-6}$
Medium-I	13,691	75	150	45	128	$0.96 \cdot 10^{-5}$
Medium-II	14,243	75	150	45	128	$1.09 \cdot 10^{-6}$
Strong-I	40,013	147	294	85	256	$4.20 \cdot 10^{-5}$
Strong-II	40,973	147	294	85	256	$<10^{-6}$

5.2 Optimized Parameters

We saw in the previous subsection that the security reduction lead to attacking a $[3n, n]$ quasi-cyclic code, for a small weight error of weight $3w$ more precisely. We also saw that in that case the decoding complexity was lower than for the $[2n, n]$ case. Modifying the weight of $\mathbf{e_r}$ does not really change drastically the decoding capacity of the modified BitFlip algorithm, but it may permit to obtain a higher complexity attack for the $[3n, n]$ matrix of the security reduction. Hence it seems a natural idea to increase the weight of $\mathbf{e_r}$ so that in that case we can still use the modified BitFlip algorithm but the practical security is reduced to decoding a random $[2n, n]$ code for weight $2w$. This is done on the parameters presented in Table 2.

Notice that without loss of generality for parameters such that $w = \mathcal{O}(\sqrt{n})$ the decoding of vector of length $3n$ with weights of the form (w, w, w), can be reduced to decoding vectors of the form (w, aw, w) for $a > 1$, simply by adding a random known vector of weight $(a - 1)w$ on the second n-length block to a (w, w, w) vector, we omit the obvious details of this proof in this short version of the paper.

Suppose the weight of $\mathbf{e_r}$ is aw (with $a > 1$) rather than w, then according to the security reduction, an attacker has to search for a word of the form (w, aw, w). For this case ($w = \mathcal{O}(\sqrt{n}) \ll n$) the best attacks corresponds to the classical ISD approach. When the the weight is regular of the form (w, w, w) the attacker will consider the same number of columns for each block, now for a weight (w, aw, w) the attacker chooses $2n$ columns but will consider more columns where the weight is aw. Let us denote by αn ($0 \le \alpha \le 1$) the number of columns for the first and third block and $(2 - 2\alpha)n$ (with $2 - 2\alpha \ge 0$) the number of columns for the second block. The asymptotic probability P that the attacker finds the error columns is hence:

$$P = (\alpha)^w \cdot (2 - 2\alpha)^{aw} \cdot (\alpha)^w.$$

For $a = 1$ with the conditions $0 \le \alpha \le 1$ and $2 - 2\alpha \ge 0$, we obtain that P is maximal for $\alpha = 2/3$ and we recover the complexity in $2^{1.75w}$, now when a increases this probability decreases and for $a = 2$ computations show that the

Table 2. Optimized parameter sets for Ouroboros in Hamming metric

Instance	Ouroboros optimized parameters					
	n	w	w_e	Threshold	Security	DFR
Low-I	4,813	41	123	27	80	$2.23 \cdot 10^{-5}$
Low-II	5,003	41	123	27	80	$2.60 \cdot 10^{-6}$
Medium-I	10,301	67	201	42	128	$1.01 \cdot 10^{-4}$
Medium-II	10,837	67	201	42	128	$<10^{-7}$
Strong-I	32,771	131	393	77	256	$<10^{-4}$
Strong-II	33,997	131	393	77	256	$<10^{-7}$

maximum P induces a complexity in 2^{2w}, hence considering the case $a = 2.1w$ and $w(\epsilon) = 0.9w$ permits to obtain $w_e \simeq 3w$ for the BitFlip algorithm, and permits to obtain that the best attacks of the system are obtained for decoding $2w$ errors for a $[2n, n]$ quasi-cyclic code. This permits to obtain better parameters (about 20% better in terms of size of public key) and which are presented in Table 2. These parameters are very similar to the parameters proposed for MDPC-McEliece.

6 Conclusion

In this paper we introduced Ouroboros: an efficient, secure and conceptually simple key exchange protocol based on coding theory. This new protocol benefits from the security proof of the HQC and RQC family based on the Alekhnovich approach, and have an IND-CPA security reduction to decoding random quasi-cyclic codes, moreover because of its inherent double circulant structure it also benefits from the simple MDPC structure and the simple BitFlip decoding algorithm, for almost the same type of parameters as MDPC codes but with better parameters than for the HQC protocol (about 40% better for the same DFR).

While the approach is presented only for the Hamming metrics, it is possible to implement a rank metric analog: Ouroboros-R. The resulting protocol also yields better parameters (about 20% better) in comparison to the RQC approach and also to benefits from the simple decoding algorithm of LRPC codes. The price to pay is a probabilistic decoding, which makes this approach especially well suited for Key Exchange. Ouroboros-R will be described into more details in an extended version of this work.

The Ouroboros protocol leads to somewhat higher public key parameters than the recent lattice-based key exchange NewHope protocol [3] but Ouroboros-R has the potential to give better parameters than the NEWHOPE protocol.

References

1. Aguilar Melchor, C., Blazy, O., Deneuville, J.C., Gaborit, P., Zémor, G.: Efficient encryption from random quasi-cyclic codes. CoRR abs/1612.05572 (2016). http://arxiv.org/abs/1612.05572. 19, 20, 21, 22, 23, 26, 28

2. Alekhnovich, M.: More on average case vs approximation complexity. In: Proceedings of 44th Symposium on Foundations of Computer Science (FOCS 2003), 11–14 October 2003, Cambridge, MA, USA, pp. 298–307 (2003). http://www.cs.toronto.edu/~toni/Courses/PCP/handouts/misha.pdf. 19, 23
3. Alkim, E., Ducas, L., Pöppelmann, T., Schwabe, P.: Post-quantum key exchange - a new hope. In: Holz, T., Savage, S. (eds.) 25th USENIX Security Symposium, USENIX Security 2016, Austin, TX, USA, 10–12 August 2016, pp. 327–343. USENIX Association (2016). https://www.usenix.org/system/files/conference/usenixsecurity16/sec16_paper_alkim.pdf. 27, 32
4. Applebaum, B., Ishai, Y., Kushilevitz, E.: Cryptography with constant input locality. In: Menezes, A. (ed.) CRYPTO 2007. LNCS, vol. 4622, pp. 92–110. Springer, Heidelberg (2007). doi:10.1007/978-3-540-74143-5_6. http://www.eng.tau.ac.il/~bennyap/pubs/input-locality-full-revised-1.pdf. 23
5. Berlekamp, E.R., McEliece, R.J., van Tilborg, H.C.: On the inherent intractability of certain coding problems. IEEE Trans. Inf. Theory 24(3), 384–386 (1978). http://authors.library.caltech.edu/5607/1/BERieeetit78.pdf. 22
6. Bernstein, D.J.: Grover vs. McEliece. In: Sendrier, N. (ed.) PQCrypto 2010. LNCS, vol. 6061, pp. 73–80. Springer, Heidelberg (2010). doi:10.1007/978-3-642-12929-2_6. https://cr.yp.to/codes/grovercode-20091123.pdf. 30
7. Bos, J.W., Costello, C., Naehrig, M., Stebila, D.: Post-quantum key exchange for the TLS protocol from the ring learning with errors problem. In: 2015 IEEE Symposium on Security and Privacy, pp. 553–570. IEEE Computer Society Press May (2015). http://eprints.qut.edu.au/86651/1/main.pdf. 27
8. Canto Torres, R., Sendrier, N.: Analysis of information set decoding for a sub-linear error weight. In: Takagi, T. (ed.) PQCrypto 2016. LNCS, vol. 9606, pp. 144–161. Springer, Cham (2016). doi:10.1007/978-3-319-29360-8_10. 30
9. Chaulet, J., Sendrier, N.: Worst case QC-MDPC decoder for McEliece cryptosystem. In: 2016 IEEE International Symposium on Information Theory (ISIT), pp. 1366–1370. IEEE (2016). https://arxiv.org/pdf/1608.06080.pdf. 24, 30
10. Ding, J.: New cryptographic constructions using generalized learning with errors problem. Cryptology ePrint Archive, Report 2012/387 (2012). http://eprint.iacr.org/2012/387.pdf. 27
11. Ding, J., Xie, X., Lin, X.: A simple provably secure key exchange scheme based on the learning with errors problem. Cryptology ePrint Archive, Report 2012/688 (2012). http://eprint.iacr.org/2012/688. 27
12. Gaborit, P.: Shorter keys for code based cryptography. In: Proceedings of the 2005 International Workshop on Coding and Cryptography (WCC 2005), pp. 81–91 (2005). http://www.unilim.fr/pages_perso/philippe.gaborit/shortIC.ps. 19
13. Hauteville, A., Tillich, J.P.: New algorithms for decoding in the rank metric and an attack on the LRPC cryptosystem. In: 2015 IEEE International Symposium on Information Theory (ISIT), pp. 2747–2751. IEEE (2015). https://arxiv.org/pdf/1504.05431.pdf. 23
14. Herranz, J., Hofheinz, D., Kiltz, E.: KEM/DEM: necessary and sufficient conditions for secure hybrid encryption. Cryptology ePrint Archive, Report 2006/265 (2006). http://eprint.iacr.org/2006/265.pdf. 27, 28
15. Misoczki, R., Tillich, J.P., Sendrier, N., Barreto, P.S.: MDPC-McEliece: new McEliece variants from moderate density parity-check codes. In: 2013 IEEE International Symposium on Information Theory Proceedings, pp. 2069–2073. IEEE (2013). https://eprint.iacr.org/2012/409.pdf. 19, 21, 24, 30

16. National Institute of Standards and Technology: Submission requirements and evaluation criteria for the post-quantum cryptography standardization process (call for proposal), December 2016. http://csrc.nist.gov/groups/ST/post-quantum-crypto/documents/call-for-proposals-final-dec-2016.pdf. 27

17. Peikert, C.: Lattice cryptography for the internet. In: Mosca, M. (ed.) PQCrypto 2014. LNCS, vol. 8772, pp. 197–219. Springer, Cham (2014). doi:10.1007/978-3-319-11659-4_12. http://web.eecs.umich.edu/~cpeikert/pubs/suite.pdf. 27

18. Sendrier, N.: Encoding information into constant weight words. In: International Symposium on Information Theory Proceedings ISIT 2005, pp. 435–438. IEEE (2005). http://ieeexplore.ieee.org/stamp/stamp.jsp?arnumber=1523371. 25

19. Sendrier, N.: Decoding one out of many. In: Yang, B.-Y. (ed.) PQCrypto 2011. LNCS, vol. 7071, pp. 51–67. Springer, Heidelberg (2011). doi:10.1007/978-3-642-25405-5_4. https://eprint.iacr.org/2011/367.pdf. 23, 30

CCA2 Key-Privacy for Code-Based Encryption in the Standard Model

Yusuke Yoshida$^{(\boxtimes)}$, Kirill Morozov, and Keisuke Tanaka

Tokyo Institute of Technology, Tokyo, Japan
yoshida.y.aw@m.titech.ac.jp

Abstract. The code-based public-key encryption schemes by McEliece and Niederreiter are famous candidates for the post-quantum world. In this work, we study key-privacy (or anonymity) for these schemes in the standard model. Specifically, we show that the following two paradigms for constructing IND-CCA2 encryption yield IK-CCA2 encryption, if the underlying primitive satisfies IK-CPA under k-repetition: (1) The Rosen-Segev construction (TCC 2009), we instantiate it with the Niederreiter scheme; (2) The Döttling et al. construction (IEEE Transactions on Information Theory 2012), we instantiate it with both the McEliece scheme and the Niederreiter scheme. As far as we know, these instantiations give the first IK-CCA2 code-based schemes in the standard model. In our proofs, we rely on an important observation by Yamakawa et al. (AAECC 2007) that the randomized McEliece encryption is IK-CPA in the standard model. As a side result, we show that the randomized Niederreiter encryption is IK-CPA as well.

Keywords: Code-based encryption · CCA2 · Key-privacy · Anonymity · Standard model

1 Introduction

Anonymity. In addition to data-privacy, key-privacy has also been studied for public-key encryption (PKE) schemes. Bellare et al. [1] first defined the notion of key-privacy or anonymity for PKE: Indistinguishability of keys (IK). Informally speaking, IK is to key-privacy what indistinguishability (IND) is to data-privacy. As with data-privacy, IK is defined against several attack scenarios such as chosen plaintext attack (CPA) and adaptive chosen ciphertext attack (CCA2). In situations when anonymity matters, both IND and IK should be examined separately, because one does not imply the other [9].

Code-Based Encryption. Security of the code-based encryption schemes by McEliece [12] and by Niederreiter [13] is guaranteed based on hardness of problems in coding theory. In this paper, we will occasionally refer to these schemes,

Y. Yoshida, K. Morozov and K. Tanaka—Supported in part by IOHK, I-System, NRI, NTT, JST CREST JPMJCR14D6, JST OPERA, and JSPS KAKENHI 17H01695, 16H01705, 15K00186.

T. Lange and T. Takagi (Eds.): PQCrypto 2017, LNCS 10346, pp. 35–50, 2017.
DOI: 10.1007/978-3-319-59879-6_3

respectively, as "McEliece" and "Niederreiter" for short. Unlike PKE schemes based on the number-theoretic assumptions such as RSA and ElGamal, the code-based encryption is believed to be secure even against quantum crypt-analysis. Therefore, the code-based encryption schemes are candidates for the post-quantum world. We note that the original McEliece and Niederreiter constructions only achieve one-wayness, but not IND-CPA.

Previous Work. In order to enhance security of the code-based encryption schemes, several conversions have been proposed. Kobara and Imai [11] studied existing generic conversions, and proposed tailored ones for the McEliece encryption. The resulting variants of the McEliece encryption satisfy IND-CCA2 security, however they are in the random oracle model. Without assuming the random oracles, Nojima et al. [14] proposed the randomized McEliece and the randomized Niederreiter encryption schemes, where the plaintext is padded with randomness, and proved their IND-CPA security.

Yamakawa et al. [17] first investigated key-privacy for the code-based encryption. They proved that the randomized McEliece satisfies IK-CPA. They also mentioned that the conversion by Kobara and Imai yields IK-CCA2 security in the random oracle model. Persichetti [15] proposed a variant of Niederreiter assuming the random oracles, and proved its IND-CCA2 and IK-CCA2 security. To our best knowledge, the IK-CCA2 code-based encryption in the standard model has not been constructed, so far.

Rosen and Segev [16] proposed k-wise products using the k-repetition paradigm for constructing IND-CCA2 PKE in the standard model. Döttling et al. [4] combined the k-wise products with the Dolev-Dwork-Naor construction [3] and applied them to the McEliece scheme in order to obtain the IND-CCA2 code-based encryption in the standard model.

Our Contribution. In this work, we first show that the randomized Niederreiter achieves IK-CPA. Then, applying the Rosen-Segev construction [16] to the Niederreiter, we gain a one-bit encryption scheme, which achieves IK-CCA2 in the standard model. In addition, applying the Döttling et al. construction [4], we gain a multi-bit encryption scheme, which also achieves IK-CCA2 in the standard model. We note that its instantiation with the McEliece scheme also achieves the IK-CCA2 security in the same manner. As far as we know, the above are the first IK-CCA2 code-based schemes in the standard model.

In Sect. 2, we review PKE, its security notions, the Niederreiter function, and related problems and assumptions. The k-repetition paradigm is introduced in Sect. 3, then we prove its key-privacy under certain assumptions in Sect. 4. In Sect. 5, we instantiate the k-repetition paradigm with Niederreiter and prove its security. An instantiation with McEliece is considered in Sect. 6.

2   Preliminaries

We start with the definitions of PKE, and then continue to the security notions for data-privacy and key-privacy.

Definition 1 (PKE). *A PKE scheme consists of a triplet of PPT algorithms* PKE = (Gen, Enc, Dec). *The key generation algorithm* Gen *takes a security parameter* 1^λ *as input, outputs a pair of public and secret keys* (pk, sk). *The encryption algorithm* Enc *takes a public-key pk and a plaintext m as input, computes a ciphertext c. The decryption algorithm* Dec *takes a secret-key sk and a ciphertext c as input, then outputs a plaintext m. We require that for any* (pk, sk) *and* m, Dec$(sk,$ Enc$(pk, m)) = m$ *holds.*

IND-CPA is one of the most natural security requirements for PKE. Intuitively, PKE is IND-CPA if a ciphertext does not leak any information on the plaintext. IND-CCA2 is a stronger notion – and a de facto standard – for PKE, which requires that even if the adversary has access to the decryption oracle, a ciphertext does not leak any information on the plaintext.

Definition 2 (IND-CPA/CCA2). *Let* PKE = (Gen, Enc, Dec) *be a public-key encryption scheme. In the IND-CPA scenario, we consider the following experiment.*

$\text{Expt}_{\text{PKE},\mathcal{A}}^{\text{IND-CPA}}(\lambda)$
$(pk, sk) \leftarrow \text{Gen}(1^\lambda)$
$(m^0, m^1, state) \leftarrow \mathcal{A}_1(pk)$
$b \leftarrow \{0, 1\}$
$c^* \leftarrow \text{Enc}(pk, m^b)$
$b' \leftarrow \mathcal{A}_2(c^*, state)$

The advantage of the adversary is defined as

$$\text{Adv}_{\text{PKE},\mathcal{A}}^{\text{IND-CPA}}(\lambda) = \left| \Pr[b = b'] - \frac{1}{2} \right|.$$

We say that PKE *is IND-CPA secure if* $\text{Adv}_{\text{PKE},\mathcal{A}}^{\text{IND-CPA}}$ *is negligible.*

The IND-CCA2 scenario is almost the same as that of IND-CPA, except that the adversary is allowed to query $c \, (\neq c^*)$ *to the decryption oracle* Dec$(sk, \cdot)$.

Key-privacy notions IK-CPA and IK-CCA2 are introduced by Bellare et al. [1]. Intuitively, if a PKE is secure in the sense of key-privacy, the adversary cannot obtain any information about who is the receiver of a given ciphertext (i.e., no information on whose public key was used for encryption).

Definition 3 (IK-CPA/CCA2). *Let* PKE = (Gen, Enc, Dec) *be a public-key encryption scheme. In the IK-CPA scenario, we consider the following experiment.*

$\text{Expt}_{\text{PKE},\mathcal{A}}^{\text{IK-CPA}}(\lambda)$
$(pk^0, sk^0), (pk^1, sk^1) \leftarrow \text{Gen}(1^\lambda)$
$(m, state) \leftarrow \mathcal{A}_1(pk^0, pk^1)$
$b \leftarrow \{0, 1\}$
$c^* \leftarrow \text{Enc}(pk^b, m)$
$b' \leftarrow \mathcal{A}_2(c^*, state)$

The advantage of the adversary is defined as

$$\mathsf{Adv}_{\mathsf{PKE},\mathcal{A}}^{\mathrm{IK\text{-}CPA}}(\lambda) = \left| \Pr[b = b'] - \frac{1}{2} \right|.$$

We say that PKE *is IK-CPA secure, if* $\mathsf{Adv}_{\mathsf{PKE},\mathcal{A}}^{\mathrm{IK\text{-}CPA}}(\lambda)$ *is negligible.*

The IK-CCA2 scenario is almost the same as that of IK-CPA, except that the adversary is allowed to query $c\ (\neq c^*)$ *to the decryption oracles:* $\mathsf{Dec}(sk^0, \cdot)$ *and* $\mathsf{Dec}(sk^1, \cdot)$.

Next, we review (one-time) signatures, which will be used in the constructions of IND-CCA2 encryption.

Definition 4 (Signature). *A signature scheme consists of the following triplet of PPT algorithms* $\mathsf{SS} = (\mathsf{SGen}, \mathsf{Sign}, \mathsf{Verify})$. *The key generation algorithm* SGen *takes a security parameter* 1^λ *as input, outputs a pair of verification and signing key* (vk, dsk). *The signing algorithm* Sign *takes a signing-key dsk and a message m as input, and then computes a signature* σ. *The verification algorithm* Verify *takes a verification-key vk, a message m, and a signature* σ *as input, then verifies whether* σ *is a valid signature of m. If valid, output 1, otherwise 0. We require that for any* (vk, dsk) *and* m, $\mathsf{Verify}(vk, m, \mathsf{Sign}(dsk, m)) = 1$ *holds.*

One-time strong existentially unforgeable under chosen message attack (OT-sEUF-CMA) is a security notion for signatures.

Definition 5 (OT-sEUF-CMA). *Let* $\mathsf{SS} = (\mathsf{SGen}, \mathsf{Sign}, \mathsf{Verify})$ *be a signature scheme. Consider the following experiment.*

$\mathsf{Expt}_{\mathsf{SS},\mathcal{A}}^{\mathrm{OT\text{-}sEUF\text{-}CMA}}(\lambda)$
$(vk, dsk) \leftarrow \mathsf{SGen}(1^\lambda)$
$(m, state) \leftarrow \mathcal{A}_1(vk)$
$\sigma \leftarrow \mathsf{Sign}(dsk, m)$
$(\hat{m}, \hat{\sigma}) \leftarrow \mathcal{A}_2(\sigma, state)$

Let **Forge** *be the event in which* $\mathcal{A}$ *outputs* $(\hat{m}, \hat{\sigma}) \neq (m, \sigma)$ *and* $\mathsf{Verify}(vk, \hat{m}, \hat{\sigma}) = 1$ *holds. The advantage of the adversary is defined by*

$$\mathsf{Adv}_{\mathsf{SS},\mathcal{A}}^{\mathrm{OT\text{-}sEUF\text{-}CMA}}(\lambda) = \Pr[\mathbf{Forge}].$$

SS *is called OT-sEUF-CMA secure if for any PPT algorithm* $\mathcal{A}$, *the advantage* $\mathsf{Adv}_{\mathsf{SS},\mathcal{A}}^{\mathrm{OT\text{-}sEUF\text{-}CMA}}(\lambda)$ *is negligible.*

The signature schemes for the post-quantum world are discussed in [2].

Code-Based Trapdoor Functions and PKE. Trapdoor function family consists of a triplet of PPT algorithms $\mathcal{F} = (\mathsf{G}, \mathsf{F}, \mathsf{F}^{-1})$. G is a generation algorithm, which takes a security parameter 1^λ, samples a function index s and a trapdoor information td corresponding to s. F is an evaluation algorithm, which takes s and x as input, computes $y = \mathsf{F}(s, x)$ deterministically, and outputs y. F^{-1} is an inversion algorithm, which takes td and y, outputs x.

Let $\mathcal{U}_l$ be the uniform distribution over $\{0,1\}^l$, let $\mathcal{U}_{r,c}$ be the uniform distribution over $r \times c$ binary matrices, and let $\mathcal{E}_{n,t}$ be the uniform distribution over binary vectors of length n and the Hamming weight t. Occasionally, we will use the same letters for denoting the respective domains, for simplicity. In the code-based encryption, parameters (n, l, t) are functions of the security parameter 1^λ.

Usually, Niederreiter is described as a (deterministic) PKE scheme. Since we will later apply the k-repetition paradigm to it, we treat Niederreiter as a trapdoor function.

Definition 6 (Niederreiter [13]**).** *The Niederreiter trapdoor function is described as a triple of algorithms* $(\mathsf{G}_{\mathsf{NR}}, \mathsf{F}_{\mathsf{NR}}, \mathsf{F}_{\mathsf{NR}}^{-1})$ *described below.*

The algorithm $\mathsf{G}_{\mathsf{NR}}(\lambda)$ *generates an* $(n - l) \times n$ *parity-check matrix* H' *of the binary irreducible* (n, l) *Goppa code with a decoding algorithm* Correct, *which corrects up to t errors; samples a random* $(n - l) \times (n - l)$ *non-singular matrix* S *and an* $n \times n$ *permutation matrix* P*; and computes the scrambled parity-check matrix* $H = SH'P$. *The algorithm* $\mathsf{G}_{\mathsf{NR}}(\lambda)$ *outputs* $s = (H, t)$ *and* $td = (S, H', P)$.

The domain of the Niederreiter function is binary row vectors of length n, *and the Hamming weight* t. *For an input* $x \in \mathcal{E}_{n,t}$, *the evaluation algorithm* $\mathsf{F}_{\mathsf{NR}}(s, x)$ *computes* $y = Hx^{\mathsf{T}}$, *where* x^{T} *denotes the transpose of* x.

The inversion algorithm $\mathsf{F}_{\mathsf{NR}}^{-1}(td, y)$ *runs* Correct *on input* $S^{-1}y = H'Px^{\mathsf{T}}$. *If* Correct *returns* Px^{T}, *then it multiplies* P^{-1} *to the output of* Correct *and outputs* x. *If* Correct *fails, then it outputs* $\perp$.

We describe problems and assumptions related to the Niederreiter function. First, we introduce the distinguishing Goppa code (DGC) problem. We use a parity-check matrix to represent the Goppa code.

Definition 7 (DGC problem). *A PPT algorithm* $\mathcal{D}$ *receives an* $(n - l) \times n$ *matrix, which is either* H *generated by the* $\mathsf{G}_{\mathsf{NR}}(\lambda)$ *or* R *chosen randomly from* $\mathcal{U}_{n-l,n}$. *The DGC problem is to distinguish, whether the given matrix is* H *or* R.

The advantage of $\mathcal{D}$ on the DGC problem is defined as

$$\mathsf{Adv}_{\mathcal{D}}^{\mathsf{DGC}}(\lambda) = |\Pr[((H, t), td) \leftarrow \mathsf{G}_{\mathsf{NR}}(1^\lambda) : \mathcal{D}(H, t) = 1]$$
$$- \Pr[R \leftarrow \mathcal{U}_{n-l,n} : \mathcal{D}(R, t) = 1]|.$$

If an irreducible binary Goppa code with low enough rate $\frac{k}{n}$ (see [5]) is used, it is believed that for any PPT algorithm $\mathcal{D}$, $\mathsf{Adv}_{\mathcal{D}}^{\mathsf{DGC}}(\lambda)$ is negligible.

It is well-known that the generator matrices can be easily computed from the parity-check matrices. Thus, the above problem can be easily re-formulated for the case of generator matrices, which are used in the McEliece encryption discussed in Sect. 6. For simplicity, we will use the above problem in Sect. 6, when referring to hardness of distinguishing Goppa codes.

Next, we introduce the syndrome decoding (SD) problem.

Definition 8 (SD problem). *The PPT algorithm* $\mathcal{A}$ *receives a random parity-check matrix and a syndrome, the problem is to find the corresponding error vector.*

The advantage of $\mathcal{A}$ on the SD problem is defined as

$$\mathsf{Adv}_{\mathcal{A}}^{\mathsf{SD}}(\lambda) = \Pr[R \leftarrow \mathcal{U}_{n-l,n}, x \leftarrow \mathcal{E}_{n,t} : \mathcal{A}(R, Rx^{\mathrm{T}}) = x].$$

The SD problem is believed to be hard. In other words, for any $\mathcal{A}$, $\mathsf{Adv}_{\mathcal{A}}^{\mathsf{SD}}(\lambda)$ is negligible.

The Niederreiter function has a useful property: Pseudorandomness. If the input x is sampled from the uniform distribution over $\mathcal{E}_{n,t}$, it is hard to distinguish the output y from a random vector u.

We say that the Niederreiter function is pseudorandom if,

$$\mathsf{Adv}_{\mathcal{D},R}^{\mathrm{pr}}(\lambda) = |\Pr[x \leftarrow \mathcal{E}_{n,t}, y = Rx^{\mathrm{T}} : \mathcal{D}(R,y) = 1] - \Pr[u \leftarrow \mathcal{U}_{n-l} : \mathcal{D}(R,u) = 1]|$$

is negligible for any PPT algorithm $\mathcal{D}$.

Lemma 1 [6]. *If the SD problem is hard, the Niederreiter function is pseudorandom.*

Nojima et al. [14] proposed IND-CPA code-based PKE schemes called the randomized McEliece encryption and the randomized Niederreiter encryption, where random padding is added to the plaintext. Specifically, the randomized Niederreiter encryption is a tuple of algorithms $\mathsf{PKE}_{\mathsf{RNR}} = (\mathsf{Gen}_{\mathsf{RNR}}, \mathsf{Enc}_{\mathsf{RNR}}, \mathsf{Dec}_{\mathsf{RNR}})$, where each algorithm works as described next. We denote concatenation of vectors by '$||$'.

$\mathsf{Gen}_{\mathsf{RNR}}(1^\lambda)$: Set $pk = s$, and $sk = td$, where $(s, td) \leftarrow \mathsf{G}_{\mathsf{NR}}(1^\lambda)$, then return (pk, sk).

$\mathsf{Enc}_{\mathsf{RNR}}(pk, m)$: The plaintext m has length n_m and weight t_m. Sample $r \in \mathcal{E}_{n_r, t_r}$ randomly, where $n_m + n_r = n$, $t_m + t_r = t$. Output the ciphertext $c = \mathsf{F}_{\mathsf{NR}}(r||m)$.

$\mathsf{Dec}_{\mathsf{RNR}}(sk, c)$: Compute $r||m = \mathsf{F}_{\mathsf{NR}}^{-1}(c)$. If $\mathsf{F}_{\mathsf{NR}}^{-1}$ fails, return $\perp$. Otherwise return m.

Theorem 1 [14]. *Assuming hardness of the DGC and the SD problems, $\mathsf{PKE}_{\mathsf{RNR}}$ is IND-CPA.*

3 k-Repetition Paradigm

Rosen and Segev [16] proposed k-wise products, which evaluate k functions on the same input. Let $\mathcal{F} = (\mathsf{G}, \mathsf{F})$ be a function family. For an integer k, k-wise products $\mathcal{F}_k = (\mathsf{G}_k, \mathsf{F}_k)$ are defined as follows.

$\mathsf{G}_k(1^\lambda)$: Invoke $\mathsf{G}(1^\lambda)$ k times to obtain s_i $(i = 1, ..., k)$ and then output $\mathbf{s} = (s_1, ..., s_k)$.

$\mathsf{F}_k(\mathbf{s}, x)$: Evaluate x with each s_i, the output is $\mathbf{y} = (y_1, ..., y_k) = (\mathsf{F}(s_1, x), ..., \mathsf{F}(s_k, x))$.

Assuming one-way trapdoor k-wise products, Rosen and Segev [16] constructed an IND-CCA2 PKE for 1-bit message using the hardcore predicates $h(\cdot)$. Before describing the IND-CCA2 scheme, we describe an IND-CPA PKE scheme for 1-bit message.

The 1-bit IND-CPA scheme $\mathsf{PKE}_{1\mathrm{cpa}} = (\mathsf{Gen}_{1\mathrm{cpa}}, \mathsf{Enc}_{1\mathrm{cpa}}, \mathsf{Dec}_{1\mathrm{cpa}})$ consists of the following algorithms.

$\mathsf{Gen}_{1\mathrm{cpa}}(1^\lambda)$: Call $\mathsf{G}_k(1^\lambda)$ to obtain $pk = \mathbf{s} = (s_1, ..., s_k)$ and $sk = (td_1, ..., td_k)$ then return (pk, sk).

$\mathsf{Enc}_{1\mathrm{cpa}}(pk, m)$: Take a plaintext m and the public key pk. Evaluating F_k on randomly chosen x, get $\mathbf{y} = \mathsf{F}_k(\mathbf{s}, x)$. Mask the plaintext with the hardcore predicate $h(\cdot)$; $c_0 = m \oplus h(\mathbf{s}, x)$. Set a ciphertext $c = (\mathbf{y}, c_0)$ and output it.

$\mathsf{Dec}_{1\mathrm{cpa}}(sk, c)$: On an input $c = ((y_1, ..., y_k), c_0)$, for all $i \in \{1, ..., k\}$, compute $x_i = \mathsf{F}^{-1}(td_i, y_i)$. If all x_i are the same, return $m = c_0 \oplus h(\mathbf{s}, x)$. Otherwise return $\bot$.

This scheme is an application of the Goldreich-Levin theorem [8] for the k-wise products. If F_k is one-way, the hardcore predicate yields IND-CPA security of this scheme.

Using twice as many keys as in the IND-CPA scheme and employing a one-time signature $\mathsf{SS} = (\mathsf{SGen}, \mathsf{Sign}, \mathsf{Verify})$, the IND-CCA2 scheme is described as follows.

Rosen and Segev [16] proposed the following 1-bit IND-CCA2 scheme denoted as $\mathsf{PKE}_{1\mathrm{cca2}} = (\mathsf{Gen}_{1\mathrm{cca2}}, \mathsf{Enc}_{1\mathrm{cca2}}, \mathsf{Dec}_{1\mathrm{cca2}})$.

$\mathsf{Gen}_{1\mathrm{cca2}}(1^\lambda)$: Call $\mathsf{G}_k(1^\lambda)$ twice to obtain $pk' = (s_{1,0}, ..., s_{k,0}, s_{1,1}, ..., s_{k,1})$, $sk' = (td_{1,0}, ..., td_{k,0}, td_{1,1}, ..., td_{k,1})$ and return (pk', sk').

$\mathsf{Enc}_{1\mathrm{cca2}}(pk', m)$: Generate a verification and signing-key pair (vk, dsk), where vk is represented as a k-bit string $(vk_1, ..., vk_k) \in \{0,1\}^k$.
Evaluating on a random input x according to vk, compute $\mathbf{y} = \mathsf{F}_k(\mathbf{s}_{vk}, x)$, where $\mathbf{s}_{vk} = (s_{1,vk_1}, ..., s_{k,vk_k})$.
Mask the plaintext m with the hardcore predicate: $c_0 = m \oplus h(\mathbf{s}_{vk}, x)$.
Compute a signature $\sigma \leftarrow \mathsf{Sign}(dsk, (\mathbf{y}, c_0))$.
Return a ciphertext $c' = (vk, \mathbf{y}, c_0, \sigma)$.

$\mathsf{Dec}_{1\mathrm{cca2}}(sk', c')$: On an input $c' = (vk, y_1, ..., y_k, c_0, \sigma)$, if we have that $\mathsf{Verify}(vk, (y_1, ..., y_k, c_0), \sigma) = 0$, return $\bot$. For all $i \in \{1, ..., k\}$, $x_i = \mathsf{F}^{-1}(td_{i,vk_i}, y_i)$.
If all x_i are the same, return $m = c_0 \oplus h(\mathbf{s}_{vk}, x)$, otherwise return $\bot$.

In this scheme, $\mathbf{y}$ is computed according to vk. However, if the length vk is too long, one can compute along its hash value $h(vk)$ instead of vk itself [16], where $h(\cdot)$ is a universal one-way hash function.

The following theorem guarantees the security of this scheme.

Theorem 2 [16]. *$\mathsf{PKE}_{1\mathrm{cca2}}$ is IND-CCA2, if F_k is one-way and SS satisfies OT-sEUF-CMA security.*

We consider an IND-CCA2 secure PKE scheme for multi-bit messages, which is a special case of the PKE proposed by Döttling et al. [4]. Note that for simplicity, the description below is slightly different from the original scheme by Döttling et al., as we use only deterministic functions in k-repetition. Before introducing the IND-CCA2 scheme, we describe an IND-CPA secure PKE for multi-bit messages.

We describe the IND-CPA scheme $\mathsf{PKE}_{\mathrm{cpa}} = (\mathsf{Gen}_{\mathrm{cpa}}, \mathsf{Enc}_{\mathrm{cpa}}, \mathsf{Dec}_{\mathrm{cpa}})$. Each algorithm works as follows.

$\mathsf{Gen}_{\mathrm{cpa}}(1^\lambda)$: Call $G_k(1^\lambda)$ to obtain $pk = \mathbf{s} = (s_1, ..., s_k)$ and $sk = (td_1, ..., td_k)$ then return (pk, sk).

$\mathsf{Enc}_{\mathrm{cpa}}(pk, m)$: Take a plaintext m and a public-key pk, padding m with randomly chosen r. Evaluating F_k on the padded plaintext, $\mathbf{y} = \mathsf{F}_k(\mathbf{s}, (m\|r))$ is obtained. Output a ciphertext $c = \mathbf{y}$.

$\mathsf{Dec}_{\mathrm{cpa}}(sk, c)$: On an input $c = (y_1, ..., y_k)$, $\forall i \in \{1, ..., k\}$, compute $(m\|r)_i = \mathsf{F}^{-1}(td_i, y_i)$. If all $(m\|r)_i$ are the same, return m. Otherwise return $\bot$.

Note that IND-CPA security of this scheme is not guaranteed in general. We must instantiate it with some concrete primitives and prove its security.

We obtain the IND-CCA2 scheme by using the same transformation as for the 1-bit scheme.

We describe the IND-CCA2 scheme $\mathsf{PKE}_{\mathrm{cca2}} = (\mathsf{Gen}_{\mathrm{cca2}}, \mathsf{Enc}_{\mathrm{cca2}}, \mathsf{Dec}_{\mathrm{cca2}})$.

$\mathsf{Gen}_{\mathrm{cca2}}(1^\lambda)$: Call $G_k(1^\lambda)$ twice to obtain $pk' = (s_{1,0}, ..., s_{k,0}, s_{1,1}, ..., s_{k,1})$, $sk' = (td_{1,0}, ..., td_{k,0}, td_{1,1}, ..., td_{k,1})$ and return (pk', sk').

$\mathsf{Enc}_{\mathrm{cca2}}(pk', m)$: Generate a verification and signing-key pair (vk, dsk), where vk is represented as a k-bit string $(vk_1, ..., vk_k) \in \{0, 1\}^k$.
Evaluate the plaintext m with a random pad r along vk;
compute $\mathbf{y} = \mathsf{F}_k(\mathbf{s}_{vk}, (m\|r))$, where $\mathbf{s}_{vk} = (s_{1,vk_1}, ..., s_{k,vk_k})$.
Compute a signature $\sigma \leftarrow \mathsf{Sign}(dsk, \mathbf{y})$.
Return a ciphertext $c' = (vk, \mathbf{y}, \sigma)$.

$\mathsf{Dec}_{\mathrm{cca2}}(sk', c')$: On an input $c' = (vk, y_1, ..., y_k, \sigma)$, if $\mathsf{Verify}(vk, (y_1, ..., y_k), \sigma) = 0$, then return $\bot$. For all $i \in \{1, ..., k\}$, $(m\|r)_i = \mathsf{F}^{-1}(td_{i,vk_i}, y_i)$. If all $(m\|r)_i$ are the same, return m. Otherwise return $\bot$.

Security of this scheme is guaranteed by the following theorem.

Theorem 3 [4]. $\mathsf{PKE}_{\mathrm{cca2}}$ is IND-CCA2, if $\mathsf{PKE}_{\mathrm{cpa}}$ is IND-CPA and SS satisfies OT-sEUF-CMA security.

4   Key-Privacy of the k-Repetition Paradigm

In this section, we show the key-privacy relation between PKE_{cpa} and PKE_{cca2}. We omit PKE_{1cpa} and PKE_{1cca2}, because they are essentially the same as the multi-bit construction.

Theorem 4. $\mathsf{PKE}_{\mathrm{cca2}}$ is IK-CCA2, if $\mathsf{PKE}_{\mathrm{cpa}}$ is IK-CPA and SS satisfies OT-sEUF-CMA security.

Proof. This proof proceeds in a similar way to that of Theorem 3. We construct a reduction algorithm $\mathcal{B}$, which attacks the IK-CPA security of PKE_{cpa}, using an adversary $\mathcal{A}$, which attacks the IK-CCA2 security of PKE_{cca2}. $\mathcal{B}$ works as follows.

Set Public-Keys. In $\mathsf{Expt}^{IK\text{-}CPA}_{\mathsf{PKE}_{cpa},\mathcal{B}}(\lambda)$, $\mathcal{B}$ receives two public-keys $pk^0 = (s^0_1, ..., s^0_k)$ and $pk^1 = (s^1_1, ..., s^1_k)$. To simulate $\mathsf{Expt}^{IK\text{-}CCA2}_{\mathsf{PKE}_{cca2},\mathcal{A}}(\lambda)$, $\mathcal{B}$ sets two public-keys of PKE_{cca2}: $pk'^0 = (s^0_{1,0}, ..., s^0_{k,0}, s^0_{1,1}, ..., s^0_{k,1})$ and $pk'^1 = (s^1_{1,0}, ..., s^1_{k,0}, s^1_{1,1}, ..., s^1_{k,1})$ as follows: $\mathcal{B}$ invokes generation algorithm of the signature scheme SGen and gets the pair (vk^*, dsk^*). Along vk^*, $\mathcal{B}$ sets $s^0_{i,vk^*_i} = s^0_i$ and $s^1_{i,vk^*_i} = s^1_i$ for all $i \in \{1, ..., k\}$. The remaining part of pk'^0 and pk'^1 are generated in $\mathcal{B}$; for all $i \in \{1, ..., k\}$, $(s^0_{i,1-vk^*_i}, td^0_{i,1-vk^*_i}) \leftarrow \mathsf{G}(1^\lambda)$, $(s^1_{i,1-vk^*_i}, td^1_{i,1-vk^*_i}) \leftarrow \mathsf{G}(1^\lambda)$.

Now, $\mathcal{B}$ has the trapdoor information related to $s^0_{i,1-vk^*_i}$ and $s^1_{i,1-vk^*_i}$. From $\mathcal{A}$'s point of view, pk'^0 and pk'^1 provided by $\mathcal{B}$ are identically distributed with respect to $\mathsf{Expt}^{IK\text{-}CCA2}_{\mathsf{PKE}_{cca2},\mathcal{A}}(\lambda)$.

Generate Challenge Ciphertext. $\mathcal{A}$ will return a plaintext m. $\mathcal{B}$ outputs this plaintext in $\mathsf{Expt}^{IK\text{-}CPA}_{\mathsf{PKE}_{cpa},\mathcal{B}}(\lambda)$. $\mathcal{B}$ receives a ciphertext of m: $c^* = \mathbf{y}$, encrypted using public-key pk^b where $b = 0$ or 1. $\mathcal{B}$ makes a signature σ^* of c^*, using dsk^*, and sends $c'^* = (vk^*, c^*, \sigma^*)$ to $\mathcal{A}$ in $\mathsf{Expt}^{IK\text{-}CCA2}_{\mathsf{PKE}_{cca2},\mathcal{A}}(\lambda)$. This ciphertext is also identically distributed with respect to $\mathsf{Expt}^{IK\text{-}CCA2}_{\mathsf{PKE}_{cca2},\mathcal{A}}(\lambda)$.

Simulate the Decryption Oracles. Since $\mathcal{A}$ is allowed to access the decryption oracles $\mathsf{Dec}_{cca2}(sk'^0, \cdot)$ and $\mathsf{Dec}_{cca2}(sk'^1, \cdot)$, $\mathcal{B}$ must simulate these oracles. The keys sk'^0 and sk'^1 should be secret keys corresponding to pk'^0 and pk'^1, respectively. However, $\mathcal{B}$ has only half of the secret keys. For all i, $\mathcal{B}$ does not know s^0_{i,vk^*_i} and s^1_{i,vk^*_i}, but $s^0_{i,1-vk^*_i}$ and $s^1_{i,1-vk^*_i}$ are generated by $\mathcal{B}$.

We denote by **Forge** the event, in which $\mathcal{A}$ submits a query $c' = (vk, c, \sigma)$ to one of the decryption oracles, such that $vk = vk^*$, and $\mathsf{Verify}(vk, c, \sigma) = 1$. The value vk^* is the verification key used when the challenge ciphertext $c'^* = (vk^*, \mathbf{y}^*, \sigma^*)$ is generated. If **Forge** occurs, the oracle simulation returns $\perp$. Otherwise, the oracle simulation acts as follows.

On a decryption query $c' = (vk, c, \sigma)$ to $\mathsf{Dec}_{cca2}(sk'^0, \cdot)$, if $\mathsf{Verify}(vk, c, \sigma) = 0$, it outputs $\perp$. If $\mathsf{Verify}(vk, c, \sigma) = 1$, since we assume that **Forge** does not occur, $vk \neq vk^*$ holds. Therefore, for some index i, $vk^*_i \neq vk_i = 1 - vk^*_i$ holds, so that $\mathcal{B}$ computes $m||r = \mathsf{F}^{-1}(s^0_{i,1-vk^*_i}, y_i)$, and if F^{-1} outputs $\perp$, it returns $\perp$. It confirms that all y_i, $(i = 1, ..., k)$ have $m||r$ as preimage and returns m. Otherwise, it returns $\perp$. The case of query to $\mathsf{Dec}_{cca2}(sk'^1, \cdot)$ is the same as $\mathsf{Dec}_{cca2}(sk'^0, \cdot)$ except that sk'^1 is used.

Finally, $\mathcal{A}$ outputs a guess b', and $\mathcal{B}$ returns this b'. Unless **Forge** occurs, $\mathcal{B}$ simulates the decryption oracles successfully. This reduction shows that

$$\Pr[b = b' \text{ in } \mathsf{Expt}^{IK\text{-}CPA}_{\mathsf{PKE}_{cpa},\mathcal{B}}(\lambda)] = \Pr[b = b' \wedge \neg\mathbf{Forge} \text{ in } \mathsf{Expt}^{IK\text{-}CCA2}_{\mathsf{PKE}_{cca2},\mathcal{A}}(\lambda)].$$

We estimate the probability that the bad event **Forge** occurs, and prove the following lemma.

Lemma 2. $\Pr[\mathbf{Forge}]$ *is negligible.*

Proof. OT-sEUF-CMA security of the signature scheme guarantees that the probability $\Pr[\mathbf{Forge}]$ is negligible. An adversary $\mathcal{B}_{\mathrm{sig}}$ is constructed using $\mathcal{A}$ that breaks OT-sEUF-CMA security of the signature scheme. We show that $\mathcal{B}_{\mathrm{sig}}$'s success probability is the probability that **Forge** occurs during the interaction between $\mathcal{A}$ and $\mathcal{B}$.

$\mathcal{B}_{\mathrm{sig}}$ simulates $\mathrm{Expt}_{\mathsf{PKE}_{\mathrm{cca2}},\mathcal{A}}^{\mathrm{IK\text{-}CCA2}}(\lambda)$, interacts with $\mathcal{A}$, and attacks OT-sEUF-CMA security of the underlying signature scheme SS.

Set Public-Keys. In this phase, $\mathcal{B}$ simulates $\mathrm{Expt}_{\mathsf{PKE}_{\mathrm{cca2}},\mathcal{A}}^{\mathrm{IK\text{-}CCA2}}(\lambda)$ and sends pk'^0 and pk'^1 to $\mathcal{A}$.

Generate Challenge Ciphertext. In $\mathrm{Expt}_{\mathsf{SS},\mathcal{B}_{\mathrm{sig}}}^{\mathrm{OT\text{-}sEUF\text{-}CMA}}(\lambda)$, $\mathcal{B}_{\mathrm{sig}}$ receives a verification-key vk^* and it also receives a plaintext m from $\mathcal{A}$. $\mathcal{B}_{\mathrm{sig}}$ flips a coin b, and computes the ciphertext $c'^* = \mathsf{Enc}_{\mathrm{cca2}}(pk'^b, m) = (vk^*, \mathbf{y}, \sigma^*)$. During computation of c'^*, σ^* is obtained using the signing query given in $\mathrm{Expt}_{\mathsf{SS},\mathcal{B}_{\mathrm{sig}}}^{\mathrm{OT\text{-}sEUF\text{-}CMA}}(\lambda)$.

Simulate the Decryption Oracles. Since $\mathcal{B}_{\mathrm{sig}}$ has all secret keys, $\mathcal{B}_{\mathrm{sig}}$ is able to answer all queries correctly. If $\mathcal{A}$ submits a query $c' = (vk, \hat{\mathbf{y}}, \hat{\sigma})$ causing **Forge**, $\mathcal{B}_{\mathrm{sig}}$ returns $\perp$ to $\mathcal{A}$ and outputs $(\hat{\mathbf{y}}, \hat{\sigma})$ as forgery.

From $\mathcal{A}$'s point of view, $\mathcal{B}_{\mathrm{sig}}$ and $\mathcal{B}$ are identical. Only when **Forge** occurs, they differ from $\mathrm{Expt}_{\mathsf{PKE}_{\mathrm{cca2}},\mathcal{A}}^{\mathrm{IK\text{-}CCA2}}(\lambda)$. This reduction shows that

$$\Pr[\mathbf{Forge} \text{ in } \mathrm{Expt}_{\mathsf{PKE}_{\mathrm{cca2}},\mathcal{B}_{\mathrm{sig}}}^{\mathrm{IK\text{-}CCA2}}(\lambda)] = \Pr[\mathbf{Forge} \text{ in } \mathrm{Expt}_{\mathsf{SS},\mathcal{A}}^{\mathrm{OT\text{-}sEUF\text{-}CMA}}(\lambda)].$$

Moreover, this probability is negligible due to the security of SS. $\square$

As a result, advantage of $\mathcal{A}$ is bounded as follows

$$\mathrm{Adv}_{\mathsf{PKE}_{\mathrm{cca2}},\mathcal{A}}^{\mathrm{IK\text{-}CCA2}}(\lambda) < \mathrm{Adv}_{\mathsf{PKE}_{\mathrm{cpa}},\mathcal{B}}^{\mathrm{IK\text{-}CPA}}(\lambda) + \mathrm{Adv}_{\mathsf{SS},\mathcal{B}_{\mathrm{sig}}}^{\mathrm{OT\text{-}sEUF\text{-}CMA}}(\lambda).$$

We conclude that $\mathsf{PKE}_{\mathrm{cca2}}$ is IK-CCA2. $\square$

5   IK-CPA/CCA2 Code-Based Encryption

In this section, we show that the randomized Niederreiter encryption $\mathsf{PKE}_{\mathrm{RNR}}$ is IK-CPA. Furthermore, $\mathsf{PKE}_{\mathrm{cpa}}$ instantiated with the Niederreiter function is also IK-CPA, and as a corollary, $\mathsf{PKE}_{\mathrm{cca2}}$ with the Niederreiter function is IK-CCA2. In the proof of the following theorem, we adapt the ideas of [17].

Theorem 5. *The randomized Niederreiter encryption is IK-CPA.*

Proof. To prove this theorem, we define a sequence of games.

First, Game0 described below is the original IK-CPA game for $\mathsf{PKE}_{\mathrm{RNR}}$. Game1 is the same as Game0, except that the parity-check matrices are replaced with random matrices.

Game0: Run $\mathsf{Gen}_{\mathsf{NR}}(1^\lambda)$ twice to get $pk^0 = H^0, pk^1 = H^1$.
$(state, m) \leftarrow \mathcal{A}_1(pk^0, pk^1)$
$b \leftarrow \{0,1\}, r \leftarrow \mathcal{E}_{n_r, t_r}$
$c^* = H^b(m||r)^{\mathrm{T}}$
$b' \leftarrow \mathcal{A}_2(state, c^*)$

Game1: Generate two random matrices and set $pk^0 = R^0, pk^1 = R^1$.
$(state, m) \leftarrow \mathcal{A}_1(pk^0, pk^1)$
$b \leftarrow \{0,1\}, r \leftarrow \mathcal{E}_{n_r, t_r}$
$c^* = R^b(m||r)^{\mathrm{T}}$
$b' \leftarrow \mathcal{A}_2(state, c^*)$

Lemma 3. *$\mathcal{A}$'s views in* Game0 *and* Game1 *are indistinguishable.*

Proof. This is proved by indistinguishability of the parity-check matrices of the Goppa code.

We can construct a reduction algorithm $\mathcal{D}_{\mathsf{DGC}}$, which tries to distinguish the parity check matrix from a random matrix. Since we replace two matrices, the difference of views in the games is bounded by twice the advantage of $\mathcal{D}_{\mathsf{DGC}}$:

$$|\Pr[\mathcal{A} \text{ outputs } 1 \mid \mathsf{Game0}] - \Pr[\mathcal{A} \text{ outputs } 1 \mid \mathsf{Game1}]| < 2\mathrm{Adv}^{\mathsf{DGC}}_{\mathcal{D}_{\mathsf{DGC}}}(\lambda).$$

□

Game1′ described below is completely the same as Game1, except that we rewrite the matrix as a concatenation of the plaintext part and the random vector part. Denoting concatenation of matrices by '|', we have

$$R^b = R^b_m | R^b_r, \quad R^b(m||r)^{\mathrm{T}} = R^b_m m^{\mathrm{T}} \oplus R^b_r r^{\mathrm{T}}.$$

Since R^b is generated uniformly at random, R^b_r is also uniformly distributed. Replacing $R^b_r r^{\mathrm{T}}$ in Game1′ with a random vector u, we obtain Game2.

Game1′: Generate random matrices and set $pk^0 = (R^0_m, R^0_r), pk^1 = (R^1_m, R^1_r)$.
$(state, m) \leftarrow \mathcal{A}_1(pk^0, pk^1)$
$b \leftarrow \{0,1\}, r \leftarrow \mathcal{E}_{n_r, t_r}$
$c^* = R^b_m m^{\mathrm{T}} \oplus R^b_r r^{\mathrm{T}}$
$b' \leftarrow \mathcal{A}_2(state, c^*)$

Game2: Generate random matrices and set $pk^0 = R^0, pk^1 = R^1$.
$(state, m) \leftarrow \mathcal{A}_1(pk^0, pk^1)$
$b \leftarrow \{0,1\}, u \leftarrow \mathcal{U}_{n-l}$
$c^* = R^b_m m^{\mathrm{T}} \oplus u$
$b' \leftarrow \mathcal{A}_2(state, c^*)$

Lemma 4. *$\mathcal{A}$'s views in* Game1′ *and* Game2 *are indistinguishable.*

Proof. This is proved by using the pseudorandomness. We can construct a reduction algorithm $\mathcal{D}_{\mathrm{pr}}$ which tries to distinguish an instance of the SD problem from a random vector, and the difference of views in the games is bounded by the advantage of $\mathcal{D}_{\mathrm{pr}}$:

$$|\Pr[\mathcal{A} \text{ outputs } 1 \mid \mathsf{Game1}'] - \Pr[\mathcal{A} \text{ outputs } 1 \mid \mathsf{Game2}]| < \mathrm{Adv}^{\mathrm{pr}}_{\mathcal{D}_{\mathrm{pr}}, R^b_r}(\lambda).$$

□

Since u is uniformly distributed, $R_m^b m^\mathrm{T} \oplus u$ is also uniformly distributed. Therefore Game2$'$ described below is completely the same as Game2.

Game2$'$: Generate random matrices and set
  $pk^0 = R^0, pk^1 = R^1$.
  $(state, m) \leftarrow \mathcal{A}_1(pk^0, pk^1)$
  $b \leftarrow \{0, 1\}, u \leftarrow \mathcal{U}_{n-l}$
  $c^* = u$
  $b' \leftarrow \mathcal{A}_2(state, c^*)$

Now, $\mathcal{A}$ has no information about b, therefore $\Pr[b = b' \mid \text{Game2}'] = \frac{1}{2}$.

Combining the lemmas shown so far, the advantage of $\mathcal{A}$ in the game of IK-CPA is bounded:

$$\mathsf{Adv}^{\text{IK-CPA}}_{\mathsf{PKE}_{\text{RNR}}, \mathcal{A}}(\lambda) < 2\mathsf{Adv}^{\text{DGC}}_{\mathcal{D}_{\text{DGC}}}(\lambda) + \mathsf{Adv}^{\text{pr}}_{\mathcal{D}_{\text{pr}}, R_r^b}(\lambda).$$

We conclude that $\mathsf{PKE}_{\text{RNR}}$ is IK-CPA. $\square$

Next, we consider the key-privacy of $\mathsf{PKE}_{\text{cpa}}$.

Theorem 6. $\mathsf{PKE}_{\text{cpa}}$ *instantiated with the Niederreiter function achieves IK-CPA.*

Proof. We prove that $\mathsf{PKE}_{\text{cpa}}$ instantiated with the Niederreiter function satisfies IK-CPA. Naturally, when repeating the Niederreiter function, we keep its parameters fixed. We define a sequence of games to prove this theorem.

Game0 described below is the original IK-CPA game for $\mathsf{PKE}_{\text{cpa}}$ instantiated with the Niederreiter function. Game1 described below is the same as Game0, except that the parity-check matrices are replaced with random matrices.

Game0: Run $\mathsf{Gen}_{\text{NR}}(1^\lambda)$ $2k$ times to obtain $pk^0 = (H_1^0, ..., H_k^0)$ and $pk^1 = (H_1^1, ..., H_k^1)$.
  $(state, m) \leftarrow \mathcal{A}_1(pk^0, pk^1)$
  $b \leftarrow \{0, 1\}, r \leftarrow \mathcal{E}_{n_r, t_r}$
  $c^* = (H_1^b(m||r)^\mathrm{T}, ..., H_k^b(m||r)^\mathrm{T})$
  $b' \leftarrow \mathcal{A}_2(state, c^*)$

Game1: Generate a random matrix $2k$ times and set $pk^0 = (R_1^0, ..., R_k^0)$, $pk^1 = (R_1^1, ..., R_k^1)$.
  $(state, m) \leftarrow \mathcal{A}_1(pk^0, pk^1)$
  $b \leftarrow \{0, 1\}, r \leftarrow \mathcal{E}_{n_r, t_r}$
  $c^* = (R_1^b(m||r)^\mathrm{T}, ..., R_k^b(m||r)^\mathrm{T})$
  $b' \leftarrow \mathcal{A}_2(state, c^*)$

Lemma 5. $\mathcal{A}$'s view in Game0 and Game1 are indistinguishable.

Proof. This is proved by the hybrid argument on the indistinguishability of the Goppa parity-check matrices.

We can construct the reduction algorithm $\mathcal{D}'_{\text{DGC}}$ similarly to $\mathcal{D}_{\text{DGC}}$. Since we replace $2k$ matrices, the difference of views in the games is bounded by $2k$ times of the advantage of $\mathcal{D}'_{\text{DGC}}$:

$$|\Pr[\mathcal{A} \text{ outputs } 1 \mid \text{Game0}] - \Pr[\mathcal{A} \text{ outputs } 1 \mid \text{Game1}]| < 2k\mathsf{Adv}^{\text{DGC}}_{\mathcal{D}'_{\text{DGC}}}(\lambda).$$

$\square$

Game1$'$ below is completely the same as Game1. Let us combine k random matrices into one big random matrix:

$$R^{0\,\mathrm{T}} = R_1^{0\,\mathrm{T}}|...|R_k^{0\,\mathrm{T}}, \quad R^{1\,\mathrm{T}} = R_1^{1\,\mathrm{T}}|...|R_k^{1\,\mathrm{T}},$$

and then divide the resulting big matrix into the plaintext part and the random vector part:

$$R^b = R_m^b|R_r^b, \quad R^b(m||r)^{\mathrm{T}} = R_m^b m^{\mathrm{T}} \oplus R_r^b r^{\mathrm{T}}.$$

Since all the matrices are uniformly distributed, the combined and divided matrices are also uniformly distributed.

Game1$'$: Generate random matrices and set
$pk^0 = (R_m^0, R_r^0), pk^1 = (R_m^1, R_r^1).$
$(state, m) \leftarrow \mathcal{A}_1(pk^0, pk^1)$
$b \leftarrow \{0, 1\}, r \leftarrow \mathcal{E}_{n_r, t_r}$
$c^* = R_m^b m^{\mathrm{T}} \oplus R_r^b r^{\mathrm{T}}$
$b' \leftarrow \mathcal{A}_2(state, c^*)$

Now, Game1$'$ in this proof is the same as that in the proof of Theorem 5, except for the parameters. Even after concatenating k matrices, the SD problem is still hard, if the parameters are chosen appropriately [7]. Therefore, the remaining part of this proof proceeds in the same way as the proof of Theorem 5. The IK-CPA advantage of $\mathcal{A}$ against PKE_{cpa} with the Niederreiter function is bounded by

$$\mathsf{Adv}_{\mathsf{PKE}_{cpa}, \mathcal{A}}^{\mathrm{IK\text{-}CPA}}(\lambda) < 2k\mathsf{Adv}_{\mathcal{D}_{\mathsf{DGC}}'}^{\mathrm{DGC}}(\lambda) + \mathsf{Adv}_{\mathcal{D}_{\mathrm{pr}}, R_r^b}^{\mathrm{pr}}(\lambda).$$

In conclusion, PKE_{cpa} instantiated with the Niederreiter function is IK-CPA. $\square$

From Theorems 4 and 6, we obtain our main result.

Corollary 1. PKE_{cca2} *instantiated with the Niederreiter function is IK-CCA2.*

6 Another Instantiation: McEliece

In this section, we introduce a variant of the McEliece encryption used in [4], where the error vector has the Bernoulli distribution. Although this introduces (negligible) decryption error, the use of this variant simplifies our security proofs. For simplicity, we refer to this variant as just "the McEliece encryption" in this section.

Definition 9 (McEliece [4,12]). *The McEliece encryption is a tuple* ($\mathsf{Gen}_{\mathsf{ME}}$, $\mathsf{Enc}_{\mathsf{ME}}, \mathsf{Dec}_{\mathsf{ME}}$). *The algorithm* $\mathsf{Gen}_{\mathsf{ME}}(\lambda)$ *generates an* $l \times n$ *generator matrix* G' *of an irreducible binary Goppa code with a decoding algorithm* Correct, *which corrects up to* t *errors. Sample a random* $l \times l$ *non-singular matrix* S *and an* $n \times n$ *permutation matrix* P. *Multiplying these two random matrices to the generator matrix, we get a scrambled generator matrix* $G = SG'P$. $\mathsf{Gen}_{\mathsf{ME}}$ *outputs* $pk = (G, t)$ *and* $sk = (S, G', P)$.

For a plaintext $x \in \{0,1\}^l$, the encryption algorithm $\mathsf{Enc_{ME}}(pk, x)$ samples an error vector $e \in \{0,1\}^n$, where each bit is chosen according to the Bernoulli distribution $\mathcal{B}_\theta$, and $\theta = \frac{t}{n} - \epsilon$ for some small $\epsilon > 0$. It outputs $y = xG \oplus e$.

The decryption algorithm $\mathsf{Dec_{ME}}(sk, y)$ computes $x = \mathsf{Correct}(yP^{-1}) \cdot S^{-1}$. If $\mathsf{Correct}$ fails, it outputs $\bot$.

Note that in the above scheme, the weight of e is lower than t with high probability, hence the decryption works correctly almost always.

Although $\mathsf{Enc_{ME}}$ is a probabilistic function, we can easily confirm that y is the output of $\mathsf{Enc_{ME}}(pk, x)$ by checking if $|wt(y - xG) - t|$ is small. Because of this property, the IND-CCA2 scheme can be instantiated with the McEliece encryption.

Security of the McEliece encryption and its variants is guaranteed based on the hardness of distinguishing the Goppa code problem (when the code is represented by a generator matrix) and the LPN problem. Let us introduce next the coding interpretation of the later problem.

Definition 10 (LPN problem). *Suppose that the PPT algorithm $\mathcal{A}$ receives a random generator matrix and a codeword distorted with the noise according to the Bernoulli distribution. The LPN problem is to decode the message corresponding to the codeword. The advantage of $\mathcal{A}$ on the LPN problem is defined by*

$$\mathsf{Adv}_{\mathcal{A}}^{\mathsf{LPN}}(\lambda) = \Pr[R \leftarrow \mathcal{U}_{l,n}, x \leftarrow \mathcal{U}_l, e \leftarrow \mathcal{B}_\theta^n : \mathcal{A}(R, xR \oplus e) = x],$$

where $\mathcal{B}_\theta^n$ denotes n values drawn independently according to the Bernoulli distribution $\mathcal{B}_\theta$.

The LPN problem is believed to be hard. In other words, for any $\mathcal{A}$, $\mathsf{Adv}_{\mathcal{A}}^{\mathsf{LPN}}(\lambda)$ is negligible.

As with the Niederreiter function, the McEliece encryption has pseudorandomness: If the input x is sampled from the uniform distribution over $\{0,1\}^l$, it is hard to distinguish a ciphertext y from a randomly sampled vector u.

Formally, for any PPT algorithm $\mathcal{D}$,

$$\mathsf{Adv}_{\mathcal{D},R}^{\mathsf{pr}}(\lambda) = |\Pr[x \leftarrow \mathcal{U}_l, e \leftarrow \mathcal{B}_\theta^n, y = xR \oplus e : \mathcal{D}(R, y) = 1]$$
$$- \Pr[u \leftarrow \mathcal{U}_n : \mathcal{D}(R, u) = 1]|$$

is negligible.

Theorem 7 [10]. *If the LPN problem is hard, the McEliece encryption with a random code is pseudorandom.*

The randomized McEliece $\mathsf{PKE_{RME}}$ is defined in the manner similar to the randomized Niederreiter: encrypting a plaintext with random padding.

Theorem 8 [14]. *Assuming hardness of the DGC problem and the LPN problem, $\mathsf{PKE_{RME}}$ is proved to be IND-CPA.*

Döttling et al. [4] showed that combining the k-repetition paradigm with the Dolev-Dwork-Naor construction [3] yields IND-CCA2 security for the McEliece encryption. We can show that this scheme also achieves IK-CCA2 security in a manner similar to that of Corollary 1.

Theorem 9. PKE_{cca2} *instantiated with the McEliece encryption is IK-CCA2.*

References

1. Bellare, M., Boldyreva, A., Desai, A., Pointcheval, D.: Key-privacy in public-key encryption. In: Boyd, C. (ed.) ASIACRYPT 2001. LNCS, vol. 2248, pp. 566–582. Springer, Heidelberg (2001). doi:10.1007/3-540-45682-1_33
2. Bernstein, D.J., Buchmann, J., Dahmen, E.: Post-Quantum Cryptography. Springer Science & Business Media, Heidelberg (2009)
3. Dolev, D., Dwork, C., Naor, M.: Nonmalleable cryptography. SIAM J. Comput. **30**(2), 391–437 (2000)
4. Döttling, N., Dowsley, R., Muller-Quade, J., Nascimento, A.C.A.: A CCA2 secure variant of the mceliece cryptosystem. IEEE Trans. Inf. Theory **58**(10), 6672–6680 (2012)
5. Faugère, J., Gauthier-Umaña, V., Otmani, A., Perret, L., Tillich, J.: A distinguisher for high rate McEliece cryptosystems. In: 2011 IEEE Information Theory Workshop, ITW 2011, Paraty, Brazil, 16–20 October 2011, pp. 282–286 (2011)
6. Fischer, J.-B., Stern, J.: An efficient pseudo-random generator provably as secure as syndrome decoding. In: Maurer, U. (ed.) EUROCRYPT 1996. LNCS, vol. 1070, pp. 245–255. Springer, Heidelberg (1996). doi:10.1007/3-540-68339-9_22
7. Freeman, D.M., Goldreich, O., Kiltz, E., Rosen, A., Segev, G.: More constructions of lossy and correlation-secure trapdoor functions. J. Cryptol. **26**(1), 39–74 (2013)
8. Goldreich, O., Levin, L.A.: A hard-core predicate for all one-way functions. In: Proceedings of the 21st Annual ACM Symposium on Theory of Computing (STOC), Seattle, Washington, USA, 14–17 May 1989, pp. 25–32 (1989)
9. Hayashi, R.: Anonymity on public-key cryptosystems. Ph.D. thesis, Tokyo Institute of Technology (2007)
10. Katz, J., Shin, J.S.: Parallel and concurrent security of the HB and HB$^+$ protocols. In: Vaudenay, S. (ed.) EUROCRYPT 2006. LNCS, vol. 4004, pp. 73–87. Springer, Heidelberg (2006). doi:10.1007/11761679_6
11. Kobara, K., Imai, H.: Semantically secure McEliece public-key cryptosystems-conversions for McEliece PKC. In: Kim, K. (ed.) PKC 2001. LNCS, vol. 1992, pp. 19–35. Springer, Heidelberg (2001). doi:10.1007/3-540-44586-2_2
12. McEliece, R.J.: A public-key cryptosystem based on algebraic coding theory. DSN Prog. Rep. **4244**, 114–116 (1978)
13. Niederreiter, H.: Knapsack-type cryptosystems and algebraic coding theory. Probl. Control Inf. Theory-Probl. Upravleniya I Teorii Informatsii **15**(2), 159–166 (1986)
14. Nojima, R., Imai, H., Kobara, K., Morozov, K.: Semantic security for the McEliece cryptosystem without random oracles. Des. Codes Crypt. **49**(1–3), 289–305 (2008)
15. Persichetti, E.: Secure and anonymous hybrid encryption from coding theory. In: Gaborit, P. (ed.) PQCrypto 2013. LNCS, vol. 7932, pp. 174–187. Springer, Heidelberg (2013). doi:10.1007/978-3-642-38616-9_12

16. Rosen, A., Segev, G.: Chosen-ciphertext security via correlated products. In: Reingold, O. (ed.) TCC 2009. LNCS, vol. 5444, pp. 419–436. Springer, Heidelberg (2009). doi:10.1007/978-3-642-00457-5_25

17. Yamakawa, S., Cui, Y., Kobara, K., Hagiwara, M., Imai, H.: On the key-privacy issue of McEliece public-key encryption. In: Boztaş, S., Lu, H.-F.F. (eds.) AAECC 2007. LNCS, vol. 4851, pp. 168–177. Springer, Heidelberg (2007). doi:10.1007/978-3-540-77224-8_21

A Reaction Attack on the QC-LDPC McEliece Cryptosystem

Tomáš Fabšič[1]([✉]), Viliam Hromada[1], Paul Stankovski[2], Pavol Zajac[1],
Qian Guo[2], and Thomas Johansson[2]

[1] Faculty of Electrical Engineering and Information Technology,
Slovak University of Technology in Bratislava,
Ilkovičova 3, 81219 Bratislava, Slovak Republic
{tomas.fabsic,viliam.hromada,pavol.zajac}@stuba.sk
[2] Department of Electrical and Information Technology,
Lund University, Lund, Sweden
{paul.stankovski,qian.guo,thomas.johansson}@eit.lth.se

Abstract. Guo et al. recently presented a reaction attack against the
QC-MDPC McEliece cryptosystem. Their attack is based on the observation that when a bit-flipping decoding algorithm is used in the QC-
MDPC McEliece, then there exists a dependence between the secret
matrix H and the failure probability of the bit-flipping algorithm. This
dependence can be exploited to reveal the matrix H which constitutes
the private key in the cryptosystem. It was conjectured that such dependence is present even when a soft-decision decoding algorithm is used
instead of a bit-flipping algorithm.

This paper shows that a similar dependence between the secret matrix
H and the failure probability of a decoding algorithm is also present in
the QC-LDPC McEliece cryptosystem. Unlike QC-MDPC McEliece, the
secret key in QC-LDPC McEliece also contains matrices S and Q in addition to the matrix H. We observe that there also exists a dependence
between the failure probability and the matrix Q. We show that these
dependences leak enough information to allow an attacker to construct a
sparse parity-check matrix for the public code. This parity-check matrix
can then be used for decrypting ciphertexts.

We tested the attack on an implementation of the QC-LDPC McEliece
using a soft-decision decoding algorithm. Thus we also confirmed that
soft-decision decoding algorithms can be vulnerable to leaking information about the secret key.

Keywords: QC-LDPC McEliece cryptosystem · Reaction attack · Soft-
decision decoding

1 Introduction

In 1978, R.J. McEliece proposed a public key cryptosystem based on coding
theory [8], now called the McEliece cryptosystem. The cryptosystem has never

T. Fabšič, V. Hromada and P. Zajac—Support by grant VEGA 1/0159/17 is
acknowledged.

T. Lange and T. Takagi (Eds.): PQCrypto 2017, LNCS 10346, pp. 51–68, 2017.
DOI: 10.1007/978-3-319-59879-6_4

been adopted widely, mainly due to the large size of the public key. The interest in the McEliece cryptosystem has, however, risen recently, since it has become a candidate for post-quantum cryptography.

In [2], Baldi and Chiaraluce proposed a variant of the McEliece cryptosystem based on quasi-cyclic low-density parity-check codes (QC-LDPC codes). Their cryptosystem is now known as the QC-LDPC McEliece cryptosystem. The use of quasi-cyclic codes in this cryptosystem allows to reduce the size of the public key. However, in [10], Otmani et al. showed that the proposed system had serious vulnerabilities. In [3], Baldi et al. proposed an amended version of the cryptosystem which was immunized against the attacks from [10]. An important role in the cryptosystem is played by matrices which are formed by blocks of circulant matrices. In [12], it was demonstrated that when the block size is chosen to be an even number a more efficient information-set decoding attack on the cryptosystem can be executed. However, this attack is not applicable when the block size is odd.

A cryptosystem related to the QC-LDPC McEliece cryptosystem, the QC-MDPC McEliece cryptosystem, was proposed by Misoczki et al. in [9]. Both QC-LDPC McEliece and QC-MDPC McEliece use an iterative decoding algorithm in their decryption procedure. Two types of iterative decoding algorithms are proposed in the literature; bit-flipping algorithms and soft-decision decoding algorithms. Both types of algorithms fail with some small probability. In [5], Guo et al. demonstrated that when the QC-MDPC McEliece cryptosystem is implemented with a bit-flipping algorithm, there exists a dependence between the secret matrix H and the failure probability of the bit-flipping algorithm. They further demonstrated that this dependence allows an attacker to recover the secret matrix H very efficiently. They conjectured that such dependence is present when a soft-decision decoding algorithm is used, as well.

In the present paper, we show that a similar dependence between the secret matrix H and the failure probability of a decoding algorithm is also present in the QC-LDPC McEliece cryptosystem. Unlike in QC-MDPC McEliece, the secret key in QC-LDPC McEliece also contains matrices S and Q in addition to the matrix H. We observe that there also exists a dependence between the failure probability and the matrix Q. We show that these dependences leak enough information to allow an attacker to construct a sparse parity-check matrix for the public code. This parity-check matrix can then be used for decrypting ciphertexts.

For our experiments we used an implementation of the QC-LDPC McEliece cryptosystem which uses a soft-decision decoding algorithm. Thus, apart from showing that an attack similar to the one in [5] can be mounted on the QC-LDPC McEliece cryptosystem, we also confirm the conjecture from [5] that these types of attacks are also possible when a soft-decision decoding algorithm is used instead of a bit-flipping algorithm.

The paper is structured as follows. In Sect. 2, we review the QC-LDPC McEliece cryptosystem, the QC-MDPC McEliece cryptosystem and the attack on the QC-MDPC McEliece from [5]. In Sect. 3, we describe a new attack on the QC-LDPC McEliece. Finally, in Sect. 4, we summarize our results and conclude the paper.

2   Preliminaries

2.1   The QC-LDPC McEliece Cryptosystem

In [2], Baldi et al. proposed a variant of the McEliece cryptosystem based on LDPC codes – the QC-LDPC McEliece cryptosystem. A part of the private key in this cryptosystem is formed by an $(n - k) \times n$ parity-check matrix H of an LDPC code able to correct t errors. The matrix H is formed by a row $\{H_0, \ldots, H_{n_0-1}\}$ of $n_0 = n/(n - k)$ binary circulant blocks of size $p \times p$, where $p = n - k$. Each block has a row weight (i.e. the number of ones in a row) equal to a number w which is small compared to p. If H_{n_0-1} is invertible, a generator matrix G for the code can be obtained as

$$G = \left[\begin{array}{c|c} \mathbf{I} & \begin{array}{c} \left(H_{n_0-1}^{-1} \cdot H_0\right)^T \\ \vdots \\ \left(H_{n_0-1}^{-1} \cdot H_{n_0-2}\right)^T \end{array} \end{array} \right].$$

The remaining part of the private key is formed by two other matrices; an invertible $k \times k$ matrix S and a sparse invertible $n \times n$ matrix Q. The matrices S and Q are formed by blocks of circulant $p \times p$ matrices. In addition, Q has a fixed row weight m. The public key is then computed as $G' = S^{-1} \cdot G \cdot Q^{-1}$.

Encryption is done as follows. Let the original message be u. Alice encrypts u as $x = u \cdot G' + e$, where e is a randomly generated error vector of length n and Hamming weight $w_H(e) = t' \leq \frac{t}{m}$.

When Bob receives the encrypted message x, he first computes

$$x' = x \cdot Q = u \cdot S^{-1} \cdot G + e \cdot Q.$$

The vector x' is a codeword of the LDPC code chosen by Bob (corresponding to the information vector $u' = u \cdot S^{-1}$), affected by the error vector $e \cdot Q$, whose maximum weight is t. Bob is able to correct all the errors with very high probability by means of LDPC decoding, thus recovering u', and then u through a post-multiplication by S.

In [10], Otmani et al. demonstrated that this cryptosystem is vulnerable to attacks which exploit the facts that Q is block-diagonal and S is sparse. In order to immunize their cryptosystem against these attacks, Baldi et al. proposed versions of the QC-LDPC McEliece cryptosystem with the matrix S dense and the matrix Q no longer block-diagonal in [3].

In [12], it was demonstrated that when the value of the block size is chosen to be an even number, a more efficient information-set decoding attack on the cryptosystem can be executed. However, this attack is not applicable when the block size is odd.

2.2   The QC-MDPC McEliece Cryptosystem

The QC-MDPC McEliece cryptosystem was proposed in [9]. This cryptosystem uses moderate density parity check (MDPC) codes, which are codes that admit a parity check matrix H^{MDPC} which is sparse, but not as sparse as in LDPC codes. The matrix H^{MDPC} again has to be quasi-cyclic, i.e. it has to be formed by a row of circulant blocks $\{H_0^{\mathrm{MDPC}}, \ldots, H_{n_0-1}^{\mathrm{MDPC}}\}$. The matrix H^{MDPC} forms the whole private key in the QC-MDPC McEliece cryptosystem. If $H_{n_0-1}^{\mathrm{MDPC}}$ is invertible, a generator matrix G^{MDPC} for the code can be obtained by the same calculation as in QC-LDPC McEliece. The matrix G^{MDPC} forms the public key for the cryptosystem.

Encryption is done as follows. Let the original message be u. Alice encrypts u as $x = u \cdot G^{\mathrm{MDPC}} + e$, where e is a randomly generated vector with the Hamming weight equal to a number of errors t^{MDPC} that the MDPC code can correct.

When Bob receives the encrypted message x, he is able to correct all the errors with very high probability by means of an LDPC decoding algorithm, thus recovering the message u.

2.3   Previous Attack on the QC-MDPC McEliece Cryptosystem

In [5], Guo et al. presented a reaction attack on the QC-MDPC McEliece cryptosystem. They demonstrate that if the QC-MDPC McEliece cryptosystem employs a bit-flipping decoding algorithm in its decryption procedure, then there exists a dangerous dependence between the probability of decoding error and the secret key.

Guo et al. demonstrate their attack on a version of the cryptosystem with two blocks in the secret parity check matrix H^{MDPC}. Since the blocks are circulant, the block H_0^{MDPC} is determined by its first row h_0^{MDPC}. They show that an attacker who sends a large number of messages encrypted by the public key and for each message learns whether it was successfully decrypted can learn distances between ones in h_0^{MDPC}. The distance between two ones in positions p_1 and p_2, $p_2 > p_1$, in h_0^{MDPC} is defined as $\min\{p_2 - p_1, p - (p_2 - p_1)\}$, where p is the length of h_0^{MDPC} (i.e. the distance is computed cyclically). With the knowledge of distances in h_0^{MDPC}, the attacker can reconstruct h_0^{MDPC} and recover the private key.

Guo et al. consider two different scenarios in their paper. In the first scenario, the attacker is allowed to choose the error vector e that is added to the message during encryption. In the second scenario, the attacker has no such freedom and the error vector is always chosen at random. Here we focus on the second scenario.

In the second scenario, the attacker sends a large number of messages containing a randomly generated error vector. The attacker then groups the messages into sets Σ_d, $d \in \{1, \ldots p/2\}$ by the following principle: a message belongs to the set Σ_d if its error vector contains the distance d. Guo et al. observe that if d is present in h_0^{MDPC}, then the estimate for the probability of decoding failure based on the set Σ_d is smaller than the estimate obtained from Σ_d when d is not present in h_0^{MDPC}. Thus, the attacker is able to learn which distances are present in h_0^{MDPC}.

3   The Attack

As in [5], we also consider an attacker who sends a large number of messages encrypted by the public key and for each message learns whether it was successfully decrypted. Similarly to the more restrictive attack scenario in [5], we assume that the attacker has no freedom to choose the error vector e that is added to the message during encryption, i.e. the error vector is always generated randomly. We will demonstrate that the attacker can learn information about the matrices H and Q which allow him to construct a sparse parity check matrix for the public code. Using this matrix, the attacker can then decrypt ciphertexts encrypted by the cryptosystem.

Similarly to [5], a special role in our attack is played by distances between ones in matrices H and Q. Following [5], we define the distance between two ones in positions p_1 and p_2, $p_2 > p_1$, in a vector of length p as $\min\{p_2 - p_1, p - (p_2 - p_1)\}$ (i.e. the distance is computed cyclically).

3.1   Learning Distances in the Matrix H - Intuition

The key observation from [5] can be loosely rephrased as: "Let e be an error vector divided into blocks of length p. Suppose that a block of e contains the distance d. If the distance d is also present in the corresponding circulant block of the matrix H^{MDPC}, then a bit-flipping algorithm fails to decode a message with error vector e less frequently."

We now analyze whether this behaviour could be utilized in attacking the QC-LDPC McEliece cryptosystem. In QC-LDPC McEliece, the decoding algorithm is not applied to e but to eQ, where Q is secret. Thus, we face the question: can the attacker learn whether a given distance d is present in eQ?

The answer to this question is positive. Suppose that the attacker knows that e has the distance d in its first block of p digits. We can think of the multiplication of e and Q as an addition of those rows of Q for which the corresponding entries in e are one. Thus, if distance d is present in e, two rows of Q, q_i and $q_{i+d \bmod p}$, will be added together in the multiplication process. Since the distance d is present in a block of length p in e and since Q is composed of circulant blocks of dimension $p \times p$, the blocks of length p in $q_{i+d \bmod p}$ are cyclic shifts of the corresponding blocks in q_i. The row q_i has m ones, with m being a small number. Thus, the vector $q_i + q_{i+d \bmod p}$ contains m pairs of ones separated by the distance d, unless an unlikely cancellation occurs. Since all the rows of Q are sparse, we can expect these pairs to remain in eQ, undisturbed by additions of further rows of Q. The attacker therefore knows that the distance d will be present in eQ.

Note that the distance d will always appear in all blocks of eQ. This means that when the attacker estimates the decoding error probability, he can only hope to learn whether the distance d is present in one of the blocks of H. Unlike the QC-MDPC case, the attacker will not learn whether d is present in one particular block of H. This could potentially make the subsequent reconstruction of H more involved. However, later we show that this is not a serious issue and that H can still be reconstructed efficiently.

These ideas give us hope that reconstruction of H is possible in the QC-LDPC McEliece cryptosystem with a bit-flipping decoding algorithm. Also, similarities between bit-flipping algorithms and soft-decision decoding algorithms give us further hope that this reconstruction is possible even for QC-LDPC McEliece with a soft-decision decoding algorithm.

3.2   Learning Distances in the Matrix Q - Intuition

The matrix H, however, forms only a part of the private key. The rest of the private key is formed by matrices S and Q. Here we argue that the attacker can even learn information about distances in the matrix Q.

Let q_i be the i-th row of Q. Suppose that the row q_1 contains a distance d in one of its blocks of length p. Suppose that the attacker knows that the error vector contains distance d in its first block of length p. Then two rows q_i and $q_{i+d \mod p}$ will be added together during the multiplication of e and Q. Since Q is composed of circulant blocks of size $p \times p$, both rows q_i and $q_{i+d \mod p}$ will contain the distance d in the same block of length p. Suppose that q_i contains the ones separated by the distance d in positions $j \times p + s$ and $j \times p + (s + d \mod p)$. Then $q_{i+d \mod p}$ will contain ones in positions $j \times p + (s + d \mod p)$ and $j \times p + (s + 2d \mod p)$. Thus, the ones in the position $j \times p + (s + d \mod p)$ will cancel in $q_i + q_{i+d \mod p}$. Since the matrix Q is very sparse, we normally expect $w_H(eQ) = m \times w_H(e)$. The cancellation described above will decrease the Hamming weight of eQ below its standard Hamming weight. Consequently, the decoding algorithm in the QC-LDPC McEliece will have to correct fewer errors than normally. Therefore we can expect the probability of the decoding error to decrease severely when e contains the distance d in its first block of length p. We can expect this effect to be present in both bit-flipping and soft-decision decoding algorithms. Thus, observing the probability of the decoding error, the attacker can learn whether the distance d is present in one of the blocks of length p of the row q_1. Again, the attacker can not learn exactly which block the distance is present in. Similarly, the attacker can learn about the presence of a distance d in rows $q_{p+1}, q_{2p+1}, \ldots, q_{(n_0-1)p+1}$.

3.3   Learning Distances - Experiments

Below, we present results of our experiments, confirming the intuition from Sects. 3.1 and 3.2. We used a version of the QC-LDPC McEliece cryptosystem with the following parameters: $n_0 = 3$, $w = 13$, $p = 8192$ and $m = 11$.[1] These values were suggested in [3] for 80-bit security. We increased the value of t' to

---

[1] These parameters were selected because they were proposed in [3]. The attack presented in this paper is equally feasible for other sets of parameters, including parameters with p odd.

48 from 40 in the original suggestion to increase the decoding error probability and make it easier to estimate. We discuss the relevance of this change in the conclusion. We constructed matrices S and Q as suggested in [3]. Thus, we constructed the matrix S so that every block in S has rows with weight approximately equal to $p/2$, with blocks along the diagonal having rows with an odd weight and blocks away from the diagonal having rows with an even weight. We obtained the matrix Q by constructing a matrix of 3×3 circulant blocks with the blocks on the diagonal having rows of weight 3 and the blocks away from the diagonal having rows of weight 4, and by randomly permuting its block-rows and block-columns.

Our implementation is based on the project BitPunch [4], which is a free standalone cryptographic library containing implementations of various variants of the McEliece cryptosystem. In our implementation, we used a soft-decision decoding algorithm from [11].

We conducted an experiment to learn what distances are present in the circulant blocks of matrices H and Q. Since the value of p in our cryptosystem was 8192, we were only interested in distances from 1 to $8192/2=4096$. To learn the distances, we used a slight variation of Algorithm 4 in [5]. Our variation of the algorithm is presented here as Algorithm 1.

Algorithm 1

INPUT: number N of ciphertexts to generate
OUTPUT: vectors a, b, u and v

---

1. $a \leftarrow$ zero-initialized vector of length $p/2$
2. $b \leftarrow$ zero-initialized vector of length $p/2$
3. $u \leftarrow$ zero-initialized vector of length $p/2$
4. $v \leftarrow$ zero-initialized vector of length $p/2$
5. $i \leftarrow 0$
6. **while** $i < N$ **do**:
   (a) generate a ciphertext c with a random error vector e
   (b) $s \leftarrow$ distances present in at least one block of length p in e
   (c) $r \leftarrow$ distances present in the first block of length p in e
   (d) $l \leftarrow 1$ if the decoding failure occurs, 0 otherwise
   (e) **for** d from 1 to $p/2$ **do**:
      i. **if** $s[d] \geq 1$ **then**:
         A. $a[d] \leftarrow a[d] + l$
         B. $b[d] \leftarrow b[d] + 1$
      ii. **if** $r[d] \geq 1$ **then**:
         A. $u[d] \leftarrow u[d] + l$
         B. $v[d] \leftarrow v[d] + 1$
   (f) $i \leftarrow i + 1$

The algorithm decrypts a large number of messages with randomly generated error vectors. The algorithm uses two vectors of counters: a and b. Each vector of counters has length 4096 and is initialized as the zero vector. After the algorithm decrypts a ciphertext c with an error vector e, the algorithm computes distances between ones in every block of length p in e. If a distance d is present in one of the blocks of e, the value of $b[d]$ is increased by 1. If a distance d is present in one of the blocks of e and there occurred a decoding error when decrypting c, the value of $a[d]$ is increased by 1. Thus, after a large number of ciphertexts is processed, the ratio $\frac{a[d]}{b[d]}$ estimates the probability of the decoding failure for ciphertexts with error vectors containing a distance d.

Our variation of the algorithm in addition uses two other vectors of counters: u and v. They again have length 4096 and are initialized as zero vectors. Vectors u and v are useful for reconstruction of the first block-row of Q. Similarly as a and b, they are updated every time the algorithm decrypts a new ciphertext. If a distance d is present in the first block of the error vector e, the value of $v[d]$ is increased by 1. If a distance d is present in the first block of e and there occurred a decoding error when decrypting the ciphertext, the value of $u[d]$ is increased by 1. Thus, after a large number of decryptions, the ratio $\frac{u[d]}{v[d]}$ estimates the probability of the decoding failure for ciphertexts with error vectors containing a distance d in its first block.

We decrypted 103 million ciphertexts. The resulting probability estimates $\frac{a[d]}{b[d]}$ are presented in Fig. 1.

If d was present in one of the circulant blocks of Q the estimates ranged from 0.095 to 0.109. If d was present in one of the circulant blocks of H the estimated probability typically ranged from 0.110 to 0.118. For four distances in H the probability was below this range but this was due to the fact that these distance were present in Q at the same time. If a distance d was present neither in Q nor in H, the estimated probability ranged from 0.115 to 0.122. Thus, our experiment confirms the expectation that the lowest probabilities are obtained for distances in Q and that probabilities for distances in H are on average lower than probabilities for distances which are neither in Q nor in H.

3.4   Distance Spectrum Reconstruction Problem

In order to explain how the attacker can reconstruct the secret matrices H and Q, we need to consider the problem of recovering a circulant matrix C, provided we only know the distances in C. This problem was already introduced in [5]. However, here we present a different approach to the problem, translating the problem into a graph problem.

Let us consider a circulant matrix C of the dimension $p \times p$. Let $P = \{p_0, p_1, \ldots, p_{w-1}\}$ be the ordered sequence of positions of ones in the first row of C. We define the distance spectrum of P as the set

$$DS(P) = \{p_i - p_j \mod p;\, p_i, p_j \in P\}.$$

Suppose we know the distance spectrum D and we want to learn the matrix C. Since every row of C gives rise to the same distance spectrum, we can only hope to learn C up to a shift of rows. Thus we can look for all sets P such that $DS(P) = D$ with the additional constraint that $p_0 = 0$. In addition, we know that the smallest distance in D must correspond to a distance between

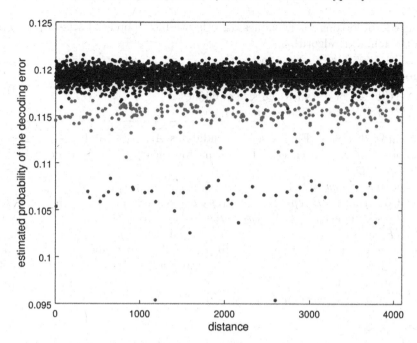

Fig. 1. Estimates of the probability of the decoding error from the experiment in Sect. 3.3. Distances in one of the circulant blocks of Q are marked in blue. Distances in one of the circulant blocks of H are marked in red. Distances which are present neither in Q nor in H are marked in black. (Color figure online)

two cyclically consecutive ones. Thus, we can add the additional constraint that $p_1 = \min(D)$.

Definition 1. *Distance spectrum reconstruction (DSR) problem: Given a set D, find all P such that $DS(P) = D$, $p_0 = 0$ and $p_1 = \min(D)$.*

It is easy to show that if a set $P = \{p_0, p_1, p_2, \ldots, p_{w-1}\}$ is a solution to the DSR problem, then so is the set

$$P' = \{p_0, p_1, p - p_{w-1} + p_1, p - p_{w-2} + p_1, \ldots, p - p_2 + p_1\}.$$

Given the spectrum D, let us define the graph G_D as follows: a set of vertices is given by the set D. Edge (d_i, d_j) exists, if and only if $d_i - d_j \mod p \in D$. If $DS(P) = D$, the induced subgraph $G_D[P]$ is a complete graph.

We will change the DSR problem into a graph problem: Given graph G_D, find a clique of w vertices, that contains vertices $\{p_0 = 0, p_1 = \min(D)\}$. From each clique, we obtain a candidate for a solution P of the DSR problem. The candidate sequence P can be verified by checking whether $DS(P) = D$ holds.

It is well known that the clique problem is NP-hard in general. In our experiments, we exploit the fact that the spectrum D and the graph G_D are sparse. In sparse graphs, we expect to find only a small number of possible w-cliques.

Instead of looking for w-cliques directly, we filter potential sets of positions with the following algorithm:

Algorithm 2

INPUT: set of distances D, size of cliques w
OUTPUT: set of candidates for w-cliques

---

1. (*Identify 3-cliques*) Find a set of candidates A: $\forall p_2 \in A$: $\{0, p_1, p_2\}$ is a 3-clique. This can be checked by testing for each $p_2 \in D \setminus \{0, p_1\}$ whether $p_2 - p_1 \in D$.
2. (*Combine 3-cliques*) Set $E = \emptyset$. For each pair (p_1, p_2), $p_2 \in A$:
   (a) Construct set B: $\forall p_3 \in B$: $\{0, p_1, p_2, p_3\}$ is a 4-clique. This can be checked by testing each $p_3 \in A \setminus \{p_2\}$, whether $p_3 - p_2 \in D$.
   (b) (*Filter 1*) If $|B| < w - 3$, try another pair (p_1, p_2).
   (c) Repeat: Remove from $C = \{0, p_1, p_2\} \cup B$ all elements that are not connected to at least $w - 1$ until either $|C| < w$, or no more elements can be removed.
   (d) (*Filter 2*) Remove all C's with $|C| < w$.
   (e) Set $E = E \cup \{C\}$.
3. Return E.

After the algorithm finishes, E contains sets of positions, that can contain an original position sequence P. Clearly, if some set $C \in E$ contains exactly w elements, it must form a w-clique: there are exactly w vertices in the induced subgraph, and each is connected to $w - 1$ other vertices. If the size of C is greater than w, we can apply further clique finding algorithms to this set.

We implemented a controlled experiment, where we tried to reconstruct a randomly generated sequence of positions. We used parameters $n = 8192, w = 13$. Out of 1000 experiments, Algorithm 2 reported surplus results (4 or 3 sets instead of the expected 2) only in 10 cases. The set of 1000 experiments with software written in Python took 558s on Intel i7-3820 CPU @ 3.60 GHz.

3.5   Reconstructing the Matrix H

Suppose that the attacker performed the experiment from Sect. 3.3. Due to the intuition presented in Sect. 3.1 he expects that if a distance d is present in one of the circulant blocks of the matrix H, then the estimate $\frac{a[d]}{b[d]}$ of the probability of the decoding error will be lower than normal. Thus he might select distances for which the estimated probability in the experiment was below some threshold and try to reconstruct the matrix H from these distances. Let D'_T be the set of distances for which the estimated probability in the experiment was below a threshold T. The attacker can create a set $D_T = \{d : d \in D'_T \text{ or } p - d \in D'_T\}$. Let P_i be the ordered sequence of positions of ones in the first row of H_i. Assuming that $DS(P_i) \subset D_T \; \forall i$, the attacker can try to solve the following variation of the DSR problem:

Problem 1. Given a set D_T, find all P such that $|P| = w$, $DS(P) \subset D_T$, $p_0 = 0$ and $p_1 = \min(DS(P))$.

If P satisfies all the conditions in the problem, it becomes a candidate for a row in one of the blocks H_i. Similarly as in the DSR problem, if a set $P = \{p_0, p_1, p_2, \ldots, p_{w-1}\}$ satisfies the conditions in Problem 1, then so does the set $P' = \{p_0, p_1, p - p_{w-1} + p_1, p - p_{w-2} + p_1, \ldots, p - p_2 + p_1\}$.

We attempted to solve Problem 1 using the data presented in Fig. 1 and the threshold $T = 0.118$. Running a variant of Algorithm 2 on a standard PC[2], we instantly obtained $n_0 = 3$ pairs of solutions (P, P'). Upon observing such result, the attacker knows that with a very high probability only one sequence in each pair (P, P') represents a row in one of the blocks H_i and for every two different pairs these sequences correspond to rows in distinct blocks H_i and H_j. Let P_1 be the set of positions of ones in the first row of H_1. If we reorder rows of H by a cyclical shift, the resulting matrix will still be a parity check matrix for the private code composed of circulant blocks. Thus the attacker can assume that the first position in P_1 is 0 and that the second position is equal to $\min(DS(P_1))$. Therefore, upon observing solutions to Problem 1 to be n_0 pairs (P, P'), the attacker obtains $(n_0!) \times 2^{n_0} \times p^{n_0-1}$ candidates for the matrix H. For the parameters from Sect. 3.3 this means obtaining approximately 2^{32} candidates.

3.6   Reconstructing the Matrix Q

Due to the intuition presented in Sect. 3.2, the attacker expects distances present in circulant blocks in the first block-row of the matrix Q to give the smallest ratios $\frac{u[d]}{v[d]}$ in the experiment from Sect. 3.3. This was the case in our experiment, where for distances present in circulant blocks in the first block-row of Q the ratio was always below 0.085, whereas for other distances it was always above 0.105. The graph of the ratios $\frac{u[d]}{v[d]}$ is presented in Fig. 2. Thus the attacker can select distances for which the ratio $\frac{u[d]}{v[d]}$ in the experiment was below some small threshold L and try to reconstruct the first block-row of the matrix Q from these distances. Let D'_L be the set of distances for which the ratio $\frac{u[d]}{v[d]}$ in the experiment was below a threshold L. Suppose that the attacker knows that the Hamming weight of rows in circulant blocks of Q is either w_1 or w_2. (this was the case in the cryptosystems proposed in [3]). Then the attacker can try to solve the following problem:

Problem 2. Given a set $D_L = \{d : d \in D'_L \text{ or } p - d \in D'_L\}$, find all P such that $|P| \in \{w_1, w_2\}$, $DS(P) \subset D_L$, $p_0 = 0$ and $p_1 = \min(DS(P))$.

If P satisfies all the conditions in the problem, it becomes a candidate for a row in one of the blocks in the first block-row of Q. Again, if a set $P =$

---

[2] In particular, we ran Algorithm 2 with inputs $D = D_{0.118}$ and $w = 13$ for all possible values of p_1. We tested candidates for p_1 in ascending order. After a candidate for p_1 was tested, it was removed from $D_{0.118}$.

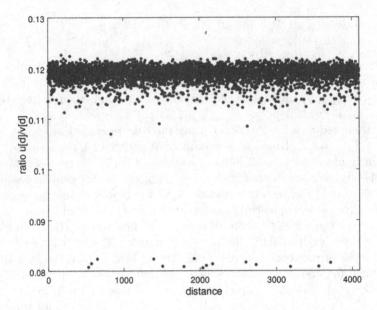

Fig. 2. Ratios $\frac{u[d]}{v[d]}$ from the experiment in Sect. 3.3. The ratios below 0.09 correspond precisely to the distances present in circulant blocks in the first block-row of Q.

$\{p_0, p_1, p_2, \ldots, p_{w-1}\}$ satisfies the conditions in Problem 2, then so does the set $P' = \{p_0, p_1, p - p_{w-1} + p_1, p - p_{w-2} + p_1, \ldots, p - p_2 + p_1\}$.

We attempted to solve Problem 2 for the set $D_{0.085}$ derived from the data from the experiment in Sect. 3.3. For the cryptosystem used in Sect. 3.3, it is a public knowledge that every block-row of Q contains two blocks with rows with the Hamming weight 4 and one block with rows with the Hamming weight 3. We found 2 pairs of sequences (P, P') of length 4. For the length 3 we found 5 pairs (P, P') which were not derived from the solutions for the length 4. This result allows the attacker to build a set of $3! \times 2^2 \times 5 \times 2 \times p^3 \approx 2^{47}$ candidates for the first block-row of Q.

Provided that suitable counters are added to Algorithm 1, the attacker can analogously build sets of candidates for other block-rows of Q. However, if the attacker wanted to combine these sets to produce one set of candidates for Q, the resulting set would be too large.

3.7 Learning to Decrypt

Instead of reconstructing the private key $\{H, S, Q\}$, the attacker can try to construct the matrix $\tilde{H} = H \times Q^T$. The matrix $\tilde{H}$ is a parity check matrix of the public code since $G' \cdot \tilde{H}^T = S^{-1} \cdot G \cdot Q^{-1} \cdot Q \cdot H^T = S^{-1} \cdot G \cdot H^T = S^{-1} \cdot 0 = 0$. The matrix $\tilde{H}$ contains at most $n_0 \times w \times m$ ones in a row. Due to the sparsity of the matrix $\tilde{H}$, the attacker can hope to use an LDPC decoding algorithm with $\tilde{H}$ to decrypt an arbitrary message encrypted by the cryptosystem.

The attacker can try to construct the first block of the matrix $\tilde{H}$. For the block $\tilde{H}_0$ it holds that $\tilde{H}_0 = \sum_{i=0}^{n_0-1} H_i \left(Q_{0i}\right)^T$. For each H_i, the set of solutions to Problem 1 contains a sequence P^i which represents a row in H_i. Since the first column of a circulant matrix is equal to its last row reversed, the transpose of a circulant matrix generates the same distance spectrum as the original matrix. Therefore, for every $\left(Q_{0i}\right)^T$, the set of solutions of Problem 2 contains a sequence $P^{Q,i}$ which represents a row in $\left(Q_{0i}\right)^T$. For the sequences P^i and $P^{Q,i}$ we consider polynomials $p^i(x)$ and $p^{Q,i}(x)$ obtained as follows: to a sequence $P = \{p_0, p_1, \ldots, p_{s-1}\}$ we allocate the polynomial $p(x) = \sum_{j=0}^{s-1} x^{p_j}$.

Next, we will use the fact that the ring of circulant binary matrices of dimension $p \times p$ is isomorphic to the ring $\mathbb{Z}_2[x]/(x^p + 1)$. The isomorphism maps a circulant matrix with the first row $(c_0, c_1, c_2, \ldots, c_{p-1})$ onto the polynomial $c(x) = c_0 + c_1 x + c_2 x^2 + \cdots + c_{p-1} x^{p-1}$. Therefore for the polynomial $\tilde{h}_0(x)$ corresponding to the block $\tilde{H}_0$ we have $\tilde{h}_0(x) = \sum_{i=0}^{n_0-1} \left(x^{\alpha_i} p^i(x)\right) \left(x^{\beta_i} p^{Q,i}(x)\right) \pmod{x^p + 1}$ for some $\alpha_i, \beta_i \in \{0, 1, \ldots, p-1\}$. Thus we have $\tilde{h}_0(x) = \sum_{i=0}^{n_0-1} x^{\gamma_i} p^i(x) p^{Q,i}(x)$ $\pmod{x^p + 1}$ for some $\gamma_i \in \{0, 1, \ldots, p-1\}$. If we reorder rows of $\tilde{H}$ by a cyclical shift, the resulting matrix will still be a parity check matrix for the public code. Thus it suffices the attacker to look for the polynomial $\tilde{h}_0(x)$ with $\gamma_0 = 0$.

Suppose that the attacker attacks the cryptosystem which we used in Sect. 3.3 and suppose that he obtains the same number of solution to Problem 1 and Problem 2 as we obtained in Sects. 3.5 and 3.6. Then the attacker can create $3! \times 2^3 \times 2^2 \times 5 \times 2 \times p^2 \approx 2^{37}$ candidates for $\tilde{h}_0(x)$.

Having obtained a number of candidates for the first row of $\tilde{H}_0$, the attacker can proceed to create a set of candidates for the first row of $\tilde{H}$. Let V be the set of candidates for the first row of $\tilde{H}_0$. For every $v \in V$, the attacker will look for words in the dual code to G' starting with v and having the Hamming weight at most $n_0 \times w \times m$. Thus the attacker can look for vectors $u^1, \ldots, u^{n_0-1} \in \mathbb{Z}_2^p$ satisfying

$$\begin{pmatrix} G'_{00} & G'_{01} & \cdots & G'_{0,n_0-1} \\ \vdots & \vdots & \ddots & \vdots \\ G'_{n_0-2,0} & G'_{n_0-2,1} & \cdots & G'_{n_0-2,n_0-1} \end{pmatrix} \begin{pmatrix} v \\ u^1 \\ \vdots \\ u^{n_0-1} \end{pmatrix} = \begin{pmatrix} 0 \\ 0 \\ \vdots \\ 0 \end{pmatrix}.$$

The equation can be rewritten as

$$\begin{pmatrix} G'_{01} & \cdots & G'_{0,n_0-1} \\ \vdots & \ddots & \vdots \\ G'_{n_0-2,1} & \cdots & G'_{n_0-2,n_0-1} \end{pmatrix} \begin{pmatrix} u^1 \\ \vdots \\ u^{n_0-1} \end{pmatrix} = \begin{pmatrix} G'_{00} \\ G'_{10} \\ G'_{20} \end{pmatrix} (v). \tag{1}$$

For the cryptosystem from Sect. 3.3 the matrix on the left-hand side of the Eq. (1) had a full rank. Therefore, for the cryptosystem from Sect. 3.3, the Eq. (1) has at most one solution for a given v. In Appendix, we consider a scenario when the matrix on the left-hand side of the Eq. (1) has each of its circulant blocks generated uniformly independently at random. We argue that for values of n_0 and the block length p relevant for the QC-LDPC McEliece cryptosystem the probability that the rank of the matrix is close to the full rank is always nontrivial. Thus it is reasonable to expect that the Eq. (1) will with a nontrivial probability have only a small number of solutions.

Note that the attacker needs to put the matrix on the left-hand side of the Eq. (1) in the reduced upper echelon form only once and can use the reduced upper echelon form for every $v \in V$. The attacker will keep only those solutions with $w_H((v, u^1, \ldots, u^{n_0-1})) \leq n_0 \times w \times m$. Each solution fully determines a candidate for the matrix $\tilde{H}$. If the resulting set of candidates for $\tilde{H}$ contains more than one element, the correct candidate can be determined by checking against a plaintext-ciphertext pair.

For the cryptosystem from Sect. 3.3, we have verified that $\tilde{H}$ can be used in a LDPC decoding algorithm to successfully decrypt ciphertexts.

4   Conclusion

We have presented a reaction attack on the QC-LDPC McEliece cryptosystem. Our attack is based on ideas from [5], where the attack on the closely related QC-MDPC McEliece cryptosystem was described. Compared to the recent attack on the QC-LDPC McEliece presented in [12], our attack has the advantage that it is feasible even when the size of circulant blocks in the cryptosystem is chosen to be odd.

We have verified the attack ideas on a version of QC-LDPC McEliece cryptosystem with parameters as proposed in [3], except for the parameter t' which we increased from 40 to 48. The parameter t' represents the number of errors added to an encoded message. Its increase resulted in the cryptosystem's probability of the decoding error to increase to approximately 0.1. This allowed us to estimate the probability of the decoding error using fewer decryptions. Consequently, we were able to break the cryptosystem after running 103 million decryptions.

In real applications the probability of the decoding error of around 0.1 would be very impractical. Thus, one would expect the QC-LDPC cryptosystem to be used with a value of t' which makes the probability of the decoding error significantly smaller. If this is the case, and if the attacker cannot inject into encoded messages a number of errors higher than t', then the attacker would need significantly more decryptions to estimate the probability of the decoding error and execute the attack. For instance, results of simulations presented in [1] (Fig. 6.1. on p. 88 in [1]) indicate that if the original value $t' = 40$ was used in the cryptosystem considered in this paper, then the probability of the decoding error would be of order 10^{-5}. Therefore, we expect that the attacker who can only send messages with $t' = 40$ errors would need 10^4 times more decryptions in order to break the cryptosystem.

In the experiments presented in this paper, we always assumed that the attacker does not have the freedom to choose what error vector is added to the message during encryption. Although we omitted the results from this paper, we also conducted experiments for the scenario where the attacker is free to choose the error vector. Similarly as in [5], we considered an attacker who for every possible distance d constructs error vectors with many pairs of ones separated by the distance d. In this case, it turns out that the attacker can break the same cryptosystem with $t' = 48$ with only 4 million decryptions.

The version of the QC-LDPC McEliece cryptosystem we used to verify our attack ideas employed a soft-decision decoding algorithm. Thus our results also confirm the conjecture from [5] that soft-decision decoding algorithms can be vulnerable to leak information about the secret parity-check matrix.

References

1. Baldi, M.: QC-LDPC Code-Based Cryptography. Springer Science & Business, Heidelberg (2014)
2. Baldi, M., Chiaraluce, F.: Cryptanalysis of a new instance of McEliece cryptosystem based on QC-LDPC codes. In: Proceedings of IEEE ISIT 2007, Nice, France, June 2007, pp. 2591–2595 (2007)
3. Baldi, M., Bodrato, M., Chiaraluce, F.: A new analysis of the McEliece cryptosystem based on QCLDPC codes. In: Ostrovsky, R., De Prisco, R., Visconti, I. (eds.) 6th International Conference on Security and Cryptography for Networks (SCN 2008). LNCS, vol. 5229, pp. 246–262. Springer, Berlin (2008)
4. BitPunch. https://github.com/FrUh/BitPunch
5. Guo, Q., Johansson, T., Stankovski, P.: A key recovery attack on MDPC with CCA security using decoding errors. In: Cheon, J.H., Takagi, T. (eds.) ASIACRYPT 2016. LNCS, vol. 10031, pp. 789–815. Springer, Heidelberg (2016). doi:10.1007/978-3-662-53887-6_29
6. Hill, R.: A First Course in Coding Theory. Oxford University Press, Oxford (1986)
7. Jungnickel, D.: Finite Fields: Structure and Arithmetics. B.I Wissenschaftsverlag, Leipzig (1993)
8. McEliece, R.J.: A public-key cryptosystem based on algebraic coding theory. Deep Space Netw. Prog. Rep. **44**, 114–116 (1978)
9. Misoczki, R., Tillich, J.-P., Sendrier, N., Barreto, P.: MDPC-McEliece: new McEliece variants from moderate density parity-check codes. In: IEEE International Symposium on Information Theory (ISIT2013), Istanbul, pp. 2069–2073 (2013)
10. Otmani, A., Tillich, J.P., Dallot, L.: Cryptanalysis of two McEliece cryptosystems based on quasi-cyclic codes. In: Proceedings of First International Conference on Symbolic Computation and Cryptography, Beijing, China, (SCC 2008) (2008)
11. Radford, M.N.: Software for Low Density Parity Check (LDPC) codes. http://www.cs.utoronto.ca/radford/ldpc.software.html
12. Shooshtari, M.K., Ahmadian-Attari, M., Johansson, T., Aref, M.R.: Cryptanalysis of McEliece cryptosystem variants based on quasi-cyclic low-density parity check codes. IET Inf. Secur. **10**(4), 194–202 (2016)

Appendix: On the Rank of a Randomly Generated Block-Circulant Matrix

In this appendix we study the rank over GF(2) of a matrix composed of $n_0 \times n_0$ randomly generated circulant blocks, the blocks being of size $p \times p$. We focus on the case when p is odd, since this ensures that the QC-LDPC McEliece cryptosystem is immune against the attack presented in [12].

Firstly, we recall some well-known facts about circulant matrices.

Fact 1 *(Proposition 1.7.1 in [7]). Consider the mapping τ which sends the circulant binary $(p \times p)$-matrix with the first row $(c_0, c_1, c_2, \ldots, c_{p-1})$ onto the polynomial $c(x) = c_0 + c_1 x + c_2 x^2 + \cdots + c_{p-1} x^{p-1}$. Then the mapping τ is an isomorphism between the ring of circulant binary $(p \times p)$-matrices and the ring $\mathbb{Z}_2[x]/(x^p + 1)$.*

Fact 2 *(p. 42 in [7]). The inverse of a non-singular circulant matrix is again circulant. A circulant binary $(p \times p)$-matrix C is non-singular if and only if $\tau(C)$ is relatively prime to $x^p + 1$.*

Let f be a polynomial in $\mathbb{Z}_2[x]/(x^p + 1)$ and let $f(x) = g(x)h(x)$ where $g(x) = \gcd(f(x), x^p + 1)$. Then $\tau^{-1}(f) = \tau^{-1}(g)\tau^{-1}(h)$. By Fact 2, $\tau^{-1}(h)$ is non-singular. Therefore $\tau^{-1}(f)$ has the same rank as $\tau^{-1}(g)$. It is well-known (e.g. Theorem 12.12 in [6]) that $\tau^{-1}(g)$ generates a cyclic code of dimension $p - d$ where d is the degree of g. Thus we have:

Fact 3. *The rank of a circulant binary $(p \times p)$-matrix C is equal to $p - d$ where d is the degree of $\gcd(\tau(C), x^p + 1)$.*

Let f and g be polynomials in $\mathbb{Z}_2[x]$, and denote by $\psi(f)$ the number of polynomials of smaller degree which are relatively prime to f in $\mathbb{Z}_2[x]$.

Fact 4 *(Theorem 1.7.5 in [7]). If $\gcd(f(x), g(x)) = 1$, then $\psi(fg) = \psi(f)\psi(g)$*

Fact 5 *(Theorem 1.7.6 in [7]). Let p be odd. Then we have*

$$\psi(x^p + 1) = 2^p \prod_{j|p} \left(1 - 2^{-o_j(2)}\right)^{\phi(j)/o_j(2)}.$$

Here $o_j(2)$ denotes the order of 2 in the group $\mathbb{Z}_j^*$ and $\phi(j)$ denotes the Euler function.

It follows that the number of $p \times p$ circulant matrices with full rank is $\psi(x^p + 1)$. Circulant $p \times p$ matrices with rank $p - 1$ are precisely the matrices whose corresponding polynomial is a product of $x + 1$ and a polynomial coprime to $\frac{x^p+1}{x+1}$ with degree less than $p - 1$. If p is odd, then $x + 1$ appears in the irreducible factorization of $x^p + 1$ only once. Thus it follows that the number of $p \times p$ circulant matrices with rank $p - 1$ is $\psi(\frac{x^p+1}{x+1}) = \psi(x^p + 1)/\psi(x + 1) = \psi(x^p + 1)$.

Now we turn to block-circulant matrices. Let $\rho(p) = \psi(x^p + 1)/2^p$.

Proposition 1. *Let p be odd. Let B be a matrix composed of $(n_0 - 1) \times (n_0 - 1)$ circulant blocks of size $p \times p$. Suppose that the blocks in B were generated uniformly and independently at random from the space of all binary circulant $p \times p$ matrices. Then*

$$P(rank(B) \geq (n_0 - 1) \times (p - 1)) \geq \prod_{i=1}^{n_0-1} \left(1 - (1 - \rho(p))^i + \rho(p)^i \right).$$

Proof. Let B_{ij} be the $p \times p$ block present in the i-th block-row and j-th block-column of B. Let $b_{ij}(x) = \tau(B_{ij})$. With probability $1 - (1 - \rho(p))^{n_0-1} + \rho(p)^{n_0-1}$ it holds that either one of the blocks in the first block-column is invertible or all blocks in the first block-column have rank $p - 1$.

Firstly, we look at the case when there exists an invertible block in the first block-column. Without loss of generality we can assume that this block is B_{11} (if not, we can swap block-rows of B). For every $i \in \{2, \ldots, n_0 - 1\}$ we can erase the block B_{i1} by adding to the i-th block-row the first block-row multiplied by $\left(B_{i1} \times B_{11}^{-1} \right)$. This corresponds to multiplying B from the left by the matrix $M_i = I_{p(n_0-1) \times p(n_0-1)} + \tilde{M}_i$, where $\tilde{M}_i$ is the matrix composed of $(n_0-1) \times (n_0-1)$ blocks of size $p \times p$ with the block $B_{i1} \times B_{11}^{-1}$ in the i-th block-row and the first block-column and with zero blocks everywhere else. Thus the resulting matrix has the same rank as B. We obtain a matrix of the form

$$\begin{pmatrix} B_{11} & B_{12} & \ldots & B_{1,n_0-1} \\ 0 & & & \\ \vdots & & \tilde{B} & \\ 0 & & & \end{pmatrix}, \tag{2}$$

where $\tilde{B}$ is a matrix composed of $(n_0 - 2) \times (n_0 - 2)$ circulant blocks of size $p \times p$. Let $\tilde{B}_{ij}$ be the $p \times p$ block present in the i-th block-row and j-th block-column of $\tilde{B}$. Then $\tilde{B}_{ij} = B_{i+1,1} \times B_{11}^{-1} \times B_{1,j+1} + B_{i+1,j+1}$. The block $B_{i+1,j+1}$ was generated independently from all other blocks in B, hence we can see $\tilde{B}_{ij}$ as a sum of $B_{i+1,j+1}$ and an independent circulant matrix. Since $B_{i+1,j+1}$ was generated uniformly at random from the space of circulant $p \times p$ matrices, $\tilde{B}_{ij}$ will, like $B_{i+1,j+1}$, have the property that each bit in its first row will be 1 with probability $1/2$ independently of other bits in its first row. Thus we can think of $\tilde{B}_{i,j}$ as of another uniformly randomly generated matrix from the space of circulant $p \times p$ matrices. Moreover, $\tilde{B}_{i,j}$ is independent of other blocks in $\tilde{B}$ and it is also independent of blocks in the first block-column of the original matrix B.

Now we consider the case when all blocks in the first block-column of B have rank $p - 1$. Then for every $b_{i1}(x)$ there exists $r_i(x) \in \mathbb{Z}_2[x]/(x^p + 1)$ such that $b_{i1}(x)r_i(x) = x + 1 \mod (x^p + 1)$ (the polynomial $r_i(x)$ can be found by the extended Euclidean algorithm). Thus for every $i \in \{2, \ldots, n_0 - 1\}$ we can erase the block B_{i1} by adding to the i-th block-row the first block-row multiplied by $\tau^{-1} \left(\frac{b_{i1}(x)}{x+1} \right) \times \tau^{-1} (r_1(x))$. By the same argument as in the previous case, this will not change the rank of B. We obtain a matrix of the form (2), where $\tilde{B}$ is again composed of $(n_0 - 2) \times (n_0 - 2)$ circulant blocks of size $p \times p$. Now we have

$\tilde{B}_{ij} = \tau^{-1}\left(\frac{b_{i+1,1}(x)}{x+1}\right) \times \tau^{-1}\left(r_1(x)\right) \times B_{1,j+1} + B_{i+1,j+1}$. By the same argument as in the previous case, we can again think of $\tilde{B}_{i,j}$ as of a uniformly randomly generated matrix from the space of circulant $p \times p$ matrices. In addition, $\tilde{B}_{i,j}$ is independent of other blocks in $\tilde{B}$ and it is also independent of blocks in the first block-column of the original matrix B.

Thus in both cases we were able to transform the matrix B to a matrix of the form (2), while preserving its rank. The submatrix $\tilde{B}$ in (2) has the same properties as the original matrix B except it contains $(n_0 - 2) \times (n_0 - 2)$ blocks instead of $(n_0-1) \times (n_0-1)$ blocks. In addition, the submatrix $\tilde{B}$ is independent of blocks in the first block-column of the original matrix B. Proceeding inductively, the statement of the proposition follows.

In the QC-LDPC McEliece cryptosystem n_0 is typically small (3 or 4, for example). Let $\alpha(p, n_0)$ be the lower bound from Proposition 1, i.e.

$$\alpha(p, n_0) = \prod_{i=1}^{n_0-1} \left(1 - (1 - \rho(p))^i + \rho(p)^i\right).$$

In Fig. 3 we present values of $\alpha(p, 4)$ for all odd p in the range from 1 to 20000. The smallest value of $\alpha(p, 4)$ in the figure is 0.11. Thus the figure shows that if $n_0 = 4$ then the probability that the rank of B is close to the full rank is nontrivial for all odd p below 20000.

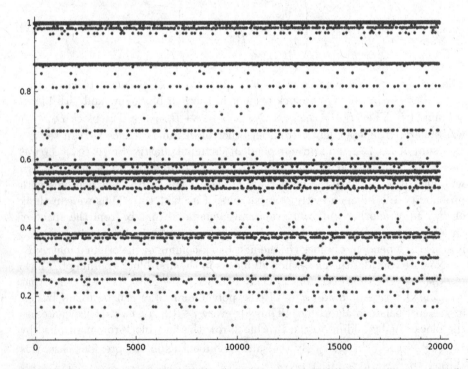

Fig. 3. Values of the lower bound $\alpha(p, 4)$ for the probability that a matrix composed of 3×3 circulant blocks of size $p \times p$ which are generated uniformly and independently at random has rank at least $3 \times (p - 1)$ for all odd p in the range from 1 to 20000.

Quantum Information Set Decoding Algorithms

Ghazal Kachigar[1] and Jean-Pierre Tillich[2(✉)]

[1] Institut de Mathématiques de Bordeaux,
. Université de Bordeaux, Talence Cedex 33405, France
`ghazal.kachigar@u-bordeaux.fr`
[2] Inria, EPI SECRET, 2 rue Simone Iff, Paris 75012, France
`jean-pierre.tillich@inria.fr`

Abstract. The security of code-based cryptosystems such as the McEliece cryptosystem relies primarily on the difficulty of decoding random linear codes. The best decoding algorithms are all improvements of an old algorithm due to Prange: they are known under the name of information set decoding techniques. It is also important to assess the security of such cryptosystems against a quantum computer. This research thread started in [23] and the best algorithm to date has been Bernstein's quantising [5] of the simplest information set decoding algorithm, namely Prange's algorithm. It consists in applying Grover's quantum search to obtain a quadratic speed-up of Prange's algorithm. In this paper, we quantise other information set decoding algorithms by using quantum walk techniques which were devised for the subset-sum problem in [6]. This results in improving the worst-case complexity of $2^{0.06035n}$ of Bernstein's algorithm to $2^{0.05869n}$ with the best algorithm presented here (where n is the codelength).

1 Introduction

As humanity's technological prowess improves, quantum computers have moved from the realm of theoretical constructs to that of objects whose consequences for our other technologies, such as cryptography, must be taken into account. Indeed, currently prevalent public-key cryptosystems such as RSA and ECDH are vulnerable to Shor's algorithm [27], which solves factorisation and the discrete logarithm problem in polynomial time. Thus, in order to find a suitable replacement, it has become necessary to study the impact of quantum computers on other candidate cryptosystems. Code-based cryptosystems such as the McEliece [21] and the Niederreiter [22] cryptosystems are such possible candidates.

Their security essentially relies on decoding a linear code. Recall that the decoding problem consists, when given a linear code $\mathcal{C}$ and a noisy codeword $c + e$, in recovering c, where c is an unknown codeword of $\mathcal{C}$ and e an unknown error of Hamming weight w. A (binary) linear code $\mathcal{C}$ of dimension k and length n is specified by a full rank binary matrix H (i.e. a parity-check matrix) of size $(n - k) \times n$ as

$$\mathcal{C} = \{c \in \mathbb{F}_2^n : Hc^T = 0\}.$$

© Springer International Publishing AG 2017
T. Lange and T. Takagi (Eds.): PQCrypto 2017, LNCS 10346, pp. 69–89, 2017.
DOI: 10.1007/978-3-319-59879-6_5

Since $H(c+e)^T = Hc^T + He^T = He^T$ the decoding problem can be rephrased as a syndome decoding problem

Problem 1 (Syndrome Decoding Problem). Given H and $s^T = He^T$, where $|e| = w$, find e.

This problem has been studied since the Sixties and despite significant efforts on this issue [2,4,7,11,19,20,24,28] the best algorithms for solving this problem [4,20] are exponential in the number of errors that have to be corrected: correcting w errors in a binary linear code of length n and dimension k has with the aforementioned algorithms a cost of $\tilde{O}(2^{\alpha(\frac{k}{n},\frac{w}{n})n})$ where $\alpha(R,w)$ is positive when R and w are both positive. All these algorithms use in a crucial way the original idea due to Prange [24] and are known under the name of Information Set Decoding (ISD) algorithms: they all take advantage of the fact that there might exist a rather large set of positions containing an information set of the code[1] that is almost error free.

All the efforts that have been spent on this problem have only managed to decrease slightly this exponent $\alpha(R,w)$. The following table gives an overview of the average time complexity of currently existing classical algorithms when w is the Gilbert-Varshamov distance $d_{GV}(n,k)$ of the code. This quantity is defined by $d_{GV}(n,k) \overset{\triangle}{=} nH_2^{-1}(1 - \frac{k}{n})$ where H_2 is the binary entropy function $H_2(x) \overset{\triangle}{=} -x\log_2(x) - (1-x)\log_2(1-x)$ and H_2^{-1} its inverse defined from $[0,1]$ to $[0,\frac{1}{2}]$. It corresponds to the largest distance for which we may still expect a unique solution to the decoding problem. If we want uniqueness of the solution, it can therefore be considered as the hardest instance of decoding. In the following table, w_{GV} is defined by the ratio $w_{GV} \overset{\triangle}{=} d_{GV}(n,k)/n$.

Author(s)	Year	$\max\limits_{0 \leq R \leq 1} \alpha(R, w_{GV})$ to 4 dec. places
Prange [24]	1962	0.1207
Dumer [11]	1991	0.1164
MMT [19]	2011	0.1114
BJMM [4]	2012	0.1019
MO [20]	2015	0.0966

The question of using quantum algorithms to speed up ISD decoding algorithms was first put forward in [23]. However, the way Grover's algorithm was used in [23, Subsect. 3.5] to speed up decoding did not allow for significant improvements over classical ISD algorithms. Later on, it was shown by Bernstein in [5] that it is possible to obtain much better speedups with Grover's

---

[1] An information set of a linear code C of dimension k is a set $\mathcal{I}$ of k positions such that when given $\{c_i : i \in \mathcal{I}\}$ the codeword c of C is specified entirely.

algorithm: by using it for finding an error-free information set, the exponent of Prange's algorithm can indeed be halved.

This paper builds upon this way of using Grover's search algorithm, as well as the quantum algorithms developped by Bernstein et al. in [6] to solve the subset sum problem more efficiently. The following table summarises the ingredients and average time complexity of the algorithm of [5] and the new quantum algorithms presented in this paper.

Author(s)	Year	Ingredients	$\max\limits_{0 \le R \le 1} \alpha(R, \omega_{\mathrm{GV}})$
Bernstein [5]	2010	Prange + Grover	0.06035
This paper	2017	Shamir-Schroeppel + Grover + QuantumWalk	0.05970
This paper	2017	MMT + "1 + 1 = 0" + Grover + QuantumWalk	0.05869

A quick calculation shows that the complexity exponent of our best quantum algorithm, $MMTQW$, fulfils $\alpha_{\mathrm{MMTQW}} \approx \frac{\alpha_{\mathrm{Dumer}}}{2} + 4.9 \times 10^{-4}$. Thus, our best quantum algorithm improves in a small but non-trivial way on [5]. Several reasons will be given throughout this paper on why it has been difficult to do better than this.

Notation. Throughout the paper, we denote by $|e|$ the Hamming weight of a vector e. We use the same notation for denoting the cardinality of a set, i.e. $|\mathscr{S}|$ denotes the cardinality of the set $\mathscr{S}$. The meaning of this notation will be clear from the context and we will use calligraphic letters to denote sets: $\mathscr{S}, \mathfrak{I}, \mathcal{M}, \ldots$. We use the standard $O\,(), \Omega\,(), \Theta\,()$ notation and use the less standard $\tilde{O}\,(), \tilde{\Omega}\,(), \tilde{\Theta}\,()$ notation to mean "$O\,(), \Omega\,(), \Theta\,()$, when we ignore logarithmic factors". Here all the quantities we are interested in are functions of the codelength n and we write $f(n) = \tilde{O}\,(g(n))$ for instance, when there exists a constant k such that $f(n) = O\left(g(n)\log^{k}(g(n))\right)$.

2   Quantum Search Algorithms

2.1   Grover Search

Grover's search algorithm [13,14] is, along with its generalisation [8] which is used in this paper, an optimal algorithm for solving the following problem with a quadratic speed-up compared to the best-possible classical algorithm.

Problem 2 (Unstructured search problem). Given a set $\mathcal{E}$ and a function $f : \mathcal{E} \rightarrow \{0, 1\}$, find an $x \in \mathcal{E}$ such that $f(x) = 1$.

In other words, we need to find an element that fulfils a certain property, and f is an oracle for deciding whether it does. Moreover, in the new results presented in this paper, f will be a quantum algorithm. If we denote by ε the proportion of elements x of $\mathcal{E}$ such that $f(x) = 1$, Grover's algorithm solves the problem above using $O(\frac{1}{\sqrt{\varepsilon}})$ queries to f, whereas in the classical setting this cannot be done with less than $O(\frac{1}{\varepsilon})$ queries. Furthermore, if the algorithm f executes in time T_f on average, the average time complexity of Grover's algorithm will be $O(\frac{T_f}{\sqrt{\varepsilon}})$.

2.2 Quantum Walk

Random Walk. Unstructured search problems as well as search problems with slightly more but still minimal structure may be recast as graph search problems.

Problem 3 (Graph search problem). Given a graph $G = (\mathcal{V}, \mathcal{E})$ and a set of vertices $\mathcal{M} \subset \mathcal{V}$, called the set of *marked elements*, find an $x \in \mathcal{M}$.

The graph search problem may then be solved using random walks (discrete-time Markov chains) on the vertices of the graph. From now on, we will take the graph to be undirected, connected, and d-regular, i.e. such that each vertex has exactly d neighbours.

Markov Chain. A Markov chain is given by an initial probability distribution v and a stochastic transition matrix M. The transition matrix of a random walk on a graph (as specified above) is obtained from the graph's adjacency matrix A by $M = \frac{1}{d}A$.

Eigenvalues and the Spectral Gap. A closer look at the eigenvalues and the eigenvectors of M is needed in order to analyse the complexity of a random walk on a graph. The eigenvalues will be noted λ_i and the corresponding eigenvectors v_i. We will admit the following points (see [10]):

  (i) all the eigenvalues lie in the interval $[-1, 1]$;
 (ii) 1 is always an eigenvalue, the corresponding eigenspace is of dimension 1;
(iii) there is a corresponding eigenvector which is also a probability distribution (namely the uniform distribution u over the vertices). It is the unique stationary distribution of the random walk.

We will suppose that the eigenvalues are ordered from largest to smallest, so that $\lambda_1 = 1$ and $v_1 = u$. An important value associated with the transition matrix of a Markov chain is its *spectral gap*, defined as $\delta \stackrel{\triangle}{=} 1 - \max_{i=2,\dots,d} |\lambda_i|$. Such a random walk on an undirected regular graph is always *reversible* and it is also *irreducible* because we have assumed that the graph is connected. The random walk is *aperiodic* in such a case if and only if the spectral gap δ is positive. In such a case, a long enough random walk in the graph converges to the uniform distribution since for all $\eta > 0$, we have $||M^k v - u|| < \eta$ for $k = \tilde{O}(1/\delta)$, where v is the initial probability distribution.

  Finding a marked element by running a Markov chain on the graph consists in the steps given in Algorithm 1.

Algorithm 1. *RandomWalk*

Input: $G = (\mathcal{E}, \mathcal{V})$, $\mathcal{M} \subset \mathcal{V}$, initial probability distribution v
Output: An element $e \in \mathcal{M}$

1 SETUP : Sample a vertex x according to v and initialise the data structure.
2 **repeat**
3   CHECK : **if** *current vertex x is marked* **then**
4 | **return** x
5 **else**
6 | **repeat**
7 | | UPDATE : Take one step of the random walk and update data structure accordingly.
8 | **until** *x is sampled according to a distribution close enough to the uniform distribution*
9

Let T_s be the cost of SETUP, T_c be the cost of CHECK and T_u be the cost of UPDATE. It follows from the preceding considerations that $\tilde{O}(1/\delta)$ steps of the random walk are sufficient to sample x according to the uniform distribution. Furthermore, if we note $\varepsilon := \frac{|\mathcal{M}|}{|\mathcal{V}|}$ the proportion of marked elements, it is readily seen that the algorithm ends after $O(1/\varepsilon)$ iterations of the outer loop. Thus the complexity of classical random walk is $T_s + \frac{1}{\varepsilon}\left(T_c + \frac{1}{\delta}T_u\right)$.

Several quantum versions of random walk algorithms have been proposed by many authors, notably Ambainis [1], Szegedy [29], and Magniez et al. [18]. A survey of these results can be found in [25]. We use here the following result.

Theorem 1 [18]. *Let M be an aperiodic, irreducible and reversible Markov chain on a graph with spectral gap δ, and $\varepsilon := \frac{|\mathcal{M}|}{|\mathcal{V}|}$ as above. Then there is a quantum walk algorithm that finds an element in $\mathcal{M}$ with cost*

$$\boxed{T_s + \frac{1}{\sqrt{\varepsilon}}\left(T_c + \frac{1}{\sqrt{\delta}}T_u\right)} \tag{1}$$

Johnson Graphs and Product Graphs. With the exception of Grover's search algorithm seen as a quantum walk algorithm, to date an overwhelming majority of quantum walk algorithms are based on Johnson graphs or a variant thereof. The decoding algorithms which shall be presented in this paper rely on cartesian products of Johnson graphs. All of these objects are defined in this section and some important properties are mentioned.

Definition 1 (Johnson graphs). *A Johnson graph $J(n, r)$ is an undirected graph whose vertices are the subsets containing r elements of a set of size n, with an edge between two vertices S and S' iff $|S \cap S'| = r - 1$. In other words, S is adjacent to S' if S' can be obtained from S by removing an element and adding a new element in its place.*

It is clear that $J(n,r)$ has $\binom{n}{r}$ vertices and is $r(n-r)$-regular. Its spectral gap is given by

$$\delta = \frac{n}{r(n-r)}. \tag{2}$$

Definition 2 (Cartesian product of graphs). *Let $G_1 = (\mathcal{V}_1, \mathcal{E}_1)$ and $G_2 = (\mathcal{V}_2, \mathcal{E}_2)$ be two graphs. Their cartesian product $G_1 \times G_2$ is the graph $G = (\mathcal{V}, \mathcal{E})$ where:*

1. *$\mathcal{V} = \mathcal{V}_1 \times \mathcal{V}_2$, i.e. $\mathcal{V} = \{v_1 v_2 \mid v_1 \in \mathcal{V}_1, v_2 \in \mathcal{V}_2\}$*
2. *$\mathcal{E} = \{(u_1 u_2, v_1 v_2) \mid (u_1 = v_1 \wedge (u_2, v_2) \in \mathcal{E}_2) \vee ((u_1, v_1) \in \mathcal{E}_1 \wedge u_2 = v_2)\}$*

The spectral gap of products of Johnson graphs is given by

Theorem 2 (Cartesian product of Johnson graphs). *Let $J(n,r) = (\mathcal{V}, \mathcal{E})$, $m \in \mathbb{N}$ and $J^m(n,r) := \times_{i=1}^{m} J(n,r) = (\mathcal{V}_m, \mathcal{E}_m)$. Then:*

1. *$J^m(n,r)$ has $\binom{n}{r}^m$ vertices and is md-regular where $d = r(n-r)$.*
2. *We will write $\delta(J)$ resp. $\delta(J^m)$ for the spectral gaps of $J(n,r)$ resp. $J^m(n,r)$. Then:*
   $\delta(J^m) \geq \frac{1}{m}\delta(J)$
3. *The random walk associated with $J^m(n,r)$ is aperiodic, irreducible and reversible for all positive m, n and $r < n$.*

This theorem is proved in the full version of the paper [17, Appendix A].

3   Generalities on Classical and Quantum Decoding

We first recall how the simplest ISD algorithm [24] and its quantised version [5] work and then give a skeleton of the structure of more sophisticated classical and quantum versions.

3.1   Prange's Algorithm and Bernstein's Algorithm

Recall that the goal is to find e of weight w given $s^T = He^T$, where H is an $(n-k) \times n$ matrix. In other words, the problem we aim to solve is finding a solution to an underdetermined linear system of $n-k$ equations in n variables and the solution is unique owing to the weight condition. Prange's algorithm is based on the following observation: if it is known that k given components of the error vector are zero, the error positions are among the $n-k$ remaining components. In other words, if we know for sure that the k corresponding variables are not involved in the linear system, then the error vector can be found by solving the resulting linear system of $n-k$ equations in $n-k$ variables in polynomial time.

The hard part is finding a correct size-k set (of indices of the components). Prange's algorithm samples such sets and solves the resulting linear equation until an error vector of weight w is found. The probability for finding such a set is of order $\Omega\left(\frac{\binom{n-k}{w}}{\binom{n}{w}}\right)$ and therefore Prange's algorithm has complexity

$$O\left(\frac{\binom{n}{w}}{\binom{n-k}{w}}\right) = \tilde{O}\left(2^{\alpha_{\text{Prange}}(R,w)n}\right)$$

where

$$\alpha_{\text{Prange}}(R,w) = H_2(\omega) - (1-R)H_2\left(\frac{\omega}{1-R}\right)$$

by using the well known formula for binomials

$$\binom{n}{w} = \tilde{\Theta}\left(2^{H_2\left(\frac{w}{n}\right)n}\right).$$

Bernstein's algorithm consists in using Grover's algorithm to find a correct size-k set. Indeed, an oracle for checking that a size-k set is correct can be obtained by following the same steps as in Prange's algorithm, i.e. deriving and solving a linear system of $n-k$ equations in $n-k$ variables and returning 1 iff the resulting error vector has weight w. Thus the complexity of Bernstein's algorithm is the square root of that of Prange's algorithm, i.e. $\alpha_{\text{Bernstein}} = \frac{\alpha_{\text{Prange}}}{2}$.

3.2   Generalised ISD Algorithms

More sophisticated classical ISD algorithms [4,7,11,12,19,20,28] generalise Prange's algorithm in the following way: they introduce a new parameter p and allow p error positions inside of the size-k set (henceforth denoted by $\mathscr{S}$). Furthermore, from Dumer's algorithm onwards, a new parameter ℓ is introduced and the set $\mathscr{S}$ is taken to be of size $k + \ell$. This event happens with probability $P_{\ell,p} \triangleq \frac{\binom{k+\ell}{p}\binom{n-k-\ell}{w-p}}{\binom{n}{w}}$. Recall now the well known fact

Proposition 1. *Assume that the restriction of H to the columns belonging to the complement of $\mathscr{S}$ is a matrix of full rank, then*

(i) *the restriction e' of the error to $\mathscr{S}$ is a solution to the syndrome decoding problem*

$$H'e'^T = s'^T. \tag{3}$$

with H' being an $\ell \times (k + \ell)$ binary matrix, $|e'| = p$ and H', s' that can be computed in polynomial time from $\mathscr{S}$, H and s;

(ii) *once we have such an e', there is a unique e whose restriction to $\mathscr{S}$ is equal to e' and which satisfies $He^T = s^T$. Such an e can be computed from e' in polynomial time.*

Remark: The condition in this proposition is met with very large probability when H is chosen uniformly at random: it fails to hold with probability which is only $O(2^{-\ell})$.

Proof. Without loss of generality assume that $\mathscr{S}$ is given by the $k + \ell$ first positions. By performing Gaussian elimination, we look for a square matrix U such that

$$UH = \begin{pmatrix} H' & 0_\ell \\ H'' & I_{n-k-\ell} \end{pmatrix}$$

That such a matrix exists is a consequence of the fact that H restricted to the last $n - k - \ell$ positions is of full rank. Write now $e = (e', e'')$ where e' is the word formed by the $k + \ell$ first entries of e. Then

$$Us^T = UHe^T = \begin{pmatrix} H'e'^T \\ H''e'^T + e''^T \end{pmatrix}.$$

If we write Us^T as $(s', s'')^T$, where s'^T is the vector formed by the ℓ first entries of Us^T, then we recover e from e' by using the fact that $H''e'^T + e''^T = s''^T$. □

From now on, we denote by Σ and h the functions that can be computed in polynomial time that are promised by this proposition, i.e.

$$s' = \Sigma(s, H, \mathscr{S})$$
$$e = h(e')$$

In other words, all these algorithms solve in a first step a new instance of the syndrome decoding problem with different parameters. The difference with the original problem is that if ℓ is small, which is the case in general, there is not a single solution anymore. However searching for all (or a large set of them) can be done more efficiently than just brute-forcing over all errors of weight p on the set $\mathscr{S}$. Once a possible solution e' to (3) is found, e is recovered as explained before. The main idea which avoids brute forcing over all possible errors of weight p on $\mathscr{S}$ is to obtain candidates e' by solving an instance of a generalised k-sum problem that we define as follows.

Problem 4 (generalised k-sum problem). Consider an Abelian group G, an arbitrary set $\mathscr{E}$, a map f from $\mathscr{E}$ to G, k subsets $\mathcal{V}_0, \mathcal{V}_1, \ldots, \mathcal{V}_{k-1}$ of $\mathscr{E}$, another map g from $\mathscr{E}^k$ to $\{0, 1\}$, and an element $S \in G$. Find a solution $(v_0, \ldots, v_{k-1}) \in \mathcal{V}_0 \times \ldots \mathcal{V}_{k-1}$ such that we have at the same time

(i) $f(v_0) + f(v_1) \cdots + f(v_{k-1}) = S$ (subset-sum condition);
(ii) $g(v_0, \ldots, v_{k-1}) = 0$ (($v_0, \ldots, v_{k-1}$) is a root of g).

Dumer's ISD algorithm, for instance, solves the 2-sum problem in the case where

$$G = \mathbb{F}_2^\ell, \quad \mathscr{E} = \mathbb{F}_2^{k+\ell}, \quad f(v) = H'v^T$$
$$\mathcal{V}_0 = \{(e_0, 0_{(k+\ell)/2}) \in \mathbb{F}_2^{k+\ell} : e_0 \in \mathbb{F}_2^{(k+\ell)/2}, |e_0| = p/2\}$$
$$\mathcal{V}_1 = \{(0_{(k+\ell)/2}, e_1) \in \mathbb{F}_2^{k+\ell} : e_1 \in \mathbb{F}_2^{(k+\ell)/2}, |e_1| = p/2\}$$

and $g(v_0, v_1) = 0$ if and only if $e = h(e')$ is of weight w where $e' = v_0 + v_1$. A solution to the 2-sum problem is then clearly a solution to the decoding problem by construction. The point is that the 2-sum problem can be solved in time which is much less than $|\mathcal{V}_0| \cdot |\mathcal{V}_1|$. For instance, this can clearly be achieved in expected time $|\mathcal{V}_0| + |\mathcal{V}_1| + \frac{|\mathcal{V}_0| \cdot |\mathcal{V}_1|}{|\mathcal{G}|}$ and space $|\mathcal{G}|$ by storing the elements v_0 of $\mathcal{V}_0$ in a hashtable at the address $f(v_0)$ and then going over all elements v_1 of the other set to check whether or not the address $S - f(v_1)$ contains an element. The term $\frac{|\mathcal{V}_0| \cdot |\mathcal{V}_1|}{|\mathcal{G}|}$ accounts for the expected number of solutions of the 2-sum problem when the elements of $\mathcal{V}_0$ and $\mathcal{V}_1$ are chosen uniformly at random in $\mathcal{E}$ (which is the assumption what we are going to make from on). This is precisely what Dumer's algorithm does. Generally, the size of $\mathcal{G}$ is chosen such that $|\mathcal{G}| = \Theta(|\mathcal{V}_i|)$ and the space and time complexity are also of this order.

Generalised ISD algorithms are thus composed of a loop in which first a set $\mathcal{S}$ is sampled and then an error vector having a certain form, namely with p error positions in $\mathcal{S}$ and $w - p$ error positions outside of $\mathcal{S}$, is sought. Thus, for each ISD algorithm A, we will denote by $Search_A$ the algorithm whose exact implementation depends on A but whose specification is always $Search_A : \mathcal{S}, H, s, w, p \rightarrow \{e \,|\, e$ has weight p on $\mathcal{S}$ and weight $w - p$ on $\overline{\mathcal{S}}$ and $s^T = He^T\} \cup \{NULL\}$, where $\mathcal{S}$ is a set of indices, H is the parity-check matrix of the code and s is the syndrome of the error we are looking for. The following pseudo-code gives the structure of a generalised ISD algorithm.

Algorithm 2. ISD_Skeleton

Input: H, s, w, p
Output: e of weight w such that $s^T = He^T$
1 **repeat**
2 $\quad$ Sample a set of indices $\mathcal{S} \subset \{1, ..., n\}$
3 $\quad$ $e \leftarrow Search_A(\mathcal{S}, H, s, w, p)$
4 **until** $|e| = w$
5 **return** e

Thus, if we note P_A the probability, dependent on the algorithm A, that the sampled set $\mathcal{S}$ is correct and that A finds e^2, and T_A the execution time of the algorithm $Search_A$, the complexity of generalised ISD algorithms is $O\left(\frac{T_A}{P_A}\right)$. To construct generalised quantum ISD algorithms, we use Bernstein's idea of using Grover search to look for a correct set $\mathcal{S}$. However, now each query made by Grover search will take time which is essentially the time complexity of $Search_A$. Consequently, the complexity of generalised quantum ISD algorithms is given by the following formula:

---

[2] In the case of Dumer's algorithm, for instance, even if the restriction of e to $\mathcal{S}$ is of weight p, Dumer's algorithm may fail to find it since it does not split evenly on both sides of the bipartition of $\mathcal{S}$.

$$O\left(\frac{T_A}{\sqrt{P_A}}\right) = O\left(\sqrt{\frac{T_A^2}{P_A}}\right). \tag{4}$$

An immediate consequence of this formula is that, in order to halve the complexity exponent of a given classical algorithm, we need a quantum algorithm whose search subroutine is "twice" as efficient.

4   Solving the Generalised 4-Sum Problem with Quantum Walks and Grover Search

4.1   The Shamir-Schroeppel Idea

As explained in Sect. 3, the more sophisticated ISD algorithms solve during the inner step an instance of the generalised k-sum problem. The issue is to get a good quantum version of the classical algorithms used to solve this problem. That this task is non trivial can already be guessed from Dumer's algorithm. Recall that it solves the generalised 2-sum problem in time and space complexity $O(V)$ when $V = |\mathcal{V}_0| = |\mathcal{V}_1| = \Theta(|\mathcal{G}|)$. The problem is that if we wanted a quadratic speedup when compared to the classical Dumer algorithm, then this would require a quantum algorithm solving the same problem in time $O\left(V^{1/2}\right)$, but this seems problematic since naive ways of quantising this algorithm stumble on the problem that the space complexity is a lower bound on the time complexity of the quantum algorithm. This strongly motivates the choice of ways of solving the 2-sum problem by using less memory. This can be done through the idea of Shamir and Schroeppel [26]. Note that the very same idea is also used for the same reason to speed up quantum algorithms for the subset sum problem in [6, Sect. 4]. To explain the idea, suppose that $\mathcal{G}$ factorises as $\mathcal{G} = \mathcal{G}_0 \times \mathcal{G}_1$ where $|\mathcal{G}_0| = \Theta(|\mathcal{G}_1|) = \Theta(|\mathcal{G}|^{1/2})$. Denote for $i \in \{0,1\}$ by π_i the projection from $\mathcal{G}$ onto $\mathcal{G}_i$ which to $g = (g_0, g_1)$ associates g_i.

The idea is to construct $f(\mathcal{V}_0)$ and $f(\mathcal{V}_1)$ themselves as $f(\mathcal{V}_0) = f(\mathcal{V}_{00}) + f(\mathcal{V}_{01})$ and $f(\mathcal{V}_1) = f(\mathcal{V}_{10}) + f(\mathcal{V}_{11})$ in such a way that the $\mathcal{V}_{ij}$'s are of size $O(V^{1/2})$ and to solve a 4-sum problem by solving various 2-sum problems. In our coding theoretic setting, it will be more convenient to explain everything directly in terms of the 4-sum problem which is given in this case by

Problem 5. Assume that $k + \ell$ and p are multiples of 4. Let

$$\mathcal{G} = \mathbb{F}_2^\ell, \quad \mathcal{E} = \mathbb{F}_2^{k+\ell}, \quad f(v) = H'v^T$$

$$\mathcal{V}_{00} \triangleq \{(e_{00}, 0_{3(k+\ell)/4}) \in \mathbb{F}_2^{k+\ell} : e_{00} \in \mathbb{F}_2^{(k+\ell)/4}, \ |e_{00}| = p/4\}$$

$$\mathcal{V}_{01} \triangleq \{(0_{(k+\ell)/4}, e_{01}, 0_{(k+\ell)/2}) \in \mathbb{F}_2^{k+\ell} : e_{01} \in \mathbb{F}_2^{(k+\ell)/4}, \ |e_{01}| = p/4\}$$

$$\mathcal{V}_{10} \triangleq \{(0_{(k+\ell)/2}, e_{10}, 0_{(k+\ell)/4}) \in \mathbb{F}_2^{k+\ell} : e_{10} \in \mathbb{F}_2^{(k+\ell)/4}, \ |e_{10}| = p/4\}$$

$$\mathcal{V}_{11} \triangleq \{(0_{3(k+\ell)/4}, e_{11}) \in \mathbb{F}_2^{k+\ell} : e_{11} \in \mathbb{F}_2^{(k+\ell)/4}, \ |e_{11}| = p/4\}$$

and S be some element in $\mathcal{G}$. Find $(v_{00}, v_{01}, v_{10}, v_{11})$ in $\mathcal{V}_{00} \times \mathcal{V}_{01} \times \mathcal{V}_{10} \times \mathcal{V}_{11}$ such that $f(v_{00}) + f(v_{01}) + f(v_{10}) + f(v_{11}) = S$ and $h(v_{00} + v_{01} + v_{10} + v_{11})$ is of weight w.

Let us explain now how the Shamir-Schroeppel idea allows us to solve the 4-sum problem in time $O(V)$ and space $O(V^{1/2})$ when the $\mathcal{V}_{ij}$'s are of order $O(V^{1/2})$, $|\mathcal{G}|$ is of order V and when $\mathcal{G}$ decomposes as the product of two groups $\mathcal{G}_0$ and $\mathcal{G}_1$ both of size $\Theta(V^{1/2})$. The basic idea is to solve for all possible $r \in \mathcal{G}_1$ the following 2-sum problems

$$\pi_1(f(v_{00})) + \pi_1(f(v_{01})) = r \tag{5}$$
$$\pi_1(f(v_{10})) + \pi_1(f(v_{11})) = \pi_1(S) - r \tag{6}$$

Once these problems are solved we are left with $O(V^{1/2}V^{1/2}/V^{1/2}) = O(V^{1/2})$ solutions to the first problem and $O(V^{1/2})$ solutions to the second. Taking any pair (v_{00}, v_{01}) solution to (5) and (v_{10}, v_{11}) solution to (6) yields a 4-tuple which is a partial solution to the 4-sum problem

$$\pi_1(f(v_{00})) + \pi_1(f(v_{01})) + \pi_1(f(v_{10})) + \pi_1(f(v_{11})) = r + \pi_1(S) - r = \pi_1(S).$$

Let $\mathcal{V}_0''$ be the set of all pairs (v_{00}, v_{01}) we have found for the first 2-sum problem (5), whereas $\mathcal{V}_1''$ is the set of all solutions to (6). To ensure that $f(v_{00}) + f(v_{01}) + f(v_{10}) + f(v_{11}) = S$ we just have to solve the following 2-sum problem

$$\underbrace{\pi_0(f(v_{00})) + \pi_0(f(v_{01}))}_{f'(v_{00}, v_{01})} + \underbrace{\pi_0(f(v_{10})) + \pi_0(f(v_{11}))}_{f'(v_{10}, v_{11})} = \pi_0(S)$$

and

$$g(v_{00}, v_{01}, v_{10}, v_{11}) = 0$$

where (v_{00}, v_{01}) is in $\mathcal{V}_0''$, (v_{10}, v_{11}) is in $\mathcal{V}_1''$ and g is the function whose root we want to find for the original 4-sum problem.

This is again of complexity $O(V^{1/2}V^{1/2}/V^{1/2}) = O(V^{1/2})$. Checking a particular value of r takes therefore $O(V^{1/2})$ operations. Since we have $\Theta(V^{1/2})$ values to check, the total complexity is $O(V^{1/2}V^{1/2}) = O(V)$, that is the same as before, but we need only $O(V^{1/2})$ memory to store all intermediate sets.

4.2   A Quantum Version of the Shamir-Schroeppel Algorithm

By following the approach of [6], we will define a quantum algorithm for solving the 4-sum problem by combining Grover search with a quantum walk with a complexity given by

Proposition 2. *Consider the generalised 4-sum problem with sets $\mathcal{V}_u$ of size V. Assume that $\mathcal{G}$ can be decomposed as $\mathcal{G} = \mathcal{G}_0 \times \mathcal{G}_1$. There is a quantum algorithm for solving the 4-sum problem running in time $\tilde{O}\left(|\mathcal{G}_1|^{1/2}V^{4/5}\right)$ as soon as $|\mathcal{G}_1| = \Omega(V^{4/5})$ and $|\mathcal{G}| = \Omega(V^{8/5})$.*

This is nothing but the idea of the algorithm [6, Sect. 4] laid out in a more general context. The idea is as in the classical algorithm to look for the right value $r \in \mathcal{G}_1$. This can be done with Grover search in time $O\left(|\mathcal{G}_1|^{1/2}\right)$ instead of $O(|\mathcal{G}_1|)$ in the classical case. The quantum walk is then used to solve the following problem:

Problem 6. Find $(v_{00}, v_{01}, v_{10}, v_{11})$ in $\mathcal{V}_{00} \times \mathcal{V}_{01} \times \mathcal{V}_{10} \times \mathcal{V}_{11}$ such that

$$\pi_1(f(v_{00})) + \pi_1(f(v_{01})) = r$$
$$\pi_1(f(v_{10})) + \pi_1(f(v_{11})) = \pi_1(S) - r$$
$$\pi_0(f(v_{00})) + \pi_0(f(v_{01})) + \pi_0(f(v_{10})) + \pi_0(f(v_{11})) = \pi_0(S)$$
$$g(v_{00}, v_{01}, v_{10}, v_{11}) = 0.$$

For this, we choose subsets $\mathcal{U}_i$'s of the $\mathcal{V}_i$'s of a same size $U = \Theta\left(V^{4/5}\right)$ and run a quantum walk on the graph whose vertices are all possible 4-tuples of sets of this kind and two 4-tuples $(\mathcal{U}_{00}, \mathcal{U}_{01}, \mathcal{U}_{10}, \mathcal{U}_{11})$ and $(\mathcal{U}'_{00}, \mathcal{U}'_{01}, \mathcal{U}'_{10}, \mathcal{U}'_{11})$ are adjacent if and only if we have for all i's but one $\mathcal{U}'_i = \mathcal{U}_i$ and for the remaining $\mathcal{U}'_i$ and $\mathcal{U}_i$ we have $|\mathcal{U}'_i \cap \mathcal{U}_i| = U - 1$. Notice that this graph is nothing but $J^4(V, U)$. By following [6, Sect. 4] it can be proved that

Proposition 3. *Under the assumptions that $|\mathcal{G}_1| = \Omega\left(V^{4/5}\right)$ and $|\mathcal{G}| = \Omega\left(V^{8/5}\right)$, it is possible to set up a data structure of size $O(U)$ to implement this quantum walk such that*
(i) setting up the data structure takes time $O(U)$;
(ii) checking whether a new 4-tuple leads to a solution to the problem above (and outputting the solution in this case) takes time $O(1)$,
(iii) updating the data structure takes time $O(\log U)$.

This proposition was first proved in [6, Sect. 4]. A proof of it can be found in the extended version of our paper [17, Sect. 4.2, p. 10]. Proposition 2 is essentially a corollary of this proposition.

Proof (Proof of Proposition 2). Recall that the cost of the quantum walk is given by $T_s + \frac{1}{\sqrt{\varepsilon}}\left(T_c + \frac{1}{\sqrt{\delta}}T_u\right)$ where $T_s, T_c, T_u, \varepsilon$ and δ are the setup cost, the check cost, the update cost, the proportion of marked elements and the spectral gap of the quantum walk. From Proposition 3, we know that $T_s = O(U) = O\left(V^{4/5}\right)$, $T_c = O(1)$, and $T_u = O(\log U)$. Recall that the spectral gap of $J(V, U)$ is equal to $\frac{V}{U(V-U)}$ by (2). This quantity is larger than $\frac{1}{U}$ and by using Theorem 2 on the cartesian product of Johnson graphs, we obtain $\delta = \Theta\left(\frac{1}{U}\right)$.

Now for the proportion of marked elements we argue as follows. If Problem 6 has a solution $(v_{00}, v_{01}, v_{10}, v_{11})$, then the probability that each of the sets $\mathcal{U}_i$ contains v_i is precisely $U/V = \Theta\left(V^{-1/5}\right)$. The probability ε that all the $\mathcal{U}_i$'s contain v_i is then $\Theta\left(V^{-4/5}\right)$. This gives a total cost of

$$O\left(V^{4/5}\right) + O\left(V^{2/5}\right)\left(O(1) + O\left(V^{2/5}\right)O(\log U)\right) = \tilde{O}\left(V^{4/5}\right).$$

When we multiply this by the cost of Grover's algorithm for finding the right r we have the aforementioned complexity.

4.3   Application to the Decoding Problem

When applying this approach to the decoding problem we obtain

Theorem 3. *We can decode $w = \omega n$ errors in a random linear code of length n and rate $R = \frac{k}{n}$ with a quantum complexity of order $\tilde{O}\left(2^{\alpha_{SSQW}(R,\omega)n}\right)$ where*

$$\alpha_{SSQW}(R,\omega) \triangleq \min_{(\pi,\lambda)\in\mathcal{R}}\left(\frac{H_2(\omega) - (1 - R - \lambda)H_2\left(\frac{\omega-\pi}{1-R-\lambda}\right) - \frac{2}{5}(R+\lambda)H_2\left(\frac{\pi}{R+\lambda}\right)}{2}\right)$$

$$\mathcal{R} \triangleq \left\{(\pi,\lambda)\in[0,\omega]\times[0,1): \lambda = \frac{2}{5}(R+\lambda)H_2\left(\frac{\pi}{R+\lambda}\right), \pi \le R+\lambda, \lambda \le 1 - R - \omega + \pi\right\}$$

Proof. Recall (see (4)) that the quantum complexity is given by

$$\tilde{O}\left(\frac{T_{SSQW}}{\sqrt{P_{SSQW}}}\right). \tag{7}$$

where T_{SSQW} is the complexity of the combination of Grover's algorithm and quantum walk solving the generalised 4-sum problem specified in Problem 6 and P_{SSQW} is the probability that the random set of $k+\ell$ positions $\mathscr{S}$ and its random partition in 4 sets of the same size that are chosen is such that all four of them contain exactly $p/4$ errors. Note that p and ℓ are chosen such that $k + \ell$ and p are divisible by 4. P_{SSQW} is given by

$$P_{SSQW} = \frac{\left(\frac{k+\ell}{4}\right)^4\left(\frac{n-k-\ell}{w-p}\right)}{\left(\frac{n}{w}\right)}$$

Therefore

$$(P_{SSQW})^{-1/2} = \tilde{O}\left(2^{\frac{H_2(\omega)-(1-R-\lambda)H_2\left(\frac{\omega-\pi}{1-R-\lambda}\right)-(R+\lambda)H_2\left(\frac{\pi}{R+\lambda}\right)}{2}n}\right) \tag{8}$$

where $\lambda \triangleq \frac{\ell}{n}$ and $\pi \triangleq \frac{p}{n}$. T_{SSQW} is given by Proposition 2:

$$T_{SSQW} = \tilde{O}\left(|\mathcal{G}_1|^{1/2}V^{4/5}\right)$$

where the sets involved in the generalised 4-sum problem are specified in Problem 6. This gives

$$V = \left(\frac{\frac{k+\ell}{4}}{\frac{p}{4}}\right)$$

We choose $\mathcal{G}_1$ as

$$\mathcal{G}_1 = \mathbb{F}_2^{\lceil\frac{\ell}{2}\rceil} \tag{9}$$

and the assumptions of Proposition 2 are verified as soon as

$$2^\ell = \Omega\left(V^{8/5}\right).$$

which amounts to

$$2^{\ell} = \Omega\left(\left(\frac{\binom{k+\ell}{4}}{\binom{p}{4}}\right)^{8/5}\right)$$

This explains the condition

$$\lambda = \frac{2}{5}(R + \lambda)H_2\left(\frac{\pi}{R + \lambda}\right) \tag{10}$$

found in the definition of the region $\mathcal{R}$. With the choices (9) and (10), we obtain

$$T_{SSQW} = \tilde{O}\left(V^{6/5}\right)$$
$$= \tilde{O}\left(2^{\frac{3}{10}(R+\lambda)H_2\left(\frac{\pi}{R+\lambda}\right)n}\right) \tag{11}$$

Substituting for P_{SSQW} and T_{SSQW} the expressions given by (8) and (11) finishes the proof of the theorem.

5   Improvements Obtained by the Representation Technique and "1 + 1 = 0"

There are two techniques that can be used to speed up the quantum algorithm of the previous section.

The Representation Technique. It was introduced in [15] to speed up algorithms for the subset-sum algorithm and used later on in [19] to improve decoding algorithms. The basic idea of the representation technique in the context of the subset-sum or decoding algorithms consists in (i) changing slightly the underlying (generalised) k-sum problem which is solved by introducing sets $\mathcal{V}_i$ for which there are (exponentially) many solutions to the problem $\sum_i f(v_i) = S$ by using redundant representations, (ii) noticing that this allows us to put additional subset-sum conditions on the solution.

In the decoding context, instead of considering sets of errors with non-overlapping support, the idea that allows us to obtain many different representations of a same solution is just to consider sets $\mathcal{V}_i$ corresponding to errors with overlapping supports. In our case, we could have taken instead of the four sets defined in the previous section the following sets

$$\mathcal{V}_{00} = \mathcal{V}_{10} \stackrel{\triangle}{=} \{(e_{00}, 0_{(k+\ell)/2}) \in \mathbb{F}_2^{k+\ell} : e_{00} \in \mathbb{F}_2^{(k+\ell)/2}, |e_{00}| = p/4\}$$

$$\mathcal{V}_{01} = \mathcal{V}_{11} \stackrel{\triangle}{=} \{(0_{(k+\ell)/2}, e_{01}) \in \mathbb{F}_2^{k+\ell} : e_{01} \in \mathbb{F}_2^{(k+\ell)/2}, |e_{01}| = p/4\}$$

Clearly a vector e of weight p can be written in many different ways as a sum $v_{00} + v_{01} + v_{10} + v_{11}$ where v_{ij} belongs to $\mathcal{V}_{ij}$. This is (essentially) due to the fact that a vector of weight p can be written in $\binom{p}{p/2} = \tilde{O}(2^p)$ ways as a sum of two vectors of weight $p/2$.

The point is that if we apply now the same algorithm as in the previous section and look for solutions to Problem 5, there is not a single value of r that leads to the right solution. Here, about 2^p values of r will do the same job. The speedup obtained by the representation technique is a consequence of this phenomenon. We can even improve on this representation technique by using the $1 + 1 = 0$ phenomenon as in [4].

The "1+1 = 0" Phenomenon. Instead of choosing the $\mathcal{V}_i$'s as explained above we will actually choose the $\mathcal{V}_i$'s as

$$\mathcal{V}_{00} = \mathcal{V}_{10} \overset{\triangle}{=} \{(e_{00}, 0_{(k+\ell)/2}) \in \mathbb{F}_2^{k+\ell} : e_{00} \in \mathbb{F}_2^{(k+\ell)/2}, \ |e_{00}| = \frac{p}{4} + \frac{\Delta p}{2}\} \quad (12)$$

$$\mathcal{V}_{01} = \mathcal{V}_{11} \overset{\triangle}{=} \{(0_{(k+\ell)/2}, e_{01}) \in \mathbb{F}_2^{k+\ell} : e_{01} \in \mathbb{F}_2^{(k+\ell)/2}, \ |e_{01}| = \frac{p}{4} + \frac{\Delta p}{2}\} \quad (13)$$

A vector e of weight p in $\mathbb{F}_2^{k+\ell}$ can indeed by represented in many ways as a sum of 2 vectors of weight $\frac{p}{2} + \Delta p$. More precisely, such a vector can be represented in $\binom{p}{p/2}\binom{k+\ell-p}{\Delta p}$ ways. Notice that this number of representations is greater than the number 2^p that we had before. This explains why choosing an appropriate positive value Δp allows us to improve on the previous choice.

The quantum algorithm for decoding follows the same pattern as in the previous section: (i) we look with Grover's search algorithm for a right set $\mathscr{S}$ of $k + \ell$ positions such that the restriction e' of the error e we look for is of weight p on this subset and then (ii) we search for e' by solving a generalised 4-sum problem with a combination of Grover's algorithm and a quantum walk. We will use for the second point the following proposition which quantifies how much we gain when there are multiple representations/solutions:

Proposition 4. *Consider the generalised 4-sum problem with sets $\mathcal{V}_u$ of size $O(V)$. Assume that G can be decomposed as $G = G_0 \times G_1 \times G_2$. Furthermore assume that there are $\Omega(|G_2|)$ solutions to the 4-sum problem and that we can fix arbitrarily the value $\pi_2(f(v_{00}) + f(v_{01}))$ of a solution to the 4-sum problem, where π_2 is the mapping from $G = G_0 \times G_1 \times G_2$ to G_2 which maps (g_0, g_1, g_2) to g_2. There is a quantum algorithm for solving the 4-sum problem running in time $\tilde{O}(|G_1|^{1/2} V^{4/5})$ as soon as $|G_1| \cdot |G_2| = \Omega(V^{4/5})$ and $|G| = \Omega(V^{8/5})$.*

Proof. Let us first introduce a few notations. We denote by π_{12} the "projection" from $G = G_0 \times G_1 \times G_2$ to $G_1 \times G_2$ which associates to (g_0, g_1, g_2) the pair (g_1, g_2) and by π_0 the projection from G to G_0 which maps (g_0, g_1, g_2) to g_0. As in the previous section, we solve with a quantum walk the following problem: we fix an element $r = (r_1, r_2)$ in $G_1 \times G_2$ and find (if it exists) $(v_{00}, v_{01}, v_{10}, v_{11})$ in $\mathcal{V}_{00} \times \mathcal{V}_{01} \times \mathcal{V}_{10} \times \mathcal{V}_{11}$ such that

$$\pi_{12}(f(v_{00})) + \pi_{12}(f(v_{01})) = r$$
$$\pi_{12}(f(v_{10})) + \pi_{12}(f(v_{11})) = \pi_{12}(S) - r$$
$$\pi_0(f(v_{00})) + \pi_0(f(v_{01})) + \pi_0(f(v_{10})) + \pi_0(f(v_{11})) = \pi_0(S)$$
$$g(v_{00}, v_{01}, v_{10}, v_{11}) = 0.$$

The difference with Proposition 2 is that we do not check all possibilities for r but just all possibilities for $r_1 \in G_1$ and fix r_2 arbitrarily. As in Proposition 2, we perform a quantum walk whose complexity is $\tilde{O}\left(V^{4/5}\right)$ to solve the aforementioned problem for a fixed r. What remains to be done is to find the right value for r_1 which is achieved by a Grover search with complexity $O\left(|G_1|^{1/2}\right)$.

By applying Proposition 4 in our decoding context, we obtain

Theorem 4. *We can decode $w = \omega n$ errors in a random linear code of length n and rate $R = \frac{k}{n}$ with a quantum complexity of order $\tilde{O}\left(2^{\alpha_{MMTQW}(R,\omega)n}\right)$ where*

$$\alpha_{MMTQW}(R,\omega) \;\triangleq\; \min_{(\pi,\Delta\pi,\lambda)\in\mathcal{R}} \left(\frac{\beta(R,\lambda,\pi,\Delta\pi) + \gamma(R,\lambda,\pi,\omega)}{2}\right)$$

with

$$\beta(R,\lambda,\pi,\Delta\pi) \;\triangleq\; \frac{6}{5}(R+\lambda)H_2\left(\frac{\pi/2+\Delta\pi}{R+\lambda}\right) - \pi - (1-R-\lambda)H_2\left(\frac{\Delta\pi}{1-R-\lambda}\right),$$

$$\gamma(R,\lambda,\pi,\omega) \;\triangleq\; H_2(\omega) - (1-R-\lambda)H_2(\frac{\omega-\pi}{1-R-\lambda}) - (R+\lambda)H_2\left(\frac{\pi}{R+\lambda}\right)$$

where $\mathcal{R}$ is the subset of elements $(\pi,\Delta\pi,\lambda)$ of $[0,\omega] \times [0,1) \times [0,1)$ that satisfy the following constraints

$$0 \le \Delta\pi \le R+\lambda-\pi$$
$$0 \le \pi \le \min(\omega, R+\lambda)$$
$$0 \le \lambda \le 1-R-\omega+\pi$$
$$\pi = 2\left((R+\lambda)H_2^{-1}\left(\frac{5\lambda}{4(R+\lambda)}\right) - \Delta\pi\right)$$

Proof. The algorithm picks random subsets $\mathscr{S}$ of size $k+\ell$ with the hope that the restriction to $\mathscr{S}$ of the error of weight w that we are looking for is of weight p. Then it solves for each of these subsets the generalised 4-sum problem where the sets $\mathcal{V}_{ij}$ are specified in (12) and (13), and $\mathcal{G}$, $\mathcal{E}$, f and g are as in Problem 6. g is in this case slightly more complicated for the sake of analysing the algorithm. We have $g(v_{00}, v_{01}, v_{10}, v_{11}) = 0$ if and only if (i) $v_{00} + v_{01} + v_{10} + v_{11}$ is of weight p (this is the additional constraint we use for the analysis of the algorithm) (ii) $f(v_{00}) + f(v_{01}) + f(v_{10}) + f(v_{11}) = \Sigma(e, H, \mathscr{S})$ and (iii) $h(v_{00} + v_{01} + v_{10} + v_{11})$ is of weight w.

From (4) we know that the quantum complexity is given by

$$\tilde{O}\left(\frac{T_{\mathrm{MMTQW}}}{\sqrt{P_{\mathrm{MMTQW}}}}\right) \tag{14}$$

where T_{MMTQW} is the complexity of the combination of Grover's algorithm and quantum walk solving the generalised 4-sum problem specified above and P_{MMTQW} is the probability that the restriction e' of the error e to $\mathscr{S}$ is of weight p and that this error can be written as $e' = v_{00} + v_{01} + v_{10} + v_{11}$ where the v_{ij} belong to $\mathcal{V}_{ij}$. It is readily verified that

$$P_{\text{MMTQW}} = \tilde{O}\left(\frac{\binom{k+\ell}{p}\binom{n-k-\ell}{w-p}}{\binom{n}{w}}\right)$$

By using asymptotic expansions of the binomial coefficients we obtain

$$(P_{\text{MMTQW}})^{-1/2} = \tilde{O}\left(2^{\frac{H_2(\omega)-(1-R-\lambda)H_2\left(\frac{\omega-\pi}{1-R-\lambda}\right)-(R+\lambda)H_2\left(\frac{\pi}{R+\lambda}\right)}{2}n}\right) \tag{15}$$

where $\lambda \overset{\triangle}{=} \frac{\ell}{n}$ and $\pi \overset{\triangle}{=} \frac{p}{n}$. To estimate T_{SSQW}, we can use Proposition 4. The point is that the number of different solutions of the generalised 4-sum problem (when there is one) is of order

$$\tilde{\Omega}\left(\binom{p}{p/2}\binom{k+\ell-p}{\Delta p}\right).$$

At this point, we observe that

$$\log_2\left(\binom{p}{p/2}\binom{k+\ell-p}{\Delta p}\right) = p + (k+\ell-p)H_2\left(\frac{\Delta p}{k+\ell-p}\right) + o(n)$$

when p, Δp, ℓ, k are all linear in n. In other words, we may use Proposition 4 with $\mathcal{G}_2 = \mathbb{F}_2^{\ell_2}$ with

$$\ell_2 \overset{\triangle}{=} p + (k+\ell-p)H_2\left(\frac{\Delta p}{k+\ell-p}\right). \tag{16}$$

We use now Proposition 4 with $\mathcal{G}_2$ chosen as explained above. V is given in this case by

$$V = \binom{\frac{k+\ell}{2}}{\frac{p}{4}+\frac{\Delta p}{2}} = \tilde{O}\left(2^{(R+\lambda)H_2\left(\frac{\pi/2+\Delta\pi}{R+\lambda}\right)n}\right)$$

where $\Delta\pi \overset{\triangle}{=} \frac{\Delta p}{n}$. We choose the size of $\mathcal{G}$ such that

$$|\mathcal{G}| = \tilde{\Theta}\left(V^{8/5}\right) \tag{17}$$

which gives

$$2^\ell = \tilde{\Theta}\left(\binom{\frac{k+\ell}{2}}{\frac{p}{4}+\frac{\Delta p}{2}}^{8/5}\right).$$

This explains why we impose

$$\lambda = \frac{8}{5}\frac{R+\lambda}{2}H_2\left(\frac{\pi/2+\Delta\pi}{R+\lambda}\right)$$

which is equivalent to the condition

$$\frac{5\lambda}{4(R+\lambda)} = H_2\left(\frac{\pi/2+\Delta\pi}{R+\lambda}\right)$$

which in turn is equivalent to the condition

$$\pi = 2\left((R+\lambda)H_2^{-1}\left(\frac{5\lambda}{4(R+\lambda)}\right) - \Delta\pi\right) \tag{18}$$

found in the definition of the region $\mathcal{R}$. The size of $\mathcal{G}_1$ is chosen such that

$$|\mathcal{G}_1| \cdot |\mathcal{G}_2| = \mathbb{F}_2^{\lceil \frac{\ell}{2} \rceil}. \tag{19}$$

By using (16) and (17), this implies

$$|\mathcal{G}_1| = \tilde{\Theta}\left(\frac{V^{4/5}}{2^{p+(k+\ell-p)H_2\left(\frac{\Delta p}{k+\ell-p}\right)}}\right) \tag{20}$$

With the choices (19) and (18), we obtain

$$\begin{aligned}
T_{\mathrm{MMTQW}} &= \tilde{O}\left(|\mathcal{G}_1|^{1/2} \cdot V^{4/5}\right) \\
&= \tilde{O}\left(\frac{V^{6/5}}{2^{\frac{p}{2}+\frac{k+\ell-p}{2}H_2\left(\frac{\Delta p}{k+\ell-p}\right)}}\right) \\
&= \tilde{O}\left(2^{\left[\frac{3}{5}(R+\lambda)H_2\left(\frac{\pi/2+\Delta\pi}{R+\lambda}\right)-\frac{\pi}{2}-\frac{R+\lambda-\pi}{2}H_2\left(\frac{\Delta\pi}{R+\lambda-\pi}\right)\right]n}\right) \tag{21}
\end{aligned}$$

Substituting for P_{MMTQW} and T_{MMTQW} the expressions given by (15) and (21) finishes the proof of the theorem.

6   Computing the Complexity Exponents

We used the software SageMath to numerically find the minima giving the complexity exponents in Theorems 3 and 4 using golden section search and a recursive version thereof for two parameters. We compare in Fig. 1 the exponents $\alpha_{\mathrm{Bernstein}}(R,\omega_{\mathrm{GV}})$, $\alpha_{SSQW}(R,\omega_{\mathrm{GV}})$ and $\alpha_{MMTQW}(R,\omega_{\mathrm{GV}})$ that we have obtained with our approach. It can be observed that there is some improvement upon $\alpha_{\mathrm{Bernstein}}$ with both algorithms especially in the range of rates between 0.3 and 0.7.

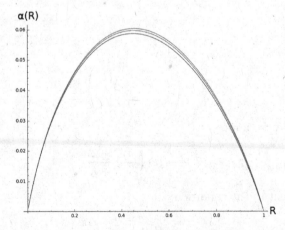

Fig. 1. $\alpha_{\mathrm{Bernstein}}$ in green, α_{SSQW} in pink, α_{MMTQW} in grey. (Color figure online)

7   Concluding Remarks

One may wonder why our best algorithm is a version of MMT's algorithm and not BJMM's algorithm or May and Ozerov's algorithm. We did try to quantise BJMM's algorithm, but it turned out to have worse time complexity than MMT's algorithm (for more details, see [16]). This seems to be due to space complexity constraints. Space complexity is indeed a lower bound on the quantum complexity of the algorithm. It has actually been shown [3, Chap. 10, Sect. 3] that BJMM's algorithm uses more space than MMT's algorithm, even when it is optimised to use the least amount of space. Moreover, it is rather insightful that in all cases, the best quantum algorithms that we have obtained here are not direct quantised versions of the original Dumer or MMT's algorithms but quantised versions of modified versions of these algorithms that use less memory than the original algorithms. The case of May and Ozerov's algorithm is also intriguing. Again the large space complexity of the original version of this algorithm makes it a very challenging task to obtain a "good" quantised version of it.

Finally, it should be noticed that while sophisticated techniques such as MMT, BJMM [4,19] or May and Ozerov [20] have managed to improve rather significantly upon the most naive ISD algorithm, namely Prange's algorithm [24], the improvement that we obtain with more sophisticated techniques is much more modest when we consider our improvements of the quantised version of the Prange algorithm [5]. Moreover, the improvements we obtain on the exponent $\alpha_{\text{Bernstein}}(R, \omega)$ are smaller when ω is smaller than ω_{GV}. Considering the techniques for proving that the exponent of classical ISD algorithms goes to the Prange exponent when the relative error weight goes to 0 [9], we conjecture that it should be possible to prove that we actually have $\lim_{\omega \to 0^+} \frac{\alpha_{\text{MMTQW}}(R,\omega)}{\alpha_{\text{Bernstein}}(R,\omega)} = 1$.

References

1. Ambainis, A.: Quantum walk algorithm for element distinctness. SIAM J. Comput. **37**, 210–239 (2007)
2. Barg, A.: Complexity issues in coding theory. In: Electronic Colloquium on Computational Complexity, October 1997
3. Becker, A.: The representation technique, applications to hard problems in cryptography. Ph.D. thesis, Université Versailles Saint-Quentin en Yvelines, October 2012
4. Becker, A., Joux, A., May, A., Meurer, A.: Decoding random binary linear codes in $2^{n/20}$: how $1 + 1 = 0$ improves information set decoding. In: Pointcheval, D., Johansson, T. (eds.) EUROCRYPT 2012. LNCS, vol. 7237, pp. 520–536. Springer, Heidelberg (2012). doi:10.1007/978-3-642-29011-4_31
5. Bernstein, D.J.: Grover vs. McEliece. In: Sendrier, N. (ed.) PQCrypto 2010. LNCS, vol. 6061, pp. 73–80. Springer, Heidelberg (2010). doi:10.1007/978-3-642-12929-2_6
6. Bernstein, D.J., Jeffery, S., Lange, T., Meurer, A.: Quantum algorithms for the subset-sum problem. In: Gaborit, P. (ed.) PQCrypto 2013. LNCS, vol. 7932, pp. 16–33. Springer, Heidelberg (2013). doi:10.1007/978-3-642-38616-9_2

7. Bernstein, D.J., Lange, T., Peters, C.: Smaller decoding exponents: ball-collision decoding. In: Rogaway, P. (ed.) CRYPTO 2011. LNCS, vol. 6841, pp. 743–760. Springer, Heidelberg (2011). doi:10.1007/978-3-642-22792-9_42
8. Boyer, M., Brassard, G., Høyer, P., Tapp, A.: Tight bounds on quantum searching. Fortsch. Phys. **46**, 493 (1998)
9. Canto Torres, R., Sendrier, N.: Analysis of information set decoding for a sub-linear error weight. In: Takagi, T. (ed.) PQCrypto 2016. LNCS, vol. 9606, pp. 144–161. Springer, Cham (2016). doi:10.1007/978-3-319-29360-8_10
10. Cvetković, D.M., Doob, M., Sachs, H.: Spectra of Graphs: Theory and Application. Academic Press, New York (1980)
11. Dumer, I.: On minimum distance decoding of linear codes. In: Proceedings of 5th Joint Soviet-Swedish International Workshop Information Theory, Moscow, pp. 50–52 (1991)
12. Finiasz, M., Sendrier, N.: Security bounds for the design of code-based cryptosystems. In: Matsui, M. (ed.) ASIACRYPT 2009. LNCS, vol. 5912, pp. 88–105. Springer, Heidelberg (2009). doi:10.1007/978-3-642-10366-7_6
13. Grover, L.K.: A fast quantum mechanical algorithm for database search. In: Proceedings 28th Annual ACM Symposium on the Theory of Computation, pp. 212–219. ACM Press, New York (1996)
14. Grover, L.K.: Quantum computers can search arbitrarily large databases by a single query. Phys. Rev. Lett. **79**, 4709–4712 (1997)
15. Howgrave-Graham, N., Joux, A.: New generic algorithms for hard knapsacks. In: Gilbert, H. (ed.) EUROCRYPT 2010. LNCS, vol. 6110, pp. 235–256. Springer, Heidelberg (2010). doi:10.1007/978-3-642-13190-5_12
16. Kachigar, G. Étude et conception d'algorithmes quantiques pour le décodage de codes linéaires. Master's thesis, Université de Rennes 1, France, September 2016
17. Kachigar, G., Tillich, J.-P.: Quantum information set decoding algorithms. preprint, arXiv:1703.00263 [cs.CR], February 2017
18. Magniez, F., Nayak, A., Roland, J., Santha, M.: Search via quantum walk. In: Proceedings of the Thirty-Ninth Annual ACM Symposium on Theory of Computing, STOC 2007, pp. 575–584 (2007)
19. May, A., Meurer, A., Thomae, E.: Decoding random linear codes in $\tilde{O}(2^{0.054n})$. In: Lee, D.H., Wang, X. (eds.) ASIACRYPT 2011. LNCS, vol. 7073, pp. 107–124. Springer, Heidelberg (2011). doi:10.1007/978-3-642-25385-0_6
20. May, A., Ozerov, I.: On computing nearest neighbors with applications to decoding of binary linear codes. In: Oswald, E., Fischlin, M. (eds.) EUROCRYPT 2015. LNCS, vol. 9056, pp. 203–228. Springer, Heidelberg (2015). doi:10.1007/978-3-662-46800-5_9
21. McEliece, R.J.: A public-key system based on algebraic coding theory, pp. 114–116. Jet Propulsion Laboratory (1978). DSN Progress Report 44
22. Niederreiter, H.: Knapsack-type cryptosystems and algebraic coding theory. Probl. Control Inf. Theory **15**(2), 159–166 (1986)
23. Overbeck, R., Sendrier, N.: Code-based cryptography. In: Bernstein, D.J., Buchmann, J., Dahmen, E. (eds.) Post-Quantum Cryptography, pp. 95–145. Springer, Heidelberg (2009)
24. Prange, E.: The use of information sets in decoding cyclic codes. IRE Trans. Inf. Theory **8**(5), 5–9 (1962)
25. Santha, M.: Quantum walk based search algorithms. In: 5th TAMC, pp. 31–46. arXiv:0808.0059 (2008)
26. Schroeppel, R., Shamir, A.: A $T = O(2^{n/2})$, $S = O(2^{n/4})$ algorithm for certain NP-complete problems. SIAM J. Comput. **10**(3), 456–464 (1981)

27. Shor, P.W.: Polynomial-time algorithms for prime factorization and discrete logarithms on a quantum computer. SIAM J. Comput. **26**(5), 1484–1509 (1997)

28. Stern, J.: A method for finding codewords of small weight. In: Cohen, G., Wolfmann, J. (eds.) Coding Theory 1988. LNCS, vol. 388, pp. 106–113. Springer, Heidelberg (1989). doi:10.1007/BFb0019850

29. Szegedy, M.: Quantum speed-up of Markov chain based algorithms. In: Proceedings of the 45th IEEE Symposium on Foundations of Computer Science, pp. 32–41 (2004)

Isogeny-Based Cryptography

Loop-Abort Faults on Supersingular Isogeny Cryptosystems

Alexandre Gélin[1]($\boxtimes$) and Benjamin Wesolowski[2]($\boxtimes$)

[1] Sorbonne Universités, UPMC Paris 6, UMR 7606, LIP6, Paris, France
`alexandre.gelin@lip6.fr`
[2] École Polytechnique Fédérale de Lausanne, EPFL IC LACAL, Lausanne,
Switzerland
`benjamin.wesolowski@epfl.ch`

Abstract. Cryptographic schemes based on supersingular isogenies have become an active area of research in the field of post-quantum cryptography. We investigate the resistance of these cryptosystems to fault injection attacks. It appears that the iterative structure of the secret isogeny computation renders these schemes vulnerable to loop-abort attacks. Loop-abort faults allow to perform a full key recovery, bypassing all the previously introduced validation methods. Therefore implementing additional countermeasures seems unavoidable for applications where physical attacks are relevant.

Keywords: Supersingular isogeny cryptosystem · Fault injection · Real-world attacks · Post-quantum cryptography

1 Introduction

Public-key cryptography, the foundation of modern communication security, is confronted to the prospect of a technology capable of breaking today's most widely deployed primitives: quantum computers of sufficient scale to run Shor's algorithm [18]. This risk has given rise to the field of post-quantum cryptography (PQC), which aims at developing new primitives that would resist cryptanalysis by both classical and quantum computers.

Cryptographic schemes based on supersingular elliptic curve isogenies were introduced in 2011 by Jao and De Feo [11] as candidates for post-quantum Diffie-Hellman key exchange (SIDH) and public-key encryption. Several other primitives have subsequently been built based on supersingular isogeny problems, such as zero-knowledge proofs of identity and signatures [6,10,12,20]. Efficient implementations of these primitives have rapidly followed: in software [5,15], in hardware [14] and on embedded systems [1].

Even though the basic version of the key exchange protocol uses ephemeral secret values (as with classical Diffie-Hellman), some of these other schemes require static secret keys for at least one party. Such static secrets constitute primary material for active attacks, and such an attack was indeed described

© Springer International Publishing AG 2017
T. Lange and T. Takagi (Eds.): PQCrypto 2017, LNCS 10346, pp. 93–106, 2017.
DOI: 10.1007/978-3-319-59879-6_6

in [9] that allows to find all n bits of the secret key with about n interactions with the victim. This attack can be prevented by the Kirkwood *et al.* [13] validation method — which is essentially a Fujisaki–Okamoto transform [8] applied in the context of supersingular isogenies.

The results of [1], together with the fact that primitives based on supersingular isogenies enjoy significantly smaller keys than the other main candidates for post-quantum cryptography, suggest that they might be well-suited for use on embedded devices. This opens new avenues of potential side-channel attacks.

In this paper, we present the first side-channel attack against supersingular isogeny-based primitives, exploiting a fault-injection technique known as loop-abort fault injection, previously introduced for pairing based cryptography [16]. The iterative structure of isogeny computations render them susceptible to loop-abort fault attacks, allowing an attacker to recover all n bits of the key, within $O(n)$ interactions with the token and a negligible amount of computation. This attack is not prevented by any of the validation methods previously discussed for isogeny-based cryptosystems. Loop-abort fault injections were proven to be feasible in practice [3], and should therefore be taken into serious consideration when implementing schemes based on supersingular isogenies in a context susceptible to physical attacks.

After a brief overview of supersingular isogeny-based cryptography in Sect. 2, we quickly discuss fault injection attacks in Sect. 3, with a particular focus on loop-abort faults. The attack is then described and analyzed in Sect. 4, while potential countermeasures are discussed in Sect. 5.

2   Cryptosystems from Supersingular Isogenies

This section recalls the necessary background and the cryptosystems based on supersingular elliptic curve isogenies introduced in [6,11].

2.1   Elliptic Curves and Isogenies

For any prime power $q = p^r$, let $\mathbf{F}_q$ denote the finite field with q elements. Let E be an elliptic curve defined over $\mathbf{F}_q$. The set $E(\overline{\mathbf{F}}_q)$ of rational points over the algebraic closure forms a group, in which the subset $E(\mathbf{F}_q)$ of $\mathbf{F}_q$-rational points forms a finite subgroup. Let E' be another elliptic curve defined over $\mathbf{F}_q$. An isogeny $E \to E'$ is a non-constant morphism sending the identity of E to the identity of E' (we then say that E' is isogenous to E). In particular, an isogeny is a surjective group homomorphism from $E(\overline{\mathbf{F}}_q)$ to $E'(\overline{\mathbf{F}}_q)$, of finite kernel. All isogenies that we consider in this paper are separable [19, Definition p. 21], so by *isogeny* we always mean *separable isogeny*. Then, the *degree* of an isogeny is simply defined as the number of points in its kernel. For any finite subgroup $G \subset E(\overline{\mathbf{F}}_q)$, there is a quotient elliptic curve E/G and the canonical projection $\pi_G : E \to E/G$ is an isogeny of degree $|G|$. In fact, any isogeny arises in this form, up to an isomorphism of the target.

2.2   Elliptic Curves for Supersingular Isogeny Schemes

Fix a reference elliptic curve E_0. In cryptographic schemes based on supersingular isogenies, the public key of Alice is, essentially, an isogenous curve E_A, and its secret is the kernel G_A of an isogeny $\varphi_A : E_0 \to E_A$. Two things appear immediately: first, Alice needs an efficient way to represent the secret kernel. Second, given E_0 and E_A, it should be difficult to find the kernel G_A. The secret isogenies are simply chosen cyclic, so that the secret is a point $P \in E_0(\mathbf{F}_q)$ generating the kernel. This means in particular that $E_0(\mathbf{F}_q)$ should contain a lot of cyclic subgroups. It follows that the traditional constraint in elliptic curve cryptography that the order of $E_0(\mathbf{F}_q)$ should have a large prime factor does not apply here: on the contrary, $|E_0(\mathbf{F}_q)|$ should be very smooth.

Let m be any positive integer; then $E[m] \subset E(\overline{\mathbf{F}}_q)$ is the subgroup of m-torsion points in $E(\overline{\mathbf{F}}_q)$. Whenever m is coprime to p, we have that $E[m]$ is isomorphic to the group $(\mathbf{Z}/m\mathbf{Z})^2$. Now, fix a prime number $\ell \neq p$, and a positive integer k. Then $E[\ell^k] \cong (\mathbf{Z}/\ell^k\mathbf{Z})^2$ contains $\ell^{k-1}(\ell+1)$ distinct cyclic subgroups of order ℓ^k. If all the points of $E[\ell^k]$ are defined over $\mathbf{F}_q$, then the set of cyclic subgroups of order ℓ^k generated by a point defined over $\mathbf{F}_q$ is sufficiently large to constitute a space of secret keys. Typically, to build the cryptographic schemes, one needs two distinct primes ℓ_A and ℓ_B (one for the keys of Alice and one for the keys of Bob). Then, the reference elliptic curve E_0 should be chosen so that

$$E_0(\mathbf{F}_q) = E_0[\ell_A^n] \oplus E_0[\ell_B^m].$$

This might be difficult to obtain, so one can simply require $E_0(\mathbf{F}_q) = E_0[\ell_A^n] \oplus E_0[\ell_B^m] \oplus F$, where the subgroup F contains a few other $\mathbf{F}_q$-rational points whose orders are coprime to ℓ_A and ℓ_B.

The schemes also require the reference curve E_0 to be supersingular — see [19, Theorem 3.1] for a few of the numerous equivalent ways to define supersingularity. The first interesting consequence is that all supersingular curves defined over $\overline{\mathbf{F}}_q$ are actually defined over $\mathbf{F}_{p^2}$. The curve E_0 is constructed as follows. The primes ℓ_A and ℓ_B are fixed (typically 2 and 3), together with some exponents n and m whose size depend on the security level. Now, one can find a cofactor f coprime to ℓ_A and ℓ_B such that $p = \ell_A^n \ell_B^m f \pm 1$ is a prime number. Bröker [4] has shown that it is easy to find an elliptic curve E_0 over $\mathbf{F}_{p^2}$ such that $|E_0(\mathbf{F}_{p^2})| = (p \mp 1)^2 = (\ell_A^n \ell_B^m f)^2$. From [2, Theorem IX.20], the group $E_0(\mathbf{F}_{p^2})$ is isomorphic to $(\mathbf{Z}/\ell_A^n \ell_B^m f\mathbf{Z})^2$, and therefore we have the desired decomposition $E_0(\mathbf{F}_{p^2}) = E_0[\ell_A^n] \oplus E_0[\ell_B^m] \oplus F$, with $F = E_0[f]$.

This choice of ℓ_A, ℓ_B, n, m, p and E_0 is fixed for the rest of the paper. We are working on the class of all elliptic curves E that are $\mathbf{F}_{p^2}$-isogenous to E_0. They are all supersingular, and by Tate's isogeny theorem [21], they all have the same number of $\mathbf{F}_{p^2}$-rational points. It follows that any such E enjoys the same decomposition

$$E(\mathbf{F}_{p^2}) = E[\ell_A^n] \oplus E[\ell_B^m] \oplus F.$$

2.3   Computing Smooth Degree Isogenies

Let $(\ell, k) \in \{(\ell_A, n), (\ell_B, m)\}$. For any elliptic curve E isogenous to E_0, the subgroup $E[\ell^k] \subset E(\mathbf{F}_{p^2})$ is a free $\mathbf{Z}/\ell^k\mathbf{Z}$-module of rank two, with a basis $\{P, Q\}$. Any point $R = c_1 P + c_2 Q$ has order ℓ^k if and only if either c_1 or c_2 is not divisible by ℓ. Any such point R of order ℓ^k induces an isogeny $\varphi_R : E \to E/\langle R \rangle$ of degree ℓ^k. As described in [6, Sect. 4.2.2], the only efficient way to compute the isogeny φ_R is as a sequence of k isogenies of degree ℓ, which can themselves be computed using Vélu's formulas [22]. We now recall that method. Set $E^0 = E$, $R^0 = R$, and for $0 \leq i < k$, recursively define

$$E^{i+1} = E^i / \langle \ell^{k-i-1} R^i \rangle,$$

$$\varphi_{i+1} : E^i \to E^{i+1} \text{ the canonical isogeny,}$$

$$R^{i+1} = \varphi_{i+1}(R^i).$$

Then, $E/\langle R \rangle = E^k$, each isogeny φ_i is of degree ℓ, and $\varphi_R = \varphi_k \circ \cdots \circ \varphi_1$. From this observation, [6, Sect. 4.2.2] describes a family of strategies to compute φ_R. These strategies allow to optimize the number of point multiplications and isogeny computations, but all boil down to computing the sequence of isogenies $(\varphi_i)_{i=1}^k$ in order.

2.4   Jao–De Feo Protocols

We present here two examples of cryptographic protocols based on supersingular isogenies: a key exchange protocol, and a public key encryption protocol. Our attack could easily be adapted to other variants of isogeny-based schemes as we target a component they all have in common: the computation by Alice of a secret isogeny.

Key Exchange. The following key exchange protocol is the first supersingular isogeny-based protocol, introduced in [11, Sect. 3.1].

Setup. Choose a prime $p = \ell_A^n \ell_B^m f \pm 1$ and an elliptic curve E_0 as in Sect. 2.2. As $E_0[\ell_A^n]$ is a free $\mathbf{Z}/\ell_A^n\mathbf{Z}$-module of rank two, let $\{P_A, Q_A\}$ be a basis[1]. Similarly, let $\{P_B, Q_B\}$ be a basis of $E_0[\ell_B^m]$.

Key exchange. Alice chooses two random elements $a_1, a_2 \in \mathbf{Z}/\ell_A^n\mathbf{Z}$, not both nilpotent[2], and Bob does the same, with $b_1, b_2 \in \mathbf{Z}/\ell_B^m\mathbf{Z}$. Let

$$R_A = a_1 P_A + a_2 Q_A,$$

$$R_B = b_1 P_B + b_2 Q_B.$$

---

[1] In [5], the pair (P_A, Q_A) does not form a basis. The protocol still works, but some caution is required (see Appendix A).

[2] Note that an element $a \in \mathbf{Z}/\ell_A^n\mathbf{Z}$ is nilpotent if and only if it is the class of a multiple of ℓ_A.

Write $E_A = E_0/\langle R_A \rangle$ and $E_B = E_0/\langle R_B \rangle$, and let $\varphi_A : E_0 \to E_A$ and $\varphi_B : E_0 \to E_B$ denote the canonical isogenies. Alice computes and publishes $(E_A, \varphi_A(P_B), \varphi_A(Q_B))$, and Bob does the same for $(E_B, \varphi_B(P_A), \varphi_B(Q_A))$. Alice can compute the j-invariant of

$$E_{AB} = E_B/\langle a_1\varphi_B(P_A) + a_2\varphi_B(Q_A) \rangle,$$

while Bob can compute the j-invariant of

$$E_{BA} = E_A/\langle b_1\varphi_A(P_B) + b_2\varphi_A(Q_B) \rangle.$$

Fortunately $E_{AB} \cong E_0/\langle R_A, R_B \rangle \cong E_{BA}$, so $j(E_{AB}) = j(E_{BA})$ is the secret shared by Alice and Bob, from which they can derive a secret key.

Public-Key Encryption. The public-key encryption scheme described in [11, Sect. 3.2] is very similar to the key exchange. Here, Bob sends an encrypted message to Alice.

Setup. As for the key exchange, choose a prime $p = \ell_A^n \ell_B^m f \pm 1$ and an elliptic curve E_0, together with bases $\{P_A, Q_A\}$ for $E_0[\ell_A^n]$ and $\{P_B, Q_B\}$ for $E_0[\ell_B^m]$. Let $\mathscr{H} = \{H_k \mid k \in K\}$ be a family of hash functions indexed by a finite set K, where each H_k is a function from $\mathbf{F}_{p^2}$ to the message space $\{0,1\}^w$.

Key generation. Choose two random elements $a_1, a_2 \in \mathbf{Z}/\ell_A^n\mathbf{Z}$, not both nilpotent. Let

$$E_A = E_0/\langle a_1 P_A + a_2 Q_A \rangle,$$

and $\varphi_A : E_0 \to E_A$ the canonical isogeny. Choose a random element $k \in K$. The public key is $(E_A, \varphi_A(P_B), \varphi_A(Q_B), k)$, and the private key is (a_1, a_2, k).

Encryption. Given a public key $(E_A, \varphi_A(P_B), \varphi_A(Q_B), k)$ and a message $m \in \{0,1\}^w$, choose two random elements $b_1, b_2 \in \mathbf{Z}/\ell_B^m\mathbf{Z}$, not both nilpotent. Fix

$$E_B = E_0/\langle b_1 P_B + b_2 Q_B \rangle,$$

and $\varphi_B : E_0 \to E_B$ the canonical isogeny, and let $E_{BA} = E_A/\langle b_1\varphi_A(P_B) + b_2\varphi_A(Q_B) \rangle$. Compute the hash value $h = H_k(j(E_{BA}))$ and $c = h \oplus m$. The ciphertext is $(E_B, \varphi_B(P_A), \varphi_B(Q_A), c)$.

Decryption. Given the ciphertext $(E_B, \varphi_B(P_A), \varphi_B(Q_A), c)$, compute

$$E_{AB} = E_B/\langle a_1\varphi_B(P_A) + a_2\varphi_B(Q_A) \rangle.$$

Let $m = H_k(j(E_{AB})) \oplus c$. Since $j(E_{AB}) = j(E_{BA})$, m is the plaintext.

Remark 1. Observe that Alice's private key (a_1, a_2) is equivalent to (ra_1, ra_2) for any r coprime to ℓ_A, since $a_1 P_A + a_2 Q_A$ and $ra_1 P_A + ra_2 Q_A$ generate the same subgroup of $E_0[\ell_A^n]$. Recall that a_1 and a_2 are not both nilpotent. Seen as integers, this means that one of them is not divisible by ℓ_A, so is invertible in $\mathbf{Z}/\ell_A^n\mathbf{Z}$. Therefore (a_1, a_2) is equivalent to either $(1, a)$ (if a_1 is coprime to ℓ_A) or to $(a, 1)$ (if a_2 is coprime to ℓ_A).

2.5   Validation Methods Against Active Attacks

Various validation methods have been introduced in order to prevent active attacks against isogeny-based protocols. Classical methods allowing to check if an elliptic curve is supersingular, or if two given points P and Q lie on the curve, have the correct order and are independent are discussed in [5]. In [9, Sect. 2.4], some validation steps are simplified, and a new one is introduced that allows Alice to gain some assurance that the two points of Bob's public-key are the images of the two base points P_A, Q_A through an isogeny of degree ℓ_B^m. The active attack of [9] allows a dishonest party to send malicious points to Alice that nevertheless pass all these validations.

The only effective countermeasure that has been proposed to prevent this attack against the key exchange protocol is to apply the Fujisaki–Okamoto transform [8], as explained in [17], which in the context of the isogeny key exchange has been discussed by Kirkwood *et al.* [13]. This validation method essentially forces Bob to send to Alice honestly generated parameters, and to prove that he has been able to compute the shared secret. More precisely, the following describes the key exchange protocol resulting from applying the Fujisaki–Okamoto transform. Here, Alice has a static secret key (a_1, a_2), and Bob — the potential adversary — generates an ephemeral key.

Bob's key generation. Bob chooses a random seed r, from which he derives his secret key $(b_1, b_2) = f(r)$ via a pseudo-random function f. He proceeds to compute his message $(E_B, \varphi_B(P_A), \varphi_B(Q_A))$ as in the regular key exchange. He computes the shared secret E_{AB} using Alice's public key $(E_A, \varphi_A(P_B), \varphi_A(Q_B))$, and derives a session key $\mathtt{sk}$ and a validation key $\mathtt{vk}$ via a key derivation function (KDF), as

$$(\mathtt{sk}, \mathtt{vk}) = \mathrm{KDF}(j(E_{AB})).$$

Key exchange. Bob sends the tuple $(E_B, \varphi_B(P_A), \varphi_B(Q_A))$ and the ciphertext $c = \mathrm{Enc}_{\mathtt{vk}}(r \oplus \mathtt{sk})$ to Alice.

Validation. Alice first derives E'_{AB}, then $\mathtt{sk}'$ and $\mathtt{vk}'$, to recover the value $r' = \mathrm{Dec}_{\mathtt{vk}'}(c) \oplus \mathtt{sk}'$. From this hypothetical seed r', she is able to recompute Bob's operations. If the result she finds coincides with the tuple $(E_B, \varphi_B(P_A), \varphi_B(Q_A))$ she has received, she terminates the protocol by accepting $\mathtt{sk}' = \mathtt{sk}$ as the shared secret. Otherwise, she returns an error.

In the fault injection attack we describe, Bob forces Alice to compute a wrong isogeny. By predicting the output of this wrong isogeny, Bob can make sure the fault is not detected by the validation, and Alice leaks some faulted information.

3   Fault Injection Attacks

Fault injection attacks are a standard kind of attacks assuming physical access to a device (Alice) using a static private key (in the present context, a pair (a_1, a_2)). They rely on the ability of the attacking party to tamper with Alice's execution of the protocol, causing her to commit errors in her computations. For the rest of the paper, we fix $\ell_A = 2$ and $\ell_B = 3$ for simplicity, but the results can easily be applied to any ℓ_A and ℓ_B.

3.1 Tampering with Bits and Bytes

The secret key is a pair of integers $a_1, a_2 \in \{1, ..., 2^n - 1\}$, such that the kernel of the secret isogeny is $R_A = a_1 P_A + a_2 Q_A$. If it is possible to force a particular bit of (a_1, a_2) to, say, 0, then the value of that bit can be recovered by checking if the faulty outcome is valid. A folklore way to make this kind of attack ineffective is to regularly randomize the representation of the secret key. In the present context, this could be done by choosing a random odd integer r each time the private key is used, and to replace (a_1, a_2) by the equivalent pair (ra_1, ra_2).

There exist mostly three ways to alter the value of a bit during execution: forcing it to 0 or 1, flipping it, or randomizing it. The simple attack above assumes that a bit can be forced to some value, but the weakest of these three assumptions is obviously the bit randomization. Under this assumption, a particular bit can be made to take a random value among 0 or 1, unknown from the attacker. This cannot be exploited in such a straightforward way as the bit-forcing assumption, but suffices for the more elaborate attack we present.

Targeting a particular bit might turn out to be difficult. Rather than a precise bit error, one could aim for a byte error (or a word error): a fault is injected in a byte, and the new value of the byte cannot be predicted by the attacker.

3.2 Implementing Loop-Aborts

A powerful way to exploit fault injections is to implement loop aborts. The weakest of the above assumptions are sufficient to force a loop to come to an end. Loop-abort faults have been introduced by Page and Vercauteren in the context of pairing based cryptography [16], and recently used by Espitau et al. [7] to attack signature schemes based on lattices. It is explained in [7, Sect. 5] that a loop-abort can simply be implemented by injecting a random fault on the loop counter — or alternatively, by skipping the jump instruction. Loop-abort faults appear to be feasible in practice, and have already been successfully performed in attacks against pairing based cryptography by Blömer et al. [3].

As any fault attack, it requires some knowledge on the structure of the implementation being targeted, to know precisely at which place and time the fault should be injected. Such structure can be recovered by combining some knowledge of the algorithms involved (and maybe of standard implementations), reverse-engineering techniques and side-channel analysis. Then, a few circumstances make loop-abort attacks easier. First, most of the possible values of the loop-counter would cause the loop to abort, so it is not necessary to target a specific bit: some imprecise randomizations should do the trick. Second, to exit the loop after k iterations, it is sufficient to tamper with the counter at any time during the execution of the k-th iteration. With that strategy, if an iteration takes time to execute, the timing of the fault injection need not be excessively precise.

4   The Loop-Abort Fault Attack

This attack takes advantage of the iterative structure of the isogeny computation, as described in Sect. 2.3. The critical point is Alice's computation of an isogeny $E \to E/\langle a_1 R + a_2 S \rangle$ based on her secret. One can inject a fault to cause Alice to compute this isogeny only partially, leaking information about the secret key (a_1, a_2).

4.1   Attack Framework

Alice takes as input the public parameters of a party who wants to initiate a secure communication, and performs her side of the protocol using a static private key (a_1, a_2). We assume that the countermeasures discussed in [9] are implemented, and in particular the Kirkwood *et al.* validation method [13], which essentially prevents attacks based on tricking Alice into computing on maliciously cooked data. Then, Alice is modeled in the form of an oracle $\mathcal{O}(E, R, S, E', b_1, b_2)$ which returns 1 if

$$j(E') = j(E/\langle a_1 R + a_2 S \rangle),$$
$$j(E) = j(E_0/\langle b_1 P_B + b_2 Q_B \rangle) \text{ and}$$
$$(R, S) = (\varphi_B(P_A), \varphi_B(Q_A))$$

and 0 otherwise. The first condition corresponds, as in the second oracle of [9, Sect. 3], to Alice taking Bob's protocol message, performing her side of the protocol, and returning an error if the shared key she finds does not coincide with Bob's. The second and third conditions account for the Kirkwood *et al.* [13] validation method: Bob can only use honestly generated parameters.

We further assume, and it is the foundation of our attack, that the attacker can make Alice abort the main loop after the k-th iteration during her computation of the isogeny $E \to E/\langle a_1 R + a_2 S \rangle$, using techniques discussed in Sect. 3.2. As described in Sect. 2.3, recall that after k iterations, Alice has computed the intermediate elliptic curve

$$E^k \cong E/\langle 2^{n-k}(a_1 R + a_2 S) \rangle$$

The fault injection is modeled by the oracle $\mathcal{O}^k(E, R, S, E', b_1, b_2)$, that returns 1 if $j(E') = j(E^k)$, $j(E) = j(E_0/\langle b_1 P_B + b_2 Q_B \rangle)$ and $(R, S) = (\varphi_B(P_A), \varphi_B(Q_A))$, and 0 otherwise.

4.2   The Attack

Alice's key (a_1, a_2) is either equivalent to $(1, a)$ (if a_1 is odd) or $(a, 1)$ (if a_2 is odd), and the attacker recover one by one the bits of a from the least significant to the most significant[3]. The attacker, playing the role of Bob, chooses a (random) secret key $(b_1, b_2) \in \{1, \cdots, 3^m\}^2$ that he is going to use for the attack. He computes $E_B = E_0/\langle b_1 P_B + b_2 Q_B \rangle$ and lets $\varphi_B : E_0 \to E_B$ be the canonical isogeny. Also write $P_A' = \varphi_B(P_A)$ and $Q_A' = \varphi_B(Q_A)$. First, the attacker needs to decide whether the key can be represented as $(1, a)$ or $(a, 1)$. We have

$$E_B^1 \cong E_B/\langle 2^{n-1}(a_1 P_A' + a_2 Q_A') \rangle$$
$$= E_B/\langle (2^{n-1} a_1 \bmod 2^n) P_A' + (2^{n-1} a_2 \bmod 2^n) Q_A' \rangle.$$

Therefore a_1 is even if and only if the first isogeny $E_B \to E_B^1$ has kernel $\langle 2^{n-1} Q_A' \rangle \subset E[2]$. This can be decided by determining the kernel $\kappa \subset E_B[2]$ of the first isogeny computed by Alice. The attacker guesses one of the three possible proper subgroups $\kappa \subset E_B[2]$, and queries the oracle $\mathcal{O}^1$ on the input $(E_B, \varphi_B(P_A'), \varphi_B(Q_A'), E_B/\kappa, b_1, b_2)$. If the output is 1, then the guess of κ was correct. If the output is 0, either the guess is incorrect or the fault injection failed. This allows simultaneously to determine if the key can be represented as $(1, a)$ or $(a, 1)$, and to determine the least significant bit of a. More precisely,

if $\kappa = \langle 2^{n-1} Q_A' \rangle$ then a_1 is even and a_2 is odd, so the key can be represented as $(a, 1)$, and the least significant bit of a is 0.

if $\kappa = \langle 2^{n-1} P_A' \rangle$ then a_2 is even and a_1 is odd, so the key can be represented as $(1, a)$, and the least significant bit of a is 0.

if $\kappa = \langle 2^{n-1}(P_A' + Q_A') \rangle$ then both a_1 and a_2 are odd, so the key can be represented as $(1, a)$, and the least significant bit of a is 1.

In the following, we assume without loss of generality that the key is represented as $(1, a)$. Now, it remains to recover all the other bits of a, from the least significant to the most significant. In order to match the structure of the attack, the bits of a are indexed from the least significant to the most significant. Observe that

$$E_B^k \cong E_B/\langle 2^{n-k}(P_A' + a Q_A') \rangle = E_B/\langle 2^{n-k} P_A' + (2^{n-k} a \bmod 2^n) Q_A' \rangle$$

only depends on the k least significant bits of a. If we know the first $k - 1$ bits of the key, we can guess the k-th one and compute the corresponding degree-ℓ^k isogeny. Then, it suffices to compare the result with the faulty outcome to determine if the guess is correct. More precisely, at the k-th step, once the $k - 1$ first bits of the key a have already been recovered, we perform the following steps:

1. Choose a guess $b \in \{0, 1\}$;
2. Compute

$$\tilde{E}_B^k = E_B/\langle 2^{n-k} P_A' + \tilde{a} 2^{n-k} Q_A' \rangle$$

where $\tilde{a} = b \cdot 2^{k-1} + (a \bmod 2^{k-1})$ is the concatenation of b with the first $k-1$ bits of a;

---

[3] Note the contrast with the simple attack of Sect. 3.1, in which the way Alice internally represents her secret key is crucial. In this more evolved attack, Alice's representation is irrelevant.

3. Query the oracle $\mathcal{O}^k$ on $\left(E_B, P'_A, Q'_A, \tilde{E}^k_B, b_1, b_2\right)$;
4. If the oracle returns 1 (*i.e.* it does not detect an error), then the k-th bit is b; otherwise, either the bit is $1 - b$, or the fault injection failed.

Assuming that the fault injection is a success (*i.e.*, the oracle $\mathcal{O}^k$ is called successfully), it is clear that the oracle returns 1 only if $\tilde{E}^k_B$ is indeed the k-th elliptic curve in the sequence of isogenies that Alice should have computed, meaning that b is a correct guess of the k-th bit of a.

4.3 Analysis of the Attack

Let μ denote the probability of successfully aborting the computation[4]. The attack above requires about $2n/\mu \approx \log_2 p/\mu$ fault injections, and as many interactions with Alice[5]. Considering that Alice is modeled as an oracle that outputs only one bit, $O(n)$ is optimal in the sense that we cannot hope to recover more than one bit of the key per interaction. The additional factor μ accounts for the potential difficulty of injecting faults. In Sect. 4.4, we describe a way to reduce the number of faults, assuming a stronger oracle which leaks more information.

To abort after k iterations, the fault must be injected during the execution of the k-th iteration. All known implementations of the isogeny computation share the same iterative structure, however the duration of an iteration is not necessarily a constant, and depends on the choice of a *strategy* — in the sense of [6, Sect. 4.2.2]. For instance, in the SIDH Library [15], the first iteration is the longest, taking about $4.0 \cdot 10^6$ CPU cycles (measured on an Intel(R) Core(TM) i7-4710MQ CPU @ 2.50 GHz), while the other iterations take between $7.9 \cdot 10^4$ and $1.8 \cdot 10^6$ CPU cycles. Finding the right moment to inject the fault can be easy if Alice is using a public implementation [5], and otherwise requires to reverse-engineer the strategy by side-channel analysis.

This attack is the first one against isogeny-based schemes that bypasses the costly Kirkwood *et al.* validation method [13]. In essence, this validation method checks these two statements: first, Bob's parameters are honestly generated (and in our attack, they indeed are), and Bob knows the shared key computed by Alice (this is precisely the guess $\tilde{E}^k_B$, which has a probability $1/2$ of being correct).

4.4 Alternative with Less Faults but Stronger Oracle

Instead of the weak oracle we have considered so far, which outputs a single bit at each call, one could also consider a more powerful oracle, closer to the first oracle of [9, Sect. 3] (but still weaker). Let $\mathcal{H}$ be a function with very rare collisions (it could be the identity, or a hash function), and consider the oracle

---

[4] For simplicity, we assume that this probability is independent of the number k of iterations after which we want to abort.

[5] More precisely, if there exists a way to determine that a fault was successful (for instance, if $\mu = 1$), we can get rid of the factor 2, because a failure brings the information that the guess is wrong, so the bit is $1 - b$.

$\mathcal{O}(E, R, S, b_1, b_2)$ which outputs $\mathcal{H}(j(E/\langle a_1 R + a_2 S \rangle))$ if $j(E) = j(E_0/\langle b_1 P_B + b_2 Q_B \rangle)$ and $(R, S) = (\varphi_B(P_A), \varphi_B(Q_A))$, and 0 otherwise. We can then hope to reduce the number of faults necessary for the attack, at the cost of additional computations.

As previously, we also define the oracle $\mathcal{O}^k(E, R, S, b_1, b_2)$ which outputs

$$\mathcal{H}(j(E/\langle 2^{n-k}(a_1 R + a_2 S)\rangle))$$

if $j(E) = j(E_0/\langle b_1 P_B + b_2 Q_B \rangle)$ and $(R, S) = (\varphi_B(P_A), \varphi_B(Q_A))$, and 0 otherwise. The idea is to consider batches of $s > 1$ bits instead of recovering one bit at a time, thereby reducing the required number of faults from n to $\lceil \frac{n}{s} \rceil$.

As in the attack of Sect. 4.2, the attacker generates parameters b_1, b_2, E_B and φ_B. Assuming the key is represented as $(1, a)$, the s least significant bits of a can be recovered as follows: call the oracle $\mathcal{O}^s(E_B, \varphi_B(P_A), \varphi_B(Q_A), b_1, b_2)$, and call the output h. Find by exhaustive search the value $x \in \{0, 1, \ldots, 2^s - 1\}$ such that $h = \mathcal{H}(E_B/\langle 2^{n-s}(P'_A + xQ'_A)\rangle)$. Unless a collision occurred in $\mathcal{H}$, this x is exactly $a \bmod 2^s$, corresponding to the s least significant bits of a. Generalizing this to the other bits is straightforward. The time complexity to find a batch of s bits clearly grows as $O(2^s)$.

Note that the Kirkwood *et al.* validation method prevents this trade-off: Alice always terminates in a non-accepting state unless Bob is able to guess in advance the value $j(\tilde{E}_{AB})$ of the (faulty) shared secret computed by Alice, bringing the probability of successfully recovering the s bits down to $\mu/2^s$.

This trade-off can be analyzed by simulating the attack in software, based on the open-source implementation of [5, 15]. The loop-abort is simulated by adding a **break** instruction at the appropriate moment. We use the default parameters that are provided, that is the curve $E : y^2 = x^3 + x$ defined over $\mathbf{F}_p$, for $p = 2^{372} 3^{239} - 1$, claimed to offer 186 bits of classical security.

Timings for various batch sizes (*i.e.*, s in the above description) are provided in Table 1. The sizes are even because the implementation of [15] computes 4-isogenies instead of 2-isogenies, so the bits have to be considered by pairs.

Table 1. Time of the computations depending on the size of the batches. The tests were run on an Intel(R) Core(TM) i7-4710MQ CPU @ 2.50 GHz.

Size of batches	2	4	6	8	10	12	14	16	18	20
Time (in seconds)	7.13	9.6	21.1	65.3	201	681	2389	7946	22809	84763
Number of faults	185	93	62	47	37	31	27	24	21	19

5   Countermeasures and Conclusion

Previously introduced validation methods are not sufficient to prevent the fault injection attack we have presented. To patch this vulnerability, it is necessary to implement new countermeasures when such a physical attack is relevant. A few generic countermeasures have already been discussed in [7].

First, simply checking after the loop if the value of the counter is exactly the expected number of iterations provides a first protection against attackers who cannot inject faults with a sufficiently high precision (for instance, attackers who can only inject random errors in a memory word). This countermeasure can be strengthened further by adding an additional (or multiple) parallel counter, and checking that both counters have the expected final value. This protects against single faults, and to some extent, against random faults.

These countermeasures are very cheap and easy to implement, as they are not related to the underlying mathematical structures but are simply meant to check that the loop completed the correct number of iterations.

Acknowledgements. This work has been supported in part by the European Union's H2020 Programme under grant agreement number ERC-669891. The second author was supported by the Swiss National Science Foundation under grant number 200021-156420.

References

1. Azarderakhsh, R., Koziel, B., Jalali, A., Kermani, M.M., Jao, D.: NEON-SIDH: efficient implementation of supersingular isogeny Diffie-Hellman key-exchange protocol on ARM. Cryptology ePrint Archive, Report 2016/669 (2016). http://eprint.iacr.org/2016/669
2. Blake, I.F., Seroussi, G., Smart, N.P.: Advances in Elliptic Curve Cryptography. London Mathematical Society Lecture Note Series, vol. 317. Cambridge University Press, Cambridge (2004)
3. Blömer, J., Gomes da Silva, R., Günther, P., Krämer, J., Seifert, J.: A practical second-order fault attack against a real-world pairing implementation. In: 2014 Workshop on Fault Diagnosis and Tolerance in Cryptography, FDTC 2014, pp. 123–136 (2014)
4. Bröker, R.: Constructing supersingular elliptic curves. J. Comb. Number Theory **1**, 269–273 (2009)
5. Costello, C., Longa, P., Naehrig, M.: Efficient algorithms for supersingular isogeny Diffie-Hellman. In: Proceedings of Advances in Cryptology - CRYPTO 2016, Part I, pp. 572–601 (2016)
6. De Feo, L., Jao, D., Plût, J.: Towards quantum-resistant cryptosystems from supersingular elliptic curve isogenies. J. Math. Cryptol. **8**(3), 209–247 (2014)
7. Espitau, T., Fouque, P.A., Gérard, B., Tibouchi, M.: Loop-abort faults on lattice-based Fiat-Shamir and hash-and-sign signatures. Cryptology ePrint Archive, Report 2016/449 (2016). http://eprint.iacr.org/2016/449
8. Fujisaki, E., Okamoto, T.: Secure integration of asymmetric and symmetric encryption schemes. In: Wiener, M. (ed.) CRYPTO 1999. LNCS, vol. 1666, pp. 537–554. Springer, Heidelberg (1999). doi:10.1007/3-540-48405-1_34
9. Galbraith, S.D., Petit, C., Shani, B., Ti, Y.B.: On the security of supersingular isogeny cryptosystems. In: Cheon, J.H., Takagi, T. (eds.) ASIACRYPT 2016. LNCS, vol. 10031, pp. 63–91. Springer, Heidelberg (2016). doi:10.1007/978-3-662-53887-6_3

10. Galbraith, S.D., Petit, C., Silva, J.: Signature schemes based on supersingular isogeny problems. Cryptology ePrint Archive, Report 2016/1154 (2016). http://eprint.iacr.org/2016/1154

11. Jao, D., Feo, L.: Towards quantum-resistant cryptosystems from supersingular elliptic curve isogenies. In: Yang, B.-Y. (ed.) PQCrypto 2011. LNCS, vol. 7071, pp. 19–34. Springer, Heidelberg (2011). doi:10.1007/978-3-642-25405-5_2

12. Jao, D., Soukharev, V.: Isogeny-based quantum-resistant undeniable signatures. In: Mosca, M. (ed.) PQCrypto 2014. LNCS, vol. 8772, pp. 160–179. Springer, Cham (2014). doi:10.1007/978-3-319-11659-4_10

13. Kirkwood, D., Lackey, B.C., McVey, J., Motley, M., Solinas, J.A., Tuller, D.: Failure is not an option: standardization issues for post-quantum key agreement on the security of supersingular isogeny cryptosystems. Workshop on Cybersecurity in a Post-Quantum World (2015). http://csrc.nist.gov/groups/ST/post-quantum-2015/presentations/session7-motley-mark.pdf

14. Koziel, B., Azarderakhsh, R., Kermani, M.M., Jao, D.: Post-quantum cryptography on FPGA based on isogenies on elliptic curves. Cryptology ePrint Archive, Report 2016/672 (2016). http://eprint.iacr.org/2016/672

15. Microsoft Security and Cryptography: SIDH Library (2016). https://www.microsoft.com/en-us/research/project/sidh-library/

16. Page, D., Vercauteren, F.: A fault attack on pairing-based cryptography. IEEE Trans. Comput. 55(9), 1075–1080 (2006)

17. Peikert, C.: Lattice cryptography for the internet. In: Mosca, M. (ed.) PQCrypto 2014. LNCS, vol. 8772, pp. 197–219. Springer, Cham (2014). doi:10.1007/978-3-319-11659-4_12

18. Shor, P.W.: Polynomial-time algorithms for prime factorization and discrete logarithms on a quantum computer. SIAM J. Comput. 26(5), 1484–1509 (1997)

19. Silverman, J.H.: The Arithmetic of Elliptic Curves. Graduate Texts in Mathematics, vol. 106, 2nd edn. Springer, New York (2009)

20. Sun, X., Tian, H., Wang, Y.: Toward quantum-resistant strong designated verifier signature from isogenies. In: 2012 Fourth International Conference on Intelligent Networking and Collaborative Systems, INCoS 2012, pp. 292–296 (2012)

21. Tate, J.: Endomorphisms of abelian varieties over finite fields. Inventiones Math. 2(2), 134–144 (1966)

22. Vélu, J.: Isogénies entre courbes elliptiques. Comptes Rendus de l'Académie des Sciences de Paris 273, 238–241 (1971)

A   When P and Q Are Not a Basis of the Torsion

The implementation proposed by [5,15] uses a pair of points P and Q in $E[\ell^k]$ that does not generate the full group $E[\ell^k]$, in order to achieve better compression. The point P is chosen to be a point of order ℓ^k, and Q is set as the image of P by the distortion map $(x, y) \mapsto (-x, iy)$ (where $i^2 = -1$).

They prove that because of this construction, when $\ell = 2$, the sum $P+Q$ has order 2^{k-1} (instead of the expected 2^k). Thus every point of the form $P + [a]Q$ for a even has order 2^k. Caution is required when applying to P and Q results that are meant to be applied to a basis of $E[2^k]$. It appears for instance in [9, Lemma 3.2], where the factor 2^{k-1} should be replaced by 2^{k-2} when using this pair (P, Q).

Also, if a is generated following the guidelines of [5] (as $a = 2m$ for $m \in \{1, 2, \ldots, 2^{k-1}\}$), then its most significant bit is superfluous. Indeed, the kernel of the first isogeny is necessarily the group generated by $[2^{k-1}]P = -[2^{k-1}]Q$. Then, the image of $P + [a]Q$ under this isogeny is the same as the image of $P + [a + 2^{k-1}]Q$. It follows that the secret a leads to the same shared secret as its reduction $a \bmod 2^{k-1}$. Therefore the secret $a = 2m$ could be chosen with $m < 2^{k-2}$.

Fault Attack on Supersingular Isogeny Cryptosystems

Yan Bo Ti[(✉)]

Mathematics Department, University of Auckland, Auckland, New Zealand
yanbo.ti@gmail.com

Abstract. We present the first fault attack on cryptosystems based on supersingular isogenies. During the computation of the auxiliary points, the attack aims to change the base point to a random point on the curve via a fault injection. We will show that this would reveal the secret isogeny with one successful perturbation with high probability. We will exhibit the attack by placing it against signature schemes and key-exchange protocols with validations in place. Our paper therefore demonstrates the need to incorporate checks in implementations of the cryptosystem.

1 Introduction

Cryptosystems based on isogenies between supersingular elliptic curves were proposed by Jao and De Feo in 2011 [13] as a candidate for cryptographic protocols in the post-quantum world. Instead of relying on the discrete logarithm problem which is susceptible to Shor's algorithm [20], it is based on the number-theoretic problem of finding isogenies between supersingular elliptic curves.

Cryptosystems based on isogenies have their genesis in an unpublished manuscript by Couveignes [8] and were later rediscovered by Rostovtsev and Stolbunov [18]. A paper by Charles, Goren and Lauter [3] then used the isogeny graphs to construct a hash function. However, Childs et al. [4] managed to find a quantum algorithm that was able to break the cryptosystems in [8,18] in sub-exponential time by reducing the problem of finding an isogeny between isogenous ordinary curves to a hidden shift problem which can be solved by a quantum algorithm (Kuperberg's algorithm [16]). The reduction is based on the abelian group action of the class group of the endomorphism ring of the elliptic curve. This action is absent in the supersingular case and hence their reduction does not apply.

Since the publication of [13], protocols such as the interactive identification protocol [9] and various signature schemes have been introduced [12,14,19,23,24] to add to the key-exchange and encryption protocols introduced in [13]. A cryptanalysis paper [11] has highlighted their vulnerability to adaptive attacks and the importance of countermeasures. Some implementation papers have introduced side-channel protection such as constant time operations [7]. However, threats posed by fault attacks have been absent in the literature.

T. Lange and T. Takagi (Eds.): PQCrypto 2017, LNCS 10346, pp. 107–122, 2017.
DOI: 10.1007/978-3-319-59879-6_7

Fault attacks exploit the leakage of sensitive information when the implementation operates under unexpected circumstances. Biehl et al. [2] extended fault attacks on RSA cryptosystems to systems using elliptic curves. Ciet and Joye [5] then refined the methods and made the attack more practical. The key insight in both papers was the absence of the a_6 elliptic curve parameter in the scalar multiplication computation. The fault changed the base point P to some P'. This meant that the output point $[\lambda]P'$, where λ is the secret, might be in a group where solving the elliptic curve discrete logarithm problem was feasible, hence allowing for the recovery of some information about λ.

In this work, we will examine the effects of changing a point P to some random P' and attempt to recover the secret, which in this case is an isogeny ϕ. The attack would be able to recover the entire secret ϕ from a single output $\phi(P')$ with high probability. This compares well against the fault attack presented in [5] where a single successful perturbation only reveals partial information of the secret. We will present a fault attack in the context of several signature schemes and key-exchange protocols. The attack would work against the countermeasure proposed by Kirkwood et al. [15] which is based on the Fujisaki–Okamoto transform. The main observation that underlies the attack is that users should never reveal the image of random points under the secret isogeny.

The main result of the paper will be presented in Sect. 3. Prior to that, Sect. 2 will cover both the mathematical notions and the cryptographic protocols required to understand this paper. In Sect. 4 we will analyse the attack and discuss its feasibility.

2   Preliminaries

2.1   Mathematical Background

Let E and E' be elliptic curves defined over a finite field $\mathbb{F}_q$ of characteristic p, then an *isogeny* between them is a non-zero morphism that maps the group identity of E to the group identity of E'. If $\phi : E \to E'$ is an isogeny, then it is a group homomorphism from $E(\overline{\mathbb{F}}_q)$ to $E'(\overline{\mathbb{F}}_q)$ [21, III.4.8] Equivalently, we are able to represent an isogeny ϕ as an algebraic morphism of the form

$$\phi(x,y) = \left(\frac{f_1(x,y)}{g_1(x,y)}, \frac{f_2(x,y)}{g_2(x,y)} \right)$$

where $\phi(\mathcal{O}) = \mathcal{O}$ and $f_i, g_i \in \mathbb{F}_q[x,y]$. In this case, we say that E and E' are *isogenous* over $\mathbb{F}_q$. The *degree* of an isogeny is defined to be its degree as an algebraic morphism and is denoted by $\deg \phi$. Isogenies with the same domain and range are known as *endomorphisms*. The map $[n] : E \to E$ given by

$$[n]P = \underbrace{P + \cdots + P}_{n \text{ times}}$$

is the multiplication-by-n map on E and is an example of an endomorphism. The kernel of this endomorphism is the set of n-torsion points which we denote by

$$E[n] = \left\{ P \in E\left(\overline{\mathbb{F}}_q\right) \mid [n]P = \mathcal{O}\right\}.$$

If $p \nmid n$, then the set of n-torsion points of an elliptic curve has the group structure $E[n] \cong \mathbb{Z}/n\mathbb{Z} \times \mathbb{Z}/n\mathbb{Z}$ [21, III.6.4].

Given an isogeny $\phi : E \to E'$, there exists a unique isogeny $\hat{\phi} : E' \to E$ such that

$$\phi \circ \hat{\phi} = [\deg \phi] = \hat{\phi} \circ \phi.$$

We call $\hat{\phi}$ the *dual isogeny* of ϕ [21, III.6.1]. Hence we can see that isogenous curves form an equivalence class.

An isogeny $\phi : E \to E'$ is *separable* if the induced extension of the function fields is separable. All of the isogenies that we will encounter in this paper will be separable. The size of the kernel of a separable isogeny is the same as the degree of the isogeny [21, III.4.10]. In fact, the link between a separable isogeny and its kernel goes deeper: the kernel of a separable isogeny uniquely defines the isogeny up to isomorphism [21, III.4.12]. To express this idea, we use the notation E/G to represent the codomain of some isogeny ϕ from E with kernel G. Given a finite subgroup G, an isogeny with kernel G can be computed using an algorithm by Vélu [22].

Given an elliptic curve E, the set of all endomorphisms over $\overline{\mathbb{F}}_q$, together with the zero isogeny, forms a ring. Addition in the ring is given by point-wise addition, and multiplication by composing endomorphisms. The endomorphism ring forms an algebra over $\mathbb{Z}$ and is of dimension at most 4 [21, III.4.2, III.7.5]. In fact $\dim_{\mathbb{Z}} \text{End } E = 2$ or 4 and in the first case, we say that E is ordinary and in the second case, we say that E is *supersingular*. For the remainder of this paper, the elliptic curves we will encounter will be supersingular.

2.2 Supersingular Isogeny Cryptosystem

In this section, we will review the key-exchange protocol, interactive identification protocol and the various signature schemes. The key-exchange and the identification protocols were first introduced in [9,13]. Thereafter, signature schemes were introduced in [12,14,24], where the latter two are based on the identification protocol.

Key-Exchange. Suppose that Alice and Bob wish to establish a shared secret. There are three steps to the protocol that will achieve this objective.

Set-up: Fix a prime p of the form $p = \ell_A^{e_A} \cdot \ell_B^{e_B} \cdot f \pm 1$ where ℓ_A and ℓ_B are small distinct primes, f is a small cofactor, and e_A and e_B are positive integers such that $\ell_A^{e_A} \approx \ell_B^{e_B}$. Now fix a supersingular elliptic curve E over $\mathbb{F}_{p^2}$ and pick bases $\{P_A, Q_A\}$ and $\{P_B, Q_B\}$ for the $\ell_A^{e_A}$ and $\ell_B^{e_B}$-torsion subgroups.

Key generation: Alice picks random elements $a_1, a_2 \in \mathbb{Z}/\ell_A^{e_A}\mathbb{Z}$, not both divisible by ℓ_A, and computes the subgroup $G_A = \langle [a_1]P_A + [a_2]Q_A \rangle$. She then uses the formula from Vélu to compute a curve $E_A = E/G_A$ and an isogeny $\phi_A : E \to E_A$, where $\ker \phi_A = G_A$. Alice also computes the points

$\phi_A(P_B)$ and $\phi_A(Q_B)$. She then sends the tuple $(E_A, \phi_A(P_B), \phi_A(Q_B))$ to Bob. Bob performs the computation mutatis mutandis on his end.

Key derivation: Upon receipt of Bob's tuple $(E_B, \phi_B(P_A), \phi_B(Q_A))$, Alice computes the subgroup $G'_A = \langle [a_1]\phi_B(P_A) + [a_2]\phi_B(Q_A) \rangle$ and uses Vélu's formula to compute the elliptic curve $E_{AB} = E_B/G'_A$. She then uses the j-invariant of E_{AB} as the shared secret. Bob proceeding likewise would also obtain the j-invariant of E_{AB} to use as the shared secret. The protocol can be summarised in Fig. 1.

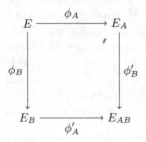

Fig. 1. Key-exchange protocol

Interactive Identification Protocol. This interactive identification protocol has four steps: set-up, commitment, challenge and response.

Set-up: Fix a prime p of the form $p = \ell_A^{e_A} \cdot \ell_B^{e_B} \cdot f \pm 1$ where ℓ_A and ℓ_B are small distinct primes, f is a small cofactor and e_A and e_B are positive integers such that $\ell_A^{e_A} \approx \ell_B^{e_B}$. Now fix a supersingular elliptic curve E over $\mathbb{F}_{p^2}$.

The prover picks a random element $S \in E[\ell_A^{e_A}]$ with order $\ell_A^{e_A}$ and computes $\phi : E \to E/\langle S \rangle = E_S$. Then, the prover generates a basis $\{P_B, Q_B\}$ for $E[\ell_B^{e_B}]$. The prover then computes and publishes the tuple

$$(E, P_B, Q_B, E_S, \phi(P_B), \phi(Q_B))$$

as the public key.

The two parties then repeat the next three steps until a security threshold is reached.

Commitment: The prover chooses random elements $r_1, r_2 \in \mathbb{Z}/\ell_B^{e_B}\mathbb{Z}$, not both divisible by ℓ_B and computes the point $R = [r_1]P_B + [r_2]Q_B$. The prover then computes the isogeny $\psi : E \to E/\langle R \rangle = E_R$ and the curve $E_{RS} = E_S/\langle \phi(R) \rangle = E_S/\langle [r_1]\phi(P_B) + [r_2]\phi(Q_B) \rangle = E/\langle R, S \rangle$. The prover sends (E_R, E_{RS}) to the verifier.

Challenge: The verifier sends the challenge bit $c \in \{0, 1\}$.

Response: In response, the prover reveals $(R, \phi(R))$[1] if $c = 0$ or $\psi(S)$ if $c = 1$. In the former case, the verifier would check that $E/\langle R \rangle \cong E_R$ and $E_S/\langle \phi(R) \rangle \cong E_{RS}$. In the latter case, the verifier checks that $E_R/\langle \psi(S) \rangle \cong E_{RS}$ (Fig. 2).

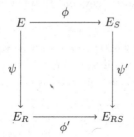

Fig. 2. Interactive identification protocol

Digital Signature Scheme. This non-interactive signature scheme is the result of applying the Fiat–Shamir transform on the interactive identification protocol presented above. This scheme was introduced in [12,24]. The signature scheme uses the output of the hash as a string of challenge bits to generate a string of responses corresponding to the challenges. The verification step then involves verifying the response in the signature for each challenge bit.

Details of the scheme are given in Appendix A.1.

Undeniable Signature Scheme. The undeniable signature scheme [14] is a "three-dimensional" analogue to key-exchange protocol which is "two-dimensional" in the sense that we consider a commutative cube instead of a commutative square. Given a signature, the scheme is able to confirm the signature if the signature is valid, or disavow an invalid signature without having to reveal a valid signature.

Details of the scheme are given in Appendix A.2.

2.3   The Kirkwood et al. Validation Method

Kirkwood et al. introduced a method to secure the key-exchange protocol of isogeny cryptosystems. This is based on the Fujisaki–Okamoto transform [10] which is also explained by Peikert [17, Sect. 5.2] and Galbraith et al. [11, Sect. 2.3]. The method allows for one party to validate the other, but for the ease of exposition, let us suppose that Alice is using a static secret and Bob needs to prove to her that he is performing the protocol correctly.

---

[1] It is also possible to compress $(R, \phi(R))$ by sending (r_1, r_2) instead (c.f. [1]). The verifier can then recover R and $\phi(R)$ given P_B, Q_B, $\phi(P_B)$ and $\phi(Q_B)$.

Bob would prove to Alice that he performed the protocol correctly by executing the key-exchange, encrypting the random seed used to generate his private key and sending this ciphertext to Alice for her to verify that the random seed leads to the correct keys.

Applied to the Jao–De Feo protocol, we will briefly explain how Bob can prove to Alice that he has executed the protocol correctly. This is especially applicable if Alice is using a static key and Bob is potentially a malicious party.

1. Alice computes and sends the public key $(E_A, \phi_A(P_B), \phi_A(Q_B))$.
2. Bob receives Alice's public key $(E_A, \phi_A(P_B), \phi_A(Q_B))$.
3. Bob obtains his random seed r_B from a random source and derives his private key using a key derivation function, KDF_1,

$$(b_1, b_2) = \text{KDF}_1(r_B).$$

   He uses the secret key to compute $G_B = \langle [b_1]P_B + [b_2]Q_B \rangle$, and uses the Vélu formula to compute ϕ_B and $E_B = E/G_B$.
4. Bob derives the shared secret $j(E_{AB})$ using his private key and Alice's public key. He then computes a session key (SK) and a validation key (VK) using a key derivation function, KDF_2,

$$SK \mid VK = \text{KDF}_2(j(E_{AB})).$$

5. Bob sends his public key $(E_B, \phi_B(P_A), \phi_B(Q_A))$ and $c_B = \text{Enc}_{VK}(r_B \oplus SK)$ to Alice.
6. Using her private key and Bob's public key, Alice computes the shared secret $j(E'_{AB})$ and derives the session and validation keys SK' and VK'. She uses these to compute
$$r'_B = \text{Dec}_{VK'}(c_B) \oplus SK'.$$

   She then computes Bob's secret keys from r'_B and recomputes all of Bob's operations and compares $(E'_B, \phi'_B(P_A), \phi'_B(Q_A))$ with $(E_B, \phi_B(P_A), \phi_B(Q_A))$. If they are equal, then Alice verifies that Bob has computed the protocol correctly and proceeds to use $SK' = SK$ for future communication with Bob. Else, the protocol terminates in a non-accepting state.

This validation method can be used for both the key-exchange and the encryption protocols. It also compels one party to reveal the secret used and so requires a change in secret keys after each verification. This protocol is summarised in Fig. 3.

3   Fault Attack

Assume that the protocol under attack reveals the x-coordinate of the image of a point under the secret isogeny. The fault attack aims to force the implementation to output the image of a random point under the secret isogeny. This would allow

Alice   Bob

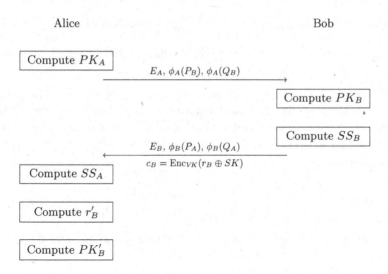

Fig. 3. The Kirkwood et al. validation method for supersingular key-exchange.

the adversary to recover the secret. We will see how this is accomplished and see the different scenarios where the fault attack may be employed.

Our first observation is that computations do not involve the y-coordinate of the points. Given a curve E and a point P, a perturbation in the x-coordinate of P would result in another point P' on the same curve over a quadratic extension. Indeed, given any x, we recover the y-coordinate of P' by solving a quadratic equation which always has a solution in $\mathbb{F}_{p^2}$. In particular, any $x \in \mathbb{F}_{p^2}$ either corresponds to a point on E or a point on its quadratic twist E'. In [7], the most efficient implementation of the cryptosystem thus far, computations do not distinguish between the curve E and its quadratic twist E', hence the isogeny will be evaluated correctly on any $x \in \mathbb{F}_{p^2}$. In a more general setting where the twists of the curves are treated separately, the faulted point will be on E with probability $1/2$ and on the twist with probability $1/2$. Hence the adversary may assume, after a series of faults, that a perturbed point will lie on E.

The perturbed point would be a random point on the curve. In Sect. 3.1, we will show how one recovers the secret isogeny given the image of the random point. This is not dissimilar to [14, Remark 3.1], where Jao and Soukharev noted that a party should never disclose any information that allows an adversary to evaluate ϕ_A on $E[\ell_A^{e_A}]$. The method to recover ϕ_A given the image of a random point in $E[\ell_A^{e_A}]$ is mentioned in [9, Sect. 5.1] and explained in detail in Sect. 3.1. In fact, we will show that a party should never reveal the image of random points under the secret isogeny.

3.1 Recovery of Isogeny from Image of Random Point

Let $E/\mathbb{F}_{p^2}$ be a supersingular elliptic curve where $p = \ell_A^{e_A} \cdot \ell_B^{e_B} \cdot f \pm 1$. Then with (P_A, Q_A), (P_B, Q_B), and (P_C, Q_C) being the generators of $E[\ell_A^{e_A}]$, $E[\ell_B^{e_B}]$, and

$E[f]$ respectively, a random point $X \in E(\mathbb{F}_{p^2})$ takes the form

$$X = [u]P_A + [v]Q_A + [w]P_B + [x]Q_B + [y]P_C + [z]Q_C$$

for some $u, v, w, x, y, z \in \mathbb{Z}$.

Now suppose that we are given the image of X under the secret isogeny ϕ_A, then we will show how one can use the knowledge of $\phi_A(X)$ to recover ϕ_A. Since ϕ_A is a group homomorphism and we know that X can be expressed as a linear combination of P_A, Q_A, P_B, Q_B, P_C, and Q_C, we have

$$\begin{aligned}
\phi_A(X) &= \phi_A([u]P_A + [v]Q_A + [w]P_B + [x]Q_B + [y]P_C + [z]Q_C) \\
&= [u]\phi_A(P_A) + [v]\phi_A(Q_A) + [w]\phi_A(P_B) \\
&\quad + [x]\phi_A(Q_B) + [y]\phi_A(P_C) + [z]\phi_A(Q_C).
\end{aligned}$$

Now our aim is to isolate a linear combination of $\phi_A(P_A)$ and $\phi_A(Q_A)$. To that end, we perform the operation

$$[\ell_B^{e_B} \cdot f]\phi_A(X) = [\ell_B^{e_B} \cdot f]([u]\phi_A(P_A) + [v]\phi_A(Q_A)) = [u']\phi_A(P_A) + [v']\phi_A(Q_A),$$

and we find ourselves in the scenario described in [14, Remark 3.1] and [9, Sect. 5.1].

Once we have $[u']\phi_A(P_A) + [v']\phi_A(Q_A)$, the subgroup generated by this point will help with the construction of the dual isogeny of ϕ_A hence recovering ϕ_A.

Lemma 1. *Let E_1 be a supersingular elliptic curve over $\mathbb{F}_{p^2}$, where $p = \ell_A^{e_A}\ell_B^{e_B}f \pm 1$. Suppose $\phi : E_1 \to E_2$ is an isogeny of degree $\ell_A^{e_A}$ with a cyclic kernel and let $\{P, Q\}$ be generators of $E_1[\ell_A^{e_A}]$. Then for any $X \in E_1[\ell_A^{e_A}]$, define $\psi : E_2 \to E'$ such that $\ker \psi = \langle \phi(X) \rangle$, then there exists some $\theta : E' \to E_1$ of degree ℓ_A^{ϵ}, $\epsilon \leq e_A$, such that*

$$\hat{\phi} = \theta \circ \psi.$$

Proof. Using [11, Lemma 1], we may suppose that $\ker \phi = \langle P + [\alpha]Q \rangle$. Hence

$$\begin{aligned}
\phi(P) &= \phi(P) - \phi(P + [\alpha]Q) \\
&= -[\alpha]\phi(Q).
\end{aligned}$$

Then expressing $X = [u]P + [v]Q$ for some u, v, we have

$$\langle \phi(X) \rangle = \langle [u]\phi(P) + [v]\phi(Q) \rangle = \langle [v - \alpha u]\phi(Q) \rangle = \langle [\ell_A^k]\phi(Q) \rangle,$$

where k is the ℓ_A-adic valuation of $(v - \alpha u)$.

Let $\psi : E_2 \to E'$ be an isogeny with kernel given by $\langle \phi(X) \rangle = \langle [\ell_A^k]\phi(Q) \rangle$. Pick any $Y \in E_1[\ell_A^{e_A}]$ and write $Y = [r]P + [s]Q$ for some r, s.

If $k = 0$, then

$$\begin{aligned}
\psi \circ \phi(Y) &= \psi(\phi([r]P + [s]Q)) \\
&= \psi([s - r\alpha]\phi(Q)) \\
&= \mathcal{O}.
\end{aligned}$$

So it is clear that $E_1[\ell_A^{e_A}] \subseteq \ker(\psi \circ \phi)$. The reverse inclusion is obvious since $\ker(\psi \circ \phi)$ does not contain any non-trivial element of order co-prime to ℓ_A. So $\psi \circ \phi = [\ell_A^{e_A}]$, which implies, by the uniqueness of the dual isogeny, that $\psi = \hat{\phi}$, and $\theta : E_1 \to E_1$ is the identity isogeny.

If $k > 0$,

$$\psi \circ \phi(Y) = \psi(\phi([r]P + [s]Q))$$
$$= \psi([s - r\alpha]\phi(Q)).$$

Note that $\psi \circ \phi(Y)$ has order at most ℓ_A^k, since

$$[\ell_A^k]\psi \circ \phi(Y) = [s - r\alpha]\psi([\ell_A^k]\phi(Q)) = \mathcal{O}.$$

Now denote by $\gamma \in \mathbb{Z}_{\geq 0}$, the ℓ_A-adic valuation of $s - r\alpha$, then

$$\mathrm{ord}(\psi \circ \phi(Y)) = \mathrm{ord}(\psi([s - r\alpha]\phi(Q)))$$
$$= \ell_A^{k-\gamma}.$$

[Note that $\epsilon = k - \gamma$.]

So choose Y such that $\gamma = 0$ and define $\theta : E' \to E_1$ such that $\ker \theta = \langle \psi \circ \phi(Y) \rangle$. Then using the above argument, we can see that $\theta \circ \psi = \hat{\phi}$. Furthermore, it is clear that $\deg \theta \leq \ell_A^{e_A}$. $\qquad\qquad \square$

The lemma tells us that given the image of a point in $E_1[\ell_A^{e_A}]$ under an $\ell_A^{e_A}$-isogeny, ϕ, we are able to find an isogeny ψ which is close to the dual isogeny of ϕ. To obtain the dual isogeny, one has to first recover θ. If ϵ is sufficiently small, one will be able to recover θ by brute force. In fact, we will examine the size of ϵ in Sect. 4 and show that ϵ is small in most cases.

Hence we have the following algorithm to recover isogenies given the image of random points.

Algorithm 1. Recovering the dual isogeny after fault injection.

Data: $\phi(X)$
Result: $\hat{\phi}$
1 Set $\lambda \leftarrow \ell_B^{e_B} \cdot f$;
2 Set $T \leftarrow [\lambda]\phi(X)$;
3 Set $\psi : E_2 \to E'$ as the isogeny with kernel T;
4 **if** $\mathrm{ord}(T) = \ell_A^{e_A}$ **then**
5 $\quad$| Return ψ;
6 **else**
7 $\quad$| Brute force for θ;
8 Return $\theta \circ \psi$;

3.2   Fault Models

We will now demonstrate the fault attack in the following scenarios:

- Interactive identification protocol
- Digital signature scheme
- Undeniable signature protocol
- Static key-exchange protocol
- Static key-exchange protocol with the Kirkwood et al. validation method

The feasibility of each of these will be discussed in Sect. 4.1

Interactive Identification Protocol and Signature Schemes. In the *interactive identification protocol*, to learn the prover's long-term secret S, the adversary needs to perturb the computation of the point $\phi(R)$. During the prover's computation, the adversary will introduce a perturbation immediately before the computation of $\phi(R)$. In particular the adversary would attempt to inject a fault into the fetching operation and cause a fault in R. This will cause the faulted point R' to be, with high probability, a point of full order. Successfully doing so would allow for the recovery of the secret isogeny ϕ. To obtain the output of the faulted point, the adversary needs the challenge bit to be 0 as described in Sect. 2.2. This would happen 50% of the time and since identification schemes typically require a large number of passes, this must happen with high probability. The adversary could check the order of the points in the responses (if the challenge bit is 0) and the faulted point would have order larger than $\ell_A^{e_A}$. Using this information, the adversary would be able to use Algorithm 1 to recover S.

Due to its similarity to the identification protocol, to learn the signer's long-term secret S in the *digital signature scheme*, the steps the adversary takes are identical to the process above. The aim now is to inject a fault during the computation of $\phi(R_i)$ (c.f. Appendix A.1) for some i's. A successful fault coinciding with the challenge bit being 0 would produce a point of order larger than $\ell_A^{e_A}$, so the adversary has to find that point in the signature by testing the orders of the points in the signature.

In the *undeniable signature protocol* the adversary will be able to learn the long term secret ϕ_A by inducing a fault in $\phi_M(P_C)$ before the computation of $\phi_{M,AM}(\phi_M(P_C))$ (c.f. Appendix A.2). Using $\phi_{M,AM}(X)$, the adversary would learn $\phi_{M,AM}$ and equivalently, $\phi_M(G_A)$. Since ϕ_M is computable from the message, the adversary would be able to recover G_A.

Static Key-Exchange Protocol. Consider the static key-exchange protocol described in Sect. 2.2. Suppose an adversary is trying to learn Alice's static secret isogeny and has the ability to cause a fault in Alice's computation. After introducing a fault in the computation of $\phi_A(P_B)$, Alice would then proceed to publish the public key tuple

$$(E_A, \phi_A(X), \phi_A(Q_B)).$$

The adversary will then be able to recover ϕ_A using Algorithm 1.

Notice that this would not be prevented by the validation method presented in Sect. 2.3. Since the validation method will only be able to detect misdemeanours carried out by Bob, it will not be able to prevent the fault attack. In particular, throughout the validation process the public key of Alice is only computed once and is never checked by the method. Hence the fault attack would not be detected by this validation and an adversary would be able to recover the secret isogeny as previously described.

Remark 1. The attack may also be implemented on the ephemeral key-exchange protocol, but in both settings the attack would cause a failure to establish a shared secret key.

3.3 Countermeasures

A simple countermeasure to this attack is to implement order checking before the publication of the auxiliary points. Another countermeasure that can be placed on the identification protocol and hence the signature scheme is the compression of the points $R, \phi(R)$ if the challenge bit is 0. Sending r_1 and r_2 allows the verifier to recompute R and $\phi(R)$ using the public keys and will prevent the adversary from learning the faulted auxiliary point. Note that the compression of $\psi(S)$ will not be useful since the attack does not attack that point.

4 Analysis of Attack

As seen in the proof of Lemma 1, to obtain the dual of the isogeny, we need $k = 0$, or failing that, have ϵ small. But since ϵ is dependent on k, we will study k instead.

We start by fixing some $\alpha \in \mathbb{Z}/\ell_A^{e_A}\mathbb{Z}$ and suppose that u and v are selected randomly in $\mathbb{Z}/\ell_A^{e_A}\mathbb{Z}$, then we have

$$\Pr\left(\ell_A^n \text{ divides } (u - \alpha v)\right) = \frac{1}{\ell_A^n}.$$

Indeed, it is clear that we can treat $\rho = u - \alpha v$ as a single random variable, so this reduces to finding $\Pr(\ell_A^n \text{ divides } \rho)$, where ρ is randomly selected from $\mathbb{Z}/\ell_A^{e_A}\mathbb{Z}$. Since one in every ℓ_A^n elements is divisible by ℓ_A^n, we have the claim.

So $k = 0$ with probability $1 - \frac{1}{\ell_A}$. More generally, $k = \kappa$ with probability $\frac{\ell_A - 1}{\ell_A^{\kappa+1}}$. So we see that the isogeny ψ obtained from the procedure in Sect. 3 will be close to being the dual isogeny and brute forcing for θ is feasible.

Lastly, we will address the issue of the faulted point $\phi(X)$ not having an order divisible by $\ell_A^{e_A}$. This would have the effect of decreasing the degree of ψ and so increase the degree of θ. But notice that we can repeat the same analysis as the above to conclude that the degree of θ would be small with high probability.

Hence we have shown that Algorithm 1 has a high probability of recovering the secret isogeny.

4.1 Feasibility of Attack Models

Let us now study the feasibility of the attacks discussed in Sect. 3.2. We will see that the attacks would work well against signature schemes but not against key-exchange protocols.

Signature Schemes. The presence of a long-term secret and the availability of auxiliary points makes the signature schemes extremely attractive for an adversary attempting a fault attack on the supersingular isogeny cryptosystem. Note that while a fault would affect the validity of the signatures, the signer will not change the long-term secret due to an invalid signature. Hence the adversary would be able to break the signature scheme. We have to add that the compression of points is an effective countermeasure that foils the attack and would also reduce the size of the responses.

Key-Exchange Protocols. Suppose that one party is using a static key in the key-exchange protocol. An adversary would be able to recover the secret isogeny if the static public key is recomputed for each exchange. However, this is unlikely to happen since $\phi_A(P_B)$ and $\phi_A(Q_B)$ will be hardcoded for efficiency.

Now suppose that the adversary is attacking the key-exchange protocol with ephemeral keys. If the secrets are not authenticated, the adversary would be able to compute $\phi_A(P_B)$, and send that in place of $\phi_A(X)$. This way, both parties would be able to derive the same shared secret. Since recovering ϕ_A from $\phi_A(X)$ can be done efficiently, and computing $\phi_A(P_B)$ is also efficient, performing the substitution before a time-out in the connection is very feasible. However, it should be noted that without authentication, it might be better to use a man-in-the-middle attack.

Acknowledgements. I am grateful to Steven Galbraith and Craig Costello for insightful conversations and comments. I would also like to thank the referees for their helpful feedback and suggestions.

References

1. Azarderakhsh, R., Jao, D., Kalach, K., Koziel, B., Leonardi, C.: Key compression for isogeny-based cryptosystems. In: Proceedings of the 3rd ACM International Workshop on ASIA Public-Key Cryptography, pp. 1–10 (2016)
2. Biehl, I., Meyer, B., Müller, V.: Differential fault attacks on elliptic curve cryptosystems. In: Bellare, M. (ed.) CRYPTO 2000. LNCS, vol. 1880, pp. 131–146. Springer, Heidelberg (2000). doi:10.1007/3-540-44598-6_8
3. Charles, D.X., Lauter, K.E., Goren, E.Z.: Cryptographic hash functions from expander graphs. J. Cryptol. **22**(1), 93–113 (2009)
4. Childs, A.M., Jao, D., Soukharev, V.: Constructing elliptic curve isogenies in quantum subexponential time. J. Math. Cryptol. **8**(1), 1–29 (2014)
5. Ciet, M., Joye, M.: Elliptic curve cryptosystems in the presence of permanent and transient faults. Des. Codes Crypt. **36**(1), 33–43 (2005)

6. Costello, C., Jao, D., Longa, P., Naehrig, M., Renes, J., Urbanik, D.: Efficient compression of SIDH public keys. In: Coron, J.-S., Nielsen, J.B. (eds.) EURO-CRYPT 2017. LNCS, vol. 10210, pp. 679–706. Springer, Cham (2017). doi:10.1007/978-3-319-56620-7_24
7. Costello, C., Longa, P., Naehrig, M.: Efficient algorithms for supersingular isogeny Diffie-Hellman. In: Robshaw, M., Katz, J. (eds.) CRYPTO 2016. LNCS, vol. 9814, pp. 572–601. Springer, Heidelberg (2016). doi:10.1007/978-3-662-53018-4_21
8. Couveignes, J.M.: Hard homogeneous spaces. IACR Cryptology ePrint Archive, 2006: 291 (2006)
9. De Feo, L., Jao, D., Plût, J.: Towards quantum-resistant cryptosystems from super-singular elliptic curve isogenies. J. Math. Cryptol. **8**(3), 209–247 (2014)
10. Fujisaki, E., Okamoto, T.: Secure integration of asymmetric and symmetric encryption schemes. In: Wiener, M. (ed.) CRYPTO 1999. LNCS, vol. 1666, pp. 537–554. Springer, Heidelberg (1999). doi:10.1007/3-540-48405-1_34
11. Galbraith, S.D., Petit, C., Shani, B., Ti, Y.B.: On the security of supersingular isogeny cryptosystems. In: Cheon, J.H., Takagi, T. (eds.) ASIACRYPT 2016. LNCS, vol. 10031, pp. 63–91. Springer, Heidelberg (2016). doi:10.1007/978-3-662-53887-6_3
12. Galbraith, S.D., Petit, C., Silva, J.: Signature schemes based on supersingular isogeny problems. Cryptology ePrint Archive, Report 2016/1154 (2016). http://eprint.iacr.org/2016/1154
13. Jao, D., De Feo, L.: Towards quantum-resistant cryptosystems from supersingular elliptic curve isogenies. In: Yang, B.-Y. (ed.) PQCrypto 2011. LNCS, vol. 7071, pp. 19–34. Springer, Heidelberg (2011). doi:10.1007/978-3-642-25405-5_2
14. Jao, D., Soukharev, V.: Isogeny-based quantum-resistant undeniable signatures. In: Mosca, M. (ed.) PQCrypto 2014. LNCS, vol. 8772, pp. 160–179. Springer, Cham (2014). doi:10.1007/978-3-319-11659-4_10
15. Kirkwood, D., Lackey, B.C., McVey, J., Motley, M., Solinas, J.A., Tuller, D.: Failure is not an option: standardization issues for post-quantum key agreement. In: Workshop on Cybersecurity in a Post-Quantum World (2015)
16. Kuperberg, G.: A subexponential-time quantum algorithm for the dihedral hidden subgroup problem. SIAM J. Comput. **35**(1), 170–188 (2005)
17. Peikert, C.: Lattice cryptography for the internet. In: Mosca, M. (ed.) PQCrypto 2014. LNCS, vol. 8772, pp. 197–219. Springer, Cham (2014). doi:10.1007/978-3-319-11659-4_12
18. Rostovtsev, A., Stolbunov, A.: Public-key cryptosystem based on isogenies. Cryptology ePrint Archive, Report 2006/145 (2006). http://eprint.iacr.org/
19. Srinath, M.S., Chandrasekaran, V.: Isogeny-based quantum-resistant undeniable blind signature scheme. Cryptology ePrint Archive, Report 2016/148 (2016). http://eprint.iacr.org/2016/148
20. Shor, P.W.: Polynomial-time algorithms for prime factorization and discrete logarithms on a quantum computer. SIAM J. Comput. **26**(5), 1484–1509 (1997)
21. Silverman, J.H.: The Arithmetic of Elliptic Curves. Graduate Texts in Mathematics, vol. 106, 2nd edn. Springer, New York (2009)
22. Vélu, J.: Isogénies entre courbes elliptiques. C.R. Acad. Sc. Paris, Série A. **273**, 238–241 (1971)
23. Xi, S., Tian, H., Wang, Y.: Toward quantum-resistant strong designated verifier signature from isogenies. Int. J. Grid Util. Comput. **5**(2), 292–296 (2012)
24. Yoo, Y., Azarderakhsh, R., Jalali, A., Jao, D., Soukharev, V.: A post-quantum digital signature scheme based on supersingular isogenies. In: Financial Crypto 2017 (2017, to appear)

A   Signature Schemes in Detail

A.1   Digital Signature Scheme

The signature scheme has three steps: key generation, signing and verifying.

Set-up and key generation: Fix a prime p of the form $p = \ell_A^{e_A} \cdot \ell_B^{e_B} \cdot f \pm 1$ where ℓ_A and ℓ_B are small distinct primes, f is a small cofactor and e_A and e_B are positive integers such that $\ell_A^{e_A} \approx \ell_B^{e_B}$. Now fix an elliptic curve E over $\mathbb{F}_{p^2}$. Next, let $t = 0.5\lfloor \log_2 p \rfloor$ and fix a hash function $H : \{0,1\}^* \to \{0,1\}^t$.

The signer picks a random element $S \in E[\ell_A^{e_A}]$ with order $\ell_A^{e_A}$ and computes $\phi : E \to E/\langle S \rangle = E_S$. The signer then generates a basis $\{P_B, Q_B\}$ for $E[\ell_B^{e_B}]$, and computes and publishes the tuple

$$(E, P_B, Q_B, E_S, \phi(P_B), \phi(Q_B))$$

as the public key.

Signing: The signer needs to produce t challenges. So for each $i = 1, \ldots, t$, choose random elements $r_{1,i}, r_{2,i} \in \mathbb{Z}/\ell_B^{e_B}\mathbb{Z}$ such that not both are divisible by ℓ_B and computes the points

$$R_i = [r_{1,i}]P_B + [r_{2,i}]Q_B,$$
$$T_i = [r_{1,i}]\phi(P_B) + [r_{2,i}]\phi(Q_B)$$

and the isogenies

$$\psi_i : E \to E/\langle R_i \rangle = E_{R_i},$$
$$\phi_i' : E_S \to E_S/\langle T_i \rangle = E_{T_i}.$$

Given a message m, the signer computes

$$h = H(m, E_{R_1}, \ldots, E_{R_t}, E_{T_1}, \ldots, E_{T_t}).$$

The bit-string of h would serve as the sequence of challenge bits.
If the i-th bit of h is 0, the signer sets $z_i = (R_i, \phi(R_i))^2$. If the i-th bit of h is 1, the signer sets $z_i = \psi_i(S)$. The signature would then be the tuple

$$(h, z_1, z_2, \ldots, z_t).$$

Verifying: To verify the signature, the verifier would use the output of the hash as the challenge bits and use the same verification procedure as seen in Sect. 2.2 to verify each z_i as the response to the challenge bits.

---

[2] It is also possible to compress z_i by sending $r_{1,i}$ and $r_{2,i}$ instead. The verifier can then recover R and $\phi(R)$ given P_B, Q_B, $\phi(P_B)$ and $\phi(Q_B)$.

A.2   Undeniable Signature Scheme

This signature scheme has three steps: key generation, signing and verifying. The last step is split into confirmation or disavowal.

Set-up and key generation: Fix a hash function $H : \{0,1\}^* \to \mathbb{Z}$. Fix a prime p of the form $p = \ell_A^{e_A} \cdot \ell_M^{e_M} \cdot \ell_C^{e_C} \cdot f \pm 1$ and fix a supersingular elliptic curve E over $\mathbb{F}_{p^2}$. Now pick bases $\{P_A, Q_A\}$, $\{P_M, Q_M\}$ and $\{P_C, Q_C\}$ for the $\ell_A^{e_A}$, $\ell_M^{e_M}$ and $\ell_C^{e_C}$-torsion points respectively. The signer then randomly picks elements $a_1, a_2 \in \mathbb{Z}/\ell_A^{e_A}\mathbb{Z}$ not both divisible by ℓ_A, computes the subgroup $G_A = \langle [a_1]P_A + [a_2]Q_A \rangle$ and uses Vélu's formula to compute $E_A = E/G_A$ and the isogeny $\phi_A : E \to E_A$. The signer computes the image of P_C and Q_C under this isogeny and publishes the tuple $(E_A, \phi_A(P_C), \phi_A(Q_C))$.

Signing: Given a message M, the signer computes the hash $h = H(M)$ and the subgroup $G_M = P_M + [h]Q_M$. Next, the signer computes the following isogenies:

- $\phi_M : E \to E_M = E/G_M$
- $\phi_{M,AM} : E_M \to E_{AM} = E/\phi_M(G_A)$
- $\phi_{A,AM} : E_A \to E_{AM} = E/\phi_A(G_M)$

The signature then consists of the tuple

$$(E_{AM}, \phi_{M,AM}(\phi_M(P_C)), \phi_{M,AM}(\phi_M(Q_C))).$$

Verification: Since this is an undeniable signature scheme, there are two components to this: the *confirmation protocol* and the *disavowal protocol*. In the former protocol, given the signature

$$(E_{AM}, \phi_{M,AM}(\phi_M(P_C)), \phi_{M,AM}(\phi_M(Q_C))),$$

the objective is to confirm E_{AM}. In the latter, given the signature (E_F, F_P, F_Q), the objective is to disavow the signature.

Confirmation:

1. The signer picks random elements $c_1, c_2 \in \mathbb{Z}/\ell_C^{e_C}\mathbb{Z}$ not both divisible by ℓ_C, computes the subgroup $G_C = \langle [c_1]P_C + [c_2]Q_C \rangle$ and computes

$$E_C = E/G_C, \qquad\qquad E_{MC} = E_M/\phi_M(G_C),$$
$$E_{AC} = E_A/\phi_A(G_C), \qquad E_{AMC} = E_{MC}/\phi_{C,MC}(G_A).$$

2. The signer publishes $(E_C, E_{AC}, E_{MC}, E_{AMC}, \phi_C(P_M) + [h]\phi_C(Q_M))$.
3. The verifier randomly selects $b \in \{0,1\}$.

   If $b = 0$: the signer outputs $\ker \phi_C$. The verifier then computes ϕ_C, $\phi_{M,MC}$, $\phi_{A,AC}$ and $\phi_F : E_F \to E_{FC}$ and checks that each isogeny maps between the curves in the commitment. The verifier also computes $\phi_{C,MC}$ and checks that it matches the commitment. If $b = 1$: the signer outputs $\ker \phi_{C,AC}$ and the verifier then computes $\phi_{MC,AMC}$, $\phi_{AC,AMC}$ and checks that E_{AMC} is the codomain.

Disavowal: The disavowal step is almost exactly the same as the confirmation step with the exception in the last step where if $b = 0$, the verifier would see that $E_{FC} \not\cong E_{AMC}$ (Fig. 4).

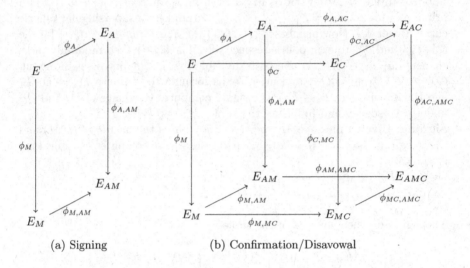

(a) Signing   (b) Confirmation/Disavowal

Fig. 4. Commutative diagrams generated during protocol

Lattice-Based Cryptography

Fast Lattice-Based Encryption: Stretching SPRING

Charles Bouillaguet[1], Claire Delaplace[1,2(✉)], Pierre-Alain Fouque[2], and Paul Kirchner[3]

[1] Univ. Lille, CNRS, Centrale Lille, UMR 9189 - CRIStAL - Centre de Recherche en Informatique Signal et Automatique de Lille, 59000 Lille, France
[2] Univ. de Rennes-1, IRISA, Rennes, France
claire.delaplace@irisa.fr
[3] Ecole Normale Supérieure, Paris, France

Abstract. The SPRING pseudo-random function (PRF) has been described by Banerjee, Brenner, Leurent, Peikert and Rosen at FSE 2014. It is quite fast, only 4.5 times slower than the AES (without hardware acceleration) when used in counter mode. SPRING is similar to the PRF of Banerjee, Peikert and Rosen from EUROCRYPT 2012, whose security relies on the hardness of the Learning With Rounding (LWR) problem, which can itself be reduced to hard lattice problems. However, there is no such chain of reductions relating SPRING to lattice problems, because it uses small parameters for efficiency reasons.

Consequently, the heuristic security of SPRING is evaluated using known attacks and the complexity of the best known algorithms for breaking the underlying hard problem.

In this paper, we revisit the efficiency and security of SPRING when used as a pseudo-random generator. We propose a new variant which is competitive with the AES in counter mode without hardware AES acceleration, and about four times slower than AES with hardware acceleration. In terms of security, we improve some previous analysis of SPRING and we estimate the security of our variant against classical algorithms and attacks. Finally, we implement our variant using AVX2 instructions, resulting in high performances on high-end desktop computers.

Keywords: Pseudo-random generator · Stream cipher · Ring-LWR · Rejection sampling

1 Introduction

Lattice-based cryptography is arguably one of the most mature proposal for post-quantum cryptography. One of the most important issue in this research direction is the size of the parameters. Indeed, when designers propose a cryptosystem whose security is related to hard lattice problems, theoretical work gives asymptotic security guarantees which are hard to assess in practice. If

T. Lange and T. Takagi (Eds.): PQCrypto 2017, LNCS 10346, pp. 125–142, 2017.
DOI: 10.1007/978-3-319-59879-6_8

we want to build a practical scheme, security safeguards can be relaxed a little. Many interesting schemes have been proposed in connection with lattice problems, ranging from the SWIFFT hash function [LMPR08] to the SPRING pseudo-random function family (PRF). Even though there is no security reduction for the latter, we can still estimate the level of security using standard algorithm for the underlying hard lattice problem on which it is based.

Symmetric primitives whose security is related to some hard computational problems have been known for a few decades. For instance, the hash function of Chaum, van Heijst and Pfitzmann is often taught as an example of a provably collision-resistant hash function (under the discrete log assumption). These "provably secure" primitives are very inefficient, and are thus rarely used in practice.

Building efficient symmetric primitives based on a well-known hard problem is therefore an interesting research direction; SWIFFT and VSH [CLS06] are two nice examples thereof. Even if there is no reduction between the security of the primitive and the hardness of the problem, this gives an intuition as to why the primitive might be secure (or not), and may help in choosing secure parameters. The SPRING PRF introduced at FSE 2014 [BBL+15] belongs to this category: the hardness of the Ring-Learning with Rounding (RLWR) problem is necessary for its security, yet an algorithm breaking SPRING cannot automatically be turned into a an algorithm that solves RLWR. Thus, SPRING is not "provably secure". As explained in Sect. 3, it does not seems to undermine the security of the scheme though.

Its performance is not horribly bad, since it is of the same order of magnitude than that of the AES. The main drawback of this primitive is the size of the key, about 8 kilobytes. Such a huge size of key require to use key derivation functions (such as HKDF) to expand a 128-bit or 256-bit key obtained after a standard key exchange protocol.

1.1   Related Work

Banerjee, Peikert and Rosen introduced in [BPR12] a new family of pseudorandom functions, that we call "BPR" in this paper, based on *rounded products* in well-chosen polynomial rings. Let n be a power of two (in this paper $n = 128$), and consider the polynomial ring:

$$R_q \stackrel{def}{=} \mathbb{Z}_q[\mathbf{x}]/\langle \mathbf{x}^n + 1 \rangle .$$

This is the ring of polynomials taken modulo $\mathbf{x}^n + 1$ and whose coefficients are taken modulo q. We denote by R_q^* the set of invertible elements in R_q. Given a positive integer k, the BPR family of PRFs is the set of functions $F_{\mathbf{a},\mathbf{s}} : \{0,1\}^k \to \{0,1\}^n$ indexed by a unit $a \in R_q^*$ and by a vector $\mathbf{s} = (\mathbf{s}_1, \ldots, \mathbf{s}_k)$ of units. The functions are defined as:

$$F_{\mathbf{a},\mathbf{s}}(x_1, \ldots, x_k) = S\left(\mathbf{a} \cdot \prod_{i=1}^{k} \mathbf{s}_i^{x_i}\right),$$

where S is a "rounding" function that maps each coefficient of the product polynomial into a single bit. The BPR family enjoys a nice security proof: its security can be reduced to the Ring-LWR problem, which is proved in [BPR12] to be equivalent to worst-case lattice problems. In [BBL+15], Banerjee *et al.* proposed and implemented an efficient yet unproven variant of the BPR family called SPRING (short for "subset-product with rounding over a **ring**"). They reduced the size of the parameters, yielding a fast implementation. However, unlike BPR, the SPRING family does not enjoy "provable security", because the choice of small parameters prevents the reduction to go through. Furthermore, in some cases, the rounding, which is the core of SPRING and BPR, may produce biased output bits, even when its input is uniformly distributed. For instance, any function rounding a coefficient in $\mathbb{Z}_{257}$ to a single bit is bound to have a very detectable bias of at least $1/257$: at the very minimum, the numbers of inputs yielding the two possible outputs differ by at least 1. In the original BPR construction, this is not a problem because the modulus is exponentially large, and thus the bias is exponentially small.

In SPRING, however, where small moduli ($q = 257$ and $q = 514$) are used for the sake of efficiency, precautions have to be taken to deal with such an eventual bias. To cope with this problem, the designers of SPRING proposed two different instantiations: SPRING-CRT and SPRING-BCH.

The first solution, SPRING-CRT, uses an even modulo $q = 514$ to make the problem disappear: $\mathbb{Z}_{514}$ can be split in two equal halves, and an unbiased "truncated" bit can be produced from $x \in \mathbb{Z}_{514}$ by checking if $x \geq 257$. It is the most efficient of the two original SPRING variants, but it is open to a subexponential attack. This attack is more efficient than trying to break the underlying hard problem using the usual algorithms. This shows that the weakening of the security guarantee provided by a reduction to hard problems can have serious consequences.

The second construction SPRING-BCH uses an odd modulus $q = 257$, which avoids the subexponential attack, but introduces a large rounding bias in the output bits. In this case, a post-processing step is added to reduce the bias using a BCH error-correcting code. The code computes linear combinations of the output bits, so that the final bias is $1/q^d = 2^{-177}$ where $d = 22$ is the minimal distance of the linear code. The downside is that the throughput is divided by two compared to SPRING-CRT. The most efficient attack against SPRING-BCH consists in detecting this small bias in the output.

Brenner *et al.* complemented these results in [BGL+14] by implementing SPRING-BCH on FPGAs and discussed the properties of SPRING in hardware implementations against side-channel attacks.

1.2   Our Contributions

We propose a simpler, faster PRG derived from SPRING and revisit the security of all these schemes. On a desktop computer, our variant, called SPRING-RS, is four times faster than SPRING-CRT, and using AVX2 instruction, it is twice more efficient than the AES-128 without AES-NI instructions and 5 times less efficient than the AES-128 with AES-NI instructions on recent CPUs.

New SPRING Variant. Our main idea to improve SPRING deals with the way the "rounding" is performed. Because it is difficult to extract a single unbiased bit from a $\mathbb{Z}_{257}$-coefficient, we use a simple form of rejection sampling:

$$S(x): \begin{cases} 0 & \text{if } x \in [0; 128) \\ 1 & \text{if } x \in [128; 256) \\ \bot & \text{if } x = 256 \end{cases}$$

This produces 0 and 1 with the same probability; the 0.4% of $\bot$ outputs are simply discarded. Applying this post-processing step with $q = 257$ makes it easy to obtain SPRING-RS, a PRG running at 0.996 times the speed of SPRING-CRT, while providing a higher level of security than SPRING-BCH. In addition, it allows for simpler implementations.

Such a technique has been used before, for instance in [Lyu09], where Luybashevsky proposes a way to generate a value independently of the secret information in an identification scheme.

An obvious downside of this approach is that the number of available output bits is not always the same. This complicates designing a PRF using this approach, because a PRF has to produce a specified number of pseudo-random output bits, regardless of the circumstances. It is nevertheless possible to build a PRF using rejection sampling. Its speed should be intermediate between that of SPRING-CRT and SPRING-BCH.

On the other hand, a PRG might be acceptable even though it produces pseudo-random bits slightly irregularly. This is for instance the case of the self-shrinking generator [MS95]. Usually a PRG is "clocked" until enough pseudo-random bits have been obtained. In this setting, the fact that the number of bits produced each time the PRG is clocked may vary is not problematic.

Rejection sampling produces unbiased outputs, and this eliminates the most efficient attack against SPRING-BCH. We thus believe that SPRING-RS is actually *more secure*, with an estimated security that we estimated around 900 bits. This much is hardly necessary, hence we decided to trade some security for speed. An obvious way to do so is to "truncate" less, for instance by extracting not one, but two, three or four bits out of a single $\mathbb{Z}_{257}$-coefficient. For each input $s \in \{0, 1\}^k$, SPRING-BCH returns a 64-bit output, while the SPRING-RS function, extracting four bits out of each coefficient, returns on average 510 bits. This increases the throughput of the PRG about 8 times, compared to SPRING-BCH.

While extracting more than one bit from a $\mathbb{Z}_{257}$-coefficient would not be immediate in the previous SPRING variants, it is extremely easy using rejection sampling. Because $\mathbb{Z}_{257}$ is "reduced" to a set of 2^8 elements, truncating to k bits boils down to keeping only the k most significant bits. We claim that SPRING-RS offers at least 128 bits of security. The best attack we could find runs in time $\approx 2^{64}$ but only succeeds with probability 2^{-900}.

As the main disadvantage of SPRING is its large key size, we also propose several way to reduce it. The first one uses a 128-bit secret key and another PRG in order to forge the secret polynomials of SPRING. The other ones use "smaller" instantiations of SPRING in a bootstrapping phase to generate the secret polynomials. We distinguish two cases. (1) In the first case, we use a SPRING instantiation with five secret polynomials to forge other secret polynomials that will be the secret key of another SPRING instantiation, and we reiterate the process until we have a $k + 1$-polynomial SPRING instantiation. In this cases, all secrets are reset at each step, and we never use the same polynomial in two different instantiations. (2) In the second case, we assume that our SPRING instantiation has circular security, and we use only the three first polynomial a, s_1, s_2 to forge the next polynomial, using this partial SPRING instantiation, and we reiterate the process until all s_i are forged. This reduces the key to 3072 bits.

More Cryptanalysis. We propose new attacks against various SPRING instantiations. The first one we present is a simple attack to distinguish the output of all SPRING variant —including ours— from uniform. This attack is a birthday attack on a small part of the internal state of the cipher, meaning that two different subset-products yield the same result. Assume that we split the input $\mathbf{x} = (x_1, \ldots, x_k)$ into $(\mathbf{w}, \mathbf{z}, x_k)$ with $\mathbf{w}$ is 1 bits and $\mathbf{z}$ is $k - 2$ bits and x_k is the last bit of $\mathbf{x}$. If we have a collision $F_{\mathbf{a},\mathbf{s}}(\mathbf{w}, \mathbf{z}, 0) = F_{\mathbf{a},\mathbf{s}}(\mathbf{w}, \mathbf{z}', 0)$, for all $\mathbf{w}$, and if we ask what is the output of $F_{a,\mathbf{s}}(\mathbf{w}, \mathbf{z}, 1)$, then it is also the output of $F_{\mathbf{a},\mathbf{s}}(\mathbf{w}, \mathbf{z}', 1)$ with probability greater than $1/2$ and we can predict the PRG. When attacking the SPRING PRFs, we can choose z, and then use the Floyd cycle detection algorithm to reduce the amount of memory needed to find the collision.

Our second original attack works in a simplified instantiation of the scheme, where the first polynomial a is known and is supposed to be identically equal to 1. In this case, we describe a lattice attack.

The third attack we present is similar to the attack of [BBL+15], where the authors consider that a whole part of the key is known, namely all $(\mathbf{s}_i)_{1 \leq i \leq k}$ and only $\mathbf{a}$ is secret. Here classical algorithms such as BKW or lattice reduction algorithms have to be considered.

Finally, we propose an algebraic attack, with the assumption that an adversary may have learned exactly which coefficients have been rejected using side-channel timing attacks. Then, he will have to solve a polynomial system, using Gröbner bases algorithms, to recover the coefficients of the secret polynomials.

We also revisit the attack presented by [BBL+15] on the SPRING-CRT instantiation and propose to use better algorithms to detect correlation using fast matrix multiplication, in Appendix A.

Implementation. Just like the designers of the original SPRING did, we implemented our variant using SIMD instructions available on most desktop CPUs. We borrow most implementation techniques from the designers of SPRING. This is in particular the case of an efficient implementation of polynomial multiplication in R_{257}^* thanks to a vectorized FFT-like algorithm using the SSE2 instruction set available in most desktop CPUs. These instructions operate on 128-bit wide "vector registers", allowing us to perform arithmetic operation on batches of eight $\mathbb{Z}_{257}$ coefficients in a single instruction.

We pushed the implementation boundary a little further by writing a new implementation of this operation using the AVX2 instruction set, providing 256-bit wide vector registers. These instructions are available on recent Intel CPUs based on the "Haswell" microarchitecture or later. Without surprise, this yields a twofold speedup and raises a few interesting programming problems.

Note that the AVX2-optimized FFT algorithm can be back-ported to all the cryptographic constructions relying on the same polynomial multiplication modulo 257, such as [BBL+15, LMPR08, LBF08], yielding the same 2× speedup. Our code is available for others to use at:

https://github.com/cbouilla/spriiiiiiiing

Table 1. Implementation results for SPRING variants, in Gray code counter mode (CTR). Speeds are presented in processor cycles per output byte. Starred numbers indicate the use of AES-NI instructions. Daggers indicate the use of AVX2 instructions.

	SPRING-BCH	SPRING-CRT	AES-CTR	SPRING-RS
ARM Cortex A7	445	[not implemented]	41	59
Core i7 "Ivy Bridge"	46	23.5	1.3*	6
Core i5 "Haswell"	19.5†	[not implemented]	0.68*	2.8†

The Table 1 give the performance of our SPRING-RS implementation, as well as previous implementation of SPRING, and compare them to the performances of the best AES implementations we could use as benchmark (we choose to compare our performances to those of AES with AES-NI instructions when we could). SPRING-RS is much faster than previous implementations of SPRING, and is about four times slower than AES with AES-NI instructions SPRING-RS is also competitive with AES without AES-NI instructions (and is even twice more efficient while using AVX2 instruction).

2   The SPRING Family of PRFs and PRGs

Ring-LWR Problem. Banerjee, Peikert and Rosen introduced in [BPR12] a derandomized version of LWE [Reg05] called Learning With Rounding (LWR), and its ring analog Ring-LWR (or RLWR), in which we are more interested here. They gave the following definition of a Ring-LWR distribution:

Definition 1. *Let n be an integer greater than 1 and let p and q be moduli such that $q \geq p \geq 2$. For $s \in R_q$, define the ring-LWR distribution to be the distribution over $R_q \times R_p$ obtained by choosing a polynomial $a \in R_q$, uniformly at random, computing $b = \lfloor s \cdot a \rceil_p$ and outputting the pair (a, b). The function $\lfloor \cdot \rceil_p : R_q \to R_p$ is a coefficient-wise rounding that maps the coefficients $b_i \in \{0, \ldots, q-1\}$ of $\sum_{i=0}^{n-1} b_i x^i$ to $\left\lfloor \frac{p \cdot b_i}{q} \right\rceil$.*

As it has been noted by the authors of [BPR12], the rounding method $\lfloor \cdot \rceil$ can be replaced by the floor or the ceiling function, without major change to the problem. For implementation purposes, we chose to use the floor function $\lfloor \cdot \rfloor$ instead. Then, in the case of SPRING, for all $a \in R_q$ computing $\lfloor a \rfloor_p$ is equivalent to keeping the $\log_2(p)$ most significant bits.

For s chosen uniformly in R_q, the decision-Ring-LWR problem is to distinguish between independent samples (a_i, b_i) drawn in the Ring-LWR distribution, and the same number of samples drawn uniformly at random in $R_q \times R_p$. While there are reductions between LWE and worst-case lattice problems, the reductions between LWR and LWE need q/p to be at least $\sqrt{n}$ [BPR12, AKPW13, BGM+15].

The SPRING Family. In [BPR12], it is proved that when a is uniform, s are independent discrete Gaussians, and when q is large enough the $F_{a,s}$ function family is a secure PRF, assuming that the Ring-LWE problem is hard on R_q. However, as described in [BBL+15], the function family does not necessarily require such a large modulus q to be a secure PRF family. Also, they show that if a weakened Ring-LWR is hard where s is uniform, one can take a small q. [BBL+15] proposed a version of the SPRING function using the parameters:

$$n = 128, \ q = 257, \ p = 2, \ k = 64.$$

In this paper, we choose the same parameters n, q and k, and we allow $p \in \{2, 4, 8, 16\}$. The choice of a larger "truncation modulus" p allows us to generate more output bits with the same amount of work. However, it reveals more information about each coefficients of the "internal state" polynomial (we return half of the bits of each coefficient when $p = 16$) so the security of the instantiation decreases as p grows, but as discussed in Sect. 3, using such parameters p should not put our system at risk. The choice of the modulus $q = 257$ is the same than in [LMPR08] for the SWIFFT hash-function. As discussed in [LMPR08], choosing q such that $q - 1$ a multiple of $2n$ allows for a fast FFT-like multiplication algorithm in R_q^*. In addition, using a Fermat prime $q = 2^{2^k} + 1$ has multiple advantages, including very efficient reduction modulo q.

2.1 SPRING-RS: Rounding with Rejection-Sampling

We introduce here a new PRG based on SPRING using rejection-sampling to eliminate the bias. Just like [BBL+15] we propose to use a counter-like mode using a Gray-code for efficiency. A Gray code is a simple way to order $\{0,1\}^k$ such that two successive values of the counter differ only by one bit. Then, when running SPRING in counter mode, we can compute the successive subset products with only one polynomial multiplication at each step. To transform the i-th value j of a Gray counter to the $(i+1)$-th, the ℓ-th bit of the counter has to be flipped, where ℓ is the number of trailing zeroes in the binary expansion of $(i+1)$.

The internal state of the PRG is therefore composed of two k-bit integers i, j and a unit polynomial $\mathbf{P}$ in R_q^*. Each time the PRG is clocked:

- i is incremented
- The ℓ-th bit of j is flipped, where ℓ is the number of trailing zeroes in i.
- The polynomial is $\mathbf{P}$ is multiplied by s_j (resp. s_j^{-1}) when the ℓ-th bit of j is 1 (resp. 0).

The initial value of $\mathbf{P}$ is the secret element $\mathbf{a}$, which is part of the key. Finally, after the internal state has been updated, a variable number of pseudorandom bits are extracted from the new value of $\mathbf{P}$.

Extracting bits from the polynomial is done by the rounding operation. We apply the following rounding function to the n coefficients of $\mathbf{P}$ in parallel:

$$\mathbb{Z}_q \longrightarrow \mathbb{Z}_p \cup \{\perp\}$$
$$S : x \mapsto \begin{cases} \perp & \text{if } x = -1 \\ \lfloor px/q \rfloor & \text{otherwise} \end{cases}$$

This results in a sequence of n symbols. The $\perp$ are then "erased" from the output, yielding a variable number of elements of $\mathbb{Z}_p$, which are appended to the pseudorandom stream.

This produces uniformly distributed outputs in $\mathbb{Z}_p$ when the inputs are uniformly distributed in $\mathbb{Z}_q$. Rejecting one of the possible value (here, -1) effectively restricts the input set to $q-1$ elements. As long as p divides $q-1$, exactly $(q-1)/p$ inputs yield each possible output.

Reducing the Size of the Key. One of the main disadvantage of SPRING is the large size of its key (8 kB). We present here several ways to reduce the size of the key for all instantiations of SPRING. The key is composed of $k+1$ secret polynomials $\mathbf{a}, s_1, \ldots, s_k$ over R_q^*. Each such polynomial requires 1024 bits:

The most intuitive and most efficient way to reduce the key size of SPRING is to use a 128-bit master secret key denoted by K_m, and use it to generate pseudorandomly the secret polynomials using... another PRG. This is a bit unsatisfying: why not use the other PRG in the first place? However, this would be beneficial if the other PRG is slow or even not cryptographically secure (consider the Mersenne Twister for instance).

In order to drop the need for another PRG, it would be natural to use SPRING to "bootstrap" itself and generate its own secret polynomials. We propose two ways to do so[1].

One possibility is to consider than the "master" key is composed of the 5 polynomials $a_0, s_{0,1}, s_{0,2}, s_{0,3}, s_{0,4}$. Then, we may evaluate the "mini-SPRING" function $F^0_{a_0,s_0}$ such that, $F^0_{a_0,s_0}(x) = S\left(a_0 \cdot \prod_{i=1}^{4} s_{0,i}^{x_i}\right)$, for all $x \in \{0,1\}^4$. Using this small instantiation of SPRING-RS with $p = 16$, we may generate up to 8192 pseudo-random bits. This is large enough to forge seven polynomials with very high probability. We call $a_1, s_{1,1}, \ldots, s_{1,6}$ these new polynomials. We reiterate the process with the mini-SPRING function $F^1_{a_1,s_1}$, and the output given by this PRG is large enough to forge between thirty and thirty-one polynomials. If we reiterate the process once more with those new polynomials, we will be able to forge the 65 polynomials $a, s_1, \ldots, s_k$ of the full SPRING-RS. Using such a trick, we can substantially reduce the size of the key (from about 8 kB to about 700 B).

It is possible to push this idea a bit further assuming the circular security of SPRING-RS. In that case, the "master" key is composed of the three secret polynomials a, s_1, s_2, and we define the nano-SPRING function $F^0_{a,s}$ such that, $F^0_{a,s}(x) = S(a \cdot s_1^{x_1} \cdot s_2^{x_2})$, for all $x \in \{0,1\}^2$. Using this small instantiation of SPRING-RS, we can generate an output long enough to forge a new polynomial. This will be the next secret polynomial, s_3. We reiterate the process with the micro-SPRING function $F^1_{a,s}$ the function such that $F^1_{a,s}(x) = S(a \cdot \prod_{i=1}^{3} s_i^{x_i})$. We do not reset the Gray Counter, as long as the previous values will only give the output of $F^0_{a,s}$. The new output thus generated is long enough to forge s_4. If we reiterate the process once more, we will get an output long enough to generate two more polynomials. We reiterate it over again —two more times should be enough— until all the s_i are forged. We never reset the Gray Counter, otherwise an adversary may know all the s_i thus obtained.

Tuning for Vector Instructions. To obtain high performance implementations on modern hardware, it is necessary to be able to exploit vector instructions. In particular, it may be beneficial to tune some aspects of the function to the underlying hardware. Let d and r be integers such that $d \cdot r = n$, and let $v_0, v_1, \ldots, v_{r-1}$ be d-wide vectors with coefficient in $\mathbb{Z}_q$ such that:

$$\begin{pmatrix} v_0 \\ v_1 \\ \vdots \\ v_{r-1} \end{pmatrix} = \begin{pmatrix} b_0 & b_1 & \cdots & b_{d-1} \\ b_d & b_{d+1} & \cdots & b_{2d-1} \\ & & \vdots & \\ b_{(r-1)d} & b_{(r-1)d+1} & \cdots & b_n \end{pmatrix}. \tag{1}$$

---

[1] As discussed in Sect. 3, SPRING seems to have a quite large level of security, even if the s_i are known. It has been asked to us why we do not choose to make part of the s_i polynomials known to reduce the size of the key. However, as shown by Table 2, it may undermine the security of SPRING, especially when $p = 16$.

Typically, d should be the width of available hardware vectors. For each vector $\mathbf{v}_i$, we apply the rounding function to all coefficients in parallel. If the resulting vector contains $\perp$, we reject the whole vector. This is illustrated in Algorithm 1. Even though this also discards "good" coefficients, it allows a performance gain, because examining individual coefficients inside a hardware vector is often very inefficient. With $d = 1$, there is no wasted output. With $d = 8$ (SSE2 instructions on Intel CPUs, or NEON instructions on ARM CPUs), about 2.7% of the good coefficients are wasted. With $d = 16$ (AVX2 instructions), this goes up to 5.7%. This loss is a small price to pay compared to the twofold speedup that we get from using twice bigger hardware vectors.

Algorithm 1. PRG based on SPRING using a rejection sampling instantiation

---

Input: $\ell \geq 0$, d the width of available hardware vectors, the secrets parameters $\tilde{\mathbf{a}} \in R_q$ and $\tilde{\mathbf{s}} \in (R_q)^k$, Fast Fourier evaluation of the secret polynomial $\mathbf{a}$ and $\mathbf{s}$.
Output: An ℓ-bits long sequence of (pseudorandom) $\mathbb{Z}_p$ elements.
  # Initialization
  $\tilde{P} \leftarrow \tilde{\mathbf{a}}$
  $P \leftarrow \text{FFT}_{128}^{-1}(\tilde{P})$
  $L \leftarrow \varepsilon$
  $i \leftarrow 0$
  $j \leftarrow 0$
  $size \leftarrow 0$
  while $size < \ell$ **do**
    # Extract output
    $(\mathbf{v}_0, \mathbf{v}_1, \ldots, \mathbf{v}_{r-1}) \leftarrow \text{DISPATCH}(P)$
    for $i = 0$ to $r - 1$ **do**
      $\mathbf{v}' \leftarrow \text{ROUNDING}(\mathbf{v_i})$
      if $\perp \notin \mathbf{v}'$ **then**
        $L \leftarrow L \| \mathbf{v}'$
        $size \leftarrow size + d \cdot \log_2(p)$
    # Update internal state
    $i \leftarrow i + 1$
    $u \leftarrow \text{COUNTTRAILINGZEROES}(i)$
    $j \leftarrow j \oplus (1 \ll u)$
    if $j \;\&\; (1 \ll u) \neq 0$ **then**
      $\tilde{P} \leftarrow \tilde{P} \cdot \tilde{\mathbf{s}}_i$
    else
      $\tilde{P} \leftarrow \tilde{P} \cdot \tilde{\mathbf{s}}_i^{-1}$
    $P \leftarrow \text{FFT}_{128}^{-1}(\tilde{P})$
  return L

We describe the full PRG in Algorithm 1. The DISPATCH procedure takes a polynomial as input, and dispatch its coefficient as in (1) in $\mathbf{v}_0, \mathbf{v}_1, \ldots, \mathbf{v}_{r-1}$, for constant parameters r and d.

A Rejection-Sampling Based PRF. It is clear that the rejection-sampling process often yields sequence of less than $n \log_2 p$ output bits. This makes it less-than-ideal to implement a PRF, which is always expected to return a specified amount of output bits. However, building a PRF is still possible if we accept a reduction in output size.

With the chosen parameters, we know that at least 96 $\mathbb{Z}_p$ elements survive the erasure process with probability greater than $1 - 2^{-156}$. Therefore, a possible yet inelegant workaround consists in making a PRF that returns the first 96 non-erased outputs. In the unlikely event that less than 96 truncated coefficients are available, the PRF output is padded with zeroes. The probability of this event is so low that it is undetectable by an adversary.

Implementing such a PRF efficiently is likely to be difficult, because of the amount of bit twiddling and juggling that is involved. Furthermore, unlike the CTR mode, we need to compute the product of many polynomials. To make this implementation efficient, we choose to store the discrete logarithms of the secret polynomials, as it was proposed in [BBL+15,BGL+14] so that the subset-product becomes a subset-sum. Each exponentiation by the final summed exponents is computed by a table look-up.

3   Security Analysis

Secure PRF and PRG over a polynomial ring R_q are described in [BPR12], assuming the hardness of Ring-LWE problem. However, for the BPR family to be secure, we need to make two assumptions:

1. The parameter q must be large (exponential in the input length k).
2. The $\mathbf{s}_i$ are drawn from the error distribution of the underlying Ring-LWE instantiation.

In [BBL+15], Banerjee *et al.* show that relaxing those statements do not seem to introduce any concrete attack against the SPRING family, and its security seems to be still very high, even thought SPRING is not provably secure. In our instantiation we slightly weaken SPRING by introducing two changes: (1) the rounding function S we use returns more bits, so more information about the internal state is returned, (2) some coefficients are rejected, so using side-channel timing attacks, an adversary may learn that some coefficients are equal to -1 (the rejected value). However, as we shall discuss in the following part, we do not think that this may undermine the security of SPRING. Finally, we believe that SPRING-RS is actually more secure than the previously proposed variants.

3.1   Birthday-Type Attack on SPRING

Let $t < k$ be such that $\log q \simeq 2^t \cdot \log p$. For all $\mathbf{x} \in \{0,1\}^k$, $\mathbf{x}$ can be decomposed in $\mathbf{x} = (\mathbf{w}||\mathbf{z}||x_k)$ with $\mathbf{w}$ t-bit wide and $\mathbf{z}$ $(k-t-1)$-bit wide. We denote by $\mathbf{b_w}$ and $\mathbf{b_z}$ the polynomials $\mathbf{b_w} := \prod_{i=1}^{i=t} \mathbf{s}_i^{x_i}$ and $\mathbf{b_z} := \prod_{i=t+1}^{i=k-1} \mathbf{s}_i^{x_i}$. Then we have:

$$F_{\mathbf{a},\mathbf{s}}(\mathbf{w}||\mathbf{z}||x_k) = S(\mathbf{a} \cdot \mathbf{b_w} \cdot \mathbf{b_z} \cdot \mathbf{s}_k^{x_k}),$$

where $S(\cdot)$ is the rounding function used by the SPRING-RS instantiation. We aim to find two $(k - t - 1)$-bit vectors $\mathbf{z}$ and $\mathbf{z}'$ such that $\mathbf{z} \neq \mathbf{z}'$ and $\mathbf{b_z} = \mathbf{b_{z'}}$. Then we will also have $\mathbf{b_z} \cdot \mathbf{s}_k = \mathbf{b_{z'}} \cdot \mathbf{s}_k$.

Notice that $\mathbf{w}$ can take 2^t different values, which are called $\mathbf{w}_0, \dots \mathbf{w}_{2^t-1}$ according to the Gray Code counter. We denote by G the function that takes as input $(\mathbf{z}||x_k) \in \{0,1\}^{k-t}$, and returns the sequence:

$$G(\mathbf{z}||x_k) := F_{\mathbf{a},\mathbf{s}}(\mathbf{w}_0||\mathbf{z}||x_k)|| \dots ||F_{\mathbf{a},\mathbf{s}}(\mathbf{w}_{2^t-1}||\mathbf{z}||x_k).$$

If no coefficient is rejected, then the output of G for a given $(\mathbf{z}||x_k)$ is a $(8 \cdot n)$-bit wide sequence ($2^t \log p = \log q = 8$). We want to find a couple $(\mathbf{z}, \mathbf{z}')$ in $\{0,1\}^{k-t-1} \times \{0,1\}^{k-t-1}$ such that $G(\mathbf{z}||x_k) = G(\mathbf{z}'||x_k)$. Then we will have $\mathbf{b_z} = \mathbf{b_{z'}}$ with high probability (actually the probability of a false positive is at most $2^{2k}/p^{2^t \cdot n} \simeq 2^{-896}$ for $p = 16$). Then, knowing $G(\mathbf{z}||x_k)$ we are able to predict $G(\mathbf{z}'||x_k)$ with high probability, and this gives us a distinguisher between SPRING-RS and the uniform distribution.

Formally, we first get the sequence generated by 2^{k-1} call to the $F_{\mathbf{a},\mathbf{s}}$ function (i.e. in this case x_k is always 0), and we store all the possible $8 \cdot n$-bit output of G in a hash table, and search for a collision inside it. Knowing that the probability that no rejection has been performed in a given $8 \cdot n$-bit sequence is $(1-1/q)^{2^t \cdot n}$, an adversary can predict that $G(\mathbf{z}'||1)$ would be equal to $G(\mathbf{z}||1)$ for some $\mathbf{z}$ and $\mathbf{z}'$ with advantage about $(1 - 1/q)^{2 \cdot n} \cdot 2^{2(k-2)}/q^n$ (Probability that no rejection sampling has been performed $\times$ probability of a collision between $G(\mathbf{z}||x_k)$ and $G(\mathbf{z}'||x_k)$), which is around 2^{-900} for the weaker instantiation of SPRING-RS (with $p = 16$).

All in all, this attack require 2^{k-1} call the SPRING function, and if we denote by ℓ the length of the bit-string thus generated. One will need to store $(\ell - 8 \cdot n + 1)$ $8 \cdot n$-bit strings in a hash table. As long as ℓ is bounded by 2^{k+8} (when $p = 16$), the total space required by this attack will be bounded by $\mathcal{O}(n \cdot 2^{k+8})$.

3.2   Lattice Attack

In this attack, we try to find back some of the secrets s_i. We present the attack on a simplified version of SPRING in which $\mathbf{a}$ is known and is equal to 1, then we have:

$$F_{\mathbf{a},\mathbf{s}}(x) = S\left(1 \cdot \prod_i \mathbf{s}_i^{x_i}\right),$$

where $\mathbf{x} \neq (0, \dots, 0)$. Assume we can apply the SPRING function on any input $\mathbf{x} = (x_1, \dots, x_k)$ which are very sparse, with only two bits i and j are set to one. Consequently, we can write equations by adding an error term e that corresponds to the missing bits.

Let $\sigma := q/p$ and $\mathbf{e}_i, \mathbf{b}_i, \mathbf{b}_{i,j}, \mathbf{e}_{i,j}$ be in R_q. Assume we get $S(\mathbf{s}_i)$ for the input that contains one bit set to one in position i for all i. We call $\mathbf{b}_i$ the output bits and $\mathbf{e}_i$ the missing bits. So, we get the corresponding equations and since we can also write $S(\mathbf{s}_i\mathbf{s}_j)$ for the following equations:

$$\mathbf{s}_i = \mathbf{b}_i + \mathbf{e}_i$$
$$\mathbf{s}_i \mathbf{s}_j = \mathbf{b}_{i,j} + \mathbf{e}_{i,j}$$

where the $\mathbf{e}_i$ values represent the least significant bits and the $\mathbf{b}_i$ values the output of the PRG. We assume here that there is no rejection so that all the $\mathbf{b}_i$ are exactly known. We have the following relation:

$$\mathbf{b}_{i,j} - \mathbf{b}_i\mathbf{b}_j - (\mathbf{s}_i\mathbf{s}_j - \mathbf{s}_i\mathbf{s}_j) = \mathbf{b}_i\mathbf{e}_j + \mathbf{b}_j\mathbf{e}_i + \mathbf{e}_i\mathbf{e}_j - \mathbf{e}_{i,j}. \tag{2}$$

Our goal is to find the $\mathbf{e}_i$ values in order to recover the secret values $\mathbf{s}_i$. We will write in (3) an equation corresponding to a closest vector problem in some lattice. In this equation, we denote by $M_\mathbf{b}$ the negacyclic matrix representing the multiplication by $\mathbf{b} = \sum_{i=0}^{n-1} p_i \mathbf{x}^i$ in the polynomial ring, formally it is a linear map defined by the multiplication of $\mathbf{b}$ in R_q in the canonical basis:

$$M_\mathbf{b} = \begin{pmatrix} p_0 & p_1 & \cdots & p_{n-1} \\ -p_{n-1} & p_0 & \cdots & p_{n-2} \\ \vdots & \ddots & \ddots & \vdots \\ -p_1 & \cdots & -p_{n-1} & p_0 \end{pmatrix}.$$

Denote by $\mathbf{\Delta}_{i,j}$ the polynomial $\mathbf{\Delta}_{i,j} := \mathbf{b}_{i,j} - \mathbf{b}_i\mathbf{b}_j$ and by $\mathbf{E}_{i,j}$ the polynomial $\mathbf{E}_{i,j} := \mathbf{e}_i\mathbf{e}_j - \mathbf{e}_{i,j}$. Let M be the block-matrix

$$M = \begin{pmatrix} 0 & M_{\mathbf{b}_i} & 0 & M_{\mathbf{b}_j} & 0 \end{pmatrix},$$

such that block i is $M_{\mathbf{b}_i}$, block j is $M_{\mathbf{b}_j}$, and the rest is 0. Then the relation 2 for all $i, j < k$ is equivalent to the system:

$$\begin{pmatrix} q & & & & \\ & \ddots & M & & \\ & & q & & \\ & & & K & \\ & & & & \ddots \\ & & & & & K \end{pmatrix} \cdot \begin{pmatrix} * \\ \mathbf{e}_0 \\ \vdots \\ \mathbf{e}_{k-1} \end{pmatrix} - \begin{pmatrix} \mathbf{\Delta}_{0,1} \\ \vdots \\ \mathbf{\Delta}_{k-2,k-1} \\ 0 \\ \vdots \\ 0 \end{pmatrix} = \begin{pmatrix} \mathbf{E}_{0,1} \\ \vdots \\ \mathbf{E}_{k-2,k-1} \\ K \cdot \mathbf{e}_0 \\ \vdots \\ K \cdot \mathbf{e}_{k-1} \end{pmatrix}, \tag{3}$$

with K chosen so that $\mathbf{E}_{i,j}$ and $K \cdot \mathbf{e}_i$ are about the same size, namely $K \approx \sigma \cdot \sqrt{n}$. To find the $\mathbf{e}_i$ we have to enumerate the lattice points of $\mathcal{L}$ in a ball of radius at least $\sigma^2 n/12\sqrt{k(k+1)/2}$. We estimate the number of false positives using the Gaussian heuristic:

$$(\sigma^2 n/12\sqrt{k(k-1)/2}\sqrt{4\pi e/n/k/(k+1)})^{k(k+1)n/2}/\det(\mathcal{L}) =$$
$$(\sigma^2\sqrt{2\pi e(k-1)/(k+1)n}/12)^{k(k+1)n/2}q^{-k(k-1)n/2}\sigma^{-kn}n^{-kn/2}$$

For our parameters with $p = 16$, the actual value is larger than $\approx 2^{1334}$ for all k and K, which is reached in $k = 2$, $K = 52$.

In fact, it is easy to see that for $\sigma^2\sqrt{n} \leq q$, there exist a k where we expect no false positives; but for q a constant times smaller, the number of false positives becomes $2^{\Omega(n)}$.

In the case one wants to attack the SPRING-RS PRF, this attack is even weaker, as only 96 coefficients of the $\mathbf{s}_i$ polynomials are returned, whether there is rejection sampling or not.

This attack can be adapted to SPRING-RS with $\mathbf{a}$ unknown, however, there would be a loss of efficiency since we need to consider the products of three terms. The version of SPRING-RS attacked here is trivially weaker than one with an unknown $\mathbf{a}$, and the attack has not been found to be efficient. Therefore, we do not detail further this case.

3.3   Partially Known Secret Key

In this part we assume that all $\mathbf{s}_i$ are known or have already been found (which is very unlikely) and we are trying to find back the secret $\mathbf{a}$. Although we do not guarantee the security of SPRING when the $\mathbf{s}_i$ are known, we show here, that the system is resistant against lattice-reduction attacks and BKW attack with a small enough p.

Let $\mathbf{x} = (x_1, \ldots, x_k)$ be in $\{0, 1\}^k$, if the $\mathbf{s}_i$ are known (even though they are not supposed to be) then the product $\mathbf{b}_\mathbf{x} := \prod_{i=1}^k \mathbf{s}_i^{x_i}$ is known. The goal is to find back $\mathbf{a}$ knowing $(\mathbf{b}_\mathbf{x}, S(\mathbf{a} \cdot \mathbf{b}_\mathbf{x}))$. So we have to solve the search Ring-LWR problem [LPR13]. An attack on SPRING-BCH is described in [BBL+15] using lattice reduction, with complexity greater than 2^{430} in time and greater than 2^{160} in space. In fact, the BKW attack appears to be more efficient. The Table 2 gives the complexity of the best attack (which is always BKW, since the noise is large), for each $p \in \{2, 4, 8, 16\}$.

Table 2. Complexity of attacking SPRING assuming the $\mathbf{s}_i$ are known, using the BKW algorithm

p	2	4	8	16
BKW	2^{163}	2^{124}	2^{97}	2^{78}

3.4   Side-Channel Leaks

An obvious drawback of rejection sampling is the irregular rate at which output is produced. It is conceivable that a timing attack could reveal some information about the internal state of the PRG. If we were optimistic about the attacker's side-channel capabilities, we could assume that she knows exactly what coefficients are rejected. We thus assume that each time a coefficient is rejected, both its location and the value of the counter x leak.

Therefore, the attacker has access to equations of the form $(\mathbf{a}\prod_i \mathbf{s}_i^{x_i})_j = -1$ over $\mathbb{Z}_q$ where the unknowns are the coefficients of $\mathbf{a}$ and $\mathbf{s}_i$. Denote by $HW(x)$ the Hamming weight of x, then each of these equations can be converted into a polynomial of degree $1 + HW(x)$ over the coefficients of $\mathbf{a}$ and all $\mathbf{s}_i$.

If the first $2^i n \log_2 p$ key-stream bits are observed, then we expect $n2^i/q$ coefficients to be rejected. This yields this many polynomial equations in $n(i + 1)$ variables, of which $n\binom{i}{d-1}/q$ are expected to be of degree d. With the chosen parameters, $i \geq 12$ is needed to obtain more equations than unknowns. With $i = 12$, we obtain the smallest possible over-determined system, with 2032 polynomial equations in 1664 unknowns, of degree mostly larger than 2. Note that the ideal spanned by these polynomial is not guaranteed to be zero-dimensional. No known technique is capable of solving arbitrary systems of polynomial equations of this size. In particular, the complexity of computing a Gröbner basis of this many equations can be roughly estimated [Fau99, BFS04]: it is about 2^{2466}.

When i grows up to 64, the system becomes more over-determined: with $i = k = 64$, the largest possible value, we obtain 2^{63} equations in 8320 variables, with degrees up to 65. Storing this amount of data is completely unpractical. Neglecting this detail, we argue that a Gröbner basis computation will crunch polynomials of degree larger than 80. As such, we expect any Gröbner basis computation to perform, amongst others, the reduction to row echelon form of a sparse matrix of size 2^{646}, a computationally unfeasible task.

4   Implementation Details

We implemented our variant of SPRING using SIMD instructions, which enabled us to perform given operations on multiple data in parallel. We propose two implementations of our scheme. The first one uses the 128-bit wide SIMD hardware vectors available in SSE2 or NEON instructions while the second one uses 256-bit wide SIMD hardware vectors and AVX2 instructions.

Most of our implementation tricks are borrowed from [BBL+15], and some of our implementations reuse parts of the code of previous SPRING variants. We refer the reader to [BBL+15] for more details. Our only innovation is the implementation of the rejection-sampling process, which is straightforward, as well as an implementation of fast polynomial multiplication using AVX2 instructions, that we describe next.

The problem comes down to computing a kind of FFT of size 128 modulo 257. We store $\mathbb{Z}_{257}$ in 16-bit words, in zero-centered representation. Using SSE2 instructions, and hardware vector registers holding 8 coefficients, a reasonable strategy is to perform one step of Cooley-Tukey recursive division, after which two size-64 FFTs have to be computed. This is done efficiently by viewing each input as an 8×8 matrix, performing 8 parallel size-8 FFTs on the rows, multiplying by the twiddle factors, transposing the matrix, and finally performing 8 parallel FFTs. The use of vector registers allows to perform the 8 parallel operations efficiently.

When AVX2 instructions are available, we have access to vector registers holding 16 coefficients. Several strategies are possible, and we describe the one we actually implemented. We view the input of a size-128 FFT as a 16×8 matrix. We perform 16 parallel size-8 FFTs on the rows, which is easy using the larger vector registers. Transposing yields a 8×16 matrix, and we need to perform 8 parallel size-16 FFTs on its rows.

This is the non-obvious part. To make full use of the large vector registers, we decided to store two rows in each vector register. Because the first pass of this size-16 FFT requires operation between adjacent rows, a bit of data juggling is necessary. We store rows 0 and 8 in the first register, rows 1 and 9 in the second, etc. This is done with the VPERM2I128 instruction. Because the last pass requires operations between rows i and $i + 8$, which is again not possible if they are in the same register, we perform the same data-juggling operation again. This puts the rows back in the right order.

Performing the rejection sampling is easy. With AVX2 instructions, we use the VPCMPEQW to perform a coefficient-wise comparison with $(-1, \ldots, -1)$, and a VPMOVMSKB to extract the result of the comparison into a 16-bit integer. It is slightly different on an ARM processor with the NEON instruction set as there is nothing like VPMOVMSKB. However, we achieve the same result, using some tricks. We first convert the int16x8_t NEON vector into a int8x16_t NEON vector, and then we ZIP the low and the high part of this vector. This gives two int8x8_t NEON vector, d0 and d1. We use the VSRI on d0 and d1 with constant 4, then we transfer the low and the high part of the obtained vector in ARM registers. Then, we obtain what we need using shift and xor. When only 128-bit vectors are available, the function is easier to program with $d = 8$ (where d is the vector width), whereas $d = 16$ is slightly more programmer-friendly when 256-bit vectors are available. This is not a very hard constraint though, as both values of d can be dealt with efficiently using both instructions sets.

5 Conclusion

In this paper, we propose to use the rejection sampling as a technique to cancel the bias in the SPRING PRF and PRG. We revisit the attack on SPRING-CRT and find new attacks on SPRING. Finally, our experimentation shows that this leads to a very efficient stream cipher, whose security is very high. We think that lattice-based cryptography can be used with high performance.

Acknowledgment. The authors are supported by the french ANR BRUTUS project.

References

[AKPW13] Alwen, J., Krenn, S., Pietrzak, K., Wichs, D.: Learning with rounding, revisited - new reduction, properties and applications. In: Canetti, R., Garay, J.A. (eds.) CRYPTO 2013. LNCS, vol. 8042, pp. 57–74. Springer, Heidelberg (2013). doi:10.1007/978-3-642-40041-4_4

[BBL+15]   Banerjee, A., Brenner, H., Leurent, G., Peikert, C., Rosen, A.: SPRING: fast pseudorandom functions from rounded ring products. In: Cid, C., Rechberger, C. (eds.) FSE 2014. LNCS, vol. 8540, pp. 38–57. Springer, Heidelberg (2015). doi:10.1007/978-3-662-46706-0_3

[BFS04]   Bardet, M., Faugere, J.-C., Salvy, B.: On the complexity of gröbner basis computation of semi-regular overdetermined algebraic equations. In: Proceedings of the International Conference on Polynomial System Solving, pp. 71–74 (2004)

[BGL+14]   Brenner, H., Gaspar, L., Leurent, G., Rosen, A., Standaert, F.-X.: FPGA implementations of SPRING. In: Batina, L., Robshaw, M. (eds.) CHES 2014. LNCS, vol. 8731, pp. 414–432. Springer, Heidelberg (2014). doi:10.1007/978-3-662-44709-3_23

[BGM+15]   Bogdanov, A., Guo, S., Masny, D., Richelson, S., Rosen, A.: On the hardness of learning with rounding over small modulus. Cryptology ePrint Archive, Report 2015/769 (2015). http://eprint.iacr.org/2015/769

[BPR12]   Banerjee, A., Peikert, C., Rosen, A.: Pseudorandom functions and lattices. In: Pointcheval, D., Johansson, T. (eds.) EUROCRYPT 2012. LNCS, vol. 7237, pp. 719–737. Springer, Heidelberg (2012). doi:10.1007/978-3-642-29011-4_42

[CLS06]   Contini, S., Lenstra, A.K., Steinfeld, R.: VSH, an efficient and provable collision-resistant hash function. In: Vaudenay, S. (ed.) EUROCRYPT 2006. LNCS, vol. 4004, pp. 165–182. Springer, Heidelberg (2006). doi:10.1007/11761679_11

[Fau99]   Faugere, J.-C.: A new efficient algorithm for computing gröbner bases (f 4). J. Pure Appl. Algebra **139**(1), 61–88 (1999)

[Gal12]   Le Gall, F.: Faster algorithms for rectangular matrix multiplication. In: 53rd FOCS, pp. 514–523. IEEE Computer Society Press, October 2012

[LBF08]   Leurent, G., Bouillaguet, C., Fouque, P.-A.: SIMD Is a Message Digest. Submission to NIST (2008)

[LMPR08]   Lyubashevsky, V., Micciancio, D., Peikert, C., Rosen, A.: SWIFFT: a modest proposal for FFT hashing. In: Nyberg, K. (ed.) FSE 2008. LNCS, vol. 5086, pp. 54–72. Springer, Heidelberg (2008). doi:10.1007/978-3-540-71039-4_4

[LPR13]   Lyubashevsky, V., Peikert, C., Regev, O.: On ideal lattices and learning with errors over rings. J. ACM (JACM) **60**(6), 43 (2013)

[Lyu09]   Lyubashevsky, V.: Fiat-Shamir with aborts: applications to lattice and factoring-based signatures. In: Matsui, M. (ed.) ASIACRYPT 2009. LNCS, vol. 5912, pp. 598–616. Springer, Heidelberg (2009). doi:10.1007/978-3-642-10366-7_35

[MS95]   Meier, W., Staffelbach, O.: The self-shrinking generator. In: Santis, A. (ed.) EUROCRYPT 1994. LNCS, vol. 950, pp. 205–214. Springer, Heidelberg (1995). doi:10.1007/BFb0053436

[Reg05]   Regev, O.: On lattices, learning with errors, random linear codes, and cryptography. In: Gabow, H.N., Fagin, R. (eds.) 37th ACM STOC, pp. 84–93. ACM Press, May 2005

A Attack on SPRING-CRT

In SPRING-CRT, the authors of [BBL+15] used a modulus $\tilde{q} = 2 \cdot q$ so that a uniform value over $\mathbb{Z}_{\bar{q}}$ can be easily transformed into a uniform value over $\mathbb{Z}_2$ using the most significant bits. However, it introduced a weakness: if we control the product over $\mathbb{Z}_2$, then the most significant bit is again biased.

Furthermore, since n is a power of two, we have over $\mathbb{F}_2$ the factorization $x^n + 1 = (x+1)^n$ and we can use this property as follows. Let κ be a power of two. Suppose we have $\mathbf{x}$ and $\mathbf{x}'$ such that for a certain index i_0, there exist i such that $x_i \neq x_i'$ and $\prod_{i \geq i_0} \mathbf{s}_i^{x_i - x_i'} = 1 \bmod (2, x^\kappa + 1)$. Furthermore, if for all $i < i_0$, $x_i = x_i'$, we have $\prod_i \mathbf{s}_i^{x_i - x_i'} = 1 \bmod (2, \mathbf{x}^\kappa + 1)$. Now, observe that the bias of $\lfloor c + 2u \rfloor_2$ for a uniform $u \in \mathbb{Z}_q$ and constant c is $(-1)^c/q$ when q is odd. Therefore, assuming $\prod_i \mathbf{s}_i^{x_i} \bmod q$ is uniform when $(x_i)_{i < i_0}$ is taken uniformly and with the same condition over $\mathbf{x}'$, we have for all $0 < t < \kappa$:

$$ bias\left(\sum_{j=0}^{n/\kappa - 1} (\lfloor a \prod_i \mathbf{s}_i^{x_i} \rfloor_2 + \lfloor a \prod_i \mathbf{s}_i^{x_i'} \rfloor_2)_{t+j\kappa} \right) = q^{-2n/\kappa}, $$

while if $\prod_i \mathbf{s}_i^{x_i - x_i'} \neq 1 \bmod (2, x^\kappa + 1)$ the other bias are null.

Then, we choose $i_0 \approx 4n/\kappa \log_2(q) + 2\ln(\kappa)$ and asks for $2^{\kappa/2} 2^{i_0}/\kappa$ blocks of values. After computing the sums over n/κ bits, it remains to find a correlation between all pairs of $2^{\kappa/2}$ vectors of 2^{i_0} bits. While [BBL+15] computed all of them naively, we can view this as multiplying matrices whose coefficient are either -1 or 1. Using the Hoeffding lemma, we conclude that we have a constant advantage.

In our case, we choose $\kappa = 64$ so that $i_0 = 72$ and the bottleneck is the multiplication of a matrix with 2^{32} rows and 2^{72} columns by its transpose.

Asymptotically, when there is $n^{72/32}$ columns for n rows, this takes time at most $O(n^{3.49})$ [Gal12]. Removing the Landau notation, this indicates (if 2^{72} is sufficiently large[2]) a time of roughly 2^{104} operations. The exact function is still unclear, but the complexity is certainly less than 2^{72-32} square matrix multiplications of size 2^{32}. Using Strassen algorithm for the square matrix multiplication gives a total of around 2^{130} operations[3].

If k is too small, then we can ask only for 2^k blocks, so that there are $\kappa 2^{k-i_0}$ rows in the matrix and the advantage $\kappa^2 2^{2(k-i_0)-\kappa}$. For $k = 64$, we choose $\kappa = 128$, $i_0 = 42$ so that there are 2^{45} rows in the matrix and the advantage is $\approx 2^{-38}$ for a complexity with Strassen's algorithm of $2^5 7^{42} \approx 2^{123}$.

Using $\kappa = \Theta(\sqrt{n\log(q)})$ for $k \geq O(\sqrt{n\log(q)})$, we get a complexity of $2^{O(\sqrt{n\log(q)})}$. This sub-exponential attack makes us wonder about the security of Ring-LWE with an even modulus.

---

[2] Since 3.49 is strictly above the number given in [Gal12], for any $\epsilon > 0$, the complexity of a multiplication is less than $\epsilon n^{3.49}$ for all sufficiently large n.

[3] [BBL+15] used $i_0 = 4n/\kappa \log_2(q)$ so that their claimed complexity is 2^{126} but this is not enough to get a constant advantage.

Revisiting TESLA in the Quantum Random Oracle Model

Erdem Alkim[1], Nina Bindel[2(✉)], Johannes Buchmann[2], Özgür Dagdelen[3],
Edward Eaton[4,5], Gus Gutoski[4(✉)], Juliane Krämer[2], and Filip Pawlega[4,5]

[1] Ege University, İzmir, Turkey
erdemalkim@gmail.com
[2] Technische Universität Darmstadt, Darmstadt, Germany
{nbindel,buchmann,jkraemer}@cdc.informatik.tu-darmstadt.de
[3] BridgingIT GmbH, Mannheim, Germany
oezdagdelen@googlemail.com
[4] ISARA Corporation, Waterloo, Canada
{ted.eaton,gus.gutoski,filip.pawlega}@isara.com
[5] University of Waterloo, Waterloo, Canada

Abstract. We study a scheme of Bai and Galbraith (CT-RSA'14), also
known as TESLA. TESLA was thought to have a tight security reduction from the learning with errors problem (LWE) in the random oracle
model (ROM). Moreover, a variant using chameleon hash functions was
lifted to the quantum random oracle model (QROM). However, both
reductions were later found to be flawed and hence it remained unre-
solved until now whether TESLA can be proven to be tightly secure in
the (Q)ROM.

In the present paper we provide an entirely new, tight security reduction for TESLA from LWE in the QROM (and thus in the ROM). Our
security reduction involves the adaptive re-programming of a quantum
oracle. Furthermore, we propose parameter sets targeting 128 bits of
security against both classical and quantum adversaries and compare
TESLA's performance with state-of-the-art signature schemes.

Keywords: Quantum random oracle · Post quantum cryptography ·
Lattice-based cryptography · Signature scheme · Tight security reduction

1 Introduction

Our interest in the present paper is in a quantum-resistant signature scheme
proposed by Bai and Galbraith [6]. Those authors argue the security of their
scheme via reductions from the *learning with errors (LWE)* and the *short integer solutions (SIS)* problems in the random oracle model (ROM). This scheme
was subsequently studied by Alkim, Bindel, Buchmann, Dagdelen, and Schwabe
under the name TESLA [4], who provided an alternate security reduction from
the LWE problem only.

© Springer International Publishing AG 2017
T. Lange and T. Takagi (Eds.): PQCrypto 2017, LNCS 10346, pp. 143–162, 2017.
DOI: 10.1007/978-3-319-59879-6_9

Since then, there have been several follow-up works on the Bai-Galbraith scheme [2,4,8,47]. Most notably, a version of the scheme called ring-TESLA, whose security is based on the ring-LWE problem [2], has the potential to evolve into a practical, quantum-resistant signature scheme that might one day see widespread use as replacement for contemporary signature schemes such as ECDSA.

In what follows, we review the concepts of tightness and the quantum random oracle model as they relate to TESLA. We then list the contributions of the present paper and discuss related work by others.

1.1 Background

Security Reduction and Parameter Choice. The security of digital signature schemes is often argued by reduction. A reductionist security argument typically proves a claim of the form, "any attacker $\mathcal{A}$ who can break the scheme can be used to build an algorithm $\mathcal{B}$ that solves some underlying hard computational problem". Hence, the security gap can be determined; it measures how much extra work $\mathcal{B}$ must perform in order to convert $\mathcal{A}$ into solving the underlying hard problem. If the run-time and probability of success of $\mathcal{B}$ are close to those of $\mathcal{A}$, *i.e.*, if the security gap is approximately 1, then the reduction is called *tight*. Achieving a small security gap, ideally a tight security reduction, is of theoretical interest in its own right, but it should also be an important consideration when selecting parameters for a concrete instantiation of a scheme. Specifically, the parameters of a signature scheme ought to be selected so that both (i) the effort needed to solve the underlying hard computational problem, and (ii) the security gap are taken into account. Hence, a tight security reduction is of advantage.

The need to instantiate schemes according to their security reductions and the role tight reductions play in these instantiations have been well argued by numerous authors. We refer the reader to [1,18,28] for a representative sample of these arguments.

The Quantum Random Oracle Model. Security arguments for the most efficient signature schemes—which therefore enjoy the most widespread real-world use—are typically presented in the ROM. (We refer to [31] by Koblitz and Menezes for discussion on why this might be the case.) The ROM postulates a truly random function that is accessible to attackers only through "black box" queries to an oracle for it—a random oracle. Any concrete proposal for a signature scheme must substitute a specific choice of hash function for the random oracle. An attacker armed with a quantum computer can be expected to evaluate that hash function in quantum superposition. Arguments that establish security even against such quantum-enabled attackers are said to hold in the quantum random oracle model (QROM).

It is conceivable that a signature scheme shown to be secure in the ROM may not be secure in the QROM. Thus, it is important that security arguments for quantum-resistant signature schemes hold not merely in the ROM, but also in the QROM.

Boneh *et al.* have proven that a security reduction in the ROM also holds in the QROM if it is *history-free* [15]. Unfortunately, many signature schemes have security reductions in the ROM that involve the *re-programming* of a random oracle; these reductions are not history-free. For these schemes, there remains a need to precisely clarify under what conditions these security reductions remain meaningful in the QROM.

Tightness in the QROM for TESLA. The security reduction presented by Bai and Galbraith for their signature scheme employs the Forking Lemma [41]. As such, it is non-tight and it involves re-programming, so it holds in the ROM but is not known to hold in the QROM.

As mentioned above, Alkim *et al.* presented an alternate security analysis for the Bai-Galbraith scheme, which they call TESLA. Their reduction is a tight reduction from LWE in the ROM. Moreover, those authors observed that their reduction can be made history-free at the cost of replacing a generic hash function with a chameleon hash function. It then follows from [15] that the history-free security reduction for TESLA holds also in the QROM. (Unfortunately, the use of a chameleon hash function would likely render any signature scheme too inefficient for widespread practical use.)

Unfortunately, a flaw in the original TESLA security reduction has been identified by the present authors. (The flaw was independently discovered by Chris Peikert.) This flaw is also present in several TESLA follow-up works, including ring-TESLA. As such, the status of the TESLA signature scheme and its derivative works has been open until now.

1.2   Our Contribution

Our primary contributions are as follows:

New security reduction. We present a new security reduction from LWE to TESLA. Our new reduction is tight. It seems that the flaw in the original tight security reduction of TESLA does not admit a fix without a huge increase in the parameters; our new reduction is a significant re-work of the entire proof.

Security in the QROM with re-programming. Our new security reduction involves the adaptive re-programming of a random oracle and hence it is not history-free. Nevertheless, we show that it holds in the QROM by applying a seminal result from quantum query complexity due to Bennet *et al.* [11]. It is possible that our approach can be abstracted so as to yield a general result on security reductions with re-programming in the QROM.

Our secondary contributions are as follows:

Parameter selection. We propose three sets of parameters for the concrete instantiation of TESLA: TESLA-0 and TESLA-1 targeting 96 and 128 bit security against a classical adversary, respectively; and TESLA-2, targeting 128 bits of security against a quantum adversary. All three parameter sets are chosen according to our (tight) security reduction.

The concrete parameter space admitted by our new security reduction is worse than that of previous reductions, but those previous reductions are either flawed or non-tight. Consequently, our proposed parameter sets lead to concrete instantiations of TESLA that are less efficient than previous proposals given in [4, 6, 47] that were not chosen according to the given security reduction.

Implementation. We provide a software implementation for the parameter sets TESLA-0 and TESLA-1. Our implementation targets Intel Haswell CPUs to provide a comparison of TESLA's performance with other signature schemes with different security levels. Unfortunately, the TESLA-2 parameter set does not seem to admit an implementation that can take advantage of the same fast parallel arithmetic instructions available on modern processors that were used in our implementations of TESLA-0 and TESLA-1, and so we do not provide a software implementation for TESLA at this parameter set. See Sect. 6 for details.

1.3   Related Work

Tightness from "Lossy" Keys. In order to avoid the non-tightness inherent in the use of the Forking Lemma, we take an approach that was introduced by Katz and Wang to obtain tightly-secure signatures from the decisional Diffie-Hellman problem [28].

The idea is to use the underlying hardness assumption to show that "real", properly-formed public keys for the signature scheme are indistinguishable from "lossy", malformed public keys. The task of forging a signature for a lossy key is then somehow proven to be intractable.

Any attacker must therefore fail to forge when given a lossy public key. Thus, any attacker who succeeds in forging a signature when given a real public key can be used to distinguish real keys from lossy keys, contradicting the underlying hardness assumption.

In the case of TESLA, the real keys are matrices A and $T = AS + E$ for some matrices S, E with small entries. (See Sect. 2.2 for a proper definition of these matrices and the LWE problem.) We call these real keys LWE yes-instances. The lossy keys are LWE no-instances: matrices A, T selected uniformly at random, so that the existence of S, E as above occurs with only negligible probability. We prove that the task of forging a TESLA signature for lossy keys is intractable, so that any TESLA forger must be able to solve the decisional LWE problem.

A Fiat-Shamir Transform for "Lossy" Identification Schemes. The TESLA signature scheme could be viewed as the result of applying the Fiat-Shamir transform to a "lossy" identification scheme based on LWE. A tight security reduction for TESLA then follows from a general theorem of Abdalla,

Fouque, Lyubashevsky, and Tibouchi (AFLT theorem) on the tight security of any signature scheme obtained in this way [1].

In order to leverage the AFLT theorem, one must propose an identification scheme and prove that it is lossy. Such a proof could be obtained by excerpting the relevant parts of our security reduction to establish the simulatability and lossiness properties of a suitably chosen identification scheme. Such an exercise might make our rather monolithic security reduction easier to digest by modularizing it and phrasing it in a familiar framework.

However, security reductions obtained by applying the AFLT theorem are guaranteed to hold only in the ROM. In order to fully recover our security reduction from this framework, one must first re-prove the AFLT theorem in the QROM. This limitation is due to the fact that the proof of the AFLT theorem involves adaptively re-programming a hash oracle. As such, it does not meet any known conditions for lifting a given proof from the ROM into the QROM.

Given that our security reduction in the QROM also involves the adaptive re-programming of a hash oracle, perhaps our approach could be mined for insights to establish the AFLT theorem in the QROM.

Other Tightly-Secure LWE or SIS Signature Schemes. Gentry *et al.* present a signature scheme with a tight security reduction from SIS in the ROM using a trapdoor construction based on possessing a secret short basis of a lattice [25]. Boneh *et al.* observed that the security reduction for this scheme is history-free, and thus holds in the QROM [15].

Boyen and Li present a signature scheme with a tight security reduction from SIS in the *standard model* [17], also using a short basis trapdoor. Since standard model security reductions do not rely on any assumptions about a random oracle, these reductions hold in the QROM.

The use of a short-basis trapdoor in a signature scheme imposes an additional constraint on the concrete parameter space admitted by that scheme's security reduction. This additional constraint on the parameters of short-basis trapdoor schemes seems to render them too inefficient for practical use. Since TESLA and its derivatives do not use a trapdoor construction, they do not suffer from this impediment.

Other than TESLA, we are aware of only one example of a signature scheme based on the Fiat-Shamir transform with a tight security reduction from LWE or SIS. Prior to Bai and Galbraith, a variant of a scheme by Lyubashevsky [33] was shown to admit a tight security reduction in the ROM by Abdalla *et al.* as part of an illustration of the aforementioned AFLT theorem [1]. An artifact of this reduction required Abdalla *et al.* to increase the parameters of the scheme, rendering it too inefficient for practical use. As mentioned earlier, security reductions produced via the AFLT theorem are not known to hold in the QROM.

Re-programming a Quantum Oracle. Adaptive reprogramming of a quantum oracle has been addressed in some specific cases. Unruh considered a re-programmed quantum oracle in order to establish the security of a quantum position verification scheme [45]. It is not clear whether Unruh's results apply to our setting.

Eaton and Song present an asymptotic result on re-programming in the QROM [24] in a context quite different from ours. Since their result is asymptotic, it does not allow for concrete parameter selection, for which the tightness of the reduction needs to be explicit.

Our approach to re-programming is independent of these previous works, though some works—such as [15,24]—do draw upon the same result by Bennet *et al.* [11] that we employ. To our knowledge we are the first to present progress on re-programming in the QROM in the context of a cryptographic scheme with potential for quantum-resistant standardization.

A Note on "Lattice-Based" Cryptography. Part of the allure of cryptosystems based on LWE or SIS is that those problems enjoy worst-case to average-case reductions from fundamental problems about lattices such as the *approximate shortest independent vectors problem (SIVP)* or the *gap shortest vector problem (GapSVP)*. (See Regev [42] or the survey of Peikert [38] and the references therein.)

These reductions suggest that the ability to solve LWE or SIS on randomly chosen instances implies the ability to solve SIVP or GapSVP, even on the hardest instances. Indeed, cryptosystems based on LWE or SIS are often referred to as *lattice-based* cryptosystems, suggesting that the security of these cryptosystems ultimately rests upon the worst-case hardness of these lattice problems.

However, as observed by Chatterjee, Koblitz, Menezes, and Sarkar, existing worst-case to average-case reductions for LWE and SIS are highly non-tight [18]. We are not aware of a proposal for a concrete instantiation of a cryptosystem based on LWE or SIS with the property that the proposed parameters were selected according to such a reduction. Instead, it is common to instantiate such cryptosystems based on the best known algorithms for solving LWE or SIS. (In addition to TESLA, see for example [5,16].)

For TESLA, we take care to instantiate the scheme according to its security reduction from LWE. However, we are unable to instantiate TESLA according to reductions from underlying lattice problems, due to the non-tightness of these reductions.

2   Preliminaries

In this section we clarify our notation used throughout the paper. We assume familiarity with the fundamentals of quantum information, such as the Dirac ket notation $|\cdot\rangle$ for pure quantum states and the density matrix formalism for mixed quantum states. (Recall that a mixed state can be viewed as a probabilistic mixture of pure states.) For background on quantum information the reader is referred to the books [29,37].

2.1   Notation

Integer scalars are denoted using Roman letters and if not stated otherwise, q is a prime integer in this paper. For any positive integer n the set $\mathbb{Z}_n$ of integers modulo n is represented by $\{-\lfloor (n-1)/2 \rfloor, \ldots, \lfloor n/2 \rfloor\}$. Fix a positive integer d and define the functions $[\cdot], [\cdot]_L : \mathbb{Z} \to \mathbb{Z}$ as follows. For any integer x let $[x]_L$ denote the representative of x in $\mathbb{Z}_{2^d}$, i.e., $x = [x]_L \pmod{2^d}$, and let $[x] = (x - [x]_L)/2^d$. Informally, $[x]_L$ is viewed as the *least significant bits* of x and $[x]$ is viewed as the *most significant bits* of x. The definitions are easily extended to vectors by applying the operators for each component. An integer vector y is *B-short* if each entry is at most B in absolute value.

Vectors with entries in $\mathbb{Z}_q$ are viewed as column vectors and denoted with lowercase Roman letters in sans-serif font, e.g., $\mathsf{y}, \mathsf{z}, \mathsf{w}$. Matrices with entries in $\mathbb{Z}_q$ are denoted with uppercase Roman letters in sans-serif font, e.g., $\mathsf{A}, \mathsf{S}, \mathsf{E}$. The transpose of a vector or a matrix is denoted by v^T or M^T, respectively. We denote by $\|\mathsf{v}\|$ the Euclidean norm of a vector v, and by $\|\mathsf{v}\|_\infty$ its infinity norm. All logarithms are base 2. With $\mathcal{D}_\sigma$, we denote the centered discrete Gaussian distribution with standard deviation σ. For a finite set S, we denote sampling the element s uniformly from S with $s \leftarrow_\$ \mathcal{U}(S)$ or simply $s \leftarrow_\$ S$.

Let χ be a distribution over $\mathbb{Z}$, then we write $x \leftarrow \chi$ if x is sampled according to χ. Moreover, we denote sampling each coordinate of a matrix $\mathsf{A} \in \mathbb{Z}^{m \times n}$ with distribution χ by $\mathsf{A} \leftarrow \chi^{m \times n}$ with $m, n \in \mathbb{Z}_{>0}$. For an algorithm $\mathcal{A}$, the value $y \leftarrow \mathcal{A}(x)$ denotes the output of $\mathcal{A}$ on input x; if $\mathcal{A}$ uses randomness then $\mathcal{A}(x)$ is a random variable. $\mathcal{A}^\chi$ denotes that $\mathcal{A}$ can request samples from the distribution χ.

2.2   The Learning with Errors Problem

Informally the (decisional) learning with errors (LWE) problem with m samples is defined as follows: Given a tuple (A, t) with $\mathsf{A} \leftarrow_\$ \mathbb{Z}_q^{m \times n}$, decide whether $\mathsf{t} \leftarrow_\$ \mathbb{Z}_q^m$ or whether $\mathsf{t} = \mathsf{As} + \mathsf{e} \pmod{q}$ for a secret $\mathsf{s} \leftarrow \mathcal{D}_\sigma^n$ and error $\mathsf{e} \leftarrow \mathcal{D}_\sigma^m$. The security of the signature scheme covered in this paper is based on the matrix version of LWE (M-LWE): Given a tuple (A, T) with $\mathsf{A} \leftarrow_\$ \mathbb{Z}_q^{m \times n}$, decide whether $\mathsf{T} \leftarrow_\$ \mathbb{Z}_q^{m \times n'}$ is chosen uniformly random or whether $\mathsf{T} = \mathsf{AS} + \mathsf{E} \pmod{q}$ for a secret $\mathsf{S} \leftarrow \mathcal{D}_\sigma^{n \times n'}$ and $\mathsf{E} \leftarrow \mathcal{D}_\sigma^{m \times n'}$. We call $(\mathsf{A}, \mathsf{T}) \in \mathbb{Z}_q^{m \times n} \times \mathbb{Z}_q^{m \times n'}$ a **yes-instance** if T is generated by selecting $\mathsf{S} = (\mathsf{s}_1, \ldots, \mathsf{s}_{n'})$ with $\mathsf{s}_1, \ldots, \mathsf{s}_{n'} \leftarrow \mathcal{D}_\sigma^n$ and $\mathsf{E} \leftarrow \mathcal{D}_\sigma^{m \times n'}$, and setting $\mathsf{T} = \mathsf{AS} + \mathsf{E} \pmod{q}$. Otherwise, when $(\mathsf{A}, \mathsf{T}) \leftarrow_\$ \mathcal{U}\left(\mathbb{Z}_q^{m \times n} \times \mathbb{Z}_q^{m \times n'}\right)$, we call (A, T) a **no-instance**. Similar concepts from the literature are also known as *lossy* [1, 10, 40] or *messy keys* [39].

We know that if an attacker can break LWE parametrized with n, m, and q in time t and with success probability ε/n', then he can solve M-LWE parametrized with n, n', m, and q in time t and with success probability ε. Intuitively this is correct since an adversary that can solve LWE has n' possibilities to solve M-LWE (see also [6, 16, 40]).

For the remainder of the paper, 'LWE' refers to the matrix version M-LWE, unless otherwise specified.

3   The Signature Scheme TESLA

In this section, we present the LWE-based signature scheme TESLA. Its original construction was proposed in 2014 by Bai and Galbraith [6]. It was later revisited by Dagdelen *et al.* [47] and by Alkim *et al.* [4].

TESLA's key generation, sign, and verify algorithms are listed informally in Algorithms 1, 2 and 3. More formal listings of these algorithms are given in Fig. 1 in Sect. 5. Our proposed concrete parameter sets are derived in Sect. 5 and listed in Table 1.

Algorithm 1. KeyGen

Input: A.
Output: Public key T, secret key (S, E).

1: Choose entries of $S \in \mathbb{Z}_q^{n \times n'}$ and $E \in \mathbb{Z}_q^{m \times n'}$ from $\mathcal{D}_\sigma$
2: If E has a row whose h largest entries sum to L or more then retry at step 1.
3: If S has a row whose h largest entries sum to L_S or more then retry at step 1.
4: $T \leftarrow AS + E$.
5: Return public key T and secret key (S, E).

TESLA is parameterized by positive integers q, m, n, n', h, d, B, L, L_S, U, a positive real σ, a hash oracle $H(\cdot)$, and the publicly available matrix $A \leftarrow_\$ \mathbb{Z}_q^{m \times n}$. Let $\mathbb{H}$ denote the set of vectors $c \in \{-1, 0, 1\}^{n'}$ with exactly h nonzero entries. For simplicity we assume that the hash oracle $H(\cdot)$ has range $\mathbb{H}$, *i.e.*, we ignore the encoding function F, cf. Table 1. We call an integer vector w *well-rounded* if w is $(\lfloor q/2 \rfloor - L)$-short and $[w]$ is $(2^d - L)$-short.

In contrast to earlier proposals [6,47], we add two additional checks. The first one is the check in Line 3 in Algorithm 1. It ensures that no coefficient of the matrix S is too large, which allows for more concrete bounds during the security reduction. The parameter L_S is chosen such that the probability of rejecting S is smaller than $2^{-\lambda}$, cf. Sect. 5. The second additional check is in Line 5 in Algorithm 2. To ensure correctness of the scheme, it checks that the absolute value of each coordinate of $Ay - Ec$ is less or equal than $\lfloor q/2 \rfloor - L$.

Algorithm 2. Sign

Input: Message μ, secret key (S, E).
Output: Signature (z, c).

1: Choose y uniformly at random among B-short vectors from $\mathbb{Z}_q^n$.
2: $c \leftarrow H([Ay], \mu)$.
3: $z \leftarrow y + Sc$.
4: If z is not $(B - U)$-short then retry at step 1.
5: If $Ay - Ec$ is not well-rounded then retry at step 1.
6: Return signature (z, c).

Algorithm 3. Verify

Input: Message μ, public key (A, T), purported signature (z, c).
Output: "Accept" or "reject".

1: If z is not $(B - U)$-short then reject.
2: If $H([Az - Tc], \mu) \neq c$ then reject.
3: Accept.

4   Security Reduction for TESLA

Our main theorem on the security of TESLA informally states that as long as M-LWE can not be solved in time t and with success probability ε then no adversary $\mathcal{A}$ exists that can forge signatures of TESLA in time t' and with success probability ε', if $\mathcal{A}$ is allowed to make at most q_h hash und q_s sign queries. The main theorem is as follows.

Theorem 1 (Security of TESLA). *Let q, m, n, n', h, d, B, L, L_S, U, σ, λ, κ be TESLA parameters that are convenient[1] (according to Definition 1 in Sect. 5.3) and that satisfy the bounds in Table 1.*

If M-LWE is (t, ε)-hard then TESLA is existentially $(t', \varepsilon', q_h, q_s)$-unforgeable against adaptively chosen message attacks with $t' \approx t$ in (i) the quantum *random oracle model with*

$$\varepsilon' < \varepsilon + \frac{3}{2^\lambda} + \frac{2^{m(d+1)+3\lambda+1}}{q^m}(q_h + q_s)^2 q_s^3 + 2(q_h + 1)\sqrt{\frac{1}{2^h \binom{n'}{h}}}, \qquad (1)$$

and in (ii) the classical *random oracle model with*

$$\varepsilon' < \varepsilon + \frac{3}{2^\lambda} + \frac{2^{m(d+1)+3\lambda+1}}{q^m}(q_h + q_s)^2 q_s^3 + q_h\frac{1}{2^h \binom{n'}{h}}. \qquad (2)$$

The proof of Theorem 1 is given in the full version of the paper. Here we present a sketch of this proof and a selection of some intermediate results we feel are the most significant technical contributions of the present manuscript.

Let $\mathcal{F}$ be a forger that forges signatures of the TESLA scheme with probability $\Pr[\text{forge}(A, T)]$, where $\text{forge}(A, T)$ denotes the event that $\mathcal{F}$ forges a signature on input (A, T), which is a yes- or a no-instance of LWE. We build an LWE-solver $\mathcal{S}$ whose run time is close to that of $\mathcal{F}$ and who solves LWE with success bias close to $\Pr[\text{forge}(A, T)]$. It then follows from the presumed hardness of LWE that $\Pr[\text{forge}(A, T)]$ must be small.

Given an LWE input (A, T), the LWE-solver $\mathcal{S}$ treats (A, T) as a TESLA public key; $\mathcal{S}$ runs $\mathcal{F}$ on input (A, T) and outputs "yes" if and only if $\mathcal{F}$ succeeds in forging a TESLA signature.

---

[1] It is not necessary that TESLA parameters be convenient in order to derive negligibly small upper bounds on ε'; the definition of convenience merely facilitates a simplified statement of those bounds.

In order to run $\mathcal{F}$, the LWE-solver $\mathcal{S}$ must respond in some way to $\mathcal{F}$'s quantum queries to the hash oracle and to $\mathcal{F}$'s classical queries to the sign oracle. Our description of $\mathcal{S}$ includes a procedure for responding to these queries.

That $\mathcal{S}$ solves LWE with success bias close to $\Pr\left[\text{forge}(\mathsf{A},\mathsf{T})\right]$ is a consequence of the following facts:

1. For yes-instances of LWE, the probability with which $\mathcal{S}$ outputs "yes" is close to $\Pr\left[\text{forge}(\mathsf{A},\mathsf{T})\right]$.
2. For no-instances of LWE, $\mathcal{F}$ successfully forges (and hence $\mathcal{S}$ outputs "yes") with only negligible probability.

4.1 Yes-Instances of LWE

We argue that $\mathcal{S}$'s responses to $\mathcal{F}$'s oracle queries are indistinguishable from the responses $\mathcal{F}$ would receive from real oracles, from which it follows that $\mathcal{S}$ reports "yes" with probability close to $\Pr\left[\text{forge}(\mathsf{A},\mathsf{T})\right]$.

Each time $\mathcal{S}$ simulates a call to the sign oracle, it must "re-program" its simulated hash oracle on one input. Because $\mathcal{F}$ is permitted to make quantum queries to the hash oracle, we must show that $\mathcal{F}$ is unlikely to notice when a quantum random oracle has been re-programmed.

To this end, let $\mathbb{Y}$ denote the set of vectors $\mathsf{y} \in \mathbb{Z}_q^n$ such that y is B-short and define the following quantities for each choice of TESLA keys $(\mathsf{A},\mathsf{T}), (\mathsf{S},\mathsf{E})$:

$\text{nwr}(\mathsf{A},\mathsf{E})$: The probability over $(\mathsf{y},\mathsf{c}) \in \mathbb{Y} \times \mathbb{H}$ that $\mathsf{Ay} - \mathsf{Ec}$ is not well-rounded.

$\text{coll}(\mathsf{A},\mathsf{E})$: The maximum over all $\mathsf{w} \in \{[\mathsf{x}] : \mathsf{x} \in \mathbb{Z}_q^m\}$ of the probability over $(\mathsf{y},\mathsf{c}) \in \mathbb{Y} \times \mathbb{H}$ that $[\mathsf{Ay} - \mathsf{Ec}] = \mathsf{w}$.

We prove the following in the full version of our paper.

Proposition 1 (Re-programming in TESLA, Informal Statement). *The following holds for each choice of TESLA keys $(\mathsf{A},\mathsf{T}), (\mathsf{S},\mathsf{E})$, each hash oracle $\mathrm{H}(\cdot)$, and each $\gamma > 0$.*

Suppose the quantum state ρ_{H} was prepared by some party $\mathcal{D}$ using t quantum queries to $\mathrm{H}(\cdot)$. Let $\mathrm{H}'(\cdot)$ be a hash oracle that agrees with $\mathrm{H}(\cdot)$ except on a small number of randomly chosen inputs $(\cdot, \mu)$ for each possible message μ. Let $\rho_{\mathrm{H}'}$ be the state prepared when $\mathcal{D}$ uses hash oracle $\mathrm{H}'(\cdot)$ instead of $\mathrm{H}(\cdot)$.

Then $\|\rho_{\mathrm{H}'} - \rho_{\mathrm{H}}\|_{\mathrm{Tr}} < \gamma$ except with probability at most

$$\frac{t^2}{\gamma^2} \cdot \frac{\text{coll}(\mathsf{A},\mathsf{E})}{1 - \text{nwr}(\mathsf{A},\mathsf{E})} \tag{3}$$

over the choice of inputs upon which $\mathrm{H}(\cdot)$ and $\mathrm{H}'(\cdot)$ differ.

We also prove bounds on $\text{nwr}(\mathsf{A},\mathsf{E})$ and $\text{coll}(\mathsf{A},\mathsf{E})$ that hold with high probability over the choice of TESLA keys $(\mathsf{A},\mathsf{T}), (\mathsf{S},\mathsf{E})$.

4.2 No-Instances of LWE

We argue that, except with negligibly small probability over the choice of hash oracle $H(\cdot)$ and LWE no-instance (A, T), a TESLA forger cannot forge a signature for (A, T) without making an intractably large number of queries to the hash oracle.

To forge a signature for message μ, a forger must find a hash input (w, μ) whose output $c = H(w, \mu)$ has the property that there exists a $(B - U)$-short $z \in \mathbb{Z}_q^n$ for which $[Az - Tc] = w$. Let $\mathbb{H}(w, A, T) \subset \mathbb{H}$ denote the set of all such c. A hash input (w, μ) is called *good* for $H(\cdot)$ and (A, T) if $H(w, \mu) \in \mathbb{H}(w, A, T)$. (Once a good hash input has been found, the forger must then somehow *find* the vector z witnessing this fact. For our purpose, we assume that the forger gets it for free.)

For each LWE no-instance (A, T), a given hash input (w, μ) is good for $H(\cdot)$ and (A, T) with probability

$$\frac{\#\mathbb{H}(w, A, T)}{\#\mathbb{H}} \tag{4}$$

over the choice of hash oracle $H(\cdot)$. In the full version of our paper, we argue that, except with negligibly small probability over the choice of $H(\cdot)$ and (A, T), the fraction of hash inputs that are good is at most the expectation over LWE no-instances (A, T) of the ratio (4), maximized over all $w \in \{[x] : x \in \mathbb{Z}_q^m\}$. We then prove the following

Proposition 2 (Good Hash Inputs are Rare). *If the TESLA parameters are convenient (according to Definition 1 in Sect. 5.3) then*

$$\operatorname*{Ex}_{(A,T)}\left[\max_{w}\left\{\frac{\#\mathbb{H}(w, A, T)}{\#\mathbb{H}}\right\}\right] \leq \frac{1}{\#\mathbb{H}}. \tag{5}$$

Thus, the fraction of good hash inputs is at most $1/\#\mathbb{H}$ except with vanishingly small probability over the choice of hash oracle $H(\cdot)$ and LWE no-instance (A, T).

Since each hash input is good with a fixed probability independent of other hash inputs, the only way to discover a good input is via search through an unstructured space. It then follows from known lower bounds for quantum search over an unstructured space that the forger cannot find a good hash input—and thus a TESLA forgery—using only q_h quantum queries to the hash oracle.

5 Selecting Parameters for TESLA

In this section we propose parameter sets for TESLA. Moreover, we present a more detailed description of TESLA in Fig. 1. Table 1 illustrates our concrete choice of parameters and Table 2 gives the hardness of the corresponding LWE instances. We propose three parameter sets: TESLA-0 that targets the same (classical) bit security of 96 bit as the instantiation proposed in [47], called DEG$^+$. TESLA-1 targets 128 bit of classical security and TESLA-2 targets 128 bit of security against quantum adversaries. Note that the parameter set DEG$^+$ was originally proposed to give 128 bit of security, *i.e.*, $\lambda = 128$, but due to new methods to estimate the bit security its bit security is now only 96 bit.

Algorithm KeyGen	Algorithm Sign

Algorithm KeyGen

INPUT: 1^λ; A, n, n', m, q, σ
OUTPUT: $(S, E, s), T$

1. $S \leftarrow_\$ \mathcal{D}_\sigma^{n \times n'}$
2. $E \leftarrow_\$ \mathcal{D}_\sigma^{m \times n'}$
3. **if** $\text{checkE}(E) = 0 \vee \text{checkS}(S) = 0$
4.   **then** Restart
5. $s \leftarrow_\$ \{0,1\}^\kappa$
6. $T \leftarrow AS + E \pmod{q}$
7. $\text{sk} \leftarrow (S, E, s), \text{pk} \leftarrow T$
8. **return** (sk, pk)

Algorithm Verify

INPUT: μ, q, z, c, A, T
OUTPUT: $\{0,1\}$

1. $c \leftarrow F(c)$
2. $w' \leftarrow Az - Tc \pmod{q}$
3. $c' \leftarrow H([w'], \mu)$
4. **if** $c' = c \wedge \|z\|_\infty \leq B - U$
5.   **then return** 1
6. **return** 0

Algorithm Sign

INPUT: μ, q, A, S, E, s
OUTPUT: (z, c)

1. $j \leftarrow 0$
2. $k \leftarrow PRF_1(s, \mu)$
3. $y \leftarrow PRF_2(k, j)$
4. $v \leftarrow Ay \pmod{q}$
5. $c \leftarrow H([v], \mu)$
6. $c \leftarrow F(c)$
7. $z \leftarrow y + Sc$
8. $w \leftarrow v - Ec \pmod{q}$
9. **if** $\|[w]_L\|_\infty > 2^{d-1} - L_E$
    $\vee \|w\|_\infty > \lfloor q/2 \rfloor - L_E \vee \|z\|_\infty > B - U$
10.   **then** $j \leftarrow j + 1$ and go to Step 1
11. **return** (z, c)

Fig. 1. Specification of the signature scheme TESLA = (KeyGen, Sign, Verify); for details of the functions checkE and checkS see the explanation of the public parameters and definition of functions.

Public Parameters and Definition of Functions. TESLA is parameterized by the dimensions n, n', m of the matrices, the size κ of the output of the hash function, and the security parameter λ with $m > n > \kappa \geq \lambda$; by the matrix $A \leftarrow_\$ \mathbb{Z}_q^{m \times n}$; by the hash function $H : \{0,1\}^* \to \{0,1\}^\kappa$, by the encoding function $F : \{0,1\}^\kappa \to \mathbb{H}$ (see [26] for more information), by the pseudo-random function $PRF_1 : \{0,1\}^\kappa \times \{0,1\}^* \to \{0,1\}^\kappa$, and the pseudo-random generator $PRF_2 : \{0,1\}^\kappa \times \mathbb{Z} \to [-B, B]^n$. The remaining values, *i.e.*, the standard deviation σ, the number h of non-zero coefficients in the output of the encoding function, the number of rounded bits d, the value B defining the interval of the randomness during Sign, the value U defining (together with B) the rejection probability during rejection sampling, and the modulus q, are derived as shown in Table 1 and described in Sect. 5.1.

Moreover, we define the functions checkE, introduced in [47, Sect. 3.2], as follows: for a matrix E, define E_i to be the i-th row of E. The function $\max_k(\cdot)$ returns the k-th largest entry of a vector. The matrix E is rejected if for any row of E it holds that $\sum_{k=1}^h \max_k(E_i)$ is greater than some bound L. We apply a similar check checkS to S: The matrix S is rejected if for any row of S it holds that $\sum_{k=1}^h \max_k(S_i)$ is greater than some bound L_S.

Remark 1 (Deterministic signature). Note that signing is deterministic for each message μ since the randomness is determined by the vector y which is deterministically computed by the secret key and the message to-be-signed. In the original scheme by Bai and Galbraith [6] the vector y was sampled uniformly random in $[-B, B]^n$. The idea to use a pseudo-random function to generate signatures deterministically was deployed several times before [9,12,28,36,46].

5.1   Derivation of System Parameters

Our security reduction for TESLA minimizes the underlying assumptions which allows us to choose secure parameters from a greater set of choices compared to [6,47]. More precisely, our parameters do not have to involve a hard instance of the SIS assumption as it was done by Bai and Galbraith [6] before. We summarize the bounds and conditions of each parameter in Table 1 and explicate the computation of some of the listed parameters in the following. Furthermore, we state the resulting key and signature sizes in the table.

Table 1. Concrete instantiation TESLA-2 of 128 bit of security against classical and quantum adversaries, and TESLA-0 of 96 bit and TESLA-1 of 128 bit of security against classical adversaries; comparison with the instantiation proposed in [47], called DEG$^+$, of 96 bit security (classically); sizes are given in kilo byte [KB]; sizes are theoretic sizes for fully compressed keys and signatures; for sizes used by our software see Table 3.

Parameter	Bound	DEG$^+$	TESLA-0	TESLA-1	TESLA-2
λ		128	96	128	128
κ		256	256	256	256
n		532	644	804	1300
n'		532	390	600	1036
m		840	3156	4972	4788
σ	$> 2\sqrt{n}$	43	55	57	73
L	$3h\sigma$ or $2.8h\sigma$, see Sect. 5.1	2322	5082	6703	17987
L_S	$14\sigma h$	-	25410	33516	89936
h	$2^h \binom{n'}{h} \geq 2^{3\lambda}$ (classically)	18	33	42	-
	$2^h \binom{n'}{h} \geq 2^{5\lambda}$ (quantumly)	-	-	-	88
B	$\geq 14n\sqrt{h}\sigma$	$2^{21} - 1$	$2^{22} - 1$	$2^{22} - 1$	$2^{24} - 1$
U	$\lceil 14\sqrt{h}\sigma \rceil$	2554	4424	5172	9588
d	$(1 - 2L/2^d)^m \geq 0.3$	23	25	26	27
q	Satisfying the bound in Eq. 7, $\geq \left(2^{m(d+1)+4\lambda+1}(q_h + q_s)^2 q_s^3\right)^{1/m}$	$2^{29} - 3$	$2^{31} - 99$	$2^{31} - 19$	40582171961 $\approx 2^{35.24}$
δ_{KeyGen}	Empirically, see Sect. 5.1	0.99	1	1	Future work
δ_{Sign}		0.314	0.307	0.154	Future work
H	$\{0,1\}^* \to \{0,1\}^\kappa$	SHA-256			
F	$\{0,1\}^\kappa \to \mathbb{H}_{n',\omega}$	see [26]			
PRF_1	$\{0,1\}^\kappa \times \{0,1\}^* \to \{0,1\}^\kappa$	-	SHA-256		
PRF_2	$\{0,1\}^\kappa \times \mathbb{Z} \to [-B,B]^n$	-	ChaCha20		
Public-key size	$mn'\lceil \log_2(q) \rceil$	1 582	4 657	11 288	21 799
Secret-key size	$(nn' + mn')\lceil \log_2(14\sigma) \rceil$	891	1 809	4 230	7 700
Signature size	$n\lceil \log_2(2(B - U)) \rceil + \kappa$	1.4	1.8	2.3	4.0

Compared to [6,47], we introduce the parameter n' as the column dimension of the secret matrices S and E to get more flexibility in the choice of parameters. The value of n' influences the parameters h (and hence B, U, q, and the encoding function F)' and the size of the secret key.

Another important parameter of the signature scheme is the value L. In the original work [6], it is set to $L = 7h\sigma$, whereas it is set to $L = 3h\sigma$ in [47]. We choose L to be roughly $L = 2.8h\sigma$. We note that the smaller the value L, the higher the probability of acceptance in the signature algorithm (Line 9, Fig. 1) becomes.

We add checkS to the key generation algorithm and the corresponding parameter L_S to bound $\|Sc\| \le L_S$ in the security reduction. We determine the value L_S such that S is rejected only with negligibly small (in the security parameter λ) probability. Hence, we do not decrease the size of the key space further. We choose L_S to be $14h\sigma$.

The acceptance probabilities of a signature δ_{Sign} and of a secret key (S, E) in Table 1 are determined experimentally.

To ensure both correctness and security of our signature scheme, we choose parameters with respect to our reduction, hence, we choose parameters such that $\epsilon' \approx \epsilon$ in Eqs. (1) and (2). We propose to choose $q_h \le 2^\lambda$ and $q_s \le 2^{\lambda/2}$, since a hash query is merely the evaluation of a publicly available function and hence the adversary can use all its computational power to make hash queries. The number of sign queries is somewhat limited since it involves more complicated operations. We refer to [30] (especially, Sect. 7) for further discussion.

5.2 Concrete Bit Security of TESLA

Choosing our parameters such that $\varepsilon \approx \varepsilon$ and $t \approx t'$ in Theorem 1 implies that we do not lose bits of security due to our security reduction. However, we lose $\lceil \log(n') \rceil$ bits of security due to the reduction from LWE to M-LWE. Hence, we have to choose an LWE instance with slightly higher bit hardness than the targeted bit security of the TESLA instances.

To estimate the classical hardness we use a recent fork [43,44] of the LWE-Estimator by Albrecht et al. [3]. The extension takes the number of given LWE samples into account.

To estimate the quantum hardness of LWE we use the same method: we use the LWE-Estimator which already includes (from commit-id b929691 on) the run time estimates for a quantumly enhanced sieving algorithm [32] as a subroutine of the lattice reduction algorithm BKZ 2.0 [20]. Moreover, we apply a recently published quantum algorithm [35] to the currently fastest enumeration estimations by Micciancio and Walter [34] and add the resulting estimations as a subroutine to be used in BKZ 2.0. We summarize the estimations using quantum sieving and quantum enumeration in Table 2.

Table 2. Estimation of the hardness of LWE instances given in TESLA-0, TESLA-1, and TESLA-2 against the decoding attack and the (dual and standard) embedding approach, in comparison to the parameter sets proposed by Dagdelen *et al.* [47], called DEG$^+$; estimations are computed using the LWE-Estimator with a restricted number of samples [3,44].

Problem	Attack	DEG$^+$	TESLA-0	TESLA-1	TESLA-2
Classical hardness [bit]					
LWE	Decoding	156	**110**	**142**	**204**
	Dual embedding	**96**	**110**	**142**	205
	Standard embedding	164	111	143	205
Post-quantum hardness [bit]					
LWE	Decoding	73	74	98	146
	Dual embedding	**61**	**71**	**94**	**142**
	Standard embedding	111	**71**	95	**142**

5.3   Convenient Parameters

We make some simplifying assumptions on the choice of TESLA parameters. These assumptions are not necessary in order to derive a negligibly small upper bound on the forger's success probability—they merely facilitate a simplified statement of the upper bound in Theorem 1 in Sect. 4.

Let $\Delta\mathbb{H}$ be the set of differences of elements in $\mathbb{H}$. That is, $\Delta\mathbb{H} \stackrel{\text{def}}{=} \{c - c' : c, c' \in \mathbb{H}\}$. In the full version of our paper we compute the size of $\Delta\mathbb{H}$, but for a trivial upper bound one can note that $\#\Delta\mathbb{H} \leq (\#\mathbb{H})^2$.

Definition 1 (Convenient TESLA Parameters). *TESLA parameters are convenient if the following bounds hold:*

$$2mL\left(\frac{1}{2^d} + \frac{1}{q}\right) + \sqrt{\frac{2^\lambda(q+1)}{(2B-1)^n}} < 1/2 \tag{6}$$

$$\#\Delta\mathbb{H}(4(B-U)-1)^n(2^{d+1}-1)^m < q^m. \tag{7}$$

All our proposed parameter sets for TESLA meet this condition.

6   Results and Comparison

To evaluate the performance of our proposed parameter sets we present a software implementation targeting the Intel Haswell microarchitecture. The starting point for our implementation is the software presented by Dagdelen *et al.* [47], which we obtained from the authors. Our software offers the same level of protection against timing attacks as the software presented in [47]. The software makes use of the fast AVX2 instructions on vectors of four double-precision floating-point numbers.

Table 3. Overview of state-of-the-art post-quantum signature schemes; signature sizes are given in byte [B], key sizes are given in kilo byte [KB]; the column "ROM?, tight?" states whether the scheme has a security reduction in the random oracle model and whether this reduction is tight; "QROM?, tight?" states the same for the quantum random oracle model; "Security (PreQ)" lists the claimed pre-quantum security level; "Security (PostQ)" lists the claimed post-quantum security level, if available

Scheme/ Software	Comp. Assum.	ROM? Tight?	QROM? Tight?	Security (PreQ)	Security (PostQ)	CPU	Key size [KB]	Sig. size [B]	Cycle counts
Selected signature schemes over standard lattices									
GPV [7,25]	SIS	Yes Yes	Yes Yes	96	59	AMD Opteron 8356 (Barcelona)	vk: 27,840 sk: 12,064	30,105	Sign: 312,800,000 Verify: 50,600,000
DEC+ [6,47]	SIS, LWE	Yes No	–	96	?	Intel Core i7-4770K (Haswell)	vk: 1,581 sk: 891	1,495	Sign: 1,203,924 Verify: 335,072
TESLA-0 (this paper)	LWE	Yes Yes	Yes Yes	96	?	Intel Core-i7-4770K (Haswell)	vk: 4,808 sk: 2,895	1,964	Sign: 27,243,747 Verify: 5,374,884
TESLA-1 (this paper)	LWE	Yes Yes	Yes Yes	128	?	Intel Core-i7-4770K (Haswell)	vk: 11,653 sk: 6,769	2,444	Sign: 143,402,231 Verify: 19,284,672
Selected signatures schemes over ideal lattices									
GPV-poly [7,25]	R-SIS	Yes Yes	Yes Yes	96	59	AMD Opteron 8356 (Barcelona)	vk: 55 sk: 26	32,972	Sign: 80,500,000 Verify: 11,500,000
GLP [26,27,47][a]	DCK	Yes No	–	75–80	?	Intel Core i5-3210M (Ivy Bridge)	vk: 1.5 sk: 0.25	1,186	Sign: 452,223 Verify: 34,004
Biss-bI [22,23][b]	R-SIS, NTRU	Yes No	–	128	?	"Intel Core @ 3.4 GHz"	vk: 7 sk: 2	1,559	Sign: ≈358,400 Verify: 102,000
Selected other post-quantum signature schemes									
SPHINCS-256 [13]	Hash collisions	Yes No[c]	No[c]	>128	128	Intel Xeon E3-1275 (Haswell)	vk: 1 sk: 1	41,000	Sign: 51,636,372 Verify: 1,451,004
Rainbow5640 [19,21][d]	MQ, EIP[e]	–	–	80	?	Intel Xeon E3-1275 (Haswell)	vk: 43 sk: 84	37	Sign: 42,700 Verify: 36,072

[a] In the benchmarks we include the improvements by Dagdelen et al. presented in [47].

[b] We report sizes of keys and signatures with "trivial" compression as explained in the text.

[c] The security of SPHINCS is reduced tightly from the hardness of finding hash collisions and non-tightly from the hardness of finding 2nd preimages in the standard model. Hence the reduction also holds in the ROM and QROM.

[d] Benchmark on Haswell CPU from [14].

[e] The security of Rainbow5640 is based on the Multivariate Quadratic polynomial (MQ) and the Extended Isomorphism of Polynomials (EIP) problem, but no security reduction has been given yet.

Table 3 gives benchmarking results for TESLA-0 and TESLA-1, and compares those benchmarks to state-of-the-art results from the literature. Due to the large values q and B of the parameter set TESLA-2, certain elements do no fit into the 53-bit mantissa of a double-precision floating point variable. Hence, we do not compare the performance of TESLA-2 in Table 3.

We obtain our benchmarks on an Intel Core-i7 4770K (Haswell) processor while disabling Turbo Boost and hyperthreading. Benchmarks of TESLA for signing are averaged over $100,000$ signatures; benchmarks of TESLA for verification are the median of 100 verifications. The reason for not reporting the median for TESLA signing performance is that because of the rejection sampling, it would be overly optimistic. For all software results we report the sizes of keys and signatures actually produced by the software, not the theoretically smallest possible sizes with full compression.[2]

As can be seen in Table 3, TESLA is several magnitudes faster and sizes are smaller than the only other lattice-based signature scheme that is also proven tightly secure in the quantum random oracle model for the same (classical) security of 96 bits. However, the signature generation and verification algorithms of TESLA-0 are much slower than the implementation of [47] for the same level of security. This is due to the large difference of the parameters chosen, $e.g.$, the matrix dimension m in TESLA-0 is 3156, while $m = 840$ in the parameter set DEG$^+$ proposed by Dagdelen $et\ al.$ [47]. Note that the parameter set TESLA-0 is chosen according to our security reduction, while the set DEG$^+$ is not chosen according to the (non-tight) security reduction given in [6].

In the (as of yet quite small) realm of signatures that offer 128 bits of post-quantum security, TESLA-2 offers an alternative to SPHINCS. Public and secret keys of TESLA-2 are much larger than SPHINCS keys, but signatures are several magnitudes smaller. The post-quantum multivariate-based signature scheme Rainbow5640 [19,21] performs best among all listed schemes but unfortunately, comes with no security reduction to its underlying problem.

Acknowledgments. We are especially grateful to Peter Schwabe for contributions to our software implementation and to the presentation of the paper. We thank Chris Peikert for pointing out a flaw in previous security reductions for TESLA in the random oracle model. We thank Steven Galbraith and anonymous reviewers for valuable feedback on an earlier version of this manuscript.

This work has been supported by the German Research Foundation (DFG) as part of project P1 within the CRC 1119 CROSSING, by TÜBITAK under 2214-A Doctoral Research Program Grant and 2211-C PhD Scholarship, by Ege University under project 2014-FEN-065, and by CryptoWorks21.

---

[2] We make an exception for BLISS. The authors of the software obviously did not spend any effort on reducing the size of signatures and keys; we report sizes with "trivial" compression through choosing native data types of appropriate sizes.

References

1. Abdalla, M., Fouque, P.-A., Lyubashevsky, V., Tibouchi, M.: Tightly-secure signatures from lossy identification schemes. In: Pointcheval, D., Johansson, T. (eds.) EUROCRYPT 2012. LNCS, vol. 7237, pp. 572–590. Springer, Heidelberg (2012). doi:10.1007/978-3-642-29011-4_34
2. Akleylek, S., Bindel, N., Buchmann, J., Krämer, J., Marson, G.A.: An efficient lattice-based signature scheme with provably secure instantiation. In: Pointcheval, D., Nitaj, A., Rachidi, T. (eds.) AFRICACRYPT 2016. LNCS, vol. 9646, pp. 44–60. Springer, Cham (2016). doi:10.1007/978-3-319-31517-1_3
3. Albrecht, M.R., Player, R., Scott, S.: On the concrete hardness of learning with errors. J. Math. Cryptol. **9**, 169–203 (2015)
4. Alkim, E., Bindel, N., Buchmann, J., Dagdelen, Ö., Schwabe, P.: TESLA: tightly-secure efficient signatures from standard lattices. Cryptology ePrint Archive, Report 2015/755, version 20161117:055833 (2015)
5. Alkim, E., Ducas, L., Pöppelmann, T., Schwabe, P.: Post-quantum key exchange–a new hope. In: 25th USENIX Security Symposium. USENIX Association (2016)
6. Bai, S., Galbraith, S.D.: An improved compression technique for signatures based on learning with errors. In: Benaloh, J. (ed.) CT-RSA 2014. LNCS, vol. 8366, pp. 28–47. Springer, Cham (2014). doi:10.1007/978-3-319-04852-9_2
7. El Bansarkhani, R., Buchmann, J.: Improvement and efficient implementation of a lattice-based signature scheme. In: Lange, T., Lauter, K., Lisoněk, P. (eds.) SAC 2013. LNCS, vol. 8282, pp. 48–67. Springer, Heidelberg (2014). doi:10.1007/978-3-662-43414-7_3
8. Barreto, P.S.L.M., Longa, P., Naehrig, M., Ricardini, J.E., Zanon, G.: Sharper ring-LWE signatures. Cryptology ePrint Archive, Report 2016/1026 (2016)
9. Barwood, G.: Digital signatures using elliptic curves. message 32f519ad.19609226@news.dial.pipex.com posted to sci.crypt (1997). http://groups.google.com/group/sci.crypt/msg/b28aba37180dd6c6
10. Bellare, M., Hofheinz, D., Yilek, S.: Possibility and impossibility results for encryption and commitment secure under selective opening. In: Joux, A. (ed.) EUROCRYPT 2009. LNCS, vol. 5479, pp. 1–35. Springer, Heidelberg (2009). doi:10.1007/978-3-642-01001-9_1
11. Bennett, C.H., Bernstein, E., Brassard, G., Vazirani, U.: Strengths and weaknesses of quantum computing. SIAM J. Comput. **26**(5), 1510–1523 (1997)
12. Bernstein, D.J., Duif, N., Lange, T., Schwabe, P., Yang, B.-Y.: High-speed high-security signatures. In: Preneel, B., Takagi, T. (eds.) CHES 2011. LNCS, vol. 6917, pp. 124–142. Springer, Heidelberg (2011). doi:10.1007/978-3-642-23951-9_9
13. Bernstein, D.J., Hopwood, D., Hülsing, A., Lange, T., Niederhagen, R., Papachristodoulou, L., Schneider, M., Schwabe, P., Wilcox-O'Hearn, Z.: SPHINCS: practical stateless hash-based signatures. In: Oswald, E., Fischlin, M. (eds.) EUROCRYPT 2015. LNCS, vol. 9056, pp. 368–397. Springer, Heidelberg (2015). doi:10.1007/978-3-662-46800-5_15
14. Bernstein, D.J., Lange, T.: eBACS: ECRYPT benchmarking of cryptographic systems. http://bench.cr.yp.to. Accessed 19 May 2015
15. Boneh, D., Dagdelen, Ö., Fischlin, M., Lehmann, A., Schaffner, C., Zhandry, M.: Random oracles in a quantum world. In: Lee, D.H., Wang, X. (eds.) ASIACRYPT 2011. LNCS, vol. 7073, pp. 41–69. Springer, Heidelberg (2011). doi:10.1007/978-3-642-25385-0_3

16. Bos, J.W., Costello, C., Ducas, L., Mironov, I., Naehrig, M., Nikolaenko, V., Raghunathan, A., Stebila, D.: Frodo: take off the ring! practical, quantum-secure key exchange from LWE. In: CCS 2016. ACM (2016)

17. Boyen, X., Li, Q.: Towards tightly secure lattice short signature and id-based encryption. In: Cheon, J.H., Takagi, T. (eds.) ASIACRYPT 2016. LNCS, vol. 10032, pp. 404–434. Springer, Heidelberg (2016). doi:10.1007/978-3-662-53890-6_14

18. Chatterjee, S., Koblitz, N., Menezes, A., Sarkar, P.: Another look at tightness II: practical issues in cryptography. Cryptology ePrint Archive, Report 2016/360 (2016)

19. Chen, A.I.-T., Chen, M.-S., Chen, T.-R., Cheng, C.-M., Ding, J., Kuo, E.L.-H., Lee, F.Y.-S., Yang, B.-Y.: SSE implementation of multivariate PKCs on modern x86 CPUs. In: Clavier, C., Gaj, K. (eds.) CHES 2009. LNCS, vol. 5747, pp. 33–48. Springer, Heidelberg (2009). doi:10.1007/978-3-642-04138-9_3

20. Chen, Y., Nguyen, P.Q.: BKZ 2.0: better lattice security estimates. In: Lee, D.H., Wang, X. (eds.) ASIACRYPT 2011. LNCS, vol. 7073, pp. 1–20. Springer, Heidelberg (2011). doi:10.1007/978-3-642-25385-0_1

21. Ding, J., Schmidt, D.: Rainbow, a new multivariable polynomial signature scheme. In: Ioannidis, J., Keromytis, A., Yung, M. (eds.) ACNS 2005. LNCS, vol. 3531, pp. 164–175. Springer, Heidelberg (2005). doi:10.1007/11496137_12

22. Ducas, L., Durmus, A., Lepoint, T., Lyubashevsky, V.: Lattice signatures and bimodal gaussians. In: Canetti, R., Garay, J.A. (eds.) CRYPTO 2013. LNCS, vol. 8042, pp. 40–56. Springer, Heidelberg (2013). doi:10.1007/978-3-642-40041-4_3

23. Ducas, L.: Accelerating bliss: the geometry of ternary polynomials. Cryptology ePrint Archive, Report 2014/874 (2014)

24. Eaton, E., Song, F.: Making existential-unforgeable signatures strongly unforgeable in the quantum random-oracle model. In: 10th Conference on the Theory of Quantum Computation, Communication and Cryptography, TQC 2015 (2015)

25. Gentry, C., Peikert, C., Vaikuntanathan, V.: Trapdoors for hard lattices and new cryptographic constructions. In: STOC 2008. ACM (2008)

26. Güneysu, T., Lyubashevsky, V., Pöppelmann, T.: Practical lattice-based cryptography: a signature scheme for embedded systems. In: Prouff, E., Schaumont, P. (eds.) CHES 2012. LNCS, vol. 7428, pp. 530–547. Springer, Heidelberg (2012). doi:10.1007/978-3-642-33027-8_31

27. Güneysu, T., Oder, T., Pöppelmann, T., Schwabe, P.: Software speed records for lattice-based signatures. In: Gaborit, P. (ed.) PQCrypto 2013. LNCS, vol. 7932, pp. 67–82. Springer, Heidelberg (2013). doi:10.1007/978-3-642-38616-9_5

28. Katz, J., Wang, N.: Efficiency improvements for signature schemes with tight security reductions. In: CCS 2003. ACM (2003)

29. Kaye, P., Laflamme, R., Mosca, M.: An Introduction to Quantum Computing. Oxford University Press Inc., New York (2007)

30. Koblitz, N., Menezes, A.: Another look at "provable security". II. In: Barua, R., Lange, T. (eds.) INDOCRYPT 2006. LNCS, vol. 4329, pp. 148–175. Springer, Heidelberg (2006). doi:10.1007/11941378_12

31. Koblitz, N., Menezes, A.: The random oracle model: a twenty-year retrospective. Des. Codes Crypt. 77(2), 587–610 (2015)

32. Laarhoven, T., Mosca, M., van de Pol, J.: Finding shortest lattice vectors faster using quantum search. Des. Codes Crypt. 77(2), 375–400 (2015)

33. Lyubashevsky, V.: Lattice signatures without trapdoors. In: Pointcheval, D., Johansson, T. (eds.) EUROCRYPT 2012. LNCS, vol. 7237, pp. 738–755. Springer, Heidelberg (2012). doi:10.1007/978-3-642-29011-4_43

34. Micciancio, D., Walter, M.: Fast lattice point enumeration with minimal overhead. In: SODA 2015. SIAM (2015)

35. Montanaro, A.: Quantum walk speedup of backtracking algorithms. arXiv preprint arXiv:1509.02374 (2016)

36. M'Raïhi, D., Naccache, D., Pointcheval, D., Vaudenay, S.: Computational alternatives to random number generators. In: Tavares, S., Meijer, H. (eds.) SAC 1998. LNCS, vol. 1556, pp. 72–80. Springer, Heidelberg (1999). doi:10.1007/3-540-48892-8_6

37. Nielsen, M.A., Chuang, I.L.: Quantum Computation and Quantum Information. Cambridge University Press, Cambridge, New York (2000)

38. Peikert, C.: A decade of lattice cryptography. Cryptology ePrint Archive, Report 2015/939 (2015)

39. Peikert, C., Vaikuntanathan, V., Waters, B.: A framework for efficient and composable oblivious transfer. In: Wagner, D. (ed.) CRYPTO 2008. LNCS, vol. 5157, pp. 554–571. Springer, Heidelberg (2008). doi:10.1007/978-3-540-85174-5_31

40. Peikert, C., Waters, B.: Lossy trapdoor functions and their applications. In: STOC 2008. ACM (2008)

41. Pointcheval, D., Stern, J.: Security proofs for signature schemes. In: Maurer, U. (ed.) EUROCRYPT 1996. LNCS, vol. 1070, pp. 387–398. Springer, Heidelberg (1996). doi:10.1007/3-540-68339-9_33

42. Regev, O.: On lattices, learning with errors, random linear codes, and cryptography. In: STOC 2005. ACM (2005)

43. Schmidt, M.: Estimation of the hardness of the learning with errors problem with a restricted number of samples. GitHub (2017). https://bitbucket.org/Ma_Schmidt/lwe-estimator

44. Schmidt, M., Bindel, N.: Estimation of the hardness of the learning with errors problem with a restricted number of samples. Cryptology ePrint Archive, Report 2017/140 (2017)

45. Unruh, D.: Quantum position verification in the random oracle model. In: Garay, J.A., Gennaro, R. (eds.) CRYPTO 2014. LNCS, vol. 8617, pp. 1–18. Springer, Heidelberg (2014). doi:10.1007/978-3-662-44381-1_1

46. Wigley, J.: Removing need for RNG in signatures. message 5gov5dpad@wapping.ecs.soton.ac.uk posted to sci.crypt (1997). http://groups.google.com/group/sci.crypt/msg/a6da45bcc8939a89

47. Dagdelen, Ö., El Bansarkhani, R., Göpfert, F., Güneysu, T., Oder, T., Pöppelmann, T., Sánchez, A.H., Schwabe, P.: High-speed signatures from standard lattices. In: Aranha, D.F., Menezes, A. (eds.) LATINCRYPT 2014. LNCS, vol. 8895, pp. 84–103. Springer, Cham (2015). doi:10.1007/978-3-319-16295-9_5

Cryptanalysis of RLWE-Based One-Pass Authenticated Key Exchange

Boru Gong[1,2] and Yunlei Zhao[1,2(✉)]

[1] Shanghai Key Laboratory of Data Science, School of Computer Science,
Fudan University, Shanghai, China
{gongboru,ylzhao}@fudan.edu.cn
[2] State Key Laboratory of Cryptology, Beijing, China

Abstract. Authenticated key exchange (AKE) plays a fundamental role in modern cryptography. Up to now, the HMQV protocol family is among the most efficient provably secure AKE protocols, which has been widely standardized and in use. Given recent advances in quantum computing, it would be desirable to develop lattice-based analogue of HMQV for the possible upcoming post-quantum era. Towards this goal, a family of AKE schemes from ideal lattice was recently proposed at Eurocrypt 2015 [ZZD+15], which could be seen as an HMQV-analogue based on the ring-LWE (RLWE) problem. It consists a two-pass variant Π_2 and a one-pass variant Π_1.

As a *supplement* to its security analysis, we propose an efficient attack against Π_1, which is referred to as the small field attack (SFA) since it fully utilizes the algebraic structure of the ring $\mathcal{R}_q$ in RLWE. The SFA attack can efficiently recover the static private key of the victim party in Π_1, *provided adversaries are allowed to register their own public keys*. Such an assumption is reasonable in practice, but may not be allowed in the security model of Π_1 [ZZD+15]. We also show that it is hard for the victim party to even detect the attack in practice.

1 Introduction

Up to now, the HMQV protocol family [LMQ+03, Kra05, YZ13] is generally considered to be the most efficient provably secure authenticated key exchange protocol family, and has been standardized and widely in use. HMQV is built upon Diffie-Hellman (DH) [DH76], and consists of two variants: two-pass HMQV, and one-pass HMQV. Although two-pass HMQV is more frequently used in practice, one-pass HMQV itself is of great value and has many applications as well. For example, it was shown in [HK11] that one-pass HMQV implies secure deniable encryption, and has natural applications to key wrapping. However, HMQV may become vulnerable in the (possible) upcoming post-quantum era. Consequently,

The full version of this work appears at Cryptology ePrint Archive, 2016/913. This research was supported in part by NSFC (Grant Nos. 61472084 and U1536205), Shanghai innovation action project No. 16DZ1100200, and Shanghai science and technology development funds No. 16JC1400801.

T. Lange and T. Takagi (Eds.): PQCrypto 2017, LNCS 10346, pp. 163–183, 2017.
DOI: 10.1007/978-3-319-59879-6_10

it would be much desirable to develop the HMQV-analogue based on lattice problems, since lattice-based cryptosystems are commonly believed to be resistant to quantum attacks. Towards this goal, an RLWE-based HMQV-analogue from ideal lattice was recently developed in [ZZDS14, ZZD+15]. Generally speaking, this RLWE-based HMQV-analogue consists of a two-pass variant Π_2 as well as a one-pass variant Π_1. In particular, the one-pass variant Π_1 is claimed in [ZZDS14, ZZD+15] to be provably secure based on the RLWE assumption *"in a weak model similar to [Kra05]"*.

In this work, we concentrate our analysis on the one-pass AKE protocol Π_1 [ZZDS14, ZZD+15]. The main contribution of this work is that we propose an *efficient* attack against Π_1, which can recover the static private key of the honest party j (*i.e.*, the responder) in Π_1, *provided that adversaries are allowed to register public keys on behalf of itself and dishonest users*. Such an assumption is reasonable in practice, but may not be allowed in the security model of Π_1 [ZZDS14, ZZD+15]. In particular, our attack against Π_1 can be well designed such that it is hard for the victim to identify the static public key of the attacker, as well as those malicious session queries made by our attacker. In addition, our attack succeeds when instantiating Π_1 with the four groups of suggested parameters proposed in [ZZD+15, ZZDS14].

The attack proposed in this work is called *small field attack* (SFA), as it fully utilizes the algebraic property of the underlying ring $c\mathcal{R}_q$ in the RLWE setting. First and foremost, by the Chinese remainder theorem (CRT), the principal ideal $q\mathcal{R}$ of $\mathcal{R}$ could be seen as the product of n distinct nonzero prime ideals $\mathfrak{q}_1, \cdots, \mathfrak{q}_n$ in $\mathcal{R}$, each of norm q that is polynomial in the security parameter. This CRT factorization of $\mathcal{R}_q = \mathcal{R}/q\mathcal{R} = \prod_i \mathcal{R}/\mathfrak{q}_i$ admits the CRT basis $\{\mathbf{c}_1, \cdots, \mathbf{c}_n\}$ for $\mathcal{R}_q$, an $\mathbb{F}_q$-basis for the free $\mathbb{F}_q$-module $\mathcal{R}_q$; What is more, $\sum u_i \mathbf{c}_i \cdot \sum v_i \mathbf{c}_i = \sum u_i v_i \cdot \mathbf{c}_i$ for every $u_i, v_i \in \mathbb{F}_q$. At a very high level, these properties of the CRT basis make it possible for us to recover, in a sequential manner, the CRT-coefficients of the static private key of the honest party j in Π_1.

Our analysis can be briefly summarized as follows, as depicted in Fig. 1.

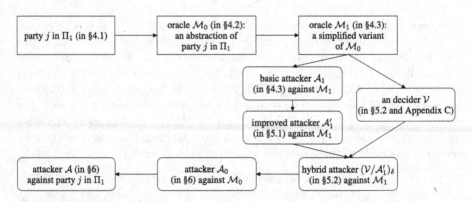

Fig. 1. The presentation organization of SFA, where the arrows indicate the order in which our analysis is carried out.

- In Sect. 4, we first review Π_1, and then abstract part of valid functionalities of party j as an oracle $\mathcal{M}_0$ with private key. To efficiently recover the static private key of party j in Π_1, it suffices to show how to recover the private key of $\mathcal{M}_0$ efficiently. To do so, we then define a simplified variant of $\mathcal{M}_0$, i.e., $\mathcal{M}_1$ with secret, which corresponds to the special case when the static public key of the attacker against $\mathcal{M}_0$ is $\mathbf{0} \in \mathcal{R}_q$ by default. Finally, a basic yet efficient attacker $\mathcal{A}_1$ is constructed that can recover the secret of $\mathcal{M}_1$.

  As a concrete instance of SFA, $\mathcal{A}_1$ implies that there exists an efficient attacker with static public key $\mathbf{0} \in \mathcal{R}_q$ who can break party j in Π_1. This basic attacker already demonstrates the insecurity of Π_1 in practice, which is, however, can be easily detected and prevented.

- In Sect. 5, we continue our analysis on $\mathcal{M}_1$ and construct an efficient attacker $(\mathcal{V}/\mathcal{A}_1')_\delta$ that can break $\mathcal{M}_1$; And, the queries made by $(\mathcal{V}/\mathcal{A}_1')_\delta$ are well designed such that it is hard for $\mathcal{M}_1$ to distinguish those malicious queries from honestly generated ones in practice.

  The attacker $(\mathcal{V}/\mathcal{A}_1')_\delta$ implies that there exists an efficient attacker, still with static public key $\mathbf{0} \in \mathcal{R}_q$, who can break party j in Π_1; Moreover, every query made by this attacker to party j is as "random-looking" as possible.

- In Sect. 6, we switch our analysis back to $\mathcal{M}_0$, and design an "undetectable" attacker $\mathcal{A}_0$ against $\mathcal{M}_0$, which is very similar to $(\mathcal{V}/\mathcal{A}_1')_\delta$ and can break $\mathcal{M}_0$ via a sequence of random-looking queries; Furthermore, motivated by the construction of $(\mathcal{V}/\mathcal{A}_1')_\delta$, the static public key of $\mathcal{A}_0$ can be well formed such that it is hard in practice for $\mathcal{M}_0$ to distinguish the static public key of $\mathcal{A}_0$ from that of an honest user.

  It follows immediately from the construction of $\mathcal{A}_0$ that we can design an "undetectable" attacker $\mathcal{A}$ that can break party j in $\overline{\Pi}_1$, and it is hard in practice for party j to identify either the static public key of $\mathcal{A}$ or those malicious queries made by $\mathcal{A}$.[1]

Security Model of Π_1. It is noteworthy that [ZZDS14, ZZD+15] do not describe precise definitions and proofs of its security claims for Π_1. Instead, some properties of this security model are discussed. For instance, it is claimed in [ZZDS14, ZZD+15] that Π_1 cannot provide forward secrecy and does not stop replays, just as the one-pass HMQV, and that Π_1 "can be proven in a weak model similar to [Kra05]"; What is more, Π_1 "can essentially be used as a KEM, and can be transformed into a CCA-secure encryption in the random oracle model by combining it with a CPA-secure symmetric-key encryption together with a MAC algorithm in a standard way (where both keys are derived from the session key in the one-pass protocol)". In addition, this CCA-secure encryption allows sender authentication and deniability.

Though some of the claims regarding the security model/proof of Π_1 are unclear to us, as far as we can see, the natural interpretation of the foregoing

---

[1] We remark that SFA does not apply to the two-pass protocol Π_2 in [ZZDS14, ZZD+15], since the static private key of party j is protected by its ephemeral private key in Π_2.

CCA-security claim about Π_1 is disproved by our SFA attack. We argue that, no matter what the precise interpretations of original security claims were, our attack shows that Π_1 is dangerous in practice, on the following grounds. In our SFA attack, it is hard to distinguish the public key registered by a malicious user from the public key honestly generated. Moreover, as the malicious user does know the private key corresponding to the registered public key, traditional mechanisms for proof-of-knowledge (POK) or proof-of-possession (POP) of private key, $e.g.$, via requiring the user to sign a random message with the registered public key, does not prevent our SFA attack. From our point of view, forbidding adversary from registering public keys on behalf of dishonest users, on the one hand, seems to be unrealistic in practice; And, on the other hand, such a security model seems to be too "weak" as naturally insecure protocol could be proved secure within.

Related Works. The work [Flu16] demonstrates, *in general*, the danger of reusing public key for RLWE-based key exchange. But there are some differences, *in nature*, between our work and [Flu16]. First, [Flu16] considers the simple scenario where the attacker only uses ephemeral public keys, while for SFA against Π_1 the attacker has to mix its public key and ephemeral public keys, making it significantly harder to attack and analyze. Second, it is easy to detect and prevent the attack proposed in [Flu16], which is in contrast to our SFA that is almost undetectable in practice. Third, our SFA critically relies on the properties of the CRT basis for $\mathcal{R}_q$, while [Flu16] employs the power basis. Though our SFA could be simplified to work in the scenario considered in [Flu16], to our knowledge, we do not know how to apply the approach of [Flu16] and its like to break Π_1. Actually, as discussed in [DARF16], no existing concrete one-pass AKE scheme was affected with attack considered in [Flu16].

2   Preliminaries

Let λ denote the security parameters throughout this work. Let $\mathbb{B} \triangleq \{0, 1\}$. For every positive integer k, let $[k]$ denote the finite set $\{1, 2, \cdots, k\} \subseteq \mathbb{Z}$. For an odd integer $p > 0$, let $\mathbb{Z}_p \triangleq \{-(p-1)/2, \cdots, (p-1)/2\}$.

Throughout this work, let $n \geq 16$ be a power-of-two, and $q = \text{poly}(\lambda)$ be a positive rational prime such that $q \equiv 1 \pmod{2n}$. When q is clear, define $q_0 \triangleq (q-1)/2$. Let $\mathbb{F}_q \triangleq \mathbb{Z}/q\mathbb{Z}$ be the finite field of prime order q, and every element in $\mathbb{F}_q$ is represented by a unique element in $\{-q_0, \cdots, q_0\}$. Let $\mathbb{F}_q^\times \triangleq \mathbb{F}_q \setminus \{0\}$.

The n-dimensional (column) vector $(u_1, \cdots, u_n)^t$ is usually abbreviated as $[u_j]_{j \in [n]}$. Let $\mathbf{0} \triangleq (0, \cdots, 0)^t \in \mathbb{F}_q^n$. When either $\mathbf{u} \in \mathbb{F}_q^n$ or $\mathbf{u} \in \mathbb{Z}^n$, let $\|\mathbf{u}\|_2$ and $\|\mathbf{u}\|_\infty$ denote the ℓ_2- and ℓ_∞-norms of $\mathbf{u}$, respectively. When n and q are clear, define the projection $\mu_j : \mathbb{F}_q^n \to \mathbb{F}_q$ for every $j \in [n]$ such that $\mu_j\left([u_j]_{j \in [n]}\right) \triangleq u_j$.

For an event E, we say that E occurs *with overwhelming probability* if $\Pr[\neg E]$ is negligible (in λ); For simplicity, the phrase "with overwhelming probability" is usually abbreviated as "*w.o.p.*" in this work. For a *finite* set S, let $x \leftarrow S$ denote a sample drawn from the *uniform* distribution over the set S.

3   The CRT Basis in the Ring-LWE Setting

Section 3.1 reviews the ring-LWE(RLWE) problem. In Sect. 3.2, the CRT basis in the RLWE setting is first recalled, followed by its algebraic properties that are essential for our small field attack.

3.1   The Ring-LWE Problem

The Rings $\mathcal{R}$ and $\mathcal{R}_q$. Let $\zeta \in \mathbb{C}$ denote a primitive $2n$-th root of unity, and its minimum polynomial over $\mathbb{Q}$ is the $2n$-th cyclotomic polynomial $\Phi_{2n}(x) \triangleq x^n + 1 \in \mathbb{Z}[x]$. Let $\mathcal{R} \triangleq \mathbb{Z}[\zeta]$ be the ring of integers in $\mathbb{Q}(\zeta)/\mathbb{Q}$. Moreover, define the principal ideal $\langle q \rangle = q\mathcal{R}$ and its associated quotient ring $\mathcal{R}_q \triangleq \mathcal{R}/q\mathcal{R}$.

In this work, each coset of $q\mathcal{R}$ in $\mathcal{R}$ is naturally represented by a *unique* element in the set $\left\{ \sum_{j \in [n]} u_j \zeta^{j-1} \,\middle|\, u_j \in \mathbb{F}_q \right\}$. Clearly every $\mathbf{u} = \sum_{j \in [n]} u_j \zeta^{j-1} \in \mathcal{R}_q$ could be identified with the vector $(u_1, \cdots, u_n)^t = [u_j]_{j \in [n]} \in \mathbb{F}_q^n$, and *vice versa*. Such identification is denoted as $\mathbf{u} \sim [u_i]_{i \in [n]}$ for simplicity. Hence, every n-dimensional vector in $\mathbb{F}_q^n$ can be regarded as an element of $\mathcal{R}_q$ in the *natural* way when necessary, *and vice versa*. It follows that the domain of the projection $\mu_j(\cdot)$ defined previously could be generalized to $\mathcal{R}_q$ in the sense that $\mu_j \left(\sum_{j \in [n]} u_j \cdot \zeta^{j-1} \right) \triangleq u_j \in \mathbb{F}_q$ for every $j \in [n]$. Moreover, let $\mu(\mathbf{u}) \triangleq [\mu_j(\mathbf{u})]_{j \in [n]}$. It is understood $\|\mathbf{u}\|_\ell \triangleq \|\mu(\mathbf{u})\|_\ell$ for $\mathbf{u} \in \mathcal{R}_q, \ell \in \{2, \infty\}$. In particular, let $\mathbf{0}$ denote both the vector $(0, \cdots, 0)^t \in \mathbb{F}_q^n$ and the zero element of $\mathcal{R}_q$ in the sequel, which would be clear from the context.

The Discrete Gaussian Distribution. Let $D_{\mathbb{Z},\alpha}$ denote the 1-dimensional *discrete* Gaussian distribution over $\mathbb{Z}$, and let $D_{\mathbb{Z}^n,\alpha}$ denote the n-dimensional *spherical* discrete Gaussian distribution over $\mathbb{Z}^n$, where each coordinate is drawn *independently* from $D_{\mathbb{Z},\alpha}$. When $\alpha = \omega(\sqrt{\log n})$, almost every sample $\varepsilon \leftarrow D_{\mathbb{Z}^n,\alpha}$ is "short" in the sense that $\|\varepsilon\|_2 \leq \alpha\sqrt{n}$ holds *w.o.p.* [Reg09,LPR13a]. For the "short" noise $\varepsilon \leftarrow D_{\mathbb{Z}^n,\alpha}$, it could be seen as an element of $\mathcal{R}$ in the natural way; Moreover, when $q > 1 + 2\alpha\sqrt{n}$, *except with negligible probability*, ε could be considered to be an element of $\mathbb{F}_q^n$ (and hence of $\mathcal{R}_q$) in the *natural* way.

Lemma 1 states the product of several "short" noises in $\mathcal{R}$ is also "short".

Lemma 1. *Let $n = \mathrm{poly}(\lambda) \geq 16$ be a power-of-two. If $\alpha_i = \omega(\sqrt{\log n})$ and $e_i \leftarrow D_{\mathbb{Z}^n,\alpha_i}$ for every $i \in \{1,2,3\}$, then every e_i could be regarded as an element of $\mathcal{R}$ w.o.p. in the natural way. Moreover, the inequalities $\|e_1 e_2\|_\infty \leq n \cdot \alpha_1 \alpha_2, \|e_1 e_2 e_3\|_\infty \leq n^2 \cdot \alpha_1 \alpha_2 \alpha_3$ holds w.o.p.* $\qquad\square$

The RLWE Problem. Here we review a *special* case of the *original* ring-LWE (RLWE) problem [LPR13a], since this special case, instead of the original one, serves as the underlying hard problem of Π_1 [ZZDS14,ZZD+15].

Each RLWE instance is parameterized by $n = n(\lambda), q = q(\lambda)$, and $\alpha = \alpha(\lambda) \geq 0$, where $n \geq 16$ is a power-of-two, q is a positive rational prime such that

$q \equiv 1 \pmod{2n}$. For every (fixed) $\mathbf{s} \in \mathcal{R}_q$, define the RLWE distribution $A_{n,q,\alpha,\mathbf{s}}$ over $\mathcal{R}_q \times \mathcal{R}_q$: every sample drawn from $A_{n,q,\alpha,\mathbf{s}}$ is of the form $(\mathbf{a}, \mathbf{b} = \mathbf{as} + 2\varepsilon)$, where $\mathbf{a} \leftarrow \mathcal{R}_q, \varepsilon \leftarrow D_{\mathbb{Z}^n,\alpha}$.

Definition 1 [LPR13a,LPR13b,DD12]. *The search variant of the RLWE problem is defined as follows: given access to arbitrarily many independent samples drawn from $A_{n,q,\alpha,s}$ for some $s \leftarrow D_{\mathbb{Z}^n,\alpha}$, the problem asks to recover $s \in \mathcal{R}_q$. In contrast, the decisional variant asks to distinguish, with non-negligible advantage, between arbitrarily many independent samples from $A_{n,q,\alpha,s}$ for $s \leftarrow D_{\mathbb{Z}^n,\alpha}$, and the same number of uniformly random and independent samples drawn from the uniform distribution over $\mathcal{R}_q \times \mathcal{R}_q$.*

3.2 The CRT Basis for $\mathcal{R}_q$ and Its Properties

The notion of the CRT basis in the RLWE setting was first proposed in [LPR13a]. Here we first review its definition and basic properties; After that, we present an algebraic property, *i.e.*, Lemma 3, regarding the CRT basis for $\mathcal{R}_q$, which would be *essential* for our efficient SFA attackers to be developed later.

When n, q are clear, let $\{\omega_1, \cdots, \omega_n\} \subseteq \mathbb{F}_q^\times$ be the set of elements in $\mathbb{F}_q^\times$ that are of multiplicative order $2n$. By assumption on q, $q\mathcal{R} = \mathfrak{q}_1 \cdots \mathfrak{q}_n \in \mathcal{R}$, where every nonzero prime ideal $\mathfrak{q}_i = \langle q, \zeta - \omega_i \rangle$ by a suitable ordering, and the norm of every $\mathfrak{q}_i$ in $\mathcal{R}$ is q. Hence, every quotient ring $\mathcal{R}/\mathfrak{q}_i$ is a finite field of prime order q, indicating $\mathcal{R}/\mathfrak{q}_i \cong \mathbb{F}_q$. As the *distinct* nonzero prime ideals $\mathfrak{q}_1, \cdots, \mathfrak{q}_n$ are necessarily pairwise coprime, it follows from the Chinese remainder theorem (CRT) that $\mathcal{R}_q = \mathcal{R}/q\mathcal{R} \cong \prod_{i \in [n]} \mathcal{R}/\mathfrak{q}_i$ under the *natural ring isomorphism* $\mathbf{u}+q\mathcal{R} \mapsto (\mathbf{u}+\mathfrak{q}_1, \cdots, \mathbf{u}+\mathfrak{q}_n)$. Stated differently, the ring $\mathcal{R}_q$ could be identified with the direct product of n *small* finite field, each of prime order $q = \text{poly}(\lambda)$. This explains how our notion of small field attack bears its name.

By the CRT factorization of $\mathcal{R}_q$, we can find n elements $\mathbf{c}_1, \cdots, \mathbf{c}_n \in \mathcal{R}$ such that $\mathbf{c}_i \equiv \delta_{i,j} \pmod{\mathfrak{q}_j}$ for every $i, j \in [n]$, where $\delta_{\cdot,\cdot}$ denotes the Kronecker delta function. Clearly $\mathbf{c}_1, \cdots, \mathbf{c}_n$ form an *integral* basis for $\mathcal{R}$, and is called *a CRT basis for $\mathcal{R}$* (relative to $\mathfrak{q}_1, \cdots, \mathfrak{q}_n$). Moreover, it is easy to see any two CRT bases for $\mathcal{R}$ (relative to $\mathfrak{q}_1, \cdots, \mathfrak{q}_n$) are *equivalent* up to mod $q\mathcal{R}$. In particular, when $\mathbf{c}_1, \cdots, \mathbf{c}_n$ fall into the set $\mathcal{R}_q = \left\{ \sum_{j \in [n]} u_j \zeta^{j-1} \,\middle|\, u_j \in \mathbb{F}_q \right\}$, they form an $\mathbb{F}_q$-basis for the free $\mathbb{F}_q$-module $\mathcal{R}_q$; By definition, this $\mathbb{F}_q$-basis is *unique* in $\mathcal{R}_q$ up to ordering, which would be called *the CRT basis for $\mathcal{R}_q$* hereafter.

Lemma 2 [LPR13a,LPR13b]. *For the CRT basis $\{\mathbf{c}_1, \cdots, \mathbf{c}_n\}$ for $\mathcal{R}_q$,*

(a) Given n, q (in unary form), the CRT basis for $\mathcal{R}_q$ could be found efficiently.
(b) Every $\mathbf{u} \in \mathcal{R}_q$ can be written uniquely as $\mathbf{u} = \sum_{i \in [n]} u_i \cdot \mathbf{c}_i$, $u_i \in \mathbb{F}_q$.
(c) For every $k \in \mathbb{F}_q, \mathbf{u} = \sum_{i \in [n]} u_i \cdot \mathbf{c}_i$ and $\mathbf{v} = \sum_{i \in [n]} v_i \cdot \mathbf{c}_i$, $u_i, v_i \in \mathbb{F}_q$, we have $k \cdot \mathbf{u} = \sum (k u_i) \mathbf{c}_i$, $\mathbf{u} + \mathbf{v} = \sum (u_i + v_i) \mathbf{c}_i$, and $\mathbf{u} \cdot \mathbf{v} = \sum (u_i v_i) \mathbf{c}_i$. ☐

Throughout this work, when n, q are clear from the context, let $\{\mathbf{c}_1, \cdots, \mathbf{c}_n\}$ denote the CRT basis for $\mathcal{R}_q$; Moreover, define $c_{i,j} \triangleq \mu_j(\mathbf{c}_i) \in \mathbb{F}_q$ for every

$i, j \in [n]$. Thus, every $\mathbf{c}_i = \sum_{j \in [n]} c_{i,j} \cdot \zeta^{j-1}$. With the CRT basis $\{\mathbf{c}_1, \cdots, \mathbf{c}_n\}$ for $\mathcal{R}_q$ in mind, define the map $\eta_i : \mathcal{R}_q \to \mathbb{F}_q$ for every $i \in [n]$, where $\eta_i \left(\sum_{i \in [n]} (u_i \cdot \mathbf{c}_i) \right) \triangleq u_i$, $u_i \in \mathbb{F}_q$. Clearly, the map $\eta_i(\cdot)$ is *well-defined* and *efficiently computable*. Every $\eta_i(\mathbf{u})$ is called a *CRT-coefficient* of $\mathbf{u} \in \mathcal{R}_q$. Finally, define $\mathsf{Dim}(\mathbf{u}) \triangleq \{i \in [n] \mid \eta_i(\mathbf{u}) \neq 0 \in \mathbb{F}_q\} \subseteq [n]$ for every $\mathbf{u} \in \mathcal{R}_q$.

Finally, we present an algebraic property of the CRT basis for $\mathcal{R}_q$, which is *essential* for our small field attacks against Π_1. The proof of this lemma is already implicit in [LPR13a, LPR13b], but we reprove it here for completeness.

Lemma 3. *For every $i, j \in [n]$, we have $c_{i,j} = c_{i,n} \cdot \omega_i^{n-j} \neq 0 \in \mathbb{F}_q$.*

Proof. Fix $i \in [n]$. For the element $\zeta \in \mathcal{R}$, we have $\zeta + \mathfrak{q}_i = \zeta + \langle q, \zeta - \omega_i \rangle = \omega_i + \langle q, \zeta - \omega_i \rangle \in \mathcal{R}/\mathfrak{q}_i$, and hence $\zeta \equiv \omega_i \cdot \mathbf{c}_i \pmod{\mathfrak{q}_i}$.

On the one hand, we have $\zeta \cdot \mathbf{c}_i = \omega_i \cdot \mathbf{c}_i = \sum_{j \in [n]} (\omega_i \cdot c_{i,j}) \zeta^{j-1} \in \mathcal{R}_q$ by Lemma 2. On the other hand, it is routine to verify

$$\zeta \cdot \mathbf{c}_i = \zeta \cdot \left(c_{i,1} + c_{i,2}\zeta + \cdots + c_{i,n}\zeta^{n-1} \right) = c_{i,n}\zeta^n + \sum_{j \in [n-1]} c_{i,j}\zeta^j = -c_{i,n} + \sum_{j \in [n-1]} c_{i,j}\zeta^j,$$

where the equality $\mathbf{0} = \Phi_{2n}(\zeta) = \zeta^n + 1 \in \mathcal{R}_q$ is implicitly applied.

As $\zeta^0, \zeta, \cdots, \zeta^{n-1}$ form an $\mathbb{F}_q$-basis for the $\mathbb{F}_q$-module $\mathcal{R}_q$, we have

$$c_{i,1} = \omega_i c_{i,2}, \quad c_{i,2} = \omega_i c_{i,3}, \quad \cdots, \quad c_{i,n-1} = \omega_i c_{i,n}, \quad -c_{i,n} = \omega_i c_{i,1};$$

Equivalently, $c_{i,j} = c_{i,n} \cdot \omega_i^{n-j} \in \mathbb{F}_q$ for every $j \in [n]$. It follows from the definition that $c_{i,n} \neq 0$, and hence $c_{i,j} \neq 0$ for every $j \in [n]$. $\square$

4   How to Attack Π_1: A Warm-Up

We first review the one-pass AKE scheme Π_1 [ZZDS14, ZZD+15] in Sect. 4.1; Then in Sect. 4.2, the honest party j in Π_1 is abstracted as an oracle $\mathcal{M}_0$ with private key, such that to efficiently recover the static private key of party j in Π_1, it suffices to show how to recover the private key of $\mathcal{M}_0$ efficiently, *provided that adversaries are allowed to register public keys on behalf of dishonest users*. Finally, we construct in Sect. 4.3 a basic yet *efficient* attacker $\mathcal{A}_1$ against the oracle $\mathcal{M}_1$, *i.e.*, a simplified variant of $\mathcal{M}_0$.

4.1   The One-Pass AKE Scheme Π_1

The one-pass AKE scheme Π_1 [ZZDS14, ZZD+15] is built upon the RLWE problem in Definition 1, where every RLWE sample is of the form $(\mathbf{a}, \mathbf{as} + 2\varepsilon)$.

In Π_1, $\mathbf{a} \leftarrow \mathcal{R}_q$ is a global public parameter, and $M > 0$ is a sufficiently large constant. As a two-party AKE scheme, users in Π_1 are represented by party i (*i.e.*, the initiator) and party j (*i.e.*, the responder), respectively. For party i: the static private key is $(\mathbf{s}_i, \mathbf{e}_i)$, where $\mathbf{s}_i, \mathbf{e}_i \leftarrow D_{\mathbb{Z}^n, \alpha}$; Its associated static public key is $\mathbf{p}_i \triangleq \mathbf{as}_i + 2\mathbf{e}_i \in \mathcal{R}_q$; And its identity issued by the Certificate Authority (CA) is $\mathbf{id}_i$. Similar notations, $\mathbf{s}_j, \mathbf{e}_j \leftarrow D_{\mathbb{Z}^n,\alpha}, \mathbf{p}_j \triangleq \mathbf{a}\mathbf{s}_j + 2\mathbf{e}_j \in \mathcal{R}_q$, and $\mathbf{id}_j$, apply to party j. Let $H_1 : \{0,1\}^* \to D_{\mathbb{Z}^n,\gamma}$ be a hash function that outputs *invertible* elements in $\mathcal{R}_q$, and $H_2 : \{0,1\}^* \to \{0,1\}^*$ be the key derivation function. Both H_1 and H_2 are regarded as random oracles in Π_1.

The following functions are essential for the Π_1 in [ZZDS14, ZZD+15], as well as for the passively-secure KE scheme in [DXL12]. First, When the prime q is clear from the context, define the function $\mathsf{Parity} : \mathbb{F}_q \to \{0,1\}$, where $\mathsf{Parity}(u) \triangleq u (\mathrm{mod}\, 2) \in \{0,1\}$. Moreover, we define the function $\mathsf{Mod} : \mathbb{F}_q \times \{0,1\} \to \{0,1\}$, where $\mathsf{Mod}(u, w) \triangleq \mathsf{Parity}((u + w \cdot q_0) \bmod q) \in \{0,1\}$. Finally, define the function $\mathsf{Cha} : \mathbb{F}_q \to \{0,1\}$, such that $\mathsf{Cha}(u) = 0$ if and only if $u \in \{-\frac{q-1}{4}, \cdots, \frac{q-1}{4}\}$; Otherwise, $\mathsf{Cha}(u) = 1$. All these functions could be easily generalized to the n-dimensional case *in the component-wise manner*.

The following lemma is *essential* both for Π_1 and for our small field attack.

Lemma 4. *For every* $u \in \mathbb{F}_q$,

(a) We always have $v \triangleq u + \mathsf{Cha}(u) \cdot q_0 \in \{-q_0/2, \cdots, +q_0/2\} \subseteq \mathbb{F}_q$.
(b) The value $\mathsf{Parity}(v) = \mathsf{Mod}(u, \mathsf{Cha}(u)) \in \mathbb{B}$ *is* immune to a short even noise *in the sense that* $\mathsf{Parity}(v) = \mathsf{Parity}(v + 2e)$ *for every* $-q_0/4 < e < q_0/4$.
(c) The value $\mathsf{Parity}(v) = \mathsf{Mod}(u, \mathsf{Cha}(u)) \in \mathbb{B}$ *is* sensitive to a short odd noise *in the sense that* $\mathsf{Parity}(v + 2e - 1) \neq \mathsf{Parity}(v) \neq \mathsf{Parity}(v + 2e + 1)$ *for every* $-q_0/4 < e < q_0/4$. □

The one-pass Π_1 [ZZDS14, ZZD+15] can be roughly described in Fig. 2.

party i

sk:($\boldsymbol{s}_i \leftarrow D_{\mathbb{Z}^n,\alpha}, \boldsymbol{e}_i \leftarrow D_{\mathbb{Z}^n,\alpha}$)
pk: $\boldsymbol{p}_i = \boldsymbol{a}\boldsymbol{s}_i + 2\boldsymbol{e}_i \in \mathcal{R}_q$

party j

sk:($\boldsymbol{s}_j \leftarrow D_{\mathbb{Z}^n,\alpha}, \boldsymbol{e}_j \leftarrow D_{\mathbb{Z}^n,\alpha}$)
pk: $\boldsymbol{p}_j = \boldsymbol{a}\boldsymbol{s}_j + 2\boldsymbol{e}_j \in \mathcal{R}_q$

ephemeral sk: $\boldsymbol{r}_i, \boldsymbol{f}_i \leftarrow D_{\mathbb{Z}^n,\beta}$;
ephemeral pk: $\boldsymbol{x}_i = \boldsymbol{a}\boldsymbol{r}_i + 2\boldsymbol{f}_i$;
$\mathbf{c} = H_1(\mathbf{id}_i, \mathbf{id}_j, \boldsymbol{x}_i)$; $\boldsymbol{g}_i \leftarrow D_{\mathbb{Z}^n,\beta}$;
$\boldsymbol{k}_i = \boldsymbol{p}_j(\boldsymbol{s}_i\mathbf{c} + \boldsymbol{r}_i) + 2\boldsymbol{g}_i$; $\boldsymbol{w}_i = \mathsf{Cha}(\boldsymbol{k}_i)$
$\sigma_i = \mathsf{Mod}(\boldsymbol{k}_i, \boldsymbol{w}_i)$;
$\mathbf{sk}_i = H_2(\mathbf{id}_i, \mathbf{id}_j, \boldsymbol{x}_i, \boldsymbol{w}_i, \sigma_i)$

$\xrightarrow{(\boldsymbol{x}_i, \boldsymbol{w}_i)}$

$\mathbf{c} = H_1(\mathbf{id}_i, \mathbf{id}_j, \boldsymbol{x}_i)$; $\boldsymbol{g}_j \leftarrow D_{\mathbb{Z}^n,\alpha}$;
$\boldsymbol{k}_j = (\boldsymbol{p}_i\mathbf{c} + \boldsymbol{x}_i)\boldsymbol{s}_j + 2\mathbf{c}\boldsymbol{g}_j$;
$\sigma_j = \mathsf{Mod}(\boldsymbol{k}_j, \boldsymbol{w}_i)$;
$\mathbf{sk}_j = H_2(\mathbf{id}_i, \mathbf{id}_j, \boldsymbol{x}_i, \boldsymbol{w}_i, \sigma_j)$

Fig. 2. General description of Π_1. Note that in the *full* description of Π_1 in [ZZDS14, ZZD+15], party i applies the rejection sampling to generate a "good" $(\mathbf{x}_i, \mathbf{w}_i)$ pair. Since the efficient SFA attacker always generates his queries *dishonestly*, this technical detail does not affect our analysis and hence is omitted here for simplicity.

Correctness/Security Analysis of Π_1. For the correctness of Π_1, It is routine to verify $\mathbf{k}_i - \mathbf{k}_j = 2\left(\mathbf{cs}_i\mathbf{e}_j + \mathbf{r}_i\mathbf{e}_j + \mathbf{g}_i - \mathbf{ce}_i\mathbf{s}_j - \mathbf{f}_i\mathbf{s}_j - \mathbf{cg}_j\right)$, and hence $\|\mathbf{k}_i - \mathbf{k}_j\|_\infty \leq 2\left(n\alpha\gamma + \beta\sqrt{n} + 2n\alpha\beta + 2n^2\alpha^2\gamma\right)$ by Lemma 1. Thus, when q is sufficiently large, $\sigma_i = \mathsf{Mod}\left(\mathbf{k}_i, \mathsf{Cha}\left(\mathbf{k}_i\right)\right) = \mathsf{Mod}\left(\mathbf{k}_j, \mathsf{Cha}\left(\mathbf{k}_i\right)\right) = \sigma_j$ holds $w.o.p.$ by Lemma 4(b). In regard to its security proof, it is claimed in [ZZDS14, ZZD+15] that when $0.97n \geq 2\lambda$, $\beta = \omega(\alpha\gamma n\sqrt{n\log n})$, $q > 203$, if Definition 1 is "hard", then Π_1 is secure "in a weak model similar to [Kra05]". In addition, four groups of parameters are suggested in [ZZD+15, ZZDS14] to instantiate Π_1.

4.2   Definition of the Oracle $\mathcal{M}_0$

To simplify our discussion on how to corrupt party j in Π_1, we define in this section an oracle $\mathcal{M}_0$ which captures some valid functionalities of party j. The oracle $\mathcal{M}_0$ is well-defined so that to corrupt party j in Π_1, it suffices to show how to construct an "undetectable" attacker against $\mathcal{M}_0$, *provided that adversaries are allowed to register public keys on behalf of dishonest users in Π_1.*

Notice that in Π_1, every time party j generates its session key by invoking $\mathsf{sk}_j \triangleq H_2(\mathsf{id}_i, \mathsf{id}_j, \mathbf{x}_i, \mathbf{w}_i, \sigma_j)$, *all the input values except σ_j are known to party i.* It follows that *except with negligible probability,* if party i is able to figure out the session key sk_j of party j correctly *before* it issues the associated session-key query to party j, then party i must be able to figure out the associated σ_j *beforehand, and vice versa.*

The foregoing observation motivates us to define an oracle $\mathcal{M}_0$ with private key, which corresponds to party j in Π_1. The private key of $\mathcal{M}_0$ is $(\mathbf{s}, \mathbf{e})$ and the associated public key is $\mathbf{p}$, where $\mathbf{s}, \mathbf{e} \leftarrow D_{\mathbb{Z}^n, \alpha}$ and $\mathbf{p} \triangleq \mathbf{a} \cdot \mathbf{s} + 2\mathbf{e} \in \mathcal{R}_q$ (recall that $\mathbf{a} \leftarrow \mathcal{R}_q$ is a global parameter in Π_1); Moreover, the identifier of $\mathcal{M}_0$ is denoted by id. On input $(\mathsf{id}^*, \mathbf{p}^*, \mathbf{x}, \mathbf{w}, \mathbf{z})$, where $\mathbf{x} \in \mathcal{R}_q, \mathbf{z}, \mathbf{w} \in \mathbb{B}^n$, and id^* denotes the identifier of the caller with static public key $\mathbf{p}^* \in \mathcal{R}_q$, the oracle $\mathcal{M}_0$ does the following: it first samples $\mathbf{g} \leftarrow D_{\mathbb{Z}^n, \alpha}$, then computes $\mathbf{c} \leftarrow H_1(\mathsf{id}^*, \mathsf{id}, \mathbf{x})$, $\mathbf{k} := (\mathbf{p}^*\mathbf{c} + \mathbf{x})\mathbf{s} + q_0\mathbf{w} + 2\mathbf{cg}$, and $\sigma := \mathsf{Parity}\left(\mathbf{k}\right) \in \mathbb{B}^n$; Finally, $\mathcal{M}_0$ returns 1 if and only if $\mathbf{z} = \sigma$; Otherwise, 0 is returned. This 1-bit oracle $\mathcal{M}_0$ is defined to capture that for every session interaction in Π_1, a malicious attacker could learn whether the session-key returned by party j is equal to the expected one or not. Clearly, such one-bit oracle is reasonable in practice.

4.3   The Oracle $\mathcal{M}_1$ and Its Associated Attacker $\mathcal{A}_1$

For the moment, we assume that there is an attacker against $\mathcal{M}_0$ with static public key $\mathbf{p}^* = \mathbf{0} \in \mathcal{R}_q$. By definition, for the input $(\mathsf{id}^*, \mathbf{p}^* = \mathbf{0}, \mathbf{x}, \mathbf{w}, \mathbf{z})$ made by this attacker, $\mathcal{M}_0$ first samples $\mathbf{g} \leftarrow D_{\mathbb{Z}^n, \alpha}$, then computes $\mathbf{c} \leftarrow H_1(\mathsf{id}^*, \mathsf{id}, \mathbf{x})$, $\mathbf{k} := (\mathbf{p}^*\mathbf{c} + \mathbf{x})\mathbf{s} + q_0\mathbf{w} + 2\mathbf{cg} = \mathbf{xs} + q_0\mathbf{w} + 2\mathbf{cg}$, and $\sigma := \mathsf{Parity}\left(\mathbf{k}\right) \in \mathbb{B}^n$; Finally, $\mathcal{M}_0$ returns 1 if and only if $\mathbf{z} = \sigma$. Notice that $\|\mathbf{cg}\|_\infty \leq n \cdot \alpha\gamma$ by Lemma 1.

This simplified analysis motivates us to define the oracle $\mathcal{M}_1$ with secret $\mathbf{s} \leftarrow D_{\mathbb{Z}^n, \alpha}$: on input $(\mathbf{x}, \mathbf{w}, \mathbf{z}) \in \mathcal{R}_q \times \mathbb{B}^n \times \mathbb{B}^n$, the oracle $\mathcal{M}_1$ first generates a small error $\varepsilon \leftarrow \mathbb{Z}_{1+2\theta}^n = \{-\theta, \cdots, \theta\}^n$, then computes $\sigma \triangleq \mathsf{Parity}\left(\mathbf{xs} + q_0\mathbf{w} + 2\varepsilon\right) \in$

$\mathbb{B}^n$, and finally returns 1 if and only if $\mathbf{z} = \sigma \in \mathbb{B}^n$; Otherwise, 0 is returned. Here, $\theta > 0$ is a constant.

Clearly, $\mathcal{M}_1$ could be seen as a simplified variant of $\mathcal{M}_0$ with $\theta = n\alpha\gamma$. And, the rest of this section is devoted to the construction of a *basic* yet efficient attacker $\mathcal{A}_1$ that, given oracle access to $\mathcal{M}_1$, can recover the secret of $\mathcal{M}_1$ *w.o.p.*

General Structure of $\mathcal{A}_1$. By properties of the CRT basis for $\mathcal{R}_q$, to recover the secret $\mathbf{s} \in \mathcal{R}_q$ of $\mathcal{M}_1$, it suffices to recover every $s_i \triangleq \eta_i(\mathbf{s}) \in \mathbb{F}_q$, $i \in [n]$. And by the search-to-decisional reduction, the recovery of s_i could be boiled down to deciding whether $s_i = \tilde{s}_i \in \mathbb{F}_q$ or not for every $\tilde{s}_i \in \mathbb{F}_q$. These observations indicate the *general structure* of our desired $\mathcal{A}_1$ as follows: the main body of $\mathcal{A}_1$ consist of an n-round loop, and the i-th round is devoted to recovering $s_i \in \mathbb{F}_q$; In the i-th round, given $s_1, \cdots, s_{i-1}$ and oracle access to $\mathcal{M}_1$, it first picks $\tilde{s}_i \leftarrow \mathbb{F}_q$ *randomly*, guesses $s_i = \tilde{s}_i \in \mathbb{F}_q$, and then verifies the correctness of this guess via a set $\mathcal{Q}_i(\tilde{s}_i)$ of queries to $\mathcal{M}_1$; The $\mathcal{Q}_i(\tilde{s}_i)$ should be carefully chosen so that the distribution of those query replies under the condition $\tilde{s}_i = s_i$ is *computationally distinguishable* from that under the condition $\tilde{s}_i \neq s_i$; When $\tilde{s}_i$ runs over $\mathbb{F}_q$, the exact value of $s_i \in \mathbb{F}_q$ would be recovered *w.o.p.*

Design of $\mathcal{Q}_i(\tilde{s}_i)$. For the moment, assume $s_1, \cdots, s_{i-1}$ have been recovered *successfully* and $\tilde{s}_i \in \mathbb{F}_q$ is fixed, and we are devoted to verifying the correctness of the guess $s_i = \tilde{s}_i$ by designing the *desired* query set $\mathcal{Q}_i(\tilde{s}_i)$. Jumping ahead,

$$\mathcal{Q}_i(\tilde{s}_i) = \left\{ \left(\mathbf{x}_k = k\mathbf{c}_i, \ \mathbf{w}_k = [w_{k,j}]_{j \in [n]}, \ \mathbf{z}_k = [z_{k,j}]_{j \in [n]} \right) \ \middle| \ k \in S_g \subseteq \mathbb{F}_q \right\},$$

where $S_g \subseteq \mathbb{F}_q$ is to be defined later. It remains to specify the $\mathbf{w}$- and $\mathbf{z}$-entries.

Under the hypothesis $s_i = \tilde{s}_i$, it is easy to set the $\mathbf{w}$- and $\mathbf{z}$-entries in $\mathcal{Q}_i(\tilde{s}_i)$, so that $\mathcal{M}_1$ returns 1 on *every* query in $\mathcal{Q}_i(\tilde{s}_i)$ when the hypothesis is correct. However, the difficulty lies in whether we can choose a "good" $\mathcal{Q}_i(\tilde{s}_i)$ such that when $s_i \neq \tilde{s}_i$, $\mathcal{M}_1$ returns 0 on *some* queries in $\mathcal{Q}_i(\tilde{s}_i)$. Given that $\mathcal{M}_1$ returns *only 1-bit information* per query, the answer to this question is *not* that easy.

Lemma 5 states we can design such a desired $\mathcal{Q}_i(\tilde{s}_i)$. Note that this lemma a special case of Lemma 8 (in Appendix A) where $H = \{0\} \subseteq \mathbb{F}_q$ and $\beta = 0$.

Lemma 5. *Let $g \in \mathbb{F}_q^{\times}$ denote a primitive element of $\mathbb{F}_q$, $S_g \triangleq \{g^r \mid r \in [d]\}$ and $d \triangleq q_0/n$. Define the aforementioned query set*

$$\mathcal{Q}_i(\tilde{s}_i) \triangleq \left\{ \left(k\mathbf{c}_i, [w_{k,j}]_{j \in [n]}, [z_{k,j}]_{j \in [n]} \right) \ \middle| \ \begin{array}{l} k \in S_g, \ j \in [n], \ u_{k,j} = \tilde{s}_i \cdot kc_{i,j}, \\ w_{k,j} = \mathsf{Cha}\left(u_{k,j}\right), z_{k,j} = \mathsf{Mod}\left(u_{k,j}, w_{k,j}\right) \end{array} \right\}$$

If $q > 1 + \max\{8\theta, 2\alpha\sqrt{n}\}$, then except with negligible probability, $s_i = \tilde{s}_i$ if and only if $\mathcal{M}_1$ returns 1 on every query in $\mathcal{Q}_i(\tilde{s}_i)$. □

The success of $\mathcal{A}_1$ is summarized in the following theorem.

Theorem 1. *When* $q > 1 + \max\{8\theta,\ 2\alpha\sqrt{n}\}$, *the efficient attacker* $\mathcal{A}_1$ *defined previously can recover the secret* s *of* $\mathcal{M}_1$ *with overwhelming probability, by making at most* $n \cdot q \cdot q_0/n = \mathrm{poly}(\lambda)$ *queries to* $\mathcal{M}_1$.   □

Remarks. First, the proof of Lemma 5 implies that the exact distribution form of the noise term ε generated by $\mathcal{M}_1$ does not matter; Only its support does. Moreover, the proof of Lemma 5 shows that the index set $S_g = \{g^r \mid r \in [d]\}$ could be replaced by *any* complete system of representatives of cosets in the quotient group $\mathbb{F}_q^\times/G$, where $G \triangleq \langle \omega_i \rangle$ is *the unique* subgroup of $\mathbb{F}_q^\times$ satisfying $|G| = 2n$. All these observations show that as a concrete instance of SFA, the basic attacker $\mathcal{A}_1$ against $\mathcal{M}_1$ is *versatile*.

The success of $\mathcal{A}_1$ relies heavily on the notion of the CRT basis $\mathbf{c}_1, \cdots, \mathbf{c}_n$ for $\mathcal{R}_q$ and its properties. Computer experiments have justified the correctness of our small field attacker $\mathcal{A}_1$ against $\mathcal{M}_1$; In particular, $\mathcal{A}_1$ succeeds when the oracle $\mathcal{M}_1$ is instantiated with these four groups of suggested parameters in [ZZD+15, ZZDS14] ($\theta := n\alpha\gamma$). Please refer to [GZ16], the full version of this work, for the pseudocode of $\mathcal{A}_1$.

The existence of $\mathcal{A}_1$ implies that there exists an efficient attacker with static public key $\mathbf{0} \in \mathcal{R}_q$ that can recover the private key of $\mathcal{M}_0$ w.o.p. Hence, $\mathcal{A}_1$ itself suffices to show the insecurity of Π_1 *in practice*.

In essence, our small field attack against Π_1 is equivalent to solving a problem that is much *harder* than the *adaptive* variant of RLWE problem, where the attacker can adaptively choose the $\mathbf{a}$-part in each RLWE sample $(\mathbf{a}, \mathbf{b})$. Although the *adaptive* RLWE can be *efficiently* solved without the CRT basis for $\mathcal{R}_q$, the CRT basis is *necessary* and plays an *essential* role in our SFA.

Although $s_1, \cdots, s_{i-1} \in \mathbb{F}_q$ are assumed known before the i-th round of $\mathcal{A}_1$, this assumption is not necessary for $\mathcal{A}_1$. Nevertheless, this assumption is *essential* for us to construct an *improved* variant of $\mathcal{A}_1$, as we shall see in Sect. 5.

5   Making Small Field Attack "Undetectable"

In this section, we continue our analysis on the oracle $\mathcal{M}_1$, and show that we can construct an efficient hybrid attacker $(\mathcal{V}/\mathcal{A}_1')_\delta$ against $\mathcal{M}_1$, whose malicious queries made to $\mathcal{M}_1$ are as "random-looking" as possible.

5.1   The Improved Attacker $\mathcal{A}_1'$ Against $\mathcal{M}_1$

Limitation of $\mathcal{A}_1$. The success of $\mathcal{A}_1$ relies on the assumption that $\mathcal{M}_1$ imposes no restrictions on the incoming queries. Intuitively, for every query made by $\mathcal{A}_1$, the $\mathbf{w}$- and $\mathbf{z}$-entries seem "random" enough; However, the algebraic structure of $\mathbf{x}$-entry is rather simple, as the $\mathbf{x}$-entry always belongs to the set $\{k\mathbf{c}_i \mid k \in \mathbb{F}_q, i \in [n]\}$ with size $nq \ll q^n$. Hence, it is easy for $\mathcal{M}_1$ to identify those malicious queries made by $\mathcal{A}_1$, and the attacker $\mathcal{A}_1$ will no longer work if the oracle $\mathcal{M}_1$ additionally requires that $\mathbf{x} \notin \{k\mathbf{c}_i \mid k \in \mathbb{F}_q, i \in [n]\}$. Such *additional* requirement seems *reasonable*, given that $nq \ll q^n$.

Construction of $\mathcal{A}_1'$. Nevertheless, we can construct an improved variant of $\mathcal{A}_1$, i.e., $\mathcal{A}_1'$, to resolve this issue. Its general structure is *almost identical* to that of $\mathcal{A}_1$, and the *only difference* lies in the choice of the query set in each round.

The design of query set in $\mathcal{A}_1'$ relies on the following two observations. First, recall that in the i-th round of $\mathcal{A}_1$, $s_1, \cdots, s_{i-1} \in \mathbb{F}_q$ are assumed to be known already; Thus, we can use these known CRT-coefficients of $\mathbf{s} \in \mathcal{R}_q$ to re-design the $\mathbf{x}$-entry so that it looks much more "complex". Moreover, by Lemma 1, the attack still succeeds if we add a "small" *even* noise into the $\mathbf{x}$-entry, *provided that q is sufficiently large*. In sum, in the i-th round, for every query made by $\mathcal{A}_1'$ to $\mathcal{M}_1$, the $\mathbf{x}$-entry is of the form $\mathbf{x} = k\mathbf{c}_i + \mathbf{h} + 2\mathbf{e}$, where $\mathbf{h} \leftarrow \{\mathbf{u} \in \mathcal{R}_q \mid \mathsf{Dim}(\mathbf{u}) = [i-1]\}$, and $\mathbf{e} \leftarrow \mathbb{Z}_{1+2\alpha'\sqrt{n}}^n$. Intuitively, the introduction of $\mathbf{h}$- and $\mathbf{e}$-parts into the $\mathbf{x}$-entry is to make the queries made by $\mathcal{A}_1'$ as "random-looking" as possible. Of course, this improvement asks us to re-design the settings of $\mathbf{w}$- and $\mathbf{z}$-entries appropriately.

It should be stressed that the $\mathbf{h}$-part cannot be drawn from the uniform distribution over $\mathcal{R}_q$: when $\mathbf{h} \leftarrow \mathcal{R}_q$, it is very likely that $\mathsf{Dim}(\mathbf{hs}) \nsubseteq [i]$, making it *impossible* for us to set $\mathbf{w}$- and $\mathbf{z}$-entries appropriately.

The following Lemma 6 characterizes the query set $\mathcal{Q}_i'(\tilde{s}_i)$ used by $\mathcal{A}_1'$ in its i-th round for every (fixed) $\tilde{s}_i \in \mathbb{F}_q$. Also, this lemma is a special case of Lemma 8 (in Appendix A) where $H = \mathbb{F}_q^\times \subseteq \mathbb{F}_q$ and $\beta = \alpha' > 0$.

Lemma 6. *Let* $g \in \mathbb{F}_q^\times$ *denote a primitive element of* $\mathbb{F}_q$, *and let* $S_g \triangleq \{g^r \mid r \in [d]\}$ *and* $d \triangleq q_0/n$. *Define the aforementioned query set* $\mathcal{Q}_i'(\tilde{s}_i)$ *as*

$$\left\{ \begin{pmatrix} k\mathbf{c}_i + \mathbf{h}_k + 2\mathbf{e}_k, \\ [w_{k,j}]_{j \in [n]}, \\ [z_{k,j}]_{j \in [n]} \end{pmatrix} \middle| \begin{array}{l} k \in S_g, \ j \in [n], \ h_{k,1}, \cdots, h_{k,i-1} \leftarrow \mathbb{F}_q^\times, \\ \mathbf{h}_k = \sum_{r \in [i-1]} h_{k,r} \mathbf{c}_r, \ \mathbf{e}_k \leftarrow \mathbb{Z}_{1+2\alpha'\sqrt{n}}^n, \\ u_{k,j} = \tilde{s}_i \cdot kc_{i,j} + \sum_{r \in [i-1]} s_r h_{k,r} c_{r,j}, \\ w_{k,j} = \mathsf{Cha}(u_{k,j}), z_{k,j} = \mathsf{Mod}(u_{k,j}, w_{k,j}) \end{array} \right\}$$

If $q > 1 + 8(\theta + n\alpha\alpha')$, *then except with negligible probability,* $s_i = \tilde{s}_i$ *if and only if* $\mathcal{M}_1$ *returns 1 on every query in* $\mathcal{Q}_i'(\tilde{s}_i)$. $\qquad\square$

The success of $\mathcal{A}_1'$ is summarized in the following theorem.

Theorem 2. *When* $q > 1 + 8(\theta + n\alpha\alpha')$, *the efficient algorithm* $\mathcal{A}_1'$ *can recover the secret of* $\mathcal{M}_1$ *w.o.p., by making at most* $n \cdot q \cdot q_0/n = \mathrm{poly}(\lambda)$ *queries to* $\mathcal{M}_1$. *Furthermore, in the* i-th *round, for every query* $(\mathbf{x}, \mathbf{w}, \mathbf{z})$ *made by* $\mathcal{A}_1'$, *the* $\mathbf{x}$-*entry is always of the form* $\mathbf{x}_0 + 2\mathbf{e}$, *where* $\mathsf{Dim}(\mathbf{x}_0) = [i]$ *and* $\mathbf{e} \in \mathbb{Z}_{1+2\alpha'\sqrt{n}}^n$. $\square$

5.2 The "Undetectable" Attacker $(\mathcal{V}/\mathcal{A}_1')_\delta$ Against $\mathcal{M}_1$

Limitation of $\mathcal{A}_1'$. To us, the most *practical* way for $\mathcal{M}_1'$ to identify those malicious queries made by $\mathcal{A}_1'$ is to analyze the algebraic structure of the $\mathbf{x}$-entry. And the $\mathbf{h}$- and $\mathbf{e}$-parts were introduced to complicate the algebraic/numeric structure of $\mathbf{x}$. Clearly, the more CRT coefficients of $\mathbf{s}$ we get, the more difficult for $\mathcal{M}_1$ to distinguish those queries made by $\mathcal{A}_1'$ from ordinary ones.

However, there is still a problem: when $\mathcal{A}_1'$ seeks to recover the *first* CRT-coefficient of $\mathbf{s}$ in its first round, $\mathbf{h} = \mathbf{0}$ and hence the $\mathbf{x}$-entry falls into the set
$$D_1 \triangleq \left\{ k \cdot \mathbf{c}_i + 2\mathbf{e} \,\middle|\, k \in \mathbb{F}_q, i \in [n], \mathbf{e} \in \mathbb{Z}_{1+2\alpha'\sqrt{n}}^n \right\} \subseteq \mathcal{R}_q,$$ which is of "small" size
compared with $\mathcal{R}_q$. It is still not hard for $\mathcal{M}_1$ to identify, and thus reject, the *first* set of queries by analyzing whether $\mathbf{x} \in D_1$ or not. Such rejection sounds "reasonable" for $\mathcal{M}_1$, given the set D_1 is of "small" size relative to $\mathcal{R}_q$. If such similar restrictions are imposed by $\mathcal{M}_1$, $\mathcal{A}_1'$ would fail since it cannot recover the first (and hence the remaining) CRT-coefficient of the secret $\mathbf{s}$.

The Hybrid Attacker $(\mathcal{V}/\mathcal{A}_1')_\delta$. Let $\mathcal{P}_1$ denote the problem of recovering the secret of $\mathcal{M}_1$. Likewise, we can define a related problem $\mathcal{P}_2$ as follows: given an index set $I \subseteq [n]$, $[\tilde{s}_i]_{i \in I} \in \mathbb{F}_q^{|I|}$, and oracle access to $\mathcal{M}_1$, decide whether $[s_i]_{i \in I} = [\tilde{s}_i]_{i \in I}$ or not. Recall that $s_i = \eta_i(\mathbf{s})$, where $\mathbf{s}$ denotes the secret of $\mathcal{M}_1$.

It turns out that we can construct an *efficient* solver $\mathcal{V}$ for the problem $\mathcal{P}_2$. Please refer to Appendix B for the construction of $\mathcal{V}$, and [GZ16] for its pseudocode. Here, it should be stressed that when solving the instance $(I, [\tilde{s}_i]_{i \in I})$ of $\mathcal{P}_2$, for every query made by $\mathcal{V}$ to $\mathcal{M}_1$, the $\mathbf{x}$-entry is always of the form $\mathbf{x}_0 + 2\mathbf{e}$, where $\mathrm{Dim}(\mathbf{x}_0) = I$ and $\mathbf{e} \in \mathbb{Z}_{1+2\alpha'\sqrt{n}}^n$.

With the help of $\mathcal{V}$, we can construct an efficient *hybrid* attacker against $\mathcal{M}_1$, which consists of two *consecutive* phases as follows:

Phase 1: First, choose a *constant* $\delta > 0$ of moderately large, and an index set $I \subseteq [n]$ of size δ *randomly*. Then, feed $\mathcal{V}$ with q^δ instances, each of the form $(I, [\tilde{s}_i]_{i \in I}), \tilde{s}_i \in \mathbb{F}_q$. In this manner, when $[\tilde{s}_i]_{i \in I}$ runs over the set $\mathbb{F}_q^\delta$, the CRT-coefficients $s_i, i \in I$, would be recovered *w.o.p.* By properties of $\mathcal{V}$, the $\mathbf{x}$-entry of every query made in this phase is always of the form $\mathbf{x}_0 + 2\mathbf{e}$, where $\mathrm{Dim}(\mathbf{x}_0) = I$, and $\mathbf{e} \leftarrow \mathbb{Z}_{1+2\alpha'\sqrt{n}}^n$. Given the randomness of I, it is *hard in practice* for $\mathcal{M}_1$ to identify those queries made by $\mathcal{V}$.

Phase 2: This phase consists of $n - \delta$ rounds, each devoted to recovering one of the remaining $n - \delta$ CRT-coefficients of $\mathbf{s}$, as we do in $\mathcal{A}_1'$. In this phase, the $\mathbf{x}$-entry of every query is always of the form $\mathbf{x}_0 + 2\mathbf{e}$ where $\mathrm{Dim}(\mathbf{x}_0) \supseteq I$ and $\mathbf{e} \leftarrow \mathbb{Z}_{1+2\alpha'\sqrt{n}}^n$, making it *harder* for $\mathcal{M}_1$ to identify those malicious queries.

The notation $(\mathcal{V}/\mathcal{A}_1')_\delta$ is applied to emphasize the structure of this attacker.

Theorem 3. *When $q > 1 + 8(\theta + n\alpha\alpha')$, there exists an attacker $(\mathcal{V}/\mathcal{A}_1')_\delta$ that can recover the secret of $\mathcal{M}_1$ w.o.p., after making $q_0\delta \cdot q^\delta + (n - \delta) \cdot q \cdot q_0/n = \mathrm{poly}(\lambda)$ queries to $\mathcal{M}_1$. And, for every query made by $(\mathcal{V}/\mathcal{A}_1')_\delta$ to $\mathcal{M}_1$, it $\mathbf{x}$-entry is always of the form $\mathbf{x} = \mathbf{x}_0 + 2\mathbf{e}$ where $|\mathrm{Dim}(\mathbf{x}_0)| \geq \delta$ and $\mathbf{e} \in \mathbb{Z}_{1+2\alpha'\sqrt{n}}^n$.* $\square$

Remarks. Some remarks are in order. First, we stress that due to the *random choice* of I, this makes it *hard in practice* for $\mathcal{M}_1$ to identify (and hence reject) those queries made by $(\mathcal{V}/\mathcal{A}_1')_\delta$. As a concrete instance of SFA, the $(\mathcal{V}/\mathcal{A}_1')_\delta$ shows that we can construct an "undetectable" attacker with static public key $\mathbf{0} \in \mathcal{R}_q$ that can efficiently recover the static private key of party j in Π_1.

Moreover, notice that the algorithms $\mathcal{A}_1'$ and $\mathcal{V}$ are firmly related to each other in essence: when $\mathcal{M}_1$ imposes no restriction on the incoming queries, $\mathcal{A}_1$ could be *adapted* to solve the problem $\mathcal{P}_2$ efficiently; Likewise, $\mathcal{V}$ can be used to recover the *whole* secret $\mathbf{s}$ of $\mathcal{M}_1$ efficiently as well.

Finally, although we could have used $\mathcal{V}$ to recover the other CRT-coefficients of $\mathbf{s}$ in Phase 2 of $(\mathcal{V}/\mathcal{A}_1')_\delta$, this is *less efficient*: roughly speaking, it takes more queries *on average* for $\mathcal{V}$ to recover one CRT-coefficient of $\mathbf{s}$ than $\mathcal{A}_1'$ does.

6   The Small Field Attack Against Π_1

In this section, we switch our analysis back to the oracle $\mathcal{M}_0$ (defined in Sect. 4.2), and construct an efficient attacker $\mathcal{A}_0$ which can recover the static private key of $\mathcal{M}_0$, after a set of queries made to $\mathcal{M}_0$; Moreover, both the static public key of $\mathcal{A}_0$ and those queries it makes to $\mathcal{M}_0$ are as "random-looking" as possible. The existence of $\mathcal{A}_0$ implies Π_1 is vulnerable to our small field attack *in practice*.

Construction of $\mathcal{A}_0$. For the oracle $\mathcal{M}_0$, to recover its private key $(\mathbf{s}, \mathbf{e})$, it suffices for $\mathcal{A}_0$ to recover $\mathbf{s} \in \mathcal{R}_q$, since $\mathbf{p} = \mathbf{a}\mathbf{s} + 2\mathbf{e} \in \mathcal{R}_q$ is made public. Moreover, it suffices for $\mathcal{A}_0$ to recover every CRT-coefficient $s_i \triangleq \eta_i(\mathbf{s})$ of $\mathbf{s} \in \mathcal{R}_q$. Recall that the "undetectable" and efficient attacker $(\mathcal{V}/\mathcal{A}_1')_\delta$ against $\mathcal{M}_1$ constructed in Sect. 5.2 implies we can already construct an efficient attacker against $\mathcal{M}_0$ *with static public key* $\mathbf{0} \in \mathcal{R}_q$, whose queries made to $\mathcal{M}_0$ are as "random-looking" as possible. Thus, the difficulty of designing $\mathcal{A}_0$ lies in how to design its static public key $\mathbf{p}^*$ that looks "random". It turns out the construction of $\mathcal{V}$ already implies how to choose a "random-looking" $\mathbf{p}^*$ for $\mathcal{A}_0$.

The *general structure* of $\mathcal{A}_0$ is defined as follows. $\mathcal{A}_0$ consists of three *consecutive* phases: *Phase 0, Phase 1*, and *Phase 2*. In Phase 0, $\mathcal{A}_0$ generates its static public/private key pair as follows: first, it chooses an integer $\delta > 0$ that is moderately large; Then, it chooses a proper index set $I \subseteq [n]$ of size δ *randomly*; After that, it samples $\mathbf{p}_0^* \leftarrow \{\mathbf{u} \in \mathcal{R}_q \mid \mathrm{Dim}\,(\mathbf{u}) = I\}$ and $\mathbf{e}_0^* \leftarrow \mathbb{Z}_{1+2\alpha'\sqrt{n}}$ uniformly at random; The static public key of $\mathcal{A}_0$ is $\mathbf{p}^* \triangleq \mathbf{p}_0^* + 2\mathbf{e}_0^*$, and its associated static private key is $(\mathbf{s}^*, \mathbf{e}^*)$, where $\mathbf{s}^* \leftarrow \mathcal{R}_q$ is drawn randomly and $\mathbf{e}^* \triangleq 2^{-1}(\mathbf{p}^* - \mathbf{a}\mathbf{s}^*)$. It should be stressed that the static public/private key pair of $\mathcal{A}_0$ is *not* honestly generated; Nevertheless, such choice is justified by the following observation: roughly speaking, every element in $\mathcal{R}_q$ is *equally* likely to be the static public key of an honest initiator in Π_1 by RLWE assumption.

The Phase 1 and Phase 2 of $\mathcal{A}_0$ are devoted to the recovery of every $s_i = \eta_i(\mathbf{s}), i \in [n]$, and their functionalities are similar to those of $(\mathcal{V}/\mathcal{A}_1')_\delta$, respectively: first Phase 1 is devoted to recovering δ CRT-coefficients of $\mathbf{s}$, *i.e.*, $\{s_i \mid i \in I\}$ where $I \subseteq [n]$ is of size δ, and Phase 2 is to recover the other ones.

The Phase 1 of $\mathcal{A}_0$ is very close to that of $(\mathcal{V}/\mathcal{A}_1')_\delta$ but with slight differences; Moreover, they share the same asymptotic time complexity, which is measured in terms of the number of queries made. The Phase 2 of $\mathcal{A}_0$ is roughly described as follows. For the moment, we assume that $I \subseteq [i-1]$ and the CRT-coefficients

$s_1, \cdots, s_{i-1} \in \mathbb{F}_q$ have already been recovered successfully, and we are about to show how $\mathcal{A}_0$ recovers a *new* CRT-coefficient of $\mathbf{s}$, say $s_i \in \mathbb{F}_q$, via a set of queries to $\mathcal{M}_0$. The general strategy is simple: first, pick $\tilde{s}_i \leftarrow \mathbb{F}_q$ randomly, and guess $s_i = \tilde{s}_i$; Then, conduct a set $\mathcal{Q}_i(\tilde{s}_i)$ of queries to $\mathcal{M}_0$ such that *except with negligible probability*, $s_i = \tilde{s}_i$ if and only if $\mathcal{M}_0$ returns 1 on every query in $\mathcal{Q}_i(\tilde{s}_i)$; When $\tilde{s}_i$ runs over $\mathbb{F}_q$, the exact value of s_i would be recovered *w.o.p.*

Jumping ahead, every query in $\mathcal{Q}_i(\tilde{s}_i)$ is of the form $(\mathtt{id}^*, \mathbf{p}^*, \mathbf{x}_k = k\mathbf{c}_i + \mathbf{h}_k + 2\mathbf{e}_k, \mathbf{w}_k, \mathbf{z}_k)$, where $k \in [q_0]$, $\mathbf{h}_k \leftarrow \{\mathbf{u} \in \mathcal{R}_q \mid \mathsf{Dim}(\mathbf{u}) = [i-1]\}$, $\mathbf{e}_k \leftarrow \mathbb{Z}^n_{1+2\alpha'\sqrt{n}}$, and $\mathbf{w}_k, \mathbf{z}_k \in \mathbb{B}^n$ are to be determined later.

By definition, on the query $(\mathtt{id}^*, \mathbf{p}^*, \mathbf{x}_k = k\mathbf{c}_i + \mathbf{h}_k + 2\mathbf{e}_k, \mathbf{w}_k, \mathbf{z}_k)$ where $\mathbf{h}_k = \sum_{r \in [i-1]} h_{k,r} \mathbf{c}_r, h_{k,r} \leftarrow \mathbb{F}_q^\times$, the oracle $\mathcal{M}_0$ first samples $\mathbf{g} \leftarrow D_{\mathbb{Z}^n, \alpha}$, then compute $\mathbf{c} \leftarrow H_1(\mathtt{id}^*, \mathtt{id}, \mathbf{x}_k)$ and

$$\mathbf{v}_k \triangleq (\mathbf{p}^*\mathbf{c} + \mathbf{x}_k) \cdot \mathbf{s} + q_0 \cdot \mathbf{w}_k + 2\mathbf{c} \cdot \mathbf{g}$$
$$= k\Delta s_i \mathbf{c}_i + (k\tilde{s}_i \mathbf{c}_i + \mathbf{p}_0^*\mathbf{c}\mathbf{s} + \mathbf{s} \cdot \mathbf{h}_k + q_0 \cdot \mathbf{w}_k) + 2\varepsilon_k$$
$$= \begin{bmatrix} \Delta s_i k c_{i,1} + \left(k\tilde{s}_i c_{i,1} + \sum_{r \in I} \eta_r(\mathbf{p}_0^*\mathbf{c}\mathbf{s})c_{r,1} + \sum_{r \in [i-1]} s_r h_{k,r} c_{r,1} + q_0 w_{k,1} \right) \\ \vdots \\ \Delta s_i k c_{i,n} + \left(k\tilde{s}_i c_{i,n} + \sum_{r \in I} \eta_r(\mathbf{p}_0^*\mathbf{c}\mathbf{s})c_{r,n} + \sum_{r \in [i-1]} s_r h_{k,r} c_{r,n} + q_0 w_{k,n} \right) \end{bmatrix} + 2 \begin{bmatrix} \varepsilon_{k,1} \\ \vdots \\ \varepsilon_{k,n} \end{bmatrix},$$

where $\Delta s_i \triangleq s_i - \tilde{s}_i$ and $\varepsilon_k \triangleq \mathbf{e}_k \mathbf{s} + \mathbf{e}_0^* \mathbf{c}\mathbf{s} + \mathbf{c}\mathbf{g} \sim [\varepsilon_{k,j}]_{j \in [n]}$. Finally, $\mathcal{M}_0$ computes $\sigma_k := \mathsf{Parity}(\mathbf{v}_k)$, and returns 1 if and only if $\sigma_k = \mathbf{z}_k$. Notice that $\mathsf{Dim}(\mathbf{p}_0^*\mathbf{c}\mathbf{s}) \subseteq \mathsf{Dim}(\mathbf{p}_0^*) = I$, making it possible for $\mathcal{A}_0$ to pre-compute every $\eta_r(\mathbf{p}_0^*\mathbf{c}\mathbf{s}), r \in I$, before issuing the query to $\mathcal{M}_0$.

It is routine to verify the correctness of the following lemma.

Lemma 7. *Let g denote a primitive element of $\mathbb{F}_q^\times$, and define $d \triangleq q_0/n, S_g \triangleq \{g^r \mid r \in [d]\}$. With the notations defined previously, if $I \subseteq [i-1]$ and $s_1, \cdots, s_{i-1}$ have been given and $q > 1 + 8(n\alpha\alpha' + n\alpha\gamma + n^2\alpha\alpha'\gamma)$, then except with negligible probability, $\Delta s_i = 0$ if and only if $\mathcal{M}_0$ returns 1 on every query in $\mathcal{Q}_i(\tilde{s}_i)$, i.e.,*

$$\left\{ \begin{pmatrix} \mathtt{id}^*, \mathbf{p}^*, \\ k\mathbf{c}_i + \mathbf{h}_k + 2\mathbf{e}_k, \\ [w_{k,j}]_{j \in [n]}, [z_{k,j}]_{j \in [n]} \end{pmatrix} \middle| \begin{array}{l} k \in S_g, \ j \in [n], \ h_{k,1}, \cdots, h_{k,i-1} \leftarrow \mathbb{F}_q^\times, \\ \mathbf{h}_k = \sum_{r \in [i-1]} h_{k,r} \mathbf{c}_r, \ \mathbf{e}_k \leftarrow \mathbb{Z}^n_{1+2\alpha'\sqrt{n}}, \\ u_{k,j} = k\tilde{s}_i c_{i,j} + \sum_{r \in I} \eta_r(\mathbf{p}_0^*\mathbf{c}\mathbf{s})c_{r,j} + \sum_{r \in [i-1]} s_r h_{k,r} c_{r,j}, \\ w_{k,j} = \mathsf{Cha}(u_{k,j}), z_{k,j} = \mathsf{Mod}(u_{k,j}, w_{k,j}) \end{array} \right\} .$$

In particular, for every query in $\mathcal{Q}_i(\tilde{s}_i)$, its $\mathbf{x}$-entry is always of the form $\mathbf{x}_0 + 2\mathbf{e}$, where $\mathsf{Dim}(\mathbf{x}_0) = [i]$ and $\mathbf{e} \in \mathbb{Z}^n_{1+2\alpha'\sqrt{n}}$. □

The correctness/efficiency of $\mathcal{A}_0$ can be easily verified. In sum, this implies the existence of the desired efficient attacker $\mathcal{A}$ against Π_1, as the following Theorem 4 indicates. Similar to $(\mathcal{V}/\mathcal{A}_1')_\delta$ and $\mathcal{A}_0$, $\mathcal{A}$ can make its session queries to party j as "random-looking" as possible by choosing an appropriate constant δ. In particular, all the four groups of parameters suggested in [ZZDS14, ZZD+15] satisfy the parameter requirement in Theorem 4, with $\alpha' := \alpha$.

Theorem 4. *With the notations defined previously, when $q > 1 + 8(n\alpha\alpha' + n\alpha\gamma + n^2\alpha\alpha'\gamma)$, there exists an efficient adversary $\mathcal{A}$ that can recover the static private* *key of the honest party j in Π_1 w.o.p., after making $\Theta(q_0\delta \cdot q^\delta + (n-\delta) \cdot q \cdot q_0/n) =$ poly(λ) queries to party j. In particular, the x-entry of every query made by $\mathcal{A}$, as well as the static public key of $\mathcal{A}$, is of the form $x_0 + 2e$, where $|\text{Dim}(x_0)| \geq \delta$ and $e \in \mathbb{Z}^n_{1+2\alpha'\sqrt{n}}$.* $\square$

Acknowledgement. We are indebted to Daniel J. Bernstein for his great shepherding efforts and for many insightful suggestions, which have significantly improved this work. We also would like to thank the anonymous PQCrypto'17 reviewers for their valuable comments.

References

[DARF16] Ding, J., Alsayigh, S., Saraswathy, R.V., Fluhrer, S.: Leakage of signal function with reused keys in RLWE key exchange. IACR Cryptology ePrint Archive, 2016/1176 (2016)

[DD12] Ducas, L., Durmus, A.: Ring-LWE in polynomial rings. In: Fischlin, M., Buchmann, J., Manulis, M. (eds.) PKC 2012. LNCS, vol. 7293, pp. 34–51. Springer, Heidelberg (2012). doi:10.1007/978-3-642-30057-8_3

[DH76] Diffie, W., Hellman, M.E.: New directions in cryptography. IEEE Trans. Inf. Theory **22**(6), 644–654 (1976)

[DXL12] Ding, J., Xie, X., Lin, X.: A simple provably secure key exchange scheme based on the learning with errors problem. IACR Cryptology ePrint Archive, 2012/688 (2012)

[Flu16] Fluhrer, S.: Cryptanalysis of ring-LWE based key exchange with key share reuse. IACR Cryptology ePrint Archive, 2016/085 (2016)

[GZ16] Gong, B. Zhao, Y.: Small field attack, and revisiting RLWE-based authenticated key exchange from Eurocrypt 15. IACR Cryptology ePrint Archive, 2016/913 (2016)

[HK11] Halevi, S., Krawczyk, H.: One-pass HMQV and asymmetric key-wrapping. In: Catalano, D., Fazio, N., Gennaro, R., Nicolosi, A. (eds.) PKC 2011. LNCS, vol. 6571, pp. 317–334. Springer, Heidelberg (2011). doi:10.1007/978-3-642-19379-8_20

[Kra05] Krawczyk, H.: HMQV: a high-performance secure diffie-hellman protocol. In: Shoup, V. (ed.) CRYPTO 2005. LNCS, vol. 3621, pp. 546–566. Springer, Heidelberg (2005). doi:10.1007/11535218_33

[LMQ+03] Law, L., Menezes, A., Qu, M., Solinas, J.A., Vanstone, S.A.: An efficient protocol for authenticated key agreement. Des. Codes Cryptogr. **28**, 119–134 (2003)

[LPR13a] Lyubashevsky, V., Peikert, C., Regev, O.: On ideal lattices and learning with errors over rings. J. ACM **60**(6), 43 (2013)

[LPR13b] Lyubashevsky, V., Peikert, C., Regev, O.: A toolkit for ring-LWE cryptography. In: Johansson, T., Nguyen, P.Q. (eds.) EUROCRYPT 2013. LNCS, vol. 7881, pp. 35–54. Springer, Heidelberg (2013). doi:10.1007/978-3-642-38348-9_3

[Reg09] Regev, O.: On lattices, learning with errors, random linear codes, and cryptography. J. ACM **56**(6), 34 (2009)

[ZZD+15] Zhang, J., Zhang, Z., Ding, J., Snook, M., Dagdelen, Ö.: Authenticated key exchange from ideal lattices. In: Oswald, E., Fischlin, M. (eds.) EUROCRYPT 2015. LNCS, vol. 9057, pp. 719–751. Springer, Heidelberg (2015). doi:10.1007/978-3-662-46803-6_24

[ZZDS14] Zhang, J., Zhang, Z., Ding, J., Snook, M.: Authenticated key exchange from ideal lattices. IACR Cryptology ePrint Archive, 2014/589 (2014)

[YZ13] Yao, A.C., Zhao, Y.: OAKE: a new family of implicitly authenticated Diffie-Hellman protocols. In: ACM CCS 2013, pp. 1113–1128 (2013)

A   Lemma 8 and Its Proof

Below we present a lemma that is *essential* both for the correctness/efficiency of $\mathcal{A}_1$ and for those of $\mathcal{A}_1'$, as indicated in Sects. 4.3 and 5.1.

Lemma 8. *Let* $g \in \mathbb{F}_q^{\times}$ *denote a primitive element of* $\mathbb{F}_q$, $S_g \triangleq \{g^r \mid r \in [d]\}$ *and* $d \triangleq q_0/n$. *Let* $\emptyset \neq H \subseteq \mathbb{F}_q$ *and* $\beta \geq 0$. *For the (fixed)* $\tilde{s}_i \in \mathbb{F}_q$, *define*

$$\mathcal{Q}_i(\tilde{s}_i) = \left\{ (kc_i + h_k + 2e_k, [w_{k,j}]_{j \in [n]}, [z_{k,j}]_{j \in [n]}) \;\middle|\; \begin{array}{l} k \in S_g, \; j \in [n], \; h_{k,1}, \cdots, h_{k,i-1} \leftarrow H, \\ h_k = \sum_{r \in [i-1]} h_{k,r} c_r, \; e_k \leftarrow \mathbb{Z}_{1+2\beta\sqrt{n}}^n, \\ u_{k,j} = \tilde{s}_i \cdot kc_{i,j} + \sum_{r \in [i-1]} s_r h_{k,r} c_{r,j}, \\ w_{k,j} = \mathsf{Cha}\,(u_{k,j}), \; z_{k,j} = \mathsf{Mod}\,(u_{k,j}, w_{k,j}) \end{array} \right\}$$

If $q > 1 + \max(8(\theta + n\alpha\beta), 2\alpha\sqrt{n})$, *then except with negligible probability,* $s_i = \tilde{s}_i$ *if and only if* $\mathcal{M}_1$ *returns 1 on every query in* $\mathcal{Q}_i'(\tilde{s}_i)$.

Proof. Let $\Delta s_i \triangleq s_i - \tilde{s}_i \in \mathbb{F}_q$. Moreover, for $\mathbf{s} \leftarrow D_{\mathbb{Z}^n, \alpha}$ and $\mathbf{e}_k \leftarrow \mathbb{Z}_{1+2\beta\sqrt{n}}^n$, define $\varepsilon_k' \triangleq \mathbf{s} \cdot \mathbf{e}_k \in \mathcal{R}_q$; By Lemma 1, the inequality $\|\varepsilon_k'\|_{\infty} \leq n\alpha\beta$ holds *w.o.p.* Moreover, by assumption there exists a $t \in [2n]$ such that $g^d = \omega_i^t, \gcd(t, d) = 1$. For the query $Q_k = (\mathbf{x}_k = kc_i + \mathbf{h}_k + 2\mathbf{e}_k, \mathbf{w}_k = [w_{k,j}]_{j \in [n]}, \mathbf{z}_k = [z_{k,j}]_{j \in [n]}) \in \mathcal{Q}_i(\tilde{s}_i)$, $\mathcal{M}_1$ first generates $\varepsilon_k \leftarrow \mathbb{Z}_{1+2\theta}^n = \{-\theta, \cdots, \theta\}^n$, and then computes

$$\mathbf{v}_k \triangleq \mathbf{s} \cdot \mathbf{x}_k + q_0 \mathbf{w}_k + 2\varepsilon_k$$
$$= \mathbf{s} \cdot (kc_i + \mathbf{h}_k + 2\mathbf{e}_k) + q_0 \mathbf{w}_k + 2\varepsilon_k$$
$$= k\Delta s_i c_i + \left(k\tilde{s}_i c_i + \sum_{r \in [i-1]} s_r h_{k,r} c_r + q_0 \mathbf{w}_k \right) + 2(\mathbf{s}e_k + \varepsilon_k)$$
$$\sim \begin{bmatrix} \Delta s_i k c_{i,1} + \left(k\tilde{s}_i c_{i,1} + \sum_{r \in [i-1]} s_r h_{k,r} c_{r,1} + q_0 w_{k,1} \right) \\ \vdots \\ \Delta s_i k c_{i,n} + \left(k\tilde{s}_i c_{i,n} + \sum_{r \in [i-1]} s_r h_{k,r} c_{r,n} + q_0 w_{k,n} \right) \end{bmatrix} + \begin{bmatrix} 2(\varepsilon_{k,1}' + \varepsilon_{k,1}) \\ \vdots \\ 2(\varepsilon_{k,n}' + \varepsilon_{k,n}) \end{bmatrix}$$
$$= \begin{bmatrix} \Delta s_i \cdot k c_{i,1} + u_{k,1} + \mathsf{Cha}\,(u_{k,1}) \cdot q_0 \\ \vdots \\ \Delta s_i \cdot k c_{i,n} + u_{k,n} + \mathsf{Cha}\,(u_{k,n}) \cdot q_0 \end{bmatrix} + \begin{bmatrix} 2(\varepsilon_{k,1}' + \varepsilon_{k,1}) \\ \vdots \\ 2(\varepsilon_{k,n}' + \varepsilon_{k,n}) \end{bmatrix},$$

where $\varepsilon_{k,j} \triangleq \mu_j(\varepsilon_k)$ and $\varepsilon_{k,j}' \triangleq \mu_j(\mathbf{s}e_k)$. Finally, if every $\mathsf{Parity}\,(v_{k,j}) = z_{k,j}$ where $v_{k,j} \triangleq \mu_j(\mathbf{v}_k)$, then $\mathcal{M}_1$ returns 1; Otherwise, $\mathcal{M}_1$ returns 0.

Notice that $u_{k,j} + \mathsf{Cha}\,(u_{k,j}) \cdot q_0 \in \{-q_0/2, \cdots, +q_0/2\}$ by Lemma 4(a). And by assumption, it is routine to see $|\varepsilon_{k,j}' + \varepsilon_{k,j}| < q_0/4$ for every $j \in [n]$.

First consider the case when $\Delta s_i = 0$. Since $|2(\varepsilon'_{k,j} + \varepsilon_{k,j})| < q_0/2$, by Lemma 4(b), it is routine to see $\mathcal{M}_1$ returns 1 on every $Q_k \in \mathcal{Q}_i(\tilde{s}_i)$.

In the sequel, we assume $\Delta s_i \neq 0$. We *claim* that $\{-1, 1\} \cap \mathsf{offset}(\Delta s_i) \neq \emptyset$, where $\mathsf{offset}(\Delta s_i) \triangleq \{\Delta s_i \cdot k c_{i,j} \mid k \in S_g, j \in [n]\}$, Since $c_{i,j} = c_{i,n} \cdot \omega_i^{n-j}$ by Lemma 3, we have $\Delta s_i \cdot k \cdot c_{i,j} = \Delta s_i c_{i,n} \cdot k \cdot \omega_i^{n-j}$. Let $\Delta s_i c_{i,n} = g^{e^*}$ where $e^* \in [q-1]$. Clearly there exists a $r^* \in [d]$ such that $d \mid (e^* + r^*)$, and $(e^* + r^*)/d \in [2n]$. Let $k^* \triangleq g^{r^*} \in S_g$. Then

$$\Delta s_i c_{i,n} \cdot k^* \cdot \omega_i^{n-j} = g^{e^* + r^*} \cdot \omega_i^{n-j} = \omega_i^{t(e^* + r^*)/d + n - j}.$$

It is easy to see there exists a $j^* \in [n]$ such that either $t(e^* + r^*)/d + n - j^* \equiv n$ (mod $2n$) or $t(e^* + r^*)/d + n - j^* \equiv 0$ (mod $2n$); Equivalently, either $\Delta s_i \cdot c_{i,n} \cdot k^* \cdot \omega_i^{n-j^*} = \omega_i^n = -1 \in \mathbb{F}_q$ or $\Delta s_i \cdot c_{i,n} \cdot k^* \cdot \omega_i^{n-j^*} = \omega_i^0 = 1 \in \mathbb{F}_q$.

When $\Delta s_i \cdot k^* \cdot c_{i,j^*} = \pm 1$, it is easy to verify that $z_{k^*,j^*} \neq \mathsf{Parity}(v_{k^*,j^*})$ by Lemma 4(c). Equivalently, the associated j^*-th equality of Q_{k^*} does not hold, and $\mathcal{M}_1$ returns 0 on the query $Q_{k^*} \in \mathcal{Q}_i(\tilde{s}_i)$. $\square$

B   Construction of $\mathcal{V}$

As indicated in Sect. 5.2, we shall construct in this appendix an efficient algorithm $\mathcal{V}$ for the problem $\mathcal{P}_2$. To simplify the following discussion, we only consider the *special* case where $I = [n]$, and it can be easily generalized to the more general case where $I \neq \emptyset$ is a *proper* subset of $[n]$.

First come some notations. Let $\Delta s_i \triangleq s_i - \tilde{s}_i$ for every $i \in [n]$. For every $j \in [n]$, define $\mathbf{a}_j \triangleq [\tilde{s}_i \cdot c_{i,j}]_{i \in [n]} \in \mathbb{F}_q^n$, and $\mathbf{b}_j \triangleq [\Delta s_i \cdot c_{i,j}]_{i \in [n]} \in \mathbb{F}_q^n$; Moreover, define $A_j(\mathbf{u}) \triangleq \langle \mathbf{u}, \mathbf{a}_j \rangle \in \mathbb{F}_q$, and $B_j(\mathbf{u}) \triangleq \langle \mathbf{u}, \mathbf{b}_j \rangle \in \mathbb{F}_q$, where $\mathbf{u} \in \mathbb{F}_q^n$. Choose $k \leftarrow [n]$ *randomly*. Define the $\mathbb{F}_q$-vector space $U_k \triangleq \{r \cdot \mathbf{a}_k \mid r \in \mathbb{F}_q\} \subseteq \mathbb{F}_q^n$. By definition, every U_k is a 1-dimensional subspace of $\mathbb{F}_q^n$, and its orthogonal complement is the $(n-1)$-dimensional subspace $U_k^\perp \triangleq \{\mathbf{v} \in \mathbb{F}_q^n \mid A_k(\mathbf{v}) = 0 \in \mathbb{F}_q\} \subseteq \mathbb{F}_q^n$. Choose an $\mathbb{F}_q$-basis for $U_k^\perp$ *randomly*, say $\mathbf{F}_k \triangleq \{\mathbf{f}_{k,1}, \cdots, \mathbf{f}_{k,n-1}\} \subseteq U_k^\perp$, such that each entry of $\mathbf{f}_{k,\ell}$ is non-zero for every $\ell \in [n-1]$. With U_k, the set $\mathbb{F}_q^n$ is partitioned into three parts: $S_1 \triangleq \mathbb{F}_q^n \setminus U_k$, $S_2 \triangleq U_k \setminus \{0\}$, and $S_3 \triangleq \{0\}$. Finally, for every $(t, \mathbf{u}) \in \mathbb{F}_q \times \mathbb{F}_q^n$, let $\tau(t, \mathbf{u})$ denote $\sum_{i \in [n]} t \mu_i(\mathbf{u}) \cdot c_i \in \mathcal{R}_q$.

Some remarks are in order. First, notice that for every $i, j \in [n]$, s_i, Δs_i and $\mathbf{b}_j$ are unknown to us. Moreover, although the map $A_j(\cdot)$ is efficiently computable, this is *not* true for $B_j(\cdot)$. Finally, recall that every $c_{i,j} \neq 0$ by Lemma 3, so the equality $[s_i]_{i \in [n]} = [\tilde{s}_i]_{i \in [n]}$ holds if and only if $\mathbf{b}_k = \mathbf{0} \in \mathbb{F}_q^n$. Since $\mathbf{0} \in S_3 \subseteq U_k$ trivially, a *necessary yet insufficient* condition for $\mathbf{b}_k = \mathbf{0}$ is: $\mathbf{b}_k \in U_k = S_2 \cup S_3$, or equivalently, $0 = \langle \mathbf{f}_{k,\ell}, \mathbf{b}_k \rangle = B_k(\mathbf{f}_{k,\ell})$ for every $\ell \in [n-1]$.

The general idea behind $\mathcal{V}$ is simple: it first makes the guess, i.e., $[s_i]_{i \in [n]} = [\tilde{s}_i]_{i \in [n]}$, and then verifies the correctness of the guess via a set $\mathcal{Q} \triangleq \mathcal{Q}_1 \cup \mathcal{Q}_2$ of queries to $\mathcal{M}_1$ such that *except with negligible probability*, the guess is correct if and only if $\mathcal{M}_1$ returns 1 on *every* query in $\mathcal{Q}$.

In more detail, $\mathcal{V}$ consists of two *consecutive* phases: Phase 1 and Phase 2.

- By issuing a set $\mathcal{Q}_1$ of queries to $\mathcal{M}_1$, *Phase 1* is devoted to deciding whether $\mathbf{b}_k \in U_k = S_2 \cup S_3$ or not;
- Conditioned on $\mathbf{b}_k \in U_k$ and hence $\mathbf{b}_k = r_0 \cdot \mathbf{a}_k$ for some $r_0 \in \mathbb{F}_q$, *Phase 2* is to decide whether $r_0 = 0$ or not, by a set $\mathcal{Q}_2$ of queries to $\mathcal{M}_1$.

It remains to design $\mathcal{Q} = \mathcal{Q}_1 \cup \mathcal{Q}_2$. Jumping ahead, for every query $(\mathbf{x}, \mathbf{w}, \mathbf{z})$ in $\mathcal{Q}$, the $\mathbf{x}$-entry is always of the form $\mathbf{x}_0 + 2\mathbf{e}$, where $\mathsf{Dim}(\mathbf{x}_0) = I = [n]$, and $\mathbf{e} \leftarrow \mathbb{Z}^n_{1+2\alpha'\sqrt{n}}$. Similar to that of $\mathcal{A}'_1$, the $\mathbf{e}$-part is introduced here to make those queries made by $\mathcal{V}$ as "random-looking" as possible.

Design of Phase 1. Jumping ahead, the query set $\mathcal{Q}_1 = \mathcal{Q}_1(\mathbf{F}_k)$ is

$$\mathcal{Q}_1(\mathbf{F}_k) = \left\{ Q_{t,\ell} = (\tau(t, \mathbf{f}_{k,\ell}) + 2\mathbf{e}_{t,\ell}, \mathbf{w}_{t,\ell}, \mathbf{z}_{t,\ell}) \,\middle|\, t \in [q_0], \ell \in [n-1], \mathbf{e}_{t,\ell} \leftarrow \mathbb{Z}^n_{1+2\alpha'\sqrt{n}} \right\}.$$

It remains to set the $\mathbf{w}_{t,\ell}$- and $\mathbf{z}_{t,\ell}$-entries.

Observe that for the query $(\tau(t, \mathbf{f}_{k,\ell}) + 2\mathbf{e}_{t,\ell}, \mathbf{w}_{t,\ell} = [w_{t,\ell,j}]_{j\in[n]}, \mathbf{z}_{t,\ell}) \in \mathcal{Q}_1(\mathbf{F}_k)$, $\mathcal{M}_1$ first generates $\varepsilon_{t,\ell} \leftarrow \mathbb{Z}^n_{1+2\theta}$, and then computes

$$\mathbf{v}_{t,\ell} \triangleq \mathbf{s} \cdot (\tau(t, \mathbf{f}_{k,\ell}) + 2\mathbf{e}_{t,\ell}) + q_0 \cdot \mathbf{w}_{t,\ell} + 2\varepsilon_{t,\ell}$$

$$= \mathbf{s} \cdot \tau(t, \mathbf{f}_{k,\ell}) + q_0 \cdot \mathbf{w}_{t,\ell} + 2(\varepsilon_{t,\ell} + \varepsilon'_{t,\ell}) \quad (\varepsilon'_{t,\ell} \triangleq \mathbf{s} \cdot \mathbf{e}_{t,\ell} \sim [\varepsilon'_{t,\ell,j}]_{j\in[n]})$$

$$\sim \begin{bmatrix} t \cdot A_1(\mathbf{f}_{k,\ell}) + t \cdot B_1(\mathbf{f}_{k,\ell}) + q_0 \cdot w_{t,\ell,1} \\ \vdots \\ t \cdot A_k(\mathbf{f}_{k,\ell}) + t \cdot B_k(\mathbf{f}_{k,\ell}) + q_0 \cdot w_{t,\ell,k} \\ \vdots \\ t \cdot A_n(\mathbf{f}_{k,\ell}) + t \cdot B_n(\mathbf{f}_{k,\ell}) + q_0 \cdot w_{t,\ell,n} \end{bmatrix} + \begin{bmatrix} 2(\varepsilon_{t,\ell,1} + \varepsilon'_{t,\ell,1}) \\ \vdots \\ 2(\varepsilon_{t,\ell,k} + \varepsilon'_{t,\ell,k}) \\ \vdots \\ 2(\varepsilon_{t,\ell,n} + \varepsilon'_{t,\ell,n}) \end{bmatrix}.$$

Notice that when $q > 1 + 8(\theta + n\alpha\alpha')$, the noise $(\varepsilon_{t,\ell} + \varepsilon'_{t,\ell})$ is "short" in the sense that $\|\varepsilon_{t,\ell} + \varepsilon'_{t,\ell}\|_\infty < q_0/4$ holds *w.o.p.* With this in mind, we can define the aforementioned query set

$$\mathcal{Q}_1(\mathbf{F}_k) \triangleq \left\{ \begin{pmatrix} \tau(t, \mathbf{f}_{k,\ell}) + 2\mathbf{e}_{t,\ell}, \\ [w_{t,\ell,j}]_{j\in[n]}, \\ [z_{t,\ell,j}]_{j\in[n]} \end{pmatrix} \,\middle|\, \begin{array}{l} t \in [q_0], \ell \in [n-1], j \in [n], \mathbf{e}_{t,\ell} \leftarrow \mathbb{Z}^n_{1+2\alpha'\sqrt{n}}, \\ u_{t,\ell,j} = tA_j(\mathbf{f}_{k,\ell}), w_{t,\ell,j} = \mathsf{Cha}(u_{t,\ell,j}), \\ z_{t,\ell,j} = \mathsf{Mod}(u_{t,\ell,j}, w_{t,\ell,j}) \end{array} \right\}$$

And this choice of $\mathcal{Q}_1(\mathbf{F}_k)$ is justified by the following lemma.

Lemma 9. *With the notations defined previously, if $q > 1 + 8(\theta + n\alpha\alpha')$, then except with negligible probability, we have*

(a) If $\mathcal{M}_1$ returns 0 on some queries in $\mathcal{Q}_1(\mathbf{F}_k)$, then $\mathbf{b}_k \neq \mathbf{0}$;
(b) If $\mathcal{M}_1$ returns 1 on every query in $\mathcal{Q}_1(\mathbf{F}_k)$, then $\mathbf{b}_k \in U_k = S_2 \cup S_3$.

Proof. First, if $\mathbf{b}_k \in S_3 = \{\mathbf{0}\}$, then our guess is correct, every $\mathbf{b}_j = \mathbf{0}$ and hence every $B_j(\cdot) = 0$; By Lemma 4(b), $\mathcal{M}_1$ returns 1 *w.o.p.* for every query in $\mathcal{Q}_1(\mathbf{F}_k)$.

Moreover, if $\mathbf{b}_k \in S_1 = \mathbb{F}^n_q \setminus U_k$, then there exists $\mathbf{f}_{k,\ell^*} \in \mathbf{F}_k$ such that $B_k(\mathbf{f}_{k,\ell^*}) \neq 0$; Moreover, there exists a $t^* \in [q_0]$ such that $t^* \cdot B_k(\mathbf{f}_{k,\ell^*}) = \pm 1$. By Lemma 4(c), for the specific query $Q_{t^*,\ell^*} \in \mathcal{Q}_1(\mathbf{F}_k)$, its associated k-th equality does not hold *w.o.p.*, and hence $\mathcal{M}_1$ returns 0 *w.o.p.* on Q_{t^*,ℓ^*}. $\square$

It should be stressed that in Phase 1, it is *not easy* to analyze the distribution of those query replies when $\mathbf{b}_k \in S_2$, which explains the necessity of Phase 2.

Design of Phase 2. In Phase 2, conditioned on the hypothesis $\mathbf{b}_k \in U_k = S_2 \cup S_3$, it remains to consider whether $\mathbf{b}_k \in S_2$ or $\mathbf{b}_k \in S_3 = \{0\}$. By hypothesis, we have $\mathbf{b}_k \in U_k = \{r \cdot \mathbf{a}_k \mid r \in \mathbb{F}_q\}$; Hence, we can assume $\mathbf{b}_k = r_0 \cdot \mathbf{a}_k$ for some $r_0 \in \mathbb{F}_q$. Then $B_k(\mathbf{u}) = r_0 \cdot A_k(\mathbf{u})$ for every $\mathbf{u} \in \mathbb{F}_q^n$. Moreover, the question now could be expressed in terms of r_0, *i.e.*, whether $r_0 = 0$ or not.

Choose $\mathbf{u}^* \leftarrow \mathcal{R}_q$ *randomly* such that $A_k(\mathbf{u}^*) = 1$ and *every entry of $\mathbf{u}^*$ is non-zero*. It follows $t \cdot A_k(\mathbf{u}^*) + t \cdot B_k(\mathbf{u}^*) = t(1 + r_0)$ for every $t \in \mathbb{F}_q$. Jumping ahead, the set $\mathcal{Q}_2 = \mathcal{Q}_2(\mathbf{u}^*)$ is

$$\mathcal{Q}_2(\mathbf{u}^*) = \left\{ Q_t' = (\tau(t, \mathbf{u}^*) + 2\mathbf{e}_t, \mathbf{w}_t, \mathbf{z}_t) \,\middle|\, t \in [q_0], \mathbf{e}_t \leftarrow \mathbb{Z}_{1 + 2\alpha'\sqrt{n}}^n \right\}.$$

It remains to set the $\mathbf{w}_t$- and $\mathbf{z}_t$-entries.

Observe that for every query $Q_t' = (\tau(t, \mathbf{u}^*) + 2\mathbf{e}_t, \mathbf{w}_t = [w_{t,j}]_{j \in [n]}, \mathbf{z}_t = [z_{t,j}]_{j \in [n]})$, $\mathcal{M}_1$ first generates $\varepsilon_t \leftarrow \mathbb{Z}_{1+2\theta}^n$, and then computes

$$
\begin{aligned}
\mathbf{v}_t' &\triangleq \mathbf{s} \cdot (\tau(t, \mathbf{u}^*) + 2\mathbf{e}_t) + q_0 \cdot \mathbf{w}_t + 2\varepsilon_t \\
&= \mathbf{s} \cdot \tau(t, \mathbf{u}^*) + q_0 \cdot \mathbf{w}_t + 2(\varepsilon_t + \varepsilon_t') \\
&\sim
\begin{bmatrix}
t \cdot A_1(\mathbf{u}^*) + t \cdot B_1(\mathbf{u}^*) + q_0 w_{t,1} \\
\vdots \\
t + t \cdot r_0 + q_0 w_{t,k} \\
\vdots \\
t \cdot A_n(\mathbf{u}^*) + t \cdot B_n(\mathbf{u}^*) + q_0 w_{t,n}
\end{bmatrix}
+
\begin{bmatrix}
2(\varepsilon_{t,1} + \varepsilon_{t,1}') \\
\vdots \\
2(\varepsilon_{t,k} + \varepsilon_{t,k}') \\
\vdots \\
2(\varepsilon_{t,n} + \varepsilon_{t,n}')
\end{bmatrix},
\end{aligned}
$$

where $\varepsilon_t' \triangleq \mathbf{s} \cdot \mathbf{e}_t \sim [\varepsilon_{t,j}']_{j \in [n]}$. Again, when $q > 1 + 8(\theta + n\alpha\alpha')$, the inequality $\|\varepsilon_t + \varepsilon_t'\|_\infty < q_0/4$ holds *w.o.p.* With this in mind, we can define

$$\mathcal{Q}_2(\mathbf{u}^*) \triangleq \left\{ \begin{pmatrix} \tau(t, \mathbf{u}^*) + 2\mathbf{e}_t, \\ [w_{t,j}]_{j \in [n]}, [z_{t,j}]_{j \in [n]} \end{pmatrix} \middle| \begin{array}{l} t \in [q_0], j \in [n], \mathbf{e}_t \leftarrow \mathbb{Z}_{1+2\alpha'\sqrt{n}}^n, u_{t,j} = tA_j(\mathbf{u}^*), \\ w_{t,j} = \mathsf{Cha}\,(u_{t,j}), z_{t,j} = \mathsf{Mod}\,(u_{t,j}, w_{t,j}) \end{array} \right\}$$

And this choice of $\mathcal{Q}_2(\mathbf{u}^*)$ is justified by the following lemma.

Lemma 10. *With the notations defined previously, if $q > 1 + 8(\theta + n\alpha\alpha')$ and $\mathbf{b}_k \in U_k$ are guaranteed, then except with negligible probability, we have $[s_i]_{i \in [n]} = [\tilde{s}_i]_{i \in [n]}$ if and only if $\mathcal{M}_1$ returns 1 on every query in $\mathcal{Q}_2(\mathbf{u}^*)$.*

Proof. First, if $[s_i]_{i \in [n]} = [\tilde{s}_i]_{i \in [n]}$, then our guess is correct, $r_0 = 0$, and every $B_j(\cdot) = 0$. By Lemma 4(b), $\mathcal{M}_1$ returns 1 on every query in $\mathcal{Q}_2(\mathbf{u}^*)$.

Conversely, if $r_0 \neq 0$, then there exists a $t^* \in [q_0]$ such that $t^* r_0 = \pm 1$. Similarly, by Lemma 4(c), $\mathcal{M}_1$ returns 0 *w.o.p.* on this specific query $Q_{t^*}' = (\tau(t^*, \mathbf{u}^*) + 2\mathbf{e}_{t^*}, \mathbf{w}_{t^*}, \mathbf{z}_{t^*}) \in \mathcal{Q}_2(\mathbf{u}^*)$. $\qquad\square$

This finishes the construction of $\mathcal{V}$, as well as its correctness analysis, for the *special* case when the index set $I = [n]$. Clearly it takes at most $n \cdot q_0 = \text{poly}(\lambda)$ queries for $\mathcal{V}$ to solve this *special* case of $\mathcal{P}_2$, indicating that $\mathcal{V}$ runs in polynomial time. Also, computer experiments have justified the correctness of $\mathcal{V}$.

Moreover, it is easy to generalize the foregoing construction such that $\mathcal{V}$ could be applied to solve the more general case of $\mathcal{P}_2$, i.e., $\emptyset \neq I \subsetneqq [n]$. In general, the number of queries made by $\mathcal{V}$ is upper-bounded by $q_0 \cdot |I| = \text{poly}(\lambda)$.

Theorem 5. *When $q > 1 + 8(\theta + n\alpha\alpha')$, it takes at most $q_0 \cdot |I|$ queries for $\mathcal{V}$ to decide whether $[s_i]_{i \in I} = [\tilde{s}_i]_{i \in I}$ or not: except with negligible probability, the equality holds if and only if $\mathcal{M}_1$ returns 1 on every query in $\mathcal{Q} = \mathcal{Q}_1 \cup \mathcal{Q}_2$. In particular, for every query in $\mathcal{Q}$, its $\boldsymbol{x}$-entry could be written as $\boldsymbol{x} = \boldsymbol{x}_0 + 2\boldsymbol{e}$ satisfying $\text{Dim}(\boldsymbol{x}_0) = I$ and $\boldsymbol{e} \in \mathbb{Z}^n_{1+2\alpha'\sqrt{n}}$.* $\qquad\square$

A Hybrid Lattice Basis Reduction and Quantum Search Attack on LWE

Florian Göpfert[2], Christine van Vredendaal[1]([✉]), and Thomas Wunderer[2]

[1] Department of Mathematics and Computer Science,
Technische Universiteit Eindhoven,
P.O. Box 513, 5600 MB Eindhoven, The Netherlands
c.v.vredendaal@tue.nl
[2] Fachbereich Informatik, Technische Universität Darmstadt,
Hochschulstraße, 10, 64289 Darmstadt, Germany
{fgoepfert,twunderer}@cdc.informatik.tu-darmstadt.de

Abstract. Recently, an increasing amount of papers proposing post-quantum schemes also provide concrete parameter sets aiming for concrete post-quantum security levels. Security evaluations of such schemes need to include all possible attacks, in particular those by quantum adversaries. In the case of lattice-based cryptography, currently existing quantum attacks are mainly classical attacks, carried out with quantum basis reduction as subroutine.

In this work, we propose a new quantum attack on the learning with errors (LWE) problem, whose hardness is the foundation for many modern lattice-based cryptographic constructions. Our quantum attack is based on Howgrave-Graham's Classical Hybrid Attack and is suitable for LWE instances in recent cryptographic proposals. We analyze its runtime complexity and optimize it over all possible choices of the attack parameters. In addition, we analyze the concrete post-quantum security levels of the parameter sets proposed for the New Hope and Frodo key exchange schemes, as well as several instances of the Lindner-Peikert encryption scheme. Our results show that – depending on the assumed basis reduction costs – our Quantum Hybrid Attack either significantly outperforms, or is at least comparable to all other attacks covered by Albrecht–Player–Scott in their work "On the concrete hardness of Learning with Errors". We further show that our Quantum Hybrid Attack improves upon the Classical Hybrid Attack in the case of LWE with binary error.

Keywords: Public-key encryption · Lattice-based cryptography · LWE · Quantum attack · Hybrid Attack

1 Introduction

Over the past decade *lattice-based cryptography* [31] has proven to be one of the most promising candidates for post-quantum cryptography. One of the reasons for this is the seemingly strong resistance it has shown against quantum attacks.

T. Lange and T. Takagi (Eds.): PQCrypto 2017, LNCS 10346, pp. 184–202, 2017.
DOI: 10.1007/978-3-319-59879-6_11

On top of this lattice-based cryptography has shown a wealth of applications (e.g., [5,15,16,19,20,30,33]). The foundation for many recent lattice-based cryptographic constructions is the *Learning with Errors* (LWE) problem [30,32,33], which is provably as hard as worst-case lattice problems [8,33].

In order to evaluate the concrete post-quantum security levels of LWE-based schemes, cryptanalysts must evaluate the best known algorithms to solve the underlying LWE problem. This evaluation must not only consider classical attacks, but attacks by adversaries with quantum computing power. So far the only existing quantum attacks on LWE are classical attacks where the basis reduction subroutine is replaced by quantum basis reduction.

In this work we present a new quantum attack on LWE: the Quantum Hybrid Attack. The attack is based on Howgrave-Graham's Classical Hybrid Attack [21], which combines lattice-based techniques such as basis reduction [14,24] with guessing techniques such as brute-force or meet-in-the-middle attack [6] (MitM). In its original form the Classical Hybrid Attack was designed to break the NTRU cryptosystem, but has recently been applied to instances of LWE with highly structured error distributions such as binary or trinary errors [11,37].

From a technical point of view our algorithm replaces the MitM-phase with a generalization of Grover's quantum search algorithm by Brassard–Hoyer–Mosca–Tapp [9]. The idea to replace this phase by Grover's search algorithm [17] was sketched in Schanck's thesis [34], but is in its original form only practical for highly structured (e.g., uniform) NTRU keys. A straightforward application of this idea to LWE Hybrid Attacks would therefore only be practical for LWE with small (uniform) error such as binary or trinary errors. In contrast, our attack is applicable for LWE with arbitrary error distribution and is particularly suitable for LWE instances in recent cryptographic proposals. This is achieved by replacing Grover's quantum search with the generalization by Brassard–Hoyer–Mosca–Tapp. For example, the time to recover r coefficients of a vector following the New Hope error distribution decreases from $2^{2.52r}$ with Grover's algorithm to $2^{1.85r}$ with the variant used for the new attack.

We also give a detailed analysis of the Quantum Hybrid Attack and optimize the attack parameters selection. We apply the new attack to the LWE key-exchange schemes New Hope [3] and Frodo [7], and the R-BinLWEenc [10] and Lindner-Peikert [25] encryption schemes, and compare it to the runtimes estimations for existing attacks given by the LWE estimator [2,35]. Depending on the assumed basis reduction costs, our Quantum Hybrid Attack either significantly outperforms, or is at least comparable to all other attacks covered by [2]. We also show that our Quantum Hybrid Attack outperforms the Classical Hybrid Attack in the case of LWE with binary errors.

1.1 Structure of the Paper

The remainder of this paper is organized as follows. In Sect. 2 we introduce lattice definitions and notations in order to explain the Classical Hybrid Attack in Sect. 3. Then in Sect. 4 we explain our improved Quantum Hybrid Attack for LWE instances with arbitrary secret and error distributions. We then analyze the runtime complexity and optimize it over the choice of the attack parameters in Sect. 5. Lastly, in Sect. 6 we apply this runtime to concrete parameter sets and compare it to existing attacks using the LWE simulator on common key-exchange and encryption schemes.

2 Preliminaries

We denote vectors by bold lower case (e.g., $\mathbf{a} \in \mathbb{Z}^n$) letters, matrices by bold uppercase letters (e.g., $\mathbf{A} \in \mathbb{Z}^{m \times n}$) and probability distributions by upper case letters (e.g., D). We use the notation $\mathbb{Z}_q$ for the quotient ring $\mathbb{Z}/q\mathbb{Z}$. By $\mathbf{a} \bmod q$ we indicate that each component of the vector is reduced modulo q to lie in the interval $[-\lceil \frac{q}{2} \rceil, \frac{q}{2})$.

For a probability distribution X, we write $x \xleftarrow{\$} X$ if an element x is sampled according to X. For every element a in the support of X, we write $x_a := \Pr[a = b | b \xleftarrow{\$} X]$. We will specifically refer to the discrete Gaussian distribution D_σ as the distribution such that

$$\forall y \in \mathbb{Z} : \Pr[x = y | x \xleftarrow{\$} D_\sigma] \sim \exp\left(-\frac{y^2}{2\sigma^2}\right).$$

For a probabilistic algorithm $\mathcal{A}$, $x \xleftarrow{\$} \mathcal{A}$ assigns the outcome of one (random) run of $\mathcal{A}$ to x.

The *Learning with Errors* (LWE) problem was introduced by Regev [33] and has been the foundation of many cryptographic constructions [30,32,33] since.

Definition 1. *Let $n, m, q \in \mathbb{Z}$ be positive integers and let D_e be a distribution on $\mathbb{Z}^m$ and D_s be a distribution on $\mathbb{Z}^n$. Let $\mathbf{s} \xleftarrow{\$} D_s$, $\mathbf{A}$ be chosen uniformly at random from $\mathbb{Z}_q^{m \times n}$, $\mathbf{e} \xleftarrow{\$} D_e$, and $\mathbf{b} = \mathbf{A}\mathbf{s} + \mathbf{e} \bmod q$. The LWE problem is the problem of recovering $\mathbf{s}$, given $(\mathbf{A}, \mathbf{b})$.*

We now review some basic definitions for lattices (for a full survey see e.g., [26]). Throughout this paper, we only consider full-rank lattices. A set $\Lambda \subset \mathbb{R}^m$ is called a *lattice* Λ in $\mathbb{R}^m$ if

$$\Lambda = \Lambda(\mathbf{B}) := \left\{ \mathbf{x} \in \mathbb{R}^m | \ \mathbf{x} = \sum_{i=1}^{m} \alpha_i \mathbf{b}_i, \text{ with } \alpha_i \in \mathbb{Z} \right\},$$

for some $\mathbb{R}$-linearly independent set $\mathbf{B} = \{\mathbf{b}_1, \ldots, \mathbf{b}_m\} \subset \mathbb{R}^m$. Such a set $\mathbf{B}$ is called a basis of the lattice Λ.

The *determinant* $\det(\Lambda)$ of a lattice Λ is defined as $\det(\Lambda) = |\det(\mathbf{B})|$, where $\mathbf{B}$ is some basis of Λ. This definition is independent of the choice of the basis.

The Hermite delta δ of a basis $\mathbf{B} = (\mathbf{b}_1, \ldots, \mathbf{b}_m)$ is defined via $\|\mathbf{b}_1\| = \delta^m \det(\Lambda)^{1/m}$.

Lattice-based cryptography is based on a variety of lattice problems that are conjectured to be hard. In the following we list the problems relevant to this work. The *Shortest Vector Problem* (SVP) is to find a shortest non-zero lattice vector, given a basis of the lattice.

The *unique Shortest Vector Problem* (uSVP) is a variant of SVP with the additional promise that the shortest non-zero lattice vector $\mathbf{y}$ is significantly shorter than all other lattice vectors that are not an integral multiple of $\mathbf{y}$.

The *Bounded Distance Decoding* (BDD) problem is the problem of given a basis of a lattice in $\mathbb{R}^m$ and a target vector $\mathbf{t} \in \mathbb{R}^m$ that is close to a lattice vector $\mathbf{v}$, find the lattice vector $\mathbf{v}$. In this work we assume that the task is to find $\mathbf{t} - \mathbf{v}$ instead of $\mathbf{v}$, which is equivalently hard.

3   The Classical Hybrid Attack

In this section, we recap the approach of solving LWE problems with the Classical Hybrid Attack, see e.g., [11,37]. The first step is to transform the LWE problem instance $\mathbf{A} \in \mathbb{Z}_q^{m \times n}, \mathbf{b} = \mathbf{As} + \mathbf{e} \in \mathbb{Z}_q^m$, into a uSVP instance. Note that a "short" $\mathbf{s}$ is necessary for this transformation to be possible. This is however a requirement that is typical for LWE instances. The second step is to then solve the resulting uSVP instance with the Hybrid Attack.

We use the following common approach [2,6,27] to transform an LWE problem into uSVP. Consider the d-dimensional lattice

$$\Lambda = \{\mathbf{x} \in \mathbb{Z}^d : (\mathbf{A}|\mathbf{I}_m| - \mathbf{b})\mathbf{x} = \mathbf{0} \bmod q\},$$

where $d = n + m + 1$. With high probability, we have $\det(\Lambda) = q^m$ [27]. Since $\mathbf{b} = \mathbf{As} + \mathbf{e}$, the vector $\mathbf{v} = (\mathbf{s}, \mathbf{e}, 1) \in \mathbb{Z}^d$ is a vector in the lattice Λ. Provided $\mathbf{v}$ is sufficiently short (again, this is typical for LWE instances), this leads to a uSVP problem in the lattice Λ. In order to apply the Hybrid Attack to the uSVP instance we need to compute a basis $\mathbf{B}'$ of Λ of the form

$$\mathbf{B}' = \begin{pmatrix} \mathbf{B} & \mathbf{C} \\ \mathbf{0} & \mathbf{I}_r \end{pmatrix} \in \mathbb{Z}^{d \times d},$$

for some $r \in \mathbb{N}$ with $r < m, n$. Wunderer [37] showed that with high probability such a basis of Λ exists and can be found efficiently.

The main idea of the Hybrid Attack is to split the short vector $\mathbf{v}$ into two parts $\mathbf{v} = (\mathbf{v}_\ell, \mathbf{v}_g)$ with $\mathbf{v}_\ell \in \mathbb{Z}^{d-r}$ and $\mathbf{v}_g \in \mathbb{Z}^r$. With this notation it holds that

$$\mathbf{v} = \begin{pmatrix} \mathbf{v}_\ell \\ \mathbf{v}_g \end{pmatrix} = \mathbf{B}' \begin{pmatrix} \mathbf{x} \\ \mathbf{v}_g \end{pmatrix} = \begin{pmatrix} \mathbf{Bx} + \mathbf{Cv}_g \\ \mathbf{v}_g \end{pmatrix},$$

for some vector $\mathbf{x} \in \mathbb{Z}^{d-r}$, which implies $\mathbf{v}_\ell - \mathbf{Bx} = \mathbf{Cv}_g$. Note that $\mathbf{Bx}$ is a lattice vector in the lattice spanned by $\mathbf{B}$, and $\mathbf{v}_\ell$ is a short vector. Consequently, if $\mathbf{v}_g$ is known, we can recover $\mathbf{v}_\ell$ by solving BDD in the lattice spanned by $\mathbf{B}$ with target vector $\mathbf{Cv}_g$. This idea results in the Hybrid Attack: loop through guesses for $\mathbf{v}_g$ and check if a guess is correct (and if so recover $\mathbf{v}_\ell$) by solving the corresponding BDD. To solve this problem Babai's Nearest Plane algorithm [4] is used. Nearest Plane runs in polynomial time, but in order to achieve a high success probability it requires a lattice basis of sufficiently good quality, which in turn has to be generated by an exponential time precomputation step (basis reduction). This makes Nearest Plane suitable for the Hybrid Attack. For every guess of $\mathbf{v}_g$ we have to solve one instance of BDD. Every such instance is a BDD in the same lattice spanned by $\mathbf{B}$, only with a different target vector. However, the most time-consuming step (basis reduction) of Nearest Plane is independent of the target vector. Consequently, we can precompute a good basis of the lattice spanned by $\mathbf{B}$ *before* looping over the possible guesses of $\mathbf{v}_g$. Therefore, we can balance the time spent on basis reduction and on guessing values for $\mathbf{v}_g$ to obtain the optimal trade-off.

As was already shown by Howgrave-Graham [21], the guessing part of the attack can be sped up using meet-in-the-middle techniques. However, this approach has three main drawbacks. First, it is only practical for highly structured LWE instances such as LWE with binary or trinary error distribution [37]. Second, its memory requirements are huge [36]. Third, the probability that collisions are actually recognized can be extremely small [37]. In this work, we show how the guessing part can be sped up by using quantum search algorithms. Our Quantum Hybrid Attack, outlined in the next section, eliminates all three drawbacks of the meet-in-the-middle approach and thus enables the Hybrid Attack to handle arbitrary error distributions of LWE.

4   The Quantum Hybrid Attack

We now introduce our new Quantum Hybrid Attack. The main idea is to use quantum search algorithms to speed up the guessing part of the classical Hybrid Attack. This section is structured as follows. We give a brief summary of Grover's quantum search algorithm and its modified version developed by Brassard-Hoyer-Mosca-Tapp [9] in Sect. 4.1. In Sect. 4.2 we show how to use this quantum search algorithm inside the Hybrid Attack to obtain a new Quantum Hybrid Attack.

4.1   Amplitude Amplification

In 1996, Grover presented a quantum algorithm that can speed up the search in unstructured databases [17]. Given a function $f : S \rightarrow \{0,1\}$ for some finite set S, we call $S_f := \{x \in \{0,1\}^d \mid f(x) = 1\}$ the set of marked elements. Grover's algorithm allows to find an element $x \in S_f$ in approximately $\frac{\pi}{4} \cdot \sqrt{|S|/|S_f|}$ evaluations of f (without any further knowledge about f), while classical algorithms require an average number of evaluations in the order of $|S|/|S_f|$.

The runtime of Grover's search algorithm is independent of how the marked elements have been chosen. The drawback is that additional information about the choice of the marked elements is not used. A generalization of Grover's search algorithm that can utilize the probability distribution on the search space was presented by Brassard–Hoyer–Mosca–Tapp [9]. Their generalization uses an additional algorithm $\mathcal{A}$ sampling from some distribution on the search space S.

Theorem 1 ([9], Theorem 3). *There exists a quantum algorithm* QSearch *with the following property. Let $\mathcal{A}$ be any quantum algorithm that uses no measurements (i.e., a unitary transformation), and let $f : S \to \{0,1\}$ be any Boolean function. Let a denote the initial success probability of $\mathcal{A}$ (i.e., $a = \Pr[f(x) = 1, x \xleftarrow{\$} \mathcal{A}]$). The algorithm* QSearch *finds a good solution using an expected number of applications of $\mathcal{A}$, $\mathcal{A}^{-1}$ and f which are in $\Theta(1/\sqrt{a})$ if $a > 0$, and otherwise runs forever.*

The quantum algorithm $\mathcal{A}$ can be constructed as follows: Given an arbitrary (efficient) probabilistic sampling algorithm, it can be easily transformed into a deterministic algorithm that gets random bits as input. This algorithm in turn can be transformed into a quantum algorithm. Instantiating this quantum algorithm with the uniform distribution as superposition for the input bits leads to the wanted algorithm $\mathcal{A}$.

Note that the complexity of the algorithm is only given asymptotically. This is only necessary because the probability a is unknown. In Appendix A, we show that the hidden constant is indeed small, and we can ignore the Landau notation in our runtime estimates.

4.2   The Attack

We now describe our new Quantum Hybrid Attack (Algorithm 2). We use the notation $\mathrm{NP_B(t)}$ to indicate that Nearest Plane is called on the target vector $\mathbf{t}$ and input basis $\mathbf{B}$. Inputs for the Quantum Hybrid Attack are an LWE instance $(\mathbf{A}, \mathbf{b}) \in \mathbb{Z}_q^{m \times n} \times \mathbb{Z}_q^m$, the LWE error distribution D_e, and the attack parameters r, δ. The algorithm first transforms the LWE instance into a uSVP instance as described in Sect. 3 and then runs *QSearch* with the function defined by Algorithm 1.

As we show in Sect. 5, it is not optimal to use the error distribution for the sampling algorithm $\mathcal{A}$ to find the solution. Instead we use the following transformed distribution.

Definition 2. *Let X be an arbitrary distribution with support S. We write $T(X)$ for the distribution defined by*

$$\forall a \in S : \Pr[a = b | b \xleftarrow{\$} T(X)] = \frac{x_a^{\frac{2}{3}}}{\sum_{c \in S} x_c^{\frac{2}{3}}}.$$

Our Quantum Hybrid Attack is presented in Algorithm 2. Recall that the attack parameter r indicates the guessing dimension and parameter δ is the Hermite delta used for basis reduction algorithms.

Algorithm 1. Function $f_{\mathbf{A},\mathbf{b},\mathbf{B},\mathbf{C}}(\mathbf{w}_g)$

1 $\mathbf{w}_\ell \leftarrow \mathrm{NP}_\mathbf{B}(\mathbf{C}\mathbf{w}_g)$;
2 Set $(\mathbf{s}',\mathbf{e}',1) = (\mathbf{w}_\ell,\mathbf{w}_g)$;
3 **if** $\mathbf{A}\mathbf{s}' + \mathbf{e}' = \mathbf{b}$ *and* $\mathbf{s}',\mathbf{e}'$ *are small* **then**
4 $\quad\lfloor$ return 1;

5 **else**
6 $\quad\lfloor$ return 0;

Algorithm 2. Quantum Hybrid Attack

Input: LWE instance $\mathbf{A} \in \mathbb{Z}_q^{m\times n}, \mathbf{b} \in \mathbb{Z}_q^m$, error distribution D_e on $\mathbb{Z}^m$, attack
  parameters $\delta \in \mathbb{R}_{>1}, r \in \mathbb{N}, r < m,n$
1 Let D be the distribution of the last r entries of the vector $(\mathbf{x},1)$, where
  $\mathbf{x} \overset{\$}{\leftarrow} D_e$;
2 Set $\mathcal{A}$ to be a quantum algorithm without measuring for the distribution $T(D)$;
3 Calculate basis $\mathbf{B}'$ of lattice $\Lambda = \{\mathbf{x} \in \mathbb{Z}^{m+n+1} : (\mathbf{A}|\mathbf{I}_m| - \mathbf{b})\mathbf{x} = \mathbf{0} \bmod q\}$ of
  form $\mathbf{B}' = \begin{pmatrix} \mathbf{B} & \mathbf{C} \\ \mathbf{0} & \mathbf{I}_r \end{pmatrix}$;
4 Perform basis reduction to reduce $\mathbf{B}$ to Hermite delta δ;
5 Let $\mathbf{v}'_g$ be the result of *QSearch* (Theorem 1) with function $f_{\mathbf{A},\mathbf{b},\mathbf{B},\mathbf{C}}$
  (Algorithm 1) and quantum algorithm $\mathcal{A}$;
6 return $(\mathrm{NP}_\mathbf{B}(\mathbf{v}'_g), \mathbf{v}'_g)$;

---

5 Analysis

In this section, we analyze the runtime complexity of the Quantum Hybrid Attack and show how to minimize it over all choices of attack parameters.

5.1 Success Probability and Number of Function Applications

In the following, we show our main result about the runtime of our Quantum Hybrid Attack.

Main Result. *For an LWE instance* $(\mathbf{A}, \mathbf{b} = \mathbf{A}\mathbf{s} + \mathbf{e})$, *let the vectors* $\mathbf{v}, \mathbf{v}_\ell, \mathbf{v}_g$, *the matrices* $\mathbf{B}, \mathbf{B}'$, *the distribution* D, *the algorithm* $\mathcal{A}$, *and the parameters* n, m, q, d, r, δ *be defined as in Sects. 3 and 4.*

The success probability p *of the Quantum Hybrid Attack is approximately*

$$p \approx \prod_{i=1}^{d-r}\left(1 - \frac{2}{B(\frac{(d-r)-1}{2},\frac{1}{2})}\int_{-1}^{\max(-r_i,-1)}(1-t^2)^{\frac{(d-r)-3}{2}}\,dt\right),$$

where $B(\cdot,\cdot)$ *denotes the Euler beta function (see [29]),*

$$r_i = \frac{R_i}{2\|\mathbf{v}_\ell\|} \quad \text{for all } i \in \{1,\ldots,d-r\},$$

and $R_1, \ldots, R_{m-r}$ denote the lengths of the Gram-Schmidt basis vectors corresponding to the basis $\mathbf{B}$.

In case of success, the expected number of applications of f, $\mathcal{A}$, and $\mathcal{A}^{-1}$ in Algorithm 2 is $\Theta(L)$, where

$$
L = \left(\sum_{x \in \mathsf{supp}(D)} d_x^{\frac{2}{3}} \right)^{\frac{3}{2}}.
$$

Furthermore, the choice of the distribution for the sampling algorithm $\mathcal{A}$ in Algorithm 4 is optimal.

We first determine the success probability of the attack. We then calculate and optimize the number of applications of f, $\mathcal{A}$, and $\mathcal{A}^{-1}$ and compare our results with Grover's search algorithm.

Success Probability. If $\mathrm{NP_B}(\mathbf{Cv}_g) = \mathbf{v}_\ell$, we have $f_{\mathbf{A},\mathbf{b},\mathbf{B},\mathbf{C}}(\mathbf{v}_g) = 1$ with overwhelming probability and *QSearch* recovers $\mathbf{v}_g$. An approximation of the probability that $\mathrm{NP_B}(\mathbf{Cv}_g) = \mathbf{v}_\ell$ is calculated in [11,37] and yields the success probability given in Theorem 1. If the components of the LWE error are distributed according to a discrete Gaussian distribution with standard deviation σ, this approximation can be replaced by the simpler (and more efficiently computable) formula

$$
\Pr\left[\mathrm{NP_B}(\mathbf{Cv}_g) = \mathbf{v}_\ell\right] = \prod_{i=1}^{d-r} \mathrm{erf}\left(\frac{R_i \sqrt{2}}{\sigma} \right) \tag{1}
$$

given by Lindner and Peikert [25].

Number of Applications of f, $\mathcal{A}$, and $\mathcal{A}^{-1}$. We now calculate the expected number of applications of f, $\mathcal{A}$ and $\mathcal{A}^{-1}$ (simply called loops in the following) in the Quantum Hybrid Attack in the case the attack is successful. We show how the choice of the sampling algorithm $\mathcal{A}$ influences the number of loops, how to minimize this number over all possible choices of $\mathcal{A}$, and that our choice in Algorithm 2 is in fact optimal. In the following, let $S = \mathsf{supp}(D)$ be a finite set. The support S is the search space of our quantum algorithm. Let $\mathcal{A}$ be the initial sampling algorithm used in the Quantum Hybrid Attack and A be the distribution with support S corresponding to $\mathcal{A}$. According to Theorem 1, for a fixed target element $x \in S$ the expected number of loops in the Quantum Hybrid Attack is roughly $(\sqrt{a_x})^{-1}$. However, since the marked element (and its probability) is not known, we can only estimate the expected number of loops

$$
L(A) = L\left((a_x)_{x \in S}\right) = \sum_{x \in S} \frac{d_x}{\sqrt{a_x}}. \tag{2}
$$

In order to minimize the runtime of the quantum search we must determine the optimal distribution A that minimizes the number of loops $L(A)$. We emphasize that minimizing the number of loops is of independent interest for any quantum search algorithm based on [9] applied in a similar way as in our attack.

Minimal Number of Loops. We first minimize the expected number of loops over all possible choices of A. Without loss of generality we assume $S = \{1, \ldots, k\}$ for some $k \in \mathbb{N}$. We minimize the expected number of loops by minimizing the function

$$L : (0,1)^k \to \mathbb{R}, \quad (a_1, \ldots, a_k) \mapsto \sum_{i=1}^{k} \frac{d_i}{\sqrt{a_i}}, \tag{3}$$

in k variables $a_1, \ldots, a_k \in (0,1)$ under the constraint

$$a_1 + \ldots + a_k = 1, \tag{4}$$

where $d_1, \ldots, d_k \in (0,1)$ are fixed. In order to minimize L under the constraints, we define the Lagrange function corresponding to L and Eq. (4)

$$\mathcal{L}(\lambda, a_1, \ldots, a_k) = \left(\sum_{i=1}^{k} \frac{d_i}{\sqrt{a_i}} \right) + \lambda \left(-1 + \sum_{i=1}^{k} a_i \right). \tag{5}$$

To find the minimum of L we need to solve the following set of $k+1$ equations

$$[E_i]_{i \in \{1, \ldots, k\}} \qquad 0 = \mathcal{L}_{a_i}(\lambda, a_1, \ldots, a_k) = -\frac{d_i}{2} a_i^{-\frac{3}{2}} + \lambda$$

$$[E_c] \qquad\qquad\qquad a_1 + \ldots + a_k = 1,$$

which gives

$$a_i = \frac{d_i^{\frac{2}{3}}}{\sum_{j=1}^{k} d_j^{\frac{2}{3}}}. \tag{6}$$

It remains to be shown that choosing the a_i according to Eq. (6) leads in fact to a local *minimum* of L under the given constraints. If this is the case, this local minimum must indeed constitute the global minimum satisfying the constraints, since it is the only local minimum and L tends to infinity as one of the a_i approaches zero (hence the problem can be restricted to a compact domain). In order to show that the a_i constitute a local minimum, we compute the determinants of the leading principal minors of the bordered Hessian matrix evaluated in the a_i

$$H = \begin{pmatrix} 0 & 1 & 1 & \ldots & 1 \\ 1 & x_1 & 0 & \ldots & 0 \\ 1 & 0 & x_2 & \ddots & \vdots \\ \vdots & \vdots & \ddots & \ddots & 0 \\ 1 & 0 & \ldots & 0 & x_k \end{pmatrix}, \quad \text{where } x_i = \frac{3d_i}{4a_i^{2.5}} > 0.$$

For $j \in \{1, \ldots, k\}$ let

$$H_j = \begin{pmatrix} 0 & 1 & 1 & \ldots & 1 \\ 1 & x_1 & 0 & \ldots & 0 \\ 1 & 0 & \ddots & \ddots & \vdots \\ \vdots & \vdots & \ddots & \ddots & 0 \\ 1 & 0 & \ldots & 0 & x_j \end{pmatrix}$$

be the leading principal minors. Using Gaussian elimination we can see the determinants of all but the first principal minors of H are given by

$$\det(H_j) = \det \begin{pmatrix} x_0 & 1 & 1 & \dots & 1 \\ 0 & x_1 & 0 & \dots & 0 \\ 0 & 0 & \ddots & \ddots & \vdots \\ 0 & \vdots & \ddots & \ddots & 0 \\ 0 & 0 & \dots & 0 & x_j \end{pmatrix} \qquad \text{where } x_0 = -\left(\sum_{i=0}^{j} \frac{1}{x_i}\right) < 0.$$

Hence all determinants of the leading principal minors of H (except the first one) are negative and thus choosing the a_i according to Eq. (6) leads in fact to a local minimum of L under the given constraints. Inserting these a_i into Eq. (3) yields the minimal number of loops

$$L_{\min} = \left(\sum_{x \in S} d_x^{\frac{2}{3}}\right)^{\frac{3}{2}}. \tag{7}$$

An Important Special Case. While Eq. (7) provides a simple formula for the minimal number of loops, evaluating it might be a computationally infeasible task for a large support S. In the following we consider the case that the support is of the form $S = S_0^r$ for some $r \in \mathbb{N}$ and smaller set S_0 and that $D = P^r$ for some distribution P on S_0. Note that this is the case for most LWE-based cryptosystems, in particular for the ones we analyze in this work. We show how in this case Eq. (7) can be evaluated by computing a sum of $|S_0|$ summands and raising it to the r-th power instead of computing a sum of $|S_0|^r$ summands. This is true since Eq. (7) can be rewritten and simplified to

$$L_{\min} = \left(\sum_{x \in S} d_x^{\frac{2}{3}}\right)^{\frac{3}{2}} = \left(\sum_{y_1 \in S_0} \cdots \sum_{y_{r-1} \in S_0} \sum_{y_r \in S_0} \prod_{i=1}^{r} p_{y_i}^{\frac{2}{3}}\right)^{\frac{3}{2}} =$$

$$= \left(\sum_{y_1 \in S_0} \cdots \sum_{y_{r-1} \in S_0} \prod_{i=1}^{r-1} p_{y_i}^{\frac{2}{3}} \left(\sum_{y_r \in S_0} p_{y_r}^{\frac{2}{3}}\right)\right)^{\frac{3}{2}} =$$

$$= \left(\sum_{y_1 \in S_0} \cdots \sum_{y_{r-1} \in S_0} \prod_{i=1}^{r-1} p_{y_i}^{\frac{2}{3}} \left(\sum_{y \in S_0} p_y^{\frac{2}{3}}\right)\right)^{\frac{3}{2}} =$$

$$= \dots = \left(\left(\sum_{y \in S_0} p_y^{\frac{2}{3}}\right)^{r}\right)^{\frac{3}{2}}, \tag{8}$$

since each of the d_x is exactly the product of r of the p_y.

Comparison with Grover's Search Algorithm. If in our Quantum Hybrid Attack the distribution D is the uniform distribution, then its complexity matches the one of Grover's search algorithm

$$L_{\min} = \left(\sum_{x \in S} d_x^{\frac{2}{3}} \right)^{\frac{3}{2}} = \left(\sum_{x \in S} \left(\frac{1}{|S|} \right)^{\frac{2}{3}} \right)^{\frac{3}{2}} = \left(|S| \frac{1}{|S|^{\frac{2}{3}}} \right)^{\frac{3}{2}} = \sqrt{|S|}.$$

For a structured search space, QSearch (see Theorem 1) gives a much better complexity. As an example we examine the distribution D on the set $S = \{-16, \ldots, 16\}^r$ used in New Hope [3]. Then $|S| = 33^r$ and using Grover's search algorithm inside the Quantum Hybrid Attack would yield a complexity of

$$L_{\text{grover}} = \sqrt{33^r} \approx 2^{2.52r}.$$

In comparison, our Quantum Hybrid Attack only has complexity

$$L_{\text{our}} = \left(\left(\sum_{i=0}^{32} p_i^{\frac{2}{3}} \right)^r \right)^{\frac{3}{2}} \approx 2^{1.85r}, \quad \text{where } p_i = \binom{32}{i} \cdot 2^{-32}.$$

For $r = 200$ entries that are guessed during the Quantum Hybrid Attack this amounts to a speedup factor of 2^{134} of our approach over using Grover's algorithm inside the Hybrid Attack. This example showcases the significant improvement of our Quantum Hybrid Attack over one that is simply using Grover's search algorithm. It also demonstrates that our new Quantum Hybrid Attack opens the possibility to apply the Hybrid Attack to larger, non-uniform search spaces.

5.2 Total Runtime of the Quantum Hybrid Attack

In this section we estimate the total runtime of the Quantum Hybrid Attack by estimating the individual cost of one application of f, $\mathcal{A}$, and $\mathcal{A}^{-1}$, the precomputation (i.e., basis reduction) cost, and combining the results with the ones of Sect. 5.1. The resulting runtime formula must then be optimized over all possible attack parameters.

Cost of f, $\mathcal{A}$, and $\mathcal{A}^{-1}$. The cost of the function f is dominated by the cost of one Nearest Plane call, which was experimentally found to be roughly $k^2/2^{1.06}$ bit operations, where k is the dimension of the lattice (in our case $k = d - r$), see [18].[1] We assume that compared to this cost, the cost of the algorithm $\mathcal{A}$ and $\mathcal{A}^{-1}$ can be neglected.

---

[1] In [18], Hirschhorn, Hoffstein, Howgrave-Graham and Whyte conservatively assume that if one has to perform multiple Nearest Plane calls with the same lattice basis (as it is the case in the Quantum Hybrid Attack), one can reduce this cost to $k/2^{1.06}$ bit operations using precomputation. However, since this speedup has not been confirmed in practice, we do not assume this linear cost for our runtime estimates. Note that assuming the linear cost instead of the quadratic one would lower the runtime of the Quantum Hybrid Attack.

Basis Reduction Cost. In the following we examine the precomputation cost of basis reduction (BKZ) to achieve a BKZ-reduced basis of quality δ. According to [2,13], the minimal block size b needed by BKZ to achieve a certain Hermite delta δ can be determined via the relation

$$\delta = (((\pi b)^{1/b} b)/(2\pi e))^{1/(2(b-1))}.$$

We assume that the number of tours t with block size b is as given in the LWE estimator [2,35]. Then the precomputation cost of BKZ with block size b in the $(d - r)$-dimensional lattice is roughly $T_{\text{red}} = t(d - r)T_{\text{SVP}_b}$, where T_{SVP_b} denotes the number of operations to solve SVP in dimension b.

The main two methods to solve SVP are *enumeration* and *sieving*. Asymptotically the runtime of sieving outperforms the one of enumeration, but the cross-over point is unknown (see e.g. the discussion in [22]). However, sieving algorithms require access to exponentially large memory (while enumeration only requires polynomial memory), which could turn out to be the limiting factor in high dimension, especially when it comes to quantum-sieving. In this work we compare the Quantum Hybrid Attack with existing attacks under two different basis reduction assumptions.

In the first model (called *quantum-sieving*) we assume that memory consumption is not a problem, sieving scales as predicted to higher dimensions and can be sped up with quantum computers as proposed by Laarhoven–Mosca–van de Pol [23] with a runtime complexity of

$$T_{\text{SVP}_b} = 2^{0.265b+16.4}.$$

From an attacker's point of view this is an optimistic prediction, so the number derived in this model can be seen as a lower bound on the hardness of the LWE instances.

The second model (*enumeration*) assumes that sieving is not practical compared to enumeration for dimensions of cryptographic size and uses an interpolation of Albrecht–Player–Scott [2] based on runtimes of enumeration given by Chen and Nguyen [14] instead. The predicted number of operations necessary to solve SVP in dimension b is given by

$$T_{\text{SVP}_b} = 2^{0.27b\ln(b)-1.019b+16.10}.$$

This methodology leads to higher runtime estimations (for both the existing attacks and the Quantum Hybrid Attack).

Total Cost and Runtime Optimization. Using these estimates we obtain that the total runtime of the Quantum Hybrid Attack is given by

$$T_{\text{total}} = \frac{T_{\text{red}} + T_{\text{hyb}}}{p},$$

where

$$T_{\text{hyb}} = \left(\sum_{x \in S} d_x^{\frac{2}{3}}\right)^{\frac{3}{2}} \cdot (d - r)^2 / 2^{1.06},$$

T_{red} is the runtime of basis reduction, and p is the success probability as given in the Main Result.

The total runtime of the attack T_{total} depends on the attack parameters r and δ and must therefore be optimized over all such choices.

6   Results

In this section, we present concrete runtime estimates of our Quantum Hybrid Attack against the New Hope [3] and Frodo [7] key exchange schemes (Sect. 6.1) and the Lindner-Peikert [25] (Sect. 6.2) and R-BinLWEenc [10] (Sect. 6.3) encryption schemes. For the comparison, we always selected the maximal number of LWE samples available for the Quantum Hybrid Attack.

6.1   New Hope and Frodo

We analyze and optimize the runtime of the Quantum Hybrid Attack against the New Hope [3] and Frodo [7] key exchange schemes and compare our results to the security levels produced by the LWE estimator for LWE instances with limited number of samples [35]. Note that the LWE estimator handles LWE instances with Gaussian distribution, while the distributions of New Hope and Frodo are only approximations of such. Therefore, for the LWE estimator we use the Gaussian distributions that are approximated. To obtain a fair comparison, we also use the approximated Gaussian distributions to determine the success probabilities according to Eq. 1.

Table 1 shows that the Quantum Hybrid is significantly faster if enumeration is used as basis reduction subroutine. If we assume that quantum-sieving is practical and behaves as predicted [23], the Quantum Hybrid and the existing attacks are comparable (see Table 2).

Table 1. Quantum security estimates for New Hope and Frodo using *enumeration* as SVP oracle. Table shows the base-two logarithm of the expected runtimes.

Attack	New hope	Frodo-592	Frodo-752	Frodo-864
Dual embedding	1346	446	485	618
Decoding	833	—	—	—
Quantum hybrid	**725**	**254**	**310**	**377**

Table 2. Quantum security estimates for New Hope and Frodo using *quantum-sieving* as SVP oracle. Table shows the base-two logarithm of the expected runtimes.

Attack	New hope	Frodo-592	Frodo-752	Frodo-864
Dual embedding	389	173	184	219
Decoding	380	—	—	—
Quantum hybrid	**384**	**171**	**189**	**221**

Note that for both, the Quantum Hybrid Attack and the LWE estimator, the results differ substantially from the claimed security levels of the schemes [3,7]. This, is not surprising, since in the spirit of guaranteeing secure post-quantum parameter sets, [3,7] aim for highly conservative security estimates.

6.2 Lindner-Peikert

In 2011, Lindner and Peikert [25] introduced an LWE-based encryption scheme. The authors give four concrete parameter sets for various security levels. Later, Albrecht–Cabarcas–Fitzpatrick–Göpfert–Schneider [1] interpolated those sets to give an asymptotic instantiation.

We analyze such instances for dimensions ranging from 256 to 1024. Note that theoretically, the discrete Gaussian distributions used in the Lindner-Peikert encryption scheme have infinite support, while our analysis requires finite support. Using a standard tailbound argument [25] one can show that with overwhelming probability the absolute value of D_σ is bounded by 14σ. We therefore assume the distributions D_σ have finite support $\{-\lceil 14\sigma \rceil, \ldots, \lceil 14\sigma \rceil\}$.

As Fig. 1 shows, the Quantum Hybrid Attack outperforms all existing attacks for *enumeration* as SVP oracle. Again, the gap between the attacks nearly vanishes when *quantum-sieving* is used. However, the Quantum Hybrid Attack seems to benefit from a slightly better asymptotic complexity (see Fig. 2). The exact hardness values are given in Appendix B.

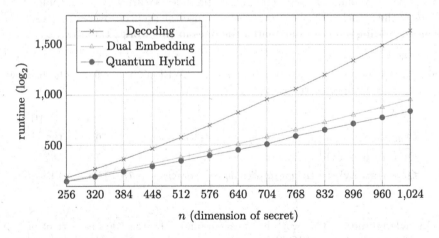

Fig. 1. Quantum security estimates for Lindner-Peikert parameter using *enumeration* as SVP oracle. Figure shows the base-two logarithm of the expected runtimes.

6.3 R-BinLWEenc

So far, all instances considered either use Gaussian errors or approximations of such. However, the Classical Hybrid Attack is most efficient on LWE with binary

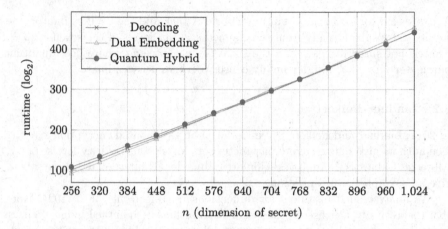

Fig. 2. Quantum security estimates for Lindner-Peikert parameter using *quantum-sieving* as SVP oracle. Figure shows the base-two logarithm of the expected runtimes.

error [11,37]. In order to compare the Classical and the Quantum Hybrid Attack, we investigate the hardness of LWE instances with binary error as used by Buchmann–Göpfert–Player–Wunderer [10] for their Lindner-Peikert-like encryption scheme.

The runtime of the Classical Hybrid Attack on binary LWE instances was estimated by Wunderer [37]. The author provides security over- and underestimates of the attack. For our comparison we use the security overestimates, since their underlying assumptions match the ones in this work (Table 3).

Table 3. Quantum security estimates for R-BinLWEEnc. Table shows the base-two logarithm of the expected runtimes.

Attack	Set-I	Set-II	Set-III
Classical hybrid estimates (*enumeration* SVP oracle)	99	90	197
Quantum hybrid (*enumeration* SVP oracle)	**82**	**75**	**167**
Quantum hybrid (*quantum-sieving* SVP oracle)	**79**	**73**	**140**

Acknowledgement. This work has been co-funded by the DFG as part of project P1 within the CRC 1119 CROSSING and supported by the Netherlands Organisation for Scientic Research (NWO) under grant 639.073.005.

References

1. Albrecht, M.R., Cabracas, D., Fitzpatrick, R., Göpfert, F., Schneider, M.: A generator for LWE and Ring-LWE instances. IACR archive (2013). https://www.iacr.org/news/files/2013-04-29lwe-generator.pdf

2. Albrecht, M.R., Player, R., Scott, S.: On the concrete hardness of learning with errors. J. Math. Crypto. **9**(3), 169–203 (2015)
3. Alkim, E., Ducas, L., Pöppelmann, T., Schwabe, P.: NewHope without reconciliation (2016). http://cryptojedi.org/papers/#newhopesimple
4. Babai, L.: On Lovász' lattice reduction and the nearest lattice point problem. Combinatorica **6**(1), 1–13 (1986)
5. Bai, S., Galbraith, S.D.: An improved compression technique for signatures based on learning with errors. In: Benaloh, J. (ed.) CT-RSA 2014. LNCS, vol. 8366, pp. 28–47. Springer, Cham (2014). doi:10.1007/978-3-319-04852-9_2
6. Bai, S., Galbraith, S.D.: Lattice decoding attacks on binary LWE. In: Susilo, W., Mu, Y. (eds.) ACISP 2014. LNCS, vol. 8544, pp. 322–337. Springer, Cham (2014). doi:10.1007/978-3-319-08344-5_21
7. Bos, J.W., Costello, C., Ducas, L., Mironov, I., Naehrig, M., Nikolaenko, V., Raghunathan, A., Stebila, D.: Frodo: take off the ring! practical, quantum-secure key exchange from LWE. In: Weippl, E.R., Katzenbeisser, S., Kruegel, C., Myers, A.C., Halevi, S. (eds.) Proceedings of the 2016 ACM SIGSAC Conference on Computer and Communications Security, Vienna, Austria, 24–28 October 2016, pp. 1006–1018. ACM (2016)
8. Brakerski, Z., Langlois, A., Peikert, C., Regev, O., Stehlé, D.: Classical hardness of learning with errors. In: Boneh, D., Roughgarden, T., Feigenbaum, J. (eds.) Symposium on Theory of Computing Conference, STOC 2013, Palo Alto, CA, USA, 1–4 June 2013, pp. 575–584. ACM (2013)
9. Brassard, G., Høyer, P., Mosca, M., Tapp, A.: Quantum amplitude amplification and estimation. In: Quantum Computation and Quantum Information: A Millennium Volume. AMS Contemporary Mathematics Series, vol. 305, pp. 53–74. American Mathematical Society (2002). Earlier version in arXiv:quant-ph/0005055
10. Buchmann, J.A., Göpfert, F., Güneysu, T., Oder, T., Pöppelmann, T.: High-performance and lightweight lattice-based public-key encryption. In: Chow, R., Saldamli, G. (eds.) Proceedings of the 2nd ACM International Workshop on IoT Privacy, Trust, and Security, CPSSAsiaCCS, Xi'an, China, 30 May–3 June 2016, pp. 2–9. ACM (2016)
11. Buchmann, J., Göpfert, F., Player, R., Wunderer, T.: On the hardness of LWE with binary error: revisiting the hybrid lattice-reduction and meet-in-the-middle attack. In: Pointcheval, D., Nitaj, A., Rachidi, T. (eds.) AFRICACRYPT 2016. LNCS, vol. 9646, pp. 24–43. Springer, Cham (2016). doi:10.1007/978-3-319-31517-1_2
12. Canetti, R., Garay, J.A. (eds.): CRYPTO 2013. LNCS, vol. 8042. Springer, Heidelberg (2013)
13. Chen, Y.: Réduction de réseau et sécurité concrete du chiffrement completement homomorphe. Ph.D. thesis, ENS-Lyon, France (2013)
14. Chen, Y., Nguyen, P.Q.: BKZ 2.0: better lattice security estimates. In: Lee, D.H., Wang, X. (eds.) ASIACRYPT 2011. LNCS, vol. 7073, pp. 1–20. Springer, Heidelberg (2011). doi:10.1007/978-3-642-25385-0_1
15. Ducas, L., Durmus, A., Lepoint, T., Lyubashevsky, V.: Lattice signatures and bimodal gaussians. In: Canetti and Garay [12], pp. 40–56
16. Gentry, C.: Fully homomorphic encryption using ideal lattices. In: Mitzenmacher [12], pp. 169–178
17. Grover, L.K.: A fast quantum mechanical algorithm for database search. In: Proceedings of the Twenty-eighth Annual ACM Symposium on Theory of Computing, STOC 1996, pp. 212–219. ACM, New York (1996)

18. Hirschhorn, P.S., Hoffstein, J., Howgrave-Graham, N., Whyte, W.: Choosing NTRUEncrypt parameters in light of combined lattice reduction and MITM approaches. In: Abdalla, M., Pointcheval, D., Fouque, P.-A., Vergnaud, D. (eds.) ACNS 2009. LNCS, vol. 5536, pp. 437–455. Springer, Heidelberg (2009). doi:10.1007/978-3-642-01957-9_27

19. Hoffstein, J., Pipher, J., Schanck, J.M., Silverman, J.H., Whyte, W.: Practical signatures from the partial fourier recovery problem. In: Boureanu, I., Owesarski, P., Vaudenay, S. (eds.) ACNS 2014. LNCS, vol. 8479, pp. 476–493. Springer, Cham (2014). doi:10.1007/978-3-319-07536-5_28

20. Hoffstein, J., Pipher, J., Silverman, J.H.: NTRU: a ring-based public key cryptosystem. In: Buhler, J.P. (ed.) ANTS 1998. LNCS, vol. 1423, pp. 267–288. Springer, Heidelberg (1998). doi:10.1007/BFb0054868

21. Howgrave-Graham, N.: A hybrid lattice-reduction and meet-in-the-middle attack against NTRU. In: Menezes, A. (ed.) CRYPTO 2007. LNCS, vol. 4622, pp. 150–169. Springer, Heidelberg (2007). doi:10.1007/978-3-540-74143-5_9

22. Laarhoven, T.: Sieving for shortest vectors in lattices using angular locality-sensitive hashing. In: Gennaro, R., Robshaw, M. (eds.) CRYPTO 2015. LNCS, vol. 9215, pp. 3–22. Springer, Heidelberg (2015). doi:10.1007/978-3-662-47989-6_1

23. Laarhoven, T., Mosca, M., van de Pol, J.: Finding shortest lattice vectors faster using quantum search. Des. Codes Crypt. $77(2)$, 375–400 (2015)

24. Lenstra, A.K., Lenstra Jr., H.W., Lovász, L.: Factoring polynomials with rational coefficients. Math. Ann. 261, 515–534 (1982)

25. Lindner, R., Peikert, C.: Better key sizes (and attacks) for LWE-based encryption. In: Kiayias, A. (ed.) CT-RSA 2011. LNCS, vol. 6558, pp. 319–339. Springer, Heidelberg (2011). doi:10.1007/978-3-642-19074-2_21

26. Micciancio, D., Goldwasser, S.: Complexity of Lattice Problems: a cryptographic perspective. The Kluwer International Series in Engineering and Computer Science, vol. 671. Kluwer Academic Publishers, Boston (2002)

27. Micciancio, D., Regev, O.: Lattice-based cryptography. In: Bernstein, D.J., Buchmann, J., Dahmen, E. (eds.) Post-Quantum Cryptography, pp. 147–191. Springer, Heidelberg (2009)

28. Mitzenmacher, M. (ed.): Proceedings of the 41st Annual ACM Symposium on Theory of Computing, STOC 2009, Bethesda, MD, USA, 31 May–2 June 2009. ACM (2009)

29. Olver, F.W.J.: NIST Handbook of Mathematical Functions. Cambridge University Press, Cambridge (2010)

30. Peikert, C.: Public-key cryptosystems from the worst-case shortest vector problem: extended abstract. In: Mitzenmacher [28], pp. 333–342

31. Peikert, C.: A decade of lattice cryptography. Found. Trends Theor. Comput. Sci. $10(4)$, 283–424 (2016)

32. Peikert, C., Waters, B.: Lossy trapdoor functions and their applications. SIAM J. Comput. $40(6)$, 1803–1844 (2011)

33. Regev, O.: On lattices, learning with errors, random linear codes, and cryptography. In: Gabow, H.N., Fagin, R. (eds.) Proceedings of the 37th Annual ACM Symposium on Theory of Computing, Baltimore, MD, USA, 22–24 May 2005, pp. 84–93. ACM (2005)

34. Schanck, J.M.: Practical Lattice Cryptosystems: NTRUEncrypt and NTRUMLS. Ph.D. thesis, University of Waterloo (2015)

35. Schmidt, M., Bindel, N.: Estimation of the hardness of the learning with errors problem with a restricted number of samples. Cryptology ePrint Archive, Report 2017/140 (2017). http://eprint.iacr.org/2017/140

36. van Vredendaal, C.: Reduced memory meet-in-the-middle attack against the NTRU private key. IACR Cryptology ePrint Archive 2016:177 (2016)
37. Wunderer, T.: Revisiting the hybrid attack: improved analysis and refined security estimates. IACR Cryptology ePrint Archive 2016:733 (2016)

A   About the constant in Theorem 1

Brassard–Hoyer–Mosca–Tapp [9] give two different results about amplitude amplification: one for known probability a, and one if a is unknown. One disadvantage of the result about amplification with unknown a is that it is an asymptotic result (see Theorem 1). Such results give a way to group algorithms into complexity classes, but are of limited value for runtime estimations on concrete instances, since the constant factor is unknown. In this section, we show that the hidden constant factor of Theorem 1 is small.

In the analysis of their algorithm with known a, Brassard–Hoyer–Mosca–Tapp show that the success probability of their quantum amplification algorithm after m rounds is given by $p = \sin^2((2m + 1)\theta_a)$ with θ_a such that $\sin^2(\theta_a) = a$.

Our goal in this section is to produce an algorithm that succeeds at least with $p = 1/2$. This leads to

$$p \geq \frac{1}{2} \Leftrightarrow \sin((2m + 1)\theta_a) \geq \frac{1}{\sqrt{2}}$$

$$\Leftrightarrow \frac{1}{4}\pi \leq (2m + 1)\theta_a \leq \frac{3}{4}\pi$$

$$\Leftrightarrow \frac{\pi}{4(2m + 1)} \leq \theta_a \leq \frac{3\pi}{4(2m + 1)}$$

$$\Leftrightarrow \sin^2\left(\frac{\pi}{4(2m + 1)}\right) \leq a \leq \sin^2\left(\frac{3\pi}{4(2m + 1)}\right)$$

Since m is big in our applications, we can approximate the bounds by

$$a \in \left[\frac{\pi^2}{64m^2}, \frac{9\pi^2}{64m^2}\right] \tag{9}$$

Assume we know that $a \in [b_{min}, b_{max}]$. In the following, we find a sequence of rounds $m_0, \ldots, m_k$ such that $[b_{min}, b_{max}] \subseteq \bigcup_i \left[\frac{\pi^2}{64m_i^2}, \frac{9\pi^2}{64m_i^2}\right]$. Given this sequence, we can find a solution as follows. We start with running the algorithm for m_0 rounds. If this succeeds, we found a solution. If not, we run the algorithm for m_1 rounds, and so on. After the last run (with m_k rounds) at least one of the algorithm calls had a success probability of at least $1/2$, so the overall success probability is at least $1/2$.

To find the sequence of m_i, we start with selecting m_0 such that $\frac{9\pi^2}{64m_0^2} = b_{max}$, which is equivalent to $m_0 = \frac{3\pi}{8\sqrt{b_{max}}}$. The other m_i are then defined iteratively by selecting m_{i+1} such that $\frac{9\pi^2}{64m_{i+1}^2} = \frac{\pi^2}{64m_i^2}$, which is equivalent to $m_{i+1} = 3m_i$, which in turn leads directly to $m_i = 3^{i+1} \frac{\pi}{8\sqrt{b_{max}}}$. The second condition of our sequence is that $\frac{\pi^2}{64m_i^2} \leq b_{min}$. A simple calculation shows that this is equivalent to $3^{2k+2} \geq \frac{b_{max}}{b_{min}}$. Finally, we take a look at the special when a is distributed according to a Gaussian distribution. By the definition of the Gaussian distribution, we have

$$\Pr[D_\sigma = x] = c \exp\left(-\frac{x^2}{2\sigma^2}\right),$$

which leads directly to $b_{min} = c$. It is common knowledge that with overwhelming probability, only elements smaller than 14σ get sampled, so we set

$$b_{max} = c \exp\left(-\frac{(14\sigma)^2}{2\sigma^2}\right) = c \exp(-98).$$

Consequently, we require $3^{2k+2} \geq \frac{c}{c\exp(-98)} = \exp(98)$, which is satisfied for $k \geq 45$ (Tables 4 and 5).

B   Hardness Tables for Lindner/Peikert LWE

Table 4. Quantum security estimates for Lindner-Peikert parameter using *enumeration* as SVP oracle. Table shows the base-two logarithm of the expected runtimes.

n	256	320	384	448	512	576	640	704	768	832	896	960	1024
Dual embedding	177	262	358	463	576	697	823	956	1058	1198	1341	1489	1640
Decoding	145	197	254	314	378	442	510	580	651	725	800	876	953
Quantum hybrid	138	186	236	288	342	397	452	508	588	649	711	772	835

Table 5. Quantum security estimates for Lindner-Peikert parameter using *enumeration* as SVP oracle. Table shows the base-two logarithm of the expected runtimes.

n	256	320	384	448	512	576	640	704	768	832	896	960	1024
Dual embedding	92	120	149	178	208	238	269	301	325	356	388	420	453
Decoding	101	127	155	182	210	239	266	295	324	353	383	412	442
Quantum hybrid	108	134	161	187	214	242	269	297	326	355	383	412	441

Multivariate Cryptography

HMFEv - An Efficient Multivariate Signature Scheme

Albrecht Petzoldt[1]([⊠]), Ming-Shing Chen[2], Jintai Ding[3], and Bo-Yin Yang[2]

[1] National Institute for Standards and Technology, Gaithersburg, MD, USA
albrecht.petzoldt@nist.gov
[2] Academia Sinica, Taipei, Taiwan
{mschen,by}@crypto.tw
[3] University of Cincinnati, Ohio, USA
jintai.ding@gmail.com

Abstract. Multivariate Cryptography, as one of the main candidates for establishing post-quantum cryptosystems, provides strong, efficient and well-understood digital signature schemes such as UOV, Rainbow, and Gui. While Gui provides very short signatures, it is, for efficiency reasons, restricted to very small finite fields, which makes it hard to scale it to higher levels of security and leads to large key sizes.

In this paper we propose a signature scheme called HMFEv ("Hidden Medium Field Equations"), which can be seen as a multivariate version of HFEv. We obtain our scheme by applying the Vinegar Variation to the MultiHFE encryption scheme of Chen et al. We show both theoretically and by experiments that our new scheme is secure against direct and Rank attacks. In contrast to other schemes of the HFE family such as Gui, HMFEv can be defined over arbitrary base fields and therefore is much more efficient in terms of both performance and memory requirements. Our scheme is therefore a good candidate for the upcoming standardization of post-quantum signature schemes.

Keywords: Post-quantum cryptography · Multivariate cryptography · Signature schemes · NIST call for proposals

1 Introduction

Multivariate Public Key Cryptosystems (MPKCs) are one of the main candidates for guaranteeing the security of communication in a quantum world [1]. Multivariate schemes are in general very fast and require only modest computational resources, which makes them attractive for the use on low cost devices like smart cards and RFID chips [3,5]. Additionally, at least in the area of digital signatures, there exists a large number of practical multivariate schemes.

The existing multivariate signature schemes can be divided into two main groups. The first are the SingleField schemes such as UOV [15] and Rainbow [11], which follow the same type of design strategy using Oil-Vinegar polynomials. We

© Springer International Publishing AG 2017
T. Lange and T. Takagi (Eds.): PQCrypto 2017, LNCS 10346, pp. 205–223, 2017.
DOI: 10.1007/978-3-319-59879-6_12

believe that these two schemes are more or less the best which can be achieved from this fundamental design.

On the other hand, we have the BigField schemes HFEv- [17] and Gui [18], which combine the HFE design with the Minus and Vinegar modifiers. These schemes make use of an HFE polynomial, whose degree D is very much affected by the size of the underlying field. We believe that, for security reasons, this degree should be chosen at least q^2+1, where q is the cardinality of the underlying field. However, during the signature generation process, we have to invert this univariate HFE polynomial and the complexity of this step can be estimated by $\mathcal{O}(D^3)$. To solve this conflict between security and efficiency, we have to build the scheme over very small finite fields such as GF(2) and GF(4). However, in this case, we have to choose the number of variables to be large, which leads to large key sizes and makes the scheme less efficient. Therefore it is a natural question, if it is possible to use large base fields such as GF(31) or GF(256) for the design of multivariate signature schemes of the HFEv- type.

In 2008, Chen et al. proposed a multivariate encryption scheme called Multi-HFE [6], which can be seen as a multivariate version of HFE. While the scheme is very efficient, its security appeared to be weak and it was broken by Bettale et al. [2] by a generalization of the Kipnis-Shamir attack against HFE using the MinRank property of the system.

In this paper, we propose a signature scheme called HMFEv ("Hidden Medium Field Equations"), which we obtain by applying the Vinegar modification to MultiHFE. We show both theoretically and by experiments that our scheme is secure against direct and Rank attacks of the Kipnis-Shamir/Bettale type and analyze the security of our scheme against other known attacks against multivariate schemes, including differential attacks [7] and Hashimotos attack against the MultiHFE encryption scheme [14].

Our scheme can be seen as an extension of the Gui and QUARTZ signature schemes. However, by enabling a flexible choice of the base field, our new scheme overcomes a fundamental practical problem in the HFEv- design. While Gui and QUARTZ are, for efficiency reasons, mainly restricted to the field GF(2), our scheme allows the choice of an arbitrary base field. This allows us to reduce the number of equations and variables in the public system significantly, which leads to smaller key sizes and more efficient signature generation and verification processes. Furthermore, this enables an easy scalability of our scheme to higher levels of security. Our scheme is therefore a very strong candidate for the upcoming standardization of post-quantum signature schemes.

The rest of this paper is organized as follows. Section 2 gives an overview of the basic concepts of multivariate cryptography. In Sect. 3 we describe the MultiHFE encryption scheme which is the basis of our construction and analyze its security and efficiency. Section 4 describes our new HMFEv signature scheme in detail. In Sect. 5 we analyze the security of our scheme, in particular its behavior against direct and rank attacks. Section 6 proposes concrete parameter sets for our scheme for different levels of security, while Sect. 7 compares our HMFEv scheme with other multivariate signature schemes such as Gui and Rainbow. In

Sect. 8 we provide implementation details of our scheme and present performance results, and Sect. 9 concludes the paper.

2   Multivariate Cryptography

The public key of a multivariate public key cryptosystem (MPKC) is a set of multivariate quadratic polynomials. The security of these schemes is based on the MQ Problem of solving such a system. The MQ problem is proven to be NP-hard even for quadratic polynomials over the field GF(2) [13] and (for $m \approx n$) believed to be hard on average (both for classical and quantum computers).

To build a public key cryptosystem based on the MQ problem, one starts with an easily invertible quadratic map $\mathcal{F} : \mathbb{F}^n \to \mathbb{F}^m$ (central map). To hide the structure of $\mathcal{F}$ in the public key, one composes it with two invertible affine (or linear) maps $\mathcal{S} : \mathbb{F}^m \to \mathbb{F}^m$ and $\mathcal{T} : \mathbb{F}^n \to \mathbb{F}^n$. The *public key* of the scheme is therefore given by $\mathcal{P} = \mathcal{S} \circ \mathcal{F} \circ \mathcal{T} : \mathbb{F}^n \to \mathbb{F}^m$. The *private key* consists of $\mathcal{S}, \mathcal{F}$ and $\mathcal{T}$ and therefore allows to invert the public key.

In this paper we concentrate on multivariate schemes of the MediumField family. For this type of schemes, one chooses two integers k and ℓ and sets $n = k \cdot \ell$. The central map $\mathcal{F}$ of the scheme is a specially chosen easily invertible polynomial map over the vector space $\mathbb{E}^k$, where $\mathbb{E}$ is a degree ℓ extension field of $\mathbb{F}$. Using an isomorphism $\phi : \mathbb{F}^\ell \to \mathbb{E}$ we can transform $\mathcal{F}$ into a map

$$\bar{\mathcal{F}} = \underbrace{(\phi^{-1} \times \cdots \times \phi^{-1})}_{k-\text{times}} \circ \mathcal{F} \circ \underbrace{(\phi \times \cdots \times \phi)}_{k-\text{times}} : \mathbb{F}^n \to \mathbb{F}^n. \tag{1}$$

from $\mathbb{F}^n$ to itself. The map $\mathcal{F}$ is chosen in such a way that the map $\bar{\mathcal{F}}$ consists of multivariate quadratic polynomials. The *public key* has the form $\mathcal{P} = \mathcal{S} \circ \bar{\mathcal{F}} \circ \mathcal{T}$ with two invertible affine maps $\mathcal{S}, \mathcal{T} : \mathbb{F}^n \to \mathbb{F}^n$, the *private key* consists of $\mathcal{S}, \mathcal{F}$ and $\mathcal{T}$.

When the map $\mathcal{F}$ is bijective, the resulting scheme can be used both for signatures and public key encryption. The standard process of signature generation/verification respectively encryption/decryption works as shown in Fig. 1.

Signature Generation: To generate a signature for a document d, one uses a hash function $\mathcal{H} : \{0,1\}^* \to \mathbb{F}^n$ to compute a hash value $\mathbf{w} = \mathcal{H}(d) \in \mathbb{F}^n$. After that, one computes recursively $\mathbf{x} = \mathcal{S}^{-1}(\mathbf{w}) \in \mathbb{F}^n$, $\mathbf{X} = (\phi \times \ldots \times \phi)(\mathbf{x}) \in \mathbb{E}^k$, $\mathbf{Y} = \mathcal{F}^{-1}(\mathbf{X}) \in \mathbb{E}^k$, $\mathbf{y} = (\phi^{-1} \times \ldots \times \phi^{-1})(\mathbf{Y}) \in \mathbb{F}^n$ and $\mathbf{z} = \mathcal{T}^{-1}(\mathbf{y})$. The signature of the document d is $\mathbf{z} \in \mathbb{F}^n$.

Signature Verification: To check, if $\mathbf{z} \in \mathbb{F}^n$ is indeed a valid signature for the document d, one computes the hash value $\mathbf{w} = \mathcal{H}(d) \in \mathbb{F}^n$ and $\mathbf{w}' = \mathcal{P}(\mathbf{z}) \in \mathbb{F}^n$. If $\mathbf{w}' = \mathbf{w}$ holds, the signature is accepted, otherwise rejected.

A good overview of existing multivariate schemes can be found in [8].

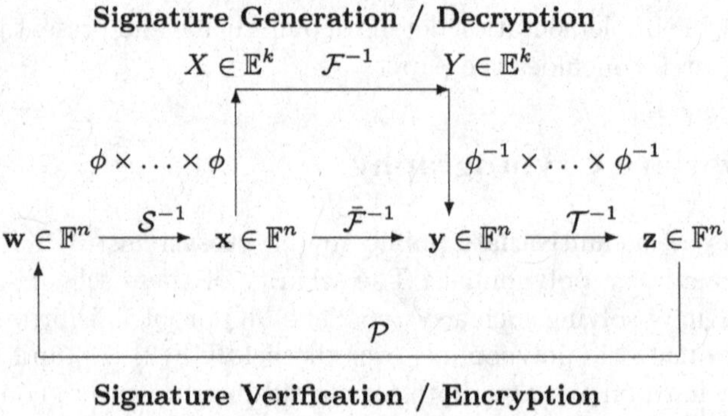

Signature Generation / Decryption

$$X \in \mathbb{E}^k \quad \mathcal{F}^{-1} \quad Y \in \mathbb{E}^k$$

$$\phi \times \ldots \times \phi \qquad\qquad \phi^{-1} \times \ldots \times \phi^{-1}$$

$$\mathbf{w} \in \mathbb{F}^n \xrightarrow{\mathcal{S}^{-1}} \mathbf{x} \in \mathbb{F}^n \xrightarrow{\bar{\mathcal{F}}^{-1}} \mathbf{y} \in \mathbb{F}^n \xrightarrow{\mathcal{T}^{-1}} \mathbf{z} \in \mathbb{F}^n$$

$$\mathcal{P}$$

Signature Verification / Encryption

Fig. 1. Workflow of multivariate MediumField schemes

3   The MultiHFE Scheme

An important example for a multivariate scheme from the MediumField family is the MultiHFE scheme of Chen et al. [6]. In its basic version, the scheme can be used both as an encryption and signature scheme.

The k components $\mathcal{F}^{(1)}, \ldots, \mathcal{F}^{(k)}$ of the central map $\mathcal{F}$ are of the form

$$\mathcal{F}^{(i)} = \sum_{r=1}^{k}\sum_{s=r}^{k} \alpha_{rs}^{(i)} \cdot X_r X_s + \sum_{r=1}^{k} \beta_r^{(i)} \cdot X_r + \gamma^{(i)} \; (i = 1, \ldots, k) \qquad (2)$$

with coefficients $\alpha_{rs}^{(i)}$, $\beta_r^{(i)}$ and $\gamma^{(i)}$ randomly chosen from $\mathbb{E}$. Note that the polynomials $\mathcal{F}^{(i)}(i = 1, \ldots, k)$ are multivariate polynomials of the HFE type with $D = 2$. The map $\bar{\mathcal{F}}$ of the MultiHFE signature scheme is defined as shown in Eq. (1) and is, due to the Frobenius isomorphism, a multivariate quadratic map over the vector space $\mathbb{F}^n$. To hide the structure of $\bar{\mathcal{F}}$ in the public key, one composes it with two invertible affine maps $\mathcal{S}$ and $\mathcal{T} : \mathbb{F}^n \to \mathbb{F}^n$. Therefore, the *public key* of the scheme is given by $\mathcal{P} = \mathcal{S} \circ \bar{\mathcal{F}} \circ \mathcal{T} : \mathbb{F}^n \to \mathbb{F}^n$; the *private key* consists of $\mathcal{S}$, $\mathcal{F}$ and $\mathcal{T}$.

Signature Generation: In order to generate a signature for a message d, one uses a hash function $\mathcal{H} : \{0,1\}^* \to \mathbb{F}^n$ to compute the hash value $\mathbf{w} = \mathcal{H}(d) \in \mathbb{F}^n$ and performs the following three steps.

1. Compute $\mathbf{x} = \mathcal{S}^{-1}(\mathbf{w}) \in \mathbb{F}^n$ and lift the result to the vector space $\mathbb{E}^k$. Denote the result by $\mathbf{X}$.
2. Invert the central map $\mathcal{F}$ to obtain $\mathbf{Y} = \mathcal{F}^{-1}(\mathbf{X}) \in \mathbb{E}^k$ and compute $\mathbf{y} = (\phi^{-1} \times \ldots \times \phi^{-1})(\mathbf{Y}) \in \mathbb{F}^n$. Since $\mathcal{F}$ is a system of k randomly chosen quadratic polynomials in k variables, we need for this step a system solver like XL [20] or a Gröbner Basis algorithm such as F_4 [12] or F_5.
3. Compute the signature $\mathbf{z} \in \mathbb{F}^n$ by $\mathbf{z} = \mathcal{T}^{-1}(\mathbf{y})$.

Signature Verification: To check, if $\mathbf{z} \in \mathbb{F}^n$ is indeed a valid signature for a message d, one computes the hash value $\mathbf{w} = \mathcal{H}(d)$ and $\mathbf{w}' = \mathcal{P}(\mathbf{z})$. If $\mathbf{w}' = \mathbf{w}$ holds, the signature is accepted, otherwise rejected.

3.1 Efficiency

The most complex step during the signing process of MultiHFE is the solution of the multivariate quadratic system $\mathcal{F}(Y_1, \ldots, Y_k) = (X_1, \ldots, X_k)$ (k equations in k variables) over the extension field $\mathbb{E}$. Since the coefficients of the system $\mathcal{F}$ are random elements of $\mathbb{E}$, we need for this step a system solver like XL [20] or a Gröbner Basis algorithm such as F_4 [12]. If the number k of equations and variables in this system is small, these algorithms can invert $\mathcal{F}$ very efficiently. However, when the parameter k gets larger, the decryption process of MultiHFE becomes very costly and the scheme therefore gets inefficient.

3.2 The Rank Attack Against HFE and MultiHFE

In [16], Kipnis and Shamir proposed a rank based attack against the univariate HFE scheme. The key idea of this attack is to lift all the maps $\mathcal{S}$, $\mathcal{P}$ and $\mathcal{T}$ to univariate maps $\mathcal{S}^\star$, $\mathcal{P}^\star$ and $\mathcal{T}^\star$ over the extension field $\mathbb{E}$. Since the rank of the central map $\mathcal{F}$ is bounded from above by $r = \lfloor \log_q(D-1) \rfloor + 1$, this enabled them to recover the private key by solving an instance of a MinRank problem. However, since computing the map $\mathcal{P}^\star$ appeared to be very costly, the attack of Kipnis and Shamir is not very efficient.

Later, Bettale et al. [2] found a way to perform the attack of Kipnis and Shamir without the need of recovering the map $\mathcal{P}^\star$. Besides improving the efficiency of the Kipnis-Shamir attack, this makes it much easier to extend the attack to MultiHFE. Due to lack of space we cannot present all the details of the attacks of Kipnis-Shamir and Bettale here and refer to the papers [2,16] for a detailed description of the attacks. Here, we just present the main results of [2].

Theorem 1. *For MultiHFE, recovering the affine transformation $\mathcal{T}$ reduces to simultaneously solving k MinRank problems over the base field.*

With this, Bettale et al. could further prove

Theorem 2. *The complexity of solving the MultiHFE MinRank problem is $\mathcal{O}(\ell^{(k+1)\omega})$ with $2 < \omega \leq 3$ being the linear algebra constant and ℓ being the degree of the field extension $\mathbb{E}|\mathbb{F}$.*

We therefore face the following problem: If the parameter k in MultiHFE is small, the scheme can be easily broken by the MinRank attack. On the other hand, if we choose k larger, the efficiency of the scheme becomes quite bad.

In the following, we show how to solve this dilemma by modifying the MultiHFE scheme.

4   The New Signature Scheme HMFEv

Let $\mathbb{F}$ be a finite field and k, ℓ and v be integers. We set $n = k \cdot \ell$. Furthermore, let $g(X) \in \mathbb{F}[X]$ be an irreducible polynomial of degree ℓ and $\mathbb{E} = \mathbb{F}[X]/g(X)$ the corresponding extension field. We define an isomorphism $\phi : \mathbb{F}^\ell \to \mathbb{E}$ by

$$\phi(x_1, \ldots, x_\ell) = \sum_{i=1}^{\ell} x_i \cdot X^{i-1}.$$

The *central map* $\mathcal{F} : \mathbb{E}^k \times \mathbb{F}^v \to \mathbb{E}^k$ of the scheme consists of k components $\mathcal{F}^{(1)}, \ldots, \mathcal{F}^{(k)}$ of the form

$$\mathcal{F}^{(i)} = \sum_{r=1}^{k} \sum_{s=r}^{k} \alpha_{rs}^{(i)} \cdot X_r X_s + \sum_{r=1}^{k} \beta_r^{(i)}(v_1, \ldots, v_v) \cdot X_r + \gamma^{(i)}(v_1, \ldots, v_v) \quad (3)$$

with coefficients $\alpha_{rs}^{(i)} \in_R \mathbb{E}$, linear functions $\beta_r^{(i)} : \mathbb{F}^v \to \mathbb{E}$ and quadratic maps $\gamma^{(i)} : \mathbb{F}^v \to \mathbb{E}$ ($i \in \{1, \ldots, k\}$).

Due to the special form of $\mathcal{F}$, the map

$$\bar{\mathcal{F}} = \underbrace{(\phi^{-1} \times \cdots \times \phi^{-1})}_{k-\text{times}} \circ \mathcal{F} \circ \underbrace{(\phi \times \cdots \times \phi}_{k-\text{times}} \times \mathrm{id}_v)$$

is a multivariate quadratic map from $\mathbb{F}^{n+v}$ to $\mathbb{F}^n$. Here, id_v is the identity map over the vector space $\mathbb{F}^v$.

To hide the structure of $\bar{\mathcal{F}}$ in the public key, we combine it with two randomly chosen invertible affine maps $\mathcal{S} : \mathbb{F}^n \to \mathbb{F}^n$ and $\mathcal{T} : \mathbb{F}^{n+v} \to \mathbb{F}^{n+v}$.

The *public key* of the scheme is given by

$$\mathcal{P} = \mathcal{S} \circ \bar{\mathcal{F}} \circ \mathcal{T} : \mathbb{F}^{n+v} \to \mathbb{F}^n,$$

the *private key* consists of $\mathcal{S}$, $\mathcal{F}$ and $\mathcal{T}$.

Signature Generation: To generate a signature for a document d, we use a hash function $\mathcal{H} : \{0,1\}^* \to \mathbb{F}^n$ to compute the hash value $\mathbf{w} = \mathcal{H}(d) \in \mathbb{F}^n$. After that, we perform the following six steps

1. Compute $\mathbf{x} = \mathcal{S}^{-1}(\mathbf{w}) \in \mathbb{F}^n$.
2. Lift the result to the vector space $\mathbb{E}^k$ by computing $\mathbf{X} = (X_1, \ldots, X_k)$ with $X_i = \phi(x_{(i-1)\cdot\ell+1}, \ldots, x_{i\cdot\ell})$ ($i = 1, \ldots, k$).
3. Choose random values for the Vinegar variables $v_1, \ldots, v_v \in \mathbb{F}$ and substitute them into the central map components to obtain the parametrized maps $\mathcal{F}_V^{(1)}, \ldots, \mathcal{F}_V^{(k)}$.
4. Use the XL-Algorithm or a Gröbner Basis method to compute $Y_1, \ldots, Y_k$ such that $\mathcal{F}_V^{(i)}(Y_1, \ldots, Y_k) = X_i$ ($i = 1, \ldots, k$).
5. Move the result down to the base field by computing $\mathbf{y} = (\phi^{-1}(Y_1), \ldots, \phi^{-1}(Y_k), v_1, \ldots, v_v) \in \mathbb{F}^{n+v}$.
6. Compute the signature $\mathbf{z} \in \mathbb{F}^{n+v}$ by $\mathbf{z} = \mathcal{T}^{-1}(\mathbf{y})$.

Signature Verification: In order to check, if $\mathbf{z} \in \mathbb{F}^{n+v}$ is indeed a valid signature for the document d, one computes $\mathbf{w} = \mathcal{H}(d)$ and $\mathbf{w}' = \mathcal{P}(\mathbf{z})$. If $\mathbf{w}' = \mathbf{w}$ holds, the signature is accepted, otherwise rejected.

5 Security

In this Section we analyze the security of our scheme. In particular we study both theoretically and using computer experiments the behavior of our scheme against direct and rank attacks.

5.1 Direct and Rank Attacks

The complexity of a direct attack is closely related to the degree of regularity of the system. Therefore the key task is to study the degree of regularity of a direct attack against our scheme.

From the work of Ding and Hodges in Crypto 2011 [10] we know that the degree of regularity of a direct attack against an HFE scheme can be estimated by looking at a single polynomial in the extension field $\mathbb{E}$, and the rank of the associated quadratic form.

In the case of HMFEv, the situation is slightly different, but still very similar. For HMFEv, the components of the public key come from several polynomials over the medium field, which are given as

$$\mathcal{F}^{(i)} = \sum_{r=1}^{k} \sum_{s=r}^{k} \alpha_{rs}^{(i)} \cdot X_r X_s + \sum_{r=1}^{k} \beta_r^{(i)}(v_1, \ldots, v_v) \cdot X_r + \gamma^{(i)}(v_1, \ldots, v_v) \ (1 \le i \le k).$$

Using the same argument as in the work of Ding and Yang in [9] we can, under the assumption of $v \le \ell$, lift each map $\mathcal{F}^{(i)}$ $(1 \le i \le k)$, which is a map from $\mathbb{E}^k \times \mathbb{F}^v$ to $\mathbb{E}$, to a map $\mathcal{F}'^{(i)}$ from $\mathbb{E}^{k+1}$ to $\mathbb{E}$. Here, the additional component in the domain comes from the use of the Vinegar variables. Then we can look at the rank of the quadratic form associated to the polynomial $\mathcal{F}'^{(i)}$ as in the case of the original Kipnis-Shamir attack.

Using the same method as in [9] we can prove

Theorem 3. *If $v \le \ell$ holds, the rank of the quadratic form associated to $\mathcal{F}'^{(i)}$ is less or equal to $k + v$.*

Proof (sketch). The main idea of the proof is to lift the central map back to a vector space of $k + 1$ copies of $\mathbb{E}$, namely $\mathbb{E}^{k+1}$, where we will use the additional copy of $\mathbb{E}$ to accommodate the Vinegar variables. Then we can use the same analysis as in [9] to derive the proof.

Under the assumption that the Vinegar maps $\beta_r^{(i)}$ look like random functions, we find that the lower bound given by Theorem 3 is tight.

From this result we directly derive a lower bound for the complexity of the MinRank attack (see Theorem 2) by

$$\text{Complexity}_{\text{MinRank}} \geq \ell^{(k+v+1)\cdot\omega}.$$ (4)

Theorem 3 allows us to use the method of [10] to derive directly.

Theorem 4. *The degree of regularity of a direct attack against an HMFEv system is, under the assumption of $v \leq \ell$, upper bounded by*

$$d_{\text{reg}} \leq \begin{cases} \frac{(q-1)(k+v-1)}{2} + 2 & \text{if } q \text{ even and } (k+v) \text{ odd} \\ \frac{(q-1)\cdot(k+v)}{2} + 2 & \text{otherwise} \end{cases}.$$ (5)

Equation (5) gives an upper bound for the degree of regularity of a direct attack against our scheme. However, in order to estimate the security of the HMFEv scheme in practice, we need to analyze if the bound given by (5) is reasonably tight. Furthermore we want to study, if, as Eq. (5) indicates, only the sum and not the concrete choice of k and v determines the degree of regularity of a direct attack against an HMFEv system. To answer these two questions, we performed a large number of experiments.

Our experiments (see in Sect. A of the appendix of this paper) show that the upper bound on the degree of regularity given by Eq. (5) is relatively tight. We could find several MHFEv instances which actually meet the upper bound and found that in most other cases the upper bound is missed only by one. Regarding the second question, we found that the concrete choice of k and v has no influence on the behavior of the scheme against direct attacks as long as k and v are not too small.

The experiments in the appendix deal with HMFEv schemes over very small fields such as GF(2) and GF(3). However, one major benefit of the HMFEv scheme is that, in contrast to HFEv-, it can be efficiently used over larger fields, too. As our experiments (see Sect. 6) show, these systems behave much more like random systems and we can reach high degrees of regularity, by which we can show the security of our scheme against direct attacks.

5.2 Quantum Attacks

In [19], Schwabe and Westerbaan showed that a binary system of n multivariate quadratic equations can be solved by a quantum computer in time

$$\text{comp}_{\text{MQquantum;GF(2)}} = 2^{n/2} \cdot 2 \cdot n^3.$$ (6)

Since our systems over GF(256) can easily be translated into systems over GF(2), this attack affects also our scheme (at least in theory). However, since this transition increases the number of variables in the system by a factor of 8, it has no major effect on the parameter selection of our scheme.

5.3   Other Attacks and a Remark on the Minus Method

Additional to direct, quantum and rank attacks, we analyzed the security of our scheme against other known attacks against multivariate schemes, including differential attacks [7] and Hashimotos attack against the original MultiHFE encryption scheme [14]. Obviously, this attack is essentially a differential symmetry attack though it is not formulated in that way. Therefore it is important to perform a solid analysis of the differential attacks for the new scheme. However, all the recent work in differential attacks indicates that it is a very special attack that is applicable ONLY to very special systems with lowest possible rank. For our scheme, this is clearly not the case and the Vinegar variables destroy efficiently all differential symmetries [4]. However, the complete analysis is very tedious, and our analysis will be presented in a subsequent paper.

Remark. A natural question here is, why we do not use the Minus method as in the case of HFEv-. There are two main reasons.

1. In contrast to the Vinegar variation, the Minus modification does not help to defend our scheme against differential attacks and Hashimotos attack against the original MultiHFE encryption scheme [14].
2. If we apply the same matrix rank method used in the proof of Theorem 3 (see also [9]) to MHFEv- (i.e. we lift the central map back to a vector space of $k+1$ copies of $\mathbb{E}$, where we use the additional copy of $\mathbb{E}$ to accommodate the Minus parameters and Vinegar variables), this directly leads to the conclusion that the MinRank should be $k+v+ak$, where a is the number of Minus equations. If we follow the above method further, we derive

$$d_{\text{reg}} \leq \begin{cases} \frac{(q-1)(k+v+ak-1)}{2} + 2 & \text{if } q \text{ even and } (k+v+ak) \text{ odd} \\ \frac{(q-1)\cdot(k+v+ak)}{2} + 2 & \text{otherwise} \end{cases} . \quad (7)$$

However our experiments show that this bound is not tight. This can be explained as follows. In the case of HFEv-, the estimate comes from using a single polynomial over the extension field, and a single polynomial already determines the whole system; in the case of MHFEv-, the system is determined by k polynomials, not by one; since our analysis considers only one of these polynomials, it does not use all the information available and therefore overestimates the degree of regularity.

This means we have a gap in the knowledge on estimating the degree of regularity in MHFEv-, which is the reason we propose the MHFEv system (i.e. only with Vinegar). This problem is very interesting and important, and we are going to deal with it in a subsequent paper.

6 Parameter Choice

In this section we consider the question how to find good parameter sets for our scheme. In particular, we aim at finding parameters for HMFEv over the fields GF(31) and GF(256).[1]

6.1 How to Choose the Parameter k?

The first question we have to answer in order to find suitable parameters for our scheme is how to choose the parameter k and therefore the number of components of the central map. Reducing the value of k will speed up the signature generation process of our scheme since it decreases the size of the multivariate quadratic system we have to solve. However, if k is too small, this might bring the security of our scheme into jeopardy.

For fields of odd characteristic (e.g. $\mathbb{F} = \mathrm{GF}(31)$) we choose the parameter k to be 2. However, in order to increase the security of our scheme against Rank attacks, we choose in this case the components of the central map $\mathcal{F}$ in a special way. Let F_1 and F_2 be the 2×2 matrices representing the homogeneous quadratic parts of the maps $\mathcal{F}^{(1)}$ and $\mathcal{F}^{(2)}$. A linear combination of F_1 and F_2 of rank 1 exists if and only if the quadratic polynomial $p(X) = \det(F_1 + X \cdot F_2) \in \mathbb{E}[X]$ has a solution. We therefore choose the coefficients of $\mathcal{F}^{(1)}$ and $\mathcal{F}^{(2)}$ in such a way that the polynomial $p(X)$ is irreducible.

For fields of even characteristic, the symmetric matrices representing the quadratic maps $\mathcal{F}^{(i)}$ contain zero elements on the main diagonal. Therefore, for $k = 2$, the rank of these matrices would be 1 and the upper linear combination of the maps $\mathcal{F}^{(1)}$ and $\mathcal{F}^{(2)}$ would actually lead to a matrix of rank 0 (i.e. no quadratic terms at all). To prevent this, we choose for fields of even characteristic the parameter k to be 3.

6.2 Experiments with Direct Attacks Against HMFEv Schemes over GF(31) and GF(256)

In Sect. 5.1 we already presented some results of experiments with the direct attack against HMFEv instances. However, in Sect. 5.1, we looked at HMFEv schemes over very small fields, for which the bound given by Eq. (5) is more or less tight. In this section we consider the question, if concrete instances of HMFEv over the larger fields GF(31) and GF(256) are hard to solve.

To do this, we created, for different parameter sets, HMFEv systems over GF(31) and GF(256) and solved these systems, after fixing v variables to obtain a determined system, with the F_4 algorithm integrated in MAGMA. The experimentswere performed on a single core of a server with 16 AMD Opteron

---

[1] The reason why we do not propose parameters for our scheme over GF(16) is the following: To defend the scheme against the quantum attack (see Sect. 5.2), we need a large number of equations over GF(16). This actually makes the schemes less efficient than HMFEv over GF(31) or GF(256).

Table 1. Experiments with the direct attack against HMFEv schemes over GF(31) and GF(256)

GF(31)	Parameters (k, ℓ, v)	$(2, 6, 4)$	$(2, 7, 4)$	$(2, 8, 4)$	Random
	m,n	12,12	14,14	16,16	16,16
	d_{reg}	14	16	18	18
	time (s)	1,911	164,089	-	-
	Memory (MB)	953	17,273	ooM	ooM
GF(256)	Parameters (k, ℓ, v)	$(3, 3, 6)$	$(3, 4, 6)$	$(3, 5, 6)$	Random
	m,n	9,9	12,12	15,15	15,15
	d_{reg}	11	14	17	17
	Time (s)	3.9	1,853	-	-
	Memory (MB)	23.7	952	ooM	ooM

processors (2.4 GHz) and 128 GB of RAM. For each parameter set we performed 10 experiments. Table 1 shows the results.

As the table shows, we can, for HMFEv instances over both GF(31) and GF(256), reach high degrees of regularity. In particular we see that, for the parameter sets proposed in the next section, the degree of regularity of a direct attack is at least 17. When solving the resulting linear systems with a sparse Wiedemann solver, we can estimate the complexity of a direct attack by

$$\text{Complexity}_{\text{direct attack}} \approx 3 \cdot \binom{n + d_{\text{reg}}}{d_{\text{reg}}}^2 \cdot \binom{n}{2}. \tag{8}$$

By substituting the value $d_{\text{reg}} = 17$ into this formula we find that the complexity of a direct attack against the HMFEv instances shown in Table 2 is beyond the claimed levels of security.

Also note that, for the underlying fields of GF(31) and GF(256), the public systems of HMFEv behave very similar to random systems. This also holds when guessing some variables before applying the F_4 algorithm (hybrid approach).

6.3 Parameters

Table 2 shows, for different levels of security (128, 192, and 256 bit) our parameter recommendations for the HMFEv signature scheme over GF(31) and GF(256). In the case of GF(31), we store one element of GF(31) in 5 bits, while 24 bits can be efficiently stored in 5 GF(31) elements.

The parameter sets given in Table 2 are chosen in such a way that the complexities of direct attacks (including hybrid approach; see Sect. 6.2), quantum attacks (see Eq. (6)) and Rank attacks (see Eq. (4)) against the given HMFEv instances are beyond the claimed levels of security. To be on the conservative side we chose, in formula (4), the linear algebra constant ω to be 2. Furthermore, in

Table 2. Parameter recommendations for the HMFEv signature scheme

Quantum security level (bit)	Parameters $(\mathbb{F}, k, \ell, v)$	Public key size (kB)	Private key size (kB)	Hash size (bit)	Signature size (bit)
128	(GF(31),2,28,12)	81.8	8.9	277	337
	(GF(256),3,15,16)	85.8	15.2	360	488
192	(GF(31),2,40,17)	234.7	20.0	396	481
	(GF(256),3,23,21)	282.1	35.0	552	720
256	(GF(31),2,55,21)	583.9	38.0	544	649
	(GF(256),3,31,26)	659.4	65.3	744	952

the case of MHFEv over GF(31), we had to take care of the fact that the public systems contain enough equations to prevent collision attacks against the hash function.

7   Comparison

The basic idea of the HMFEv signature scheme is very similar to that of Gui [18]: by applying the Vinegar modification it is possible to increase both the security and the efficiency of the scheme significantly. However, there are at least three major advantages of our scheme compared to Gui.

Key Sizes: First, for efficiency reasons, the Gui signature scheme is mainly restricted to the field GF(2). This leads to a large number of variables in the scheme and therefore to large key sizes. On the other hand, the HMFEv signature scheme can be defined over larger fields, too. This enables us to decrease the number of variables in the system and therefore reduces the public key size of the scheme significantly (see Table 3).

Simplicity and Efficiency: Secondly, for the parameter sets recommended in [18], the output size of the HFEv- public key is only 90 bit. Therefore, in order to defend the HFEv- signature scheme against collision attacks, the authors of Gui had to create a specially designed signature generation process for their scheme which inverts the HFEv- core map several times. Since the design of Gui requires the single HFEv- systems to have exactly one solution, generating one single Gui signature implies about 11 inversions of the HFEv- map, which leads to a relatively low performance of Gui. In the case of the HMFEv scheme, we do not need this multiple inversion of the core map, which makes the signature generation process of our scheme much faster and easier to implement. Furthermore, since the number of variables in the public systems of Gui is much larger than for our scheme, the evaluation of the HMFEv public systems and therefore the verification process of our scheme is much cheaper. This advantage of our scheme is increased by the fact that, during the verification process of Gui, we have to evaluate the public system several times.

Scalability: The third major advantage of the HMFEv scheme is that, in contrast to other HFEv- based schemes like Gui, the scheme can be scaled much easier to higher levels of security. For example, in order to obtain a quantum security level of 256 bit, we need an internal state of at least 457 bit (see Eq. (6)), which means that we need at least 457 variables over $GF(2)$. This would lead to key sizes which are completely impractical (see Table 3). In the case of HMFEv, the necessary increase of the number of variables is far less drastical. Alternatively, we can increase the size of the internal state simply by choosing a larger base field. For both strategies, the resulting increase of the key size is far less significant.

Table 3 compares, for different levels of security, the HMFEv and Gui signature schemes with respect to key and signature sizes. Note here that the parameters proposed in [18] are not chosen to provide quantum security. In order to provide a fair comparison, we therefore extrapolated the parameters of [18] to meet the quantum security levels. For better comparison, Table 3 also shows key and signature sizes of Rainbow.

Table 3. Comparison of our scheme with other multivariate signature schemes

Quantum security level (bit)		Public key size (kB)	Private key size (kB)	Signature size (bit)
80	Rainbow (GF(256),17,13,13)	25.1	19.9	344
	Gui (GF(2),120,9,3,3,2)	110.7	3.8	129
	HMFEv (GF(31),2,18,8)	**22.5**	**3.5**	**218**
	HMFEv (GF(256),3,9,12)	**21.6**	**6.0**	**312**
128	Rainbow (GF(256),36,21,22)	136.0	102.5	632
	Gui (GF(2),212,9,3,4,2)	592.8	11.6	222
	HMFEv (GF(31),2,28,12)	**81.8**	**8.9**	**337**
	HMFEv (GF(256),3,15,16)	**85.8**	**15.2**	**488**
256	Rainbow (GF(256),86,45,46)	1,415.7	1,046.3	1,416
	Gui (GF(2),464,9,7,8,2)	6,253.7	56.4	488
	HMFEv (GF(31),2,55,21)	**583.9**	**38.0**	**649**
	HMFEv (GF(256),3,31,26)	**659.4**	**65.3**	**952**

As Table 3 shows, the key sizes of our scheme are much smaller than that of Rainbow and Gui (especially for high levels of (quantum) security). The reason for this is that our scheme combines the main advantages of Rainbow and Gui: similar to Rainbow, we can use the HMFEv scheme over large finite fields, which reduces the number of equations needed in the public system. Similar to Gui, our scheme has a small blow up factor between the number of equations and the number of variables of about 1.25 (for Rainbow, this factor is about 1.8). This reduces both key and signature sizes significantly.

8 Implementation

In this section we provide some implementation details for our scheme and present performance results. In particular, we describe here

- how to efficiently invert the central map $\mathcal{F}$ and
- how to perform arithmetic operations in $\mathbb{F}$ and $\mathbb{E}$ efficiently.

8.1   Inversion of the Central Map $\mathcal{F}$

The most costly step during the signature generation process of our scheme is the inversion of the central equation $\mathcal{F}_V(\mathbf{Y}) = \mathbf{X}$, which is given as a system of k multivariate quadratic equations in k variables over the extension field $\mathbb{E}$. Since the coefficients of this system are random $\mathbb{E}$-elements, we need a system solver such as XL or a Gröbner Basis algorithm for this step.

Obviously, the complexity of solving the system $\mathcal{F}_V(\mathbf{Y}) = \mathbf{X}$ and therefore the complexity of the signature generation process depends mainly on the choice of the parameter k. A small value of k will reduce the number of $\mathbb{E}$-multiplications in this process. However, it also leads to large extension fields and therefore increases the cost of a single $\mathbb{E}$-multiplication. Furthermore, choosing k too small might weaken the security of our scheme (see Sect. 6.1).

To find the optimal parameter k for our scheme, we therefore have to analyze the process of inverting the central map $\mathcal{F}_V$ in more detail. Let the multivariate system $\mathcal{F}_V$ be given by the k multivariate quadratic maps $\mathcal{F}_V^{(1)}, \dots, \mathcal{F}_V^{(k)} : \mathbb{E}^k \to \mathbb{E}$. As we find, the process of solving the multivariate system $\mathcal{F}_V(\mathbf{Y}) = \mathbf{X}$ consists mainly of two parts:

1. (**Gröbner Basis step**) Find a univariate polynomial $p : \mathbb{E} \to \mathbb{E}$ in the ideal $\langle \mathcal{F}_V^{(1)}, \dots, \mathcal{F}_V^{(k)} \rangle$.
2. (**Solving step**) Solve the polynomial p by Berlekamp's algorithm.

In the following we analyze, for different values of k, these two steps in detail. For this, we fix the number $n = k \cdot \ell$ to $n = 48$ and choose $k \in \{2, 3, 4\}$. Inverting the system $\mathcal{F}_V$ therefore relates to

- solving a system of 2 quadratic equations in 2 variables over $\mathbb{F}^{24}$ or
- solving a system of 3 quadratic equations in 3 variables over $\mathbb{F}^{16}$ or
- solving a system of 4 quadratic equations in 4 variables over $\mathbb{F}^{12}$.

For $k = 2, 3$, we use for the first part a specially designed Gröbner Basis method tailored for the occasion. In the case of 2 quadratic equations in 2 variables, we run in the Gröbner Basis step successively 2 Gaussian eliminations on matrices of size 5×9 and 7×10. By doing so, we obtain a single variable equation p of degree 4. To perform this step, we need about $5 \cdot (11 + 12) + 7 \cdot 8 \cdot 4 = 339$ multiplications over the field $\mathbb{F}^{24}$.

In the Solving step, we have to solve the univariate equation p of degree 4 over the field $\mathbb{F}^{24}$. This takes about $6 \cdot 4^2 \cdot 24 = 2{,}304$ multiplications over the field $\mathbb{F}^{24}$. One can see that the overall complexity is dominated by the Solving step.

In the case of 3 quadratic equations in 3 variables, we run in the Gröbner Basis step successively 3 Gaussian eliminations on matrices of size 11×19, 8×16

and 5×13 with many zero elements to derive a single variable equation of degree 8. For this we need about $1{,}700$ $\mathbb{F}^{16}$-multiplications.

Then we solve this single variable equation of degree 8 over $\mathbb{F}^{16}$. This requires about $6 \cdot 8^2 \cdot 16 = 6{,}144$ $\mathbb{F}^{16}$-multiplications. One can see that the Solving step again dominates the complexity.

In the case of 4 quadratic equations in 4 variables, the situation is too complicated to do it by hand and we use the F_4 algorithm directly. In this case, we run successively Gaussian eliminations on matrices of size $19 \times 34, 41 \times 50, 42 \times 50$ and 35×48, which requires about $2 \cdot 50^3 = 250{,}000$ $\mathbb{F}^{12}$ multiplications. By doing so, we obtain a single variable equation p of degree 16.

In the Solving step, we have to solve this univariate equation p over the field $\mathbb{F}^{12}$, which requires about $6 \cdot 16^2 \cdot 12 = 18{,}432$ multiplications. One can see that here the solving of the single variable equation does not dominate the complexity anymore.

8.2   Arithmetic over Finite Fields

Evaluating the public map requires first to generate all monomials, and then the computation of the inner products between coefficient and monomial vectors. The first step requires $n(n + 1)/2$ field multiplications. The second part is much more important and requires $mn(n + 3)/2$ multiplications in the base field and nearly as many additions (or XORs) to accumulate the results.

Arithmetic in GF(256) is done via the table-lookup instruction VPSHUFB. This instruction allows 32 simultaneous lookups from a table of 16 elements, which allows for easy scalar-vector multiplications of GF(16) elements using log-exp tables. Every 32 GF(16) multiplications then take two VPSHUFB instructions and an add in addition to the required VPXOR, since we store the public key in log form. Finally we put together multiplications of GF(256) for the public key using four multiplications in GF(16) (schoolbook method).

The main computation in big binary fields uses PCLMULQDQ and schoolbook methods, because on recent processors this instruction is really fast. We also use lazy reductions, which means that we often do not reduce to the lowest degree. A time-constant complete reduction is performed after the entire operation.

Arithmetics in GF(31) use AVX2 instructions (and following that SSSE3 instructions). For best use of our resources, we use a YMM register to represent a vector of 16 or 32 coefficients in the public key to be multiplied by two monomials. Values for two monomials each time are also expanded into an YMM register. The actual arithmetic uses the VPMADDUSBW instruction to multiply two pairs of byte values (one signed, one unsigned) into signed 16-bit values, and add them together all in one cycle. This requires us to ensure that input monomials are in $0, \ldots, 31$ and the coefficients in $-15, \ldots, 15$. We add together 32 results of VPMADDUSBW each time, which keeps the result between -32767 and 32766. We can then reduce the results again to numbers between 0 and 31. Arithmetic operations in extension fields over GF(31) are performed in straight schoolbook form and do not use VPMADDUSBW instructions, because the sizes are not convenient for it.

Table 4 shows the running time of the signature generation and verification processes of our scheme for 80 and 128 bit quantum security. For comparison, we also provide here the running time of Gui [18]. Note again that the parameters of Gui were not chosen for quantum security. We expect the Gui parameters for 80 bit classical security to have about 62 bit quantum security. Similarly, the Gui parameters for 120 bit classical security provide 83 bit quantum security. Furthermore we want to emphasize that the implementation of [18] was far more optimized than ours (use of special processor instructions etc.). All the schemes listed in the table run on an Intel Xeon E3-1245 (Sandy Bridge) processor with 3.4 GHz.

Table 4. Comparison of the efficiency of HMFEv and Gui

Quantum security level (bit)		Sign. gen. time (ms)	Verification time (ms)
62	Gui (GF(2),96,5,6,6)	0.07	0.02
	Gui(GF(2),95,9,5,5)	0.18	0.02
	Gui(GF(2),94,17,4,4)	0.73	0.02
80	**HMFEv (GF(31),2,18,8)**	**0.131**	**0.0085**
	HMFEv (GF(256),3,9,12)	**0.261**	**0.0236**
83	Gui(127,9,4,6,2)	0.28	0.015
128	**HMFEv (GF(31),2,28,12)**	**0.259**	**0.0259**
	HMFEv (GF(256),3,15,16)	**0.443**	**0.063**

As the table shows, the performance of our scheme is at least comparable with that of Gui (note here that the Gui parameters provide significantly less security). Since, for increasing security level, the Gui parameters increase much faster than the parameters of our scheme, we believe that, for higher levels of security, our scheme will be much faster than Gui.

9 Conclusion

In this paper we proposed a new multivariate signature scheme called HMFEv which is obtained by applying the Vinegar modification to the MultiHFE scheme of Chen et al. [6]. By using this variation, we are able to reduce the number of components in the central map of the scheme and therefore to increase the efficiency significantly. We studied the security of our scheme against direct and rank attacks both theoretically and experimentally and showed that our scheme can not be attacked using differential methods or Hashimotos attack against the original MultiHFE scheme. We showed that our scheme is much more efficient than the Gui and Rainbow signature schemes with regard to key and signature sizes.

Future work includes in particular the further optimization of the implementation to enable a better comparison of our results with those from [18] as well as a careful study on the effects of applying the Minus modification on HMFEv.

Acknowledgments. The third author is partially supported by NIST. The second and fourth authors would like to thank Academia Sinica for the second author's Investigator Award and Taiwan's Ministry of Science and Technology grant MoST-105-2923-E-001-003-MY3. We want to thank the anonymous reviewers for their valuable comments which helped to improve this paper.

Disclaimer. Certain algorithms and commercial products are identified in this paper to foster understanding. Such identification does not imply recommendation or endorsement by NIST, nor does it imply that the algorithms or products identified are necessarily the best available for the purpose.

References

1. Bernstein, D.J., Buchmann, J., Dahmen, E. (eds.): Post Quantum Cryptography. Springer, Heidelberg (2009)
2. Bettale, L., Faugère, J.C., Perret, L.: Cryptanalysis of HFE, multi-HFE and variants for odd and even characteristic. Des. Codes Cryptogr. **69**(1), 1–52 (2013)
3. Bogdanov, A., Eisenbarth, T., Rupp, A., Wolf, C.: Time-area optimized public-key engines: $\mathcal{MQ}$-cryptosystems as replacement for elliptic curves? In: Oswald, E., Rohatgi, P. (eds.) CHES 2008. LNCS, vol. 5154, pp. 45–61. Springer, Heidelberg (2008). doi:10.1007/978-3-540-85053-3_4
4. Cartor, R., Gipson, R., Smith-Tone, D., Vates, J.: On the differential security of the HFEv- signature primitive. In: Takagi, T. (ed.) PQCrypto 2016. LNCS, vol. 9606, pp. 162–181. Springer, Cham (2016). doi:10.1007/978-3-319-29360-8_11
5. Chen, A.I.-T., Chen, M.-S., Chen, T.-R., Cheng, C.-M., Ding, J., Kuo, E.L.-H., Lee, F.Y.-S., Yang, B.-Y.: SSE implementation of multivariate PKCs on modern x86 CPUs. In: Clavier, C., Gaj, K. (eds.) CHES 2009. LNCS, vol. 5747, pp. 33–48. Springer, Heidelberg (2009). doi:10.1007/978-3-642-04138-9_3
6. Chen, C.H.O., Chen, M.S., Ding, J., Werner, F., Yang, B.Y.: Odd-char multivariate Hidden Field Equations. IACR eprint (2008). http://eprint.iacr.org/2008/543
7. Daniels, T., Smith-Tone, D.: Differential properties of the HFE cryptosystem. In: Mosca, M. (ed.) PQCrypto 2014. LNCS, vol. 8772, pp. 59–75. Springer, Cham (2014). doi:10.1007/978-3-319-11659-4_4
8. Ding, J., Gower, J.E., Schmidt, D.S.: Multivariate Public Key Cryptosystems. Springer, New York (2006)
9. Ding, J., Yang, B.-Y.: Degree of regularity for HFEv and HFEv-. In: Gaborit, P. (ed.) PQCrypto 2013. LNCS, vol. 7932, pp. 52–66. Springer, Heidelberg (2013). doi:10.1007/978-3-642-38616-9_4
10. Ding, J., Hodges, T.J.: Inverting HFE systems is quasi-polynomial for all fields. In: Rogaway, P. (ed.) CRYPTO 2011. LNCS, vol. 6841, pp. 724–742. Springer, Heidelberg (2011). doi:10.1007/978-3-642-22792-9_41
11. Ding, J., Schmidt, D.: Rainbow, a new multivariable polynomial signature scheme. In: Ioannidis, J., Keromytis, A., Yung, M. (eds.) ACNS 2005. LNCS, vol. 3531, pp. 164–175. Springer, Heidelberg (2005). doi:10.1007/11496137_12

12. Faugère, J.C.: A new efficient algorithm for computing Gröbner bases (F4). J. Pure Appl. Algebra **139**, 61–88 (1999)
13. Garey, M.R., Johnson, D.S.: Computers and Intractability: A Guide to the Theory of NP-Completeness. W.H. Freeman and Company, New York (1979)
14. Hashimoto, Y.: Cryptanalysis of Multi HFE. IACR eprint (2015). http://eprint. iacr.org/2015/1160.pdf
15. Kipnis, A., Patarin, J., Goubin, L.: Unbalanced oil and vinegar signature schemes. In: Stern, J. (ed.) EUROCRYPT 1999. LNCS, vol. 1592, pp. 206–222. Springer, Heidelberg (1999). doi:10.1007/3-540-48910-X_15
16. Kipnis, A., Shamir, A.: Cryptanalysis of the HFE public key cryptosystem by relinearization. In: Wiener, M. (ed.) CRYPTO 1999. LNCS, vol. 1666, pp. 19–30. Springer, Heidelberg (1999). doi:10.1007/3-540-48405-1_2
17. Patarin, J., Courtois, N., Goubin, L.: QUARTZ, 128-bit long digital signatures. In: Naccache, D. (ed.) CT-RSA 2001. LNCS, vol. 2020, pp. 282–297. Springer, Heidelberg (2001). doi:10.1007/3-540-45353-9_21
18. Petzoldt, A., Chen, M.-S., Yang, B.-Y., Tao, C., Ding, J.: Design principles for HFEv- based multivariate signature schemes. In: Iwata, T., Cheon, J.H. (eds.) ASIACRYPT 2015. LNCS, vol. 9452, pp. 311–334. Springer, Heidelberg (2015). doi:10.1007/978-3-662-48797-6_14
19. Schwabe, P., Westerbaan, B.: Solving binary MQ with Grovers algorithm. https:// cryptojedi.org/papers/mqgrover-20160901.pdf
20. Yang, B.-Y., Chen, J.-M.: Theoretical analysis of XL over small fields. In: Wang, H., Pieprzyk, J., Varadharajan, V. (eds.) ACISP 2004. LNCS, vol. 3108, pp. 277–288. Springer, Heidelberg (2004). doi:10.1007/978-3-540-27800-9_24

A   Results of Our Computer Experiments with the Direct Attack Against HMFEv Systems over Small Fields

In this section we present the results of our computer experiments with the direct attack against HMFEv schemes over small fields. In particular, we wanted to answer the questions

1. Is the concrete choice of k and v (or only their sum) important for the degree of regularity of a direct attack against the scheme? and
2. Is the upper bound on d_{reg} given by Eq. (5) reasonably tight?

In order to answer the first question, we performed experiments of the following type: For fixed values of q and $s = k + v$, we varied the values of k and v. We then created the public systems of the corresponding HMFEv instances (for different values of ℓ) and solved these systems using the F_4 algorithm integrated in MAGMA. The experiments were (like all the experiments presented in this paper) performed on a server with 16 AMD Opteron cores (2.4 GHz) and 128 GB of RAM. However, as MAGMA is not parallelizable, our programs use only one core.

In our experiments, we fixed the field $\mathbb{F}$ to be GF(2) and the sum $s = k + v$ to be 9. We varied v in the interval $I = \{0, \ldots, 8\}$ and created HMFEv(GF(2), $s - v$, ℓ, v) instances (for increasing values of ℓ). After that, we fixed v of the variables to get a determined system and solved the resulting public systems by the F_4 algorithm integrated in MAGMA. Table 5 shows, for $v \in I$, the highest degree of regularity we observed in these experiments. For each parameter set, we performed 10 experiments.

Table 5. Degree of regularity of HMFEv systems over GF(2) with $k + v = 9$

v	0	1	2	3	4	5	6	7	8
k	9	8	7	6	5	4	3	2	1
d_{reg}	3	4	4	5	5	5	5	5	4

As the experiments show, the concrete ratio between k and v has, as long as we choose v and k not too small, no influence on the degree of regularity of solving the public systems of HMFEv. For HMFEv schemes over larger fields the importance of the concrete choice of k and v decreases further, since those systems behave much more like random systems (see Sect. 6.2). We therefore choose, in order to increase the efficiency of our scheme, the parameter $k \in \{2, 3\}$ and increase v to reach the required level of security.

Is the Upper Bound on d_{reg} Given by Eq. (5) Reasonably Tight?

In order to answer this second question, we created for fixed values of q, k and v and varying values of ℓ public systems of HMFEv and solved them with the F_4 algorithm integrated in MAGMA. We increased the value of ℓ and therefore the numbers of equations and variables in the system until we reached the upper bound of (5) or ran out of memory.

It is obvious that we can only hope to find such systems for small field sizes. We therefore restricted to values of $q \in \{2, 3\}$.

By doing so, we identified the following "tight" instances of HMFEv

Scheme	Upper bound on d_{reg} (Eq. (5))	Experimental result
HMFEv(GF(2),1,ℓ,2)	3	3 for $\ell \geq 9(n \geq 9)$
HMFEv(GF(2),2,ℓ,3)	4	4 for $\ell \geq 9(n \geq 18)$
HMFEv(GF(2),3,ℓ,4)	5	5 for $\ell \geq 10(n \geq 30)$
HMFEv(GF(3),1,ℓ,2)	5	5 for $\ell \geq 18(n \geq 18)$

For most other HMFEv instances with $q \in \{2, 3\}$ and $k + v \leq 9$ we missed the upper bound given by Eq. (5) only by 1.

We believe that, also for these systems, we could have reached the upper bound given by Eq. (5) by increasing the parameter ℓ further. However, we did not have the necessary memory resources to solve HMFEv systems with more than 35 equations.

MQ Signatures for PKI

Alan Szepieniec[(⊠)], Ward Beullens, and Bart Preneel

imec-COSIC KU Leuven, Leuven, Belgium
{alan.szepieniec,bart.preneel}@esat.kuleuven.be,
ward.beullens@student.kuleuven.be

Abstract. It is well known that multivariate quadratic (MQ) digital signature schemes have small signatures but huge public keys. However, in some settings, such as public key infrastructure (PKI), both variables are important. This paper explains how to transform any MQ signature scheme into one with a much smaller public key at the cost of a larger signature. The transformation aims to reduce the combined size of the public key and signature and this metric is improved significantly. The security of our transformation reduces to that of the underlying MQ signature scheme in the random oracle model. It is possible to decrease signature sizes even further but then its security is related to the conjectured hardness of a new problem, the Approximate MQ Problem (AMQ).

Keywords: Multivariate quadratic · Public key infrastructure · Signature · Random oracle · Post-quantum · Hard problem

1 Introduction

Post-quantum cryptography is gaining in popularity in recent years, largely due to the promise of Shor's algorithms to break most deployed public-key cryptography as soon as large enough quantum computers are built [25]. For instance, NIST [17] is looking to standardize one or more quantum-resistant public-key cryptographic algorithms [18]. The EU-funded PQCRYPTO project aims to develop a portfolio of fast and highly secure implementations of post-quantum cryptosystems [28]. The conference of the same name has been held semi-anually since 2006 with larger turnouts every edition [2]. Perhaps the most noteworthy illustration of the increased consideration afforded to post-quantum cryptography is the experimental but successful adoption of the New Hope key establishment algorithm by Google in Chrome browsers [1,15].

While certainly a step forward, the deployment of the New Hope key establishment algorithm only protects users against passive eavesdroppers. An active attacker can launch a man-in-the-middle attack and fool Alice and Bob into establishing a secure channel with the *attacker*, rather than directly with one other. Alice and Bob can *sign* their messages to guarantee authenticity and thus foil the attack. However, this countermeasure does not fundamentally solve the problem as it requires that either Alice or Bob knows the other's public key, or at the very least is capable of verifying its authenticity when they receive it.

T. Lange and T. Takagi (Eds.): PQCrypto 2017, LNCS 10346, pp. 224–240, 2017.
DOI: 10.1007/978-3-319-59879-6_13

Public Key Infrastructure (PKI) solves this problem with certificates that authenticate the transmitted public key. The certificate itself is a linked list of public keys and signatures, where each signature authenticates the next public key under the previous one. The first public key in this link is the root public key of a Certificate Authority (CA), which in the case of web traffic is built into the user's browser.

The transmission of the certificate constitutes a significant bandwidth cost in any key establishment protocol and should consequently be minimized. However, most current proposals for post-quantum signatures do not seem to take this particular use case into account. By and large, post-quantum signature schemes fall into two camps. In camp (1) public keys are small but the signatures are huge. This is the case for hash-based signatures such as SPHINCS [3] and signatures based on non-interactive zero-knowledge proofs such as the MQ-based SSH protocol [24] and the subsequent MQDSS [7] or Stern's code-based identification scheme [27]. By contrast, in camp (2) the signatures are small but the public keys are huge, such as is the case for well-known MQ signature schemes such as UOV [14] or HFEv^- [19,21] but also notably the code-based trapdoor schemes such as CFS and derivates [8]. The odd exception to this polarization is the lattice-based BLISS [10] whose public keys and signatures clock in at roughly the same size.

In the case of PKI, only the root public key is not transmitted as part of the certificate as it is assumed to be present on the client already. For this purpose, camp (2) is ideal as it increases the certificate size by the smallest amount. At the other end of the chain, the public key should be small as it is transmitted every time; but more importantly its signature generation algorithm should be fast as it must produce new signatures every time the protocol runs — in contrast to the certificate itself, which can be copied straight from memory. Therefore, fast representatives from camp (1) or the odd exception between camps seem more suited for the tail end of the chain. In the middle of the chain, signatures are generated relatively infrequently and the chief concern is not so much the cost of the signature generation algorithm but rather the sizes of the public keys and signatures. Between these two size variables, one should not minimize one at the expense of the other, but rather *both variables at the same time*.

Figure 1 plots several signature schemes and their positions in the quarter plane spanned by the signature size and public key size axes. While ECDSA enjoys both very short signatures and public keys, it offers zero security against quantum computers.

In this paper we present a generic transformation that turns MQ signature schemes — whose public keys are huge and whose signatures are small — into a new signature scheme with smaller public keys and larger signatures. The objective is a new signature scheme whose public keys pk and signatures s solve

$$\min(|\mathsf{pk}| + |s|). \tag{1}$$

It should be noted that it is easy to transform any representative from camp (2) to one from camp (1) using hash functions. Just replace the public key with

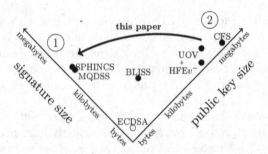

Fig. 1. Diagram of various digital signature schemes laid out according to signature and public key size.

its hash digest, and include the original public key as part of the new signatures. This naïve transformation does not improve the target quantity. However, as there is no equivalent reverse transformation, it shows perhaps that camp (2) is the more fruitful starting point.

Indeed, our transform can be thought of as applying the above naïve transformation and stopping half-way. Instead of including the entire original public key in the signatures, we *include only a small portion* of it — but just enough to keep the verification procedure meaningful. Which portion is to be included, is decided by the random oracle after being queried with the signature. Lastly, a small set of Merkle tree paths ending in linearly homomorphic MACs allows the verifier to verify that the released portion of the original public key matches the Merkle root, which is the new public key.

It is possible to choose parameters for which our transform generates a new signature scheme whose security reduces cleanly to that of the underlying MQ signature scheme. For parameters that lead to even smaller signatures we have no security proof but we are able to relate forgery to a hard problem called the *Approximate MQ Problem* (AMQ), which generalizes the MQ problem to allow erroneous solutions, as long as the errors live in a consistent small-dimension subspace. We offer several arguments supporting the hardness of the AMQ Problem.

2   Preliminaries

Random Oracle Model. We use a hash function in our construction. For the purpose of proving security we model it by a *random oracle*, which is a random function $H : \{0,1\}^* \rightarrow \{0,1\}^\kappa$ with a fixed output length, typically equal to the security parameter. If necessary, the random oracle's output space can be lifted to any finite set X. We use subscripts to differentiate the random oracles associated with different output spaces. A security proof relying on the modelling of hash function as random oracles is said to hold in the *random oracle model*.

Signature Scheme. A public key signature scheme is defined as a triple of polynomial-time algorithms (KeyGen, Sign, Verify). The probabilistic key generation algorithm takes the security level κ (in unary notation) and produces a secret and public key: $\mathsf{KeyGen}(1^\kappa) = (\mathsf{sk}, \mathsf{pk})$; the signature generation algorithm produces a signature: $s = \mathsf{Sign}(\mathsf{sk}, m) \in \{0,1\}^*$. The verification algorithm takes the public key, the message and the signature and decides if the signature is valid: $\mathsf{Verify}(\mathsf{pk}, m, s) \in \{0,1\}$. The signature scheme is *correct* if signing a message with the secret key produces a valid signature under the matching public key:

$$(\mathsf{sk}, \mathsf{pk}) = \mathsf{KeyGen}(1^\kappa) \quad \Rightarrow \quad \forall m \in \{0,1\}^* . \mathsf{Verify}(\mathsf{pk}, m, \mathsf{Sign}(\mathsf{sk}, m)) = 1.$$

Security is defined with respect to the Existential Unforgeability under Chosen Message Attack (EUF-CMA) game [12] between the adversary $\mathcal{A}$ and the challenger $\mathcal{C}$, both polynomial-time Turing machines. The challenger generates a key pair and sends the public key to the adversary. The adversary is allowed to make a polynomial number of queries $m_i, i \in \{1, \ldots, q\}, q \leq \kappa^c$ for some c, which the challenger signs using the secret key and sends back: $s_i \leftarrow \mathsf{Sign}(\mathsf{sk}, m_i)$. At the end of the game, the adversary must produce a pair of values (m', s') where m' was not queried before: $m' \notin \{m_i\}_{i=1}^q$. The adversary wins if $\mathsf{Verify}(\mathsf{pk}, m', s') = 1$. A signature scheme is secure in the EUF-CMA model if for all quantum polynomial-time adversaries $\mathcal{A}$, the probability of winning is negligible, *i.e.*, drops faster than any polynomial's reciprocal:

$$\forall c > 1 . \exists N \in \mathbb{N} . \forall \kappa > N . \forall \mathcal{A} .$$

$$\Pr \left[\begin{matrix} \mathsf{Verify}(\mathsf{pk}, m', s') = 1 \\ \wedge \, m' \notin \{m_i\}_{i=1}^q \end{matrix} \middle| \begin{matrix} (\mathsf{sk}, \mathsf{pk}) \leftarrow \mathsf{KeyGen}(1^\kappa) \\ (\{m_i, s_i\}_{i=1}^{q < \kappa^c}, m', s') \leftarrow \langle \mathcal{C}(\mathsf{sk}), \mathcal{A}\rangle(\mathsf{pk}) \end{matrix} \right] \leq \frac{1}{\kappa^c}.$$

3   Multivariate Quadratic Signature Schemes

Multivariate quadratic (MQ) cryptosystems rely on the cryptographic hardness of the MQ Problem, which asks to find a satisfying solution $\mathbf{x} \in \mathbb{F}_q^n$ to a list of m multivariate quadratic polynomials $\mathcal{P} \in (\mathbb{F}_q[\mathbf{x}])^m$. This problem is **NP**-hard as well as empirically hard on average, requiring an exponential running time for solution by state-of-the-art algorithms whenever $m \approx n$. This paper, and all other MQ-based cryptography, assumes that the MQ Problem is hard.

MQ Problem. Given: a list of m multivariate quadratic polynomials $\mathcal{P}(\mathbf{x}) = (p_1(\mathbf{x}), \ldots, p_m(\mathbf{x}))^\mathsf{T}$ over a finite field $\mathbb{F}_q$ in n variables $(x_1, \ldots, x_n)^\mathsf{T} = \mathbf{x} \in \mathbb{F}_q^n$. Find an assignment to $\mathbf{x}$ that satisfies $p_1(\mathbf{x}) = \ldots = p_m(\mathbf{x}) = 0$. We write MQ to denote the problem class and $\mathsf{MQ}[m, n]$ to make the parameters explicit.

MQ Assumption. If $m \approx n$, there is no polynomial-time quantum computer that solves generic instances of $\mathsf{MQ}[m, n]$.

The MQ signature schemes considered in this paper have public keys that contain a trapdoor. The signature verification algorithm consists of evaluating the public key $\mathcal{P}$ in the signature $\mathbf{s} \in \mathbb{F}_q^n$, and checking whether this evaluation results in the hash of the message $m \in \{0,1\}^*$ lifted to $\mathbb{F}_q^m$: $\mathcal{P}(\mathbf{s}) \stackrel{?}{=} \mathsf{H}(m)$. In order to sign a message, the signer must know a secret decomposition of $\mathcal{P}$ into $\mathcal{P} = T \circ \mathcal{F} \circ S$ where T and S are affine and where $\mathcal{F}$ is efficiently invertible[1]. Therefore, in addition to the MQ Problem, these signature schemes rely on the Extended Isomorphism of Polynomials (EIP) Problem, which asks to recover the factorization $T, \mathcal{F}, S$ from $\mathcal{P}$ (Fig. 2).

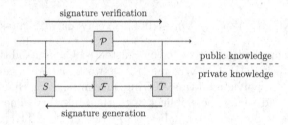

Fig. 2. Schematic representation of multivariate quadratic signature schemes.

The EIP problem is not hard in general. Rather, the central map $\mathcal{F}$ requires careful design to resist all known attacks. We recommend relying on the HFEv[-] [21] or UOV [14] signature schemes, as these have remained unbroken for close to two decades. We omit a formal treatment of the EIP problem as it is not relevant to our transformation and it is assumed to be hard for the underlying signature scheme anyway.

3.1 Approximate MQ

Unfortunately, not all instances of our construction have a clean reduction towards the underlying MQ signature scheme. Instead, we relate their security to a new computational problem called the *Approximate MQ Problem* (AMQ for short). Roughly speaking, the AMQ Problem is a weaker variant of the MQ problem where the solution does not have to be exact; rather, the errors have to live in a subspace of small dimension.

AMQ Problem. Let $m, n, v, r \in \mathbb{N}$ be integers with $r < m$ and $r < v$. Given a list of m multivariate quadratic polynomials $\mathcal{P}(\mathbf{x}) = (p_1(\mathbf{x}), \ldots, p_m(\mathbf{x}))^{\mathsf{T}}$ over a finite field $\mathbb{F}_q$ in n variables $(x_1, \ldots, x_n)^{\mathsf{T}} = \mathbf{x} \in \mathbb{F}_q^n$, and a list of v target vectors $\mathbf{y}_1, \ldots, \mathbf{y}_v \in \mathbb{F}_q^m$. Find a list of v vectors $\mathbf{x}_1, \ldots, \mathbf{x}_v \in \mathbb{F}_q^n$ such that

$$\mathsf{dim} \, \langle \{\mathcal{P}(\mathbf{x}_i) - \mathbf{y}_i\}_{i=1}^{v} \rangle \leq r.$$

We write AMQ to denote the problem class and write $\mathsf{AMQ}[m, n, v, r]$ to make the parameters explicit.

Obviously, we have $\mathsf{MQ}[m, n] \equiv \mathsf{AMQ}[m, n, v, 0]$. Other trivial reductions include $\mathsf{AMQ}[m, n, v, r+1] \leq \mathsf{AMQ}[m, n, v, r]$; $\mathsf{AMQ}[m, n, v, r] \leq \mathsf{MQ}[m, n]$; $\mathsf{AMQ}[m, n, v, r] \leq \mathsf{AMQ}[m+1, n, v, r]$; and $\mathsf{AMQ}[m, n, v, r] \leq \mathsf{AMQ}[m, n, v+1, r]$.

---

[1] If $n > m$, which is necessary for MQ signature schemes, any image is likely to have multiple inverses. By "efficiently invertible" we mean that there is an efficient algorithm to sample from the inverse set of any given image.

Unfortunately, we know of no reduction showing that AMQ with $r \geq 1$ is at least as hard as another hard problem. Nevertheless, we argue that it is a hard problem by detailing three algorithms to solve it, each with an exponential running time, assuming $v \gg m \gg r$.

Exhaustive Search. Modelling $\mathcal{P}$ as a random function, we have that a random choice of $\mathbf{x}_i$ will lie in a subspace of dimension r with probability $1/q^{(m-r)}$. The first r vectors $\mathbf{x}_1, \ldots, \mathbf{x}_r$ can be chosen at random and the next $v - r$ vectors should be chosen such that $\forall i \in \{r+1, \ldots, v\} . \mathcal{P}(\mathbf{x}_i) - \mathbf{y}_i \in \langle \{\mathcal{P}(\mathbf{x}_j) - \mathbf{y}_j\}_{j=1}^r \rangle$. This strategy takes about $O(q^{m-r})$ time.

Grover. A large asymptotical work factor can be saved by running the algorithm on a quantum computer, employing Grover's algorithm [13] or its generalization by the name of amplitude amplification [6]. The probability of $\mathcal{P}(\mathbf{x}_i) - \mathbf{y}_i$ lying in a targeted space of dimension r is still $1/q^{(m-r)}$ but a quantum search will find one in roughly $O(q^{(m-r)/2})$ steps.

Algebraic. This strategy attempts to repeatedly find one extra vector $\mathbf{x}_{r+i}$ by running a Gröbner basis algorithm such as F4 [11] or XL [9], or a hybrid approach [4,5]. Introduce r new indeterminates z_j for $j \in \{1, \ldots, r\}$ and in addition to the n variables $\mathbf{x}_{r+i}$. Then require that $\dot{z}_1(\mathcal{P}(\mathbf{x}_1) - \mathbf{y}_1) + \ldots + z_r(\mathcal{P}(\mathbf{x}_r) - \mathbf{y}_r) + \mathcal{P}(\mathbf{x}_{r+i}) - \mathbf{y}_{r+i} = 0$. After applying a linear transformation, this is equivalent to an instance of the MQ Problem with n variables and $m - r$ equations, *i.e.*, $\mathsf{AMQ}[m, n, v, r] \leq \mathsf{MQ}[m - r, n]$. A similar search for $\mathbf{x}_1, \ldots, \mathbf{x}_v$ *simultaneously* will lead to a *cubic* system with a number of equations and variables that scale linearly in v.

It is clear that the AMQ problem gets easier as r approaches $\min(m, v)$. The algorithms above suggest that the complexity of a solution should be exponential in $m - r$, assuming v is large enough.

4   Construction

We now describe a transform that turns an MQ signature scheme (ORIGINAL. KeyGen, ORIGINAL.Sign, ORIGINAL.Verify) into another one (NEW.KeyGen, NEW. Sign, NEW.Verify) that has a smaller public key but larger signatures. The objective is to minimize $|\mathsf{pk}| + |s|$ (public key size plus signature size) subject to guaranteeing κ bits of security against attackers. In the following we denote by $\mathcal{P} \in (\mathbb{F}_q[\mathbf{x}])^m$ the list of polynomials of the original public key and by pk its representation as a bit string.

Only Transmit a Randomly Chosen Part of Public Key. New signatures consist of σ original signatures $\mathbf{s}_1, \ldots, \mathbf{s}_\sigma$ along with some information to verify them. The main idea is that it is not necessary to transmit the entire public key for this verification. Instead, it suffices to include a small number of randomly chosen linear combinations of polynomials of $\mathcal{P}$ in each signature. So besides the

σ original signatures, part of the new signature consists of a list of α quadratic polynomials $\mathcal{R}(\mathbf{x}) : \mathbb{F}_q^n \rightarrow \mathbb{F}_q^\alpha$ derived from the original public key as $\mathcal{R}(\mathbf{x}) = \mathbf{t}\mathcal{P}(\mathbf{x})$, where $\mathbf{t} \in \mathbb{F}_q^{\alpha \times m}$ is a randomly chosen matrix.

At the time of verifying the new signature, $\mathcal{P}$ might be unknown. Nevertheless, $\mathcal{R}(\mathbf{x})$ is known so it can be used instead to obtain some level of assurance of the signatures' validity. In particular, if $\mathbf{s}$ is a valid signature for document d, i.e., $\mathcal{P}(\mathbf{s}) = \mathsf{H}_1(d)$, then the same holds after multiplication by $\mathbf{t}$, i.e., $\mathcal{R}(\mathbf{s}) = \mathbf{t}\mathcal{P}(\mathbf{s}) = \mathbf{t}\mathsf{H}_1(d)$. The matrix $\mathbf{t}$ is chosen *after* the σ signatures $\mathbf{s}_1, \ldots, \mathbf{s}_\sigma$ are fixed by passing them through a hash function $\mathsf{H}_2 : \{0,1\}^* \rightarrow \{0,1\}^\kappa$ whose output is lifted to the space of $\alpha \times m$ matrices: $\mathbf{t} \leftarrow \mathsf{H}_2(d\|\mathbf{s}_1\| \cdots \|\mathbf{s}_\sigma)$. This delayed choice strategy forces the signer to produce signatures honestly, because any invalid signature has probability $1/q^\alpha$ of passing this test. This probability can be made negligible by choosing the parameter α sufficiently large.

Alternatively, one can keep α by increasing the number σ of original signatures $\mathbf{s}_1, \ldots, \mathbf{s}_\sigma$ on documents deterministically derived from d as $\mathbf{s}_i = \mathsf{Sign}(\mathsf{sk}, d\|i)$ for $i \in \{1, \ldots, \sigma\}$. The probability that a set of signatures $\mathbf{s}_1, \ldots, \mathbf{s}_\sigma$ all satisfy $\mathcal{R}(s_i) = \mathbf{t}\mathsf{H}_1(d\|i)$ for a randomly chosen $\mathbf{t}$ is then $1/q^{\alpha D}$, where $D \leq \sigma$ is the dimension of the subspace spanned by the errors $\mathcal{P}(s_i) - \mathsf{H}(d\|i)$. We then have to rely on the hardness of the AMQ problem, because it should be infeasible to forge the signatures $\mathbf{s}_1, \cdots, \mathbf{s}_\sigma$ such that D is small.

Assure the Validity of $\mathcal{R}(\mathbf{x})$. Using $\mathcal{R}(\mathbf{x})$ instead of $\mathcal{P}(\mathbf{x})$ introduces a new attack strategy: to forge signatures for a polynomial system $\mathcal{R}(\mathbf{x})$ that is not at all related to $\mathcal{P}(\mathbf{x})$. To block this attack, we need to add some information to the signature such that the verifier can check that $\mathcal{R}(\mathbf{x}) = \mathbf{t}\mathcal{P}(\mathbf{x})$. An obvious way to do this is committing to $\mathcal{P}(\mathbf{x})$ in the public key and revealing it in the signature, but this would lead to a huge signature and defeat the purpose of our construction. Instead, we compute MAC (message authentication code) polynomials to authenticate $\mathcal{R}(\mathbf{x})$.

Fix any ordering of monomials and consider the list of $N = n(n+1)/2 + n + 1$ coefficients of $p_i(\mathbf{x})$, the ith polynomial of the original public key. Group these elements into $\lceil N/k \rceil$ adjacent tuples of k elements each, padding with zeros if necessary. Interpret these k-tuples as coefficients in $\mathbb{F}_{q^k}$ of a polynomial $\hat{p}_i(z) \in \mathbb{F}_{q^k}[z]$. Let $\hat{\mathcal{P}}(z)$ denote the vector of these MAC polynomials: $\hat{\mathcal{P}}(z) = (\hat{p}_i(z))_{i=0}^{m-1}$. Apply the same operation to the α polynomials of $\mathcal{R}(\mathbf{x})$ to obtain $\hat{\mathcal{R}}(z) \in (\mathbb{F}_{q^k}[z])^\alpha$. The following diagram commutes:

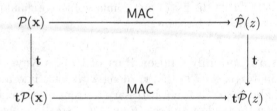

In other words, we have that $\mathsf{MAC}(\mathsf{t}\mathcal{P}(\mathbf{x})) = \mathsf{t}\mathsf{MAC}(\mathcal{P}(\mathbf{x}))$. The public key represents a commitment to the evaluation of $\hat{\mathcal{P}}(z)$ in a large number τ of points $r \in Z \subset \mathbb{F}_{q^k}$. A signature reveals the evaluation of $\hat{\mathcal{P}}$ in a small number ϑ of randomly chosen points $r \in O \subset Z$, and the verifier can check for all $r \in O$ whether $\hat{\mathcal{R}}(r) = \mathsf{t}\hat{\mathcal{P}}(r)$. Since $\hat{\mathcal{R}}(z) - \mathsf{t}\hat{\mathcal{P}}(z)$ are α polynomials of degree at most $\lceil N/k \rceil - 1$ there are at most $\lceil N/k \rceil - 1$ values of $r \in \mathbb{F}_{q^k}$ for which this equality holds when $\hat{\mathcal{R}}(z) \neq \mathsf{t}\hat{\mathcal{P}}(z)$. Therefore, if the equality holds for enough randomly chosen values $r \in O$, this assures the verifier that $\mathcal{R}(\mathbf{x}) = \mathsf{t}\mathcal{P}(\mathbf{x})$. Exactly which evaluations are revealed is determined by the hash value of $d\|\mathbf{s}_1\| \cdots \|\mathbf{s}_\sigma\|\mathcal{R}(\mathbf{x})$, i.e., $O = \mathsf{H}_3(d\|\mathbf{s}_1\| \cdots \|\mathbf{s}_\sigma\|\mathcal{R}(\mathbf{x}))$. For an incorrect $\mathcal{R}(\mathbf{x})$ at most $\lceil N/k \rceil - 1$ values of $r \in \mathbb{F}_{q^k}$ can satisfy $\hat{\mathcal{R}}(r) = \mathsf{t}\hat{\mathcal{P}}(r)$. Therefore the probability that an incorrect $\mathcal{R}(\mathbf{x})$ passes the tests is bounded above by $\left(\frac{\lceil N/k \rceil - 1}{\tau} \right)^\vartheta$. The parameters τ and ϑ have to be chosen so that this probability is negligible.

To save space, put the $\tau = \#Z$ evaluations of $\hat{\mathcal{P}}(z)$ as leaves into a Merkle tree. The public key is the root of this Merkle tree: it commits to all evaluations of $\hat{\mathcal{P}}(z)$. Revealing a single evaluation of $\hat{\mathcal{P}}(z)$ requires $(\log_2 \tau) - 2$ hash values to trace and verify the path from the given point to the root (Fig. 3).

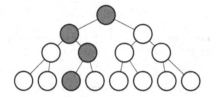

Fig. 3. Merkle tree with one opened path. The length of the path is logarithmic in the number of leafs.

We do not cover the exact implementation of the Merkle tree and instead invoke the following procedures abstractly. Merkle.generate_tree takes a list of 2^k (for some $k \in \mathbb{N}$) objects and generates the entire Merkle tree from them, returning the tree as its output. Merkle.root takes the tree and outputs its root node. Merkle.open_path takes the tree and leaf node and outputs that leaf along with all hashes needed to merge branches and travel to the root. Merkle.verify takes a root node and a path and verifies that both belong to the same tree.

While our transformation borrows the Merkle tree construction from hash-based signature schemes, we would like to stress that this is for compression only. In particular, reusing the same Merkle path for different signature poses no security threat as the transformed signature scheme is still stateless.

4.1 Summary

Figures 4, 5 and 6 present pseudocode for the new key generation, signature generation, and signature verification algorithms. Aside from the standard parameter names for MQ cryptosystems, we also rely on the following parameters or shorthand forms:

N — number of columns of the Macaulay matrix of $\mathcal{P}$, equal to $n(n+3)/2+1$.
σ — number of original signatures to include in the new signature;
α — number of polynomials to include in the new signature;
τ — number of MAC values; must be a power of two and $\tau \geq N$ must hold;
k — degree of the extension field $\mathbb{F}_{q^k}$ such that $\#\mathbb{F}_{q^k} \geq \tau$;
ϑ — number of Merkle paths to open; ϑ must be greater than 1;
Z — A subset of $\mathbb{F}_{q^k}$ that contains τ elements.

---

algorithm NEW.KeyGen
input: 1^κ — the security parameter in unary representation
output: sk$'$ — new secret key
        pk$'$ – new public key
1: $(\mathsf{pk}, \mathsf{sk}) \leftarrow \mathsf{ORIGINAL.KeyGen}(1^\kappa)$
2: **for** i from 0 to $m-1$ **do:**   ▷ obtain MAC polynomials $\hat{\mathcal{P}}(z)$
3:    **for** j from 0 to $\lceil N/k \rceil - 1$ **do:**
4:       $c_j \leftarrow$ cast coeffs$(p_i(\mathbf{x}))[jk : (j+1)k - 1]$ to $\mathbb{F}_{q^k}$
5:    **end**
6:    $p_i(z) \leftarrow \sum_{j=0}^{\lceil N/k \rceil - 1} c_j z^j$
7: **end**
8: $\hat{\mathcal{P}}(z) \leftarrow (\hat{p}_i(z))_{i=0}^{m-1}$
9: mt $\leftarrow$ Merkle.generate_tree$(\{\hat{\mathcal{P}}(r)\}_{r \in Z})$ ▷ evaluate $\hat{\mathcal{P}}(z)$ in Z and Merkleize
10: pk$' \leftarrow$ Merkle.root(mt)
11: sk$' \leftarrow (\mathsf{sk}, \mathcal{P}(\mathbf{x}), \mathsf{mt})$

Fig. 4. New key generation algorithm.

---

algorithm NEW.Sign
input: sk$'$ — secret key
      $d \in \{0,1\}^*$ — document to be signed
output: s' — signature for d
1: sk, $\mathcal{P}(\mathbf{x})$, mt $\leftarrow$ sk$'$
2: **for** i from 1 to σ **do:**   ▷ generate σ original signatures
3:    $s_i \leftarrow \mathsf{ORIGINAL.Sign}(\mathsf{sk}, d\|i)$
4: **end**
5: $\mathbf{t} \leftarrow \mathsf{H_2}(d\|s_1\| \cdots \|s_\sigma)$
6: $\mathcal{R}(\mathbf{x}) \leftarrow \mathbf{t}^\mathsf{T} \mathcal{P}(\mathbf{x})$ ▷ get verification polynomials $\mathcal{R}(\mathbf{x})$
7: $O \leftarrow \mathsf{H_3}(d\|s_1\| \cdots \|s_\sigma\|\mathcal{R}(\mathbf{x}))$ such that $O \subset Z$ and $\#O = \vartheta$
8: open paths $\leftarrow$ empty_list
9: **for** r in O **do:**   ▷ open indicated Merkle paths for MACs
10:    open paths.append(Merkle.open_path(mt, $\hat{\mathcal{P}}(r)$))
11: **end**
12: $s' \leftarrow (s_1, \ldots, s_\sigma, \mathcal{R}(\mathbf{x}), \text{open paths})$

Fig. 5. New signature generation algorithm.

---

algorithm NEW.Verify
input: pk′ — public key
$\quad\quad\quad d \in \{0, 1\}^*$ — document
$\quad\quad\quad s'$ — signature on document
output: True or False
1: $s_1, \ldots, s_\sigma, \mathcal{R}(\mathbf{x})$, open paths ← s'
2: $\mathbf{t}$ ← $\mathsf{H}_2(d\|s_1\|\ldots\|s_\sigma)$
3: **for** i **from** 1 **to** σ **do:** $\triangleright$ verify original signatures against $\mathcal{R}(\mathbf{x})$
4: $\quad$ $\mathbf{s}_i$ ← cast s_i to $\mathbb{F}_q^n$
5: $\quad$ **if** $\mathcal{R}(\mathbf{s}_i) \neq \mathbf{t}\mathsf{H}_1(d\|i)$
6: $\quad\quad$ **return** False
7: $\quad$ **end**
8: **end**
9: **for** j **from** 1 **to** α **do:** $\triangleright$ obtain MAC polynomials $\hat{\mathcal{R}}(z)$
10: $\quad$ **for** i **from** 0 **to** $\lceil N/k \rceil - 1$ **do:**
11: $\quad\quad$ a_i ← cast $\mathsf{coeffs}(r_j(\mathbf{x}))[ik : (i+1)k - 1]$ to $\mathbb{F}_{q^k}$
12: $\quad$ **end**
13: $\quad$ $\hat{r}_j(z)$ ← $\sum_{i=0}^{\lceil N/k \rceil - 1} a_i z^i$
14: **end**
15: $\hat{\mathcal{R}}(z)$ ← $(\hat{r}_j(z))_{j=1}^\alpha$
16: O ← $\mathsf{H}_3(d\|s_1\|\cdots\|s_\sigma\|\mathcal{R}(\mathbf{x}))$ such that $O \subset Z$ and $\#O = \vartheta$
17: **for** i **from** 1 **to** $\#O$ **do:** $\triangleright$ validate $\hat{\mathcal{R}}(z)$ against opened Merkle paths
18: $\quad$ $\hat{\mathcal{P}}(r)$, mp ← open paths[i]
19: $\quad$ **if** Merkle.verify(pk′, mp) = False **or** $\hat{\mathcal{R}}(O[i]) \neq \mathbf{t}^\mathsf{T}\hat{\mathcal{P}}(r)$
20: $\quad\quad$ **return** False
21: $\quad$ **end**
22: **end**
23: **return** True

Fig. 6. New signature verification algorithm.

5 Security

Security of the construction for large enough α is shown through a sequence of games reduction [26], going from an adversary winning the EUF-CMA game of the new scheme to one that wins the same game but associated with the original MQ signature scheme. Our reduction works in two steps. The intermediate game is also an EUF-CMA game but against a hybrid scheme defined as follows:

- HYBRID.KeyGen is identical to ORIGINAL.KeyGen. No MACs are generated.
- HYBRID.Sign retains steps 1–6 from NEW.Sign and drops the opened paths from the signature in step 12.
- HYBRID.Verify retains steps 1–8 from NEW.Verify and instead of verifying the MAC (steps 9–19) verifies that $\mathcal{R}(\mathbf{x}) = \mathbf{t}^\mathsf{T}\mathcal{P}(\mathbf{x})$ because the public key $\mathcal{P}(\mathbf{x})$ is now known and there is no longer any need to rely on the MACs.

Theorem 1. *If there is an adversary A against EUF-CMA-NEW in time T with Q random oracle queries and with success probability ϵ, then there is an adversary B^A that wins EUF-CMA-HYB in time $O(T)$ and with success probability at least*

$$\epsilon - (Q + 1) \left(\frac{\lceil N/k \rceil - 1}{\tau} \right)^{\vartheta} - 2\tau(Q+1)/2^{\kappa}.$$

Theorem 2. *If there is an adversary A against EUF-CMA-HYB in time T with Q random oracle queries and with success probability ϵ then there exists an adversary B^A against EUF-CMA-ORIGINAL in time $O(T)$ with success probability at least $\epsilon - (Q + 1) \left(\frac{1}{q} \right)^{\alpha}$.*

Due to the space constraint, we defer the proofs to Appendix A. In both cases the simulated algorithm has unbridled access to the real random oracle; the simulator does not measure nor compute on queries or responses. The set of challenge-response pairs of the random oracle is random but fixed before the protocol starts. While the simulator algorithm works in the quantum random oracle model, the proof of the lower bound on the success probability models the queries as classical messages and therefore only holds in the classical random oracle model. Nevertheless, we believe that the success probability can still be proven to be significant in the quantum random oracle model.

Theorems 1 and 2 give a tight reduction of EUF-CMA-NEW to EUF-CMA-ORIGINAL if we select parameters such that $((\lceil N/k \rceil - 1)/\tau)^{\vartheta} < 2^{-\kappa}$ and $q^{-\alpha} < 2^{-\kappa}$ and the resulting scheme will be provably as secure as the underlying MQ signature scheme. If we choose α to be smaller and compensate with a larger σ then the conditions on τ and ϑ are identical but Theorem 2 fails to produce a winning adversary. Instead we must rely on the hardness of AMQ for small r.

If the adversary wishes to produce a forgery then he must query H_2 on $d \| s_1 \| \cdots \| s_\sigma$ and obtain a *suitable* $t \in \mathbb{F}_q^{\alpha \times m}$, where suitable means $\forall j \, . \, t\mathcal{P}(s_j) = tH_1(d\|j)$ even though, potentially, $\exists j \, . \, \mathcal{P}(s_j) \neq H_1(d\|j)$. The probability of obtaining a suitable t is $q^{-\alpha r}$, where $r = \dim\langle\{\ldots, \mathcal{P}(s_j) - H_1(d\|j), \ldots\}\rangle$. So if the adversary can generate small-dimension AMQ solutions, then he can generate forgeries.

We have tried to find a formal reduction-based proof showing that the hardness of AMQ (for small r) is sufficient in addition to necessary. However, this task seems very non-trivial. Therefore, we leave the exact security of this parameter choice as an open problem.

6   Discussion

The public key contains only the Merkle root, and hence $|pk| = \kappa$. By contrast, a signature contains σ original-scheme signatures $s_1, \ldots, s_\sigma$; α quadratic polynomials $\mathcal{R}(x)$; and ϑ Merkle paths of depth $\log_2 \tau$ ending in an element of $\mathbb{F}_{q^k}^m$. Consequently, $|s| = (\sigma n + \alpha N + \vartheta m k) \lceil \log_2 q \rceil + \vartheta(\log_2 \tau - 2)\kappa$.

Two constraints should be satisfied in order to guarantee at least κ bits of security. First, the MAC should be unforgeable: $\left(\frac{\lceil N/k \rceil - 1}{\tau} \right)^{\vartheta} \leq 2^{-\kappa}$. A larger τ is slower but generates smaller signatures. Second, forging approximate signatures should be hard. The case $\sigma = 1$ requires that $\alpha \geq \lceil \frac{\kappa}{\log_2 q} \rceil$ and is provably secure. In contrast, smaller α does not lead to a concrete security estimate even if the AMQ Problem is hard. In this case we need at least $\alpha\sigma \geq \lceil \frac{\kappa}{\log_2 q} \rceil$ to be safe against a trivial brute force attack. Table 1 presents several viable parameter choices and compares the schemes before and after transformation.

In the case of UOV, our technique is perfectly compatible with the compression technique of Petzoldt *et al.* [22], where the first $v(v + 1)/2 + ov$ columns of the Macaulay matrix are generated from a pseudorandom generator and a short seed. The same number of coefficients can be dropped from $\mathcal{R}(\mathbf{x})$, and the smaller degree of $\hat{\mathcal{R}}(z)$ requires fewer opened Merkle paths. This combination shrinks signatures even more while only increasing the public key by κ bits.

Table 1. Comparison of public key and signature size of HFEv$^-$ and UOV (with compression) before and after applying our transformation. The recommended parameters were drawn from the Gui signature scheme [21] and Petzoldt's dissertation [20]. In all cases, $\tau = 2^{20}$.

Scheme	Parameters	Sec. lvl.	|pk|	|s|
Original HFEv$^-$	$q = 2, n = 98, m = 90$	80	56.8 kB	98 bits
Transformed	$\alpha = 1, \sigma = 80, k = 21, \vartheta = 7$	?	80 bits	4.4 kB
Original HFEv$^-$	$q = 2, n = 133, m = 123$	120	139.2 kB	123 bits
Transformed	$\alpha = 1, \sigma = 120, k = 21, \vartheta = 11$	?	120 bits	9.4 kB
UOVrand	$q = 256, n = 135, m = 45$	128	45.5 kB	1080 bits
Transformed	$\alpha = 16, \sigma = 1, k = 3, \vartheta = 12$	128	256 bits	21.3 kB
UOVrand	$q = 256, n = 210, m = 70$	192	169.9 kB	1 680 bits
Transformed	$\alpha = 24, \sigma = 1, k = 3, \vartheta = 19$	192	384 bits	70.4 kB
UOVrand	$q = 256, n = 285, m = 95$	256	423.0 kB	2 280 bits
Transformed	$\alpha = 32, \sigma = 1, k = 3, \vartheta = 28$	256	512 bits	166.3 kB

The shrinkage is the most striking for $\sigma > 1$, in which case α can be small. However, this requires the AMQ Problem to be hard and offers no provable security. There is another possibility: security takes no hit when α is kept reasonably small and we choose a larger q instead. Unfortunately, not all MQ signature schemes can be adapted as-is to a larger field.

We close with a note on the flexibility of our construction. As we presented the transform, the entire public key is replaced by a single Merkle root. However, some applications prefer to minimize the signature size while having a fixed and insufficient allowance for the public key. In this scenario, one can apply the Merkle tree MAC construction to only the second half of the public key's Macaulay matrix, and present the other half with the Merkle root as the new public key. Similarly, it is somewhat redundant to reduce the public key to a single Merkle root if both its children are released in nearly every signature. It is better to compute 2^δ separate trees of height $\log_2 \tau - \delta$ and shrink the signatures a little by tracing a shorter path for each MAC, at the expense of a factor-2^δ larger public key.

Acknowledgements. The authors would like to thank the reviewers for their helpful feedback. This work was supported in part by the Research Council KU Leuven: C16/15/058. In addition, this work was supported by the European Commission through the ICT programme under contract FP7-ICT-2013-10-SEP-210076296 PRACTICE, through the Horizon 2020 research and innovation programme under grant agreement No. H2020-ICT-2014-644371 WITDOM and H2020-ICT-2014-645622 PQCRYPTO. Alan Szepieniec is being supported by a doctoral grant from the Flemish Agency for Innovation and Entrepreneurship (VLAIO, formerly IWT).

References

1. Alkim, E., Ducas, L., Pöppelmann, T., Schwabe, P.: Post-quantum key exchange - a new hope. In: Holz, T., Savage, S. (eds.) 25th USENIX Security Symposium, USENIX Security 2016, Austin, TX, USA, 10–12 August 2016, pp. 327–343. USENIX Association (2016). https://www.usenix.org/conference/usenixsecurity16/technical-sessions/presentation/alkim
2. Bernstein, D.J., Buchmann, J., Ding, J., Goubin, L., Lange, T., Nguyen, P., Okamoto, T., Salvail, L., Silverberg, A., Silverman, J., Stam, M., Wolf, C. (eds.): Proceedings of International Workshop on Post-Quantum Cryptography, PQCrypto 2006, Leuven, Belgium, 23–26 May 2006 (2006). http://postquantum.cr.yp.to/
3. Bernstein, D.J., et al.: SPHINCS: practical stateless hash-based signatures. In: Oswald, E., Fischlin, M. (eds.) EUROCRYPT 2015. LNCS, vol. 9056, pp. 368–397. Springer, Heidelberg (2015). http://dx.doi.org/10.1007/978-3-662-46800-5_15
4. Bettale, L., Faugère, J., Perret, L.: Hybrid approach for solving multivariate systems over finite fields. J. Math. Cryptol. **3**(3), 177–197 (2009). http://dx.doi.org/10.1515/JMC.2009.009
5. Bettale, L., Faugère, J., Perret, L.: Solving polynomial systems over finite fields: improved analysis of the hybrid approach. In: van der Hoeven, J., van Hoeij, M. (eds.) International Symposium on Symbolic and Algebraic Computation, ISSAC 2012, Grenoble, France, 22–25 July 2012, pp. 67–74. ACM (2012). http://doi.acm.org/10.1145/2442829.2442843
6. Brassard, G., Hoyer, P., Mosca, M., Tapp, A.: Quantum amplitude amplification and estimation (2000). arXiv preprint quant-ph/0005055 https://arxiv.org/abs/quant-ph/0005055
7. Chen, M.-S., Hülsing, A., Rijneveld, J., Samardjiska, S., Schwabe, P.: From 5-pass $\mathcal{MQ}$-based identification to $\mathcal{MQ}$-based signatures. In: Cheon, J.H., Takagi, T. (eds.) ASIACRYPT 2016. LNCS, vol. 10032, pp. 135–165. Springer, Heidelberg (2016). http://dx.doi.org/10.1007/978-3-662-53890-6_5
8. Courtois, N.T., Finiasz, M., Sendrier, N.: How to achieve a McEliece-based digital signature scheme. In: Boyd, C. (ed.) ASIACRYPT 2001. LNCS, vol. 2248, pp. 157–174. Springer, Heidelberg (2001). http://dx.doi.org/10.1007/3-540-45682-1_10
9. Courtois, N., Klimov, A., Patarin, J., Shamir, A.: Efficient algorithms for solving overdefined systems of multivariate polynomial equations. In: Preneel, B. (ed.) EUROCRYPT 2000. LNCS, vol. 1807, pp. 392–407. Springer, Heidelberg (2000). http://dx.doi.org/10.1007/3-540-45539-6_27

10. Ducas, L., Durmus, A., Lepoint, T., Lyubashevsky, V.: Lattice signatures and bimodal gaussians. In: Canetti, R., Garay, J.A. (eds.) CRYPTO 2013. LNCS, vol. 8042, pp. 40–56. Springer, Heidelberg (2013). http://dx.doi.org/10.1007/978-3-642-40041-4_3

11. Faugère, J.C.: A new efficient algorithm for computing Gröbner bases (F 4). J. Pure Appl. Algebra **139**(1), 61–88 (1999)

12. Goldwasser, S., Micali, S., Rivest, R.L.: A digital signature scheme secure against adaptive chosen-message attacks. SIAM J. Comput. **17**(2), 281–308 (1988). http://dx.doi.org/10.1137/0217017

13. Grover, L.K.: A fast quantum mechanical algorithm for database search. In: Miller, G.L. (ed.) Proceedings of the Twenty-Eighth Annual ACM Symposium on the Theory of Computing, Philadelphia, Pennsylvania, USA, 22–24 May 1996, pp. 212–219. ACM (1996). http://doi.acm.org/10.1145/237814.237866

14. Kipnis, A., Patarin, J., Goubin, L.: Unbalanced Oil and Vinegar Signature Schemes. In: Stern, J. (ed.) EUROCRYPT 1999. LNCS, vol. 1592, pp. 206–222. Springer, Heidelberg (1999). http://dx.doi.org/10.1007/3-540-48910-X_15

15. Braithwaite, M.: Google: Experimenting with post-quantum cryptography (2016). https://security.googleblog.com/2016/07/experimenting-with-post-quantum.html

16. Maurer, U.M. (ed.): EUROCRYPT 1996. LNCS, vol. 1070. Springer, Heidelberg (1996). doi:10.1007/3-540-68339-9

17. http://csrc.nist.gov/groups/ST/toolkit/

18. National Institute for Standards and Technology (NIST): Post-quantum crypto standardization (2016). http://csrc.nist.gov/groups/ST/post-quantum-crypto/

19. Patarin, J.: Hidden fields equations (HFE) and isomorphisms of polynomials (IP): two new families of asymmetric algorithms. In: Maurer [16], pp. 33–48. http://dx.doi.org/10.1007/3-540-68339-9_4

20. Petzoldt, A.: Selecting and reducing key sizes for multivariate cryptography, July 2013. http://tuprints.ulb.tu-darmstadt.de/3523/

21. Petzoldt, A., Chen, M.-S., Yang, B.-Y., Tao, C., Ding, J.: Design principles for HFEv- based multivariate signature schemes. In: Iwata, T., Cheon, J.H. (eds.) ASIACRYPT 2015. LNCS, vol. 9452, pp. 311–334. Springer, Heidelberg (2015). http://dx.doi.org/10.1007/978-3-662-48797-6_14

22. Petzoldt, A., Thomae, E., Bulygin, S., Wolf, C.: Small public keys and fast verification for Multivariate Quadratic public key systems. In: Preneel, B., Takagi, T. (eds.) CHES 2011. LNCS, vol. 6917, pp. 475–490. Springer, Heidelberg (2011). http://dx.doi.org/10.1007/978-3-642-23951-9_31

23. Rogaway, P. (ed.): CRYPTO 2011. LNCS, vol. 6841. Springer, Heidelberg (2011). http://dx.doi.org/10.1007/978-3-642-22792-9

24. Sakumoto, K., Shirai, T., Hiwatari, H.: Public-key identification schemes based on multivariate quadratic polynomials. In: Rogaway [23], pp. 706–723. http://dx.doi.org/10.1007/978-3-642-22792-9_40

25. Shor, P.W.: Polynomial time algorithms for discrete logarithms and factoring on a quantum computer. In: Adleman, L.M., Huang, M.-D. (eds.) ANTS 1994. LNCS, vol. 877, pp. 289–289. Springer, Heidelberg (1994). http://dx.doi.org/10.1007/3-540-58691-1_68

26. Shoup, V.: Sequences of games: a tool for taming complexity in security proofs. IACR Cryptology ePrint Archive 2004/332 (2004). http://eprint.iacr.org/2004/332

27. Stern, J.: A new identification scheme based on syndrome decoding. In: Stinson, D.R. (ed.) CRYPTO 1993. LNCS, vol. 773, pp. 13–21. Springer, Heidelberg (1994). http://dx.doi.org/10.1007/3-540-48329-2_2

28. PQCRYPTO ICT-645622 (2015). http://pqcrypto.eu.org/

A   Proofs

A.1   Proof of Theorem 1

Theorem 1. If there is an adversary A against EUF-CMA-NEW in time T with Q random oracle queries and with success probability ϵ, then there is an adversary B^A that wins EUF-CMA-HYB in time $O(T)$ and success probability at least $\epsilon - (Q+1) \left(\frac{\lceil N/k \rceil - 1}{\tau} \right)^{\vartheta} - 2\tau(Q+1)/2^{\kappa}$.

Proof. Firstly, we describe how the adversary B^A plays the EUF-CMA-HYB game. We denote by C the challenger for the EUF-CMA-HYB game. The EUF-CMA-HYB game begins when our adversary B^A receives the public key pk $= \mathcal{P}(\mathbf{x})$ from the challenger C. Upon receiving this message, the hybrid adversary B^A runs steps 5–12 of NEW.KeyGen to produce a new public key pk$'$ and Merkle tree mt. The public key pk$'$ is sent to the EUF-CMA-NEW adversary A.

Whenever A requests a message $d_i \in \{0,1\}^*$ be signed, B^A requests C to sign the message d_i. Then, C responds with the signature $s_i = (\mathbf{s}_1, \ldots, \mathbf{s}_\sigma, \mathcal{R}(\mathbf{x}))$. At this point A^B runs steps 7–12 of NEW.Sign to compute O and open the associated Merkle paths necessary to complete the signature, which he then sends to A. After making some message-queries, A terminates his end of the protocol by producing a message-signature pair (d, s). The adversary B^A simply drops the Merkle paths from the signature s to get a signature s' for the hybrid signature scheme and sends the message-signature (d, s') on to the challenger C.

It is clear that B^A runs with overhead linear in the number of signing queries done by A, so the overhead is $O(T)$. We show that B^A wins the EUF-CMA-HYB game with probability at least $\epsilon - (Q+1) \left(\frac{\lceil N/k \rceil - 1}{\tau} \right)^{\vartheta} - 2\tau(Q+1)/2^{\kappa}$, where Q is the number of random oracle queries made by A.

Our adversary B^A wins the EUF-CMA-HYB game if the message-signature pair (d, s') it outputs is a valid signature for the hybrid signature scheme and if B^A has not queried C to sign d before. This is the case if the message-signature pair (d, s) output by A wins the EUF-CMA-NEW game and the polynomial map included in s is correct, meaning that if $s = (\mathbf{s}_1, \cdots, \mathbf{s}_\sigma, \mathcal{R}(x))$ and $\mathbf{t} = \mathsf{H}_2(d\|\mathbf{s}_1\| \cdots \|\mathbf{s}_\sigma)$, then $\mathcal{R}(x) = \mathbf{t}\mathcal{P}(x)$.

By assumption the first event occurs with probability ϵ. We finish the proof by showing that that the probability that the first event occurs, but the second event fails is bounded by $2\tau(Q+1)/2^{\kappa} + (Q+1) \left(\frac{\lceil N/k \rceil - 1}{\tau} \right)^{\vartheta}$.

Assume the message-signature pair (d, s) that is output by A wins the EUF-CMA-NEW game. First consider the case where for one of the $r \in O$ the leaf of the merkle paths corresponding to r in s is not equal to $\hat{\mathcal{P}}(r)$. Since s is a valid signature for the new signature scheme this means that A has forged a valid merkle path that ends in the merkle root. This requires finding a second preimage to one of the $2\tau - 1$ values in the Merkle tree. The probability that any algorithm does that is bounded by $2\tau(Q+1)/2^\kappa$, so in the rest of the proof we can assume that all the leaves included in the signature are valid.

Without loss of generality we can assume that A only outputs a message-signature pair (d, s) with $s = (\mathbf{s}_1, \cdots, \mathbf{s}_\sigma, \mathcal{R}(\mathbf{x}), \mathsf{open\ paths})$ after having queried the random oracle H_3 for its value at $d\|\mathbf{s}_1\|\cdots\|\mathbf{s}_\sigma\|\mathcal{R}(\mathbf{x})$. Indeed, if this is not the case A can be transformed into an adversary that does this at the cost of only one extra random oracle query. Let $d^{(i)}\|\mathbf{s}_1^{(i)}\|\cdots\|\mathbf{s}_1^{(i)}\|\mathcal{R}^{(i)}$ for i running from 1 to $Q + 1$ be all the values of this form that A has queried H_3 for. Then A can only output a message-signature pair which is a valid pair and such that $\mathcal{R}(\mathbf{x}) \neq \mathbf{t}\mathcal{P}(\mathbf{x})$ if this is true for one of the message pairs $(d^{(i)}, s^{(i)})$. But for any message-signature pair (d, s) the probability that for a randomly chosen elements $r \in Z$ we have that $\hat{\mathcal{R}}(r) = \mathbf{t}\hat{\mathcal{P}}(r)$ is either 1 in the case that $\mathcal{R}(\mathbf{x}) = \mathbf{t}\mathcal{P}(\mathbf{x})$, or bounded by $\left(\frac{\lceil N/k\rceil - 1}{\tau}\right)$ otherwise. This is so because if $\mathcal{R}(\mathbf{x}) \neq \mathbf{t}\mathcal{P}(\mathbf{x})$, then $\hat{\mathcal{R}}(z) \neq \mathbf{t}\hat{\mathcal{P}}(z)$, so the list of polynomials $\hat{\mathcal{R}}(z) - \mathbf{t}\hat{\mathcal{P}}(z)$ contains at least one nonzero polynomial of degree at most $\lceil N/k\rceil - 1$, so it has at most $\lceil N/k\rceil - 1$ zeros in Z. The probability that a zero is chosen randomly from Z is therefore at most $\left(\frac{\lceil N/k\rceil - 1}{\tau}\right)$.

Since ϑ elements of Z are chosen randomly and independently by the random oracle H_3 the probability that a message-signature pair (d, s) for which $\mathcal{R}(\mathbf{x}) \neq \mathbf{t}\mathcal{P}(\mathbf{x})$ is valid for the new signature scheme is at most $\left(\frac{\lceil N/k\rceil - 1}{\tau}\right)^\vartheta$. The union bound implies that the probability that for any $1 \leq i \leq Q + 1$ the message-signature pair $(d^{(i)}, s^{(i)})$ is valid and $\mathcal{R}^{(i)}(\mathbf{x}) \neq \mathbf{t}^{(i)}\mathcal{P}(\mathbf{x})$ is bounded by $(Q + 1)\left(\frac{\lceil N/k\rceil - 1}{\tau}\right)^\vartheta$. The probability that A outputs such a signature pair is also bounded by this probability. $\square$

A.2   Proof of Theorem 2

Theorem 2. If there is an adversary A against EUF-CMA-HYB in time T with Q random oracle queries and with success probability ϵ then there exists an adversary B^A against EUF-CMA-ORIGINAL in time $O(T)$ with success probability at least $\epsilon - (Q + 1)\left(\frac{1}{q}\right)^\alpha$.

Proof. Firstly, we describe how the adversary B^A plays the EUF-CMA-ORIGINAL game. We denote by C the challenger for the EUF-CMA-ORIGINAL game. The EUF-CMA-ORIGINAL game begins when the challenger C sends the public key $\mathsf{pk} = \mathcal{P}(\mathbf{x})$ to B^A. This is also the public key under the hybrid scheme, so B^A sends it to the adversary A to initiate the EUF-CMA-HYB game.

Whenever the adversary A requests a message $d_i \in \{0, 1\}^*$ be signed, B^A requests C to sign the messages $d_i\|1, \ldots, d_i\|\sigma$. Then, C responds with signatures $\mathbf{s}_i^{(1)}, \ldots, \mathbf{s}_i^{(\sigma)}$. Using this set of σ original scheme signatures, the B^A runs steps

5 and 6 of NEW.Sign to compute $\mathcal{R}(\mathbf{x})$. He then sends $s_i = (\mathbf{s}_i^{(1)}, \ldots, \mathbf{s}_i^{(\sigma)}, \mathcal{R}(\mathbf{x}))$ to A.

After making some message queries A terminates the protocol by producing a pair (d, s). Let $s = (\mathbf{s}_1, \cdots, \mathbf{s}_\sigma, \mathcal{R}(x))$, then B^A sends the message-signature pair $(d\|1, \mathbf{s}_1)$ to C. (Any one of the pairs $(d\|i, \mathbf{s}_i)$ would do the job).

It is clear that B^A runs with overhead linear in the number of signing queries done by A, so the overhead is $O(T)$. We show that B^A wins the EUF-CMA-ORIGINAL game with probability at least $\epsilon - (Q+1)q^{-\alpha}$, where Q is the number of random oracle queries made by A.

Our adversary B^A wins the EUF-CMA-HYB game if the message-signature pair (d, s') it outputs is a valid signature for the hybrid signature scheme and if B^A has not queried C to sign d before. This is the case if the message-signature pair (d, s) outputted by A wins the EUF-CMA-HYB game and $\mathcal{P}(\mathbf{s}_1) = \mathsf{H}_1(d\|1)$.

By assumption the first event occurs with probability ϵ. We finish the proof by showing that the probability that the first event occurs, but the second event fails is bounded by $(Q+1)q^{-\alpha}$.

Without loss of generality we can assume that A only outputs a message-signature pair (d, s) with $s = (\mathbf{s}_1, \cdots, \mathbf{s}_\sigma, \mathcal{R}(\mathbf{x}))$ after having queried the random oracle H_2 for its value at $d\|\mathbf{s}_1\|\cdots\|\mathbf{s}_\sigma$. Indeed, if this is not the case A can be transformed into an adversary that does this at the cost of only one extra random oracle query. Let $d^{(i)}\|\mathbf{s}_1^{(i)}\|\cdots\|\mathbf{s}_1^{(i)}$ for i running from 1 to $(Q+1)$ be all the values of this form that A has queried H_2 for. Then A can only output a message-signature pair which is valid and such that $\mathcal{P}(\mathbf{s}_1) \neq \mathsf{H}_1(d\|1)$ if this is true for one of the message pairs $(d^{(i)}, s^{(i)})$. But, for any message-signature pair (d, s) the probability that for a random $\mathbf{t} \in \mathbb{F}_q^{\alpha \times m}$ we have that $\mathbf{t}\mathcal{P}(\mathbf{s}_1) = \mathbf{t}\mathsf{H}_1(d\|1)$ is either 1 in the case that $\mathcal{P}(\mathbf{s}_1) = \mathsf{H}_1(d\|1)$, or $q^{-\alpha}$ otherwise. This is so because if $\mathcal{P}(\mathbf{s}_1) \neq \mathsf{H}_1(d\|1)$, then $\mathcal{P}(\mathbf{s}_1) - \mathsf{H}_1(d\|1)$ is a nonzero vector in $\mathbb{F}_q^m$. The probability that a nonzero vector is in the kernel of a randomly chosen matrix $\mathbf{t} \in \mathbb{F}_q^{\alpha \times m}$ is exactly $q^{-\alpha}$.

Since $\mathbf{t}$ is 'chosen randomly by the random oracle H_2 the probability that a message-signature pair (d, s) for which $\mathcal{P}(\mathbf{s}_1) \neq \mathsf{H}_1(d\|1)$ is valid for the new signature scheme is $q^{-\alpha}$. The union bound implies that the probability that for any $1 \leq i \leq Q+1$ the message-signature pair $(d^{(i)}, s^{(i)})$ is valid and $\mathcal{P}(\mathbf{s}_1) \neq \mathsf{H}_1(d\|1)$ is bounded by $(Q+1)q^{-\alpha}$. The probability that A outputs such a signature pair is also bounded by this probability.   □

An Updated Security Analysis of PFLASH

Ryann Cartor[1] and Daniel Smith-Tone[1,2(✉)]

[1] Department of Mathematics, University of Louisville, Louisville, KY, USA
ryann.cartor@louisville.edu, daniel.smith@nist.gov
[2] National Institute of Standards and Technology, Gaithersburg, MD, USA

Abstract. One application in post-quantum cryptography that appears especially difficult is security for low-power or no-power devices. One of the early champions in this arena was SFLASH, which was recommended by NESSIE for implementation in smart cards due to its extreme speed, low power requirements, and the ease of resistance to side-channel attacks. This heroship swiftly ended with the attack on SFLASH by Dubois et al. in 2007. Shortly thereafter, an old suggestion re-emerged: fixing the values of some of the input variables. The resulting scheme known as PFLASH is nearly as fast as the original SFLASH and retains many of its desirable properties but without the differential weakness, at least for some parameters.

PFLASH can naturally be considered a form of high degree HFE^- scheme, and as such, is subject to any attack exploiting the low rank of the central map in HFE^-. Recently, a new attack has been presented that affects HFE^- for many practical parameters. This development invites the investigation of the security of PFLASH against these techniques.

In this vein, we expand and update the security analysis of PFLASH by proving that the entropy of the key space is not greatly reduced by choosing parameters that are provably secure against differential adversaries. We further compute the complexity of the new HFE^- attack on instances of PFLASH and conclude that PFLASH is secure against this avenue of attack as well. Thus PFLASH remains a secure and attractive option for implementation in low power environments.

Keywords: Multivariate cryptography · HFE · PFLASH · Discrete differential · MinRank

1 Introduction

In December of 2016, the National Institute of Standards and Technology (NIST) published an open call for proposals for new post-quantum standards for some of the most critical security applications in digital communication infrastructure, see [1]. The post-quantum technologies this project aspires to vet and standardize are designed to be secure against adversaries with access to quantum computing devices—machines capable of acheiving exponential speed-up over classical computers on certain problems, see [2].

© Springer International Publishing AG 2017 (outside the US)
T. Lange and T. Takagi (Eds.): PQCrypto 2017, LNCS 10346, pp. 241–254, 2017.
DOI: 10.1007/978-3-319-59879-6_14

Many avenues to post-quantum security are developing, including techniques from lattice theory, coding theory and algebraic geometry. Each of these areas enjoy hard computational problems that have been studied extensively and have histories going back many decades. They also share the common trait that the fundamental computational problems in these fields have no known significant speed-up in the quantum paradigm.

One of the hard computational problems on which the security of many post-quantum cryptosystems is based is the problem of solving systems of multivariate equations. Generically, solving systems of multivariate quadratic equations is hard, so a valid technique for constructing a cryptosystem is to find a class of quadratic vector-valued functions on a vector space that is easy to invert, and transform it into a system that appears random.

Both of these tasks present challenges. The standard technique for the second task is computing a morphism of the system in an attempt to remove the properties allowing the system to be inverted. Techniques for the prior task are more varied, and in this work our focus is on a particular big field scheme.

1.1 Prior Work

The progenitor of all "big field" schemes is commonly known as C^*, or the Matsumoto-Imai scheme, see [3]. This scheme exploits the vector space structure of extension fields to provide two versions of a function—a vector-valued version which is quadratic over the base field, and a monomial function whose input and output lie in the extension field. The cryptanalysis of this scheme by Patarin in [4] inspired many big field constructions.

In [5], Patarin introduced the Hidden Field Equations (HFE) cryptosystem, a natural generalization of the monomial based C^* in which the monomial map is replaced with a low degree polynomial. Also described in the above work is the minus modifier—the removal of public equations—which can be applied to both HFE, producing HFE$^-$, and to C^*, creating C^{*-}.

A popular iteration of C^{*-} was SFLASH, see [6], which was very efficient, but unfortunately insecure. An attack by Dubois et al. in [7] broke SFLASH by way of a symmetric differential relation present in the central monomial map.

In [8], a way to resist the attack on SFLASH is presented. The augmentation of the scheme, known as projection, fixes the value of d of the input variables producing a scheme we now call PFLASH. PFLASH is still a very fast signature scheme and is amenable to low-power environments without sacrificing side-channel resistance. This projected C^{*-} system is shown to resist differential cryptanalysis for restricted parameters, that is, when the degree is bounded by $q^{n/2-d}$, in [9] and is fully specified with paractical parameters in [10].

Since the design of PFLASH there have been a number of cryptanalytic developments in the big field venue. The development of differential invariant attacks in [11] and their further application in [12] are examples of advancement in this active area. Furthermore, the improved efficiency of the Kipnis-Shamir (KS) attack of [13] presented in [14] is directly impactful to PFLASH, as one can consider PFLASH as a possibly high degree but still low rank version of HFE$^-$.

1.2 Our Contribution

We expand and update the analysis in [9,10] proving resistance to differential and rank techniques for the vast majority of parameters, and verifying that the provably secure key spaces are not as severely limited as the previous works suggest. This improvement is directly impactful, providing further assurance that attacks based on equivalent keys cannot weaken PFLASH.

The degree bound restriction in [9] reduces the dimension of possible private keys by a factor of more than two. Our updated differential analysis verifies the security of the scheme when the central map has no degree bound, and thus assures us that very little entropy is lost in the key space when restricting to parameters that are provably secure against differential adversaries.

In [10], an argument for the resistance of PFLASH to the technique of [14, Sect. 8.2] when PFLASH is considered as a low degree projected HFE⁻ scheme is provided. We make this assessment more robust by also considering the possibility of an adversary attempting to remove the projection modifier from PFLASH considering it to be a higher rank HFE⁻ scheme. Whereas in the former case, the attack is impossible, in the latter case, the algebraic structure allows the possibility that the attack can succeed; however, the complexity of the attack is directly computed and shown to be infeasible.

1.3 Organization

The paper is organized as follows. The next section introduces the notion of big field schemes and provides the description of those schemes relevant to this work, namely, C^*, $PFLASH$ and HFE. In the following section, we review the cryptanalytic techniques that have proven most successful in attacking big field schemes. The subsequent two sections provide a new proof of security against differential attacks for PFLASH, first by analyzing the projected C^* primitive and then by extending these results to the full scheme. We then conclude, noting parameter choices for PFLASH and discussing applications of the scheme.

2 Big Field Schemes

Many multivariate cryptosystems utilize the structure of a degree n extension $\mathbb{K}$ of a finite field $\mathbb{F}_q$ as an $\mathbb{F}_q$-algebra. Such cryptosystems are collectively known as "big field" schemes. To emphasize a choice of basis, one chooses an $\mathbb{F}_q$-vector space isomorphism $\phi : \mathbb{F}_q^n \to \mathbb{K}$. There is then an equivalence between systems F of n quadratic polynomials in n variables over $\mathbb{F}$ and univariate polynomials of the form

$$f(x) = \sum_{0 \le i \le j < n} \alpha_{ij} x^{q^i + q^j}$$

over $\mathbb{K}$ given by $F = \phi^{-1} \circ f \circ \phi$.

To hide the structure of an easily invertible map, the standard technique is to apply an isomorphism of polynomials to mask the choice of basis for the input and output of f.

Definition 1. *A polynomial morphism between two systems of polynomials is a pair of affine maps (T, U) such that $G = T \circ F \circ U$. If both T and U are invertible, then the morphism is said to be an isomorphism and F and G are said to be isomorphic.*

Thus, for big field schemes, the construction of a public key can be summarized with the following diagram.

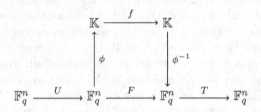

2.1 C^*

Matsumoto and Imai discovered massively multivariate cryptography, introducing the scheme now known as C^* at Eurocrypt '88. The $C^*(q, n)$ scheme is a big field construction in which the vector-valued representation of a quadratic monomial map $f(x) = x^{q^\theta + 1}$ is hidden by an isomorphism. Thus the public key is given by $P = T \circ \phi^{-1} \circ f \circ \phi \circ U$.

The C^* scheme was originally envisioned for encryption, but could quite apparently be applied in either encryption or digital signatures. To encrypt (or to verify a signature), one simply computes the output of the public function P. To decrypt (or to sign), the preimage must be determined successively for each of the components of the private key, all of which can be computed efficiently. The interesting step, the inversion of f can be accomplished by noticing that if $b(q^\theta + 1) = 1 \pmod{q^n - 1}$, then $(x^{q^\theta + 1})^b = x$.

2.2   PFLASH

The PFLASH scheme is a particular parametrization of a projected C^{*-} scheme. The projection and minus modifiers were both originally suggested in reference to C^* in [15]. The idea of projection is to fix the value of d input variables to change the simplicity of the central map. Thus the composition of the projection and the affine map U form a projection onto a codimension d hyperplane. The minus modification removes r equations from the public key. Thus the composition of this projection with T has corank r. The public key of PFLASH(q, n, r, d) is given by $P = \pi_r \circ T \circ \phi^{-1} \circ f \circ \phi \circ U \circ \pi_d$.

We note that the public key is no longer isomorphic to the private monomial function. Instead there is merely a polynomial morphism between the central map and the public key. Since it is well-known that the morphism of polynomials problem is NP-hard, see [16], there is some hope that the information lost to the public key may secure the scheme.

Mechanically, the scheme works as a digital signature primitive as follows. Verification is accomplished by evaluating the public polynomials at the signature. Signing is done by finding preimages of each of the private maps. To find a preimage of $\pi_r \circ T\phi^{-1}$, randomly append r values to the message, then apply T^{-1} and ϕ. Once f is inverted, an element in the preimage of $\phi \circ U$ and in the image of π_d is selected as the signature.

2.3   HFE

Hidden Field Equation (HFE) scheme of [5] is a generalization of the C^* construction, in which the monomial map is replaced by a more general polynomial with a degree bound D. Given the degree n extension $\mathbb{F} \subseteq \mathbb{K}$ we choose a quadratic polynomial $f : \mathbb{K} \to \mathbb{K}$ of degree bound D. Thus f has the form:

$$f(x) = \sum_{\substack{i \leq j \\ q^i + q^j \leq D}} \alpha_{i,j} x^{q^i + q^j} + \sum_{\substack{i \\ q^i \leq D}} \beta_i x^{q^i} + \gamma,$$

where $\alpha_{i,j}, \beta_i, \gamma \in \mathbb{K}$. The public key is then constructed via the isomorphism:

$$P = T \circ \phi^{-1} \circ f \circ \phi \circ U.$$

Inversion is accomplished by first taking a ciphertext $y = P(x)$, computing $v = T^{-1}(y)$, solving $v = f(u)$ for u via the Berlekamp algorithm, see [17], and then recovering $x = U^{-1}(u)$.

3   Cryptanalyses of Big Field Schemes

The big field multivariate cryptosystems have an extensive history in cryptanalysis. Several techniques have been developed that illustrate that it is very difficult to hide efficient inversion of a system. These techniques can largely be grouped into two categories: those based on differential propertys and those based on rank properties.

3.1   Differential Techniques

By breaking "big field" schemes and also inspiring modifiers, differential attacks have been instrumental in the development and analysis of multivariate public key cryptography. Given a field map f, the discrete differential is defined by $Df(a, x) = f(a + x) - f(a) - f(x) + f(0)$. As an operator on $\mathbb{K}$, D is $\mathbb{K}$-linear and reduces the complexity while increasing the dimension of a function. For example, the differential of an affine map is zero, the differential of a quadratic map is bilinear, the differential of a cubic map is bi-quadratic, etc.

Patarin's linearization equations attack of [4] can be viewed as a differential attack as follows. The differential of the C^* monomial $f(x) = x^{q^\theta + 1}$ is symmetric in characteristic two; hence, it is zero on the diagonal, $Df(x, x) = 0$. Therefore setting $v = f(u)$ we have

$$0 = Df(v, f(u)) = vu^{q^{2\theta}+q^{\theta}} + v^{q^{\theta}}u^{q^{\theta}+1}$$
$$= u^{q^{\theta}}(vu^{q^{2\theta}} + uv^{q^{\theta}}),$$

and whether or not $u = 0$, the right factor must be zero; thus, we obtain a bilinear relation between u and v. Setting $u = Ux$ and $v = T^{-1}y$, we obtain a bilinear relation between plaintext and ciphertext pairs: the linearization equations. Indeed even the higher order linearization equations (HOLEs) attacks pioneered in [18] can similarly be derived via differentials.

Another notable application of symmetric differential techniques in cryptanalysis is the attack on SFLASH of [7]. This attack exploits the fact that C^* polynomials are multiplicative. Specifically, $f(x) = x^{q^{\theta}+1}$ exhibits a differential symmetry.

Definition 2. *A function $f : \mathbb{K} \to \mathbb{K}$ has a differential symmetry if there exists a pair of $\mathbb{F}$-linear maps $L, \Lambda_L : \mathbb{K} \to \mathbb{K}$ such that*

$$Df(La, x) + Df(a, Lx) = \Lambda_L Df(a, x).$$

The attack uses the fact that left-multiplication maps of elements in $\mathbb{K}$ satisfy the above relation. This equality provides a criterion for the derivation of such maps, and via a linear algebra distillation technique, such a map can be efficiently recovered, and a full rank key derived.

It is important to note that once such a symmetry inducing linear map is discovered, there is no need to recover a full rank private key; an attack can be mounted directly with the recovered representation of the extension field multiplicative structure. Thus, even if a central map does not have a differential symmetry, it is possible that a minus-modified version of the scheme might; thus, an attack may be mounted directly on the choice of representation of the big field. This fact is the basis for the direct analysis of minus-modified schemes of [19, 20].

It was shown in [21] that a quadratic map can only have the symmetry of Definition 2 with L a representation of left-multiplication by a field element when f is multiplicative; that is, when f has only one quadratic monomial. Later it was shown in [9] that the only linear maps L satisfying the above relation for C^* are the multiplication maps.

This famous cryptanalysis incited a more careful analysis of a technique originally proposed at ASIACRYPT 1998 in [15] and further suggested after the attack in [8]. The idea is to use projection, that is, to fix some of the input values, to make U singular. PFLASH, whose parameters are defined in [10], is a particular parametrization of this structure. This change nullifies the basis of the differential symmetric attack as proven in [9] for a certain parameter set. In the resulting scheme, a pC^{*-} scheme, the central map can be made to no longer admit any symmetry. The parameter set which is provably secure against a differential adversary appears quite small, however, and considering the fact that such a scheme can be considered a special case of HFE$^-$ with perhaps a larger degree bound but an even smaller rank, it is necessary to review the rank structure of such schemes as well.

3.2   Rank Techniques

The first significant cryptanalysis of HFE was the Kipnis-Shamir (KS) attack of [13]. The attack is based on the fact that as a quadratic form over the extension field, the public key has low rank. This attack was significantly improved in [14], where minors modeling, instead of the original modeling of the rank property by Kipnis and Shamir, and Gröbner basis techniques are employed. The result is that the security of HFE is polynomial in the degree of the extension $\mathbb{K}$ over $\mathbb{F}_q$.

PFLASH can easily be characterized as an HFE$^-$ scheme with a more efficient inversion process. This characterization is possible by absorbing the projection into the central monomial map to make a more general polynomial. As an HFE$^-$ scheme, the rank of the central map is still 2, thus the central map has a very strong property. The minus modifier, however, provably increases the rank of the public key.

One may even consider PFLASH to be an HFE instance if we append zero polynomials to the public key. In this case, one should suspect that the rank of the central map would be quite high, rendering attacks such as [13,14] infeasible. Still, a theoretical verification of this intuition is absent in the literature.

4   Updated Differential Analysis of Projected Primitive

As discussed in [9], we may assume that the projection mapping is tied to f and consider differential symmetries of $f \circ \pi$ where π is chosen in a basis such that $deg(\pi) = q^d$. Clearly, if $f \circ \pi$ has a differential symmetry then the equation $Df(Ma, \pi x) + Df(\pi a, Mx) = \Lambda_M Df(\pi a, \pi x)$ is satisfied for some M. We can express this relation with matrix multiplication, namely

$$a^\top (\Pi^\top \mathbf{Df} M)x + a^\top (M^\top \mathbf{Df} \Pi)x = \Lambda_M [a^\top (\Pi^\top \mathbf{Df} \Pi)x],$$

where $\mathbf{Df}$ is the matrix representing Df as a bilinear form over $\mathbb{K}$, having one in the $(0, \theta)$ and $(\theta, 0)$ coordinates and zero elsewhere, where $\Pi x = \sum_{i=0}^d \beta_i x^{q^i}$ and where $Mx = \sum_{i=0}^{n-1} m_i x^{q^i}$.

Examining this equation, we see that $a^\top (\Pi^\top \mathbf{Df} M)x + a^\top (M^\top \mathbf{Df} \Pi)x$ will have nonzero entries restricted to certain coordinates depending only on d and θ, see Fig. 1. Similarly, the right hand side of the equation, $\Pi^\top \mathbf{Df} \Pi$, has a structure dependent upon d and θ, see Fig. 2. Notice, the graphs may look different depending on the choice of θ and d.

The strategy for finding conditions on π, M and Λ_M for the existence of such a symmetry is then to find coordinates in which one side of this matrix equation is zero while the other side involves only a single unknown coefficient of M or

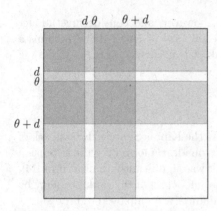

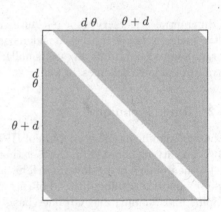

Fig. 1. The shape of the matrix representation over $\mathbb{K}$ of $Df(Ma, \pi x) + Df(\pi a, Mx)$. Shaded regions correspond to possibly nonzero values.

Fig. 2. The shape of the matrix representation of $\Lambda_M Df(\pi a, \pi x)$ over $\mathbb{K}$. Shaded regions correspond to possibly nonzero values.

Λ_M. While this system of equations is nonlinear in the coefficients of π, it is linear in both the unknown coefficients of M and those of Λ_M.

The system contains many more equations than variables, but certainly generates a positive dimensional ideal. The reason is that for any fixed π, $M = a\pi$ for any $a \in \mathbb{F}_q$ generates a solution. On the other hand, for a fixed π and a fixed θ, the above system becomes linear with the number of nonzero equations depending on both d and θ. Even in the best case, the number of equations is far larger than the number of variables. Since the coefficients of π are the only source of randomness for this system of linear equations, the great number of equations are not independent in a probabilistic sense. Therefore, probabilistic arguments are difficult, though extensive experiments show that the solution space is generally one dimensional.

Luckily, we can do better by bootstrapping the result of [9]. Specifically, we examine the case when $\theta > \frac{n}{2}$.

Lemma 1. $f(x^{q^\rho}) = f(x)^{q^\rho}$ when $f(x) = x^{q^\theta + 1}$

Proof. $f(x^{q^\rho}) = (x^{q^\rho})^{q^\theta + 1} = x^{(q^\theta + 1)q^\rho} = \left(x^{q^\theta + 1} \right)^{q^\rho} = f(x)^{q^\rho}$

Consider the special case of Lemma 1 when $\rho = -\theta$. After applying this map to the output of **Df**, the nonzero terms, originally in the $(\theta, 0)$ and $(0, \theta)$ coordinates, are transported to the $(0, -\theta)$ and $(-\theta, 0)$ coordinates, respectively. This observation leads to the following theorem, revealing that most parameters of PFLASH are provably secure against a differential adversary.

Theorem 1. *Let $f(x) = x^{q^\theta + 1}$ be a C^* map, and let M and $\pi x := \sum_{i=0}^{d} x^{q^i}$ be linear. Suppose that f satisfies the symmetric relation:*

$$Df(Ma, \pi x) + Df(\pi a, Mx) = \Lambda_M Df(\pi a, \pi x).$$

If $d < min\{\frac{n}{2} - \theta, |n - 3\theta|, \theta - 1\}$, or if $d < \{\theta - \frac{n}{2}, |2n - 3\theta|, n - \theta - 1\}$, then $M = M_\sigma \circ \pi$ for some $\sigma \in k$.

Proof. Assume $Df(Ma, \pi x) + Df(\pi a, Mx) = \Lambda_M Df(\pi a, \pi x)$ holds true. Then, we have two cases.

(1) $\theta < \frac{n}{2}$

By [9, Theorem 3], we are done.

(2) $\theta > \frac{n}{2}$

Let $\tilde{f}(x) = f(x)^{q^{-\theta}} = f\left(x^{q^{-\theta}}\right)$

We have,

$$Df(Ma, \pi x) + Df(\pi a, Mx) = \Lambda_M Df(\pi a, \pi x)$$

$$[Df(Ma, \pi x) + Df(\pi a, Mx)]^{q^{-\theta}} = [\Lambda_M Df(\pi a, \pi x)]^{q^{-\theta}}$$

$$[Df(Ma, \pi x) + Df(\pi a, Mx)]^{q^{-\theta}} = L_\theta^{-1} \Lambda_M Df(\pi a, \pi x)$$

Let L_θ represent the map that raises terms to the θth power. We can use the definition of the discrete differential to expand the left hand side of the equation. By linearity, we can distribute the exponent $q^{-\theta}$ to each term. After applying our lemma we get the following,

$$\tilde{f}(Ma + \pi x) + \tilde{f}(Ma) + \tilde{f}(\pi x) + \tilde{f}(\pi a + Mx) + \tilde{f}(\pi a) + \tilde{f}(Mx) = L_\theta^{-1} \Lambda_M Df(\pi a, \pi x)$$

By adding $0 = 2\tilde{f}(0)$ to the left and applying $I = L_\theta L_\theta^{-1}$ to the right we get,

$$D\tilde{f}(Ma, \pi x) + D\tilde{f}(\pi a, Mx) = L_\theta^{-1} \Lambda_M (L_\theta L_\theta^{-1}) Df(\pi a, \pi x)$$

And by the lemma we have,

$$D\tilde{f}(Ma, \pi x) + D\tilde{f}(\pi a, Mx) = L_\theta^{-1} \Lambda_M L_\theta D\tilde{f}(\pi a, \pi x)$$

We now have a relation on $\tilde{f}(x)$ where $-\theta + d < \frac{n}{2}$. Now we can apply [9, Theorem 3] to conclude that $M = M_\sigma \circ \pi$ for some $\sigma \in k$.

We note that the existence of a differential symmetry on $f \circ \pi$ implies a solution of the equation in Theorem 1 as well as the commutativity of M_σ and π. Since the commutativity of M_σ and π requires that π is L-linear, where $\mathbb{F}_q \subseteq L \subseteq k$ and $\sigma \in L$, for any nontrivial differential symmetry to exist, $(d, n) > 1$. Thus, there is a most desirable value of d from an efficiency and security standpoint: $d = 1$.

Let us specifically consider this most desired value $d = 1$. Then the only restriction on θ for provable differential security is

$$\theta \in \left(2, \frac{n-1}{3}\right) \cup \left(\frac{n+1}{3}, \frac{n}{2} - 1\right) \cup \left(\frac{n}{2} + 1, \frac{2n-1}{3}\right) \cup \left(\frac{2n+1}{3}, n - 2\right).$$

Furthermore, since $\theta = \frac{n}{2}$ always produces a many-to-one map in any characteristic, the restriction to provably secure parameters for PFLASH eliminates at most four possible values for θ for all extension degrees n.

5   Extension to PFLASH

We now generalize the analysis of the previous section in application to PFLASH. First we derive a heuristic argument for bootstrapping the provable security of the composition $f \circ \pi$ to statistical security for the projected primitive. We then clarify the resistance of PFLASH to analysis as an HFE$^-$ scheme. Finally, we derive security bounds for various PFLASH parameters.

5.1   Differential Analysis

As mentioned in Sect. 3, proof that differential symmetries do not exist for the central map of a scheme verifies that a differential adversary cannot recover a full rank key. Such a proof does not, however, verify that a differential adversary cannot find a symmetry revealing the extension field multiplicative structure and directly attack the scheme.

To illustrate this principal, imagine a high degree variant of HFE in which the central map has the form $f(x) = x^{q^\theta+1} + \pi_2(Q(x))$ over an extension of degree $2n$, where π_2 is a rank n projection onto the complement of the subfield of size q^n and Q is an arbitrary quadratic. Then any minus variant in which the image of π_2 is the kernel of T is a C^{*-} public key, but one with multiplicative symmetry. In particular, any map L representing muliplication by an element in the intermediate extension of degree n would satisfy

$$D(T \circ f \circ U)(U^{-1}La, x) + D(T \circ f \circ U)(a, U^{-1}Lx) = (L^{q^\theta} + L)D(T \circ f \circ U)(a, x).$$

Thus the minus scheme has a multiplicative symmetry even though the original scheme provably does not. In fact, even more strongly, we have computed functions of the form of f above over a degree 6 extension of $GF(2)$ for which no linear differential symmetry of any form exists, but under projection onto the degree 3 subfield, the *multiplicative* symmetry is exhibited.

In the case of PFLASH, we may attempt the strategy of the previous section for proving security. We may always model the removal of r equations as the application of a polynomial $\pi(x) = \sum_{i=0}^{r} a_i x^{q^i}$ to the central map. If only a few equations are removed, then the analysis proceeds just like in [19], because $f \circ \pi$ is a low rank albeit high degree polynomial. Since no parameters suggested for PSFLASH are near this range, however, this analysis does not apply. When we perform this analysis with $r \approx \frac{n}{3}$ and $f \circ \pi$, however, the methods of the previous section fail to generate a provably secure class of private keys.

Fortunately, there is an easy heuristic argument revealing a simple relationship between symmetries of the central map and symmetries of a map with the minus modifier that shows that symmetry should be statistically no more likely for any minus modified scheme than for the original. Let T' be the minus projection composed with the inclusion mapping with domain $\mathbb{F}_q^{n-r}$ and codomain $\mathbb{K}$. Suppose that $T' \circ f \circ \pi$ has a differential symmetry. Then

$$D(T' \circ f)(\pi a, Mx) + D(T' \circ f)(Ma, \pi x) = \Lambda_M D(T' \circ f)(\pi a, \pi x)$$
$$T'[Df(\pi a, Mx) + Df(Ma, \pi x)] = \Lambda_M T' Df(\pi a, \pi x).$$

Since the left is clearly in $T'\mathbb{K}$, the right must be as well. Thus, with high probability, that is, when $Span_{a,x}(Df(\pi a, \pi x)) = \mathbb{K}$, we have that $\Lambda_M T'\mathbb{K} = T'\mathbb{K}$. We know from linear algebra that in this case there exists at least one invertible transformation Λ'_M such that $\Lambda_M T' = T'\Lambda'_M$. Therefore, we obtain the relation

$$Df(\pi a, Mx) + Df(Ma, \pi x) = \Lambda'_M Df(\pi a, \pi x) \; (mod \; ker(T')). \tag{1}$$

Clearly, this argument is not reversible for any Λ'_M satisfying (1); therefore, we cannot in general conclude that the scheme with the minus modifier inherits any differential symmetry from the central map. On the other hand, satisfying (1) imposes $n - r$ constraints on Λ_M, while the "commuting" of Λ_M with T' imposes another r constraints. Thus, the existence of a symmetry in the minus case imposes the same number of constraints on Λ_M as for the central map and so we expect the probability of the existence of a differential symmetry to be no higher than for the central map.

5.2 Rank Analysis

One can consider PFLASH to be a high degree version of HFE$^-$ by absorbing the projection of the variables into the central map. Notice that the rank of the composition is still only two, thus PFLASH must achieve its security from the minus modifier.

Recently, in [22], a key recovery attack valid for all parameters of HFE$^-$ is presented. For an HFE$^-$ instance with parameters (q, n, D, r), the complexity is noted as $\mathcal{O}(\binom{n + \lceil log_q(D) \rceil + 1}{\lceil log_q(D) \rceil + r + 1}^\omega)$.

In application to PFLASH, there are two things to note about this attack. First, the attack produces an equivalent HFE$^-$ key, not a pC^{*-} key. This fact may not limit the attack, because it will still recover a central map of rank two of the form $f \circ \pi$ which we may then attack as a pC^* scheme in the manner of [23]. Second, the quantity $\lceil log_q(D) \rceil$ in the complexity estimate is derived from the rank structure that the degree bound of HFE implies, not directly from the degree bound itself. Thus, the rank of the C^* monomial, which is two, plays the role of $\lceil log_q(D) \rceil$ in the application of the techniques of [22] to PFLASH.

In fact, instances of PFLASH with quite inappropriate but still large parameters can be broken with this method. In particular we note that for a PFLASH$(256, 44, 3, 1)$ that the complexity of the attack is roughly estimated $44^{(3+2+1)\omega} \sim 2^{78}$. For large values of r, however, such as in all parameter sets in [10], this attack is infeasible. For example, the smallest parameters suggested in [10] still resist this attack to dozens of orders of magnitude beyond brute force. Thus, for sensible parameters with r sufficiently large, PFLASH is secure.

5.3 Security Estimates

Now with a refined security analysis, we can eliminate differential attacks for a larger set of parameters, thus doubling the entropy of the key space for PFLASH.

In addition, with the complexity estimate of $\mathcal{O}(n^{(r+3)\omega})$ and practical values of r, PFLASH is quite secure against the new attack on HFE$^-$ schemes. In conjunction with the invariant analysis of [10], we conclude that the security of PFLASH is determined by its resistance to algebraic and brute force attacks.

Viewing PFLASH as an HFE$^-$ scheme, we may use the bound in [24] to estimate the degree of regularity of PFLASH. This upper bound can be computed

$$\frac{(q-1)(R+r)}{2}+2,$$

where R is the rank of the central map; in the case of PFLASH, this quantity is two. Though this is an upper bound, empirical evidence suggests that it is tight for random systems of rank R. Thus the degree of regularity is far too high for practical schemes to be weakened. Furthermore, direct algebraic attacks for large schemes are impractical even with smaller complexity bounds because the space complexity of the best algorithms are too large to be practical.

Therefore, we corroborate the claims of [10] that brute force collision attacks are the greatest threat to PFLASH schemes. The evidence from our increase of the entropy of the key space and the verification that PFLASH resists recent weaknesses revealed in HFE$^-$ suggest the security levels in Table 1 (all of which are in agreement with [10]).

Table 1. Security levels for standard parameters of PFLASH

Scheme	Public key (bytes)	Security (bits)
PFLASH(16, 62, 22, 1)	39,040	80
PFLASH(16, 74, 22, 1)	72,124	104
PFLASH(16, 94, 30, 1)	142,848	128

6   Conclusion

The history of PFLASH intersects with most of the major advances in design and cryptanalysis in asymmetric multivariate cryptography. Interestingly, essentially all of the major cryptanalytic techniques that have proven successful in attacking multivariate schemes are relevant for PFLASH, and so any security metric for the scheme must inherently be complex. In spite of all of the tools available to an adversary, PFLASH remains secure.

Our analysis expands upon and complements previous analysis of PFLASH. We verify that the entropy of the key space is not significantly reduced by selecting parameters for which differential security is provable. We further verify security against new developments in rank analysis relevant to schemes employing the minus modifier. We conclude that any attack that fundamentally reduces the security of PFLASH below the brute force bound must include techniques as of yet undeveloped.

In venues for which speed, digest size, storage and power are severe limitations PFLASH seems to be one of the most performant options. When one considers devices in which no public key needs to be transported, such as some applications of smart cards, PFLASH is a leading candidate. In light of the security assurance this analysis provides, PFLASH appears ready for deployment.

References

1. Cryptographic Technology Group: Submission requirements and evaluation criteria for the post-quantum cryptography standardization process. NIST CSRC (2016). http://csrc.nist.gov/groups/ST/post-quantum-crypto/documents/call-for-proposals-final-dec-2016.pdf
2. Shor, P.W.: Polynomial-time algorithms for prime factorization and discrete logarithms on a quantum computer. SIAM J. Sci. Stat. Comp. **26**, 1484 (1997)
3. Matsumoto, T., Imai, H.: Public quadratic polynomial-tuples for efficient signature-verification and message-encryption. In: Barstow, D., et al. (eds.) EUROCRYPT 1988. LNCS, vol. 330, pp. 419–453. Springer, Heidelberg (1988). doi:10.1007/3-540-45961-8_39
4. Patarin, J.: Cryptanalysis of the matsumoto and imai public key scheme of Eurocrypt'88. In: Coppersmith, D. (ed.) CRYPTO 1995. LNCS, vol. 963, pp. 248–261. Springer, Heidelberg (1995). doi:10.1007/3-540-44750-4_20
5. Patarin, J.: Hidden fields equations (HFE) and isomorphisms of polynomials (IP): two new families of asymmetric algorithms. In: Maurer, U. (ed.) EUROCRYPT 1996. LNCS, vol. 1070, pp. 33–48. Springer, Heidelberg (1996). doi:10.1007/3-540-68339-9_4
6. Patarin, J., Courtois, N., Goubin, L.: FLASH, a fast multivariate signature algorithm. In: Naccache, D. (ed.) CT-RSA 2001. LNCS, vol. 2020, pp. 298–307. Springer, Heidelberg (2001). doi:10.1007/3-540-45353-9_22
7. Dubois, V., Fouque, P.-A., Shamir, A., Stern, J.: Practical cryptanalysis of SFLASH. In: Menezes, A. (ed.) CRYPTO 2007. LNCS, vol. 4622, pp. 1–12. Springer, Heidelberg (2007). doi:10.1007/978-3-540-74143-5_1
8. Ding, J., Dubois, V., Yang, B.-Y., Chen, O.C.-H., Cheng, C.-M.: Could SFLASH be repaired? In: Aceto, L., Damgård, I., Goldberg, L.A., Halldórsson, M.M., Ingólfsdóttir, A., Walukiewicz, I. (eds.) ICALP 2008. LNCS, vol. 5126, pp. 691–701. Springer, Heidelberg (2008). doi:10.1007/978-3-540-70583-3_56
9. Smith-Tone, D.: On the differential security of multivariate public key cryptosystems. In: Yang, B.-Y. (ed.) PQCrypto 2011. LNCS, vol. 7071, pp. 130–142. Springer, Heidelberg (2011). doi:10.1007/978-3-642-25405-5_9
10. Chen, M.S., Yang, B.Y., Smith-Tone, D.: PFLASH - secure asymmetric signatures on smart cards. In: Lightweight Cryptography Workshop (2015). http://csrc.nist.gov/groups/ST/lwc-workshop.2015/papers/session3-smith-tone-paper.pdf
11. Moody, D., Perlner, R.A., Smith-Tone, D.: An asymptotically optimal structural attack on the ABC multivariate encryption scheme. In: [25] pp. 180–196 (2014)
12. Moody, D., Perlner, R.A., Smith-Tone, D.: Key recovery attack on the cubic ABC simple matrix multivariate encryption scheme. In: Lange, T., Takagi, T. (eds.) PQCrypto 2017. LNCS, vol. 10346, pp. 241–254. Springer, Cham (2017)
13. Kipnis, A., Shamir, A.: Cryptanalysis of the HFE public key cryptosystem by relinearization. In: Wiener, M. (ed.) CRYPTO 1999. LNCS, vol. 1666, pp. 19–30. Springer, Heidelberg (1999). doi:10.1007/3-540-48405-1_2

14. Bettale, L., Faugère, J., Perret, L.: Cryptanalysis of HFE, multi-HFE and variants for odd and even characteristic. Des. Codes Crypt. **69**, 1–52 (2013)
15. Patarin, J., Goubin, L., Courtois, N.: C^*_{-+} and HM: variations around two schemes of T. Matsumoto and H. Imai. In: Ohta, K., Pei, D. (eds.) ASIACRYPT 1998. LNCS, vol. 1514, pp. 35–50. Springer, Heidelberg (1998). doi:10.1007/3-540-49649-1_4
16. Patarin, J., Goubin, L., Courtois, N.: Improved algorithms for isomorphisms of polynomials. In: Nyberg, K. (ed.) EUROCRYPT 1998. LNCS, vol. 1403, pp. 184–200. Springer, Heidelberg (1998). doi:10.1007/BFb0054126
17. Berlekamp, E.R.: Factoring polynomials over large finite fields. Math. Comput. **24**, 713–735 (1970)
18. Ding, J., Hu, L., Nie, X., Li, J., Wagner, J.: High order linearization equation (HOLE) attack on multivariate public key cryptosystems. In: Okamoto, T., Wang, X. (eds.) PKC 2007. LNCS, vol. 4450, pp. 233–248. Springer, Heidelberg (2007). doi:10.1007/978-3-540-71677-8_16
19. Daniels, T., Smith-Tone, D.: Differential properties of the HFE cryptosystem. In: [25], pp. 59–75 (2014)
20. Cartor, R., Gipson, R., Smith-Tone, D., Vates, J.: On the differential security of the HFEv- signature primitive. In: Takagi, T. (ed.) PQCrypto 2016. LNCS, vol. 9606, pp. 162–181. Springer, Cham (2016). doi:10.1007/978-3-319-29360-8_11
21. Smith-Tone, D.: Properties of the discrete differential with cryptographic applications. In: Sendrier, N. (ed.) PQCrypto 2010. LNCS, vol. 6061, pp. 1–12. Springer, Heidelberg (2010). doi:10.1007/978-3-642-12929-2_1
22. Vates, J., Smith-Tone, D.: Key recovery attack for all parameters of HFE-. In: Lange, T., Takagi, T. (eds.) PQCrypto 2017. LNCS, vol. 10346, pp. 272–288. Springer, Cham (2017)
23. Billet, O., Macario-Rat, G.: Cryptanalysis of the square cryptosystems. In: Matsui, M. (ed.) ASIACRYPT 2009. LNCS, vol. 5912, pp. 451–468. Springer, Heidelberg (2009). doi:10.1007/978-3-642-10366-7_27
24. Ding, J., Kleinjung, T.: Degree of regularity for HFE-. IACR Cryptology ePrint Archive 2011, p. 570 (2011)
25. Mosca, M. (ed.): PQCrypto 2014. LNCS, vol. 8772. Springer, Cham (2014)

Improved Attacks for Characteristic-2 Parameters of the Cubic ABC Simple Matrix Encryption Scheme

Dustin Moody[1(✉)], Ray Perlner[1], and Daniel Smith-Tone[1,2]

[1] National Institute of Standards and Technology, Gaithersburg, MD, USA
{dustin.moody,ray.perlner,daniel.smith}@nist.gov
[2] Department of Mathematics, University of Louisville, Louisville, KY, USA

Abstract. In the last few years multivariate public key cryptography has experienced an infusion of new ideas for encryption. Among these new strategies is the ABC Simple Matrix family of encryption schemes which utilize the structure of a large matrix algebra to construct effectively invertible systems of nonlinear equations hidden by an isomorphism of polynomials. One promising approach to cryptanalyzing these schemes has been structural cryptanalysis, based on applying a strategy similar to MinRank attacks to the discrete differential. These attacks however have been significantly more expensive when applied to parameters using fields of characteristic 2, which have been the most common choice for published parameters. This disparity is especially great for the cubic version of the Simple Matrix Encryption Scheme.

In this work, we demonstrate a technique that can be used to implement a structural attack which is as efficient against parameters of characteristic 2 as are attacks against analogous parameters over higher characteristic fields. This attack demonstrates that, not only is the cubic simple matrix scheme susceptible to structural attacks, but that the published parameters claiming 80 bits of security are less secure than claimed (albeit only slightly.) Similar techniques can also be applied to improve structural attacks against the original Simple Matrix Encryption scheme, but they represent only a modest improvement over previous structural attacks. This work therefore demonstrates that choosing a field of characteristic 2 for the Simple Matrix Encryption Scheme or its cubic variant will not provide any additional security value.

Keywords: Multivariate public key cryptography · Differential invariant · MinRank · Encryption

1 Introduction

The National Institute of Standards and Technology (NIST) is currently engaged in an effort to update the public key infrastructure, providing alternatives to the

© Springer International Publishing AG 2017 (outside the US)
T. Lange and T. Takagi (Eds.): PQCrypto 2017, LNCS 10346, pp. 255–271, 2017.
DOI: 10.1007/978-3-319-59879-6_15

classical public key schemes based on arithmetic constructions. The discovery by Peter Shor in the 1990s of efficient algorithms for factoring and computing discrete logarithms, see [1], accelerated research towards building the necessary class of computers, those that Feynman famously suggested in [2]: quantum computers. There has been growing interest among scientists in our discipline in the years since, to provide protocols and algorithms that are post-quantum, that is, secure in the quantum model of computing. The recent publication by (NIST), see [3], of a call for proposals for post-quantum standards directly addresses the challenge of migration towards a more diverse collection of tools for our public key infrastructure.

Public key schemes based on the difficulty of inverting nonlinear systems of equations provide one possibility for post-quantum security. Multivariate Public Key Cryptography (MPKC) is a reasonable option because the problem of solving systems of nonlinear equations, even if only quadratic, is known to be NP-complete; thus, the generic problem is likely beyond the reach of quantum adversaries. Furthermore, there are a variety of standard techniques to metamorphosize multivariate schemes, to introduce new properties, to enhance security, to reduce power consumption, to resist side-channel analysis, etc.

There are numerous long-lived multivariate digital signature schemes. All of UOV [4], HFE- [5], and HFEv- [6] have been studied for around two decades. Moreover, some of the above schemes have optimizations which have strong theoretical support or have stood unbroken in the literature for some time. Notable among these are UOV, which has a cyclic variant [7] that dramatically reduces the key size, and Gui [8], an HFEv- scheme, that, due to tighter bounds on the complexity of algebraically solving the underlying system of equations, see [9], has much more aggressive parameters than QUARTZ, see [6].

Multivariate public key encryption, however, has a much rockier history. Several attempts at multivariate encryption, see [10,11] for example, have been shown to be weak based on rank or differential weaknesses. Recently, a new framework for developing secure multivariate encryption schemes has surfaces, drawing on the idea that it may impose sufficiently few restrictions on a multivariate map to be merely an injective map into a much larger codomain instead of being essentially a permutation. A few interesting attempts to achieve multivariate encryption have originated from this thought. ZHFE, see [12], the quadratic and cubic variants of the ABC Simple Matrix Scheme, see [13,14], and Extension Field Cancellation, see [15], all use fundamentally new structures for the derivation of an encryption system.

A few of the above schemes have already suffered some setbacks. A questionable rank property in the public key of ZHFE presented in [16] makes this scheme appear dubious, while it was shown that the quadratic Simple Matrix structure leaves the signature of a differential invariant in the public key which is exploited in [17] to effect an attack.

The case of the Cubic Simple Matrix encryption scheme is more interesting; the authors in [14] present a heuristic argument for security and suggest the possibility of provable security for the scheme. These provable security claims were undermined in [18], however, with the presentation of a key recovery attack on a full scale version of the Cubic Simple Matrix encryption scheme. The complexity of the attack was on the order of q^{s+2} for characteristic $p > 3$, q^{s+3} for characteristic 3, and q^{2s+6} for characteristic 2. Here s is the dimension of the matrices in the scheme, and q is the cardinality of the finite field used. This technique was an extension and augmentation of the technique of [17], and similarly exploited a differential invariant property of the core map to perform a key recovery attack. Nonetheless, the much higher complexity of this attack for characteristic 2 left open the possibility that there may be some security advantage to using a cubic ABC map over a field with characteristic 2.

In this paper, we present an attack whose complexity is on the order of q^{s+2} for all characteristics. Similar techniques can also improve the complexity of attacks against characteristic 2 parameters for the original quadratic version of the ABC cryptosystem, from q^{s+4} (reported in [17]) to q^{s+2}.

Specifically, our technique improves the complexity of attacking CubicABC ($q = 2^8$, $s = 7$), designed for 80-bit security, from the horrendous value of 2^{177} in [18] to approximately 2^{88} operations, the same as the direct algebraic attack complexity reported in [14]. More convincing is our attack on CubicABC($q = 2^8$, $s = 8$), designed for 100-bit security. We break the scheme in approximately 2^{98} operations. Furthermore, the attack is fully parallelizable and requires very little memory; hence, our technique is asymptotically far more efficient than algebraic attacks, the basis for the original security estimation. Thus, the security claims in [14] not only fail to hold in the odd characteristic case, they fail to hold in characteristic two as well.

The paper is organized as follows. In the next section, we present the structure of the Cubic ABC Simple Matrix encryption scheme. In the following section, the fingerprint of the matrix algebra used in the construction of the ABC scheme is exposed. In the subsequent section, the effect of this structure on minrank calculations is determined. We then calculate the complexity of the full attack including the linear algebra steps required for full key recovery. Finally, we review these results and discuss the security of the Cubic ABC scheme and its quadratic counterpart moving forward.

2   The Cubic ABC Matrix Encryption Scheme

In [14], the Cubic ABC Matrix encryption scheme is proposed. The motivation behind the scheme is to use a large matrix algebra over a finite field to construct an easily invertible cubic map. The construction uses matrix multiplication to combine random linear and quadratic formulae into cubic formulae in a way that allows a user with knowledge of the structure of the matrix algebra and the polynomial isomorphism used to compose the scheme to invert the map.

Let $k = \mathbb{F}_q$ be a finite field. Linear forms and variables over k will be denoted with lower case letters. Vectors of any dimension over k will be denoted with bold font, $\mathbf{v}$. Fix $s \in \mathbb{N}$ and set $n = s^2$ and $m = 2s^2$. An element of a matrix ring $M_d(k)$ or the linear transformations they represent, will be denoted by upper case letters, such as M. When the entries of the matrix are being considered functions of a variable, the matrix will be denoted $M(\mathbf{x})$. Let $\phi : M_{s \times 2s}(k) \rightarrow k^{2s^2}$ represent the vector space isomorphism sending a matrix to the column vector consisting of the concatenation of its rows. The output of this map, being a vector, will be written with bold font; however, to indicate the relationship to its matrix preimage, it will be denoted with an upper case letter, such as $\mathbf{M}$.

The scheme utilizes an isomorphism of polynomials to hide the internal structure. Let $\mathbf{x} = [x_1, x_2, \ldots, x_n]^T \in k^n$ denote plaintext while $\mathbf{y} = [y_1, \ldots, y_m] \in k^m$ denotes ciphertext. Fix two invertible linear transformations $T \in M_m(k)$ and $U \in M_n(k)$. (One may use affine transformations, but there is no security or performance benefit in doing so.) Denote the input and output of the central map by $\mathbf{u} = U\mathbf{x}$ and $\mathbf{v} = T^{-1}(\mathbf{y})$.

The construction of the central map is as follows. Define three $s \times s$ matrices A, B, and C in the following way:

$$A = \begin{bmatrix} p_1 & p_2 & \cdots & p_s \\ p_{s+1} & p_{s+2} & \cdots & p_{2s} \\ \vdots & \vdots & \ddots & \vdots \\ p_{s^2-s+1} & p_{s^2-s+2} & \cdots & p_{s^2} \end{bmatrix}, B = \begin{bmatrix} b_1 & b_2 & \cdots & b_s \\ b_{s+1} & b_{s+2} & \cdots & b_{2s} \\ \vdots & \vdots & \ddots & \vdots \\ b_{s^2-s+1} & b_{s^2-s+2} & \cdots & b_{s^2} \end{bmatrix},$$

and

$$C = \begin{bmatrix} c_1 & c_2 & \cdots & c_s \\ c_{s+1} & c_{s+2} & \cdots & c_{2s} \\ \vdots & \vdots & \ddots & \vdots \\ c_{s^2-s+1} & c_{s^2-s+2} & \cdots & c_{s^2} \end{bmatrix}.$$

Here the p_i are quadratic forms on $\mathbf{u}$ chosen independently and uniformly at random from among all quadratic forms and the b_i and c_i are linear forms on $\mathbf{u}$ chosen independently and uniformly at random from among all linear forms.

We define two $s \times s$ matrices $E_1 = AB$ and $E_2 = AC$. Since A is quadratic and B and C are linear in u_i, E_1 and E_2 are cubic in the u_i. The central map $\mathcal{E}$ is defined by

$$\mathcal{E} = \phi \circ (E_1 \| E_2).$$

Thus $\mathcal{E}$ is an m dimensional vector of cubic forms in $\mathbf{u}$. Finally, the public key is given by $\mathcal{F} = T \circ \mathcal{E} \circ U$.

Encryption with this system is standard: given a plaintext $(x_1, \ldots, x_n)$, compute $(y_1, \ldots, y_m) = \mathcal{F}(x_1, \ldots, x_n)$. Decryption is somewhat more complicated.

To decrypt, one inverts each of the private maps in turn: apply T^{-1}, invert $\mathcal{E}$, and apply U^{-1}. To "invert" $\mathcal{E}$, one assumes that $A(\mathbf{u})$ is invertible, and forms a matrix

$$A^{-1}(\mathbf{u}) = \begin{bmatrix} w_1 & w_2 & \cdots & w_s \\ w_{s+1} & w_{s+2} & \cdots & w_{2s} \\ \vdots & \vdots & \ddots & \vdots \\ w_{s^2-s+1} & w_{s^2-s+2} & \cdots & w_{s^2} \end{bmatrix},$$

where the w_i are indeterminants. Then collectinging the relations $A^{-1}(\mathbf{u})$ $E_1(\mathbf{u}) = B(\mathbf{u})$ and $A^{-1}(\mathbf{u})E_2(\mathbf{u}) = C(\mathbf{u})$, we have $m = 2s^2$ linear equations in $2n = 2s^2$ unknowns w_i and u_i. Using, for example, Gaussian elimination one can eliminate all of the variables w_i and most of the u_i. The resulting relations can be substituted back into $E_1(\mathbf{u})$ and $E_2(\mathbf{u})$ to obtain a large system of equations in very few variables which can be solved efficiently in a variety of ways.

3   The Structure of the Cubic ABC Scheme

3.1   Column Band Spaces

Each component of the central $\mathcal{E}(\mathbf{u}) = E_1(\mathbf{u})\|E_2(\mathbf{u})$ map may be written as:

$$\mathcal{E}_{(i-1)s+j} = \sum_{l=1}^{s} p_{(i-1)s+l} b_{(l-1)s+j},$$

for the E_1 equations, and likewise, for the E_2 equations:

$$\mathcal{E}_{s^2+(i-1)s+j} = \sum_{l=1}^{s} p_{(i-1)s+l} c_{(l-1)s+j}$$

where i and j run from 1 to s.

Consider the s sets of s polynomials that form the columns of E_1, i.e. for each $j \in \{1, \ldots, s\}$ consider $(\mathcal{E}_j, \mathcal{E}_{s+j}, \ldots, \mathcal{E}_{s^2-s+j})$. With high probability, the linear forms $b_j, b_{s+j}, \ldots, b_{s^2-s+j}$ are linearly independent, and if so the polynomials may be re-expressed, using a linear change of variables to $(u'_1, \ldots u'_{s^2})$ where $u'_i = b_{(i-1)s+j}$ for $i = 1, \ldots, s$. After the change of variables, the only cubic monomials contained in $(\mathcal{E}_j, \mathcal{E}_{s+j}, \ldots, \mathcal{E}_{s^2-s+j})$ will be those containing at least one factor of $u'_1, \ldots, u'_s$. We can make a similar change of variables to reveal structure in the s sets of s polynomials that form the columns of E_2: Setting $u'_i = c_{(i-1)s+j}$ for $i = 1, \ldots, s$ and a fixed j, the only cubic monomials contained in $(\mathcal{E}_{s^2+j}, \mathcal{E}_{s^2+s+j}, \ldots, \mathcal{E}_{2s^2-s+j})$ will be those containing at least one factor of $u'_1, \ldots, u'_s$.

More generally, we can make a similar change of variables to reveal structure in any of a large family of s dimensional subspaces of the span of the component polynomials of E_1 and E_2, which we will call column band spaces in analogy to the band spaces used to analyze the quadratic ABC cryptosystem in [17]. Each family is defined by a fixed linear combination, (β, γ), of the columns of E_1 and E_2:

Definition 1. *The column band space defined by the $2s$-dimensional linear form (β, γ) is the space of cubic maps, $\mathcal{B}_{\beta,\gamma}$, given by:*

$$\mathcal{B}_{\beta,\gamma} = Span(\mathcal{E}_{\beta,\gamma,1}, \ldots, \mathcal{E}_{\beta,\gamma,s}),$$

where

$$\mathcal{E}_{\beta,\gamma,i} = \sum_{j=1}^{s} (\beta_j \mathcal{E}_{(i-1)s+j} + \gamma_j \mathcal{E}_{s^2+(i-1)s+j})$$

$$= \sum_{l=1}^{s} \left(p_{(i-1)s+l} \sum_{j=1}^{s} \left(\beta_j b_{(l-1)s+j} + \gamma_j c_{(l-1)s+j} \right) \right).$$

Note that under a change of variables

$$(x_1, \ldots, x_{s^2}) \xmapsto{M} (u'_1, \ldots u'_{s^2}), \text{ where } u'_i = \sum_{j=1}^{s} \left(\beta_j b_{(i-1)s+j} + \gamma_j c_{(i-1)s+j} \right) \text{ for } i = 1, \ldots, s,$$

the only cubic monomials contained in the elements of $\mathcal{B}_{\beta,\gamma}$ will be those containing at least one factor of $u'_1, \ldots, u'_s$.

In such a basis, the third formal derivative, or the 3-tensor of third partial derivatives

$$D^3 \mathcal{E} = \sum_{i,j,k} \frac{\partial^3 \mathcal{E}}{\partial u'_i \partial u'_j \partial u'_k} du'_i \otimes du'_j \otimes du'_k,$$

of any map $\mathcal{E} \in \mathcal{B}_{\beta,\gamma}$ has a special block form, see Fig. 1. This tensor is the same as the one used for the attack in [18], although in that case it was computed using the discrete differential. There are, however, a number of disadvantages to using this 3-tensor to represent the structural features of cubic ABC. In particular, when defined over a field of characteristic 2, the symmetry of the 3-tensor results in the loss of any information about coefficients for monomials of the form $x_i^2 x_j$, since the 3rd derivatave of such a monomial is always 0. We will therefore use a different tool to express the structure of cubic ABC.

Using the same u' basis as above, we see that the gradient $\nabla_{u'} \mathcal{E}$ produces a covector of quadratic forms, which can be though of as a quadratic map that takes any vector w of the form

$$(0, \ldots, 0, u'_{s+1}(\mathbf{w}), \ldots, u'_{s^2}(\mathbf{w}))^{\top},$$

to a covector of the form

$$(y(u'_1), \ldots, y(u'_s), 0, \ldots, 0).$$

Note that, by the chain rule, we can relate $\nabla_{u'} \mathcal{E} = \left[\frac{\partial \mathcal{E}}{\partial u'_1}, \ldots, \frac{\partial \mathcal{E}}{\partial u'_{s^2}} \right]$ to the formal derivative defined over the public basis:

$$\nabla \mathcal{E} = \left[\frac{\partial \mathcal{E}}{\partial x_1}, \ldots, \frac{\partial \mathcal{E}}{\partial x_{s^2}} \right] = \nabla_{u'} \mathcal{E} \left[\frac{du'_j}{dx_i} \right]_{i,j}$$

using the nonsingular change of basis matrix whose entries are $\frac{du'_j}{dx_i}$. We can therefore conclude that even defined over the public basis, the first formal derivative of any map $\mathcal{E} \in \mathcal{B}_{\beta,\gamma}$ is a quadratic map that takes an $s^2 - s$ dimensional space of vectors to an s dimensional space of covectors.

We will define the term "band kernel" to describe this $s^2 - s$ dimensional space of vectors (including $\mathbf{w}$) which are mapped to an s dimensonal image space by the first formal derivative of $\mathcal{E}$.

Definition 2. *The band kernel of* $\mathcal{B}_{\beta,\gamma}$, *denoted* $\mathcal{BK}_{\beta,\gamma}$, *is the space of vectors* x, *such that*

$$u_i' = \sum_{j=1}^{s} \left(\beta_j b_{(i-1)s+j}(x) + \gamma_j c_{(i-1)s+j}(x) \right) = 0,$$

for $i = 1, \ldots, s$.

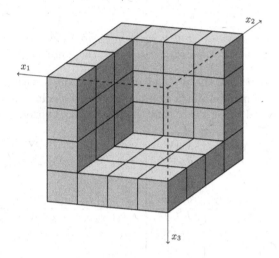

Fig. 1. 3-tensor structure of the third formal derivative of a band space map. Solid regions correspond to nonzero coefficients. Transparent regions correspond to zero coefficients.

4   A Variant of MinRank Exploiting the Column Band Space Structure

A minrank-like attack may be used to locate the column band space maps defined in the previous section. In this case, the attack proceeds by selecting s^2-dimensional vectors $\mathbf{w}_1$ and $\mathbf{w}_2$, setting

$$\sum_{i=1}^{2s^2} t_i \nabla \mathcal{E}_i(\mathbf{w}_1) = 0,$$

$$\sum_{i=1}^{2s^2} t_i \nabla \mathcal{E}_i(\mathbf{w}_2) = 0, \qquad (1)$$

and then solving for the t_i. The attack succeeds when $\sum_{i=1}^{2s^2} t_i \mathcal{E}_i \in \mathcal{B}_{\beta,\gamma}$, and $\mathbf{x}_1$ and $\mathbf{x}_2$ are within the corresponding band kernel. If these conditions are met, then the 2-tensors

$$\sum_{i=1}^{2s^2} t_i \mathbf{H}(\mathcal{E}_i)(\mathbf{w}_1) \text{ and } \sum_{i=1}^{2s^2} t_i \mathbf{H}(\mathcal{E}_i)(\mathbf{w}_2),$$

will have rank at most $2s$ (see Fig. 2), and this will be easily detectable. Here $\mathbf{H}(\mathcal{E}_i)$ is the Hessian matrix

$$\mathbf{H}(\mathcal{E}_i) := \begin{bmatrix} \frac{\partial^2 \mathcal{E}_i}{\partial x_1^2} & \frac{\partial^2 \mathcal{E}_i}{\partial x_1 \partial x_2} & \cdots & \frac{\partial^2 \mathcal{E}_i}{\partial x_1 \partial x_n} \\ \frac{\partial^2 \mathcal{E}_i}{\partial x_1 \partial x_2} & \frac{\partial^2 \mathcal{E}_i}{\partial x_2^2} & \cdots & \frac{\partial^2 \mathcal{E}_i}{\partial x_1 \partial x_n} \\ \vdots & \vdots & \ddots & \vdots \\ \frac{\partial^2 \mathcal{E}_i}{\partial x_n \partial x_1} & \frac{\partial^2 \mathcal{E}_i}{\partial x_n \partial x_2} & \cdots & \frac{\partial^2 \mathcal{E}_i}{\partial x_n^2} \end{bmatrix}.$$

Theorem 1. *The probability that 2 randomly chosen vectors, $\mathbf{w}_1$ and $\mathbf{w}_2$, are both in the band kernel of some band space $\mathcal{B}_{\beta,\gamma}$ is approximately $\frac{1}{q-1}$.*

Proof. The condition that the $\mathbf{w}_1$ and $\mathbf{w}_2$ are contained within a band kernel is that there be a nontrivial linear combination of the columns of the following matrix which is equal to zero (i.e. that the matrix has nonzero column corank):

$$\begin{bmatrix} b_1(\mathbf{w}_1) & b_2(\mathbf{w}_1) & \cdots & b_s(\mathbf{w}_1) & c_1(\mathbf{w}_1) & c_2(\mathbf{w}_1) & \cdots & c_s(\mathbf{w}_1) \\ b_{s+1}(\mathbf{w}_1) & b_{s+2}(\mathbf{w}_1) & \cdots & b_{2s}(\mathbf{w}_1) & c_{s+1}(\mathbf{w}_1) & c_{s+2}(\mathbf{w}_1) & \cdots & c_{2s}(\mathbf{w}_1) \\ \vdots & \vdots & \ddots & \vdots & \vdots & \vdots & \ddots & \vdots \\ b_{s^2-s+1}(\mathbf{w}_1) & b_{s^2-s+2}(\mathbf{w}_1) & \cdots & b_{s^2}(\mathbf{w}_1) & c_{s^2-s+1}(\mathbf{w}_1) & c_{s^2-s+2}(\mathbf{w}_1) & \cdots & c_{s^2}(\mathbf{w}_1) \\ b_1(\mathbf{w}_2) & b_2(\mathbf{w}_2) & \cdots & b_s(\mathbf{w}_2) & c_1(\mathbf{w}_2) & c_2(\mathbf{w}_2) & \cdots & c_s(\mathbf{w}_2) \\ b_{s+1}(\mathbf{w}_2) & b_{s+2}(\mathbf{w}_2) & \cdots & b_{2s}(\mathbf{w}_2) & c_{s+1}(\mathbf{w}_2) & c_{s+2}(\mathbf{w}_2) & \cdots & c_{2s}(\mathbf{w}_2) \\ \vdots & \vdots & \ddots & \vdots & \vdots & \vdots & \ddots & \vdots \\ b_{s^2-s+1}(\mathbf{w}_2) & b_{s^2-s+2}(\mathbf{w}_2) & \cdots & b_{s^2}(\mathbf{w}_2) & c_{s^2-s+1}(\mathbf{w}_2) & c_{s^2-s+2}(\mathbf{w}_2) & \cdots & c_{s^2}(\mathbf{w}_2) \end{bmatrix}.$$

The matrix is a uniformly random $2s \times 2s$ matrix, which has nonzero column corank with probability approximately $\frac{1}{q-1}$. □

Theorem 2. *If $\mathbf{w}_1$ and $\mathbf{w}_2$ are chosen in such a way that they are both in the band kernel of a column band space $\mathcal{B}_{\beta,\gamma}$, and they are linearly independent from one another and statistically independent from the private quadratic forms, $p_{(i-1)s+j}$ in the matrix A, then $\mathbf{w}_1$ and $\mathbf{w}_2$ are both in the kernel of the first formal derivative of some column band space map, $\mathcal{E} = \sum_{\mathcal{E}_{\beta,\gamma,i} \in \mathcal{B}_{\beta,\gamma}} \tau_i \mathcal{E}_{\beta,\gamma,i}$ with probability approximately $\frac{1}{(q-1)q^s}$.*

Proof. An $\mathcal{E}$ meeting the above condition exists iff there is a nontrivial solution to the following system of equations

$$\begin{aligned} \sum_{\mathcal{E}_{\beta,\gamma,i} \in \mathcal{B}_{\beta,\gamma}} \tau_i \nabla \mathcal{E}_{\beta,\gamma,i}(\mathbf{w}_1) = 0, \\ \sum_{\mathcal{E}_{\beta,\gamma,i} \in \mathcal{B}_{\beta,\gamma}} \tau_i \nabla \mathcal{E}_{\beta,\gamma,i}(\mathbf{w}_2) = 0. \end{aligned} \qquad (2)$$

We may express our band space maps in a basis (e.g. the u_i' basis used in Definition 2) where the first s basis vectors are chosen to be outside the band kernel, and the remaining $s^2 - s$ basis vectors are chosen from within the band kernel. Combining this with Definition 1, we see that the band space maps can be written as

$$\mathcal{E}_{\beta,\gamma,i} = \sum_{j=1}^{s} p_{(i-1)s+j} u'_j.$$

Note that $\mathbf{w}_1$ and $\mathbf{w}_2$ are band kernel vectors, and so for both vectors we have that $u'_j = 0$ for $j = 1, \ldots, s$. Therefore, in such a basis, the only formal derivatives of $\mathcal{E}$ that can be nonzero are $\frac{\partial \mathcal{E}}{\partial u'_r} = p_{(i-1)s+j}$ for $j = 1, \ldots, s$. Thus in order for there to be a nontrivial solution to Eq. (2), it is necessary and sufficient that $\sum_{i=1}^{s} \tau_i p_{(i-1)s+j}(\mathbf{w}_k) = 0$ for $j = 1, \ldots, s$ and $k = 1, 2$. This condition will be satisfied if and only if the following $2s \times s$ matrix has nonzero column corank:

$$\begin{bmatrix} p_1(\mathbf{w}_1) & p_{s+1}(\mathbf{w}_1) & \cdots & p_{s^2-s+1}(\mathbf{w}_1) \\ p_2(\mathbf{w}_1) & p_{s+2}(\mathbf{w}_1) & \cdots & p_{s^2-s+2}(\mathbf{w}_1) \\ \vdots & \vdots & \ddots & \vdots \\ p_s(\mathbf{w}_1) & p_{2s}(\mathbf{w}_1) & \cdots & p_{s^2}(\mathbf{w}_1). \\ p_1(\mathbf{w}_2) & p_{s+1}(\mathbf{w}_2) & \cdots & p_{s^2-s+1}(\mathbf{w}_2) \\ p_2(\mathbf{w}_2) & p_{s+2}(\mathbf{w}_2) & \cdots & p_{s^2-s+2}(\mathbf{w}_2) \\ \vdots & \vdots & \ddots & \vdots \\ p_s(\mathbf{w}_2) & p_{2s}(\mathbf{w}_2) & \cdots & p_{s^2}(\mathbf{w}_2) \end{bmatrix}.$$

This matrix is a random matrix over $k = \mathbb{F}_q$, which has nonzero column corank with probability approximately $\frac{1}{(q-1)q^s}$, for practical parameters. $\square$

Combining the results of Theorems 1 and 2, we find that for a random choice of the vectors $\mathbf{w}_1$ and $\mathbf{w}_2$, there is a column band space map among the solutions of Eq. (1) with probability approximately $\frac{1}{(q-1)^2 q^s}$. It may be somewhat undesirable to choose $\mathbf{w}_1$ and $\mathbf{w}_1$ completely randomly, however. The naïve algorithm for constructing the coefficients of Eq. (1) for a random choice of $\mathbf{w}_1$ and $\mathbf{w}_2$ requires on the order of s^8 field operations. This can be reduced to s^6 operations if we make sure that each new choice of $\mathbf{w}_1$ and $\mathbf{w}_2$ differs from the previous choice at only a single coordinate. Then, rather than recomputing Eq. (1) from scratch, we can use the previous values of the coefficients and we will only need to include corrections for the monomials that contain the variable that was changed from the previous iteration. Over a large number of iterations, the distribution of $\mathbf{w}_1$ and $\mathbf{w}_2$ should still be sufficiently close to random that the probability of success for the attack will not be meaningfully altered.

One final factor which may increase the cost of attacks is the expected dimension of the solution space of Eq. (1). If this space has a high dimension, then the attack will be slowed down since the attacker much search through a large number of spurious solutions to find a real solution (i.e. one where $\sum_{i=1}^{2s^2} t_i \mathbf{H}(\mathcal{E}_i)(\mathbf{w}_l)$ has rank at most $2s$ for $l = 1, 2$). Fortunately, Eq. (1) is a system of $2s^2$ equations in $2s^2$ variables and it generally has a 0-dimensional space of solutions. The lone exception occurs for characteristic 3. In this case, there are two linear dependencies among the equations, given by $\mathbf{w}_1 [\nabla \mathcal{E}_i(\mathbf{w}_1)]^\top = 0$ and $\mathbf{w}_2 [\nabla \mathcal{E}_i(\mathbf{w}_2)]^\top = 0$. In this situation we would therefore expect a 2-dimensional solution space. We can, however, recover two additional linear constraints on the t_i's by also requiring:

$$\sum_{i=1}^{2s^2} t_i \mathcal{E}_i(\mathbf{w}_l) = 0, \text{ for } l = 1, 2.$$

When these additional linear constraints are added to those given by Eq. (1), the expected dimension of the solution space drops back to 0. We can therefore assess the cost of the above attack at approximately $s^6 q^{s+2}$, regardless of the characteristic.

5 Application to the Quadratic ABC Scheme

A similar technique was used to attack the original quadratic version of the ABC cryptosytem in [17]. While this technique was expressed in terms of the discrete differential, it can also be expressed using the formal derivative. In that case, the attack proceeds by selecting two random vectors $\mathbf{w}_1$ and $\mathbf{w}_2$, and solving an equation identical to Eq. (1) for t_i, where the $\mathcal{E}_i$ are quadratic rather than cubic. The attack succeeds when $\sum_{i=1}^{2s^2} t_i \mathbf{H}(\mathcal{E}_i)$ has low rank.

When this attack is applied to parameters chosen over a field with characteristic 2, it is less efficient for the same reason as the basic attack given in the previous section is less efficient for the characteristic 3 parameters: the $2s^2$ linear equations given by Eq. (1) have three linear dependencies given by $\mathbf{w}_1 [\nabla \mathcal{E}_i(\mathbf{w}_1)]^\top = 0$, $\mathbf{w}_2 [\nabla \mathcal{E}_i(\mathbf{w}_2)]^\top = 0$, and $\mathbf{w}_1 [\nabla \mathcal{E}_i(\mathbf{w}_2)]^\top + \mathbf{w}_2 [\nabla \mathcal{E}_i(\mathbf{w}_1)]^\top = 0$, and the attacker must generally search through a 3-dimensional solution space of spurious solutions in order to find a 1-dimensional space of useful solutions. As a result, the complexity of the attack for characteristic 2 is $s^{2\omega} q^{s+4}$, instead of $s^{2\omega} q^{s+2}$, as it is for all other characteristics. ($\omega \approx 2.373$ is the linear algebra constant.)

However, just as with cubic ABC parameters of characteristic 3, we can add two additional linear constraints and reduce the expected dimension of the solution space to 1:

$$\sum_{i=1}^{2s^2} t_i \mathcal{E}_i(\mathbf{w}_l) = 0, \text{ for } l = 1, 2.$$

Thus, we can also reduce the attack complexity for quadratic ABC parameters with characteristic 2 to $s^{2\omega} q^{s+2}$.

6 Completing the Key Recovery

Once the MinRank instance is solved, key extraction proceeds in a similar manner to [18, Sect. 6] in the cubic case and [17, Sect. 6]. Here we discuss the cubic version.

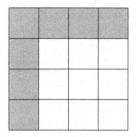

Fig. 2. Structure of $\mathbf{H}(\mathcal{E})(\mathbf{w})$ when $\mathcal{E} \in \mathcal{B}_{\beta,\gamma}$ and $\mathbf{w}$ is in the band kernel corresponding to the band space $\mathcal{B}_{\beta,\gamma}$. The shaded region corresponds to nonzero coefficients.

First, note that U is not a critical element of the scheme. If A is a random matrix of quadratic forms and B and C are random matrices of linear forms, then so are $A \circ U$, $B \circ U$ and $C \circ U$ for any full rank map U. Thus, since $T \circ \phi(AB\|AC) \circ U = T \circ \phi((A \circ U)(B \circ U)\|(A \circ U)(C \circ U))$, we may absorb the action of U into A, B, and C, and consider the public key to be of the form

$$P(\mathbf{x}) = T \circ \phi(AB\|AC)(\mathbf{x}).$$

Let $\mathcal{E} \in \mathcal{B}_{\beta,\gamma}$, and consider $\mathbf{H}(\mathcal{E})$. For $\mathbf{w}_1$ and $\mathbf{w}_2$ in the band kernel corresponding to $\mathcal{B}_{\beta,\gamma}$, there is a basis in which both $\mathbf{H}(\mathcal{E})(\mathbf{w}_1)$ and $\mathbf{H}(\mathcal{E})(\mathbf{w}_2)$ have the form illustrated in Fig. 2. Thus, for $s \geq 3$, with high probability the kernels of both maps are contained in the corresponding band kernel $\mathcal{B}_{\beta,\gamma}$, and $\mathrm{span}\{\ker(\mathbf{H}(\mathcal{E})(\mathbf{w}_1)), \ker(\mathbf{H}(\mathcal{E})(\mathbf{w}_2))\} = \mathcal{B}_{\beta,\gamma}$.

Given the basis for an $s^2 - s$ dimensional band kernel $\mathcal{BK}$, we may choose a basis $\{v_1, \ldots, v_s\}$ for the subspace of the dual space vanishing on $\mathcal{BK}$. We can also find a basis $\mathcal{E}_{v_1}, \ldots, \mathcal{E}_{v_s}$ for the band space itself by solving the linear system

$$\sum_{\mathcal{E}_i} \tau_i \mathcal{E}_i(\mathbf{w}_1) = 0,$$

$$\sum_{\mathcal{E}_i} \tau_i \mathcal{E}_i(\mathbf{w}_2) = 0,$$

$$\vdots = \vdots$$

$$\sum_{\mathcal{E}_i} \tau_i \mathcal{E}_i(\mathbf{w}_t) = 0,$$

where $t \approx 2s^2$ and $\mathbf{w}_i$ is in the band kernel.

Since the basis $\mathcal{E}_{v_1}, \ldots, \mathcal{E}_{v_s}$ is in a single band space, there exists an element $\begin{bmatrix} b'_1 \cdots b'_s \end{bmatrix}^{\top}$ in $\mathrm{ColumnSpace}(B\|C)$, and two matrices Ω_1 and Ω_2 such that

$$\Omega_1 A \left(\Omega_2 \begin{bmatrix} b'_1 \\ \vdots \\ b'_s \end{bmatrix} \right) =: A' \left(\begin{bmatrix} v_1 \\ \vdots \\ v_s \end{bmatrix} \right) = \begin{bmatrix} \mathcal{E}_{v_1} \\ \vdots \\ \mathcal{E}_{v_s} \end{bmatrix}.$$

Solving the above system of equations over $\mathbb{F}_q[x_1, \ldots, x_{s^2}]$ uniquely determines A' in the quotient $\mathbb{F}_q[x_1, \ldots, x_{s^2}]/\langle v_1, \ldots, v_s \rangle$. To recover all of A', note that the above system is part of an equivalent key

$$\mathcal{F} = T' \circ A'(B'\|C')$$

where $\begin{bmatrix} v_1 & \cdots & v_s \end{bmatrix}^\top$ is the first column of B'.

Applying T'^{-1} to both sides and inserting the information we know we may construct the system

$$A'(B'\|C') = T'^{-1}\mathcal{F}. \tag{3}$$

Solving this system of equations modulo $\langle v_1, \ldots, v_s \rangle$ for B', C' and T'^{-1} we can recover a space of solutions, which we will restrict by arbitrarily fixing the value of T'^{-1}. Note that the elements of T'^{-1} are constant polynomials, and therefore $T'^{-1}(\mathrm{mod}\langle v_1, \ldots, v_s \rangle)$ is the same as T'^{-1}. Thus, for any choice of T'^{-1} in this space, the second column of $T'^{-1}\mathcal{F}$ is a basis for a band space. Moreover, the elements $v'_{s+1}, \ldots, v'_{2s}$ of the second column of $B'(\mathrm{mod}\langle v_1, \ldots, v_s \rangle)$ are the image, modulo $\langle v_1, \ldots, v_s \rangle$, of linear forms vanishing on the corresponding band kernel. Therefore, we obtain the equality

$$\left(\bigcap_{i=1}^{s} \ker(v_i) \right) \bigcap \left(\bigcap_{i=s+1}^{2s} \ker(v'_i) \right) = \mathcal{BK}_2 \cap \mathcal{BK}_1,$$

the intersection of the band kernels of our two band spaces.

We can reconstruct the full band kernel of this second band space using the same method we used to obtain our first band kernel. We take a map $\mathcal{E}_2$ from the second column of $T'^{-1}\mathcal{F}$, and two vectors $\mathbf{w}_a$ and $\mathbf{w}_b$ from $\mathcal{BK}_2 \cap \mathcal{BK}_1$, and we compute $\mathcal{BK}_2 = \mathrm{span}\{\ker(\mathbf{H}(\mathcal{E}_2)(\mathbf{w}_a) \cup \ker(\mathbf{H}(\mathcal{E}_2)(\mathbf{w}_b)\}$. We can now solve for the second column of B', $\begin{bmatrix} v_{s+1} & \cdots & v_{2s} \end{bmatrix}^\top$, uniquely over $\mathbb{F}_q[x_1, \ldots, x_{s^2}]$ (NOT modulo $\langle v_1, \ldots, v_s \rangle$) by solving the following system of linear equations:

$$v_i \equiv v'_i \mathrm{mod}\langle v_1, \ldots, v_s \rangle,$$
$$v_i(\mathbf{w}_1) = 0,$$
$$v_i(\mathbf{w}_2) = 0,$$
$$\vdots = \vdots$$
$$v_i(\mathbf{w}_{s^2-s}) = 0,$$

where $i = s+1, \ldots, 2s$, and $\{\mathbf{w}_1, \ldots, \mathbf{w}_{s^2-s}\}$ is a basis for $\mathcal{BK}_2$. We can now solve for A' (again, uniquely over $\mathbb{F}_q[x_1, \ldots, x_{s^2}]$) by solving:

$$A' \left(\begin{bmatrix} v_1 \\ \vdots \\ v_s \end{bmatrix} \right) \equiv \begin{bmatrix} \mathcal{E}_{v_1} \\ \vdots \\ \mathcal{E}_{v_s} \end{bmatrix} \mathrm{mod}\langle v_1, \ldots, v_s \rangle,$$

$$A'\left(\begin{bmatrix} v_{s+1} \\ \vdots \\ v_{2s} \end{bmatrix}\right) \equiv \begin{bmatrix} \mathcal{E}_{v_{s+1}} \\ \vdots \\ \mathcal{E}_{v_{2s}} \end{bmatrix} \mathrm{mod}\langle v_{s+1}, \dots, v_{2s}\rangle,$$

where $\begin{bmatrix} \mathcal{E}_{v_{s+1}} & \cdots & \mathcal{E}_{v_{2s}} \end{bmatrix}^{\top}$ is the second column of $T'^{-1}\mathcal{F}$. This allows us to solve Eq. (3) for the rest of B' and C', completing the attack.

The primary cost of the attack involves finding the band space map. The rest of the key recovery is additive in complexity and dominated by the band space map recovery; thus the total complexity of the attack is of the same order as the band space map recovery. Hence, the cost of private key extraction is approximately $q^{s+2}s^6$ for all characteristics.

The original parameters of Cubic ABC were designed for a security level of 80-bits and 100-bits. Since NIST has been recommending a security level of 112-bits since 2015, see [19], these figures may be a bit out of date. In fact, our attack seems more effective for larger parameter sets than small.

We note that our attack breaks CubicABC($q = 2^8, s = 7$), designed for 80-bit security, in approximately 2^{88} operations. More convincingly, our attack breaks CubicABC($q = 2^8, s = 8$), designed for 100-bit security, in approximately 2^{98} operations, indicating that for parameters as small as these, we have already crossed the threshold of algebraic attack efficiency. Furthermore, the attack is fully parallelizable and requires very little memory. Hence, this technique is asymptotically far more efficient than algebraic attacks, the basis for the original security estimation in [14].

In the case of the quadratic ABC scheme, the original 86-bit secure parameters ABC($q = 2^8, s = 8$). The attack complexity with the new methodology presented here is 2^{87}, just above the claimed level. We note, however, that the authors of [13] supplied additional parameters using odd characteristic in their presentation at PQCRYPTO 2013, see [20], with a claimed security level of 108-bits. This scheme, ABC($q = 127, s = 8$) offers resistance only to the level of 2^{77} to our slight improvement in technique over that of [17]. Thus, our attack definitively breaks these parameters.

7   Comparison with Minors Methods

The MinRank problem has been a central computational challenge related to the security of various multivariate schemes since the beginning of the century, and as discussed in the previous section, is the primary bottleneck of our attack. There are two main disparate techniques for solving MinRank.

The first technique, which we employ here, can be called "linear algebra search." The linear algebra search technique randomly selects vectors $\mathbf{x}_1, \dots, \mathbf{x}_\ell \in k^n$ in an attempt to solve a system of equations of the form:

$$\left(\sum_{i=1}^{m} t_i \mathbf{M}_i\right) \mathbf{x}_j = \mathbf{0} \text{ for } j \in \{1, \dots, \ell\}.$$

The technique is essentially free in terms of memory, but is exponential in q, the size of k. The linear algebra search can benefit from certain exponential speedups depending on the structure of the equations. In particular, the linear algebra search is exponentially faster in the case of "interlaced kernels" as specified in [21] or in the case of differential invariants, as in the case of the original ABC scheme, see [17].

The second technique is known as minors modeling. Given an instance of minrank, $\mathbf{M}_1, \ldots, \mathbf{M}_m$ with target rank r, construct the matrix

$$\sum_{i=1}^{m} y_i \mathbf{M}_i,$$

with entries in $k[y_1, \ldots, y_m]$. Since there is an assignment of values of the y_i in k such that the resulting matrix has rank r, via the Finite Field Nullstellensatz, the system of $r + 1 \times r + 1$ minors of this matrix, along with the field equations $y_i^q - y_i$, form a positive dimensional ideal. Fixing a variable to a nonzero value by adding another equation, say $y_1 - 1$ still statistically results in a nonempty variety containing solutions to the MinRank problem.

The complexity of the minors modeling technique is dependent upon the degree of regularity of the minors system, though this can easily be seen for large systems to be $r + 1$, since for sufficiently large schemes the application of a Gröbner basis algorithm is equivalent to linearization. Thus the complexity is $\mathcal{O}\left(\binom{m+r+1}{r+1}^{\omega}\right)$, where ω is the linear algebra constant. A serious drawback of this technique is memory usage, which also nontrivially complicates the practical time complexity. The space complexity of the minors approach can be roughly estimated as $\mathcal{O}\left(\binom{m+r}{r+1}^2\right)$.

To make a direct comparison of these techniques for the MinRank portion of the attack, we use the parameters $q = 2^8$ and $s = 8$ discussed in the previous section. Recall that the linear algebra search technique requires memory on the order of $s^4 q = 2^{20}$ and that the time complexity is about 2^{87}. For the minors modeling method, the space complexity can be computed from the above estimates using $m = 2s^2 = 128$ and $r = 2s = 16$ to be about 2^{144}, roughly the square root of the number of subatomic particles in the universe, and the time complexity is 2^{172}. We thus conclude that for such small values of q that the linear algebra search, due to the interlaced nature of the kernels, is far more efficient. Furthermore, for ABC schemes, it is questionable whether the memory constraints for the minors approach can ever be realistic.

8   Experiments

Using SAGE [22], we performed some experiments as a sanity check to confirm the efficiency of our ideas on small scale variants of the Cubic ABC scheme. The computer used has a 64 bit quad-core Intel i7 processor, with clock cycle 2.8 GHz. Rather than considering the full attack, we were most interested in confirming our complexity estimates on the most costly step in the attack, the MinRank instance. Given as input the finite field size q, and the scheme parameter s, we computed the average number of vectors v required to be sampled in order for the rank of the 2-tensor $\mathbf{H}(\mathcal{E})(v)$ to fall to $2s$. As explained in Sect. 4, when the rank falls to this level, we have identified the subspace differential invariant structure of the scheme which can then be exploited to attack the scheme.

As this paper is only concerned with binary fields, we ran experiments with $q = 2, 4$ and 8. We found that for $s = 3$ and $q = 2, 4$, or 8, with high probability only a single vector was needed before the rank fell to $2s$. For $s = 4$ and $s = 5$, the computations were only feasible in SAGE for $q = 2$ and $q = 4$. The average values obtained are presented in Table 1 below. Note that for $q = 4$ and $s = 5$ the average value is based on a small number of samples as the computation time was quite lengthy.

Table 1. Average number of vectors needed for the rank to fall to $2s$ versus the predicted values.

	$s = 4$	$(q - 1)^2 q^s$	$s = 5$	$(q - 1)^2 q^s$
$q = 2$	24	16	35	32
$q = 4$	1962	2304	7021	9216

In comparison, our previous experiments [18] were only able to obtain data for $q = 2$ and $s = 4, 5$. The average number of vectors needed in the $s = 4$ case was 244, while for $s = 5$, the average number in our experiments was 994 (with the predicted values being 256 and 1024).

9 Conclusion

The ABC schemes offer an interesting new technique for the construction of multivariate public key schemes. Previously, we have used the multiplicative structure of an extension field to generate an efficiently invertible map. Schemes built on such a construct are known as "big field" schemes. The ABC framework is essentially a "large structure" or perhaps "large algebra" scheme, depending on multiplication from a matrix algebra over the base field. Since the only simple algebras are either matrix algebras or field extensions, we seem to have exhausted the possibilities. Interestingly, MinRank techniques seem optimal in this setting, at least asymptotically in the dimension of the extension.

Also interesting to note is the fact that the authors present in [14] a heuristic security argument for the provable security of the scheme and reinforce the notion of provable security in this venue at the presentation of the scheme at [23]. Unfortunately, this analysis does not contribute a sound conclusion, as demonstrated by the methodology of [18]. With our improved attack, we rule out the possibility that the cubic variant of ABC offers any security advantage over the original quadratic scheme. Likewise, our improved attack on quadratic ABC eliminates any security benefit associated with characteristic-2 parameters in the quadratic case.

References

1. Shor, P.W.: Polynomial-time algorithms for prime factorization and discrete logarithms on a quantum computer. SIAM J. Sci. Stat. Comp. **26**, 1484 (1997)
2. Feynman, R.P.: Simulating physics with computers. Int. J. Theor. Phys. **21**, 467–488 (1982)
3. Group, C.T.: Submission requirements and evaluation criteria for the post-quantum cryptogra-phy standardization process. NIST CSRC (2016). http://csrc.nist.gov/groups/ST/post-quantum-crypto/documents/call-for-proposals-nal-dec-2016.pdf
4. Kipnis, A., Patarin, J., Goubin, L.: Unbalanced oil and vinegar signature schemes. In: Stern, J. (ed.) EUROCRYPT 1999. LNCS, vol. 1592, pp. 206–222. Springer, Heidelberg (1999). doi:10.1007/3-540-48910-X_15
5. Patarin, J., Goubin, L., Courtois, N.: C_{-+}^{*} and HM: variations around two schemes of T. Matsumoto and H. Imai. In: Ohta, K., Pei, D. (eds.) ASIACRYPT 1998. LNCS, vol. 1514, pp. 35–50. Springer, Heidelberg (1998). doi:10.1007/3-540-49649-1_4
6. Patarin, J., Courtois, N., Goubin, L.: QUARTZ, 128-bit long digital signatures. In: Naccache, D. (ed.) CT-RSA 2001. LNCS, vol. 2020, pp. 282–297. Springer, Heidelberg (2001). doi:10.1007/3-540-45353-9_21
7. Petzoldt, A., Bulygin, S., Buchmann, J.: CyclicRainbow – a multivariate signature scheme with a partially cyclic public key. In: Gong, G., Gupta, K.C. (eds.) INDOCRYPT 2010. LNCS, vol. 6498, pp. 33–48. Springer, Heidelberg (2010). doi:10.1007/978-3-642-17401-8_4
8. Petzoldt, A., Chen, M.-S., Yang, B.-Y., Tao, C., Ding, J.: Design principles for HFEv- based multivariate signature schemes. In: Iwata, T., Cheon, J.H. (eds.) ASIACRYPT 2015. LNCS, vol. 9452, pp. 311–334. Springer, Heidelberg (2015). doi:10.1007/978-3-662-48797-6_14
9. Ding, J., Yang, B.-Y.: Degree of regularity for HFEv and HFEv-. In: Gaborit, P. (ed.) PQCrypto 2013. LNCS, vol. 7932, pp. 52–66. Springer, Heidelberg (2013). doi:10.1007/978-3-642-38616-9_4
10. Goubin, L., Courtois, N.T.: Cryptanalysis of the TTM cryptosystem. In: Okamoto, T. (ed.) ASIACRYPT 2000. LNCS, vol. 1976, pp. 44–57. Springer, Heidelberg (2000). doi:10.1007/3-540-44448-3_4
11. Tsujii, S., Gotaishi, M., Tadaki, K., Fujita, R.: Proposal of a signature scheme based on STS trapdoor. In: Sendrier, N. (ed.) PQCrypto 2010. LNCS, vol. 6061, pp. 201–217. Springer, Heidelberg (2010). doi:10.1007/978-3-642-12929-2_15
12. Porras, J., Baena, J., Ding, J.: ZHFE, a new multivariate public key encryption scheme. In: [23], pp. 229–245 (2014)
13. Tao, C., Diene, A., Tang, S., Ding, J.: Simple matrix scheme for encryption. In: [24], pp. 231–242 (2013)
14. Ding, J., Petzoldt, A., Wang, L.: The cubic simple matrix encryption scheme. In: [23], pp. 76–87 (2014)
15. Szepieniec, A., Ding, J., Preneel, B.: Extension field cancellation: a new central trapdoor for multivariate quadratic systems. In: [25], pp. 182–196 (2016)

16. Perlner, R.A., Smith-Tone, D.: Security analysis and key modification for ZHFE. In: [25], pp. 197–212 (2016)
17. Moody, D., Perlner, R.A., Smith-Tone, D.: An asymptotically optimal structural attack on the ABC multivariate encryption scheme. In: [23], pp. 180–196 (2014)
18. Moody, D., Perlner, R.A., Smith-Tone, D.: Key recovery attack on the cubic ABC simple matrix multivariate encryption scheme. In: Lange, T., Takagi, T. (eds.) PQCrypto 2017. LNCS, vol. 10346, pp. 255–271. Springer, Cham (2017)
19. Barker, E., Roginsky, A.: Transitions: recommendation for transitioning the use of cryptographic algorithms and key lengths. NIST Special Publication (2015). http://nvlpubs.nist.gov/nistpubs/SpecialPublications/NIST.Spp.800-131Ar1.pdf
20. Diene, A., Tao, C., Ding, J.: Simple matrix scheme for encryption (ABC). In: PQCRYPTO 2013 (2013). http://pqcrypto2013.xlim.fr/slides/05-06-2013/Diene.pdf
21. Yang, B.-Y., Chen, J.-M.: Building secure tame-like multivariate public-key cryptosystems: the new TTS. In: Boyd, C., González Nieto, J.M. (eds.) ACISP 2005. LNCS, vol. 3574, pp. 518–531. Springer, Heidelberg (2005). doi:10.1007/11506157_43
22. Developers, T.S.: SageMath, the Sage Mathematics Software System (SAGE, Version 7.2) (2016). http://www.sagemath.org
23. Mosca, M. (ed.): PQCrypto 2014. LNCS, vol. 8772. Springer, Cham (2014). doi:10.1007/978-3-319-11659-4
24. Gaborit, P. (ed.): PQCrypto 2013. LNCS, vol. 7932. Springer, Heidelberg (2013). doi:10.1007/978-3-642-38616-9
25. Takagi, T. (ed.): PQCrypto 2016. LNCS, vol. 9606. Springer, Cham (2016). doi:10.1007/978-3-319-29360-8

Key Recovery Attack
for All Parameters of HFE-

Jeremy Vates[1] and Daniel Smith-Tone[1,2(✉)]

[1] Department of Mathematics, University of Louisville, Louisville, KY, USA
jeremy.vates@louisville.edu, daniel.smith@nist.gov
[2] National Institute of Standards and Technology, Gaithersburg, MD, USA

Abstract. Recently, by an interesting confluence, multivariate schemes with the minus modifier have received attention as candidates for multivariate encryption. Among these candidates is the twenty year old HFE$^-$ scheme originally envisioned as a possible candidate for both encryption and digital signatures, depending on the number of public equations removed.

HFE has received a great deal of attention and a variety of cryptanalyses over the years; however, HFE$^-$ has escaped these assaults. The direct algebraic attack that broke HFE Challenge I is provably more complex on HFE$^-$, and even after two decades HFE Challenge II is daunting, though not achieving a security level we may find acceptable today. The minors modeling approach to the Kipnis-Shamir (KS) attack is very efficient for HFE, but fails when the number of equations removed is greater than one. Thus it seems reasonable to use HFE$^-$ for encryption with two equations removed.

This strategy may not be quite secure, however, as our new approach shows. We derive a new key recovery attack still based on the minors modeling approach that succeeds for all parameters of HFE$^-$. The attack is polynomial in the degree of the extension, though of higher degree than the original minors modeling KS-attack. As an example, the complexity of key recovery for HFE$^-(q = 31, n = 36, D = 1922, a = 2)$ is 2^{52}. Even more convincingly, the complexity of key recovery for HFE Challenge-2, an HFE$^-(16, 36, 4352, 4)$ scheme, is feasible, costing around 2^{67} operations. Thus, the parameter choices for HFE$^-$ for both digital signatures and, particularly, for encryption must be re-examined.

Keywords: Multivariate cryptography · *HFE* · Encryption · MinRank · Q-rank

1 Introduction

In the 1990s, several important developments in the history of asymmetric cryptography occured. Among these discoveries, and of the greatest significance to

© Springer International Publishing AG 2017 (outside the US)
T. Lange and T. Takagi (Eds.): PQCrypto 2017, LNCS 10346, pp. 272–288, 2017.
DOI: 10.1007/978-3-319-59879-6_16

forward-thinking cryptographers, was the discovery by Peter Shor of polynomial time algorithms for factoring and computing discrete logarithms on a quantum computer, see [1]. In the years since that time, we have witnessed quantum computing become a reality, while *large-scale* quantum computing has transmogrified from a dream into what many of us now see as an inevitability, if not an impending phenomenon. The call for proposals by the National Institute of Standards and Technology (NIST), see [2], charges our community with the task of protecting the integrity and confidentiality of our critical data in this time of tremendous change.

The 1990s also beheld an explosive development in public key technologies relying on mathematics of a less linear character than number theory. In particular, multivariate public key cryptography (MPKC) produced numerous schemes for public key encryption and digital signatures in the late 1990s. These schemes further fuelled the development of computational algebraic geometry, and seem to have inspired the advancement of some of the symbolic algebra techniques we now apply to all areas of post-quantum cryptography, that is, cryptography designed with quantum computers in mind.

Armed with new tools and a more developed theory, many multivariate schemes were cryptanalyzed; in particular, secure multivariate encryption seemed particularly challenging. The purpose of this disquisition is to cryptanalyze an old digital signature scheme that has been repurposed to achieve multivariate encryption.

1.1 Recent History

While the ancestor of all of the "large structure" schemes is the C^* scheme of Matsumoto and Imai, see [3], the more direct parent of multivariate encryption schemes of today is HFE, see [4]. The idea behind such systems is to define a large associative algebra over a finite field and utilize its multiplication to construct maps that are quadratic when expressed over the base field.

There have been many proposals in this area in the last five years. The Simple Matrix Schemes, see [5] for the quadratic version and [6] for the cubic version, are constructed via multiplication in a large matrix algebra over the base field. ZHFE, see [7] and Extension Field Cancellation, see [8], just as HFE, utilize the structure of an extension field in the derivation of their public keys.

Many of these "large structure" schemes have effective cryptanalyses that either break or limit the efficiency of the schemes. HFE, in its various iterations, has been cryptanalyzed via direct algebraic attack, see [9], via an attack exploiting Q-rank known as the Kipnis-Shamir, or KS, attack, see [10], and via a fusion of these techniques utilizing an alternative modeling of the Q-rank property, see [11]. The Quadratic Simple Matrix Scheme is made less efficient for parameters meeting NIST's current suggested security levels in [12], while the Cubic Simple Matrix Scheme is broken for such parameters in [13]. In addition, a low Q-rank property for ZHFE is discovered in [14] which calls in to question the security of the scheme. In light of such an array of cryptanalyses for multivariate encryption schemes, the question of whether the correct strategy is being employed is very relevant.

Interestingly, at PQCRYPTO 2016 and the winter school prior to the conference, three independent teams of researchers in MPKC related the same idea: the idea of using the minus modifier in encryption. In fairness, the concept of using the minus modifier in encryption is not new; it was suggested as early as in the proposal of HFE. The convergence on this strategy is surprising because it is common knowledge that either the number of equations removed is too large for effective, or even fault-tolerant, encryption, or that the scheme must have parameters that are too large for the system to be efficient. The three techniques are presented in the articles [14] and [8] and in the presentation [15].

While both of the techniques in [14] and [8] are very new schemes, HFE$^-$ has been well studied for over twenty years. Using HFE$^-$ for encryption is more complicated than using the scheme for digital signatures, so careful review of theory is critical for this application.

1.2 Previous Analysis

There are a few results in the literature that are relevant in the analysis of HFE$^-$. These articles address the security of the scheme against algebraic, differential and rank attacks.

In [16], the degree of regularity for the public key of HFE$^-$ schemes is derived. The result shows that the upper bound on the degree of regularity of the public key when a equations is removed is about $\frac{a(q-1)}{2}$ higher than the same bound for a comparable HFE scheme over $GF(q)$.

In [17], information theoretic proofs of security against differential adversaries are derived for HFE$^-$. The consequence of this work is that attacks of the flavor of the attack on SFLASH, see [18], using symmetry and attacks in the manner of the attack on the Simple Matrix Scheme, see [12], exploiting invariants are not relevant for HFE$^-$.

In the other direction, in [11, Sect. 8.1], an attack on weak parameters of HFE$^-$ with asymptotic complexity of $\mathcal{O}(n^{(\lceil log_q(D) \rceil + 1)\omega})$ is derived, where n is the degree of the extension, D is the degree bound for HFE and ω is the linear algebra constant. The caveat here is that the attack is only successful against HFE$^-$ if only a single equation is removed. This restriction on the attack technique is fundamental and is due to theory, not computational feasibility. The existence of the attack, however, implies that at least two equations must be removed for reasonable parameters, and thus q must be quite small for encryption.

1.3 Our Contribution

We present a key recovery attack on HFE$^-$ that works for any HFE$^-$ public key. The attack is based on the Q-rank of the public key instead of the Q-rank of the private central map as in [11].

The attack works by performing key extraction on a related HFE scheme and then converting the private key of the related scheme into an equivalent private key for the HFE$^-$ scheme. The complexity of the attack is dominated by the

HFE key extraction phase and is on the order of $\mathcal{O}\left(\binom{n+\lceil log_q(D)\rceil+1}{\lceil log_q(D)\rceil+a+1}^{\omega}\right)$, where D is the degree bound of the central HFE polynomial, a is the number of removed equations and ω is the linear algebra constant, for all practical parameters. We note that this value implies that the minus modification of HFE adds at most $a\omega log_2(n)$ bits of security for any parameters, though we find that it is much less for many practical parameters.

1.4 Organization

The paper is organized as follows. In the next section, we present isomorphisms of polynomials and describe the structure of HFE and HFE$^-$. The following section reviews the Q-rank of ideals in polynomial rings and discusses invariant properties of Q-rank and min-Q-rank. In Sect. 4, we review more carefully the previous cryptanalyses of HFE and HFE$^-$ that are relevant to our technique. The subsequent section contains our cryptanalysis of HFE$^-$. Then, in Sect. 6, we conduct a careful complexity analysis of our attack, followed by our experimental results in the following section. Finally, we conclude, noting the affect these results have on parameter selection for HFE$^-$.

2 HFE Variants

Numerous multivariate cryptosystems fall into a category known as "big field" schemes exploiting the vector space structure of a degree n extension $\mathbb{K}$ over $\mathbb{F}_q$. Let $\phi : \mathbb{F}_q^n \to \mathbb{K}$ be an $\mathbb{F}_q$-vector space isomoprhism. Since a generator of $Gal_{\mathbb{F}_q}(\mathbb{K})$ is the Frobenius automorphism, $x \mapsto x^q$, for every monomial map of the form $f(x) = x^{q^i+q^j}$ in $\mathbb{K}$, $\phi^{-1} \circ f \circ \phi$ is a vector-valued quadratic function over $\mathbb{F}_q$. By counting, one can see that any vector-valued quadratic map on $\mathbb{F}_q^n$ is thusly isomorphic to a sum of such monomials. Consequently, any quadratic map f over $\mathbb{K}$ can be written as a vector-valued map, F, over $\mathbb{F}_q$. Throughout this work, for any map $g : \mathbb{K} \to \mathbb{K}$, we denote by G the quantity $\phi^{-1} \circ g \circ \phi$.

This equivalence allows us to construct cryptosystems in conjunction with the following concept, the of isomorphisms of polynomials.

Definition 1. *Two vector-valued multivariate polynomials F and G are said to be* isomorphic *if there exist two affine maps T, U such that $G = T \circ F \circ U$.*

The equivalence and isomorphism marry in a method commonly referred to as the butterfly construction. Given a vector space isomorphism $\phi : \mathbb{F}_q^n \to \mathbb{K}$ and an efficiently invertible map $f : \mathbb{K} \to \mathbb{K}$, we compose two affine transformations $T, U : \mathbb{F}_q^n \to \mathbb{F}_q^n$ in order to obscure our choice of basis for the input and output. This construction generates a vector-valued map $P = T \circ \phi^{-1} \circ f \circ \phi \circ U$.

$$\begin{array}{ccc}
\mathbb{K} & \xrightarrow{\ f\ } & \mathbb{K} \\
{\scriptstyle \phi}\uparrow & & \downarrow{\scriptstyle \phi^{-1}} \\
\mathbb{F}_q^n \xrightarrow{\ U\ } \mathbb{F}_q^n & \xrightarrow{\ F\ } & \mathbb{F}_q^n \xrightarrow{\ T\ } \mathbb{F}_q^n
\end{array}$$

The Hidden Field Equation Scheme was first introduced by Patarin in [4]. This scheme is an improvement on the well known C^* construction of [19], where a general polynomial with degree bound D is used in place of the C^*'s central monomial map.

Explicitly, one chooses a quadratic map $f : \mathbb{K} \to \mathbb{K}$ of the form:

$$f(x) = \sum_{\substack{i \leq j \\ q^i + q^j \leq D}} \alpha_{i,j} x^{q^i + q^j} + \sum_{\substack{i \\ q^i \leq D}} \beta_i x^{q^i} + \gamma,$$

where the coefficients $\alpha_{i,j}, \beta_i, \gamma \in \mathbb{K}$ and the degree bound D is sufficiently low for efficient inversion.

The public key is computed as $P = T \circ F \circ U$. Inversion is accomplished by first taking a cipher text $y = P(x)$, computing $v = T^{-1}(y)$, solving $\phi(v) = f(u)$ for u via the Berlekamp algorithm, see [20], and then recovering $x = U^{-1}(\phi^{-1}(u))$.

HFE$^-$ uses the HFE primitive f along with a projection Π that removes a equations from the public key. The public key is $P_\Pi = \Pi \circ T \circ F \circ U$.

3   Q-Rank

A critical quantity tied to the security of big field schemes is the Q-rank (or more correctly, the min-Q-rank) of the public key.

Definition 2. *The Q-rank of any quadratic map $f(\overline{x})$ on $\mathbb{F}_q^n$ is the rank of the quadratic form $\phi^{-1} \circ f \circ \phi$ in $\mathbb{K}[X_0, \ldots, X_{n-1}]$ via the identification $X_i = \phi(\overline{x})^{q^i}$.*

Quadratic form equivalence corresponds to matrix congruence, and thus the definition of the rank of a quadratic form is typically given as the minimum number of variables required to express an equivalent quadratic form. Since congruent matrices have the same rank, this quantity is equal to the rank of the matrix representation of this quadratic form, even in characteristic 2, where the quadratics x^{2q^i} are additive, but not linear for $q > 2$.

Q-rank is invariant under one-sided isomorphisms $f \mapsto f \circ U$, but is not invariant under isomorphisms of polynomials in general. The quantity that is often meant by the term Q-rank, but more properly called min-Q-rank, is the minimum Q-rank among all nonzero linear images of f. This min-Q-rank is invariant under isomorphisms of polynomials and is the quantity relevant for cryptanalysis.

4   Previous Cryptanalysis of HFE

HFE has been cryptanalyzed via a few techniques in the over twenty years since its inception. The principal analyses are the Kipnis-Shamir (KS) attack of [10], the direct algebraic attack of [9], and the minors modeling approach of the KS-attack of [11].

The KS-attack is a key recovery attack exploiting the fact that the quadratic form representing the central map F over $\mathbb{K}$ is of low rank. Specfically, considering an odd characteristic case, we may write the homogeneous quadratic part of F as

$$\begin{bmatrix} x & x^q & \cdots & x^{q^{n-1}} \end{bmatrix} \begin{bmatrix} \alpha_{0,0} & \alpha'_{0,1} & \cdots & \alpha'_{0,d-1} & 0 \cdots 0 \\ \alpha'_{0,1} & \alpha_{1,1} & \cdots & \alpha'_{1,d-1} & 0 \cdots 0 \\ \vdots & \vdots & \ddots & \vdots & \vdots \ddots \vdots \\ \alpha'_{0,d-1} & \alpha'_{1,d-1} & \cdots & \alpha_{d-1,d-1} & 0 \cdots 0 \\ 0 & 0 & \cdots & 0 & 0 \cdots 0 \\ \vdots & \vdots & \ddots & \vdots & \vdots \ddots \vdots \\ 0 & 0 & \cdots & 0 & 0 \cdots 0 \end{bmatrix} \begin{bmatrix} x \\ x^q \\ \vdots \\ x^{q^{n-1}} \end{bmatrix},$$

where $\alpha'_{i,j} = \frac{1}{2}\alpha_{i,j}$ and $d = \lceil log_q(D) \rceil$. Using polynomial interpolation, the public key can be expressed as a quadratic polynomial G over a degree n extension, and it is known that there is a linear map T^{-1} such that $T^{-1} \circ G$ has rank d, thus there is a rank d matrix that is a $\mathbb{K}$-linear combination of the Frobenius powers of G. This turns recovery of the transformation T into the solution of a MinRank problem over $\mathbb{K}$.

In contrast to the KS-attack, the Gröbner basis attack of Faugère in [9], is a direct algebraic attack on HFE using the F4 Gröbner basis algorithm. The attack succeeds in breaking HFE Challenge 1, see [4]. The success is primarily due to the fact that the coefficients of the central map in HFE Challenge 1 were very poorly chosen. The scheme is defined over $GF(2)$ and uses only a degree 80 extension. Thus the scheme fails to brute force analysis with complexity at worst 2^{80}. The very small base field drastically limits the number of monomials of degree d and makes Gröbner basis techniques extremely powerful.

The key recovery attack of [11] combines these two approaches with some significant improvements. First, via a very clever construction, it is shown that a $\mathbb{K}$-linear combination of the *public* polynomials has low rank as a quadratic form over $\mathbb{K}$. Second, setting the unknown coefficients in $\mathbb{K}$ as variables, the polynomials representing $(d + 1) \times (d + 1)$ minors of such a linear combination, which must be zero due to the rank property, reside in $\mathbb{F}_q[t]$. Thus a Gröbner basis needs to be computed over $\mathbb{F}_q$ and the variety computed over $\mathbb{K}$. This technique is called minors modeling and dramatically improves the efficiency of the KS-attack. The complexity of the KS-attack with minors modeling is asymptotically $\mathcal{O}(n^{(\lceil log_q(D) \rceil + 1)\omega})$, where $2 \leq \omega \leq 3$ is the linear algebra constant.

The effect of the minus modifier on these schemes is worthy of notice. For the direct algebraic attack, the fact that the degree of regularity for a subsystem is lower bounded by the degree of regularity of the entire system shows that the minus modifier introduces no weakness. In particular, the degree of regularity of HFE$^-$ is investigated in [16] where it is shown that the best known upper bound on the degree of regularity for HFE increases with each equation removed. For the KS-attack with either the original modeling or the minors modeling, it suffices to note that though there is a method of reconstructing a single removed equation, it is not true in general that there is a rank $\lceil log_q(D) \rceil$ $\mathbb{K}$-quadratic form in the linear span of the public key; thus, these attacks fail if the number of equations removed is at least two.

5   Key Recovery for HFE⁻

In this section we explain our key recovery attack on HFE⁻. The process is broken down into two main steps. The first is finding a related HFE instance of the HFE⁻ public key. This related instance will then be the focus. Then we discuss how to systematically solve for an equivalent private key for the original HFE⁻ scheme.

5.1   Reduction of HFE⁻ to HFE

Recall that by imposing the field equations we may always assume that any affine variety associated with HFE is contained in the finite field $\mathbb{K}$. Then we may use the following definition.

Definition 3 (see Definition 1, [17]). *The* minimal polynomial, *of the algebraic set* $V \subseteq \mathbb{K}$ *is given by*

$$\mathcal{M}_V := \prod_{v \in V} (x - v).$$

Equivalently, $\mathcal{M}_V$ *is the generator of the principal ideal* $I(V)$, *the intersection of the maximal ideals* $\langle x - v \rangle$ *for all* $v \in V$.

Recall that the public key of an HFE⁻ scheme is constructed by truncating a full rank linear combination of the central polynomials. That is, with parenthetical emphasis, $P = \Pi(T \circ F \circ U)$. We now show that this singular linear transformation can be transported "past" the invertible transformation T and "absorbed" by the central map.

Lemma 1. *Let* $\Pi \circ T$ *be a corank* a *linear transformation on* $\mathbb{F}_q^n$. *There exist both a nonsingular linear transformation* S *and a degree* q^a *linear polynomial* π *such that* $\Pi \circ T = S \circ \phi^{-1} \circ \pi \circ \phi$.

Proof. Let V be the kernel of $\Pi \circ T$ and let $\pi = \mathcal{M}_V$. Note that $|V| = q^a$, thus $\mathcal{M}_V(x)$ has degree q^a and is of the form

$$x^{q^a} + c_{a-1}x^{q^{a-1}} + \cdots + c_1 x^q + c_0 x \text{ where } c_i \in \mathbb{K} \tag{1}$$

Now let $B_V = \{b_{n-a}, b_{n-a+1}, \ldots, b_{n-1}\}$ be a basis for V and extend this to a basis $B = \{b_0, \ldots, b_{n-1}\}$ of $\mathbb{F}_q^n$. Let M be the matrix transporting from the standard basis to B. Clearly the matrix representations of both $M^{-1}(\Pi \circ T)M$ and $M^{-1}(\phi^{-1} \circ \pi \circ \phi)M$ have the last a columns of 0.

Observe that there exist invertible matrices A and A', corresponding to row operations, such that both $AM^{-1}(\Pi \circ T)M$ and $A'M^{-1}(\phi^{-1} \circ \pi \circ \phi)M$ are in reduced echelon form; that is:

$$AM^{-1}(\Pi \circ T)M = \left[\begin{array}{c|c} I & 0 \\ \hline 0 & 0 \end{array}\right] = A'M^{-1}(\phi^{-1} \circ \pi \circ \phi)M \tag{2}$$

Solving for $\Pi \circ T$, we obtain

$$MA^{-1}A'M^{-1}(\phi^{-1} \circ \pi \circ \phi) = \Pi \circ T. \tag{3}$$

Let $S = MA^{-1}A'M^{-1}$ and the lemma is proven.

Lemma 1 suggests the possibility of considering an HFE$^-$ public key as a full rank basis for the low rank image of a quadratic map. In fact, Lemma 1 is powerful enough to maintain a low degree bound for this map.

Theorem 1. *Let P be the public key of an HFE$^-(q, n, D, a)$ scheme. Then*

$$P' := P\|\{p_{n-a}, p_{n-a+1} \ldots, p_{n-1}\}$$

is a public key of an HFE$(q, n, q^a D)$ scheme for any choice of $p_i \in Span(P)$ where $i \in \{n - a, n - a + 1, \ldots, n - 1\}$.

Proof. Let P be a public key for HFE$^-(q, n, D, a)$. Observe that P has the following form, $P = \Pi \circ T \circ F \circ U$ where $T, U : \mathbb{F}_q^n \to \mathbb{F}_q^n$ are affine transformations applied to an HFE(q, n, D) central map F. Let Π' be the natural embedding of Π as a linear map $\mathbb{F}_q^n \to \mathbb{F}_q^n$ obtained by composing the inclusion mapping $\mathbb{F}_q^{n-a} \hookrightarrow \mathbb{F}_q^n$. By Lemma 1, we can rewrite $P\|\{0, 0, \ldots 0\}$ in the following way:

$$P\|\{0, 0, \ldots 0\} = \Pi' \circ T \circ \phi^{-1} \circ f \circ \phi \circ U = S \circ \phi^{-1} \circ (\pi \circ f) \circ \phi \circ U, \tag{4}$$

where S is nonsingular and π is a linear polynomial of degree q^a.

Observe that $P\|\{0, 0, \ldots 0\}$ now has the structure of an HFE$(q, n - a, q^a D)$, since the degree bound is increased by a factor of q^a; that is, $deg(\pi(f)) = deg(\pi)deg(f)$. Finally, construct $P' = P\|\{p_{n-a}, p_{n-a+1}, \ldots, p_{n-1}\}$ where $p_i \in Span(P)$, possibly 0. Since the composition A of elementary row operations produces P' from $P\|\{0, 0 \ldots, 0\}$, we obtain an HFE$(q, n, q^a D)$ key, $(AS, \pi \circ f, U)$.

Theorem 1 indicates that HFE$^-$, in some sense, *is* HFE with merely a slightly higher degree bound. Thus it is sensible to discuss recovering an equivalent key for an instance of HFE$^-$ as an HFE scheme. We can, in fact, do more and recover an equivalent HFE$^-$ key.

5.2 Key Recovery

Any HFE key recovery oracle $\mathcal{O}$, when given a public key P of an HFE instance recovers a private key of HFE "shape." By Theorem 1, such an oracle can recover a private key for the augmented public key P' which is also of HFE shape. We now show, however, that in this case, the key derived from $\mathcal{O}$ must preserve more structure.

Theorem 2. *Let P be a public key for an instance of HFE$^-(q,n,D,a)$ and let $P' = P\|\{p_{n-a}, p_{n-a+1}\cdots, p_{n-1}\}$ be a corresponding HFE(q,n,q^aD) public key. Further, let (T', f', U') be any private key of P'. Then the representation of f' as a quadratic form over $\mathbb{K}$ is block diagonal of the form:*

$$\mathbf{F'} = \begin{bmatrix} F'_1 & 0 \\ 0 & 0 \end{bmatrix}, \tag{5}$$

where $F'_1 = [f_{i,j}]_{i,j}$ is $(\lceil log_q(D) \rceil + a) \times (\lceil log_q(D) \rceil + a)$ and has the property that $f_{i,j} = 0$ if $|i - j| \geq \lceil log_q(D) \rceil$. That is, F'_1 has only a diagonal "band" of nonzero values of width $2\lceil log_q(D) \rceil - 1$.

Proof. Let (T, f, U) be a private key for P as an instance of HFE$^-(q,n,D,a)$. By Theorem 1, one private key of P' has the form (T', f', U') where $f' = \pi \circ f$ and

$$\pi(x) = \sum_{i=0}^{a} b_i x^{q^i}.$$

Therefore,

$$f'(x) = \pi \circ f(x) = \sum_{\substack{i \leq j \\ q^i + q^j \leq D}} \sum_{\ell=0}^{a} b_\ell \alpha_{i,j}^{q^\ell} x^{q^{i+\ell} + q^{j+\ell}}$$

$$= \sum_{\substack{i,j \leq \lceil log_q(D) + a \rceil \\ |i-j| < \lceil log_q(D) \rceil}} f_{i,j} x^{q^i + q^j}$$

Thus there exists one private key of the required form.

Denote by Frob$_i$ the map raising all entries of a vector to the power q^i and let M_b be the linear map $x \mapsto bx$ for $b \in \mathbb{K}$. By the homogeneous case of [11, Theorem 4], for any second private key (T'', f'', U'') of P', we have for some integer $0 \leq k < n$ and for some $a, b \in \mathbb{K}$ that

$$F'' = \text{Frob}_k \circ M_b \circ F' \circ M_a \circ \text{Frob}_{n-k}.$$

It is straightforward to check that the representation of F'' as a quadratic form has the shape of (5) with nonzero entries restricted to $|i - j| < \lceil log_q(D) \rceil$.

Armed with Theorem 2, we are prepared to perform a full key recovery for an instance $P = \Pi \circ T \circ \phi^{-1} \circ f \circ \phi \circ U$ of HFE$^-$. The strategy is simple. By way of Theorem 1, there exists an HFE instance with an equivalent public key. That is, there exists a $P' = T' \circ \phi^{-1} \circ f' \circ \phi \circ U'$ with T', U' invertible, f' of degree bounded by $q^a D$, and where the first $n - a$ public equations in P' form P while the remaining a equations are in the $\mathbb{F}_q$-linear span of P. We perform a key recovery on this instance of HFE via the best known attack, the KS-attack with minors modeling of [11]. Finally, we can recover a central map of degree bound D by way of the following theorem.

Theorem 3. *Let (T, f, U) be an HFE$^-$$(q, n, D, a)$ private key and let (T', f', U') be an equivalent HFE$(q, n, q^a D)$ key. Then a linear map T'' and a quadratic map f'' of degree bound D such that $\Pi \circ T'' \circ \phi^{-1} \circ f'' \circ \phi \circ U' = \Pi \circ T \circ \phi^{-1} \circ f \circ \phi \circ U$ can be recovered by solving two linear systems, the first of dimension a and the second of dimension $\binom{\lceil \log_q(D) \rceil}{2}$.*

Proof. Let (T, f, U) be an HFE$^-$$(q, n, D, a)$ private key and let (T', f', U') be an equivalent HFE$(q, n, q^a D)$ key. Let $\mathbf{F}'$ denote the matrix representation of f' as a quadratic form over $\mathbb{K}$. Finally, let $d = \lceil \log_q(D) \rceil$. By Theorem 2, $\mathbf{F}'$ has the diagonal band shape of width $2d - 1$. From the proof of Theorem 1, there exists a linear map $\pi(x) = \sum_{i=0}^{a} p_i x^{q^i}$, where we may sacrifice monicity and insist $p_0 = 1$ for convenience, and a degree bound D quadratic function f'' such that the composition $\pi(f'') = f'$. Let $\mathbf{F}'' = (f''_{i,j})_{i,j}$ and $\widehat{\pi \mathbf{F}''}$ denote the matrix representations of f'' and $\pi \circ f''$, respectively, as quadratic forms over $\mathbb{K}$. Then we have $\mathbf{F}' = \widehat{\pi \mathbf{F}''}$. The (i, j)th entry of $\widehat{\pi \mathbf{F}''}$ is of the form

$$\sum_{\ell=0}^{a} p_\ell (f''_{i-\ell, j-\ell})^{q^\ell},$$

thus, since $\mathbf{F}'$ is known, we obtain a bilinear system of equations in the unknowns p_i and $f''_{i,j}$.

The insistence that $p_0 = 1$ allows us to recover the values of $f''_{0,j}$ without cost. We then note that due to the fact that $f''_{i,j} = 0$ when $\max\{i, j\} \geq d$, the $(i, i + d - 1)$th coefficients of $\widehat{\pi \mathbf{F}''}$ are $p_i (f''_{0,d-1})^{q^i}$ for $0 \leq i \leq a$. Thus, since $f''_{0,d-1}$ is known, we obtain *a* linear system of equations $f'_{i,i+d-1} = p_i (f''_{0,d-1})^{q^i}$ for $1 \leq i \leq a$ in the unknowns p_i, and can therefore solve for π. Once the values of p_i are known, the system of equations becomes linear in $f''_{i,j}$ for $i > 0$. Solving for the remaining unknown values can be done simply with the upper triangular segment from $(1, 1)$ to $(d - 1, d - 1)$, of size $\binom{d}{2}$.

To illustrate the attack in all of its steps, we have prepared a toy example in Appendix A.

6   Complexity of Attack

In this section we derive a tight complexity estimate of the key recovery attack for HFE$^-$ of Sect. 5. First, we expound upon the relationship between the computational complexity of HFE$^-$ key recovery and that of HFE key recovery.

Theorem 4. *Let $\mathcal{O}$ be an HFE key recovery oracle that can recover a private key for any instance of HFE(q, n, D) in time $t(q, n, D)$. Then an equivalent HFE key for HFE$^-$$(q, n, D, a)$ can be recovered by $\mathcal{O}$ in time $t(q, n, q^a D)$.*

Proof. Let P be the public key for an instance of HFE$^-$$(q, n, D, a)$. Then make the following construction: $P' = P \| \{p_{n-a}, p_{n-a+1} \ldots, p_{n-1}\}$ where $p_i \in Span(P)$. By Theorem 1, P' is an instance of $HFE(q, n, q^a D)$. Thus $\mathcal{O}$ recovers an equivalent HFE key in time $t(q, n, q^a D)$.

Table 1. The degree of regularity of the system arising from minors modeling on HFE$^-(q, n, D, a)$ with $a = 2$, $\lceil log_q(D) \rceil$ as indicated, and n sufficiently large.

$\lceil log_q(D) \rceil$	2	3	4	5	6
d_{reg}	5	6	7	8	9

Thus, the complexity of deriving a key for the associated HFE scheme is bounded by the complexity of the best key recovery algorithm for HFE with a degree bound a factor of q^a larger. By Theorem 3, converting the recovered specially structured HFE$(q, n, q^a D)$ key into an equivalent HFE$^-(q, n, D, a)$ scheme is of complexity on the order of $\lceil log_q(D) \rceil^{2\omega}$. Since this quantity is very small, the key conversion is instantaneous for all practical parameters. Hence the complexity of the entire attack is bounded by $t(q, n, q^a D)$ from Theorem 4.

We can achieve a tight practical bound when specifying the oracle. Using the minors modeling approach to the KS-attack, which is the currently most successful algebraic attack on HFE, we can accurately determine the complexity of HFE$^-$ key recovery. Just as in HFE, the complexity of the attack is dominated by the MinRank calculation.

Proposition 1. *Let $d = \lceil log_q(D) \rceil$. The degree of regularity of the MinRank instance with parameters $(n, a + d, n - a)$ arising from minors modeling on the public key of HFE$^-(q, n, D, a)$ is the degree of the first negative term in the series*

$$H_r(t) = (1 - t)^{(n-a-d)^2 - n + a} \frac{det(\mathbf{A_{a+d}})}{t^{\binom{a+d}{2}}},$$

where $\mathbf{A_{a+d}}$ is the $(a + d) \times (a + d)$ matrix whose (i, j)-th entry is

$$a_{i,j} = \sum_{\ell=0}^{n - max\{i,j\}} \binom{n - i}{\ell} \binom{n - j}{\ell} t^\ell.$$

Proposition 1 follows immediately from [21, Corollary 3], which relies on the genericity conjecture [21, Conjecture 1] which is related to Fröberg's Conjecture, see [22]. With this proposition we can derive the degree of regularity for the MinRank instances for larger systems as well. Focusing on the case in which $a = 2$ we summarize the data in Table 1.

From these data we are prepared to make the following conjecture:

Conjecture 1. *The degree of regularity of the MinRank instance with parameters $(n, a + d, n - a)$ arising from minors modeling on the public key of HFE$^-(q, n, D, a)$ is*

$$d_{reg} = a + d + 1,$$

for all sufficiently large n.

Finally, under the above conjecture, we derive the complexity of our key recovery technique for HFE$^-$.

Theorem 5. *The complexity of key recovery for HFE$^-$(q, n, D, a) using the minors modeling variant of the KS-attack is*

$$\mathcal{O}\left(\binom{n - a + d_{reg}}{d_{reg}}^{\omega}\right) \sim \mathcal{O}\left(\binom{n + \lceil log_q(D) \rceil + 1}{\lceil log_q(D) \rceil + a + 1}^{\omega}\right).$$

7 Experimental Results

We ran a series of experiments with Magma, see [23], on a 3.2 GHz Intel® Xeon™ CPU, testing the attack for a variety of values of q, n and D. In all cases, a valid private key was recovered. Table 2 summarizes some of our results for the asymptotically most costly step, the MinRank attack. The data support our complexity estimate of $\mathcal{O}\left(\binom{n + \lceil log_q(D) \rceil + 1}{\lceil log_q(D) \rceil + a + 1}^{\omega}\right)$.

Table 2. Average time (in ms) for 100 instances of the MinRank attack on HFE$^-$($3, n, 3^2 + 3^2 = 18, a$) for various values of n and a.

a	$n = 8$	$n = 9$	$n = 10$	$n = 11$	$n = 12$
0	37	94	235	575	1269
1	166	535	1572	3653	3374
2	764	1254	6148	26260	97838

8 Conclusion

The HFE$^-$ scheme is a central figure in the development of multivariate cryptography over the last twenty years, inspiring the development of several cryptostystems. Finally, the scheme has revealed a vulnerability significant enough to affect the necessary parameters for the signature algorithm. For example, our attack breaks the HFE$^-$($31, 36, 1922, 2$) primitive in about 2^{52} operations. For an even characteristic example, consider HFE Challenge-2, HFE$^-$($16, 36, 4352, 4$). Our attack breaks HFE Challenge-2 in roughly 2^{67} operations. This efficiency far outperforms any other cryptanalysis and implies that even larger parameters are needed for security. Considering the 2015 suggestion of NIST in [24] that we migrate to 112-bit security, secure parameters for such an HFE$^-$ scheme will be very large, indeed.

Moreover, the use of HFE$^-$ for encryption, in light of this attack, seems very tricky. Presumably the choice of very large and very inefficient instances of HFE$^-$ over very large and very inefficient instances of HFE for encryption is to slightly enhance the efficiency of the scheme by lowering the degree bound. Against our attack, however, lowering $\lceil log_q(D) \rceil$ by x requires a corresponding increase in a by x to achieve *a slightly smaller* security level. This is due to the fact that this transformation preserves the degree of regularity of the MinRank system, but reduces the number of variables by a. Thus, it is reasonable to question the extent of the benefit of using HFE$^-$ over HFE for encryption.

References

1. Shor, P.W.: Polynomial-time algorithms for prime factorization and discrete logarithms on a quantum computer. SIAM J. Sci. Stat. Comp. **26**, 1484 (1997)
2. Group, C.T.: Submission requirements and evaluation criteria for the post-quantum cryptography standardization process. NIST CSRC (2016). http://csrc.nist.gov/groups/ST/post-quantum-crypto/documents/call-forproposals-nal-dec-2016.pdf
3. Matsumoto, T., Imai, H.: Public quadratic polynomial-tuples for efficient signature-verification and message-encryption. In: Barstow, D., et al. (eds.) EUROCRYPT 1988. LNCS, vol. 330, pp. 419–453. Springer, Heidelberg (1988). doi:10.1007/3-540-45961-8_39
4. Patarin, J.: Hidden fields equations (HFE) and isomorphisms of polynomials (IP): two new families of asymmetric algorithms. In: Maurer, U. (ed.) EUROCRYPT 1996. LNCS, vol. 1070, pp. 33–48. Springer, Heidelberg (1996). doi:10.1007/3-540-68339-9_4
5. Tao, C., Diene, A., Tang, S., Ding, J.: Simple matrix scheme for encryption. In: Gaborit, P. (ed.) PQCrypto 2013. LNCS, vol. 7932, pp. 231–242. Springer, Heidelberg (2013). doi:10.1007/978-3-642-38616-9_16
6. Ding, J., Petzoldt, A., Wang, L.: The cubic simple matrix encryption scheme. In: [25], pp. 76–87 (2014)
7. Porras, J., Baena, J., Ding, J.: ZHFE, A new multivariate public key encryption scheme. In: [25], pp. 229–245 (2014)
8. Szepieniec, A., Ding, J., Preneel, B.: Extension field cancellation: a new central trapdoor for multivariate quadratic systems. In: [26], pp. 182–196 (2016)
9. Faugère, J.-C., Joux, A.: Algebraic cryptanalysis of hidden field equation (HFE) cryptosystems using Gröbner bases. In: Boneh, D. (ed.) CRYPTO 2003. LNCS, vol. 2729, pp. 44–60. Springer, Heidelberg (2003). doi:10.1007/978-3-540-45146-4_3
10. Kipnis, A., Shamir, A.: Cryptanalysis of the HFE public key cryptosystem by relinearization. In: Wiener, M. (ed.) CRYPTO 1999. LNCS, vol. 1666, pp. 19–30. Springer, Heidelberg (1999). doi:10.1007/3-540-48405-1_2
11. Bettale, L., Faugère, J., Perret, L.: Cryptanalysis of HFE, multi-HFE and variants for odd and even characteristic. Des. Codes Crypt. **69**, 1–52 (2013)
12. Moody, D., Perlner, R.A., Smith-Tone, D.: An asymptotically optimal structural attack on the ABC multivariate encryption scheme. In: [25], pp. 180–196 (2014)
13. Moody, D., Perlner, R.A., Smith-Tone, D.: Key recovery attack on the cubic ABC simple matrix multivariate encryption scheme. PQCrypto 2017. LNCS, vol. 10346, pp. 272–288. Springer, Cham (2017)
14. Perlner, R.A., Smith-Tone, D.: Security analysis and key modification for ZHFE. In: [26], pp. 197–212 (2016)
15. Perret, L.: Grobner basis techniques in post-quantum cryptography. Presentation - Post-Quantum Cryptography - 7th International Workshop, PQCrypto 2016, Fukuoka, Japan, 24–26 February 2016. https://www.youtube.com/watch?v=0q957wj6w2I
16. Ding, J., Kleinjung, T.: Degree of regularity for HFE-. IACR Cryptology ePrint Archive 2011, p. 570 (2011)
17. Daniels, T., Smith-Tone, D.: Differential properties of the HFE cryptosystem. In: [25], pp. 59–75 (2014)
18. Dubois, V., Fouque, P.-A., Shamir, A., Stern, J.: Practical cryptanalysis of SFLASH. In: Menezes, A. (ed.) CRYPTO 2007. LNCS, vol. 4622, pp. 1–12. Springer, Heidelberg (2007). doi:10.1007/978-3-540-74143-5_1

19. Matsumoto, T., Imai, H.: Public quadratic polynomial-tuples for efficient signature-verification and message-encryption. In: Barstow, D., et al. (eds.) EUROCRYPT 1988. LNCS, vol. 330, pp. 419–453. Springer, Heidelberg (1988). doi:10.1007/3-540-45961-8_39
20. Berlekamp, E.R.: Factoring polynomials over large finite fields. Math. Comput. **24**, 713–735 (1970)
21. Faugère, J., Din, M.S.E., Spaenlehauer, P.: Computing loci of rank defects of linear matrices using Gröbner bases and applications to cryptology. In: Koepf, W., (ed.) Symbolic and Algebraic Computation, International Symposium, ISSAC 2010, Proceedings, Munich, Germany, 25–28 July 2010, pp. 257–264. ACM (2010)
22. Fröberg, R.: An inequality for Hilbert series of graded algebras. Math. Scand. **56**, 117–144 (1985)
23. Bosma, W., Cannon, J., Playoust, C.: The Magma algebra system. I. The user language. J. Symbolic Comput. **24**, 235–265 (1997). Computational algebra and number theory, London (1993)
24. Barker, E., Roginsky, A.: Transitions: recommendation for transitioning the use of cryptographic algorithms and key lengths. NIST Special Publication (2015). http://nvlpubs.nist.gov/nistpubs/SpecialPublications/NIST.SP.800-131Ar1.pdf
25. Mosca, M. (ed.): PQCrypto 2014. LNCS, vol. 8772. Springer, Cham (2014). doi:10.1007/978-3-319-11659-4
26. Takagi, T. (ed.): PQCrypto 2016. LNCS, vol. 9606. Springer, Cham (2016). doi:10.1007/978-3-319-29360-8

A   Toy Example

To illustrate the attack, we present a complete key recovery for a small odd prime field instance of HFE$^-$. We simplify the exposition by considering a homogeneous key.

Let $q = 7$, $n = 8$, $D = 14$ and $a = 2$. We construct the degree n extension $\mathbb{K} = \mathbb{F}_7[x]/\langle x^8 + 4x^3 + 6x^2 + 2x + 3\rangle$ and let $b \in \mathbb{K}$ be a fixed root of this irreducible polynomial.

We randomly select $f : \mathbb{K} \to \mathbb{K}$ of degree D,

$$f(x) = b^{4100689}x^{14} + b^{1093971}x^8 + b^{5273323}x^2,$$

and two invertible linear transformations T and U:

$$T = \begin{bmatrix} 2 & 1 & 0 & 3 & 5 & 0 & 3 & 2 \\ 6 & 2 & 1 & 3 & 4 & 2 & 5 & 1 \\ 0 & 2 & 5 & 1 & 3 & 1 & 4 & 3 \\ 3 & 2 & 6 & 4 & 5 & 3 & 4 & 4 \\ 6 & 4 & 2 & 1 & 0 & 5 & 0 & 0 \\ 0 & 3 & 3 & 6 & 5 & 1 & 1 & 3 \\ 0 & 3 & 0 & 4 & 3 & 6 & 1 & 5 \\ 4 & 3 & 2 & 6 & 1 & 1 & 6 & 3 \end{bmatrix}, \text{ and } U = \begin{bmatrix} 5 & 1 & 4 & 1 & 4 & 2 & 5 & 3 \\ 0 & 6 & 1 & 5 & 3 & 5 & 3 & 2 \\ 3 & 3 & 5 & 0 & 3 & 4 & 2 & 2 \\ 4 & 0 & 5 & 4 & 0 & 6 & 4 & 1 \\ 2 & 6 & 4 & 0 & 0 & 5 & 3 & 5 \\ 0 & 2 & 4 & 0 & 2 & 0 & 6 & 5 \\ 4 & 3 & 0 & 3 & 3 & 2 & 2 & 6 \\ 6 & 2 & 5 & 3 & 5 & 4 & 0 & 0 \end{bmatrix}.$$

Since $b^{1093971}/2 = b^{4937171}$, we have

$$F = \begin{bmatrix} b^{5273323} & b^{4937171} & 0\,0\,0\,0\,0\,0 \\ b^{4937171} & b^{4100689} & 0\,0\,0\,0\,0\,0 \\ 0 & 0 & 0\,0\,0\,0\,0\,0 \\ 0 & 0 & 0\,0\,0\,0\,0\,0 \\ 0 & 0 & 0\,0\,0\,0\,0\,0 \\ 0 & 0 & 0\,0\,0\,0\,0\,0 \\ 0 & 0 & 0\,0\,0\,0\,0\,0 \\ 0 & 0 & 0\,0\,0\,0\,0\,0 \end{bmatrix}.$$

We fix $\Pi : \mathbb{F}_q^8 \to \mathbb{F}_q^6$, the projection onto the first 6 coordinates. Then the public key $P = \Pi \circ T \circ F \circ U$ in matrix form over $\mathbb{F}_q$ is given by:

$$P_0 = \begin{bmatrix} 5\,6\,3\,6\,6\,0\,4\,2 \\ 6\,0\,1\,3\,3\,5\,2\,1 \\ 3\,1\,4\,0\,6\,0\,4\,4 \\ 6\,3\,0\,3\,0\,2\,3\,1 \\ 6\,3\,6\,0\,4\,2\,2\,4 \\ 0\,5\,0\,2\,2\,2\,5\,1 \\ 4\,2\,4\,3\,2\,5\,1\,5 \\ 2\,1\,4\,1\,4\,1\,5\,2 \end{bmatrix}, P_1 = \begin{bmatrix} 1\,6\,1\,5\,4\,2\,2\,2 \\ 6\,5\,4\,4\,0\,1\,6\,2 \\ 1\,4\,3\,5\,6\,2\,1\,1 \\ 5\,4\,5\,2\,2\,3\,1\,5 \\ 4\,0\,6\,2\,2\,1\,2\,4 \\ 2\,1\,2\,3\,1\,6\,2\,6 \\ 2\,6\,1\,1\,2\,2\,5\,6 \\ 2\,2\,1\,5\,4\,6\,6\,2 \end{bmatrix}, P_2 = \begin{bmatrix} 2\,5\,2\,2\,2\,3\,3\,2 \\ 5\,1\,2\,1\,3\,2\,5\,4 \\ 2\,2\,2\,1\,6\,2\,1\,0 \\ 2\,1\,1\,4\,4\,5\,2\,3 \\ 2\,3\,6\,4\,4\,5\,2\,2 \\ 3\,2\,2\,5\,5\,3\,4\,6 \\ 3\,5\,1\,2\,2\,4\,5\,5 \\ 2\,4\,0\,3\,2\,6\,5\,2 \end{bmatrix},$$

$$P_3 = \begin{bmatrix} 1\,6\,6\,4\,0\,0\,3\,4 \\ 6\,2\,5\,5\,4\,5\,5\,6 \\ 6\,5\,4\,6\,3\,6\,4\,2 \\ 4\,5\,6\,4\,5\,2\,4\,5 \\ 0\,4\,3\,5\,6\,3\,6\,0 \\ 0\,5\,6\,2\,3\,2\,4\,1 \\ 3\,5\,4\,4\,6\,4\,4\,4 \\ 4\,6\,2\,5\,0\,1\,4\,0 \end{bmatrix}, P_4 = \begin{bmatrix} 4\,4\,5\,2\,6\,6\,5\,2 \\ 4\,4\,0\,0\,3\,4\,1\,6 \\ 5\,0\,5\,3\,3\,0\,1\,0 \\ 2\,0\,3\,4\,1\,3\,3\,2 \\ 6\,3\,3\,1\,6\,5\,0\,1 \\ 6\,4\,0\,3\,5\,4\,6\,0 \\ 5\,1\,1\,3\,0\,6\,2\,6 \\ 2\,6\,0\,2\,1\,0\,6\,4 \end{bmatrix}, P_5 = \begin{bmatrix} 0\,2\,6\,1\,6\,2\,3\,4 \\ 2\,4\,2\,0\,3\,1\,5\,0 \\ 6\,2\,5\,1\,4\,3\,1\,1 \\ 1\,0\,1\,5\,0\,0\,3\,0 \\ 6\,3\,4\,0\,1\,4\,1\,4 \\ 2\,1\,3\,0\,4\,5\,5\,5 \\ 3\,5\,1\,3\,1\,5\,1\,2 \\ 4\,0\,1\,0\,4\,5\,2\,6 \end{bmatrix}.$$

A.1   Recovering a Related HFE Key

This step in key recovery is a slight adaptation of the program of [11]. First, we recover the related private key of Theorem 2. To do this, we solve the MinRank instance on the above $6 = n - 2$ $n \times n$ matrices with target rank $\lceil \log_q(D) \rceil + a = 2 + 2 = 4$. We may fix one variable to make the ideal generated by the 5×5 minors zero-dimensional. There are $n = 8$ solutions, each of which consists of the Frobenius powers of the coordinates of

$$v = (1, b^{5656746}, b^{3011516}, b^{3024303}, b^{1178564}, b^{1443785}).$$

The combination $L = \sum_{i=0}^{5} v_i P_i$ is now a rank 4 matrix with entries in $\mathbb{K}$.

We next form $\widehat{v}$ from v by appending $a = 2$ random nonzero values from $\mathbb{K}$ to v. Now we compute

$$\phi^{-1} T'^{-1} \circ \phi = \sum_{i=0}^{8} \widehat{v}_i x^{q^i}.$$

Next we let K_i be the left kernel matrix of the $n - i$th Frobenius power of L for $i = 0, 1, \ldots, a + 1$. We then recover a vector w simultaneously in the right kernel of K_i for all i. For this example, each such element is a multiple in $\mathbb{K}$ of

$$w = (b^{4849804}, b^{3264357}, b^{4466027}, b^{638698}, b^{2449742}, b^{4337472}, b^{2752502}, b^{1186132}).$$

Then we may compute

$$\phi^{-1} \circ U \circ \phi = \sum_{i=0}^{8} w_i x^{q^i}.$$

At this point we can recover $\phi^{-1} \circ f' \circ \phi = T'^{-1} \circ P \circ U'^{-1}$, and have a full private key for the related instance HFE(7, 8, 686). The transformations T' and U' and the matrix representation of f' as a quadratic form over $\mathbb{K}$ are given by

$$T' = \begin{bmatrix} 1 & 4 & 4 & 5 & 4 & 5 & 5 & 2 \\ 0 & 6 & 6 & 0 & 4 & 4 & 5 & 5 \\ 0 & 5 & 0 & 4 & 2 & 0 & 0 & 3 \\ 0 & 4 & 4 & 2 & 5 & 6 & 6 & 6 \\ 0 & 3 & 6 & 2 & 5 & 6 & 0 & 0 \\ 0 & 2 & 0 & 4 & 4 & 6 & 2 & 2 \\ 0 & 1 & 5 & 5 & 0 & 5 & 2 & 6 \\ 0 & 3 & 3 & 3 & 6 & 5 & 2 & 2 \end{bmatrix}, U' = \begin{bmatrix} 6 & 2 & 1 & 4 & 4 & 4 & 1 & 6 \\ 1 & 6 & 0 & 2 & 3 & 0 & 4 & 2 \\ 2 & 5 & 3 & 6 & 3 & 3 & 0 & 4 \\ 0 & 5 & 6 & 5 & 4 & 1 & 4 & 2 \\ 6 & 5 & 3 & 5 & 4 & 6 & 3 & 2 \\ 0 & 4 & 6 & 1 & 4 & 0 & 1 & 5 \\ 6 & 0 & 2 & 3 & 6 & 5 & 6 & 3 \\ 5 & 2 & 0 & 4 & 1 & 2 & 4 & 5 \end{bmatrix}$$

$$F' = \begin{bmatrix} b^{416522} & b^{5402526} & 0 & 0 & 0 & 0 & 0 & 0 \\ b^{5402426} & b^{3093518} & b^{5177024} & 0 & 0 & 0 & 0 & 0 \\ 0 & b^{5177024} & b^{5689467} & b^{5706144} & 0 & 0 & 0 & 0 \\ 0 & 0 & b^{5706144} & b^{3464750} & 0 & 0 & 0 & 0 \\ 0 & 0 & 0 & 0 & 0 & 0 & 0 & 0 \\ 0 & 0 & 0 & 0 & 0 & 0 & 0 & 0 \\ 0 & 0 & 0 & 0 & 0 & 0 & 0 & 0 \\ 0 & 0 & 0 & 0 & 0 & 0 & 0 & 0 \end{bmatrix}.$$

A.2 Recovery of Equivalent HFE$^-$ Key

Now we describe the full key recovery given the related HFE key. We know that there exists a degree $D = 14$ map $f''(x) = f''_{0,0} x^2 + 2f''_{0,1} x^8 + f''_{1,1} x^{14}$ with associated quadratic form

$$F'' = \begin{bmatrix} f''_{0,0} & f''_{0,1} & 0 & 0 & 0 & 0 & 0 & 0 \\ f''_{0,1} & f''_{1,1} & 0 & 0 & 0 & 0 & 0 & 0 \\ 0 & 0 & 0 & 0 & 0 & 0 & 0 & 0 \\ 0 & 0 & 0 & 0 & 0 & 0 & 0 & 0 \\ 0 & 0 & 0 & 0 & 0 & 0 & 0 & 0 \\ 0 & 0 & 0 & 0 & 0 & 0 & 0 & 0 \\ 0 & 0 & 0 & 0 & 0 & 0 & 0 & 0 \\ 0 & 0 & 0 & 0 & 0 & 0 & 0 & 0 \end{bmatrix},$$

and a polynomial $\pi(x) = x + p_1 x^7 + p_2 x^{49}$ such that $f' = \pi \circ f''$. Thus we obtain the bilinear system of equations by equating $\mathbf{F}'$ to:

$$\widehat{\pi \mathbf{F}''} = \begin{bmatrix} f''_{0,0} & f''_{0,1} & 0 & 0 & 0\,0\,0\,0 \\ f''_{0,1} & f''_{1,1} + p_1(f''_{0,0})^7 & p_1(f''_{0,1})^7 & 0 & 0\,0\,0\,0 \\ 0 & p_1(f''_{0,1})^7 & p_1(f''_{1,1})^7 + p_2(f''_{0,0})^{49} & p_2(f''_{0,1})^{49} & 0\,0\,0\,0 \\ 0 & 0 & p_2(f''_{0,1})^{49} & p_2(f''_{1,1})^{49} & 0\,0\,0\,0 \\ 0 & 0 & 0 & 0 & 0\,0\,0\,0 \\ 0 & 0 & 0 & 0 & 0\,0\,0\,0 \\ 0 & 0 & 0 & 0 & 0\,0\,0\,0 \\ 0 & 0 & 0 & 0 & 0\,0\,0\,0 \end{bmatrix}.$$

We clearly have the values of $f''_{0,0}$ and $f''_{0,1}$. Then the equations on the highest diagonal are linear in p_i. We obtain $\pi = x + b^{1948142} x^7 + b^{398370} x^{49}$ and continue to solve the now linear system to recover $f''(x) = b^{416522} x^2 + b^{1559326} x^8 + b^{1121420} x^{14}$.

We then obtain the matrix form of π over $\mathbb{F}_q$ and compose with T':

$$\widehat{\pi} = \begin{bmatrix} 2\,6\,6\,0\,2\,2\,5\,5 \\ 6\,3\,5\,3\,1\,4\,5\,0 \\ 5\,2\,6\,0\,6\,6\,6\,1 \\ 1\,1\,3\,6\,4\,1\,1\,6 \\ 5\,6\,2\,4\,6\,6\,1\,6 \\ 5\,3\,1\,5\,0\,1\,0\,4 \\ 3\,2\,1\,3\,3\,1\,3\,5 \\ 4\,2\,1\,1\,1\,4\,4\,2 \end{bmatrix}, T' \circ \widehat{\pi} = \begin{bmatrix} 0\,0\,1\,2\,0\,5\,4\,0 \\ 1\,2\,4\,4\,2\,1\,0\,4 \\ 0\,2\,2\,1\,1\,6\,1\,0 \\ 3\,3\,1\,0\,6\,3\,2\,0 \\ 0\,1\,3\,1\,0\,2\,2\,2 \\ 3\,4\,5\,0\,1\,3\,4\,2 \\ 0\,0\,0\,0\,0\,0\,0\,0 \\ 0\,0\,0\,0\,0\,0\,0\,0 \end{bmatrix}.$$

Replacing the last two rows of $T' \circ \widehat{\pi}$ to make a full rank matrix produces T''. Then the original public key P is equal to $\Pi \circ T'' \circ \phi^{-1} \circ f'' \circ \phi \circ U'$.

Key Recovery Attack for ZHFE

Daniel Cabarcas[1], Daniel Smith-Tone[2,3], and Javier A. Verbel[1(✉)]

[1] Universidad Nacional de Colombia, Sede Medellín, Medellín, Colombia
{dcabarc,javerbelh}@unal.edu.co
[2] University of Louisville, Louisville, USA
daniel-c.smith@louisville.edu, daniel.smith@nist.gov
[3] National Institute of Standards and Technology, Gaithersburg, USA

Abstract. At PQCRYPTO 2014, Porras, Baena and Ding introduced ZHFE, an interesting new technique for multivariate post-quantum encryption. The scheme is a generalization of HFE in which a single low degree polynomial in the central map is replaced by a pair of high degree polynomials with a low degree cubic polynomial contained in the ideal they generate. We present a key recovery attack for ZHFE based on the independent discoveries of the low rank property of ZHFE by Verbel and by Perlner and Smith-Tone. Thus, although the two central maps of ZHFE have high degree, their low rank property makes ZHFE vulnerable to the Kipnis-Shamir (KS) rank attack. We adapt KS attack pioneered by Bettale, Faugère and Perret in application to HFE, and asymptotically break ZHFE.

Keywords: Multivariate public key cryptography · Encryption schemes · ZHFE

1 Introduction

The fundamental problem of solving systems of nonlinear equations is thousands of years old and has been very influential in the development of algebra and number theory. In the realm of cryptography, the task of solving systems of nonlinear, often quadratic, equations is a principal challenge which is relevant in the analysis of many primitives, both in the symmetric and asymmetric setting. This basic problem is the basis of numerous public key schemes, which, in principle, add to the diversity of public key options. The subdiscipline of cryptography concerned with this family of cryptosystems is usually called Multivariate Public Key Cryptography (MPKC).

In addition to the benefit of creating a more robust toolkit of public key primitives, the advent of MPKC offers a potential solution to the problem of securing communication against quantum adversaries, adversaries with access to a sophisticated quantum computer. Since Peter Shor discovered in the mid 90s, see [25], algorithms for factoring and computing discrete logarithms on a quantum computer, a dedicated community has been emmersed in the challenge of securing data from quantum adversaries. In December 2016 the National

© Springer International Publishing AG 2017
T. Lange and T. Takagi (Eds.): PQCrypto 2017, LNCS 10346, pp. 289–308, 2017.
DOI: 10.1007/978-3-319-59879-6_17

Institute of Standards and Technology (NIST) published a call for proposals for post-quantum standards from the international community, putting a figurative spotlight on public key cryptography useful in an era with quantum computing technology. In light of this focus from NIST, the cryptometry and cryptanalysis of post-quantum schemes is not simply an academic matter.

While there are several secure, performant, and well-studied multivariate signature schemes, see [5,9,16,21], for example, there are very few unbroken multivariate encryption schemes in the current cryptonomy. Surprisingly, this general absence of secure and long-lived encryption schemes is primarily due to a small array of extremely effective cryptanalytic techniques.

Broadly, we can categorize attacks on multivariate cryptosystems as either direct algebraic, directly inverting the multivariate public key via Gröbner basis calculation, differential, exploiting some symmetric or invariant structure exhibited by the differential of the private key, or rank, recovering a low rank equivalent private key structure by solving an instance of MinRank, i.e. finding a low rank map in a space of linear maps derived from the public key. These basic tools form the core of modern multivariate cryptanalysis and the algebraic objects related to them are of great interest, not only theoretically, but also for use in cryptometry, see for example, [2,4,6,7,10,11,14,18,22,26].

In the last few years, a few novel techniques for the construction of multivariate encryption schemes have been proposed. The idea is to retain statistical injectivity while relaxing the structure of the public key by doubling the dimension of the codomain. The schemes ABC Simple Matrix, and Cubic Simple Matrix, proposed in [8,28], are based on a large matrix algebra over a finite field. The ZHFE scheme, proposed in [24] (with a significant key generation improvement from [1]) is based on high degree polynomials F and $\tilde{F}$ over an extension field. Decryption in the later is possible, by the existence of a low degree polynomial Ψ in the ideal generated by F and $\tilde{F}$.

The ABC Simple Matrix and Cubic Simple Matrix encryption schemes have been shown vulnerable to differential attacks, see [18,19]. Moreover, in [23] and independently in [29] a trivial upper bound on the Q-rank, or quadratic rank, of ZHFE is provided, further calling into question whether the design strategy of enlarging the dimension of the codomain of the public key is an effective way of achieving multivariate encryption.

On the other hand, in [30], a new security estimate is provided for the original parameters of ZHFE. The paper not only purports to prove the security of ZHFE against the attack methodology of Kipnis and Shamir on low Q-rank schemes, see [17], it also improves the estimate of the degree of regularity of the public key of ZHFE, indicating that the security level of the original parameters is at least 2^{96} instead of the original claim of 2^{80}. In particular, their bound on the complexity of the KS attack on ZHFE is 2^{138}, placing this attack well out of the realm of possibility.

In this paper we revise such claims making the impossible plausible. We detail a full key recovery attack, that works with high probability from the public key alone, and test its effectiveness for small parameters. Our attack adapts the techniques first introduced in [17] and later improved in [2], to recover low rank central maps. Furthermore, we show how to recover a low degree polynomial equivalent to Ψ, that can be used to decrypt.

Our complexity analysis of the attack demonstrates that ZHFE is also asymptotically broken, revealing an error in the analysis of [30]. Specifically, we find that the expected complexity of the Kipnis-Shamir attack on this scheme is $\mathcal{O}\left(n^{(\lceil \log_q(D)\rceil+2)\omega}\right)$, where D is the degree bound in ZHFE and ω is the linear algebra constant, instead of the complexity $\mathcal{O}\left(n^{2(\lceil \log_q(D)\rceil+2)\omega}\right)$ as reported in [30]. Our empirical data from an implementation of this attack support our complexity estimate. This correction in the complexity estimate reveals that the attack is plausible for the original parameters, with a complexity much lower than 2^{138} as claimed in [30].

The article is organized as follows. In the next section, we describe the ZHFE construction and discuss the encryption scheme. In the subsequent section, we outline our attack, describing our notation, our proof of the existence of a low rank equivalent private key, reduce the task of recovering a low rank central polynomial to a MinRank problem, and state how to construct a fully functional equivalent key from it. In the following section, we derive the complexity of our attack, and present our experimental data supporting our complexity bound. A detailed comparison of our analysis to previous MinRank analysis and a toy example are provided in the appendices for space reasons. In the last section, we conclude that ZHFE is broken and discuss the current landscape of multivariate public key encryption.

2   The ZHFE Encryption Scheme

The ZHFE encryption scheme was introduced in [24] based on the idea that a high degree central map may resist cryptanalysis in the style of [2]. The hope of the authors was that having a high degree central map may result in high Q-rank.

Let $\mathbb{F}$ be a finite field of order q. Let $\mathbb{K}$ be a degree n extension of $\mathbb{F}$. Large Roman letters near the end of the alphabet denote indeterminants over $\mathbb{K}$. Small Roman letters near the end of the alphabet denote indeterminants over $\mathbb{F}$. An underlined letter denotes a vector over $\mathbb{F}$, e.g. $\underline{v} = (v_1, \ldots, v_n)$. A small bold letter denotes a vector over $\mathbb{K}$, e.g. $\mathbf{u} = (u_0, \ldots, u_{n-1})$. Small Roman letters near $f, g, h, \ldots$ denote polynomials over $\mathbb{F}$. Large Roman letters near $F, G, H, \ldots$ denote polynomials over $\mathbb{K}$. Large bold letters denote matrices; the field in which coefficients reside will be specified, but may always be considered to be included in $\mathbb{K}$. The function $\mathrm{Frob}_k()$ takes as argument a polynomial or a matrix. For polynomials it returns the polynomial with its coefficient raised to k-th Frobenius power, and for matrices it raises each entry of the matrix to k-th Frobenius power.

Fix an element $y \in \mathbb{K}$ whose orbit under the Frobenius map $y \mapsto y^q$ is of order n. We define the canonical $\mathbb{F}$-vector space isomorphism $\varphi : \mathbb{F}^n \to \mathbb{K}$ defined by $\varphi(\underline{a}) = \sum_{i=0}^{n-1} a_i y^{q^i}$. We further define $\varphi_2 = \varphi \times \varphi$.

The construction of the central map of ZHFE is quite simple. Let F and $\tilde{F}$ high degree HFE polynomials. Without loss of the generality of analysis, we focus on the homogeneous case. One formally declares the following relation over $\mathbb{K}$:

$$\Psi = X\left(\alpha_1 F^{q^0} + \cdots + \alpha_n F^{q^{n-1}} + \beta_1 \tilde{F}^{q^0} + \cdots + \beta_n \tilde{F}^{q^{n-1}}\right)$$
$$+ X^q\left(\alpha_{n+1} F^{q^0} + \cdots + \alpha_{2n} F^{q^{n-1}} + \beta_{n+1}\tilde{F}^{q^0} + \cdots + \beta_{2n}\tilde{F}^{q^{n-1}}\right),$$

where juxtaposition represents multiplication in $\mathbb{K}$ and where Ψ is constrained to have degree less than a bound D. By its construction, Ψ has the form

$$\Psi(X) = \sum_{i=0}^{1} \sum_{\substack{i \leq j \leq k \\ q^i + q^j + q^k \leq D}} a_{i,j,k} X^{q^i + q^j + q^k}.$$

One may then arbitrarily choose the coefficients α_i and β_i and solve the resulting linear system for the unknown coefficients of F and $\tilde{F}$. Even making an arbitrary selection of the coefficients $a_{i,j,k}$ of Ψ, we have an underdefined system and have a large solution space for maps F and $\tilde{F}$.

The private key is given by $\Pi = (G, S, T)$ where $G = (F, \tilde{F})$, $S \in End(\mathbb{F}^n)$ and $T \in End(\mathbb{F}^{2n})$. The public key is constructed via

$$P = T \circ \varphi_2 \circ G \circ \varphi^{-1} \circ S.$$

Encryption is accomplished by simply evaluating P at the plaintext $\underline{x} \in \mathbb{F}^n$. The interesting step in decryption is inverting the central map, G. Notice that if $G(X) = (Y_1, Y_2)$ then the following relation holds:

$$\Psi(X) = X\left(\alpha_1 Y_1 + \alpha_2 Y_1^q + \cdots \alpha_n Y_1^{q^{n-1}} + \beta_1 Y_2 + \cdots + \beta_n Y_2^{q^{n-1}}\right)$$
$$+ X^q\left(\alpha_{n+1} Y_1 + \alpha_{n+2} Y_1^q + \cdots \alpha_{2n} Y_1^{q^{n-1}} + \beta_{n+1} Y_2 + \cdots + \beta_{2n} Y_2^{q^{n-1}}\right).$$

Since this equation is of degree bounded by D, solutions X can be found efficiently using Berlekamp's Algorithm. While it is possible that there may be multiple solutions to this equation, it is very unlikely; furthermore, the public key can be used to determine the actual preimage.

3   Key Recovery Attack for ZHFE

In this section we describe a key recovery attack for ZHFE using the MinRank approach. We first show that with high probability there exist linear combinations of Frobenius powers of the core polynomials F and $\tilde{F}$ of low rank. Then, we show that such linear combinations can be efficiently extracted from the public key. Finally, we describe how to construct a low degree polynomial Ψ' from those low rank polynomials.

3.1 Existence of a Low Rank Equivalent Key

Fix the representation $a \overset{\Phi}{\mapsto} (a, a^q, \ldots, a^{q^{n-1}})$ of $\mathbb{K}$. Then the image $\Phi(\mathbb{K}) = \mathbb{A} = \{(a, a^q, \ldots, a^{q^{n-1}}) : a \in \mathbb{K}\}$ is a one-dimensional $\mathbb{K}$-algebra. We define $\mathbf{M}_n$ by $\mathbf{M}_n = \Phi \circ \varphi$. Using the element y defined in Sect. 2, we recover an explicit representation of $\mathbf{M}_n \in \mathcal{M}_{n \times n}(\mathbb{K})$:

$$\mathbf{M}_n = \begin{pmatrix} 1 & 1 & \cdots & 1 \\ y & y^q & & y^{q^{n-1}} \\ \vdots & & \ddots & \\ y^{n-1} & y^{(n-1)q} & & y^{(n-1)q^{n-1}} \end{pmatrix}.$$

It is well known that the matrix $\mathbf{M}_n$ is invertible. The following proposition is a particular case of Proposition 4 in [2].

Proposition 1. *Let* $M_{2n} = \begin{pmatrix} M_n & 0 \\ 0 & M_n \end{pmatrix}$. *Then the function* $\varphi_2 = \mathbb{K}^2 \to \mathbb{F}^{2n}$ *can be expressed as* $(X, Y) \mapsto (X, X^q, \ldots, X^{q^{n-1}}, Y, Y^q, \ldots, Y^{q^{n-1}}) M_{2n}^{-1}$, *and its inverse* $\varphi_2^{-1} : \mathbb{F}^{2n} \to \mathbb{K}^2$ *as* $(x_1, \ldots, x_{2n}) \mapsto (X_1, X_{n+1})$, *where* $(X_1, \ldots, X_{2n}) = (x_1, \ldots, x_{2n}) M_{2n}$

Two private keys are equivalent if they build the same public key, that is:

Definition 1. *Let* $\Pi = (G, S, T)$, *and* $\Pi' = (G', S', T')$ *be private ZHFE keys. We say that* Π *and* Π' *are equivalent if*

$$T' \circ \varphi_2 \circ G' \circ \varphi^{-1} \circ S' = T \circ \varphi_2 \circ G \circ \varphi^{-1} \circ S.$$

We show that given an instance of ZHFE with public key $P = T \circ (\varphi \times \varphi) \circ (F, \tilde{F}) \circ \varphi^{-1} \circ S$ and private key $\Pi = (G, S, T)$, with high probability, there exists an equivalent key $\Pi' = (G', S', T')$, where the polynomials $G' = (F', \tilde{F}')$ have low rank associated matrices. We only consider linear transformations and homogeneous polynomials. This case can be easily adapted to affine transformations and general HFE polynomial.

It was noted by Perlner and Smith-Tone [23] and independently by Verbel [29] that there exists a linear transformation of ZHFE's core map $G = (F, \tilde{F})$ with low rank associated matrices. Recall that for each ZHFE private key (G, S, T), $G = (F, \tilde{F})$, there are scalars $\alpha_1, \ldots, \alpha_{2n}, \beta_1, \ldots, \beta_{2n}$ in the big field $\mathbb{K}$ such that the function

$$\Psi = X \left(\alpha_1 F^{q^0} + \cdots + \alpha_n F^{q^{n-1}} + \beta_1 \tilde{F}^{q^0} + \cdots + \beta_n \tilde{F}^{q^{n-1}} \right)$$
$$+ X^q \left(\alpha_{n+1} F^{q^0} + \cdots + \alpha_{2n} F^{q^{n-1}} + \beta_{n+1} \tilde{F}^{q^0} + \cdots + \beta_{2n} \tilde{F}^{q^{n-1}} \right),$$

has degree less than a small integer D. Notice that for $s \in \{0, 1\}$ the polynomial,

$$X^{q^s} \left(\alpha_{sn+1} F^{q^0} + \cdots + \alpha_{sn+n} F^{q^{n-1}} + \beta_{sn+1} \tilde{F}^{q^0} + \cdots + \beta_{sn+n} \tilde{F}^{q^{n-1}} \right)$$

has HFE shape and its non-zero monomials with degree greater than D have the form $ZX^{q^0+q^1+q^j}$, with $Z \in \mathbb{K}$ and j an integer. Consequently, in each case the matrix associated with that polynomial has rank less than or equal to $\lceil \log_q D \rceil + 1$ and a particular form of tail shown in A.2.

Let L be the function from $\mathbb{K}^2$ to $\mathbb{K}^2$ given by $L(X,Y) = (L_1(X,Y), L_2(X,Y))$, such that

$$L_1(X,Y) = \sum_{i=1}^n \alpha_i X^{q^{i-1}} + \sum_{i=1}^n \beta_i Y^{q^{i-1}}, \; L_2(X,Y) = \sum_{i=1}^n \alpha_{n+i} X^{q^{i-1}} + \sum_{i=1}^n \beta_{n+i} Y^{q^{i-1}}.$$

Notice that L is a linear transformation of the vector space $\mathbb{K}^2$ over $\mathbb{F}$. From the above observation, the matrices associated with the polynomials in $L \circ G$ are of low rank (less than or equal to $r + 1 = \lceil \log_q D \rceil + 1$). Furthermore, if L is invertible, then $(L \circ G, S, T \circ R)$ is an equivalent key to (G, S, T), with $R = \varphi_2 \circ L^{-1} \circ \varphi_2^{-1}$ and the matrices associated with the core polynomials $L \circ G$ are of low rank. Indeed

$$(T \circ R) \circ \varphi_2 \circ (L \circ G) \circ \varphi^{-1} \circ S = T \circ \varphi_2 \circ (L^{-1} \circ \varphi_2^{-1} \circ \varphi_2 \circ L) \circ G \circ \varphi^{-1} \circ S$$
$$= T \circ \varphi_2 \circ G \circ \varphi^{-1} \circ S.$$

For the above assertion to make sense, the function R must be an invertible linear transformation from $\mathbb{F}^{2n}$ to $\mathbb{F}^{2n}$, and this is only possible if L^{-1} is well defined. It is easy to see that if the coefficients $\alpha_1, \ldots, \alpha_{2n}, \beta_1, \ldots, \beta_{2n}$ are chosen uniformly at random in $\mathbb{K}$, the probability that L is invertible is very high (see [29] for more details).

Were L singular as suggested in [23], a different approach is also possible. Defining the linear transformation $R' = \varphi_2 \circ L \circ \varphi_2^{-1} \circ T^{-1}$ and with the public key $P = T \circ \varphi_2 \circ G \circ \varphi^{-1} \circ S$, we have $R' \circ P = \varphi_2 \circ (L \circ G) \circ \varphi^{-1} \circ S$. Thus, $R' \circ P$ has low rank core polynomials $L \circ G$. We will further consider this case at the end of Sect. 3.2. From now on, we assume L is invertible which happens with high probability for the scheme as originally proposed.

3.2   Finding a Low Rank Core Polynomial

In the previous section we saw that, with high probability a ZHFE public key P has at least one private key (G', S', T') such that the matrices associated with the polynomials in G' have low rank. We now discuss how from the public key P, we can obtain such an equivalent key and how to further exploit it to decrypt without knowing the secret key.

Let P be a ZHFE public key and let us assume there exists an equivalent key (G', S', T'), with low rank core map $G' = (H, \tilde{H})$, so that $P = T' \circ \varphi_2 \circ G' \circ \varphi^{-1} \circ S'$. Let $\mathbf{H}$ and $\tilde{\mathbf{H}}$ be the low rank $(r+1$, with $r = \lceil \log_q D \rceil)$ matrices associated with H and $\tilde{H}$.

Note that the above relation implies that, algebraically, ZHFE is similar to a high degree (but still low rank) version of multi-HFE. Thus, we may suspect that all of the consequences of low rank derived in [2] apply. In fact, our attack on ZHFE, though related, has some subtle but significant distinctions from the cryptanalysis of multi-HFE. The details of the MinRank attack follow.

Using the notation $\mathbf{H}^{*k} \in \mathcal{M}_{n \times n}(\mathbb{K})$ to represent the matrix associated with the k-th Frobenius power of a polynomial H with matrix $\mathbf{H} = [a_{i,j}]$, it is easy to see that the (i,j)-th entry of $\mathbf{H}^{*k}$ is $a_{i-k,j-k}^{q^k}$ (indices are modulo n).

Now we use the property on the matrices $\mathbf{M}_n$ and $\mathbf{M}_{2n}$ to deduce a useful relation between the matrices associated with the low rank polynomials $\mathfrak{H} = \varphi_2 \circ (H, \tilde{H}) \circ \varphi^{-1} = (h_1, \ldots, h_{2n})$ and the matrices $\mathbf{H}^{*k}$'s. The following Lemma follows from Lemma 2 in [2].

Lemma 1. *Let* $(\boldsymbol{H}_1, \ldots, \boldsymbol{H}_{2n}) \in (\mathcal{M}_{n \times n}(\mathbb{F}))^{2n}$ *be the matrices associated with the quadratic polynomials* $\varphi_2 \circ (H, \tilde{H}) \circ \varphi^{-1} = (h_1, \ldots, h_{2n}) \in (\mathbb{F}[x_1, \ldots, x_n])^{2n}$, *i.e.* $h_i = \underline{x} \boldsymbol{H}_i \underline{x}^\top$ *for all* i, $1 \leq i \leq n$. *It holds that*

$$(\boldsymbol{H}_1, \ldots, \boldsymbol{H}_{2n}) =$$

$$(\boldsymbol{M}_n \boldsymbol{H}^{*0} \boldsymbol{M}_n^\top, \ldots, \boldsymbol{M}_n \boldsymbol{H}^{*n-1} \boldsymbol{M}_n^\top, \boldsymbol{M}_n \tilde{\boldsymbol{H}}^{*0} \boldsymbol{M}_n^\top, \ldots, \boldsymbol{M}_n \tilde{\boldsymbol{H}}^{*n-1} \boldsymbol{M}_n^\top) \boldsymbol{M}_{2n}^{-1}$$

Let $(\mathbf{P}_1, \ldots, \mathbf{P}_{2n}) \in (\mathcal{M}_{n \times n}(\mathbb{F}))^{2n}$ be the matrices associated with the quadratic public polynomials. Then,

$$P(\underline{x}) = T(\mathfrak{H}(S(\underline{x})))$$
$$(\underline{x} \mathbf{P}_1 \underline{x}^\top, \ldots, \underline{x} \mathbf{P}_{2n} \underline{x}^\top) = (h_1(\underline{x}\mathbf{S}), \ldots, h_{2n}(\underline{x}\mathbf{S}))\mathbf{T} \tag{1}$$
$$(\underline{x} \mathbf{P}_1 \underline{x}^\top, \ldots, \underline{x} \mathbf{P}_{2n} \underline{x}^\top) = (\underline{x} \mathbf{S} \mathbf{H}_1 \mathbf{S}^\top \underline{x}^\top, \ldots, \underline{x} \mathbf{S} \mathbf{H}_{2n} \mathbf{S}^\top \underline{x}^\top)\mathbf{T},$$

where $\mathbf{S} \in \mathcal{M}_{n \times n}(\mathbb{F})$ and $\mathbf{T} \in \mathcal{M}_{2n \times 2n}(\mathbb{F})$. Using this relation and Lemma 1, we can derive a simultaneous MinRank problem on the matrices associated with the public polynomials, which lie in $\mathcal{M}_{n \times n}(\mathbb{F})$, the solutions of which lie in the extension field $\mathbb{K}$. This result is similar to, but has consequential differences from, [2, Theorem 2].

Theorem 1. *Given the notation above, for any instance of ZHFE, calculating* $U = T^{-1} M_{2n} \in \mathcal{M}_{2n \times 2n}(\mathbb{K})$ *for some equivalent key* (G', S', T') *reduces to solving a MinRank instance with rank* $r + 1$ *and* $k = 2n$ *on the public matrices* $(P_1, \ldots, P_{2n}) \in \mathcal{M}_{n \times n}(\mathbb{F})$. *The solutions of this MinRank instance lie in* $\mathbb{K}^n$.

Proof. By Eq. (1) and Lemma 1,

$$(\mathbf{P}_1, \ldots, \mathbf{P}_{2n})\mathbf{U} =$$

$$(\mathbf{W}\mathbf{H}^{*0}\mathbf{W}^\top, \ldots, \mathbf{W}\mathbf{H}^{*n-1}\mathbf{W}^\top, \mathbf{W}\tilde{\mathbf{H}}^{*0}\mathbf{W}^\top, \ldots, \mathbf{W}\tilde{\mathbf{H}}^{*n-1}\mathbf{W}^\top), \tag{2}$$

where, $\mathbf{W} = \mathbf{S}\mathbf{M}_n \in \mathcal{M}_{n \times n}(\mathbb{K})$ and $\mathbf{U} = \mathbf{T}^{-1}\mathbf{M}_{2n} \in \mathcal{M}_{2n \times 2n}(\mathbb{K})$. If $\mathbf{U} = [u_{i,j}]$, by (2) we get the following equations

$$\sum_{i=0}^{2n-1} u_{i,0}\mathbf{P}_{i+1} = \mathbf{W}\mathbf{H}\mathbf{W}^\top, \text{ and } \sum_{i=0}^{2n-1} u_{i,n}\mathbf{P}_{i+1} = \mathbf{W}\tilde{\mathbf{H}}\mathbf{W}^\top. \tag{3}$$

Since $\mathbf{H}$ has rank $r+1$ and $\mathbf{W}$ is an invertible matrix, the rank of $\mathbf{WHW}^{\top}$ is also $r+1$ (similarly for $\tilde{\mathbf{H}}$). Consequently, the last equation implies that the vectors $\mathbf{u} = (u_{0,0}, \ldots, u_{2n-1,0})$ and $\mathbf{v} = (u_{0,n}, \ldots, u_{2n-1,n})$ are solutions (called the original solutions) for the MinRank problem associated with the $k = 2n$ public symmetric matrices $(\mathbf{P}_1, \ldots, \mathbf{P}_{2n})$ and the integer $r+1$.

An immediate consequence of Theorem 1 is that if we solve that MinRank problem we get the matrix associated with a linear combination of the Frobenius powers of H and $\tilde{H}$ composed with $\varphi^{-1} \circ S$. We must next analyze the space of solutions of the MinRank problem for ZHFE and complete the key extraction.

3.3   Finding Solution from a MinRank Problem

From the previous section we know that there are at least two solution $\mathbf{u}$ and $\mathbf{v}$ (the original solutions) for the MinRank problem associated with ZHFE. In this part we show that every nonzero linear combination of a Frobenius power of the original solutions, i.e., $\alpha \mathbf{u}^{q^k} + \beta \mathbf{v}^{q^k}$, is also solution for the MinRank problem associated with ZHFE.

First of all, note that for each nonzero vector $(a_{00}, a_{10}) \in \mathbb{K} \times \mathbb{K}$ there is another vector $(a_{01}, a_{11}) \in \mathbb{K} \times \mathbb{K}$ such that the matrix $A^* = \begin{bmatrix} a_{00} & a_{10} \\ a_{01} & a_{11} \end{bmatrix}$ is an invertible matrix. If $\mathcal{A}$ is the linear transformation associated with A^*, from [2, Proposition 7] the private key (G'', S'', T'') with

$$G'' = \mathrm{Frob}_k \circ \mathcal{A} \circ (H, \tilde{H}) \circ \mathrm{Frob}_{n-k}$$
$$T'' = T' \circ \varphi_2 \circ \mathcal{A}^{-1} \circ \mathrm{Frob}_{n-k} \circ \varphi_2^{-1}$$
$$S'' = \varphi \circ \mathrm{Frob}_k \circ \varphi^{-1} \circ S',$$

is equivalent to (G', S', T'). From Proposition 8 in [2], we know that the matrix associated with $\varphi_2 \circ \mathcal{A} \circ \varphi_2^{-1}$ is $\mathbf{M}_{2n} \widehat{A^*} \mathbf{M}_{2n}^{-1}$, where $\widehat{A^*} = \left[\begin{array}{c|c} A_{00} & A_{01} \\ \hline A_{10} & A_{11} \end{array} \right]$ and $A_{ij} =$ $\mathrm{Diag}(a_{ij}, a_{ij}^q, \ldots, a_{ij}^{q^{n-1}})$.

Also, from Proposition 10 in [2], the matrix associated with $\varphi_2 \circ \mathrm{Frob}_{n-k} \circ \varphi_2^{-1}$ is $\mathbf{M}_{2n} \mathbf{P}_{2,n-k} \mathbf{M}_{2n}^{-1}$, where $\mathbf{P}_{N,k} = \mathrm{Diag}(\mathbf{R}_{n,k}, \ldots, \mathbf{R}_{n,k})(N \text{ times})$, and $\mathbf{R}_{n,k}$ is the $n \times n$ matrix of a k positions left-rotation. So the matrices associated with $H', \tilde{H}'$ (where $G'' := (H', \tilde{H}')$), T''^{-1} and S'' are respectively

$$\mathbf{H}' = a_{00} \mathrm{Frob}_k(\mathbf{H}) + a_{01} \mathrm{Frob}_k(\tilde{\mathbf{H}}),$$
$$\tilde{\mathbf{H}}' = a_{10} \mathrm{Frob}_k(\mathbf{H}) + a_{11} \mathrm{Frob}_k(\tilde{\mathbf{H}}),$$
$$\mathbf{T}''^{-1} = \mathbf{T}'^{-1} \mathbf{M}_{2n} \mathbf{P}_{2,k} \widehat{A^*} \mathbf{M}_{2n}^{-1},$$
$$\mathbf{S}'' = \mathbf{S}' \mathbf{M}_{2n} \mathbf{P}_{1,k} \mathbf{M}_{2n}^{-1}.$$

As Rank $(\mathbf{H}') \le r+1$, (similarly for $\tilde{\mathbf{H}}'$), from Eq. (3) we get that all columns of $\mathbf{T}''^{-1} \mathbf{M}_{2n}$ are solutions of the MinRank problem associated with the public matrices $(\mathbf{P}_1, \ldots, \mathbf{P}_{2n})$ and $r+1$. Note that $\mathbf{T}''^{-1} \mathbf{M}_{2n} = \mathbf{U} \mathbf{P}_{2,k} \widehat{A^*}$, so the first column of $\mathbf{UP}_{2,k}\widehat{A^*}$, namely $a_{00}\mathbf{u}^{q^k} + a_{10}\mathbf{v}^{q^k}$, is in particular a solution for such MinRank problem. Moreover, we expect most solutions to be of this form because the system is very overdetermined. Our experiments confirm this latest claim (see Sect. 4).

So far we know that there are many equivalent keys like (G'', T'', S''). In the following, we explain how we can find one of them. First, we solve the MinRank problem, and use the vector solution $\mathbf{u}' = a_{00}\mathbf{u}^{q^k} + a_{10}\mathbf{v}^{q^k} = (u'_1, \ldots, u'_{2n})$ to compute $\mathbf{K}' = \ker\left(\sum_{i=0}^{2n-1} u'_i \mathbf{P}_{i+1}\right)$. Next, we find another solution $\mathbf{v}' = (v'_0, \ldots, v'_{2n-1})$ to the MinRank problem by solving the linear system,

$$\mathbf{K}'\left(\sum_{i=0}^{2n-1} x_i \mathbf{P}_{i+1}\right) = \mathbf{0}_{(n-r)\times n}.$$

Again, we expect that the new solution $\mathbf{v}'$ preserves the form as a linear combination of the Frobenius power of the original solutions, i.e., $\mathbf{v}' = a_{01}\mathbf{u}^{q^{k_1}} + a_{11}\mathbf{v}^{q^{k_1}}$. Moreover, we claim that both founded solutions come from the same Frobenius power, i.e., $k_1 = k$. Indeed, if $\mathbf{u} = (u_0, \ldots, u_{2n-1})$ (one of the original solutions) and we set $\mathbf{K} = \ker\left(\sum_{i=0}^{2n-1} u_i \mathbf{P}_{i+1}\right)$, Theorem 6 in [2] give us $\mathbf{K}' = \mathrm{Frob}_k(\mathbf{K}) = \mathrm{Frob}_{k_1}(\mathbf{K})$, hence, if $\mathbf{K}$ has at least one entry in $\mathbb{K} \setminus \mathbb{F}$, then $k_1 = k$.

It is easy to see that the probability that $\mathbf{A} = [a_{ij}]$, $i, j = 0, 1$ is invertible is high. In that case, we already know that the matrix $\mathbf{T}''$, such that, $\mathbf{T}''^{-1} = \mathbf{U}''\mathbf{M}_{2n}^{-1}$, with $\mathbf{U}'' := [\mathbf{u}' | \cdots | \mathbf{u}'^{q^{n-1}} | \mathbf{v}' | \cdots | \mathbf{v}'^{q^{n-1}}]$ is part of an equivalent key. In the rest of this section we show how to find the other two elements of the already fixed equivalent key.

Once an equivalent key has been fixed, our second target is to find $\mathbf{W}'' := \mathbf{S}''\mathbf{M}_n$. Keeping in mind that $\sum_{i=0}^{2n-1} u'_i \mathbf{P}_{i+1} = \mathbf{W}''\mathbf{H}'\mathbf{W}''^{\top}$, and $\mathbf{W}''$ is invertible, we get $\ker(\mathbf{H}') = \mathbf{K}'\mathbf{W}''$. Assuming $\mathbf{H}'$ has the shape

$$\left[\begin{array}{c|c} \mathbf{A} & \mathbf{B}^T \\ \hline \mathbf{B} & \mathbf{0}_{(n-r)\times(n-r)} \end{array}\right],$$

where $\mathbf{A}$ is a full rank $r \times r$ matrix, and $\mathbf{B}$ is a rank one $(n-r) \times r$ matrix, it is easy to see that $\ker(\mathbf{H}')$ is of the form $[\mathbf{0}_{(n-r-1)\times r} \mid \mathbf{C}]$, where $\mathbf{C}$ is a full rank $(n-r-1) \times (n-r)$ matrix. Thus $\mathbf{K}'\mathbf{W}''$ has its first r columns set to zero. In particular, if $\mathbf{w}$ is the first column of $\mathbf{W}''$, then $\mathbf{K}'\mathbf{w} = 0$ leads to a linear system of $n - r - 1$ equations in n variables. Such a system might have spurious solutions that do not correspond to a matrix of the form $\mathbf{W}'' = \mathbf{S}''\mathbf{M}_n$. In order to get more equations we can use Frobenius powers of $\mathbf{K}'$. For $j = 0, \ldots, n-1$,

$$\mathrm{Frob}_j(\mathbf{K}') = \ker\left(\sum_{i=0}^{2n-1} u_{i,j}\mathbf{P}_{i+1}\right) = \ker\left(\mathbf{W}''\mathbf{H}'^{*j}\mathbf{W}''^{\top}\right) = \ker\left(\mathbf{W}''\mathbf{H}'^{*j}\right),$$

hence $\ker(\mathbf{H}'^{*j}) = \mathrm{Frob}_j(\mathbf{K}')\mathbf{W}''$. Moreover, $\ker(\mathbf{H}'^{*j})$ has r zero columns indexed by $j + 1, \ldots, j + r + 1 \mod n$. Therefore, for $j = n - r, \ldots, n - 1$,

$\mathrm{Frob}_j(\mathbf{K}')\mathbf{w} = 0$ and each of these contributes $n - r - 1$ equations in the same n variables. Note that we only need one column of $\mathbf{W}''$ to build the rest of the matrix.

Once $\mathbf{U}''$ and $\mathbf{W}''$ are recovered, we might find the core polynomials by using the following equations

$$\mathbf{H}' = \mathbf{W}''^{-1}\left(\sum_{i=0}^{2n-1} u'_i\mathbf{P}_{i+1}\right)\mathbf{W}''^{-t} \quad \text{and} \quad \tilde{\mathbf{H}}' = \mathbf{W}''^{-1}\left(\sum_{i=0}^{2n-1} v'_i\mathbf{P}_{i+1}\right)\mathbf{W}''^{-t}.$$

At this point, we are not able to decrypt a ciphertext because the recovered core polynomials $\mathbf{H}'$ and $\tilde{\mathbf{H}}'$ would have high degree. But fortunately $\mathbf{H}'$ and $\tilde{\mathbf{H}}'$ satisfy the following equations

$$a_{11}\mathbf{H}' - a_{01}\tilde{\mathbf{H}}' = (a_{11}a_{00} - a_{01}a_{10})\,\mathrm{Frob}_k(\mathbf{H}) = \det(A^*)\,\mathrm{Frob}_k(\mathbf{H}), \quad \text{and}$$

$$-a_{10}\mathbf{H}' + a_{00}\tilde{\mathbf{H}}' = (-a_{01}a_{10} + a_{11}a_{00})\,\mathrm{Frob}_k(\tilde{\mathbf{H}}) = \det(A^*)\,\mathrm{Frob}_k(\tilde{\mathbf{H}}),$$

where the a'_{ij}s are the ones given by the equivalent key already fixed by $\mathbf{T}''$. Consequently, if we would know the a'_{ij}s, we could derive a low degree polynomial (useful to invert H' and $\tilde{H}'$) as shown in the next equation

$$X(a_{11}H' - a_{01}\tilde{H}') + X^q(-a_{10}H' + a_{00}\tilde{H}') =$$

$$\det(A^*)\left[X\,\mathrm{Frob}_k(H) + X^q\,\mathrm{Frob}_k(\tilde{H})\right] =$$

$$\det(A^*)\,\mathrm{Frob}_k(\Psi).$$

Setting $\mathbf{H}' = [h_{ij}]$ and $\tilde{\mathbf{H}}' := [\tilde{h}_{ij}]$, we try to find a_{00}, a_{01}, a_{10}, and a_{11} by first solving the overdetemined systems

$$\begin{bmatrix} h_{1,r+1} & h_{1,r+2} & \cdots & h_{1,n-1} & h_{1,n} \\ \tilde{h}_{1,r+1} & \tilde{h}_{1,r+2} & \cdots & \tilde{h}_{1,n-1} & \tilde{h}_{1,n} \end{bmatrix}^{\mathsf{T}} \begin{bmatrix} x_0 \\ x_1 \end{bmatrix} = \mathbf{0}, \quad \text{and}$$

$$\begin{bmatrix} h_{2,r+1} & h_{2,r+2} & \cdots & h_{2,n-1} & h_{2,n} \\ \tilde{h}_{2,r+1} & \tilde{h}_{2,r+2} & \cdots & \tilde{h}_{2,n-1} & \tilde{h}_{2,n} \end{bmatrix}^{\mathsf{T}} \begin{bmatrix} y_0 \\ y_1 \end{bmatrix} = \mathbf{0}.$$

For n large enough we expect that both solution spaces are one-dimensional, i.e., our expected solution are of the form

$$\begin{bmatrix} x_0 \\ x_1 \end{bmatrix} = \alpha \begin{bmatrix} a_{11} \\ -a_{01} \end{bmatrix}, \quad \begin{bmatrix} y_0 \\ y_1 \end{bmatrix} = \beta \begin{bmatrix} -a_{10} \\ a_{00} \end{bmatrix}.$$

for some $\alpha, \beta \in \mathbb{K}$. Then, we compute

$$\alpha a_{11}H' - \alpha a_{01}\tilde{H}' = \alpha\det(A^*)\,\mathrm{Frob}_k(H), \quad \text{and}$$

$$-\beta a_{10}H' + \beta a_{00}\tilde{H}' = \beta\det(A^*)\,\mathrm{Frob}_k(\tilde{H}),$$

and by solving a linear system, we can get α, β, and our low degree polynomial

$$\Psi'' := \gamma\det(A^*)\,\mathrm{Frob}_k(\Psi), \quad \text{with } \gamma \in \mathbb{K}.$$

If L is singular, as we mentioned at the end of Sect. 3, $R' \circ P$ has low rank, Even thought we do not know R', we know that all columns of $\mathbf{R}'\mathbf{M}_{2n}$ are solutions of the MinRank problem associated with the public matrices $\mathbf{P}_1, \ldots, \mathbf{P}_{2n}$) and $r+1$. So, solving that MinRank problem, we can build an equivalent R' and equivalent private key for $R' \circ P$. Therefore to invert an image of a ciphertext $y = P(x)$ we simply compute $y' = R'(y)$ and use the recovered equivalent private key $R' \circ P$ to find preimages of y'.

4   Experimental Results and Complexity

In order to experimentally verify our attack, we generated ZHFE instances for different parameters and carried out the full attack. We were able to solve the MinRank problem associated with each instance of ZHFE and then we recovered an equivalent key for every solved MinRank problem. We also recovered the low degree polynomial Ψ''. Every time we successfully solved the MinRank problem, we were able to carry out the rest of the attack. This confirms that most solutions for such MinRank problem are of the form $a_{00}\mathbf{u}^{q^k} + a_{10}\mathbf{v}^{q^k}$. For these experiments we used the fast key generation method proposed by Porras et al. [24], so we need to keep in mind that n must be even and the relation $q + 2q^{r-1} < D \leq q^r$ must be satisfied. The experiments were performed using Magma v2.21-1 [3] on a server with a processor Intel(R) Xeon(R) CPU E5-2609 0 @ 2.40 GHz, running Linux CentOS release 6.6.

Table 1. MinRank attack to ZHFE

			Minors		KS	
q	r	n	CPU time [s]	Memory [MB]	CPU time [s]	Memory [MB]
7	2	8	255	4216	280	439
7	2	12	3111	59651	1272	752
7	2	16			5487	2537
17	2	8	277	5034	299	503
17	2	12	3584	68731	1330	817
17	2	16			6157	2800

Table 1 shows the time and memory required for the attacks using either the Kipnis-Shamir modeling or the minors modeling for solving the MinRank. These few data measures suggests that the Kipnis-Shamir modeling is more efficient. The Kipnis-Shamir modeling yields a bilinear system of $n(n - r - 1)$ equations in $(n - r - 1)(r + 1) + 2n$ variables. The Groebner Basis computation on every reported instance with $r = 2$ had a falling degree of 4. It follows that under this modeling the resulting system is not bi-regular as defined in [12]. To the best of our knowledge, there is no tight bound in the literature for the falling degree for the system that arises from the Kipnis-Shamir modeling.

Alternatively, the minors modeling yields a system of $\binom{n}{r+2}^2$ equations in $2n$ variables, whose complexity can be studied as in [2]. Assuming the conjecture about regularity in [13], the Hilbert series of the minors model ideal is

$$HS(t) = (1-t)^{(n-R)^2-2n}\frac{\det A(t)}{t^{\binom{R}{2}}},$$

where R is the target matrix rank (in our case $R = r+1$) and $A(t) = [a_{i,j}(t)]$ is the $R \times R$ matrix defined by $a_{i,j} = \sum_{\ell=0}^{n-\max(i,j)} \binom{n-i}{\ell}\binom{n-j}{\ell}t^\ell$. The degree of regularity is then given by the index of the first negative coefficient of $HS(t)$.

In comparison to the Hilbert Series in the multi-HFE case discussed in [2], the only difference is the $2n$ term in the exponent of $1-t$ (simply n in their case). This does not affect significantly the analysis thereafter. For example, if we define $H_R(t) = (1-t)^{(n-R)^2-2n}\det A(t)$, we can compute

$$H_1(t) = 1 + nt - \frac{1}{4}n(n-4)(n+1)^2t^2 + \mathcal{O}(t^3).$$

Note that the coefficient of 1 and t are positive and that the coefficient of t^2 is negative for $n > 4$. So the degree of regularity is $2 = R+1 = r+2$. Similarly, with $r = 1$, $R = 2$, the degree of regularity is $3 = R+1 = r+2$ for $n > 5.88$, with $r = 2$, $R = 3$, the degree of regularity is 4 for $n > 7.71$, and with $r = 3$, $R = 4$, the degree of regularity is 5 for $n > 9.54$. We thus adventure to claim that the degree of regularity of the minors modeling of the min-rank problem arising from the attack on ZHFE is less or equal to $r+2$ for all cases of interest. It follows that the complexity is $\mathcal{O}\left(\binom{2n+r+2}{r+2}\right)^\omega \sim \mathcal{O}\left(n^{(r+2)\omega}\right)$, where $2 < \omega < 3$ is the linear algebra constant. This is polynomial in n for r constant. Even if r is a logarithmic function of n, the complexity is barely superpolynomial in n.

It is worth spelling out the practical consequences of the above analysis. The expected degree of regularity $r+2$ is also the degree of the minors. Thus, for n large enough, these minors span the whole degree $r+2$ polynomial ring's subspace. Therefore, to solve this system it suffices to gather enough minors and linearly reduce them among themselves. No Groebner basis algorithm is necessary. Moreover, in practice two variables can be fixed to 0 and 1, thus we just need to row-reduce a $\binom{2n+r}{r+2}$ square matrix.

4.1 Comparison to Previous MinRank Analysis

It has been noted in [24,30], for example, that we may consider ZHFE to be a high degree instance of multi-HFE with two branches, i.e. $(X_1, X_2) \mapsto (F_1(X_1), F_2(X_2))$. This intuition is, however, mistaken. If we regard ZHFE as an instance of multi-HFE with $N = 2$, we must impose the relation $X_1 = X_2$, which considerably changes the rank analysis. This fact is missing from the discussion of the KS-attack complexity in both [24], before the low Q-rank property was discovered and in [30] after the low Q-rank property of ZHFE was announced in [23].

Although our complexity analysis is quite similar to the analysis of the multi-HFE attack of [2], there are, however, a few important distinctions that arise and elucidate the disparity between the complexity reported in [30] and our derived complexity. First, in multi-HFE, with N branches, the number of variables over the extension field required to express the quadratic function is N; thus the dimension of matrices required to construct a matrix representation for the central map is Nn, see [2, Proposition 5]. In ZHFE, a single variable is required over the extension field, and thus dimension n matrices are all that is required. Another distinction is that the rank bound for multi-HFE is due to a simultaneous degree bound in each of N variables over the extension field, producing a rank bound on the dimension Nn matrices of NR, where R is the rank, see [2, Lemma 3]. In ZHFE, the rank bound is due to the degree bound on Ψ, and only applies to a single variable; thus the rank bound is merely $R = r + 1$ where $r = \lceil \log_q(D) \rceil$. Moreover, the minrank instance involves twice as many matrices in relation to the dimension of the matrices when compared with the minrank instances arising in multi-HFE. A final important distinction is that after the simultaneous MinRank is solved, an extra step, the derivation of an equivalent Ψ map, is required to recover a full private key.

These distinctions lead to vastly different complexity estimates on the KS-attack with minors modeling for ZHFE. In [30], the complexity of the KS-attack is reported as $\mathcal{O}(n^{2(R+1)\omega})$ citing the complexity estimate in [2]. Indeed, the complexity would be $\mathcal{O}(n^{(2R+1)\omega})$ for the KS-attack on a multi-HFE instance with Q-rank R according to [2, Proposition 13]. We are uncertain where the extra power of ω enters the analysis of [30]. We also note that the asymptotic complexity estimate of $\mathcal{O}\left(n^{(2\lfloor \log_q(D) \rfloor + 8)\omega}\right)$ used to estimate the complexity of the minors approach to the Kipnis-Shamir attack for the parameters ZHFE $(7, 55, 105)$ is not in agreement with the formula $\mathcal{O}\left(n^{(2s+6)\omega}\right)$. This discrepancy is due to the fact that $q + 2q^{s-1} < D \leq q + 2q^s$ implies that $s = \lfloor \log_q(D) \rfloor$ and thus $s \neq \lfloor \log_q(D) \rfloor + 1$, as was claimed.

The reality is that the analysis in [2, Proposition 13] is related but not directly applicable to ZHFE since ZHFE does *not* correspond to multi-HFE with $N = 2$. Using an analysis analogous to the techniques in [2, Sect. 7], we derive above, using rank $R = r + 1$, an estimate of $\mathcal{O}\left(\binom{2n+r+2}{r+2}\right)^\omega$. Using the proposed parameters $q = 7$, $n = 55$, and $D = 105$, which imply $r = 3$, the bottle neck of the attack is to reduce a matrix of size about 150 million over $\mathbb{F}_7$. The precise number of operations this would take depends on several factors. A rough estimate would be between 2^{76} with $\omega = 2.8$ and 2^{81} with $\omega = 3$.

5   Conclusion

We have shown a key recovery attack on the ZHFE encryption scheme. The details provided leave no doubt about its effectiveness. The asymptotic analysis shows the scheme vulnerable even for larger parameters. The rank structure of the central polynomials has proven too difficult to mask. Though the concept of

ZHFE was directly inspired by a desire to avoid rank weakness, ZHFE succumbed to rank weaknesses.

Nevertheless, the idea of an injective multivariate trapdoor function may be viable, though ZHFE is not the correct technique. The landscape for multivariate public key encryption remains fairly bleak at this time. Fundamentally new ideas must emerge to realize the goal of secure multivariate encryption.

Acknowledgements. This work was partially supported by "Fondo Nacional de Financiamiento para la Ciencia, la Tecnología y la Innovación Francisco José de Caldas", Colciencias (Colombia), Project No. 111865842333 and Contract No. 049-2015. We would like to thank Ludovic Perret and John B. Baena for useful discussions. We would also like to thank the reviewers of PQCrypto for some constructive reviews and suggestions.

References

1. Baena, J.B., Cabarcas, D., Escudero, D.E., Porras-Barrera, J., Verbel, J.A.: Efficient ZHFE key generation. In: Takagi [27], pp. 213–232. http://dx.doi.org/10.1007/978-3-319-29360-8_14

2. Bettale, L., Faugère, J.C., Perret, L.: Cryptanalysis of HFE, multi-HFE and variants for odd and even characteristic. Des. Codes Crypt. **69**(1), 1–52 (2013)

3. Bosma, W., Cannon, J., Playoust, C.: The Magma algebra system I. The user language. J. Symbolic Comput. **24**(3–4), 235–265 (1997). http://dx.doi.org/10.1006/jsco.1996.0125, computational algebra and number theory (London, 1993)

4. Cartor, R., Gipson, R., Smith-Tone, D., Vates, J.: On the differential security of the HFEV- signature primitive. In: Takagi [27], pp. 162–181. http://dx.doi.org/10.1007/978-3-319-29360-8_11

5. Chen, M.S., Yang, B.Y., Smith-Tone, D.: PFLASH - secure asymmetric signatures on smart cards. In: Lightweight Cryptography Workshop 2015 (2015). http://csrc.nist.gov/groups/ST/lwc-workshop.2015/papers/session3-smith-tone-paper.pdf

6. Daniels, T., Smith-Tone, D.: Differential properties of the HFE cryptosystem. In: Mosca [20] , pp. 59–75. http://dx.doi.org/10.1007/978-3-319-11659-4_4

7. Ding, J., Hodges, T.J.: Inverting HFE systems is quasi-polynomial for all fields. In: Rogaway, P. (ed.) CRYPTO 2011. LNCS, vol. 6841, pp. 724–742. Springer, Heidelberg (2011). http://dx.doi.org/10.1007/978-3-642-22792-9_41

8. Ding, J., Petzoldt, A., Wang, L.: The cubic simple matrix encryption scheme. In: Mosca [20], pp. 76–87. http://dx.doi.org/10.1007/978-3-319-11659-4_5

9. Ding, J., Schmidt, D.: Rainbow, a new multivariable polynomial signature scheme. In: Ioannidis, J., Keromytis, A., Yung, M. (eds.) ACNS 2005. LNCS, vol. 3531, pp. 164–175. Springer, Heidelberg (2005). http://dx.doi.org/10.1007/11496137_12

10. Ding, J., Yang, B.Y.: Degree of regularity for HFEV and HFEV. In: Gaborit [15], pp. 52–66. http://dx.doi.org/10.1007/978-3-642-38616-9

11. Dubois, V., Gama, N.: The degree of regularity of HFE systems. In: Abe, M. (ed.) ASIACRYPT 2010. LNCS, vol. 6477, pp. 557–576. Springer, Heidelberg (2010). http://dx.doi.org/10.1007/978-3-642-17373-8_32

12. Faugère, J.C., Din, M.S.E., Spaenlehauer, P.J.: Gröbner bases of bihomogeneous ideals generated by polynomials of bidegree: algorithms and complexity. J. Symbolic Comput. **46**(4), 406–437 (2011)

13. Faugère, J.C., El Din, M.S., Spaenlehauer, P.J.: Computing loci of rank defects of linear matrices using gröbner bases and applications to cryptology. In: Proceedings of the 2010 International Symposium on Symbolic and Algebraic Computation, ISSAC 2010, pp. 257–264. ACM, New York (2010)

14. Faugère, J.-C., Gligoroski, D., Perret, L., Samardjiska, S., Thomae, E.: A polynomial-time key-recovery attack on MQQ cryptosystems. In: Katz, J. (ed.) PKC 2015. LNCS, vol. 9020, pp. 150–174. Springer, Heidelberg (2015). http://dx.doi.org/10.1007/978-3-662-46447-2_7

15. Gaborit, P. (ed.): PQCrypto 2013. LNCS, vol. 7932. Springer, Heidelberg (2013). http://dx.doi.org/10.1007/978-3-642-38616-9

16. Kipnis, A., Patarin, J., Goubin, L.: Unbalanced oil and vinegar signature schemes. In: Stern, J. (ed.) EUROCRYPT 1999. LNCS, vol. 1592, pp. 206–222. Springer, Heidelberg (1999). http://dx.doi.org/10.1007/3-540-48910-X_15

17. Kipnis, A., Shamir, A.: Cryptanalysis of the HFE public key cryptosystem by relinearization. In: Wiener, M. (ed.) CRYPTO 1999. LNCS, vol. 1666, pp. 19–30. Springer, Heidelberg (1999). doi:10.1007/3-540-48405-1_2

18. Moody, D., Perlner, R.A., Smith-Tone, D.: An asymptotically optimal structural attack on the ABC multivariate encryption scheme. In: Mosca [20], pp. 180–196. http://dx.doi.org/10.1007/978-3-319-11659-4_11

19. Moody, D., Perlner, R.A., Smith-Tone, D.: Key recovery attack on the cubic ABC simple matrix multivariate encryption scheme. In: Lange, T., Takagi, T. (eds.) PQCrypto 2017. LNCS, vol. 10346, pp. 289–308. Springer, Cham (2017)

20. Mosca, M. (ed.): PQCrypto 2014. LNCS, vol. 8772. Springer, Cham (2014). http://dx.doi.org/10.1007/978-3-319-11659-4

21. Patarin, J., Courtois, N., Goubin, L.: QUARTZ, 128-bit long digital signatures. In: Naccache, D. (ed.) CT-RSA 2001. LNCS, vol. 2020, pp. 282–297. Springer, Heidelberg (2001). http://dx.doi.org/10.1007/3-540-45353-9_21

22. Perlner, R.A., Smith-Tone, D.: A classification of differential invariants for multivariate post-quantum cryptosystems. In: Gaborit [15], pp. 165–173. http://dx.doi.org/10.1007/978-3-642-38616-9

23. Perlner, R.A., Smith-Tone, D.: Security analysis and key modification for ZHFE. In: Takagi[27], pp. 197–212. http://dx.doi.org/10.1007/978-3-319-29360-8_13

24. Porras, J., Baena, J., Ding, J.: ZHFE, a new multivariate public key encryption scheme. In: Mosca, M. (ed.) PQCrypto 2014. LNCS, vol. 8772, pp. 229–245. Springer, Cham (2014). doi:10.1007/978-3-319-11659-4_14

25. Shor, P.W.: Polynomial-time algorithms for prime factorization and discrete logarithms on a quantum computer. SIAM Rev. **41**(2), 303–332 (1999). (electronic)

26. Smith-Tone, D.: On the differential security of multivariate public key cryptosystems. In: Yang, B.-Y. (ed.) PQCrypto 2011. LNCS, vol. 7071, pp. 130–142. Springer, Heidelberg (2011). doi:10.1007/978-3-642-25405-5_9

27. Takagi, T. (ed.): PQCrypto 2016. LNCS, vol. 9606. Springer, Cham (2016). http://dx.doi.org/10.1007/978-3-319-29360-8

28. Tao, C., Diene, A., Tang, S., Ding, J.: Simple matrix scheme for encryption. In: Gaborit [15], pp. 231–242. http://dx.doi.org/10.1007/978-3-642-38616-9

29. Verbel, J.A.: Efficiency and security of ZHFE. Master's thesis, Universidad Nacional de Colombia, Sede Medellín (2016)

30. Zhang, W., Tan, C.H.: On the security and key generation of the ZHFE encryption scheme. In: Ogawa, K., Yoshioka, K. (eds.) IWSEC 2016. LNCS, vol. 9836, pp. 289–304. Springer, Cham (2016). doi:10.1007/978-3-319-44524-3_17

A   Appendix

A.1   Toy Example

We provide a small example of the MinRank attack for ZHFE with parameters $n = 8$, $q = 3$ and $D = 9$. The small field is $\mathbb{F} = \mathbb{F}_q$, the extension field is $\mathbb{K} = \mathbb{F}/\langle g(y)\rangle$, where $g(y) = y^8 + 2y^5 + y^4 + 2y^2 + 2y + 2 \in \mathbb{F}[y]$, and b is a primitive root of the irreducible polynomial $g(y)$.

For ease of presentation, we consider a homogeneous public key and linear transformations. An easy adaptation for the general case can be done following the ideas expressed in [2].

The matrices associated with our private key $\left((F,\tilde{F}), S, T\right)$ are

$$\mathbf{F} = \begin{pmatrix} b^{827} & b^{4873} & b^{3298} & b^{211} & b^{1824} & b^{5374} & b^{6155} & b^{2404} \\ b^{4873} & b^{5172} & b^{1526} & b^{1317} & b^{2727} & b^{1863} & b^{3546} & b^{5876} \\ b^{3298} & b^{1526} & b^{1842} & b^{3540} & b^{2647} & b^{2349} & b^{4599} & b^{2987} \\ b^{211} & b^{1317} & b^{3540} & b^{5242} & b^{5758} & b^{4705} & b^{2663} & b^{4097} \\ b^{1824} & b^{2727} & b^{2647} & b^{5758} & b^{4629} & b^{5792} & b^{5196} & b^{666} \\ b^{5374} & b^{1863} & b^{2349} & b^{4705} & b^{5792} & b^{6318} & b^{4937} & b^{6150} \\ b^{6155} & b^{3546} & b^{4599} & b^{2663} & b^{5196} & b^{4937} & b^{2275} & b^{1436} \\ b^{2404} & b^{5876} & b^{2987} & b^{4097} & b^{666} & b^{6150} & b^{1436} & b^{4721} \end{pmatrix}, \mathbf{S} = \begin{pmatrix} 0 & 0 & 2 & 2 & 2 & 2 & 1 & 2 \\ 0 & 1 & 0 & 1 & 0 & 1 & 0 & 1 \\ 2 & 1 & 1 & 0 & 0 & 2 & 2 & 2 \\ 1 & 2 & 2 & 1 & 1 & 1 & 0 & 2 \\ 0 & 2 & 1 & 2 & 0 & 1 & 0 & 2 \\ 0 & 1 & 1 & 0 & 1 & 2 & 2 & 0 \\ 0 & 1 & 2 & 1 & 2 & 1 & 0 & 0 \\ 2 & 1 & 0 & 2 & 2 & 1 & 0 & 2 \end{pmatrix}$$

$$\tilde{\mathbf{F}} = \begin{pmatrix} b^{5574} & b^{2257} & b^{4540} & b^{880} & b^{2073} & b^{4932} & b^{3441} & b^{5482} \\ b^{2257} & b^{301} & b^{5824} & b^{5391} & b^{1155} & b^{1678} & b^{572} & b^{3108} \\ b^{4540} & b^{5824} & b^{5208} & b^{3763} & b^{6074} & b^{2097} & b^{3074} & b^{139} \\ b^{880} & b^{5391} & b^{3763} & b^{125} & b^{2055} & b^{1763} & b^{1168} & b^{4512} \\ b^{2073} & b^{1155} & b^{6074} & b^{2055} & b^{5080} & b^{1720} & b^{5820} & b^{5832} \\ b^{4932} & b^{1678} & b^{2097} & b^{1763} & b^{1720} & b^{5850} & b^{1822} & b^{5443} \\ b^{3441} & b^{572} & b^{3074} & b^{1168} & b^{5820} & b^{1822} & b^{2857} & b^{939} \\ b^{5482} & b^{3108} & b^{139} & b^{4512} & b^{5832} & b^{5443} & b^{939} & b^{1665} \end{pmatrix}$$

and $\mathbf{T} = [\mathbf{T}_1 | \mathbf{T}_2]$, where

$$\mathbf{T1} = \begin{pmatrix} 0 & 2 & 2 & 1 & 0 & 1 & 0 & 1 & 1 & 0 & 1 & 1 & 0 & 1 & 1 & 1 \\ 2 & 2 & 0 & 2 & 2 & 1 & 2 & 2 & 2 & 2 & 0 & 1 & 2 & 2 & 0 & 0 \\ 2 & 0 & 2 & 0 & 2 & 0 & 2 & 2 & 2 & 1 & 1 & 0 & 1 & 2 & 1 & 0 \\ 1 & 1 & 0 & 0 & 0 & 1 & 1 & 1 & 1 & 1 & 1 & 0 & 1 & 0 & 1 & 1 \\ 1 & 0 & 1 & 2 & 2 & 1 & 2 & 0 & 2 & 2 & 1 & 0 & 0 & 0 & 1 & 2 \\ 0 & 1 & 1 & 1 & 2 & 1 & 2 & 0 & 0 & 0 & 1 & 2 & 1 & 1 & 0 & 0 \\ 0 & 1 & 2 & 2 & 1 & 0 & 2 & 2 & 1 & 2 & 2 & 1 & 0 & 2 & 2 & 1 \\ 2 & 0 & 0 & 1 & 2 & 2 & 2 & 2 & 2 & 1 & 0 & 1 & 1 & 0 & 1 \end{pmatrix}^{\mathsf{T}}, \mathbf{T2} = \begin{pmatrix} 2 & 1 & 0 & 2 & 0 & 0 & 1 & 1 & 0 & 1 & 1 & 0 & 0 & 0 & 1 & 0 \\ 2 & 0 & 0 & 0 & 1 & 0 & 2 & 2 & 1 & 1 & 1 & 1 & 1 & 2 & 0 & 0 \\ 1 & 2 & 2 & 2 & 0 & 0 & 2 & 0 & 0 & 2 & 1 & 1 & 1 & 1 & 2 \\ 2 & 0 & 1 & 1 & 1 & 2 & 1 & 2 & 1 & 1 & 2 & 2 & 1 & 2 & 0 & 1 \\ 0 & 1 & 1 & 1 & 1 & 0 & 0 & 1 & 0 & 0 & 1 & 2 & 2 & 0 & 1 & 0 \\ 0 & 1 & 0 & 1 & 2 & 2 & 0 & 1 & 0 & 0 & 2 & 2 & 0 & 1 & 0 & 1 \\ 1 & 2 & 0 & 0 & 2 & 0 & 0 & 0 & 0 & 1 & 1 & 0 & 2 & 0 & 0 & 1 \\ 0 & 2 & 0 & 0 & 2 & 0 & 2 & 2 & 2 & 0 & 2 & 0 & 2 & 1 & 2 & 0 \end{pmatrix}^{\mathsf{T}}$$

This private key gives us a public key represented by the matrices $\mathbf{P}_1, \mathbf{P}_2, \ldots, \mathbf{P}_{2n}$.

$$
\mathbf{P}_1 = \begin{pmatrix} 0&0&2&0&2&1&0&2 \\ 0&2&1&2&2&2&0&1 \\ 2&1&0&1&0&0&0&1 \\ 0&2&1&1&2&2&1&2 \\ 2&2&0&2&0&2&2&0 \\ 1&2&0&2&2&0&0&2 \\ 0&0&0&1&2&0&0&0 \\ 2&1&1&2&0&2&0&0 \end{pmatrix}, \mathbf{P}_2 = \begin{pmatrix} 2&1&0&1&1&0&2&0 \\ 1&0&2&0&0&0&0&2 \\ 0&2&0&2&0&0&2&1 \\ 1&0&2&1&1&0&0&1 \\ 1&0&0&1&1&0&0&1 \\ 0&0&0&0&0&2&1&0 \\ 2&0&2&0&0&1&0&1 \\ 0&2&1&1&1&0&1&2 \end{pmatrix}, \mathbf{P}_3 = \begin{pmatrix} 1&0&0&0&2&1&1&1 \\ 0&2&1&2&1&1&2&1 \\ 0&1&1&2&0&1&1&2 \\ 0&2&2&1&2&2&1&1 \\ 2&1&0&2&2&0&0&2 \\ 1&1&1&2&0&0&1&0 \\ 1&2&1&1&0&1&2&2 \\ 1&1&2&1&2&0&2&0 \end{pmatrix}, \mathbf{P}_4 = \begin{pmatrix} 0&1&2&2&2&1&1&0 \\ 1&0&0&2&0&2&0&2 \\ 2&0&1&0&2&0&2&2 \\ 2&2&0&0&2&2&2&2 \\ 2&0&2&2&0&2&1&0 \\ 1&2&0&2&2&0&1&0 \\ 1&0&2&2&1&1&1&0 \\ 0&2&2&2&0&0&0&1 \end{pmatrix},
$$

$$
\mathbf{P}_5 = \begin{pmatrix} 2&0&1&1&1&0&2&1 \\ 0&1&2&0&0&0&2&1 \\ 1&2&2&0&0&0&1&0 \\ 1&0&0&1&2&1&0&0 \\ 1&0&0&2&1&1&2&1 \\ 0&0&0&1&1&0&0&1 \\ 2&2&1&0&2&0&0&2 \\ 1&1&0&0&1&1&2&0 \end{pmatrix}, \mathbf{P}_6 = \begin{pmatrix} 0&1&1&0&0&2&1&1 \\ 1&2&2&2&2&2&1&2 \\ 1&2&0&1&1&2&0&2 \\ 0&2&1&0&2&1&2&0 \\ 0&2&1&2&0&2&0&1 \\ 2&2&2&1&2&2&1&2 \\ 1&1&0&2&0&1&2&0 \\ 1&2&2&0&1&2&0&2 \end{pmatrix}, \mathbf{P}_7 = \begin{pmatrix} 0&1&2&2&1&2&2&0 \\ 1&1&2&2&0&1&0&0 \\ 2&2&0&1&2&1&1&0 \\ 2&2&1&1&0&1&1&2 \\ 1&0&2&0&0&2&2&2 \\ 2&1&1&1&2&0&0&1 \\ 2&0&1&1&2&0&0&0 \\ 0&0&0&2&2&1&0&0 \end{pmatrix}, \mathbf{P}_8 = \begin{pmatrix} 1&2&0&0&0&2&0&2 \\ 2&1&0&2&1&1&0&1 \\ 0&0&2&1&0&1&1&1 \\ 0&2&1&0&1&1&1&0 \\ 0&1&0&1&1&1&0&1 \\ 2&1&1&0&1&2&2&1 \\ 0&0&1&0&0&2&2&1 \\ 2&1&1&1&1&1&1&0 \end{pmatrix},
$$

$$
\mathbf{P}_9 = \begin{pmatrix} 2&0&2&1&2&0&1&0 \\ 0&0&0&1&1&2&1&2 \\ 2&0&1&2&1&2&2&2 \\ 1&1&2&1&2&2&2&0 \\ 2&1&1&2&0&1&0&1 \\ 0&2&0&2&1&2&2&1 \\ 1&1&2&2&0&2&0&2 \\ 0&2&2&0&1&1&2&2 \end{pmatrix}, \mathbf{P}_{10} = \begin{pmatrix} 0&2&0&0&0&0&1&1 \\ 2&2&2&2&0&1&1&1 \\ 0&2&1&2&2&0&1&0 \\ 0&2&2&1&1&1&0&1 \\ 0&0&2&1&1&0&1&1 \\ 0&1&0&1&0&1&1&0 \\ 1&1&1&0&1&1&2&0 \\ 1&1&0&1&1&0&0&1 \end{pmatrix}, \mathbf{P}_{11} = \begin{pmatrix} 0&0&0&2&2&2&0&1 \\ 0&0&2&0&1&2&0&1 \\ 0&2&2&0&1&2&2&1 \\ 2&0&0&0&2&2&1&0 \\ 2&1&1&2&2&1&1&1 \\ 2&2&2&1&0&0&0&1 \\ 0&0&2&1&1&0&1&2 \\ 1&1&1&0&1&1&2&2 \end{pmatrix}, \mathbf{P}_{12} = \begin{pmatrix} 0&2&1&0&2&1&1&0 \\ 2&1&0&1&2&1&1&2 \\ 1&0&0&1&0&0&1&2 \\ 0&1&1&2&2&2&1&1 \\ 2&2&0&2&2&0&2&2 \\ 1&1&0&2&0&2&0&2 \\ 1&1&1&1&2&2&0&2 \\ 0&2&2&1&2&2&2&0 \end{pmatrix},
$$

$$
\mathbf{P}_{13} = \begin{pmatrix} 2&0&0&0&2&1&1&0 \\ 0&1&1&2&0&1&1&0 \\ 0&1&1&0&2&1&2&1 \\ 0&2&0&2&1&1&2&2 \\ 2&0&2&1&2&0&2&2 \\ 1&1&1&1&0&2&1&2 \\ 1&1&2&2&2&1&1&0 \\ 0&0&1&2&2&2&0&0 \end{pmatrix}, \mathbf{P}_{14} = \begin{pmatrix} 1&0&0&1&0&2&1&0 \\ 0&0&2&2&0&1&0&0 \\ 0&2&0&2&1&0&1&1 \\ 1&2&2&2&0&1&0&2 \\ 0&0&1&0&0&0&0&2 \\ 2&1&0&1&0&2&0&1 \\ 1&0&1&0&0&0&1&2 \\ 0&0&1&2&2&1&2&0 \end{pmatrix}, \mathbf{P}_{15} = \begin{pmatrix} 1&0&2&2&2&1&1&0 \\ 0&2&2&0&2&1&0&2 \\ 2&2&2&1&2&1&2&0 \\ 2&0&1&1&2&1&2&0 \\ 2&2&2&2&0&0&2&0 \\ 1&1&1&1&0&2&0&2 \\ 1&0&2&2&2&0&1&2 \\ 0&2&0&0&0&2&2&0 \end{pmatrix}, \mathbf{P}_{16} = \begin{pmatrix} 1&1&0&0&1&1&0&0 \\ 1&1&2&1&0&1&0&1 \\ 0&2&1&2&1&0&1&2 \\ 0&1&2&2&0&2&1&0 \\ 1&0&1&0&1&0&0&0 \\ 1&1&0&2&0&2&1&0 \\ 0&0&1&1&0&1&2&1 \\ 0&1&2&0&0&0&1&1 \end{pmatrix}.
$$

Recovering T: The first and harder step to recover an equivalent linear transformation T is to solve the MinRank problem associated with the public matrices $\mathbf{P}_1, \ldots, \mathbf{P}_{16}$ and $r + 1$, with $r = \lceil \log_q D \rceil = 2$. Using the minors modeling, we construct a degree 4 polynomial system in $2n$ variables. We can fix the two first coordinates of the vector $\mathbf{u}'' = (u'_0, u'_1, \ldots, u'_7)$ as 1 and 0 respectively. A solution for this system is

$$
\mathbf{u}' = (1, 0, b^{5854}, b^{4879}, b^{2843}, b^{2676}, b^{6279}, b^{1845}, b^{6102}, b^{5619}, b^{5448}, b^{6022}, b^{1721}, b^{2632}, b^{3738}, b^{6170}).
$$

Next we compute

$$
\mathbf{K}' = \ker \left(\sum_{i=0}^{2n-1} u'_i \mathbf{P}_{i+1} \right) = \begin{pmatrix} 1&0&0&0&0&b^{6158}&b^{1567}&b^{6415} \\ 0&1&0&0&0&b^{3943}&b^{4591}&b^{95} \\ 0&0&1&0&0&b^{4461}&b^{4216}&b^{3027} \\ 0&0&0&1&0&b^{3577}&b^{5899}&b^{1096} \\ 0&0&0&0&1&b^{6554}&b^{4266}&b^{907} \end{pmatrix},
$$

and by solving the linear system

$$
\mathbf{K}' \left(\sum_{i=0}^{2n-1} x_i \mathbf{P}_{i+1} \right) = \mathbf{0}_{(n-r) \times n},
$$

we get another solution

$$\mathbf{v}' := (b^{1519}, b^{4750}, b^{4454}, b^{3326}, b^{2077}, b^{4519}, b^{3525}, b^{1978}, b^{5511}, b^{315}, b^{715}, b^{4722}, b^{5003}, b^{1895}, b^{2665}, b^{4505}).$$

Once we have two solution for the MinRank problem we compute

$$\mathbf{T}''^{-1} = \mathbf{U}''\mathbf{M}_{16}^{-1},$$

with $\mathbf{U}'' := [\mathbf{u}'|\cdots|\mathbf{u}'^{q^{n-1}}|\mathbf{v}'|\cdots|\mathbf{v}'^{q^{n-1}}]$, invert the output matrix to obtain $\mathbf{T}'' = [\mathbf{T}_1''|\mathbf{T}_2'']$, with

$$\mathbf{T}_1'' = \begin{pmatrix} 2\,0\,2\,1\,1\,0\,1\,0 \\ 1\,2\,2\,2\,0\,2\,0\,0 \\ 1\,1\,0\,2\,0\,0\,0\,2 \\ 2\,2\,1\,2\,0\,1\,0\,0 \\ 0\,2\,2\,0\,2\,0\,0\,0 \\ 2\,1\,0\,1\,1\,2\,0\,0 \\ 2\,1\,1\,1\,1\,1\,0\,0 \\ 2\,2\,1\,0\,2\,1\,0\,1 \\ 0\,0\,2\,0\,0\,1\,2\,0 \\ 1\,2\,2\,0\,0\,0\,0\,1 \\ 0\,1\,1\,2\,2\,2\,2\,2 \\ 2\,2\,0\,1\,0\,1\,2\,1 \\ 1\,0\,0\,1\,1\,0\,0\,1 \\ 1\,2\,2\,1\,1\,2\,1\,0 \\ 1\,0\,0\,1\,1\,0\,1\,0 \\ 0\,0\,2\,0\,2\,2\,1\,1 \end{pmatrix}, \mathbf{T}_2'' = \begin{pmatrix} 1\,1\,0\,0\,2\,1\,1\,1 \\ 1\,0\,0\,1\,0\,2\,1\,1 \\ 2\,1\,1\,2\,2\,1\,1\,0 \\ 1\,2\,2\,1\,2\,2\,0\,0 \\ 0\,1\,1\,2\,0\,1\,2\,1 \\ 2\,0\,2\,1\,2\,0\,1\,2 \\ 2\,0\,2\,2\,2\,0\,2\,1 \\ 2\,2\,1\,0\,2\,2\,0\,1 \\ 2\,1\,0\,1\,2\,1\,1\,0 \\ 0\,1\,2\,1\,0\,2\,1\,1 \\ 2\,2\,2\,1\,1\,0\,1\,2 \\ 0\,0\,0\,0\,1\,2\,2\,0 \\ 0\,2\,0\,0\,2\,1\,1\,0 \\ 0\,1\,2\,0\,1\,1\,2\,1 \\ 1\,2\,0\,2\,0\,1\,2\,1 \\ 1\,2\,0\,0\,0\,1\,1\,0 \end{pmatrix}$$

Recovering S: To find $\mathbf{W}'' := \mathbf{S}''\mathbf{M}_n = [\mathbf{w}''|\mathbf{w}''^q|\cdots|\mathbf{w}''^{q^{n-1}}]$, we find its first column $\mathbf{w}''$, which satisfy $\text{Frob}_{j+1}(\mathbf{K}')\mathbf{w}'' = \mathbf{0}$, for $j = n - r, \ldots, n - 1 = 7, 8$.

By solving the overdetermined system

$$\begin{pmatrix} \mathbf{K}' \\ \text{Frob}_7(\mathbf{K}') \end{pmatrix} \mathbf{w}'' = \begin{pmatrix} 1\,0\,0\,0\,0\; b^{6158}\; b^{1567}\; b^{6415} \\ 0\,1\,0\,0\,0\; b^{3943}\; b^{4591}\; b^{95} \\ 0\,0\,1\,0\,0\; b^{4461}\; b^{4216}\; b^{3027} \\ 0\,0\,0\,1\,0\; b^{3577}\; b^{5899}\; b^{1096} \\ 0\,0\,0\,0\,1\; b^{6554}\; b^{4266}\; b^{907} \\ 1\,0\,0\,0\,0\; b^{6426}\; b^{2709}\; b^{4325} \\ 0\,1\,0\,0\,0\; b^{3501}\; b^{3717}\; b^{4405} \\ 0\,0\,1\,0\,0\; b^{1487}\; b^{3592}\; b^{1009} \\ 0\,0\,0\,1\,0\; b^{3379}\; b^{4153}\; b^{2552} \\ 0\,0\,0\,0\,1\; b^{6558}\; b^{1422}\; b^{2489} \end{pmatrix} \mathbf{w}'' = \mathbf{0},$$

we obtain $\mathbf{w}'' = (b^{929}, b^{2174}, b^{2323}, b^{4231}, b^{3677}, b^{6313}, b^{2372}, b^{3245})$. We then compute

$$
\mathbf{W}'' = \begin{pmatrix}
b^{929} & b^{2787} & b^{1801} & b^{5403} & b^{3089} & b^{2707} & b^{1561} & b^{4683} \\
b^{2174} & b^{6522} & b^{6446} & b^{6218} & b^{5534} & b^{3482} & b^{3886} & b^{5098} \\
b^{2323} & b^{409} & b^{1227} & b^{3681} & b^{4483} & b^{329} & b^{987} & b^{2961} \\
b^{4231} & b^{6133} & b^{5279} & b^{2717} & b^{1591} & b^{4773} & b^{1199} & b^{3597} \\
b^{3677} & b^{4471} & b^{293} & b^{879} & b^{2637} & b^{1351} & b^{4053} & b^{5599} \\
b^{6313} & b^{5819} & b^{4337} & b^{6451} & b^{6233} & b^{5579} & b^{3617} & b^{4291} \\
b^{2372} & b^{556} & b^{1668} & b^{5004} & b^{1892} & b^{5676} & b^{3908} & b^{5164} \\
b^{3245} & b^{3175} & b^{2965} & b^{2335} & b^{445} & b^{1335} & b^{4005} & b^{5455}
\end{pmatrix},
$$

and

$$
\mathbf{S}'' = \mathbf{W}''\mathbf{M}_8^{-1} = \begin{pmatrix}
2 & 2 & 2 & 1 & 2 & 0 & 0 & 2 \\
1 & 2 & 1 & 1 & 2 & 0 & 1 & 2 \\
2 & 1 & 0 & 2 & 0 & 2 & 1 & 0 \\
2 & 2 & 1 & 1 & 2 & 1 & 2 & 2 \\
0 & 2 & 1 & 2 & 0 & 0 & 0 & 2 \\
1 & 0 & 1 & 0 & 1 & 1 & 1 & 2 \\
1 & 0 & 2 & 0 & 1 & 2 & 2 & 0 \\
0 & 1 & 1 & 0 & 2 & 2 & 0 & 1
\end{pmatrix}
$$

Recovering Core Polynomials: To find our equivalent core polynomials H' and $\tilde{H}'$ we calculate $\mathbf{H}' = \mathbf{W}''^{-1}\left(\sum_{i=0}^{7} u'_i \mathbf{P}_{i+1}\right)\mathbf{W}''^{-t}$ as well as the value of $\tilde{\mathbf{H}}' = \mathbf{W}''^{-1}\left(\sum_{i=0}^{7} v'_i \mathbf{P}_{i+1}\right)\mathbf{W}''^{-t}$ and obtain

$$
\mathbf{H}' = \begin{pmatrix}
b^{2287} & b^{992} & b^{5159} & b^{4953} & b^{4144} & b^{6518} & b^{3920} & b^{4127} \\
b^{992} & b^{5165} & b^{5229} & b^{5023} & b^{4214} & b^{28} & b^{3990} & b^{4197} \\
b^{5159} & b^{5229} & 0 & 0 & 0 & 0 & 0 & 0 \\
b^{4953} & b^{5023} & 0 & 0 & 0 & 0 & 0 & 0 \\
b^{4144} & b^{4214} & 0 & 0 & 0 & 0 & 0 & 0 \\
b^{6518} & b^{28} & 0 & 0 & 0 & 0 & 0 & 0 \\
b^{3920} & b^{3990} & 0 & 0 & 0 & 0 & 0 & 0 \\
b^{4127} & b^{4197} & 0 & 0 & 0 & 0 & 0 & 0
\end{pmatrix},
$$

$$
\tilde{\mathbf{H}}' = \begin{pmatrix}
b^{87} & b^{1874} & b^{3075} & b^{2869} & b^{2060} & b^{4434} & b^{1836} & b^{2043} \\
b^{1874} & b^{6189} & b^{1832} & b^{1626} & b^{817} & b^{3191} & b^{593} & b^{800} \\
b^{3075} & b^{1832} & 0 & 0 & 0 & 0 & 0 & 0 \\
b^{2869} & b^{1626} & 0 & 0 & 0 & 0 & 0 & 0 \\
b^{2060} & b^{817} & 0 & 0 & 0 & 0 & 0 & 0 \\
b^{4434} & b^{3191} & 0 & 0 & 0 & 0 & 0 & 0 \\
b^{1836} & b^{593} & 0 & 0 & 0 & 0 & 0 & 0 \\
b^{2043} & b^{800} & 0 & 0 & 0 & 0 & 0 & 0
\end{pmatrix}
$$

Recovering the Low Degree Polynomial: Once the core polynomials $\mathbf{H}' = [h_{ij}]$, $\tilde{\mathbf{H}}' = [\tilde{h}_{ij}]$ are recovered, our target is to build the low degree polynomial Ψ'' fundamental for the attacker to be able decrypt. So, we solve the following overdetermined systems

$$\begin{bmatrix} h_{1,r+1} & h_{1,r+2} & \cdots & h_{1,n-1} & h_{1,n} \\ \tilde{h}_{1,r+1} & \tilde{h}_{1,r+2} & \cdots & \tilde{h}_{1,n-1} & \tilde{h}_{1,n} \end{bmatrix}^{\top} \begin{bmatrix} x_0 \\ x_1 \end{bmatrix} = \begin{bmatrix} b^{5159} & b^{4953} & b^{4144} & b^{6518} & b^{3920} & b^{4127} \\ b^{3075} & b^{2869} & b^{2060} & b^{4434} & b^{1836} & b^{2043} \end{bmatrix}^{\top} \begin{bmatrix} x_0 \\ x_1 \end{bmatrix} = \mathbf{0},$$

$$\begin{bmatrix} h_{2,r+1} & h_{2,r+2} & \cdots & h_{2,n-1} & h_{2,n} \\ \tilde{h}_{2,r+1} & \tilde{h}_{2,r+2} & \cdots & \tilde{h}_{2,n-1} & \tilde{h}_{2,n} \end{bmatrix}^{\top} \begin{bmatrix} y_0 \\ y_1 \end{bmatrix} = \begin{bmatrix} b^{5229} & b^{5023} & b^{4214} & b^{28} & b^{3990} & b^{4197} \\ b^{1832} & b^{1626} & b^{817} & b^{3191} & b^{593} & b^{800} \end{bmatrix}^{\top} \begin{bmatrix} y_0 \\ y_1 \end{bmatrix} = \mathbf{0},$$

and we obtain the solutions $[x_0, x_1]^{\top} = [b^{1418}, b^{222}]^{\top}$ and $[y_0, y_1]^{\top} = [b^{2162}, b^{2279}]^{\top}$. Then, we compute $b^{1418}\mathbf{H}' + b^{222}\tilde{\mathbf{H}}'$ and $b^{2162}\mathbf{H}' + b^{2279}\tilde{\mathbf{H}}'$ obtaining respectively

$$\begin{pmatrix} b^{106} & b^{6092} & 0 & 0 & 0 & 0 & 0 & 0 \\ b^{6092} & b^{3643} & b^{4437} & b^{4231} & b^{3422} & b^{5796} & b^{3198} & b^{3405} \\ 0 & b^{4437} & 0 & 0 & 0 & 0 & 0 & 0 \\ 0 & b^{4231} & 0 & 0 & 0 & 0 & 0 & 0 \\ 0 & b^{3422} & 0 & 0 & 0 & 0 & 0 & 0 \\ 0 & b^{5796} & 0 & 0 & 0 & 0 & 0 & 0 \\ 0 & b^{3198} & 0 & 0 & 0 & 0 & 0 & 0 \\ 0 & b^{3405} & 0 & 0 & 0 & 0 & 0 & 0 \end{pmatrix}, \begin{pmatrix} b^{1294} & b^{536} & b^{3144} & b^{2938} & b^{2129} & b^{4403} & b^{1905} & b^{2112} \\ b^{536} & b^{844} & 0 & 0 & 0 & 0 & 0 & 0 \\ b^{3144} & 0 & 0 & 0 & 0 & 0 & 0 & 0 \\ b^{2938} & 0 & 0 & 0 & 0 & 0 & 0 & 0 \\ b^{2129} & 0 & 0 & 0 & 0 & 0 & 0 & 0 \\ b^{4503} & 0 & 0 & 0 & 0 & 0 & 0 & 0 \\ b^{1905} & 0 & 0 & 0 & 0 & 0 & 0 & 0 \\ b^{2112} & 0 & 0 & 0 & 0 & 0 & 0 & 0 \end{pmatrix}.$$

Finally, we form the system

$$\begin{bmatrix} b^{4437} & b^{4231} & b^{3422} & b^{5796} & b^{3198} & b^{3405} \\ b^{3144} & b^{2938} & b^{2129} & b^{4403} & b^{1905} & b^{2112} \end{bmatrix}^{\top} \begin{bmatrix} z_0 \\ z_1 \end{bmatrix} = \mathbf{0},$$

we a solution $[z_0,\ z_1]^{\top} = [b^{1024},\ b^{5597}]^{\top}$, and we use it to compute our low degree polynomial,

$$\Psi'' = b^{1024} X (b^{1418} H' + b^{222} \tilde{H}') + X^q (b^{2162} H' + b^{2279} \tilde{H}')$$
$$= b^{6441} X^9 + b^{2097} X^7 + b^{852} X^5 + b^{1130} X^3$$

A.2   Low Rank Matrix Forms

Case $s = 0$.   Case $s = 1$.

Quantum Algorithms

Post-quantum RSA

Daniel J. Bernstein[1,2]([✉]), Nadia Heninger[3], Paul Lou[3], and Luke Valenta[3]

[1] Department of Computer Science,
University of Illinois at Chicago,
Chicago, IL 60607–7045, USA
djb@cr.yp.to
[2] Department of Mathematics and Computer Science,
Technische Universiteit Eindhoven,
P.O. Box 513, 5600 MB Eindhoven, The Netherlands
[3] Computer and Information Science Department,
University of Pennsylvania,
Philadelphia, PA 19103, USA
{nadiah,plou,lukev}@seas.upenn.edu

Abstract. This paper proposes RSA parameters for which (1) key generation, encryption, decryption, signing, and verification are feasible on today's computers while (2) all known attacks are infeasible, even assuming highly scalable quantum computers. As part of the performance analysis, this paper introduces a new algorithm to generate a batch of primes. As part of the attack analysis, this paper introduces a new quantum factorization algorithm that is often much faster than Shor's algorithm and much faster than pre-quantum factorization algorithms. Initial pqRSA implementation results are provided.

Keywords: Post-quantum cryptography · RSA scalability · Shor's algorithm · ECM · Grover's algorithm · Make RSA Great Again

Author list in alphabetical order; see https://www.ams.org/profession/leaders/culture/CultureStatement04.pdf. This work was supported by the Commission of the European Communities through the Horizon 2020 program under project number 645622 (PQCRYPTO) and project number 645421 (ECRYPT-CSA); by the Netherlands Organisation for Scientific Research (NWO) under grant 639.073.005; by the U.S. National Institute of Standards and Technology under grant 60NANB10D263; by the U.S. National Science Foundation under grants 1314919, 1408734, 1505799, and 1513671; and by a gift from Cisco. P. Lou was supported by the Rachleff Scholars program at the University of Pennsylvania. We are grateful to Cisco for donating much of the hardware used for our experiments. "Any opinions, findings, and conclusions or recommendations expressed in this material are those of the author(s) and do not necessarily reflect the views of the National Science Foundation" (or other funding agencies). Permanent ID of this document: aaf273785255fe95feca9484e74c7833. Date: 2017.04.23.

© Springer International Publishing AG 2017
T. Lange and T. Takagi (Eds.): PQCrypto 2017, LNCS 10346, pp. 311–329, 2017.
DOI: 10.1007/978-3-319-59879-6_18

1   Introduction

The 1994 publication of Shor's algorithm prompted widespread claims that quantum computers would kill cryptography, or at least public-key cryptography. For example:

- [15]: "Nobody knows exactly when quantum computing will become a reality, but when and if it does, it will signal the end of traditional cryptography".
- [37]: "If quantum computers exist one day, Shor's results will make all current known public-key cryptographic systems useless".
- [29]: "It is already proven that quantum computers will allow to break public key cryptography."
- [20]: "When the first quantum factoring devices are built the security of public-key crypstosystems [*sic*] will vanish."

But these claims go far beyond the actual limits of Shor's algorithm, and subsequent research into quantum cryptanalysis has done little to close the gap. The conventional wisdom among researchers in post-quantum cryptography is that quantum computers will kill RSA and ECC but will not kill hash-based cryptography, code-based cryptography, lattice-based cryptography, or multivariate-quadratic-equations cryptography.

Contents of This Paper. Is it actually true that quantum computers will kill RSA?

The question here is not whether quantum computers will be built, or will be affordable for attackers. This paper assumes that astonishingly scalable quantum computers will be built, making a qubit operation as inexpensive as a bit operation. Under this assumption, Shor's algorithm easily breaks RSA *as used on the Internet today*. The question is whether RSA parameters can be adjusted so that all known quantum attack algorithms are infeasible while encryption and decryption remain feasible.

The conventional wisdom is that Shor's algorithm factors an RSA public key n almost as quickly as the legitimate RSA user can decrypt. Decryption uses an exponentiation modulo n; Shor's algorithm uses a quantum exponentiation modulo n. There are some small overheads in Shor's algorithm—for example, the exponent is double-length—but these overheads create only a very small gap between the cost of decryption and the cost of factorization. (Shor speculated in [48, Sect. 3] that faster quantum algorithms for modular exponentiation "could even make breaking RSA on a quantum computer asymptotically faster than encrypting with RSA on a classical computer"; however, no such algorithms have been found.)

The main point of this paper is that standard techniques for speeding up RSA, when pushed to their extremes, create a much larger gap between the legitimate user's costs and the attacker's costs. Specifically, for this paper's version of RSA, the attack cost is essentially *quadratic* in the usage cost.

These extremes require a careful analysis of quantum algorithms for integer factorization. As part of this security analysis, this paper introduces a new quantum factorization algorithm, GEECM, that is often much faster than Shor's algorithm and all pre-quantum factorization algorithms. See Sect. 2. GEECM turns out to be one of the main constraints upon parameter selection for post-quantum RSA.

These extremes also require a careful analysis of algorithms for the basic RSA operations. See Sect. 3. As part of this performance analysis, this paper introduces a new algorithm to generate a large batch of independent uniform random primes more efficiently than any known algorithm to generate such primes one at a time.

Section 4 reports initial implementation results for RSA parameters large enough to push all known quantum attacks above 2^{100} qubit operations. These results include successful completion of the most expensive operation in post-quantum RSA, namely generating a 1-terabyte public key.

Evaluation and Comparison. Post-quantum RSA does not qualify as secure under old-fashioned security definitions requiring asymptotic security against polynomial-time adversaries. However, post-quantum RSA does appear to provide a reasonable level of concrete security.

Note that, for theoretical purposes, it is possible that (1) there are no public-key encryption systems secure against polynomial-time quantum adversaries but (2) there *are* public-key encryption systems secure against, e.g., essentially-linear-time quantum adversaries. Post-quantum RSA is a candidate for the second category.

One might think that the quadratic security of post-quantum RSA is no better than the well-known quadratic security of Merkle's original public-key system. However, the well-known quadratic security is against *pre-quantum* attackers, not against *post-quantum* attackers. The analyses by Brassard and Salvail in [17], and by Brassard, Høyer, Kalach, Kaplan, Laplante, and Salvail in [16], indicate that more complicated variants of Merkle's original public-key system can achieve exponents close to 1.5 against quantum computers, but this is far below the exponent 2 achieved by post-quantum RSA. Concretely, $(2^{100})^{1/1.5}$ is approximately 100000 times larger than $(2^{100})^{1/2}$.

Post-quantum RSA is not what one would call lightweight cryptography: the cost of each new encryption or decryption is on the scale of \$1 of computer time, many orders of magnitude more expensive than pre-quantum RSA. However, if this is the least expensive way to protect high-security information against being recorded by an adversary today and decrypted by future quantum computers, then it should be of interest to some users. One can draw an analogy here with fully homomorphic encryption: something expensive might nevertheless be useful if it is the least expensive way to achieve the user's desired security goal.

Code-based cryptography and lattice-based cryptography have been studied for many years and *appear* to provide secure encryption at far less expense than post-quantum RSA. However, one can reasonably argue that triple encryption with code-based cryptography, lattice-based cryptography, and post-quantum RSA, for users who can afford it, provides a higher level of confidence than only two of the mechanisms. Post-quantum RSA is also quite unusual in allowing post-quantum encryption, signatures, and more advanced cryptographic functionality such as blind signatures to be provided in a familiar way by a single unified mechanism, a multiplicatively homomorphic trapdoor permutation.

Obviously the overall use case for post-quantum RSA relies heavily on the faint possibility of dramatic improvements in attacks against a broad range of alternatives. But the same criticism applies even more strongly to, e.g., the proposals in [16]. More importantly, it is interesting to see that the conventional wisdom is wrong, and that RSA has enough flexibility to survive the advent of quantum computers—beaten, bruised, and limping, perhaps, but not dead.

Future Work. There is a line of work suggesting big secrets as a protection against limited- volume side-channel attacks and limited-volume exfiltration by malware. As a recent example, Shamir is quoted in [7] as saying that he wants the file containing the Coca-Cola secret "to be a terabyte, which cannot be [easily] exfiltrated". A terabyte takes only a few hours to transmit over a gigabit-per-second link, but the basic idea of this line of work is that there are sometimes limits on time and/or bandwidth in side channels and exfiltration channels, and that these limits could stop the attacker from extracting the desired secrets. It would be interesting to analyze the extent to which the secrets in post-quantum RSA provide this type of protection. Beware, however, that a positive answer could be undermined by other parts of the system that have not put the same attention into expanding their data.

Our batch prime-generation algorithm suggests that, to help reduce energy consumption and protect the environment, all users of RSA—including users of traditional pre-quantum RSA—should delegate their key-generation computations to NIST or another trusted third party. This speed improvement would also allow users to generate new RSA keys and erase old RSA keys more frequently, limiting the damage of key theft.[1] However, all trusted-third-party protocols raise security questions (see, e.g., [19,24]), and there are significant costs to all known techniques to securely distribute or delegate RSA computations. The challenge here is to show that secure multi-user RSA key generation can be carried out more efficiently than one-user-at-a-time RSA key generation.

Another natural direction of followup work is integration of post-quantum RSA into standard Internet protocols such as TLS. This integration is conceptually straightforward but requires tackling many systems-level challenges, such as various limitations on the RSA key sizes allowed in cryptographic libraries.

Acknowledgments. Thanks to Christian Grothoff for pointing out the application to post-quantum blind signatures. Thanks to Joshua Fried for extensive help with the compute cluster. Thanks to Daniel Genkin for pointing out the

---

[1] If the goal is merely to protect past traffic against complete key theft ("forward secrecy") then a user can obtain a speedup by generating many RSA keys in advance, and erasing each key soon after it is first *used*. But erasing each key soon after it has been *generated* is sometimes advertised as helping protect future traffic against limited types of compromise. Furthermore, batching across many users provides larger speedups.

possibility that post-quantum RSA naturally provides extra side-channel protection. Thanks to Ahto Truu for pointing out a typo in the math. Thanks to anonymous referees for their helpful comments, including asking about [47,52]. Thanks to Tanja Lange for encouragement and many helpful comments during several years of development of this paper.

2   Post-quantum Factorization

For every modern variant of RSA, including the variants considered in this paper, the best attacks known are factorization algorithms. This section analyzes the post-quantum complexity of integer factorization.

There have been some papers analyzing and improving the complexity of Shor's algorithm; see, e.g., [56]. However, the literature does not seem to contain any broader study of quantum factorization algorithms. There seems to be an implicit assumption that—once large enough quantum computers are available—Shor's algorithm supersedes the entire previous literature on integer factorization, rendering all previous factorization algorithms obsolete, so studying the complexity of factorization in a post-quantum world is tantamount to studying the complexity of Shor's algorithm.

The main point of this section is that post-quantum factorization is actually a much richer subject. It should be obvious that previous algorithms are not always superseded by Shor's algorithm: as a trivial example, an integer divisible by 2 or 3 or 5 is much more efficiently detected by trial division than by Shor's algorithm. Perhaps less obvious is that there are quantum factorization algorithms that are, for many integers, much faster than Shor's algorithm *and* much faster than all known pre-quantum algorithms. These algorithms turn out to be important for post-quantum RSA, as discussed in Sect. 3.

Overview of Pre-quantum Integer Factorization. There are two important classes of factorization algorithms. The first class consists of algorithms that are particularly fast at finding small primes: e.g., trial division, the rho method [40], the $p - 1$ method [39], the $p + 1$ method [55], and the elliptic-curve method (ECM) [35].

Each of these algorithms can be rephrased, without serious loss of efficiency, as a **ring algorithm** that composes the ring operations $0, 1, +, -, \cdot$ to produce a large integer divisible by many small primes. By carrying out the same sequence of operations modulo a target integer n and computing the greatest common divisor of the result with n, one sees whether n is divisible by any of the same primes. For example, trial division up through y has essentially the same performance as computing $\gcd\{n, 2 \cdot 3 \cdot 5 \cdots y\}$; as another example, m steps of the rho method compute $\gcd\{n, (\rho_2 - \rho_1)(\rho_4 - \rho_2)(\rho_6 - \rho_3) \cdots (\rho_{2m} - \rho_m)\}$ with $\rho_1 = 1$ and $\rho_{i+1} = \rho_i^2 + 10$.

The importance of ring operations is that carrying them out modulo n has the effect of carrying them out modulo every prime p dividing n; i.e., $\mathbf{Z}/n \to \mathbf{Z}/p$ is a ring morphism. To measure the speed and effectiveness of a ring algorithm one sees how many operations are carried out by the algorithm and how many primes p of various sizes divide the output. The size of n is almost irrelevant, except that each ring operation modulo n costs $(\lg n)^{1+o(1)}$ bit operations.

The second class consists of **congruence-combining algorithms**: e.g., the continued-fraction method [33], the quadratic sieve [41], and the number-field sieve (NFS) [34]. These algorithms multiply various congruences modulo n to obtain a congruence of the form $a^2 \equiv b^2 \pmod{n}$, and then hope that $\gcd\{n, a - b\}$ is a nontrivial factor of n. These algorithms are not usefully viewed as ring algorithms (the congruences modulo n are produced in a way that depends on n) and are not particularly fast at finding small primes.

For large n the best congruence-combining algorithm appears to be NFS, which (conjecturally) uses $2^{(\lg n)^{1/3+o(1)}}$ bit operations. For comparison, ECM uses $2^{(\lg y)^{1/2+o(1)}}$ ring operations if ECM parameters are chosen to (conjecturally) find every prime $p \leq y$. Evidently ECM uses fewer bit operations than NFS to find sufficiently small primes p; the cutoff is $2^{(\lg n)^{2/3+o(1)}}$.

Shor's Algorithm. Shor begins with a circuit to compute the function $x \mapsto (x, 3^x \bmod n)$, where x is an integer having about $2 \lg n$ bits. Exponentiation uses about $2 \lg n$ multiplications modulo n, and the best multiplication methods known use $(\lg n)^{1+o(1)}$ bit operations, so exponentiation uses $(\lg n)^{2+o(1)}$ bit operations.

A standard conversion produces a quantum circuit that uses $(\lg n)^{2+o(1)}$ qubit operations to evaluate the same function on a quantum superposition of inputs. With a small extra overhead (applying a quantum Fourier transform to the output, sampling, et al.) Shor finds the period of this function, i.e., the order of 3 modulo n. This order is a divisor, typically a large divisor, of $\varphi(n) = \#(\mathbf{Z}/n)^*$, and factoring n with this information is a standard exercise. In the rare case that 3 has small order modulo n, one can replace 3 with a random number—preferably a small random number to save time in exponentiation.

There is a tremendous gap between the $(\lg n)^{2+o(1)}$ qubit operations used by Shor and the $2^{(\lg n)^{1/3+o(1)}}$ bit operations used by NFS. Of course, for the moment qubit operations seem impossibly expensive compared to bit operations, but post-quantum cryptography looks ahead to a future where qubit operations are affordable at a large scale. In this future it seems that congruence-combining algorithms will be of little, if any, interest.

On the other hand, Shor's algorithm is not competitive with ring algorithms at finding small primes. Even if a qubit operation is as inexpensive as a bit operation, Shor's $(\lg n)^{2+o(1)}$ qubit operations are as expensive as $(\lg n)^{1+o(1)}$ ring operations. ECM's $2^{(\lg y)^{1/2+o(1)}}$ ring operations are better than this for sufficiently small primes. The cutoff is $2^{(\lg \lg n)^{2+o(1)}}$.

Some Wishful Thinking. One might think that Shor's algorithm can be tweaked to take advantage of a small prime divisor p of n: the function $x \mapsto 3^x \bmod p$ has small period, and this period should be visible for x having only about $2 \lg p$ bits, rather than the $2 \lg n$ bits used by Shor. This would save a factor of 2 even in the most extreme case $p \approx \sqrt{n}$.

The difficulty is that one is not given the function $x \mapsto 3^x \bmod p$. The function $x \mapsto 3^x \bmod n$ has a small pseudo-period, in the sense that shifting the input produces a related output, but one is also not given this relation.

If there were a fast way to detect pseudo-periods with respect to unknown relations then one could drastically speed up Shor's algorithm by finding the pseudo-period p of the simpler function $x \mapsto x \bmod n$. If x is limited to $2 \lg p < \lg n$ bits then this function is simply the identity function $x \mapsto x$, independent of n, so there would have to be some other way for the algorithm to learn about n. These obstacles seem insurmountable.

A Quantum Ring Algorithm: GEECM. A more productive approach is to take the best pre-quantum algorithms for finding small primes, and to accelerate those algorithms using quantum techniques.

Under standard conjectures, ECM finds primes $p \leq y$ using $2^{(\lg y)^{1/2+o(1)}}$ ring operations, as mentioned above; the rho method finds primes $p \leq y$ using $y^{1/2+o(1)}$ ring operations; and trial division (in its classic form) finds primes $p \leq y$ using $y^{1+o(1)}$ ring operations. Evidently ECM supersedes the rho method and trial division as y grows. The cutoff is generally stated (on the basis of more detailed analyses of the $o(1)$) to be below 2^{30}, and the primes of interest in this paper are much larger, so this paper focuses on ECM.

(There are occasional primes for which the $p-1$ and $p+1$ methods are faster than ECM, but the primes of interest in this paper are randomly generated. Most of the comments in this section generalize to hyperelliptic curves, but genus-≥ 2-hyperelliptic-curve methods have always been slightly slower than ECM.)

The state-of-the-art variant of ECM is EECM (ECM using Edwards curves), introduced by Bernstein, Birkner, Lange, and Peters in [12]. EECM chooses an Edwards curve $x^2 + y^2 = 1 + dx^2y^2$ over $\mathbf{Q}$, or more generally a twisted Edwards curve, with a known non-torsion point P; EECM also chooses a large integer s and uses the Edwards addition law to compute the sth multiple of P on the curve, and in particular the x-coordinate $x(sP)$, represented as a fraction of integers. The output of the ring algorithm is the numerator of this fraction. Overall the computation takes $(7 + o(1)) \lg s$ multiplications (more than half of which are squarings) and a comparable number of additions and subtractions. For optimized curve choices and further details see [5,11,12,14,22].

If s is chosen as $\mathrm{lcm}\{1, 2, \ldots, z\}$ then $\lg s \approx 1.4z$ so this curve computation uses about $10z$ multiplications. If $z \in L^{c+o(1)}$ as $y \rightarrow \infty$, where $L = \exp\sqrt{\log y \log \log y}$ and c is a positive real constant, then standard conjectures imply that each prime $p \leq y$ is found by this curve with probability $1/L^{1/2c+o(1)}$. Standard conjectures also imply that curves are almost independent, so by trying $L^{1/2c+o(1)}$ curves one finds each prime p with high probability. The total cost of trying all these curves is $L^{c+1/2c+o(1)}$ ring operations. The expression $c + 1/2c$ takes its minimum value $\sqrt{2}$ for $c = 1/\sqrt{2}$; the total cost is then $L^{\sqrt{2}+o(1)}$ ring operations.

This paper introduces GEECM (Grover plus EECM), which uses quantum computers as follows to accelerate the same EECM computation. Recall that Grover's method accelerates searching for roots of functions: if the inputs to a function f are roots of f with probability $1/R$, then classical searching performs (on average) R evaluations of f, while Grover's method performs about $\sqrt{R}$ quantum evaluations of f. Consider, in particular, the function f whose input is an EECM curve choice, and whose output is 0 exactly when the EECM result for that curve choice has a nontrivial factor in common with n. EECM finds a root of f by classical searching; GEECM finds a root of f by Grover's method. If s and z are chosen as above then the inputs to f are roots of f with probability $1/L^{1/2c+o(1)}$, so GEECM uses just $L^{1/4c+o(1)}$ quantum evaluations of f, for a total of $L^{c+1/4c+o(1)}$ quantum ring operations. The expression $c + 1/4c$ takes its minimum value 1 for $c = 1/2$; the total cost is then just $L^{1+o(1)}$ ring operations.

To summarize, GEECM reduces the number of ring operations from $L^{\sqrt{2}+o(1)}$ to $L^{1+o(1)}$, where $L = \exp\sqrt{\log y \log\log y}$. For the same number of operations, GEECM increases $\log y$ by a factor $2 + o(1)$, almost doubling the number of bits of primes that can be found.

3   RSA Scalability

Obviously a post-quantum RSA public key n will need to be quite large to resist the attacks described in Sect. 2. This section analyzes the scalability of the best algorithms available for RSA key generation, encryption, decryption, signature generation, and signature verification.

Small Exponents. The fundamental RSA public-key operation is computing an eth power modulo n. This modular exponentiation uses approximately $\lg e$ squarings modulo n, and, thanks to standard windowing techniques, $o(\lg e)$ extra multiplications modulo n.

In the original RSA paper [43], e was a random number with as many bits as n. Rabin in [42] suggested instead using a small constant e, and said that $e = 2$ is "several hundred times faster." Rabin's speedup factor grows as $\Theta(\lg n)$, making it particularly important for the large sizes of n considered in this paper.

The slower but simpler choice $e = 3$ was deployed in a variety of real-world applications. The much slower alternative $e = 65537$ subsequently became popular as a means of compensating for poor choices of RSA message-randomization mechanisms, but with proper randomization no attacks against $e = 3$ are known that are faster than factorization.

For simplicity this paper also focuses on $e = 3$. Computing an eth power modulo n then takes one squaring modulo n and one general multiplication modulo n. Each of these steps takes just $(\lg n)^{1+o(1)}$ bit operations using standard fast-multiplication techniques; see below for further discussion. Notice that $(\lg n)^{1+o(1)}$ is asymptotically far below the $(\lg n)^{2+o(1)}$ cost of Shor's algorithm.

Many Primes. The fundamental RSA secret-key operation is computing an eth root modulo n. For $e = 3$ one chooses n as a product of distinct primes congruent to 2 modulo 3; then the inverse of $x \mapsto x^3 \bmod n$ is $x \mapsto x^d \bmod n$, where $d = (1 + 2\prod_{p|n}(p-1))/3$. Unfortunately, d is not a small exponent—it has approximately $\lg n$ bits.

A classic speedup in the computation of $x^d \bmod n$ is to compute $x^d \bmod p$ and $x^d \bmod q$, where p and q are the prime divisors of n, and to combine them into $x^d \bmod n$ by a suitably explicit form of the Chinese remainder theorem. Fermat's identity $x^p \bmod p = x \bmod p$ further implies that $x^d \bmod p = x^{d \bmod (p-1)} \bmod p$ (since $d \bmod (p-1) \geq 1$) and similarly $x^d \bmod q = x^{d \bmod (q-1)} \bmod q$. The exponents $d \bmod (p-1)$ and $d \bmod (q-1)$ have only half as many bits as n; the exponentiation $x^d \bmod n$ is thus replaced by two exponentiations with half-size exponents and half-size moduli.

If n is a product of more primes, say $k \geq 3$ primes, then the same speedup becomes even more effective, using k exponentiations with $(1/k)$-size exponents and $(1/k)$-size moduli. Prime generation also becomes much easier since the primes are smaller. Of course, if primes are too small then the attacker can find them using the ring algorithms discussed in the previous section—specifically EECM before quantum computers, and GEECM after quantum computers.

What matters for this paper is how multi-prime RSA scales to much larger moduli n. Before quantum computers the top threats are EECM and NFS, and balancing these threats implies that each prime p has $(\lg n)^{2/3+o(1)}$ bits (see above), i.e., that $k \in (\lg n)^{1/3+o(1)}$. After quantum computers the top threats are GEECM and Shor's algorithm, and balancing these threats implies that each prime p has just $(\lg \lg n)^{2+o(1)}$ bits, i.e., that $k \in (\lg n)/(\lg \lg n)^{2+o(1)}$. RSA key generation, decryption, and signature generation then take $(\lg n)^{1+o(1)}$ bit operations; see below for further discussion.

Key Generation. To recap: A k-prime exponent-3 RSA public key n is a product of k distinct primes p congruent to 2 modulo 3. In particular, a post-quantum RSA public key n is a product of k distinct primes p congruent to 2 modulo 3, where each prime p has $(\lg \lg n)^{2+o(1)}$ bits.

Standard prime-generation techniques use $(\lg p)^{3+o(1)}$ bit operations. See, e.g., [6, Sect. 3] and [38, Sect. 4.5]. The point is that one must try about $\log p$ random numbers before finding a prime, and checking primality has similar cost to a single exponentiation modulo p.

A standard speedup is to check whether p is divisible by any primes up through some limit, say y. The chance of a random integer surviving this divisibility test is approximately $1/\log y$, reducing the original pool of $\log p$ random numbers to $(\log p)/\log y$ random numbers and saving an overall factor of $\log y$ *if* the trial division is not a bottleneck. The conventional view is that keeping the cost of trial division under control requires y to be chosen as a polynomial in $\lg p$, saving a factor of only $\Theta(\lg \lg p)$ and thus still requiring $(\lg p)^{3+o(1)}$ bit operations.

A nonstandard speedup is to replace trial division (or sieving) by batch trial division [8] or batch smoothness detection [9]. The algorithm of [9] reads a finite sequence S of positive integers and a finite set P of primes, and finds "the largest P-smooth divisor of each integer in S" using just $b(\lg b)^{2+o(1)}$ bit operations, where b is the total number of bits in P and S. In particular, if P is the set of primes up through y, and S is a sequence of $\Theta(y/\lg p)$ integers each having $\Theta(\lg p)$ bits, then b is $\Theta(y)$ and this algorithm uses just $y(\lg y)^{2+o(1)}$ bit operations, i.e., $(\lg p)(\lg y)^{2+o(1)}$ bit operations for each element of S. Larger sequences S can trivially be split into sequences of size $\Theta(y/\lg p)$, producing the same performance per element of S.

To do even better, assume that the original size of S is at least 2^{2^α}, and apply batch smoothness detection successively for $y = 2^{2^0}$, $y = 2^{2^1}$, $y = 2^{2^2}$, and so on through $y = 2^{2^\alpha}$. Each step weeds out about half of the remaining elements of S as composites; the next step costs about four times as much per element but is applied to only half as many elements. The total cost is just $(\lg p)(2^\alpha)^{1+o(1)}$ bit operations for each of the original elements of S. Each of the original elements has probability about $1/2^\alpha$ of surviving this process and incurring an exponentiation, which costs $(\lg p)^{2+o(1)}$ bit operations. Choosing $2^\alpha \in (\lg p)^{0.5+o(1)}$ balances these costs as $(\lg p)^{1.5+o(1)}$ for each of the original elements of S, i.e., $(\lg p)^{2.5+o(1)}$ for each prime generated.

In the context of post-quantum RSA the assumption about the original size of S is satisfied: one has to generate $(\lg n)^{1+o(1)}$ primes, so the original size of S is $(\lg n)^{1+o(1)}$, which is at least 2^{2^α} for $2^\alpha \in (1 + o(1))\lg\lg n$; this choice of α satisfies $2^\alpha \in (\lg p)^{0.5+o(1)}$ since $\lg p \in (\lg\lg n)^{2+o(1)}$. The primes are also balanced, in the sense that $(\lg n)/k \in (\lg p)^{1+o(1)}$ for each p, so generating k primes in this way uses $k(\lg p)^{2.5+o(1)} = (\lg n)(\lg p)^{1.5+o(1)} = (\lg n)(\lg\lg n)^{3+o(1)}$ bit operations.

Computing n by multiplying these primes uses only $(\lg n)(\lg\lg n)^{2+o(1)}$ bit operations using standard fast-arithmetic techniques; see, e.g., [10, Sect. 12]. At this level of detail it does not matter whether one uses the classic Schönhage–Strassen multiplication algorithm [46], Fürer's multiplication algorithm [21], or the Harvey–van der Hoeven–Lecerf multiplication algorithm [27].

The total number of bit operations for key generation is essentially linear in $\lg n$. For comparison, the usual picture is that prime generation is vastly more expensive than any of the other steps in RSA.

One can try to further accelerate key generation using Takagi's idea [52] of choosing n as $p^{k-1}q$. We point out two reasons that this is worrisome. The first reason is lattice attacks [13]. The second reason is that any nth power modulo n has small order, namely some divisor of $(p-1)(q-1)$; Shor's algorithm finds the order at relatively high speed once the nth power is computed.

Encryption and Decryption. There are many different RSA encryption mechanisms in the literature. The oldest mechanisms use RSA to directly encrypt a user's message; this requires careful padding and scrambling of the message. Newer mechanisms generate a secret key (for example, an AES key), use the secret key to encrypt and authenticate the user's message, and use RSA to encrypt the secret key; this allows simpler padding, since the secret key is already randomized. The newest mechanisms such as Shoup's "RSA-KEM" [51] simply use RSA to encrypt $\lg n$ bits of random data, hash the random data to obtain a secret key, and use the secret key to encrypt and authenticate the user's message; this does not require any padding. For simplicity this paper takes the last approach.

Generating large amounts of truly random data is expensive. Fortunately, truly random data can be simulated by pseudorandom data produced by a stream cipher from a much smaller key. (Even better, slight deficiencies in the randomness of the cipher key do not compromise security.) The literature contains several scalable ciphers that produce a $\Theta(b)$-bit block of output from a $\Theta(b)$-bit key, with a conjectured 2^b security level, using $b^{2+o(1)}$ bit operations (and even fewer for some ciphers), i.e., $b^{1+o(1)}$ bit operations for each output bit. In the context of post-quantum RSA one has $b \in \Theta(\lg\lg n)$ so generating $\lg n$ pseudorandom bits costs $(\lg n)(\lg\lg n)^{1+o(1)}$ bit operations. The same ciphers can also be converted into hash functions with only a constant-factor loss in efficiency, so hashing the bits also costs $(\lg n)(\lg\lg n)^{1+o(1)}$ bit operations.

Multiplication also takes $(\lg n)(\lg\lg n)^{1+o(1)}$ bit operations. Squaring, reduction modulo n, multiplication, and another reduction modulo n together take $(\lg n)(\lg\lg n)^{1+o(1)}$ bit operations. The overall cost of RSA encryption is therefore $(\lg n)(\lg\lg n)^{1+o(1)}$ bit operations plus the cost of encrypting and authenticating the user's message under the resulting secret key.

Decryption is more complicated but not much slower; it works as follows. First reduce the ciphertext modulo all of the prime divisors of n. This takes $(\lg n)(\lg\lg n)^{2+o(1)}$ bit operations using a remainder tree or a scaled remainder tree; see, e.g., [10, Sect. 18]. Then compute a cube root modulo each prime. A cube root modulo p takes $(\lg p)^{2+o(1)}$ bit operations, so all of the cube roots together take $(\lg n)(\lg\lg n)^{2+o(1)}$ bit operations. Then reconstruct the cube root modulo n. This takes $(\lg n)(\lg\lg n)^{2+o(1)}$ bit operations using fast interpolation techniques; see, e.g., [10, Sect. 23]. Finally hash the cube root. The overall cost of RSA decryption is $(\lg n)(\lg\lg n)^{2+o(1)}$ bit operations, plus the cost of verifying and decrypting the user's message under the resulting secret key.

Shamir in [47] proposed decrypting modulo just one prime, and choosing plaintexts to be smaller than primes. However, this requires exponents to be much larger for security, and in the context of post-quantum RSA this slows down encryption by vastly more than it speeds up decryption. A more interesting variant, which we do not explore further, is to use a significant fraction of the primes to decrypt a plaintext having $(\lg n)/(\lg\lg n)^{0.5+o(1)}$ bits; this should reduce the total cost of encryption and decryption to $(\lg n)(\lg\lg n)^{1.5+o(1)}$ bit operations with a properly chosen exponent.

Signature Generation and Verification. Standard padding schemes for RSA signatures involve the same operations discussed above, such as hashing to a short string and using a stream cipher to expand the short string to a long string.

The final speeds are, unsurprisingly, $(\lg n)(\lg\lg n)^{2+o(1)}$ bit operations to generate a signature and $(\lg n)(\lg\lg n)^{1+o(1)}$ bit operations to verify a signature, plus the cost of hashing the user's message.

4   Concrete Parameters and Initial Implementation

Summarizing what we've learned so far: Shor's algorithm takes $(\lg n)^{2+o(1)}$ qubit operations to factor n. If the prime divisors of n are too small then GEECM becomes a larger threat than Shor's algorithm; protecting against GEECM requires each prime to have $(\lg \lg n)^{2+o(1)}$ bits. Section 3 showed that, under this constraint, all of the RSA operations can be carried out using $(\lg n)(\lg \lg n)^{O(1)}$ bit operations; the $O(1)$ is $3 + o(1)$ for key generation, $2 + o(1)$ for decryption and signature generation, and $1 + o(1)$ for encryption and signature verification.

These asymptotics do not imply anything about any particular size of n. This section looks at performance in more detail, and in particular reports successful generation of a 1-terabyte post-quantum RSA key built from 4096-bit primes.

Prime Sizes and Key Sizes. Before looking at performance, we explain why these sizes (1-terabyte key, 4096-bit primes) provide ample security.

A 1-terabyte key n has 2^{43} bits, so Shor's algorithm uses 2^{44} multiplications modulo n. We have not found literature analyzing the cost of circuits for optimized FFT-based multiplication at this scale, so we extrapolate as follows.

The recent speed records from Harvey–van der Hoeven–Lecerf [28] for multiplication of degree-2^{21} polynomials over a particularly favorable finite field, $\mathbf{F}_{2^{60}}$, use 640 ms on a 3.4 GHz CPU core. More than half of the cycles are performing 128-bit vector xor, and more than 10% of the cycles are performing 64×64-bit polynomial multiplications, according to [28, Sect. 3.3], for a total of approximately 2^{40} bit operations to multiply 2^{27}-bit inputs.

Imagine that the same 2^{13} ratio scales directly from 2^{27}-bit inputs to 2^{43}-bit inputs; that integer multiplication uses as few bit operations as binary-polynomial multiplication; that reduction modulo n does not cost anything; and that there are no overheads for switching from bit operations to reversible qubit operations inside a realistic quantum-computer architecture. (For comparison, the ratio in [56] is more than 2^{20} for 2^{20}-bit inputs.) Each multiplication modulo n inside Shor's algorithm then uses 2^{56} qubit operations, and overall Shor's algorithm consumes an astonishing 2^{100} qubit operations.

We caution the reader that this is only a preliminary estimate. A thorough analysis would have to account for several overheads mentioned above; for the number of Shor iterations required; for known techniques to reduce the number of iterations; for techniques to use slightly fewer multiplications per iteration; and for the latest improvements in integer-multiplication algorithms.

As for prime sizes: Standard pre-quantum cost analyses conclude that 4096-bit RSA keys provide roughly 2^{140} security against all available algorithms. ECM is well known to be inferior to NFS at such sizes; evidently it uses even more than 2^{140} bit operations to find 2048-bit primes. ECM would be even slower against a much larger modulus, simply because arithmetic is slower. However, the speedup from ECM to GEECM reduces the post-quantum security level of 2048-bit primes. Rather than engaging in a detailed analysis of this loss, we move up to 4096-bit primes, obviously putting GEECM far out of reach.

Table 4.1. Encryption and decryption times—We measure wall clock time in seconds on lattice0 for encryption and the three stages of decryption: reducing the ciphertext modulo each prime factor, computing a cube root modulo each prime, and reconstructing the plaintext modulo the product.

Key size	Bytes	Encryption	Decryption		
			Rem. tree	Cube root	CRT tree
1 MB	2^{20}	0.3	0.2	4.8	25.0
10 MB	$2^{23.3}$	5	6	18	262
100 MB	$2^{26.6}$	77	261	177	2851
1 GB	2^{30}	654	812	1765	33586
4 GB	2^{32}	3123	2318	8931	101309
8 GB	2^{33}	6689	7214	17266	212215
16 GB	2^{34}	18183	20420	34376	476798
32 GB	2^{35}	29464	62729	62567	N/A
128 GB	2^{37}	150975	N/A	N/A	N/A
256 GB	2^{38}	362015	N/A	N/A	N/A

Implementation. We now discuss our implementation of post-quantum RSA. Our main result is successful generation of a 1-terabyte exponent-3 RSA key consisting of 4096-bit primes. We also have preliminary results for encryption and decryption, although so far only for smaller sizes.

Our computations were performed on a heterogeneous cluster. We give a description of the machines in Appendix A. The memory-intensive portions of our computations were carried out a single machine running Ubuntu with 24 cores at 3.40 GHz (4 Intel Xeon E7-8893 v2 processors), 3 terabytes of DRAM, and 4.9 terabytes of swap memory built from enterprise SSDs. We will refer to this machine as lattice0 below. We measured memory consumption and overall runtime for bignum multiplications using GNU's Multiple Precision (GMP) Library [26]. We encountered a number of software limits and bugs, which we detail in Appendix A.

Prime Generation. Generating a 1-terabyte exponent-3 RSA key requires 2^{31} 4096-bit primes that are congruent to 2 mod 3. To efficiently generate such a large number of primes, our implementation first applies the batched smoothness detection technique discussed in Sect. 3 to an input collection of random 4096-bit numbers. We then use the Fermat congruence primality test to produce our final set of primes. While we do not *prove* that each number in the final output is prime, this test is sufficient to guarantee with high confidence that all of the 4096-bit numbers in the final output are prime. See [31] for quantitative upper bounds on the error probability.

We found that first filtering for random numbers congruent to 5 mod 6, and then applying batch sieving with the successive bounds $y = 2^{10}$ and $y = 2^{20}$ worked well in practice. Our heterogeneous cluster was able to generate primes at a rate of 750–1585 primes per core-hour. Generating all 2^{31} primes took approximately 1,975,000 core-hours. In calendar time, prime generation completed in four months running on spare compute capacity of a 1,400-core cluster.

Product Tree. After we successfully generated 2^{31} 4096-bit primes, we used a product tree to compute the 1-terabyte public RSA key. We distributed individual multiplications across our heterogeneous cluster to reduce the wall-clock time. We first multiplied batches of 8 million primes and wrote their products out to disk. Each subsequent single-threaded multiplication job read two integers from disk and wrote their product back to disk. Running times varied due to different CPU types and non-pqRSA related jobs sharing cache space. Once the integers reached 256 GB in size, we finished computing the product on lattice0. The aggregate wall-clock time used by individual multiply jobs was about 1,239,626 s, and the elapsed time for the terabyte key generation was about four days. The final multiplication of two 512 GB integers took 176,223 s in wall-clock time, using 3.166 TB of RAM and 2.5 TB of swap storage.

Encryption. We implemented RSA encryption using RSA-KEM, as described in Sect. 3. With the exponent $e = 3$, we found that a simple square-and-reduce using GMP's mpz_mult and mpz_mod was almost twice as fast as using the modular exponentiation function mpz_powm. Each operation was single-threaded. We were able to complete RSA encryption for modulus sizes up to 2 terabits, as shown in Table 4.1. For the 2 TB (256 GB) encryption, the longest multiplication took 13 h, modular reduction took 40 h, and in total encryption took a little over 100 h.

Decryption. We implemented RSA decryption as described in Sect. 3. Table 4.1 gives wall-clock timings for the three computational steps in decryption, each parallelized across 48 threads. Precomputing the entire product and remainder tree for a terabyte-sized key and storing it to disk would have taken 32 TB of disk space, so instead we recomputed portions of the trees on the fly. The reported timings for the remainder tree step in Table 4.1 include the time it takes to recompute both the product and remainder tree with a batch size of 8 million primes. Using a batch size of 8 million primes was roughly twice as fast as using a batch size of 2 million primes. We obtained experimental results for decryption of messages for key sizes of up to 16 GB.

References

1. — (no editor): Second International Conference on Quantum, Nano, and Micro Technologies, ICQNM 2008, 10–15 February 2008, Sainte Luce, Martinique, French Caribbean. IEEE Computer Society (2008). See [17]
2. — (no editor): Kernel BUG at mm/huge_memory.c:1798! (2012). http://linux-kernel.2935.n7.nabble.com/kernel-BUG-at-mm-huge-memory-c-1798-td5740 29.html. Citations in this document: §A
3. — (no editor): Proceedings of the 23rd USENIX Security Symposium, 20–22 August 2014, San Diego, CA, USA. USENIX (2014). See [19]

4. Abdalla, M., Barreto, P.S.L.M. (eds.): LATINCRYPT 2010. LNCS, vol. 6212. Springer, Heidelberg (2010). doi:10.1007/978-3-642-14712-8. See [11]

5. Barbulescu, R., Bos, J.W., Bouvier, C., Kleinjung, T., Montgomery, P.L.: Finding ECM-friendly curves through a study of Galois properties. In: ANTS-X: Proceedings of the Tenth Algorithmic Number Theory Symposium, pp. 63–86 (2013). http://msp.org/obs/2013/1/p04.xhtml. Citations in this document: §2

6. Beauchemin, P., Brassard, G., Crépeau, C., Goutier, C., Pomerance, C.: The generation of random numbers that are probably prime. J. Cryptol. 1, 53–64 (1988). https://math.dartmouth.edu/~carlp/probprime.pdf. Citations in this document: §3

7. Bellare, M., Kane, D., Rogaway, P.: Big-key symmetric encryption: resisting key exfiltration. In: [44], pp. 373–402 (2016). https://eprint.iacr.org/2016/541.pdf. Citations in this document: §1

8. Bernstein, D.J.: How to find small factors of integers (2002). https://cr.yp.to/papers.html#sf. Citations in this document: §3

9. Bernstein, D.J.: How to find smooth parts of integers (2004). https://cr.yp.to/papers.html#smoothparts. Citations in this document: §3, §3

10. Bernstein, D.J.: Fast multiplication and its applications. In: [18], pp. 325–384 (2008). https://cr.yp.to/papers.html#multapps. Citations in this document: §3,§3,§3

11. Bernstein, D.J., Birkner, P., Lange, T.: Starfish on strike. In: LATINCRYPT 2010 [4], pp. 61–80 (2010). https://eprint.iacr.org/2010/367. Citations in this document: §2

12. Bernstein, D.J., Birkner, P., Lange, T., Peters, C.: ECM using Edwards curves (2008). https://eprint.iacr.org/2008/016. Citations in this document: §2, §2

13. Boneh, D., Durfee, G., Howgrave-Graham, N.: Factoring $N = p^r q$ for large r. In: [54], pp. 326–337 (1999). http://crypto.stanford.edu/dabo/abstracts/prq.html. Citations in this document: §3

14. Bos, J.W., Kleinjung, T.: ECM at work pages. In: ASIACRYPT 2012 [53], pp. 467–484 (2012). https://eprint.iacr.org/2012/089. Citations in this document: §2

15. Boukhonine, S.: Cryptography: a security tool of the information age (1998). https://pdfs.semanticscholar.org/3932/8253d692f791b37c425e776f6cee0b8c3e56.pdf. Citations in this document: §1

16. Brassard, G., Høyer, P., Kalach, K., Kaplan, M., Laplante, S., Salvail, L.: Merkle puzzles in a quantum world. In: CRYPTO 2011 [45], pp. 391–410 (2011). https://arxiv.org/abs/1108.2316. Citations in this document: §1,§1

17. Brassard, G., Salvail, L.: Quantum Merkle puzzles. In: ICQNM 2008 [1], pp. 76–79 (2008). Citations in this document: §1

18. Buhler, J.P., Stevenhagen, P.: Surveys in Algorithmic Number Theory. Mathematical Sciences Research Institute Publications, vol. 44. Cambridge University Press, New York (2008). See [10]

19. Checkoway, S., Fredrikson, M., Niederhagen, R., Everspaugh, A., Green, M., Lange, T., Ristenpart, T., Bernstein, D.J., Maskiewicz, J., Shacham, H.: On the practical exploitability of Dual EC in TLS implementations. In: USENIX Security 2014 [3] (2014). https://projectbullrun.org/dual-ec/index.html. Citations in this document: §1

20. Ekert, A.: Quantum cryptoanalysis–introduction (2010). http://www.qi.damtp.cam.ac.uk/node/69. Citations in this document: §1

21. Fürer, M.: Faster integer multiplication. In: [30], pp. 57–66 (2007). https://www.cse.psu.edu/~furer/. Citations in this document: §3

22. Gélin, A., Kleinjung, T., Lenstra, A.K.: Parametrizations for families of ECM-friendly curves (2016). https://eprint.iacr.org/2016/1092. Citations in this document: §2

23. Goldwasser, S. (ed.): 35th Annual IEEE Symposium on the Foundations of Computer Science. Proceedings of the IEEE Symposium Held in Santa Fe, NM, 20–22 November 1994. IEEE (1994). ISBN 0–8186-6580-7. MR 98h:68008. See [48]

24. Goodin, D.: Symantec employees fired for issuing rogue HTTPS certificate for Google (2015). https://arstechnica.com/security/2015/09/symantec-employees-fired-for-issuing-rogue-https-certificate-for-google/. Citations in this document: §1

25. Granlund, T.: GMP integer size limitation (2012). https://gmplib.org/list-archives/gmp-discuss/2012-April/005020.html. Citations in this document: §A

26. Granlund, T., The GMP Development Team: GNU MP: The GNU Multiple Precision Arithmetic Library (2015). https://gmplib.org/. Citations in this document: §4

27. Harvey, D., van der Hoeven, J., Lecerf, G.: Even faster integer multiplication. J. Complex. **36**, 1–30 (2016). https://arxiv.org/abs/1407.3360. Citations in this document: §3

28. Harvey, D., van der Hoeven, J., Lecerf, G.: Fast polynomial multiplication over $F_{2^{60}}$. In: Proceedings of ISSAC 2016 (2016, to appear). https://hal.archives-ouvertes.fr/hal-01265278. Citations in this document: §4, §4

29. ID Quantique: Future-proof data confidentiality with quantum cryptography (2005). https://classic-web.archive.org/web/20070728200504/, http://www.idquantique.com/products/files/vectis-future.pdf. Citations in this document: §4

30. Johnson, D.S., Feige, U. (eds.): Proceedings of the 39th Annual ACM Symposium on Theory of Computing, San Diego, California, USA, 11–13 June 2007. Association for Computing Machinery, New York (2007). ISBN 978-1-59593-631-8. See [21]

31. Kim, S.H.,. Pomerance, C.: The probability that a random probable prime is composite. Math. Comput. **53**, 721–741 (1989). https://math.dartmouth.edu/~carlp/PDF/paper72.pdf. Citations in this document: §4

32. Krawczyk, H. (ed.): CRYPTO 1998. LNCS, vol. 1462. Springer, Heidelberg (1998). doi:10.1007/BFb0055715. ISBN 3-540-64892-5. MR 99i:94059. See [52]

33. Lehmer, D.H., Powers, R.E.: On factoring large numbers. Bull. Am. Math. Soc. **37**, 770–776 (1931). Citations in this document: §2

34. Lenstra, A.K., Lenstra Jr., H.W. (eds.): The Development of the Number Field Sieve. LNM, vol. 1554. Springer, Heidelberg (1993). doi:10.1007/BFb0091534. ISBN 3-540-57013-6. MR 96m:11116. Citations in this document: §2

35. Lenstra Jr., H.W.: Factoring integers with elliptic curves. Ann. Math. **126**, 649–673 (1987). MR 89g:11125. Citations in this document: §2

36. Lenstra Jr., H.W., Tijdeman, R.: Computational Methods in Number Theory I. Mathematical Centre Tracts, vol. 154. Mathematisch Centrum, Amsterdam (1982). ISBN 90-6196-248-X. MR 84c:10002. See [41]

37. Leprévost, F.: The end of public key cryptography or does God play dices? PricewaterhouseCoopers Cryptogr. Centre Excell. Q. J. (1999). http://tinyurl.com/jdkkxc3. Citations in this document: §2

38. Maurer, U.M.: Fast generation of prime numbers and secure public-key cryptographic parameters. J. Cryptol. **8**, 123–155 (1995). http://link.springer.com/article/10.1007/BF00202269. Citations in this document: §2

39. Pollard, J.M.: Theorems on factorization and primality testing. Proc. Camb. Philos. Soc. **76**, 521–528 (1974). MR 50 #6992. Citations in this document: §2

40. Pollard, J.M.: A Monte Carlo method for factorization. BIT **15**, 331–334 (1975). MR 52 #13611. Citations in this document: §2

41. Pomerance, C.: Analysis and comparison of some integer factoring algorithms. In: [36], pp. 89–139 (1982). MR 84i:10005. Citations in this document: §2

42. Rabin, M.O.: Digitalized signatures and public-key functions as intractableas factorization. Technical report 212, MIT Laboratory for Computer Science (1979). https://archive.org/details/bitsavers_mitlcstrMI_457188. Citations in this document: §3

43. Rivest, R.L., Shamir, A., Adleman, L.M.: A method for obtaining digital signatures and public-key cryptosystems. Commun. ACM **21**, 120–126 (1978). ISSN 0001-0782. Citations in this document: §3

44. Robshaw, M., Katz, J. (eds.): CRYPTO 2016. LNCS, vol. 9814. Springer, Heidelberg (2016). doi:10.1007/978-3-662-53018-4. ISBN 978-3-662-53017-7. See [7]

45. Rogaway, P. (ed.): CRYPTO 2011. LNCS, vol. 6841. Springer, Heidelberg (2011). doi:10.1007/978-3-642-22792-9. See [16]

46. Schönhage, A., Strassen, V.: Schnelle Multiplikation großer Zahlen. Computing **7**, 281–292 (1971). http://link.springer.com/article/10.1007/BF02242355. Citations in this document: §3

47. Shamir, S.: RSA for paranoids. CryptoBytes **1** (1995). http://citeseerx.ist.psu.edu/viewdoc/download?doi=10.1.1.154.5763&rep=rep1&type=pdf. Citations in this document: §1,§3

48. Shor, P.W.: Algorithms for quantum computation: discrete logarithms and factoring. In: [23], pp. 124–134 (1994). See also newer version [49]. MR 1489242. Citations in this document: §1

49. Shor, P.W.: Polynomial-time algorithms for prime factorization and discrete logarithms on a quantum computer (1995). See also older version [48]; see also newer version [50]. https://arxiv.org/abs/quant-ph/9508027v2

50. Shor, P.W.: Polynomial-time algorithms for prime factorization and discrete logarithms on a quantum computer. SIAM J. Comput. **26**, 1484–1509 (1997). See also older version [49]. MR 98i:11108

51. Shoup, V.: A proposal for an ISO standard for public key encryption (version 2.1) (2001). http://www.shoup.net/papers. Citations in this document: §3

52. Takagi, T.: Fast RSA-type cryptosystem modulo $p^k q$. In: [32], pp. 318–326 (1998). http://imi.kyushu-u.ac.jp/takagi/takagi/publications/cr98.ps. Citations in this document: §1, §3

53. Wang, X., Sako, K. (eds.): ASIACRYPT 2012. LNCS, vol. 7658. Springer, Heidelberg (2012). doi:10.1007/978-3-642-34961-4. ISBN 978-3-642-34960-7. See [14]

54. Wiener, M. (ed.): CRYPTO 1999. LNCS, vol. 1666. Springer, Heidelberg (1999). doi:10.1007/3-540-48405-1. ISBN 3-540-66347-9. MR 2000h:94003. See [13]

55. Williams, H.C.: A $p + 1$ method of factoring. Math. Comput. **39**, 225–234 (1982). MR 83h:10016. Citations in this document: §2

56. Zalka, C.: Fast versions of Shor's quantum factoring algorithm (1998). https://arxiv.org/abs/quant-ph/9806084. Citations in this document: §2, §4

57. Zimmermann, P.: About memory-usage of mpz_mul (2016). https://gmplib.org/list-archives/gmp-discuss/2016-June/006009.html. Citations in this document: §A

Table A.1. Time per product-tree level in key generation—We record the time for each product-tree level in a 1-terabyte key generation using `lattice0`. Level 1 takes 1,953,125,000 4096-bit numbers as input, and produces 976,562,500 8192-bit numbers as output. Level 31 takes two 500 GB numbers and multiplies them to create the final 1 TB output.

Level	Time (s)	Level	Time (s)	Level	Time (s)	Level	Time (s)
1	4417.1	9	750.3	17	2121.7	25	4482.4
2	4039.3	10	1035.7	18	2188.4	26	5548.5
3	312.9	11	918.1	19	2392.1	27	9019.0
4	2709.8	12	1078.5	20	2463.8	28	16453.6
5	446.5	13	1180.3	21	2485.0	29	32835.6
6	1003.4	14	1291.4	22	2533.5	30	69089.7
7	647.7	15	1402.2	23	2632.7	31	123100.4
8	998.7	16	1503.6	24	3078.2		

A   Appendix: Implementation Barriers and Details

Extending GMP's Integer Capacity. The GMP library uses hard-coded 32-bit integers to represent sizes in multiple locations in the library. Without any modifications, GMP supports 2^{37}-bit integers on 64-bit machines [25]. To represent large values, we extended GMP's capacity from 32-bit integers to 64-bit integers by changing the data typing in GMP's integer structure, `mpz`. Namely, we changed `mpz_size` and `mpz_alloc` from `int` types to `int64_t` types. To accommodate increased memory usage, we increased the bound for GMP's memory allocation for the `mpz` struct in `realloc.c` to `LLONG_MAX`. The final modifications we made were to create binary-format I/O functions for 64-bit `mpz`s, namely in `mpz_inp_out.c` and `mpz_out_raw.c`.

Impact of Swapping. We initially evaluated the performance of our product-tree implementation by generating a "dummy key", a terabyte product of random 4096-bit integers. During this product computation, we counted instructions per CPU cycle (IPCs) with the command `perf stat -e instructions,cycles -a sleep 1` to measure the lost performance caused by swapping. When no swapping occurred, the machine had about 2 instructions per cycle, but upon swapping, the instructions per cycles dropped as low as 0.37 instructions per cycle and held around 0.5 to 1.2 instructions per cycle.

GMP Memory Consumption. GMP's memory consumption is another concern. High RAM and swap usage at higher levels in the product tree are attributed to GMP's FFT implementation. According to GMP's developers, their FFT implementation consumes about $8n$ bytes of temporary memory space for an $n \cdot n$ product where n is the byte size of the factors [57]. This massive consumption of memory also triggered a known race condition in the Linux kernel [2]. The bug was found in the `huge_memory.c` code. There are numerous bug reports for variants of the same bug on various mainline Linux systems

Table A.2. Heterogeneous compute cluster—The experiments in this paper were carried out on a heterogeneous cluster.

Name	CPU type	Physical cores	RAM	Count
lattice0	3.40 GHz Intel Xeon E7-8893 v2	quad 6-core	3 TB	1
raminator	2.60 GHz Intel Xeon E7-4860 v2	quad 12-core	1 TB	1
siv-1-[1-8]	2.50 GHz Intel Xeon E5-2680 v3	dual 12-core	512 GB	8
lattice[1-6]	2.30 GHz Intel Xeon E5-2699 v3	dual 18-core	256 GB	6
siv-[2-3]-[1-8]	2.20 GHz Intel Xeon E5-2699 v4	dual 22-core	512 GB	16
utah[1-4]	2.20 GHz Intel Xeon E5-2699 v4	dual 22-core	512 GB	4

throughout the past six years. Disabling transparent huge pages avoided the transparent_hugepage code in the kernel.

Measurements for 1-Terabyte Key Product Tree. In Table A.1, we show the wall-clock time for each level of computing a 1-terabyte product tree. Levels far down in the product tree are easily parallelized. We carried out the entire computation on lattice0 using 48 threads. The computation used a peak of 3.16 TB of RAM and 2.22 TB of swap memory, and completed in 356,709 s, or approximately 4 days, in wall-clock time.

Heterogeneous Cluster Description. See Table A.2.

B   Credits for Multi-prime RSA

The idea of using RSA with more than two primes is most commonly credited to Collins, Hopkins, Langford, and Sabin, who received patent 5848159 in 1998 for "RSA with several primes":

> The invention, allowing 4 primes each about 150 digits long to obtain a 600 digit n, instead of two primes about 350 [*sic*] digits long, results in a marked improvement in computer performance. For, not only are primes that are 150 digits in size easier to find and verify than ones on the order of 350 digits, but by applying techniques the inventors derive from the Chinese Remainder Theorem (CRT), public key cryptography calculations for encryption and decryption are completed much faster— even if performed serially on a single processor system.

However, the same idea had already appeared in the original RSA patent in 1983:

> In alternative embodiments, the present invention may use a modulus n which is a product of three or more primes (not necessarily distinct). Decoding may be performed modulo each of the prime factors of n and the results combined using "Chinese remaindering" or any equivalent method to obtain the result modulo n.

In any event, both of these patents have now expired, so they will not interfere with the deployment of post-quantum RSA.

A Low-Resource Quantum Factoring Algorithm

Daniel J. Bernstein[1,2]($\boxtimes$), Jean-François Biasse[3]($\boxtimes$), and Michele Mosca[4,5,6]($\boxtimes$)

[1] Department of Computer Science,
University of Illinois at Chicago, Chicago, USA
[2] Department of Mathematics and Computer Science,
Technische Universiteit Eindhoven,
Eindhoven, The Netherlands
djb@cr.yp.to
[3] Department of Mathematics and Statistics,
University of South Florida, Tampa, USA
biasse@usf.edu
[4] Institute for Quantum Computing and Department of Combinatorics
and Optimization, University of Waterloo, Waterloo, Canada
mmosca@uwaterloo.ca
[5] Perimeter Institute for Theoretical Physics, Waterloo, Canada
[6] Canadian Institute for Advanced Research, Toronto, Canada

Abstract. In this paper, we present a factoring algorithm that, assuming standard heuristics, uses just $(\log N)^{2/3+o(1)}$ qubits to factor an integer N in time $L^{q+o(1)}$ where $L = \exp((\log N)^{1/3}(\log \log N)^{2/3})$ and $q = \sqrt[3]{8/3} \approx 1.387$. For comparison, the lowest asymptotic time complexity for known pre-quantum factoring algorithms, assuming standard heuristics, is $L^{p+o(1)}$ where $p > 1.9$. The new time complexity is asymptotically worse than Shor's algorithm, but the qubit requirements are asymptotically better, so it may be possible to physically implement it sooner.

1 Introduction

The two main families of public-key primitives in widespread use today rely on the presumed hardness of the RSA problem [22] or the discrete-logarithm

Author list in alphabetical order; see https://www.ams.org/profession/leaders/culture/CultureStatement04.pdf. This work was supported by the Commission of the European Communities through the Horizon 2020 program under project 645622 (PQCRYPTO), by the U.S. National Science Foundation under grants 1018836 and 1314919, by the Netherlands Organisation for Scientific Research (NWO) under grant 639.073.005, by NIST under grant 60NANB17D184, by the Simons Foundation under grant 430128; by NSERC; by CFI; and by ORF. IQC and the Perimeter Institute are supported in part by the Government of Canada and the Province of Ontario. "Any opinions, findings, and conclusions or recommendations expressed in this material are those of the author(s) and do not necessarily reflect the views of the National Science Foundation" (or other funding agencies). Permanent ID of this document: d4969875ec8996389d6dd1271c032a204f7bbc42. Date: 2017.04.19.

© Springer International Publishing AG 2017
T. Lange and T. Takagi (Eds.): PQCrypto 2017, LNCS 10346, pp. 330–346, 2017.
DOI: 10.1007/978-3-319-59879-6_19

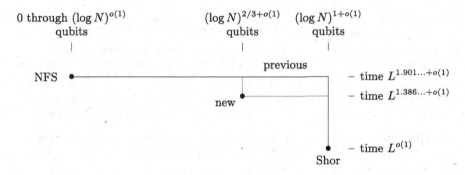

Fig. 1. Tradeoffs between factorization time and number of logical qubits; i.e., evolution of time as more and more qubits become available.

problem [13] respectively. Shor's algorithm [25] provides an efficient solution to both the factorization problem and the discrete-logarithm problem, thus breaking these primitives, assuming that the attacker has a large general-purpose quantum computer.

Shor's algorithm has motivated a new field of research, post-quantum cryptography, consisting of cryptographic primitives designed to resist quantum attacks. It is clear that the main public-key primitives will have to be replaced before the practical realization of large-scale quantum computers. However, the precise time line remains an important open question that can have significant economic consequences. In particular, the community needs to predict the point in time when quantum computers will threaten commonly deployed RSA key sizes, whether through Shor's algorithm or any other quantum factoring algorithm.

An obvious obstruction to the implementation of Shor's algorithm is the number of qubits necessary to run it. The number of qubits used by Shor's algorithm is $\Theta(\log N)$, where N is the integer being factored; i.e., the number of qubits grows linearly with the number of bits in N. There has been some effort to reduce the Θ constant; see, e.g., [27], [4], [24], [3], and [26].

1.1. Contributions of This Paper. We present a factoring algorithm that, assuming standard heuristics, uses a *sublinear* number of qubits, specifically $(\log N)^{2/3+o(1)}$ qubits, to factor N in time $L^{q+o(1)}$ where $q = \sqrt[3]{8/3} \approx 1.387$ and $L = \exp((\log N)^{1/3}(\log\log N)^{2/3})$ see Fig. 1.

To put this in perspective: The lowest asymptotic time complexity for known pre-quantum (0-qubit) factoring algorithms, assuming standard heuristics, is $L^{p+o(1)}$ where $p = \sqrt[3]{92 + 26\sqrt{13}}/3 \approx 1.902$. This exponent p is from a 1993 algorithm by Coppersmith [12], slightly improving upon the exponent $\sqrt[3]{64/9} \approx 1.923$ from [18].

The new time complexity is asymptotically worse than Shor's algorithm, but the qubit requirements are asymptotically better, so it may be possible to physically implement the new algorithm sooner than Shor's algorithm.

The fact that we use fewer qubits than Shor's algorithm *for all sufficiently large key sizes* does not answer the question of whether we use fewer qubits than Shor's algorithm to break, e.g., common 2048-bit RSA keys. Optimization of exact qubit requirements for this algorithm is a challenging open problem.

1.2. Discrete Logarithms. The same idea can also be used for multiplicative-group discrete logarithms. (On the other hand, the idea has no obvious impact upon the number of qubits needed for elliptic-curve discrete logarithms.)

Specifically, the idea of NFS has been adapted to solving discrete-logarithm problems in the multiplicative group of any prime field. See [14,23] for early work and [2] for the latest optimizations.

The first stage of these algorithms computes discrete logarithms of many small numbers in the field. The best pre-quantum complexity known for this stage is $L^{p+o(1)}$. Here $p \approx 1.902$ as before, and the N used in defining L is replaced by the number of elements of the field. The idea of our factoring algorithm adapts straightforwardly to this context, reducing the cost of the first stage to $L^{q+o(1)}$, where $q \approx 1.387$ as before.

The second stage deduces the discrete logarithm of the target. This stage takes time $L^{d+o(1)}$ where $d \approx 1.232$. If many discrete-logarithm problems are posed for the same field then this second stage is the bottleneck (since the first stage is reused for all targets), and we have not found a way to speed up this stage using sublinear quantum resources. On the other hand, if there are relatively few targets then the first stage is the bottleneck.

There is a fast-moving literature (see, e.g., [20]) on pre-quantum techniques to solve discrete-logarithm problems in the multiplicative group of *extension fields*. We expect our approach to combine productively with these techniques, but we have not attempted to analyze the details or the resulting costs.

1.3. Notes on Fault Tolerance. Our primary cost metrics are time and the number of *logical* qubits. Beware, however, that an improved tradeoff between these metrics does not guarantee an improved tradeoff between time and the number of *physical* qubits.

In what Gottesman calls the "standard version" (see [15]) of the threshold theorem for fault-tolerant quantum computing, a logical circuit using Q qubits and containing T gates is converted into a fault-tolerant circuit using $Q(\log QT)^{O(1)}$ physical qubits. This bound is too weak to say anything useful about our algorithm: for us $\log T$ is $(\log N)^{1/3+o(1)}$, so all the bound says is that the resulting fault-tolerant circuit uses $(\log N)^{O(1)}$ physical qubits.

Gottesman in [15] introduced a different approach to fault-tolerant quantum computing, encoding Q logical qubits as just $O(Q)$ physical qubits, without much overhead in the number of qubit operations. However, Gottesman's analysis is focused on the case that T is in $Q^{O(1)}$. While extending the analysis to larger T may yield useful results in terms of quantum overhead, it is important to note that Gottesman explicitly disregards the cost of pre-quantum computation (for decoding error-correcting codes), while we take all computations into account.

To factor in time $L^{q+o(1)}$ with a sublinear number of physical qubits, it would be enough to encode Q logical qubits as, e.g., $Q^{1.49+o(1)}$ physical qubits, with time overhead at most $\exp(Q^{0.49+o(1)})$ and with logical error rate at most $1/\exp(Q^{0.51+o(1)})$. We leave this as another challenge.

1.4. Notation. We use the standard abbreviation "$\mathbb{Z}/M$" for the quotient $\mathbb{Z}/M\mathbb{Z}$.

2 Factoring Integers with NFS

The number-field sieve (NFS) is a factoring method introduced by Pollard [21] and subsequently improved by many authors. NFS produced the $L^{p+o(1)}$ asymptotic speed record mentioned above; it was also used for the latest RSA factorization record, the successful factorization of a 768-bit RSA modulus [17]. Our $L^{q+o(1)}$ algorithm, described in Section 3, uses quantum techniques to accelerate the relation-collection step in NFS.

This section gives a high-level description of NFS. For simplicity we restrict attention to the version of NFS introduced by Buhler, Lenstra, and Pomerance in [10], without the subsequent multi-field improvement [12] from Coppersmith (which does not seem to produce a better exponent in our context).

NFS begins as follows. Assume that N is an odd positive integer. Compute $m = \lfloor N^{1/d} \rfloor$; here $d \geq 2$ is an integer parameter optimized below. Assume that $N > 2^{d^2}$; then $N < 2m^d$ by [10, Proposition 3.2]. Write N in base m as $m^d + c_{d-1}m^{d-1} + \cdots + c_1 m + c_0$ where each of $c_{d-1}, \ldots, c_1, c_0$ is between 0 and $m-1$. Define $f = X^d + c_{d-1}X^{d-1} + \cdots + c_1 X + c_0 \in \mathbb{Z}[X]$, so that $f(m) = N$. Check whether f is irreducible; if not then the factorization of f immediately reveals a nontrivial factorization of N, as noted in [10, Section 3].

Let α be a root of f, and let ϕ be the ring homomorphism $\sum_i a_i\alpha^i \mapsto \sum_i a_i m^i$ from $\mathbb{Z}[\alpha]$ to $\mathbb{Z}/N$. Find, as explained below, a nontrivial set S of pairs (a, b) such that the following two properties hold simultaneously:

"rational side": $\qquad \displaystyle\prod_{(a,b)\in S}(a+bm)$ is a square X^2 in $\mathbb{Z}$,

"algebraic side": $\qquad f'(\alpha)^2 \displaystyle\prod_{(a,b)\in S}(a+b\alpha)$ is a square β^2 in $\mathbb{Z}[\alpha]$.

Then compute $Y = \phi(\beta)$. Note that $Y^2 = \phi(\beta^2) = \phi(f'(\alpha))^2 \prod \phi(a+b\alpha) = f'(m)^2 \prod(a+bm) = (f'(m)X)^2$ in $\mathbb{Z}/N$ since $\phi(a+b\alpha) = a+bm$ in $\mathbb{Z}/N$. Check whether $\gcd\{N, Y - f'(m)X\}$ is a nontrivial factor of N.

NFS actually produces many sets S at negligible extra cost, leading to many such potential factorizations. Conjecturally every odd positive integer N is factored by this procedure into products of prime powers.

2.1. Finding Squares on the Rational Side. Consider first the simpler problem of finding S such that $\prod_{(a,b)\in S}(a+bm)$ is a square. NFS handles this as follows.

Define an integer as "y-smooth" when it is not divisible by any primes $>y$. Here the "smoothness bound" y is a parameter optimized below.

Find many y-smooth integers of the form $a + bm$, and combine these y-smooth integers to form a square. More specifically, search through the space

$$U = \{(a,b): \quad a, b \in \mathbb{Z}, \quad \gcd\{a,b\} = 1, \quad |a| \leq u, \quad 0 < b \leq u\},$$

where u is another parameter optimized below. For each $(a, b) \in U$ such that $a + bm$ is y-smooth, factor $a + bm$ as $(-1)^{e_0} p_1^{e_1} \cdots p_B^{e_B}$ where $p_1 < \cdots < p_B$ are the primes $\leq y$, and compute the exponent vector

$$e(a, b) = (e_0 \bmod 2, \ldots, e_B \bmod 2) \in \mathbb{F}_2^{B+1}.$$

If there are at least $B + 2$ such pairs (a_i, b_i) then the vectors $e(a_i, b_i)$ must have a nontrivial linear dependency: linear algebra reveals bits $x_i \in \mathbb{F}_2$, not all zero, such that $\sum_i x_i e(a_i, b_i) = 0$ in $\mathbb{F}_2^{B+1}$, which directly yields a square $\prod_{i:x_i \neq 0} (a_i + b_i m)$.

2.2. Finding Squares on the Algebraic Side. The search for S such that $f'(\alpha)^2 \prod_{(a,b) \in S}(a + b\alpha)$ is a square is handled similarly.

Define $g(a, b) = (-b)^d f(-a/b) = a^d - c_{d-1} a^{d-1} b + \cdots + c_1 a(-b)^{d-1} + c_0(-b)^d$. Search for pairs (a, b) in the same space U such that $g(a, b)$ is y-smooth.

There is a standard definition of an exponent vector $e'(a, b) \in \mathbb{F}_2^{B'+B''}$ for any such pair (a, b). This vector has the following properties: if $f'(\alpha)^2 \prod_{(a,b) \in S}(a + b\alpha)$ is a square then $\sum_{(a,b) \in S} e'(a, b) = 0$; conversely, if $\sum_{(a,b) \in S} e'(a, b) = 0$ then $f'(\alpha)^2 \prod_{(a,b) \in S}(a + b\alpha)$ is a square, assuming standard heuristics; the vector length $B' + B''$, like $B + 1$, is approximately $y/\log y$; and e' is not difficult to compute. See [10, Sections 5 and 8] for the detailed definition of e', involving ideals and quadratic characters of $\mathbb{Z}[\alpha]$; the point of $g(a, b)$ is that $\mathcal{N}(a + b\alpha) = g(a, b)$, where $\mathcal{N}$ is the norm map from $\mathbb{Z}[\alpha]$ to $\mathbb{Z}$.

2.3. Overall Algorithm. Algorithm 1 combines all of these steps. It searches through U for pairs (a, b) such that both $a + bm$ and $g(a, b)$ are y-smooth, i.e., such that $(a + bm)g(a, b)$ is y-smooth. If there are enough such pairs (a, b) then linear algebra finds a nontrivial linear dependency between the vectors $(e(a, b), e'(a, b)) \in \mathbb{F}_2^{B+1+B'+B''}$, i.e., a set S of pairs (a, b) such that both $\prod_{(a,b) \in S}(a + bm)$ and $f'(\alpha)^2 \prod_{(a,b) \in S}(a + b\alpha)$ are squares.

By generating some further pairs (a, b) one obtains more linear dependencies, obtaining further sets S as noted above. For simplicity we omit this refinement from the algorithm statement.

3   Accelerating NFS Using Quantum Search

The main loop in Algorithm 1 searches for y-smooth integers $(a + bm)g(a, b)$, where (a, b) ranges through a set U of size $u^{2+o(1)}$. If the number of y-smooth integers $(a + bm)g(a, b)$ is at least $B + 2 + B' + B''$ then the algorithm is

Algorithm 1. Conventional NFS

Input: Odd positive integer N and parameters d, y, u with $N > 2^{d^2}$.
Output: A divisor of N (conjecturally often nontrivial when N is not a prime power).
1: Compute $m = \lfloor N^{1/d} \rfloor$.
2: Write N in base m as $m^d + c_{d-1}m^{d-1} + \cdots + c_1 m + c_0$.
3: Define $f = X^d + c_{d-1}X^{d-1} + \cdots + c_1 X + c_0 \in \mathbb{Z}[X]$.
4: If f has a proper factor h in $\mathbb{Z}[X]$, return $h(m)$.
5: Define $g(a, b) = a^d - c_{d-1}a^{d-1}b + \cdots + c_1 a(-b)^{d-1} + c_0(-b)^d$.
6: **for** each $(a, b) \in \mathbb{Z} \times \mathbb{Z}$ with $\gcd\{a, b\} = 1$, $|a| \leq u$, $0 < b \leq u$ **do**
7:   **if** $a + bm$ and $g(a, b)$ are y-smooth **then**
8:     Compute the vector $(e(a, b), e'(a, b)) \in \mathbb{F}_2^{B+1+B'+B''}$.
9:   **end if**
10: **end for**
11: If these vectors are linearly independent, return 1.
12: Find a nonempty subset S of $\{(a, b)\}$ where the corresponding vectors have sum 0.
13: Compute $X = \sqrt{\prod_{(a,b) \in S}(a + bm)}$ and $\beta = \sqrt{f'(\alpha)^2 \prod_{(a,b) \in S}(a + \alpha b)}$.
14: **return** $\gcd\{N, \phi(\beta) - f'(m)X\}$.

guaranteed to find a linear dependency, and conjecturally has a good chance of factoring N. This cutoff $B + 2 + B' + B''$ is in $y^{1+o(1)}$, and standard parameter choices are tuned so that there are in fact this many y-smooth values.

Algorithm 2 uses Grover's algorithm for the same search. Other steps of the algorithm remain unchanged. In this section we analyze the impact of this speedup upon the overall complexity of NFS.

The main appeal of this algorithm, compared to Shor's algorithm, is as follows. When NFS parameters are optimized, the number of bits in $(a + bm)g(a, b)$ is at most $(\log N)^{2/3+o(1)}$. With careful attention to reversible algorithm design (see Sections 4, 5, and 6) we fit the entire algorithm into $(\log N)^{2/3+o(1)}$ qubits. This is asymptotically *sublinear* in the length of N.

Note that our optimization here is for time. We would not be surprised if allowing a somewhat larger exponent of L in the time allows a constant-factor improvement in the number of qubits, but establishing this requires solving the challenging qubit-optimization problem mentioned in Section 1.

3.1. Complexity Analysis. The following analysis shows, under the same heuristics used for previous NFS analyses, that the optimal time exponent q for this algorithm is $\sqrt[3]{8/3}$. As in the conventional NFS analysis by Buhler, Lenstra, and Pomerance [10], we choose

- $y \in L^{\beta+o(1)}$,
- $u \in L^{\epsilon+o(1)}$, and
- $d \in (\delta + o(1))(\log N)^{1/3}(\log \log N)^{-1/3}$,

where β, ϵ, δ are positive real numbers and $L = \exp((\log N)^{1/3}(\log \log N)^{2/3})$. Conventional NFS takes $\epsilon = \beta$, but we end up with ϵ larger than β; specifically, our optimization will produce $\beta = \sqrt[3]{1/3}$, $\epsilon = \sqrt[3]{9/8}$, and $\delta = \sqrt[3]{8/3}$.

Algorithm 2. New: NFS accelerated using quantum search

Input: Odd positive integer N and parameters d, y, u with $N > 2^{d^2}$.
Output: A divisor of N (conjecturally often nontrivial when N is not a prime power).
1: Compute $m = \lfloor N^{1/d} \rfloor$.
2: Write N in base m as $m^d + c_{d-1}m^{d-1} + \cdots + c_1 m + c_0$.
3: Define $f = X^d + c_{d-1}X^{d-1} + \cdots + c_1 X + c_0 \in \mathbb{Z}[X]$.
4: If f has a proper factor h in $\mathbb{Z}[X]$, return $h(m)$.
5: Define $g(a,b) = a^d - c_{d-1}a^{d-1}b + \cdots + c_1 a(-b)^{d-1} + c_0(-b)^d$.
6: Use Grover's algorithm to search for all $(a,b) \in \mathbb{Z} \times \mathbb{Z}$ with $\gcd\{a,b\} = 1$, $|a| \leq u$, $0 < b \leq u$ such that $a + bm$ and $g(a,b)$ are y-smooth.
7: **for** each such (a,b) **do**
8:    Compute the vector $(e(a,b), e'(a,b)) \in \mathbb{F}_2^{B+1+B'+B''}$.
9: **end for**
10: If these vectors are linearly independent, return 1.
11: Find a nonempty subset S of $\{(a,b)\}$ where the corresponding vectors have sum 0.
12: Compute $X = \sqrt{\prod_{(a,b) \in S}(a + bm)}$ and $\beta = \sqrt{f'(\alpha)^2 \prod_{(a,b) \in S}(a + \alpha b)}$.
13: **return** $\gcd\{N, \phi(\beta) - f'(m)X\}$.

The quantities $a + bm$ and $g(a,b)$ that we wish to be smooth are bounded in absolute value by, respectively, $u + uN^{1/d} \leq 2uN^{1/d}$ and $(d+1)N^{1/d}u^d$. Their product is thus bounded by $x = 2(d+1)N^{2/d}u^{d+1}$. Note that

$$\log x = \log(2(d+1)) + \frac{2}{d}\log N + (d+1)\log u$$

$$\in \left(\frac{2}{\delta} + \delta\epsilon + o(1)\right)(\log N)^{2/3}(\log\log N)^{1/3}.$$

A uniform random integer in $[1, x]$ has y-smoothness probability $v^{-v(1+o(1))}$, where

$$v = \frac{\log x}{\log y} \in \frac{1}{\beta}\left(\frac{2}{\delta} + \delta\epsilon + o(1)\right)(\log N)^{1/3}(\log\log N)^{-1/3}.$$

We have $\log v \in (1/3 + o(1))\log\log N$ so this smoothness probability is

$$\exp(-(1+o(1))v\log v) = \exp\left(-\frac{1}{3\beta}\left(\frac{2}{\delta} + \delta\epsilon + o(1)\right)(\log N)^{1/3}(\log\log N)^{2/3}\right),$$

i.e., $L^{-(2/\delta+\delta\epsilon+o(1))/3\beta}$. We heuristically assume that the same asymptotic holds for the smoothness probability of the products $(a + bm)g(a,b)$.

The search space has size $u^{2+o(1)} = L^{2\epsilon+o(1)}$ and needs to contain $y^{1+o(1)} = L^{\beta+o(1)}$ smooth products. We thus need $2\epsilon - (2/\delta + \delta\epsilon)/3\beta \geq \beta$ for the algorithm to work as $N \to \infty$; i.e., we need $2 > \delta/3\beta$ and $\epsilon \geq (\beta + 2/3\beta\delta)/(2 - \delta/3\beta)$.

There is no point in taking ϵ larger than this cutoff, so we assume from now on that $\epsilon = (\beta + 2/3\beta\delta)/(2 - \delta/3\beta)$. (In this equality case we also need to take a large enough $o(1)$ for u to ensure enough smooth products, but this affects only the $o(1)$ in the final complexity.) The smoothness probability is now $L^{-2\epsilon+\beta+o(1)}$.

The conventional pre-quantum complexity analysis continues by saying that searching $L^{2\epsilon+o(1)}$ integers takes time $L^{2\epsilon+o(1)}$. We instead search with Grover's algorithm. Specifically, we partition the search space U in any systematic fashion into $L^{\beta+o(1)}$ parts, each of size $L^{2\epsilon-\beta+o(1)}$, each (with overwhelming probability) producing $L^{o(1)}$ smooth values. Grover's algorithm takes time $L^{\epsilon-\beta/2+o(1)}$ to search each part, for total time just $L^{\epsilon+\beta/2+o(1)}$.

Linear algebra takes time $L^{2\beta+o(1)}$. The pre-quantum-search exponent 2ϵ is balanced against 2β when $\epsilon = \beta$, i.e., $\beta^2 - \beta\delta/3 - 2/3\delta = 0$, forcing $\beta = (\delta + \sqrt{\delta^2 + 24/\delta})/6$ since $\delta - \sqrt{\delta^2 - 24/\delta}$ is negative. It is now a simple calculus exercise to see that taking $\delta = \sqrt[3]{3}$ produces the minimum $\beta = \sqrt[3]{8/9}$, satisfying the requirement $2 > \delta/3\beta$, and thus total time $L^{\sqrt[3]{64/9}+o(1)}$, roughly $L^{1.923}$.

Our quantum-search exponent $\epsilon + \beta/2$ is balanced against 2β when $\epsilon = 3\beta/2$, i.e., $\beta^2 - \beta\delta/4 - 1/3\delta = 0$, forcing $\beta = (\delta + \sqrt{\delta^2 + 64/3\delta})/8$. This time the calculus exercise produces $\delta = \sqrt[3]{8/3}$ and the minimum $\beta = \sqrt[3]{1/3}$, again satisfying $2 > \delta/3\beta$, and thus total time $L^{\sqrt[3]{8/3}+o(1)}$, roughly $L^{1.387}$.

Note that a more realistic cost model for two-dimensional NFS circuits was used in [7], assigning a higher cost $L^{2.5\beta+o(1)}$ to linear algebra and ending up with exponent approximately 1.976 for conventional NFS. An analogous analysis of our algorithm ends up with exponent approximately 1.456.

4   A Quantum Relation Search

This section presents an algorithm to find a λ-bit string s such that $F(s)$ is y-smooth. If many such strings exist then the algorithm makes a random choice; if no such string exists then the algorithm fails.

We assume that $F(s)$ is an integer between $-x$ and x for each λ-bit string s. We also assume that $\log y \in \Theta(\lambda)$; that $\log x \in (\log y)^{2+o(1)}$; and that the function F is computable by a reversible $(\log x)^{1+o(1)}$-bit circuit in time $2^{o(\lambda)}$.

Our time budget for the search algorithm is $2^{(0.5+o(1))\lambda}$. Our qubit budget is $(\log x)^{1+o(1)} = \lambda^{2+o(1)}$.

4.1. ECM as a Subroutine. The usual pre-quantum approach is as follows. Lenstra's elliptic-curve method (ECM) [19], assuming standard heuristics and again assuming $\log x \in (\log y)^{2+o(1)}$, takes time $\exp((\log y)^{1/2+o(1)})$ and space $O(\log x)$ to find all primes $\leq y$ dividing a nonzero input integer in $[-x, x]$. By trial division, within the same space, one sees whether the integer is y-smooth.

Generic techniques due to Bennett [5] convert any algorithm taking time T and space S into a reversible algorithm taking time $T^{1+\epsilon}$ and space $O(S \log T)$. For us $T^{1+\epsilon} \in y^{o(1)} = 2^{o(\lambda)}$ and $S \log T \in (\log x)(\log y)^{1/2+o(1)} = (\log x)^{5/4+o(1)}$. Applying Grover's algorithm then takes time $2^{(0.5+o(1))\lambda}$ using $(\log x)^{5/4+o(1)}$ qubits. This is beyond our budget. (The NFS application takes time $L^{q+o(1)}$ using $(\log N)^{5/6+o(1)}$ qubits, which meets our goal of sublinearity but is not as strong as we would like.)

4.2. Shor as a Subroutine. To do better we replace the ECM subroutine with Shor's factoring method. We emphasize that here Shor is being applied only to integers between $-x$ and x; these are asymptotically much smaller than N.

Recall that, to find y-smooth integers $F(s)$, Grover's search algorithm uses a quantum circuit $U_{F,y}$ such that

- $U_{F,y}|s\rangle = -|s\rangle$ if $F(s)$ is y-smooth.
- $U_{F,y}|s\rangle = |s\rangle$ if $F(s)$ is not y-smooth.

This circuit does not need to be derived from a pre-quantum circuit; it can carry out quantum computations, such as Shor's algorithm. The main challenge is to minimize the number of qubits used to compute $U_{F,y}$, while staying within a $2^{o(\lambda)}$ time bound. Grover's algorithm then takes time $2^{(0.5+o(1))\lambda}$.

Section 5 explains how to apply Shor's algorithm to a superposition of odd positive integers, factoring with significant probability each integer that is not a power of a prime. Section 6 explains how to use Shor's algorithm repeatedly to recognize y-smooth integers.

4.3. Application to NFS. For our NFS application in Section 3, we choose an even integer λ so that $2^\lambda \in L^{2\epsilon-\beta+o(1)}$. We map λ-bit strings s to pairs (a, b) in a straightforward way, choosing a range of $2^{\lambda/2}$ consecutive integers a within $[-u, u]$ and a range of $2^{\lambda/2}$ consecutive integers b within $[1, u]$. We define x and y as in the previous section, and we define $F(s)$ as $(a + bm)g(a, b)$. The assumptions of this section are satisfied.

The algorithm in this section finds a, b in these ranges such that $(a + bm)g(a, b)$ is y-smooth. The algorithm takes time $2^{(0.5+o(1))\lambda} = L^{\epsilon-\beta/2+o(1)}$ and works with $(\log x)^{1+o(1)} = (\log N)^{2/3+o(1)}$ qubits as desired. Repeating the same algorithm $L^{o(1)}$ times finds all such pairs (a, b) with overwhelming probability. (This is overkill: Section 3 needs enough pairs to find a nontrivial linear dependency but does not need to find *all* pairs.) Repeating for $L^{\beta+o(1)}$ ranges covers all pairs (a, b) in the set U defined in the previous section. That set omits pairs (a, b) with $\gcd\{a, b\} > 1$; we simply discard such pairs.

5   Shor's Factorization Method in Superposition

The conventional view is that Shor's algorithm is applied to *one* odd positive integer $M \in [1, x]$, obtaining a (hopefully nontrivial) divisor M_1 of M. We instead factor a *superposition* of inputs M, obtaining a *superposition* of divisors M_1 of M. This changes costs: in particular, Shor's original algorithm uses $(\log x)^{2+o(1)}$ qubits when it is run in superposition.

This section reviews the relevant features of Shor's algorithm, and explains a variant of the algorithm that fits into $(\log x)^{1+o(1)}$ qubits even when run in superposition. This section also explains a further variant (applicable to both the conventional case and the superposition case) that often finds more factors at the same cost.

5.1. Review of Shor's Algorithm. Shor starts with some a coprime to M and precomputes $a^2 \bmod M$, $a^4 \bmod M$, $a^8 \bmod M$, etc., along with their inverses.

Shor then carries out a quantum computation, ending with a measurement, yielding an approximation $z/2^m$ of a fraction of the form k/r, where r is the order of a modulo M.

If m is chosen large enough, at least twice the number of bits of M, then, with probability $\Omega(1/\log\log M)$, the largest denominator below M in the continued fraction of $z/2^m$ will be exactly r. "Probability" here implicitly assumes that the random variable a is uniformly distributed in $(\mathbb{Z}/M)^*$.

One can switch to more reliable methods of finding r, improving the probability to $\Omega(1)$ at constant overhead, as discussed in, e.g., [11, 25]. For us Shor's original method is adequate: the $\log\log$ factor is subsumed by $(\log x)^{o(1)}$.

Usually r is even. Shor then finishes by computing $M_1 = \gcd\{M, a^{r/2} - 1\}$.

5.2. Shor in Superposition Without Many Qubits.

Using the same method to factor a superposition of inputs M means that we also need to execute the selection of a, the precomputation of $a^2 \bmod M$ etc., the continued-fraction computation, and the computation of $\gcd\{M, a^{r/2} - 1\}$ in superposition. We need to be careful here to fit these computations into our space budget, just $(\log x)^{1+o(1)}$ qubits.

As an example of what can go wrong, consider the seemingly trivial first step in typical statements of Shor's algorithm, namely generating an integer a uniformly at random between 1 and $M - 1$ (assuming $M > 1$). The textbook implementation of this step is rejection sampling: generate $b = \lceil \log_2 x \rceil$ random bits; interpret those bits as an integer R between 0 and $2^b - 1$; restart if $R \geq (M - 1)\lfloor 2^b/(M - 1)\rfloor$; compute $a = 1 + (R \bmod M - 1)$. The restart happens with probability $<1/2$, so on average <2 values of R are required.

The obvious way to handle a superposition of M is to choose in advance how many R's to generate, and to choose this number to be large, so that failures cannot be expected to occur. In the context of NFS, generating $(\log N)^{1/3+o(1)}$ values of R is adequate, for a total of $(\log N)^{1+o(1)}$ random bits. This might not sound like a problem, but storing this number of qubits is beyond our budget.

We instead generate one value of R and define $a = 1 + (R \bmod M - 1)$, skipping the rejection step. This cannot reduce the success probability of Shor's algorithm by more than a factor 2. We could bring this factor arbitrarily close to 1 by generating a few more bits in R, but a factor 2 is already not a problem for us: it is subsumed by $(\log x)^{o(1)}$ at the level of detail of our analysis.

Furthermore, there is no reason for us to store R in superposition: we use one R for all choices of M, so we do not need to spend qubits storing it. We do vary R across the multiple Shor calls explained in Section 6, so that each M is overwhelmingly likely to be factored; i.e., the function of M defined by our choice of the sequence of R is overwhelmingly likely to equal the desired function of M, recognizing whether or not M is y-smooth.

There is a more serious problem with the precomputation in Shor's algorithm: Shor uses a quadratic number, $(\log x)^{2+o(1)}$, of bits to store the sequence $a^2 \bmod M$, $a^4 \bmod M$, etc. This precomputation is important for Shor's method of computing $a^e \bmod M$ with e in superposition: namely, Shor uses the ith bit of

e to control a multiplication by $a^i \bmod M$ and then to control a multiplication by $1/a^i \bmod M$ (used to erase the previous temporary value).

We use, instead of Shor's strategy, a conventional pre-quantum "square and multiply" exponentiation algorithm taking time $(\log x)^{O(1)}$ and space $O(\log x)$. Bennett's generic conversion then produces a reversible algorithm taking time $(\log x)^{O(1)}$ and space $O(\log x \log \log x)$, i.e., space $(\log x)^{1+o(1)}$ as desired.

Finally, standard pre-quantum algorithms take time $(\log x)^{O(1)}$ to compute continued fractions, m-bit powers modulo M, gcd, and inverses mod M, all in space $O(\log x)$. Again generic conversion produces reversible algorithms for the same computations taking time $(\log x)^{O(1)}$ and space $O(\log x \log \log x)$.

5.3. Further Factorization for Free.

We point out an easy tweak to Shor's algorithm that, starting from r, often finds more factors of an odd integer M in the same time (and space), and that is also much more reliable at separating any particular prime divisors of M from each other. (See also [16] for some other post-r tweaks that do not provide the same reliability but that sometimes help.)

Understanding this tweak requires a review of the probability that r produces a nontrivial divisor $M_1 = \gcd\{M, a^{r/2} - 1\}$ of M. Assume that M has prime factorization $p_1^{e_1} p_2^{e_2} \cdots p_f^{e_f}$, and write $(p_j - 1)p_j^{e_j - 1}$ as $2^{t_j} u_j$ where u_j is odd. By assumption M is odd so each $t_j \geq 1$. The group $(\mathbb{Z}/M)^*$ is isomorphic to the product of the groups $\mathbb{Z}/2^{t_1}, \mathbb{Z}/2^{t_2}, \ldots, \mathbb{Z}/2^{t_f}, \mathbb{Z}/u_1, \ldots, \mathbb{Z}/u_f$; choosing a uniform random element $a \in (\mathbb{Z}/M)^*$ is equivalent to choosing independent uniform random elements $x_1, x_2, \ldots, x_f, y_1, y_2, \ldots, y_f$ of these groups.

Write the order of x_j as 2^{c_j}, and write the order of y_j as d_j. The order r of a is then $2^{\max\{c_1, \ldots, c_f\}} d$, where d is an odd integer, namely $\operatorname{lcm}\{d_1, \ldots, d_f\}$. Note that c_j is t_j with probability $1/2$; $t_j - 1$ with probability $1/4$; and so on through 1 and 0, each with probability $1/2^{t_j}$. For any particular value of c_1, the chance that $c_2 = c_1$ is at most $1/2$, and similarly for c_3 etc., so the chance of all of $c_1, \ldots, c_f$ being identical is at most $1/2^{f-1}$.

Assume from now on that $c_1, \ldots, c_f$ are not identical. Then $\max\{c_1, \ldots, c_f\} > 0$ so r is even. By construction $a^r = 1$ in $(\mathbb{Z}/M)^*$, so $a^r = 1$ in $(\mathbb{Z}/p_j^{e_j})^*$, so $a^{r/2} = \pm 1$ in $(\mathbb{Z}/p_j^{e_j})^*$. The case $+1$ occurs exactly when $(r/2)x_j = 0$ in $\mathbb{Z}/2^{t_j}$, i.e., when $c_j < \max\{c_1, \ldots, c_f\}$; so $M_1 = \gcd\{M, a^{r/2} - 1\}$ is divisible by p_j exactly when $c_j < \max\{c_1, \ldots, c_f\}$.

In other words, computing M_1 splits the prime divisors p_j of M into two nonempty classes: those for which $c_j < \max\{c_1, \ldots, c_f\}$, and those for which $c_j = \max\{c_1, \ldots, c_f\}$. Hence M is nontrivially factored into M_1 and M/M_1.

Our tweak (inspired by "strong probable prime" tests [1]) is to compute

$$\gcd\{M, a^{r/2} + 1\}, \gcd\{M, a^{r/4} + 1\}, \gcd\{M, a^{r/8} + 1\}, \ldots,$$
$$\gcd\{M, a^d + 1\}, \gcd\{M, a^d - 1\}.$$

These divisors of M have product exactly M and fit into essentially the same space as M. This splits the prime divisors into more classes, namely those for which $c_j = \max\{c_1, \ldots, c_f\}$, those for which $c_j = \max\{c_1, \ldots, c_f\} - 1$, those for which $c_j = \max\{c_1, \ldots, c_f\} - 2$, and so on, ending with those for which $c_j = 0$.

Shor's algorithm is unlikely to split p_i from p_j when t_i and t_j are significantly below $\max\{t_1, \ldots, t_f\}$. For example, if $f = 3$ and $(t_1, t_2, t_3) = (20, 3, 2)$, then c_1 is almost always larger than c_2 and c_3, so Shor's algorithm will almost always factor M into $p_1^{e_1}$ and $p_2^{e_2} p_3^{e_3}$. For our tweak, each pair (i, j) with $i \neq j$ has chance at least 50% of being split, since $c_i = c_j$ with probability at most 50%.

We also briefly mention a different way to avoid biases towards particular primes, namely to change the group used in Shor's algorithm from $(\mathbb{Z}/N)^*$ to a randomly selected elliptic-curve group $E(\mathbb{Z}/N)$. This is analogous to the change in [19] from the $p - 1$ factorization method to ECM.

6   Recognizing Smooth Integers

We present two constructions of fast quantum circuits $U_{F,y}$ usable in Section 4. Recall that the job of $U_{F,y}$, given a superposition of inputs s, is to recognize for each s whether $F(s) \in \{-x, \ldots, x\}$ is y-smooth.

6.1. Parallel Construction. Starting with $M = F(s)$, declare non-smoothness if $M = 0$. Otherwise replace M by its absolute value, and remove all powers of 2 from M. From now on, M is an odd positive integer.

Use the tweaked version of Shor's algorithm presented in Section 5.3 to obtain a factorization of M into various divisors. Repeat this t times, where $t \in (\log x)^{o(1)}$ is a parameter chosen below, obtaining t factorizations of M. This consumes $(\log x)^{1+o(1)}$ qubits.

Use the algorithm of [8] to factor all the divisors, and thus also M, into coprimes. Use the algorithm of [6] (or, alternatively, [9]) to write each of the coprimes as a maximal power of a root. Note that if all the roots are $\leq y$ then M has been proven to be y-smooth; save one bit indicating whether this is the case. These algorithms take time and space $(\log x)^{1+o(1)}$, so reversible versions take time $(\log x)^{1+\epsilon+o(1)}$ and space $(\log x)^{1+o(1)}$.

If M is in fact y-smooth but this algorithm fails to prove it, then one of the roots is $>y$, and thus contains two distinct prime divisors p, q of M. This means that all t factorizations of M failed to split p from q.

There are at most $\log_2 M \leq \log_2 x$ prime divisors of M, and thus fewer than $(\log_2 x)^2$ pairs of distinct prime divisors. Fix a pair (p, q). Recall that each run of Shor's algorithm has probability $\Omega(1/\log\log x)$ of finding r. For the tweaked version, given that r is found, there is conditional probability $\geq 1/2$ of splitting p from q, and thus probability $\Omega(1/\log\log x)$ of splitting p from q. The probability of a failed split after t repetitions is thus $1/\exp(\Omega(t/\log\log x))$. Now let (p, q) vary: the total probability is below $(\log_2 x)^2/\exp(\Omega(t/\log\log x))$. We choose t just large enough for this probability bound to be below $1/4$; then $t \in (\log\log x)^{2+o(1)}$, so $t \in (\log x)^{o(1)}$ as claimed above.

We now uncompute everything except for the qubit indicating whether M was proven y-smooth. We then reuse the same temporary storage to repeat the entire procedure T times, accumulating T independent proof qubits. Together these qubits reliably indicate whether M is y-smooth; the failure probability is at most $1/4^T$. We take T as, e.g., $(\log N)^{1/2+o(1)}$, consuming only $(\log N)^{1/2+o(1)}$

qubits and reducing the failure probability to $1/\exp((\log N)^{1/2+o(1)})$. This failure probability can safely be ignored, since all our computations take time at most $\exp((\log N)^{1/3+o(1)})$.

6.2. Serial Construction.

As an alternative approach, we apply Shor's algorithm *serially*. First we use Shor's algorithm to split M into two factors, then we use Shor's algorithm to split the largest factor that remains, etc.

Like the parallel approach, this serial approach runs Shor's algorithm on a superposition of odd positive integers M, as explained in Section 5, after reducing to the odd case. Unlike the parallel approach, this serial approach does not need the tweak from Section 5.3: it is enough here to have a significant probability of splitting M whenever M is not a power of a prime. This serial approach also does not need factorization into coprimes as a subroutine.

As in the parallel approach, factoring M into factors $\leq y$ proves that M is y-smooth; and it is sufficient to achieve, e.g., probability $3/4$ of finding a proof when a proof exists, since an outer loop can then amplify the proof-finding probability. An advantage of the serial approach is that this outer loop is unnecessary: we simply repeat Shor's algorithm enough times (see below) that every y-smooth input integer will, with overwhelming probability, be factored into factors $\leq y$. The parallel approach could not afford the qubits for so many repetitions.

This serial approach requires care at three points. First, Shor's algorithm—as we have stated it—has no chance of factoring powers of primes. If the largest factor that remains is (e.g.) p^2, where p is prime, then Shor's algorithm will repeatedly try and fail to factor p^2. Postprocessing the list of factors to find powers, as in the parallel construction, will split p^2, but if the list also contains a product $qr > y$ then the overall algorithm will not recognize M as smooth.

To avoid this case we incorporate power detection into each run of Shor's algorithm. As noted above, there are pre-quantum power-detection algorithms that take time and space $(\log x)^{1+o(1)}$, so reversible versions take time $(\log x)^{1+\epsilon+o(1)}$ and space $(\log x)^{1+o(1)}$.

(Whether this case needs to be avoided is a different question. It seems unlikely that prime powers larger than y are common, and it seems unlikely that throwing away smooth numbers with such factors noticeably affects the performance of NFS. But we prefer to have subroutines that always work, so that such questions do not need to be asked.)

Second, we need to ensure that we have run Shor's algorithm enough times. A y-smooth positive integer $M \leq x$ will have many factors: at least $(\log M)/\log y$, and perhaps as many as $\log_2 x$. A product $\leq y$ does not need to be factored further, but Shor's algorithm will need to succeed many times before the largest factor is so small.

We maintain a list of integers >1 whose product is M. Initially this list contains simply M (unless $M = 1$, in which case the list is empty). An iteration of the algorithm uses power detection, followed by Shor's algorithm, to try to split the largest element of the list into ≥ 2 factors, each factor being >1. We define the iteration to be successful if either (1) this splitting succeeds—this happens fewer than $\log_2 x$ times, since each splitting increases the list size—or (2) the largest element of the list is prime.

Each iteration succeeds with probability $\Omega(1/\log\log x)$. Specifically: If the largest element of the list is prime, then the iteration succeeds by definition. If the largest element of the list is a square, cube, etc., then power detection succeeds. Otherwise Shor's algorithm succeeds with probability $\Omega(1/\log\log x)$.

We run t iterations. We choose t to guarantee that, except with probability $O(1/x)$, there are at least $\log_2 x$ successful iterations—which cannot all be splittings, so the largest element of the list must be prime, and then this largest element is $\leq y$ if and only if M is y-smooth. Concretely, we choose t with a $\Theta(\log\log x)$ factor accounting for the success probability of each iteration, a $\log_2 x$ factor for the number of successful iterations desired, and a further constant factor to be able to apply a Chernoff-type bound on the overall failure probability; see Appendix A. Note that $t \in (\log x)^{1+o(1)}$.

Third, we need to record enough information for each iteration to be reversible, and we need to do this while still fitting into $(\log x)^{1+o(1)}$ qubits.

Along with the list of factors of M, we keep a journal of actions taken by the iterations. Each iteration produces exactly one journal entry. An iteration that splits the ith list entry into two factors, replacing it by one factor at position i in the list and one factor added to the end of the list, records a journal entry $(2, i)$. More generally, an iteration that splits the ith list entry into $k \geq 2$ factors (e.g., splitting p^3 into p, p, p) records a journal entry (k, i). Reversing this iteration means multiplying the last $k - 1$ entries of the list into the ith entry of the list, removing those $k - 1$ entries, and removing the journal entry. An iteration that does not split the list records a journal entry $(0, 0)$.

The list always has at most $\log_2 x$ entries, so recording a journal entry takes $O(\log\log x)$ bits. The total number of journal entries is $t \in (\log x)^{1+o(1)}$, so the total journal size is $(\log x)^{1+o(1)}$.

References

1. Artjuhov, M.M.: Certain criteria for primality of numbers connected with the little Fermat theorem. Acta Arith. **12**, 355–364 (1966)
2. Barbulescu, R.: Algorithms of discrete logarithm in finite fields. Thesis, Université de Lorraine, December 2013. https://tel.archives-ouvertes.fr/tel-00925228
3. Beauregard, S.: Circuit for Shor's algorithm using $2n + 3$ qubits. Quantum Inf. Comput. **3**(2), 175–185 (2003)
4. Beckman, D., Chari, A.N., Devabhaktuni, S., Preskill, J.: Efficient networks for quantum factoring. Phys. Rev. A **54**, 1034–1063 (1996)
5. Bennett, C.H.: Time/space trade-offs for reversible computation. SIAM J. Comput. **18**(4), 766–776 (1989)
6. Bernstein, D.J.: Detecting perfect powers in essentially linear time. Math. Comput. **67**(223), 1253–1283 (1998)
7. Bernstein, D.J.: Circuits for integer factorization: a proposal (2001). https://cr.yp.to/papers.html#nfscircuit
8. Bernstein, D.J.: Factoring into coprimes in essentially linear time. J. Algorithms **54**(1), 1–30 (2005)

9. Bernstein, D.J., Lenstra Jr., H.W., Pila, J.: Detecting perfect powers by factoring into coprimes. Math. Comput. **76**(257), 385–388 (2007)

10. Buhler, J.P., Lenstra Jr., H.W., Pomerance, C.: Factoring integers with the number field sieve. In: Lenstra, A.K., Lenstra Jr., H.W. (eds.) The development of the number field sieve. LNM, vol. 1554, pp. 50–94. Springer, Heidelberg (1993). doi:10. 1007/BFb0091539

11. Cleve, R., Ekert, A., Macchiavello, C., Mosca, M.: Quantum algorithms revisited. In: Proceedings of the Royal Society of London A: Mathematical, Physical and Engineering Sciences, vol. 454. The Royal Society (1998)

12. Coppersmith, D.: Modifications to the number field sieve. J. Cryptol. **6**(3), 169–180 (1993)

13. Diffie, W., Hellman, M.: New directions in cryptography. IEEE Trans. Inf. Soc. **22**(6), 644–654 (1976)

14. Gordon, D.: Discrete logarithms in GF(p) using the number field sieve. SIAM J. Discret. Math. **6**, 124–138 (1993)

15. Gottesman, D.: Fault-tolerant quantum computation with constant overhead. Quantum Inf. Comput. **14**(15–16), 1338–1372 (2014). https://arxiv.org/pdf/1310.2984

16. Grosshans, F., Lawson, T., Morain, F., Smith, B.: Factoring safe semiprimes with a single quantum query (2015). http://arxiv.org/abs/1511.04385

17. Kleinjung, T., Aoki, K., Franke, J., Lenstra, A.K., Thomé, E., Bos, J.W., Gaudry, P., Kruppa, A., Montgomery, P.L., Osvik, D.A., Riele, H., Timofeev, A., Zimmermann, P.: Factorization of a 768-bit RSA modulus. In: Rabin, T. (ed.) CRYPTO 2010. LNCS, vol. 6223, pp. 333–350. Springer, Heidelberg (2010). doi:10.1007/978-3-642-14623-7_18

18. Lenstra, A.K., Lenstra Jr., H.W., Manasse, M.S., Pollard, J.M.: The number field sieve. In: STOC 1990: Proceedings of the Twenty-Second Annual ACM Symposium on Theory of Computing, pp. 564–572. ACM, New York (1990)

19. Lenstra Jr., H.W.: Factoring integers with elliptic curves. Ann. Math. (2) **126**(3), 649–673 (1987)

20. Menezes, A., Sarkar, P., Singh, S.: Challenges with assessing the impact of NFS advances on the security of pairing-based cryptography. In: Proceedings of Mycrypt 2016 (2016, to appear). https://eprint.iacr.org/2016/1102

21. Pollard, J.M.: Factoring with cubic integers. In: Lenstra, A.K., Lenstra Jr., H.W. (eds.) The development of the number field sieve. LNM, vol. 1554, pp. 4–10. Springer, Heidelberg (1993). doi:10.1007/BFb0091536

22. Rivest, R.L., Shamir, A., Adleman, L.M.: A method for obtaining digital signatures and public-key cryptosystems. Commun. ACM **21**(2), 120–126 (1978)

23. Schirokauer, O.: Discrete logarithms and local units. Philos. Trans. Phys. Sci. Eng. **345**, 409–423 (1993)

24. Seifert, J.-P.: Using fewer qubits in Shor's factorization algorithm via simultaneous diophantine approximation. In: Naccache, D. (ed.) CT-RSA 2001. LNCS, vol. 2020, pp. 319–327. Springer, Heidelberg (2001). doi:10.1007/3-540-45353-9_24

25. Shor, P.: Polynomial-time algorithms for prime factorization and discrete logarithms on a quantum computer. SIAM J. Comput. **26**(5), 1484–1509 (1997)

26. Takahashi, Y., Kunihiro, N.: A quantum circuit for Shor's factoring algorithm using $2n + 2$ qubits. Quantum Inf. Comput. **6**(2), 184–192 (2006)

27. Vedral, V., Barenco, A., Ekert, A.: Quantum networks for elementary arithmetic operations. Phys. Rev. A **54**, 147–153 (1996)

A   Number of Iterations for the Serial Construction

This appendix justifies the claim in Section 6 that choosing a sufficiently large $t \in O(\log x \log \log x)$ produces at least $\log_2 x$ successful iterations except with probability $O(1/x)$.

We abstract and generalize the situation in Section 6 as follows. The algorithm state evolves through t iterations: from state S_0, to state $S_1 = A_1(S_0)$, to state $S_2 = A_2(S_1)$, and so on through state $S_t = A_t(S_{t-1})$. We are given a positive real number p and a guarantee that each iteration is successful with probability *at least* p. Our objective is to put an upper bound on the chance that there are fewer than s successful iterations.

More formally: Fix a finite set X. (The algorithm state at each moment will be an element of this set.) Also fix a function $f : X \to \mathbb{Z}$. (For each algorithm state S, the value $f(S)$ is the total number of successes that occurred as part of producing this algorithm state; we augment the algorithm state if necessary to count the number of successes.) Finally, fix a positive real number p.

Let A be a random function from X to X. (This will be what the algorithm does in one iteration.) Note that "random" does not mean "uniform random"; we are not assuming that A is uniformly distributed over the space of functions from X to X.

Define A as **admissible** if the following two conditions are both satisfied:

- $f(A(S)) - f(S) \in \{0, 1\}$ for each $S \in X$.
- $q(A, S) \geq p$ for each $S \in X$, where $q(A, S)$ by definition is the probability that $f(A(S)) - f(S) = 1$.

(In other words, no matter what the starting state S is, an A iteration starting from S has probability at least p of being successful.)

Let t be a positive integer. (This is the number of iterations in the algorithm.) Let $A_1, A_2, \ldots, A_t$ be independent admissible random functions from X to X. (A_i is what the algorithm does in the ith iteration; concretely, these functions are independent if the coin flips used in the ith iteration of the algorithm are independent of the coin flips used in the jth iteration whenever $i \neq j$.)

Let S_0 be a random element of X. (This is the initial algorithm state.) Note that again we are not assuming a uniform distribution. Recursively define $S_i = A_i(S_{i-1})$ for each $i \in \{1, 2, \ldots, t\}$. ($S_i$ is the state of the algorithm after i iterations.)

Proposition 1. *Let s be a positive real number. Assume that $tp \geq s$. Then $f(S_t) - f(S_0) \leq s$ with probability at most $\exp(-(1 - s/tp)^2 tp/2)$.*

In other words, except with probability at most $\exp(-(1 - s/tp)^2 tp/2)$, there are more than s successes in t iterations.

In the application in Section 6, we take $p \in \Omega(1/\log \log x)$ to match the analysis of Shor's algorithm; we take $s = \log_2 x$; and we compute t as an integer between, say, $(4 \log_2 x)/p$ and $(4 \log_2 x)/p + 1.5$. (Taking a gap noticeably larger than 1 means that we can compute t from a low-precision approximation to

$(4 \log_2 x)/p$.) Then $t \in O(\log x \log \log x)$. The condition $tp \geq s$ in the proposition is satisfied, so there are more than $\log_2 x$ successes in t iterations, except with probability at most $\exp(-(1-s/tp)^2 tp/2)$. The quantity tp is at least $4 \log_2 x$, and the quantity $1 - s/tp$ is at least $3/4$, so $(1-s/tp)^2 tp/2 \geq (9/8) \log_2 x > 1.6 \log x$, so the probability is below $1/x^{1.6}$.

Proof. Chernoff's bound says that if $v_1, v_2, \ldots, v_t$ are *independent* random elements of $\{0, 1\}$, with probabilities $\mu_1, \mu_2, \ldots, \mu_t$ respectively of being 1 and with $\mu = \mu_1 + \mu_2 + \cdots + \mu_t$, then the probability that $v_1 + v_2 + \cdots + v_t \leq \delta\mu$ is at most $\exp(-(1 - \delta)^2 \mu/2)$ for $0 < \delta \leq 1$.

It is tempting at this point to define $v_i = f(S_i) - f(S_{i-1})$, but then there is no reason for $v_1, v_2, \ldots, v_t$ to be independent.

Instead flip independent coins $c_1, c_2, \ldots, c_t$, where $c_i = 1$ with probability $p/q(A_i, S_{i-1})$ and $c_i = 0$ otherwise. Define $v_i = c_i(f(S_i) - f(S_{i-1}))$.

By assumption $S_i = A_i(S_{i-1})$, so $f(S_i) - f(S_{i-1}) = f(A_i(S_{i-1})) - f(S_{i-1})$. This difference is 1 with probability exactly $q(A_i, S_{i-1})$, and 0 otherwise. Hence v_i is 1 with probability exactly p, and 0 otherwise. This is also true conditioned upon $v_1, v_2, \ldots, v_{i-1}$, since A_i and c_i are independent of $v_1, v_2, \ldots, v_{i-1}$; hence $v_1, v_2, \ldots, v_t$ are independent.

Now substitute $\mu_1 = \mu_2 = \cdots = \mu_t = p$, $\mu = tp$, and $\delta = s/tp$ in Chernoff's bound: we have $0 < \delta \leq 1$ (since $0 < s \leq tp$), so the probability that $v_1 + v_2 + \cdots + v_t \leq s$ is at most $\exp(-(1 - s/tp)^2 tp/2)$.

Note that $v_i \leq f(S_i) - f(S_{i-1})$, so $v_1 + v_2 + \cdots + v_t \leq f(S_t) - f(S_0)$. Hence the probability that $f(S_t) - f(S_0) \leq s$ is at most $\exp(-(1 - s/tp)^2 tp/2)$ as claimed. □

Quantum Algorithms for Computing Short Discrete Logarithms and Factoring RSA Integers

Martin Ekerå[1,2($\boxtimes$)] and Johan Håstad[1]

[1] KTH Royal Institute of Technology, 100 44 Stockholm, Sweden
{ekera,johanh}@kth.se
[2] Swedish NCSA, Swedish Armed Forces, 107 85 Stockholm, Sweden

Abstract. We generalize the quantum algorithm for computing short discrete logarithms previously introduced by Ekerå [2] so as to allow for various tradeoffs between the number of times that the algorithm need be executed on the one hand, and the complexity of the algorithm and the requirements it imposes on the quantum computer on the other hand. Furthermore, we describe applications of algorithms for computing short discrete logarithms. In particular, we show how other important problems such as those of factoring RSA integers and of finding the order of groups under side information may be recast as short discrete logarithm problems. This gives rise to an algorithm for factoring RSA integers that is less complex than Shor's general factoring algorithm in the sense that it imposes smaller requirements on the quantum computer. In both our algorithm and Shor's algorithm, the main hurdle is to compute a modular exponentiation in superposition. When factoring an n bit integer, the exponent is of length $2n$ bits in Shor's algorithm, compared to slightly more than $n/2$ bits in our algorithm.

Keywords: Discrete logarithms · Factoring · RSA · Shor's algorithms

1 Introduction

In a groundbreaking paper [8] from 1994, subsequently extended and revised in a later publication [9], Shor introduced polynomial time quantum computer algorithms for factoring integers over $\mathbb{Z}$ and for computing discrete logarithms in the multiplicative group $\mathbb{F}_p^*$ of the finite field $\mathbb{F}_p$.

Although Shor's algorithm for computing discrete logarithms was originally described for $\mathbb{F}_p^*$, it may be generalized to any finite cyclic group, provided the group operation may be implemented efficiently using quantum circuits.

1.1 Recent Work

Ekerå [2] has introduced a modified version of Shor's algorithm for computing short discrete logarithms in finite cyclic groups.

© Springer International Publishing AG 2017
T. Lange and T. Takagi (Eds.): PQCrypto 2017, LNCS 10346, pp. 347–363, 2017.
DOI: 10.1007/978-3-319-59879-6_20

Unlike Shor's original algorithm, this modified algorithm does not require the order of the group to be known. It only requires the logarithm to be short; i.e. it requires the logarithm to be small in relation to the group order.

The modified algorithm is less complex than Shor's general algorithm when the logarithm is short. This is because the main hurdle in both algorithms is to compute a modular exponentiation in superposition.

In the case where the group order is of length l bits and the logarithm sought is of length $m \lll l$ bits, Ekerå's algorithm exponentiates two elements to exponents of size $2m$ bits and m bits respectively. In Shor's algorithm, both exponents are instead of size $l \ggg m$ bits.

This difference is important since it is seemingly hard to build and operate large and complex quantum computers. If the complexity of a quantum algorithm may be reduced, in terms of the requirements that it imposes on the quantum computer, this could potentially mean the difference between being able to execute the algorithm and not being able to execute the algorithm.

1.2   Our Contributions

In the first part of this paper, we generalize the algorithm of Ekerå by considering the setting where the quantum algorithm is executed multiple times to yield multiple partial results. We then combine these partial results using lattice-based techniques in a classical post-processing stage to yield the discrete logarithm.

This enables us to further reduce the size of the exponent to only slightly more than m bits. Furthermore, this enables us to make tradeoffs between the number of times that the quantum algorithm need be executed on the one hand, and the complexity of the algorithm and the requirements that it imposes on the quantum computer on the other hand.

In the second part of this paper, we describe applications for our algorithm for computing short discrete logarithms. In particular, we show how the problems of factoring RSA integers and of finding the order of groups under side information may be recast as short discrete logarithm problems. By RSA integer we mean an integer that is the product of two primes of similar size.

This immediately gives rise to an algorithm for factoring RSA integers that is less complex than Shor's original general factoring algorithm in terms of the requirements that it imposes on the quantum computer. When factoring an n bit integer using Shor's order finding algorithm, an exponentiation is performed to an exponent of length $2n$ bits. In our algorithm, the corresponding exponent is instead of length $(\frac{1}{2} + \frac{1}{s})n$ bits where $s \geq 1$ is a parameter that may assume any small integer value. The exponent length is hence reduced from $2n$ bits to slightly more than $n/2$ bits.

1.3   Related Work

In an earlier work, unknown to us at the time of developing these results, Seifert [7] proposed to execute Shor's order finding algorithm multiple times with a smaller range of exponents to obtain a set of partial results, and to compute the order from this set using simultaneous Diophantine approximation techniques. He gives an algorithm that uses an exponent of length slightly more than n bits when factoring an n bit RSA integer.

Seifert does not give all details in his analysis of the algorithm but several of his ideas parallel those of ours. In this work, however, we further reduce the length of the exponent to slightly more than $n/2$ bits by casting the RSA factoring problem as a short discrete logarithm problem and solving it using our generalized algorithm. The fact that we do not have any modular reductions in the exponent makes for a simpler and more transparent proof.

1.4   Overview

In the next section, we introduce notation that is used throughout the paper, and in Sect. 3 we describe our generalized algorithm for computing short discrete logarithms, briefly discuss its applications, and describe its advantage.

We proceed to describe algorithms for factoring RSA integers in Sect. 4 and for finding the order of group elements under side information in Sect. 5. Both of these algorithms are based upon the generalized algorithm for computing short discrete logarithms introduced in Sect. 3.

2   Notation

In this section, we introduce some notation used throughout this paper.

- $u \bmod n$ denotes u reduced modulo n and constrained to $0 \le u \bmod n < n$.
- $\{u\}_n$ denotes u reduced modulo n and constrained to $-n/2 \le \{u\}_n < n/2$.
- $\lfloor u \rceil$ denotes u rounded to the closest integer.
- $|a + ib| = \sqrt{a^2 + b^2}$ where $a, b \in \mathbb{R}$ denotes the Euclidean norm of $a + ib$.
- $|\boldsymbol{u}|$ denotes the Euclidean norm of the vector $\boldsymbol{u} = (u_0, \ldots, u_{n-1}) \in \mathbb{R}^n$.

3   Computing Short Discrete Logarithms

In this section, we describe a generalization of the algorithm for computing short discrete logarithms previously introduced by Ekerå [2].

3.1   The Discrete Logarithm Problem

Let $\mathbb{G}$ under $\odot$ be a group of order r generated by g, and let

$$x = [d]\, g = \underbrace{g \odot g \odot \cdots \odot g \odot g}_{d \text{ times}}.$$

Given x, a generator g and a description of $\mathbb{G}$ and $\odot$ the discrete logarithm problem is to compute $d = \log_g x$.

The bracket notation that we have introduced above is commonly used in the literature to denote repeated application of the group operation regardless of whether the group is written multiplicatively or additively.

3.2 Algorithm Overview

The generalized algorithm for computing short discrete logarithms consists of two stages; an initial quantum stage and a classical post-processing stage.

The initial quantum stage is described in terms of a quantum algorithm, see Sect. 3.3, that upon input of g and $x = [d]\,g$ yields a pair (j, k). The classical post-processing stage is described in terms of a classical algorithm, see Sect. 3.9, that upon input of $s \geq 1$ "good" pairs computes and returns d.

The parameter s determines the number of good pairs (j, k) required to successfully compute d. It furthermore controls the sizes of the index registers in the algorithm, and thereby the complexity of executing the algorithm on a quantum computer and the sizes of and amount of information on d contained in the two components j, k of each pair.

In the special case where $s = 1$ the generalized algorithm is identical to the algorithm in [2]. A single good pair then suffices to compute d.

By allowing s to be increased, the generalized algorithm enables a tradeoff to be made between the requirements imposed by the algorithm on the quantum computer on the one hand, and the number of times it needs to be executed and the complexity of the classical post-processing stage on the other hand.

We think of s as a small constant. Thus, when we analyze the complexity of the algorithm, and in particular the parts of the algorithm that are executed classically, we can neglect constants that depend on s.

3.3 The Quantum Algorithm

Let m be the smallest integer such that $0 < d < 2^m$ and let ℓ be an integer close to m/s. Provided that the order r of g is at least $2^{\ell+m} + 2^\ell d$, the quantum algorithm described in this section will upon input of g and $x = [d]\,g$ compute and output a pair (j, k).

A set of such pairs is then input to the classical algorithm to recover d.

1. Let

$$
|\Psi\rangle = \frac{1}{\sqrt{2^{2\ell+m}}} \sum_{a=0}^{2^{\ell+m}-1} \sum_{b=0}^{2^\ell-1} |a\rangle|b\rangle|0\rangle .
$$

2. Compute $[a]\,g \odot [-b]\,x$ and store the result in the third register

$$
|\Psi\rangle = \frac{1}{\sqrt{2^{2\ell+m}}} \sum_{a=0}^{2^{\ell+m}-1} \sum_{b=0}^{2^\ell-1} |a, b, [a - bd]\,g\rangle .
$$

3. Compute a QFT of size $2^{\ell+m}$ of the first register and a QFT of size 2^ℓ of the second register to obtain

$$
|\Psi\rangle = \frac{1}{2^{2\ell+m}} \sum_{a, j=0}^{2^{\ell+m}-1} \sum_{b, k=0}^{2^\ell-1} e^{2\pi i\,(aj+2^m bk)/2^{\ell+m}} |j, k, [a - bd]\,g\rangle .
$$

4. Observe the system in a measurement to obtain (j, k) and $[e]\,g$.

3.4   Analysis of the Probability Distribution

When the system above is observed, the state $|\,j, k, [e]\,g\,\rangle$, where $e = a - bd$, is obtained with probability

$$\frac{1}{2^{2(2\ell+m)}} \cdot \left|\sum_a \sum_b \exp\left[\frac{2\pi i}{2^{\ell+m}}(aj + 2^m bk)\right]\right|^2 \tag{1}$$

where the sum is over all pairs (a, b) that produce this specific e. Note that the assumption that the order $r \geq 2^{\ell+m} + 2^\ell d$ implies that no reduction modulo r occurs when e is computed.

Since $e = a - bd$ we have $a = e + bd$. Substituting a for this expression in (1), extracting the term containing e, and centering b around zero yields

$$\frac{1}{2^{2(2\ell+m)}} \cdot \left|\sum_b \exp\left[\frac{2\pi i}{2^{\ell+m}}(b - 2^{\ell-1})\{dj + 2^m k\}_{2^{\ell+m}}\right]\right|^2 \tag{2}$$

where the sum is over all b in $\{\, 0 \leq b < 2^\ell \mid 0 \leq a = e + bd < 2^{\ell+m}\,\}$.

Note that a modular reduction by $2^{\ell+m}$ has furthermore been introduced. This is possible since adding or subtracting multiples of $2^{\ell+m}$ has no effect; it is equivalent to shifting the phase angle by a multiple of 2π.

3.5   The Notion of Constructive Interference

The claim below summarizes the notion of constructive interference that we use to lower-bound the success probability.

Claim 1. *Let* θ_j *for* $0 \leq j < N$ *be phase angles such that* $|\theta_j| \leq \frac{\pi}{4}$. *Then*

$$\left|\sum_{j=0}^{N-1} e^{i\theta_j}\right|^2 \geq \frac{N^2}{2}.$$

Proof.

$$\left|\sum_{j=0}^{N-1} e^{i\theta_j}\right|^2 = \left|\sum_{j=0}^{N-1}(\cos\theta_j + i\sin\theta_j)\right|^2 \geq \left|\sum_{j=0}^{N-1}\cos\theta_j\right|^2 \geq \frac{N^2}{2}$$

since for j *on the interval* $0 \leq j < N$ *we have* $|\theta_j| \leq \frac{\pi}{4}$ *which implies that* $\frac{1}{\sqrt{2}} \leq \cos\theta_j \leq 1$ *and so the claim follows.* □

3.6   The Notion of a Good Pair (j, k)

By Claim 1 the sum in Eq. (2) is large when $|\{dj + 2^m k\}_{2^{\ell+m}}| \leq 2^{m-2}$ since this condition implies that the angle is less than or equal to $\pi/4$.

This observation serves as our motivation for introducing the below notion of a good pair, and for proceeding in the following sections to lower-bound the number of good pairs and the probability of obtaining any specific good pair.

Definition 1. *A pair* (j, k), *where* j *and* k *are integers such that* $0 \leq j < 2^{\ell+m}$ *and* $0 \leq k < 2^{\ell}$, *is said to be* good *if* $|\{dj + 2^m k\}_{2^{\ell+m}}| \leq 2^{m-2}$.

Note that j uniquely defines k as k gives the ℓ high order bits of dj modulo $2^{\ell+m}$ or more specifically as $k = -\lfloor (dj \bmod 2^{\ell+m})/2^m \rceil \bmod 2^{\ell}$.

3.7   Lower-Bounding the Number of Good Pairs (j, k)

Lemma 1. *There are at least* $2^{\ell+m-1}$ *different* j *such that there is a* k *such that* (j, k) *is a good pair.*

Proof. For a good pair

$$|\{dj + 2^m k\}_{2^{\ell+m}}| = |\{dj\}_{2^m}| \leq 2^{m-2} \tag{3}$$

and for each j that satisfies (3) there is a unique k such that (j, k) is good.

Let 2^κ be the greatest power of two that divides d. Since $0 < d < 2^m$ it must be that $\kappa \leq m - 1$. As j runs through all integers $0 \leq j < 2^{\ell+m}$, the function $dj \bmod 2^m$ assumes the value of each multiple of 2^κ exactly $2^{\ell+\kappa}$ times.

Assume that $\kappa = m - 1$. Then the only possible values are 0 and 2^{m-1}. Only zero gives rise to a good pair. With multiplicity there are $2^{\ell+\kappa} = 2^{\ell+m-1}$ integers j such that (j, k) is a good pair. Assume that $\kappa < m - 1$. Then only the $2 \cdot 2^{m-\kappa-2} + 1$ values congruent to values on $[-2^{m-2}, 2^{m-2}]$ are such that $|\{dj\}_{2^m}| \leq 2^{m-2}$. With multiplicity $2^{\ell+\kappa}$ there are $2^{\ell+\kappa} \cdot (2 \cdot 2^{m-\kappa-2} + 1) \geq 2^{\ell+m-1}$ integers j such that (j, k) is a good pair. In both cases there are at least $2^{\ell+m-1}$ good pairs and so the lemma follows.   □

3.8   Lower-Bounding the Probability of a Good Pair (j, k)

To lower-bound the probability of a good pair we first need to lower-bound the number of pairs (a, b) that yield a certain e.

Definition 2. *Let* T_e *denote the number of pairs* (a, b) *such that* $e = a - bd$ *where* a, b *are integers on the intervals* $0 \leq a < 2^{\ell+m}$ *and* $0 \leq b < 2^{\ell}$.

Claim 2.

$$\sum_{e=-2^{\ell+m}}^{2^{\ell+m}-1} T_e = 2^{2\ell+m}.$$

Proof. Since a, b may independently assume $2^{\ell+m}$ and 2^ℓ values, there are $2^{2\ell+m}$ distinct pairs (a, b). From this fact, and from the fact that $|e = a - bd| < 2^{\ell+m}$ since $0 \leq a < 2^{\ell+m}$, $0 \leq b < 2^\ell$ and $0 < d < 2^m$, the claim follows.   □

Claim 3.

$$\sum_{e=-2^{\ell+m}}^{2^{\ell+m}-1} T_e^2 \geq 2^{3\ell+m-1}.$$

Proof. This follows from the Cauchy–Schwarz inequality and Claim 2 since

$$2^{2(2\ell+m)} = \left(\sum_{e=-2^{\ell+m}}^{2^{\ell+m}-1} T_e \right)^2 \leq \left(\sum_{e=-2^{\ell+m}}^{2^{\ell+m}-1} 1^2 \right) \left(\sum_{e=-2^{\ell+m}}^{2^{\ell+m}-1} T_e^2 \right).$$

$\square$

We are now ready to demonstrate a lower-bound on the probability of obtaining a good pair using the above definition and claims.

Lemma 2. *The probability of obtaining any specific good pair (j, k) from a single execution of the algorithm in Sect. 3.3 is at least $2^{-m-\ell-2}$.*

Proof. For a good pair

$$\left| \frac{2\pi}{2^{\ell+m}} (b - 2^{\ell-1}) \{dj + 2^m k\}_{2^{\ell+m}} \right| \leq \frac{2\pi}{2^{\ell+2}} |b - 2^{\ell-1}| \leq \frac{\pi}{4}$$

for any integer b on the interval $0 \leq b < 2^\ell$. It therefore follows from Claim 1 that the probability of observing (j, k) and $[e]\,g$ is at least

$$\frac{1}{2^{2(2\ell+m)}} \cdot \left| \sum_b \exp\left[\frac{2\pi i}{2^{\ell+m}} (b - 2^{\ell-1}) \{dj + 2^m k\}_{2^{\ell+m}} \right] \right|^2 \geq \frac{T_e^2}{2 \cdot 2^{2(2\ell+m)}}$$

Summing this over all e and using Claim 3 yields

$$\sum_{e=-2^{\ell+m}}^{2^{\ell+m}-1} \frac{T_e^2}{2 \cdot 2^{2(2\ell+m)}} \geq 2^{-m-\ell-2}$$

from which the lemma follows.

$\square$

We note that by Lemmas 1 and 2 the probability of the algorithm yielding a good pair as a result of a single execution is at least 2^{-3}.

3.9   Computing d from a Set of s Good Pairs

In this section, we specify a classical algorithm that upon input of a set of s distinct good pairs $\{(j_1, k_1), \ldots, (j_s, k_s)\}$, that result from multiple executions of the algorithm in Sect. 3.3, computes and outputs d.

Definition 3. *Let L be the integer lattice generated by the row span of*

$$\begin{bmatrix} j_1 & j_2 & \cdots & j_s & 1 \\ 2^{\ell+m} & 0 & \cdots & 0 & 0 \\ 0 & 2^{\ell+m} & \cdots & 0 & 0 \\ \vdots & \vdots & \ddots & \vdots & \vdots \\ 0 & 0 & \cdots & 2^{\ell+m} & 0 \end{bmatrix}.$$

The algorithm proceeds as follows to recover d from $\{(j_1, k_1), \ldots, (j_s, k_s)\}$.

1. Let $\boldsymbol{v} = (\{-2^m k_1\}_{2^{\ell+m}}, \ldots, \{-2^m k_s\}_{2^{\ell+m}}, 0) \in \mathbb{Z}^{s+1}$.
   For all vectors $\boldsymbol{u} \in L$ such that

$$|\boldsymbol{u} - \boldsymbol{v}| < \sqrt{s/2^4 + 1} \cdot 2^m$$

   test if the last component of $\boldsymbol{u}$ is d by checking if $x = [d]\, g$. If so return d.
2. If d is not found in step 1 or the search is infeasible the algorithm fails.

As s is a small constant, all vectors close to $\boldsymbol{v}$ can be explored efficiently.

The most straightforward way to explore all vectors close to $\boldsymbol{v}$ is to first compute a reduced basis for L using standard basis reduction techniques such as Lenstra-Lenstra-Lovász (LLL) [4]. The reduced basis may then be used to find the vector in L closest to $\boldsymbol{v}$, and to explore the neighborhood of this vector in L by adding and subtracting vectors from the basis. There are however more efficient ways to enumerate the vectors in lattices, see for instance the work of Micciancio and Walter [5].

One problem that remains to be addressed is that there may theoretically exist many vectors in L that are close to $\boldsymbol{v}$. In Lemma 3 in the next section we demonstrate that this is not the case with high probability.

3.10   Rationale and Analysis

For any $m_1, \ldots, m_s \in \mathbb{Z}$ the vector

$$\boldsymbol{u} = (\{dj_1\}_{2^{\ell+m}} + m_1 2^{\ell+m}, \ldots, \{dj_s\}_{2^{\ell+m}} + m_s 2^{\ell+m}, d) \in L.$$

The above algorithm performs an exhaustive search of all vectors in L at distance at most $\sqrt{s/2^4 + 1} \cdot 2^m$ from $\boldsymbol{v}$ to find $\boldsymbol{u}$ for some $m_1, \ldots, m_s$. It then recovers d as the second component of $\boldsymbol{u}$. The search will succeed in finding $\boldsymbol{u}$ since

$$|\boldsymbol{u} - \boldsymbol{v}| = \sqrt{d^2 + \sum_{i=1}^{s} (\{dj_i\}_{2^{\ell+m}} + m_i\, 2^{\ell+m} - \{-2^m k_i\}_{2^{\ell+m}})^2}$$

$$= \sqrt{d^2 + \sum_{i=1}^{s} (\{dj_i + 2^m k_i\}_{2^{\ell+m}})^2} < \sqrt{s/2^4 + 1} \cdot 2^m$$

since $0 < d < 2^m$ and $|\{dj + 2^m k\}_{2^{\ell+m}}| \leq 2^{m-2}$ by the definition of a good pair, and since $m_1, \ldots, m_s$ may be freely selected to obtain equality.

Whether the search is computationally feasible depends on the number of vectors in L that lie within distance $\sqrt{s/2^4 + 1} \cdot 2^m$ of $\boldsymbol{v}$. This number is related to the norm of the shortest vector in the lattice.

Note that the determinant of L is $2^{(\ell+m)s} \approx 2^{m(s+1)}$. As the lattice is $s+1$-dimensional we would expect the shortest vector to be of length about 2^m. This is indeed true with high probability.

Lemma 3. *The probability that L contains a vector $u = (u_1, \ldots u_{s+1})$ with $|u_i| < 2^{m-3}$ for $1 \leq i \leq s+1$ is bounded by 2^{-s-1}.*

Proof. Take any integer u with all coordinates strictly bounded by 2^{m-3}.

If 2^κ is the largest power of two that divides u_{s+1} then u_i must also be divisible by 2^κ for u to belong to any lattice in the family. By family we mean all lattices on the same form and degree as L, see Definition 3. If it this is true for all i then u belongs to L for $2^{s\kappa}$ different values of $(j_i)_{i=1}^s$.

There are $2^{(m-2-\kappa)(s+1)}$ vectors u with all coordinates divisible by 2^κ and bounded in absolute value by 2^{m-3}. We conclude that the total number of lattices L that contain such a short vector is bounded by

$$\sum_\kappa 2^{(m-2-\kappa)(s+1)} \cdot 2^{\kappa s} \leq 2^{1+(m-2)(s+1)}.$$

As the number of s-tuples of good j is at least $2^{s(\ell+m-1)}$, the lemma follows. □

Lemma 3 shows that with good probability the number of lattice points such that $|u - v| < \sqrt{s/2^4 + 1} \cdot 2^m$ is a constant that only depends on s and thus we can efficiently find all such vectors.

3.11   Building a Set of s Good Pairs

The probability of a single execution of the quantum algorithm in Sect. 3.3 yielding a good pair is at least 2^{-3} by Lemmas 1 and 2. Hence, if we execute the quantum algorithm $t = 8s$ times, we obtain a set of t pairs that we expect contains at least s good pairs.

In theory, we may then recover d by executing the classical algorithm in Sect. 3.9 with respect to all $\binom{t}{s}$ subsets of s pairs selected from this set. Since s is a constant, this approach implies a constant factor overhead in the classical part of the algorithm. It does not affect the quantum part of the algorithm. We summarize these ideas in Theorem 4 below.

In practice, however, we suspect that it may be easier to recover d. First of all, we remark that we have only established a lower bound on the probability that a good pair is yielded by the algorithm. This bound is not tight and we expect the actual probability to be higher than is indicated by the bound.

Secondly, we have only analyzed the probability of the classical algorithm in Sect. 3.9 recovering d under the assumption that all s pairs in the set input are good. It might however well turn out to be true that the algorithm will succeed in recovering d even if not all pairs in the input set are good.

3.12   Main Result

In this subsection we summarize the above discussion in a main theorem. Again, we stress that the approach outlined in the theorem is conservative.

Theorem 4. *Let d be an integer on $0 < d < 2^m$, let $s \geq 1$ be a fixed integer, let ℓ be an integer close to m/s and let g be a generator of a finite cyclic group of order $r \geq 2^{\ell+m} + 2^\ell d$. Then there exists a quantum algorithm that yields a pair as output when executed with g and $x = [d] g$ as input. The main operation in this algorithm is an exponentiation of g in superposition to an exponent of length $\ell + m$ bits. If this algorithm is executed cs times for some small constant c to yield a set of pairs S, then there exists a polynomial time classical algorithm that computes d if executed with all unordered subsets of s pairs from S as input.*

The proof of the quantum part of Theorem 4 follows from the above discussion.

Again, we remind the reader that s is a small constant. The complexity of the algorithm would otherwise be exponential in s. Furthermore, we note that the order r of the group need not be explicitly known. It suffices that the above requirement on r is met. Note furthermore that it must be possible to implement the group operation efficiently on a quantum computer.

3.13   The Advantage of Our Algorithm

The advantage of using our algorithm to compute short discrete logarithms in comparison to using Shor's general algorithm is that our algorithm imposes smaller requirements on the quantum computer.

To explain in which respects our algorithm imposes smaller requirements on the quantum computer, we first note that in both our algorithm and Shor's algorithm the quantum stages consist of two modular exponentiations followed by the computation of two QFTs, see Figs. 1 and 2 in the appendix.

Except for the reduction in the exponent lengths and in the sizes of the QFTs in our algorithm compared to Shor's algorithm, the quantum stages of the two algorithms are identical. The advantage provided by our algorithm over Shor's algorithm when the logarithm is short stems from these reductions.

Second, we note that a QFT may be computed efficiently when the size is a power of two as described by Shor [8,9]. In fact, the QFTs may be computed on-the-fly using only a single control qubit as we will elaborate on in further detail below. Hence, the main hurdle is the modular exponentiation. For a more in-depth discussion, see for instance the work by Cleve and Watrous [1].

The standard quantum algorithm for exponentiating a fixed group element as described by Shor [9] is to classically pre-compute consecutive powers of the two elements, and to construct quantum circuits for combining these pre-computed powers with generic group elements under the group operation. These circuits are then executed in sequence controlled by one or more qubits in a separate index register. The classical counterpart to this algorithm is the square-and-multiply algorithm, or the double-and-add algorithm, if the group is written additively.

Assuming the standard algorithm is used to implement the exponentiation, the number of such group operations that need be implemented in the quantum circuit is reduced by a constant factor directly proportional to the reduction in the exponent length. The reduction in the number of group operations that need be implemented in the circuit implies a corresponding reduction both in the circuit depth and in the time required to execute the circuit, which translates into a reduction in the time that the quantum system need be kept coherent.

As for the register of qubits used to control the group operations, its size is reduced by a constant factor in implementations where a distinct qubit is used to control each group operation. However, it is possible to use a single control qubit to control all group operations, as described by Mosca and Ekert [6]. In such implementations, the number of qubits required to implement our algorithm compared to Shor's algorithm is not reduced.

As is evident from the above discussion, the advantage of using our algorithm to compute short discrete logarithms compared to using Shor's general algorithm depends on how the algorithms are implemented, but it always stems from the reduction in the length of the exponents and in the sizes of the QFTs.

3.14   Implementation Remarks

It should be explicitly stated that we describe our algorithm mathematically in this paper in terms of it using two index registers, and in terms of the quantum system being initialized, of a circuit then being executed, and of the system then being observed in a measurement.

This algorithm description, whilst being useful when seeking to understand and analyze the algorithm, is not necessarily representative of the manner in which the algorithm would be implemented in practice. To base comparisons solely upon this description without taking implementation details into account may prove misleading. This was demonstrated in the previous section.

Furthermore, it should be stated that there are various papers on how Shor's algorithm may be implemented in the literature. Many of these ideas carry over to our algorithm since the quantum stages are very similar.

3.15   Applications

Quantum algorithms for computing short discrete logarithms have cryptanalytic applications with respect to cryptanalysis of schemes in which the security relies on the intractability of the short discrete logarithm problem.

A concrete example of such an application is to attack Diffie-Hellman over finite fields when safe prime groups are used in conjunction with short exponents.

The existence of efficient specialized algorithms for computing short discrete logarithms on quantum computers should be taken into account when selecting and comparing domain parameters for asymmetric cryptographic schemes that rely on the computational intractability of the discrete logarithm problem.

For further details, the reader is referred to the extended rationale in [2] and to the references to the literature provided in that paper.

4 Factoring RSA Integers

In this section we describe how the RSA integer factoring problem may be recast as a short discrete logarithm problem by using ideas from Håstad et al. [3], and the fact that our algorithm does not require the group order to be known.

This immediately gives rise to an algorithm for factoring RSA integers that imposes smaller requirements on the quantum computer than Shor's general factoring algorithm.

4.1 The RSA Integer Factoring Problem

Let $p, q \neq p$ be two random odd primes such that $2^{n-1} < p, q < 2^n$. The RSA integer factoring problem is then to factor $N = pq$ into p and q.

4.2 The Factoring Algorithm

Consider the multiplicative group $\mathbb{Z}_N^*$ to the ring of integers modulo N. This group has order $\phi(N) = (p-1)(q-1)$. Let $\mathbb{G}$ be some cyclic subgroup to $\mathbb{Z}_N^*$.

Then $\mathbb{G}$ has order $\phi(N)/t$ for some $t \mid \phi(N)$ such that $t \geq \gcd(p-1, q-1)$. In what follows below, we assume that $\phi(N)/t > (p + q - 2)/2$.

1. Let g be a generator of $\mathbb{G}$. Compute $x = g^{(N-1)/2}$. Then $x \equiv g^{(p+q-2)/2}$.
2. Compute the short discrete logarithm $d = (p + q - 2)/2$ from g and x.
3. Compute p and q by solving the quadratic equation

$$N = (2d - q + 2)q = 2(d+1)q - q^2$$

where we use that $2d + 2 = p + q$. This yields

$$p, q = c \pm \sqrt{c^2 - N} \quad \text{where} \quad c = d + 1.$$

We obtain p or q depending on the choice of sign.

To understand why we obtain a short logarithm, note that

$$N - 1 = pq - 1 = (p - 1) + (q - 1) + (p - 1)(q - 1)$$

from which it follows that $(N - 1)/2 \equiv (p + q - 2)/2 \mod \phi(N)/t$ provided that the above assumption that $\phi(N)/t > (p + q - 2)/2$ is met.

The only remaining difficulties are the selection of the generator in step 1 and the computation of the short discrete logarithm in step 2.

In step 1 we may pick any cyclic subgroup $\mathbb{G}$ to $\mathbb{Z}_N^*$ for as long as its order $\phi(N)/t$ is sufficiently large. It suffices that $\phi(N)/t > (p + q - 2)/2$ and that the discrete logarithm can be computed, see Sect. 4.2 below for more information.

This implies that we may simply select an element g uniformly at random on the interval $1 < g < N - 1$ and use it as the generator.

To compute the short discrete logarithm in step 2, we use the algorithm in Sect. 3. This algorithm requires that the order

$$\phi(N)/t \geq 2^{\ell+m} + 2^\ell d \quad \Rightarrow \quad \phi(N)/t \geq 2^{\ell+m+1}$$

where we have used that $0 < d < 2^m$. We note that

$$2^n \leq d = (p + q - 2)/2 < 2^{n+1} \quad \Rightarrow \quad m = n + 1.$$

Furthermore, we note that $\phi(N) = (p-1)(q-1) \geq 2^{2(n-1)}$ which implies

$$\phi(N)/t \geq 2^{2(n-1)}/t \geq 2^{\ell+m+1} = 2^{\ell+n+2} \quad \Rightarrow \quad t < 2^{2(n-1)-(n+\ell+2)} = 2^{n-\ell-4}.$$

Recall that $\ell = m/s = (n + 1)/s$ where $s \geq 1$. For random p and q, and a randomly selected cyclic subgroup to $\mathbb{Z}_N^*$, the requirement $t < 2^{n-\ell-4}$ is hence met with overwhelming probability for any $s > 1$.

We remark that further optimizations are possible. For instance the size of the logarithm may be reduced by computing $x = g^{(N-1)/2-2^n}$ since $p, q > 2^{n-1}$.

4.3 Generalizations

We note that the algorithm proposed in this section can be generalized.

In particular, we note that we need not assume that the two factors are of the same length in bits. It suffices that the difference in length between the two factors is not too great for a short discrete logarithm problem to arise.

4.4 The Advantage of Our Algorithm

The advantage of using our algorithm to factor RSA integers in comparison to using Shor's general integer factoring algorithm is that our algorithm imposes smaller requirements on the quantum computer.

To compute two exponentiations with respect to different base elements and two QFTs, as in the discrete logarithm algorithms previously described, is not significantly different from computing a single larger exponentiation followed by a single QFT of large size, as in Shor's order finding algorithm that is the quantum part of Shor's factoring algorithm. For more information, see [8,9] and the quantum circuits in Figs. 1, 2 and 3 in the appendix.

In analogy with the situation in Sect. 3.13, the advantage of our algorithm over Shor's algorithm is again obtained by the total exponent length and the total size of the QFT being reduced by a constant factor.

5 Order Finding Under Side Information

In this section, we briefly consider the problem of computing the order of a cyclic group $\mathbb{G}$ when a generator g for the group is available and when side information is available in the form of an estimate of the group order.

Let $\mathbb{G}$ be a cyclic group of order r. Let r_0 be a known approximation of the order such that $0 \leq r - r_0 < 2^m$. The problem of computing the order r under the side information r_0 may then be recast as a short discrete logarithm problem:

1. Let g be a generator of $\mathbb{G}$. Compute $x = g^{-r_0}$. Then $x \equiv g^{r-r_0}$.
2. Compute the short discrete logarithm $d = r - r_0$ from g and x.
3. Compute the order $r = d + r_0$.

6   Summary and Conclusion

We have generalized the quantum algorithm for computing short discrete logarithms previously introduced by Ekerå [2] so as to allow for various tradeoffs between the number of times that the algorithm need be executed on the one hand, and the complexity of the algorithm and the requirements it imposes on the quantum computer on the other hand.

In the case where the group order is of length l bits and the logarithm sought is of length $m \lll l$ bits, Ekerå's algorithm exponentiates two elements to exponents of size $2m$ bits and m bits respectively. In Shor's algorithm for computing discrete logarithms, both exponents are instead of size l bits. Our generalized algorithm reduces this to $\ell + m$ and ℓ bits where $\ell \approx m/s$ and $s \geq 1$ is a small integer constant. For $s = 1$ our algorithm is identical to Ekerå's algorithm.

These algorithms have immediate cryptanalytic applications with respect to cryptanalysis of schemes in which the security rests on the intractability of the short discrete logarithm problem. Furthermore, we have described additional applications for algorithms for computing short discrete logarithms.

In particular, we have shown how other important problems such as those of factoring RSA integers and of finding the order of groups under side information may be recast as short discrete logarithm problems. This immediately gives rise to an algorithm for factoring RSA integers that is less complex than Shor's general factoring algorithm in the sense that it imposes smaller requirements on the quantum computer.

In both our algorithm and Shor's algorithm, the main hurdle is to compute a modular exponentiation in superposition. When factoring an n bit integer, the exponent is of length $2n$ bits in Shor's algorithm, compared to slightly more than $n/2$ bits in our algorithm. We have made essentially two optimizations that give rise to this improvement:

First, we gain a factor of two by re-writing the factoring problem as a short discrete logarithm problem and solving it using our algorithm for computing short discrete logarithms. One way to see this is that we know an approximation N of the order $\phi(N)$. This gives us a short discrete logarithm problem and our algorithm for solving it does not require the order to be known beforehand.

Second, we gain a factor of two by executing the quantum algorithm multiple times to yield a set of partial results. We then recover the discrete logarithm d from this set in a classical post-processing step. The classical algorithm uses lattice-based techniques.

Acknowledgments. Support for this work was provided by the Swedish NCSA, that is a part of the Swedish Armed Forces, and by the Swedish Research Council (VR). We are grateful to Lennart Brynielsson for many interesting discussions on the topic of this paper. The input of the referees and of Rainer Steinwandt was also helpful.

A   Appendix

In this appendix we provide graphical visualizations of some of the quantum circuits described earlier so as to facilitate the reader's comprehension.

All circuits below use the standard algorithm for exponentiation and one control qubit for each group operation as described in Sect. 3.13. Recall that a single qubit may be used to control all operations as described by Mosca and Ekert [6]. This reduces the topmost registers in the figures to a single qubit.

We assume below that t qubits is sufficient to represent group elements and to perform the required group operations. Furthermore, we introduce the controlled operator U_v that upon input of $|u\rangle$ where $u, v \in \mathbb{G}$ outputs $|u \odot v\rangle$ if the control qubit is $|1\rangle$ and $|u\rangle$ otherwise.

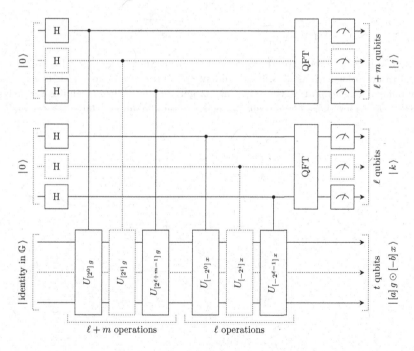

Fig. 1. A quantum circuit for the quantum stage in the algorithm for computing short discrete logarithms described in Sect. 3.

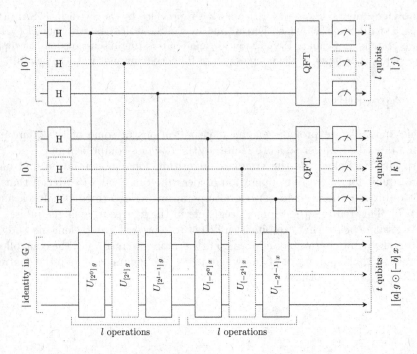

Fig. 2. A quantum circuit for the quantum stage in Shor's algorithm for computing general discrete logarithms [2,8,9]. It is identical to the circuit in Fig. 1, except that the exponent lengths and register sizes are larger. In this figure, l denotes the length in bits of the order of $\mathbb{G}$. The circuit in Fig. 1 has an advantage when $l \ggg \ell + m/2$.

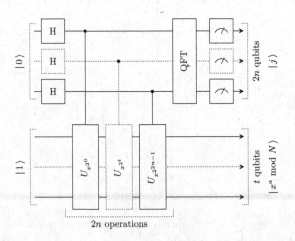

Fig. 3. A quantum circuit for the quantum stage in the order finding algorithm that is part of Shor's factoring algorithm [8,9]. In this figure, x is a random integer, n denotes the length in bits of the integer N to be factored and we assume $\mathbb{G} \subseteq \mathbb{Z}_N^*$.

References

1. Cleve, R., Watrous, J.: Fast parallel circuits for the quantum Fourier transform. In: Proceedings of the 41st Annual Symposium on Foundations of Computer Science, pp. 526–536 (2000)
2. Ekerå, M.: Modifying Shor's algorithm to compute short discrete logarithms. Cryptology ePrint Archive, Report 2016/1128 (2016)
3. Håstad, J., Schrift, A., Shamir, A.: The discrete logarithm modulo a composite hides O(n) bits. J. Comput. Syst. Sci. **47**(3), 376–404 (1993)
4. Lenstra, H.W., Lenstra, A.K., Lovász, L.: Factoring polynomials with rational coefficients. Math. Ann. **261**, 515–534 (1982)
5. Micciancio, D., Walter, M.: Fast lattice point enumeration with minimal overhead. In: Proceedings of the Twenty-Sixth Annual ACM-SIAM Symposium on Discrete Algorithms, pp. 276–294 (2015)
6. Mosca, M., Ekert, A.: The hidden subgroup problem and eigenvalue estimation on a quantum computer. In: Williams, C.P. (ed.) QCQC 1998. LNCS, vol. 1509, pp. 174–188. Springer, Heidelberg (1999). doi:10.1007/3-540-49208-9_15
7. Seifert, J.-P.: Using fewer qubits in Shor's factorization algorithm via simultaneous diophantine approximation. In: Naccache, D. (ed.) CT-RSA 2001. LNCS, vol. 2020, pp. 319–327. Springer, Heidelberg (2001). doi:10.1007/3-540-45353-9_24
8. Shor, P.W.: Algorithms for quantum computation: discrete logarithms and factoring. In: Proceedings of the 35th Annual Symposium on Foundations of Computer Science, pp. 124–134 (1994)
9. Shor, P.W.: Polynomial-time algorithms for prime factorization and discrete logarithms on a quantum computer. SIAM J. Comput. **26**(5), 1484–1509 (1997)

Security Models

XOR of PRPs in a Quantum World

Bart Mennink[1,2($\boxtimes$)] and Alan Szepieniec[3]

[1] Digital Security Group, Radboud University, Nijmegen, The Netherlands
b.mennink@cs.ru.nl
[2] CWI, Amsterdam, The Netherlands
[3] imec-COSIC KU Leuven, Leuven, Belgium
alan.szepieniec@esat.kuleuven.be

Abstract. In the classical world, the XOR of pseudorandom permutations $E_{k_1} \oplus \cdots \oplus E_{k_r}$ for $r \geq 2$ is a well-established way to design a pseudorandom function with "optimal" security: security up to approximately $\min\{|K|, |X|\}$ queries, where K and X are the key and state space of the block cipher E. We investigate security of this construction against adversaries who have access to quantum computers. We first present a key recovery attack in $|K|^{r/(r+1)}$ complexity. The attack relies on a clever application of a claw-finding algorithm and testifies of a significant gap with the classical setting where 2 pseudorandom permutations already yield optimal security. Next, we perform a quantum security analysis of the construction, and prove that it achieves security up to $\min\{|K|^{1/2}/r, |X|\}$ queries. The analysis relies on a generic characterization of classical and quantum distinguishers and a universal transformation of classical security proofs to the quantum setting that is of general interest.

Keywords: XOR of pseudorandom permutations · Classical · Quantum · Claw-finding · Proof transformation

1 Introduction

PRP to PRF Conversion. Block ciphers are omnipresent in cryptographic literature, and their security is usually measured in the degree to which they approximate a pseudorandom permutation (PRP). However, in many cases, one prefers to reason with pseudorandom functions instead. A simple example of this is the counter mode encryption. Using a block cipher $E : K \times X \to X$, counter mode encrypts a message $M = M_1 \cdots M_\ell \in X^\ell$ as

$$C_i = E_k(\text{ctr} + i) \oplus M_i \text{ for } i = 1, \ldots, \ell, \tag{1}$$

for a carefully selected counter ctr. If E_k behaves like a random permutation, it is straightforward to observe a bias: an adversary that keeps all message blocks the same will never see colliding ciphertext blocks. However, if we consider E_k to behave like a random function, the ciphertext will always be perfectly random,

© Springer International Publishing AG 2017
T. Lange and T. Takagi (Eds.): PQCrypto 2017, LNCS 10346, pp. 367–383, 2017.
DOI: 10.1007/978-3-319-59879-6_21

and distinguishing counter mode from random reduces to distinguishing E_k from a random function. The trick to view a PRP as a PRF is called the "PRP-PRF-switch," and it finds myriad applications in existing symmetric key security proofs (e.g., [3,10,18,22,26,36,40,41,46]).

The PRP-PRF-switch only guarantees tight birthday bound security: security up to $\min\{|K|,|X|^{1/2}\}$ queries [7,8,20,23]. The same bound applies to counter mode. Suppose we *replace* E_k with $E_{k_1} \oplus E_{k_2}$ for two secret keys k_1, k_2 (this is in fact a simplified case of the CENC mode by Iwata [24,25]):

$$C_i = E_{k_1}(\text{ctr} + i) \oplus E_{k_2}(\text{ctr} + i) \oplus M_i \text{ for } i = 1, \ldots, \ell. \tag{2}$$

In a steady line of research set out in '99 [6,16,33,39,43,44],[1] Patarin finally proved in 2010 [44] that $E_{k_1} \oplus E_{k_2}$ behaves like a random function up to query complexity $\min\{|K|,|X|\}$, well beyond the classical $\min\{|K|,|X|^{1/2}\}$ birthday level of the PRP-PRF-switch. This result almost immediately implies security up to about $\min\{|K|,|X|\}$ queries for this case of CENC, and more generally demonstrates well the relevance of beyond birthday level security of the PRP to PRF conversion.

Quantum Security. Computers exploiting the physical properties of quantum particles seem to promise dramatic speedups for certain problems. The growing branch of *post-quantum cryptography* [9] focuses chiefly on public key cryptosystems and aims to offer immunity to Shor's quantum algorithm for integer factorization and discrete logarithms [50]. Within this branch it is tacitly assumed that symmetric cryptographic primitives remain largely unaffected by the advent of quantum computers: a doubling of the key length will suffice to protect against Grover's search algorithm [19]. Among other things we show that this tacit assumption is false: it is possible to outperform Grover in certain circumstances even without achieving the exponential speedup promised by Shor.

For modes that operate *on top of* symmetric cryptographic primitives, various attacks have been mounted recently [2,28,30,31], but all explicitly require the attack *and the cryptographic algorithm itself* to be run on a quantum computer. In our estimation this model is uninteresting because it requires sophisticated users in order to be relevant; as opposed to offering simple users protection against sophisticated attacks.

The current reality is that secret keys are stored in classical hardware and are hence incapable of sustaining quantum superposition or entanglement. Consequently, while the attacker may have classical query access to keyed primitives, there can be *no quantum interaction with secret key material*. Nevertheless, the attacker *is* allowed to evaluate offline and in quantum superposition any publicly known circuit, such as block ciphers—as long as it provides its own guess, in superposition or not, at the secret key.

---

[1] This list omits research on the XOR of *public* permutations [37,39].

PRP-PRF-Conversion in Quantum Computers. Recently, Zhandry [54] considered the PRP-PRF-switch in case the adversary has quantum access to the secret key material, and he proves tight $|X|^{1/3}$ security. His analysis builds upon two of his earlier observations from [53]. Zhandry likewise considered transitions from QPRGs to QPRFs in [53] and QPRPFs to QPRPs [55]. To our knowledge, this work is the first to generically study the XOR of multiple PRPs in a quantum setting, online *or* offline.

We first present a quantum key recovery attack against the XOR of r PRPs in $|K|^{r/(r+1)}$ complexity. This attack is performed *without* quantum interaction with secret key material, and as such, it stands in sharp contrast with the state of the art in the classical world where optimal $\min\{|K|, |X|\}$ security is achieved already for $r = 2$. The attack internally runs the quantum claw-finding algorithm of Tani [52] in a sophisticated way to recover the key of the r PRPs.[2] In order to eliminate false positives, the algorithm incorporates a threshold τ. We prove that, if the PRPs are perfect permutations, for $\tau = O(r)$ the number of false positives is 0 with high probability. In case the PRP is instantiated with an off-the-shelf block cipher (such as AES), a slightly higher threshold may be required.

As a second contribution, we present a quantum security analysis of the XOR of r PRPs, and prove that the construction achieves security up to around $\min\{|K|^{1/2}/r, |X|\}$ queries by a quantum distinguisher with only classical access to the keyed primitives. At the core of the security proof lies a fresh perspective on (i) how to formalize classical and quantum distinguishers, (ii) how classical proofs compare with quantum proofs, and (iii) how classical proofs can be *used* in a quantum setting. The observations show particularly that a large part of classical security reductionist proofs can be lifted to the quantum setting almost verbatim: for our result on the XOR of PRPs we immediately rely on a classical security proof by Patarin [43,44], but the techniques carry over to a broader spectrum of existing security proofs. For example, the techniques can be used *in turn* to argue quantum security of counter mode of Eq. (1), CENC of Eq. (2), and many more schemes whose security analysis is in the standard model [1,4,5,18, 22,26,29,32,34,41,46,47,49].[3] We remark that Hallgren et al. [21] and Song [51] already considered how to lift classical security proofs to the quantum world. However, their focus was on adversaries with quantum interaction to the secret key material, making the conditions stricter and the lifting harder to verify. We focus on the setting where the secret key material is stored in classical hardware, and our lifting conditions are easily verified.

Admittedly, the gap between our attack and our security bound is not tight. Informally, this gap is caused by a specific step in the analysis that upper bounds the success probability of guessing the secrets key of the r PRPs by r times the

---

[2] An earlier, yet unrelated and less profound, application of claw finding to cascaded encryption appeared by Kaplan [27].

[3] The lifting does not apply to ideal-model proofs, such as the ones used for sponge functions [3,40], Even-Mansour constructions [11,14], and some tweakable block cipher designs [17,38], which is because in ideal-model proofs the adversary has quantum query access to idealized primitives.

success probability of guessing one of the keys (the step is in fact more technical, cf., Eq. (13) in the proof of Theorem 2). While this step is conventional in classical security proofs as it gives a fairly insignificant loss; for distinguishers that can make quantum evaluations the loss is more severe. In Sect. 6 we discuss various paths towards potentially resolving this step.

2   Preliminaries

For two sets X, Y, by $\mathsf{Func}(X, Y)$ we denote the set of all functions from X to Y and by $\mathsf{Perm}(X)$ the set of all permutations on X. We denote by $x \xleftarrow{\$} X$ the uniformly random drawing of an element x from X. For a positive natural number $r \geq 1$, $\binom{X}{r}$ denotes the set of unordered subsets of X of size r with no duplicates. For two bit strings x and y of equal length, $x \oplus y$ denotes their bitwise exclusive OR (XOR). For two integers $m \geq n \geq 1$, we denote by $m^{\underline{n}} = m(m-1)\cdots(m-n+1) = \frac{m!}{(m-n)!}$ the falling factorial power.

2.1   Security Notions

PRP Security. A block cipher $E : K \times X \to X$ is a family of permutations $E(k, \cdot)$ indexed by a key $k \in K$. Its security is measured by considering a distinguisher $\mathcal{D}$ that has forward query access to either $E_k(\cdot) := E(k, \cdot)$ for a randomly drawn key $k \xleftarrow{\$} K$, or to a random permutation $\pi \xleftarrow{\$} \mathsf{Perm}(X)$. Its goal is to distinguish both worlds, and after its interaction it outputs 0 or 1, referring to the guessed oracle.

Definition 1 (PRP Security). *Let $E : K \times X \to X$ be a block cipher. The PRP (pseudorandom permutation) advantage of a distinguisher $\mathcal{D}$ is defined as*

$$\mathsf{Adv}_E^{\mathrm{prp}}(\mathcal{D}) = \left| \mathbf{P}\left(\mathcal{D}^{E_k} = 1\right) - \mathbf{P}\left(\mathcal{D}^{\pi} = 1\right) \right|,$$

where the probabilities are taken over $k \xleftarrow{\$} K$, $\pi \xleftarrow{\$} \mathsf{Perm}(X)$, and the randomness of $\mathcal{D}$.

For a set of distinguishers $\mathbb{D}$, we define

$$\mathsf{Adv}_E^{\mathrm{prp}}(\mathbb{D}) = \sup_{\mathcal{D} \in \mathbb{D}} \mathsf{Adv}_E^{\mathrm{prp}}(\mathcal{D}).$$

The set of distinguishers $\mathbb{D}$ is typically parameterized by certain complexity parameters, and contains the set of all distinguishers that are bounded by these complexities. In Sect. 3 we elaborate on distinguishers and their complexities.

We remark that block ciphers are often considered in a slightly stronger security model, namely SPRP (strong pseudorandom permutation) security, where the distinguisher can query its oracle in forward as well as in inverse direction. However, for the analysis in this work, SPRP security is inconsequential. We need only consider the weak security notion, PRP security.

PRF Security. Let $F : K \times X \to Y$ be a family of functions $F(k, \cdot)$ from $X \to Y$ indexed by a key $k \in K$. Its security as a family of random functions is defined similarly as the SPRP security, with the difference that distinguisher $\mathcal{D}$ now has oracle access to either $F_k(\cdot) := F(k, \cdot)$ for a randomly drawn key $k \xleftarrow{\$} K$, or to a random function $\rho \xleftarrow{\$} \mathsf{Func}(X, Y)$.

Definition 2 (PRF Security). *Let $F : K \times X \to Y$ be a family of functions. The PRF (pseudorandom function) advantage of a distinguisher $\mathcal{D}$ is defined as*

$$\mathsf{Adv}_F^{\mathrm{prf}}(\mathcal{D}) = \left| \mathbf{P}\left(\mathcal{D}^{F_k} = 1\right) - \mathbf{P}\left(\mathcal{D}^\rho = 1\right) \right|,$$

where the probabilities are taken over $k \xleftarrow{\$} K$, $\rho \xleftarrow{\$} \mathsf{Func}(X, Y)$, and the randomness of $\mathcal{D}$.

As before, for a set of distinguishers $\mathbb{D}$, we define

$$\mathsf{Adv}_F^{\mathrm{prf}}(\mathbb{D}) = \sup_{\mathcal{D} \in \mathbb{D}} \mathsf{Adv}_F^{\mathrm{prf}}(\mathcal{D}).$$

We remark that in above definition, the key set can be anything. Typically, K is a set of bit strings, but in this work we will also apply the analysis to the case where K is a set of functions. For example, consider $F : \mathsf{Perm}(X) \times X \to X$, defined as $F(\pi, x) = \pi(x) \oplus x$. This definition of F is a family of functions indexed by "key" π and for every key it represents a Davies-Meyer-like random function. The probabilities in the PRF security advantage are in this case taken over $\pi \xleftarrow{\$} \mathsf{Perm}(X)$ and $\rho \xleftarrow{\$} \mathsf{Func}(X, X)$.

2.2   XOR of PRPs

Let $E : K \times X \to X$ be a block cipher, and let $r \geq 1$ be a positive natural number. The "XOR of r permutations" is the function $F_r : K^r \times X \to X$ defined as

$$F_r(\mathbf{k}, x) = E_{k_1}(x) \oplus \cdots \oplus E_{k_r}(x) =: z, \tag{3}$$

where $\mathbf{k} = (k_1, \ldots, k_r)$. The function F_r is visually depicted in Fig. 1.

The terminology is a bit misleading for $r = 1$ (there is no such thing as the "XOR of 1 permutation"), but we have opted this naming for the sake of generality. The case of $r = 1$ is in fact the "PRP-to-PRF-switch" [7,8,20,23].

2.3   Idealized XOR of PRPs

We also consider an idealized version of F_r that is not based on an underlying block cipher, but is instead keyed via r random permutations. In more detail, for a positive natural number $r \geq 1$ we define $F_r^{\mathrm{id}} : \mathsf{Perm}(X)^r \times X \to X$ as

$$F_r^{\mathrm{id}}(\boldsymbol{\pi}, x) = \pi_1(x) \oplus \cdots \oplus \pi_r(x) =: z, \tag{4}$$

where $\boldsymbol{\pi} = (\pi_1, \ldots, \pi_r)$.

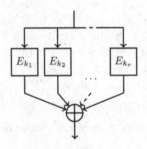

Fig. 1. XOR of r permutations.

2.4   Quantum Claw-Finding

The claw-finding problem centers around the following goal: given two functions $f : X \to Z$ and $g : Y \to Z$, determine whether a tuple $(x, y) \in X \times Y$ such that $f(x) = g(y)$ exists, and find this "claw." Quantum algorithms for solving the claw-problem are usually a function of $M = |X|$ and $N = |Y|$, and we denote the problem by $\mathsf{claw}(M, N)$. We follow the work of Tani [52], that uses quantum walks to solve the problem and that builds upon a list of earlier results on quantum claw-finding [12,13,35,56]. Tani describes an optimal algorithm for discovering a claw in the following number of evaluations of f and g:

$$\mathcal{Q}(\mathsf{claw}(M, N)) = \begin{cases} O\left((M \cdot N)^{1/3}\right) & \text{if } N \le M < N^2, \\ O\left(M^{1/2}\right) & \text{if } M \ge N^2. \end{cases} \tag{5}$$

We remark that Tani [52] derives this algorithm as a special case of a generalized problem that aims at deriving p evaluations of f and q evaluations of g that satisfy a pre-described relation R. More formally, denote by $\mathsf{relation}_{p,q,R}(M, N)$ the problem of discovering a tuple $(x_1, \ldots, x_p, y_1, \ldots, y_q) \in X^p \times Y^q$ such that $(f(x_1), \ldots, f(x_p), g(y_1), \ldots, g(y_q)) \in R$.[4] Tani's relation-finding algorithm solves the problem in the following number of evaluations of f and g:

$$\mathcal{Q}(\mathsf{relation}_{p,q,R}(M, N)) = \begin{cases} O\left((M^p \cdot N^q)^{1/(p+q+1)}\right) & \text{if } N \le M < N^{1+1/p}, \\ O\left(M^{p/(p+1)}\right) & \text{if } M \ge N^{1+1/p}. \end{cases} \tag{6}$$

Note that $\mathsf{claw}(M, N)$ is equivalent to $\mathsf{relation}_{1,1,R}(M, N)$ if we define R as the equality relation.

3   Modeling Quantum Distinguishers

Consider a security measurement $\mathsf{Adv}(\cdot)$ (*e.g.*, $\mathsf{Adv}_E^{\mathrm{prp}}(\cdot)$ or $\mathsf{Adv}_F^{\mathrm{prf}}(\cdot)$). For a family of distinguishers $\mathbb{D}$, we define

$$\mathsf{Adv}(\mathbb{D}) = \sup_{\mathcal{D} \in \mathbb{D}} \mathsf{Adv}(\mathcal{D}).$$

---

[4] Tani [52] uses a slightly different naming: (p, q)-$\mathsf{subset}(M, N)$.

The complexity of a distinguisher is typically bounded in two parameters: data or *online* complexity $q \geq 0$, and time or *offline* complexity $t \geq 0$.[5] Data complexity measures the number of oracle queries the distinguisher can make to its oracle. Time complexity bounds the number of other activities that $\mathcal{D}$ can do, and it can use its time for anything it wants: making coffee, solving sudokus, or, on a more serious note, making evaluations of underlying unkeyed primitives. For example, if we consider the XOR of PRPs of (3) and a distinguisher that tries to separate F_r from a random function ρ in terms of Definition 2, the online complexity measures the number of queries to the oracle $\mathcal{O} \in \{F_r, \rho\}$. As F_r internally uses a block cipher E, which is a known construction, the distinguisher can evaluate E offline. These evaluations are counted by the offline complexity.

Note the small abuse of terminology here: *time complexity* refers to the number of *time steps* that are available to the distinguisher, while *offline complexity* refers to the number of *evaluations of E* that the distinguisher can make offline. This abuse retains generality, as these numbers only differ by a small constant factor. For example, assume that one evaluation of E always takes at least t_E time. We simply rescale to $t_E = 1$ and assume that the time spent on other computations is negligible in this number. This makes the time and offline complexity equivalent.

We have so far bounded the distinguisher to data and time complexities q and t. Another distinction can be made depending on the *type of access* the distinguisher has to its oracle: quantum, printed as $\hat{q}$ or $\hat{t}$ (with hat), or classical, printed as q or t (without hat). In more detail, we will adopt the following notations:

- $\mathbb{D}(q, t)$ is the set of all distinguishers that can make q classical oracle queries and t classical offline evaluations,
- $\mathbb{D}(q, \hat{t})$ is the set of all distinguishers that can make q classical oracle queries and t quantum offline evaluations,
- $\mathbb{D}(\hat{q}, \hat{t})$ is the set of all distinguishers that can make q quantum oracle queries and t quantum offline evaluations.

There is little point in considering the remaining set $\mathbb{D}(\hat{q}, t)$, where the distinguisher can make quantum oracle queries but only classical offline evaluations.

Note how the difference between $\mathbb{D}(\hat{q}, \hat{t})$ and $\mathbb{D}(q, \hat{t})$ effectively pinpoints the difference between quantum adversaries with quantum access or with classical access to the oracle. The former set includes in particular distinguishers based on Simon's or Shor's quantum algorithms and that require quantum oracle access; whereas the latter set covers distinguishers based on Grover's algorithm and that therefore require only classical oracle access. In this work we do not consider the former set, and instead restrict our focus on quantum adversaries which only have classical oracle access to the keyed primitives. This models the scenario where the secret key is stored in classical memory but where the adversary employs a quantum computer to perform its attack.

---

[5] Throughout this work, we ignore a third measurement, memory, and assume that the distinguisher has sufficient memory available at all times.

We will consider a final set of distinguishers:

- $\mathbb{D}(q, \infty)$, the set of all distinguishers that can make q classical oracle queries and that have *unbounded computational power*.

Note that by definition, we have for any $q, t \geq 0$ (see also Fig. 2):

$$\mathbb{D}(q, t) \subseteq \mathbb{D}(q, \hat{t}) \subseteq \mathbb{D}(q, \infty). \tag{7}$$

Both $\mathbb{D}(q, t)$ and $\mathbb{D}(q, \infty)$ appear in non-quantum literature frequently. As a matter of fact, a customary way to perform classical standard-model security analysis goes along the following lines (see, e.g., [1,4,5,18,22,26,29,32,34,41, 46,47,49] for just a few examples): consider a scheme $\mathcal{S}$ that internally uses a primitive $\mathcal{P}$, where the key k to the scheme is fed to the primitive. Consider a distinguisher with complexities (q, t). As a first step, we replace $\mathcal{P}_k$ by its ideal equivalent $\mathcal{I}$. This step "costs" us the standard-model security of $\mathcal{P}_k$ against a distinguisher with complexities $(O(q), O(t))$ (the exact complexities depend on the number of times $\mathcal{S}$ invokes $\mathcal{P}$ per evaluation). What is left is the scheme $\mathcal{S}$ *keyed* by ideal secret primitive $\mathcal{I}$, and the only way for a distinguisher to gain any information about the construction is through queries to the construction. Therefore, the distinguisher is given unlimited computational power, and security is solely measured by the number of queries to the online oracle: the scheme is evaluated against a distinguisher with complexities (q, ∞). More formally, we thus obtain:

$$\mathsf{Adv}_{\mathcal{S}^{\mathcal{P}_k}}(\mathbb{D}(q, t)) \leq \mathsf{Adv}_{\mathcal{P}_k}(\mathbb{D}(O(q), O(t))) + \mathsf{Adv}_{\mathcal{S}^{\mathcal{I}}}(\mathbb{D}(q, \infty)),$$

where the corresponding security notions depend on the type of scheme $\mathcal{S}$ and type of primitive $\mathcal{P}$, and are omitted from the equation. The security of the primitive $\mathcal{P}_k$ is often not evaluated further, it for instance corresponds to the PRP security of AES. The other two advantage terms, on the other hand, *are* considered.

Equation (7) confirms that many non-quantum research on distinguishers with unbounded computational power directly covers distinguishers that can make quantum offline evaluations. We will use this observation in Sect. 5, but the observation has many more applications. As a matter of fact, virtually any standard-model security proof can be lifted to quantum security up to reasonable assumptions, including recently introduced authenticated encryption schemes [1, 4,22,26,41,46,47] and MAC functions [5,18,34]. The approach does not apply to security proofs that are a priori ideal-model, such as the analyses of sponge functions [40], Even-Mansour [11,14], and others. This is mostly due to the fact that in ideal-model security analyses, both the construction and the primitive are idealized and accessible by the distinguishers through queries: q stands for queries to the construction and t queries to the primitive, and the distinguishers have unbounded time complexity. Once evaluated in a quantum setting, part of the queries—namely the primitive queries—should be considered quantum.

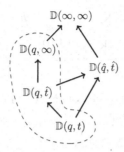

$$\mathbb{D}(\infty, \infty)$$
$$\mathbb{D}(q, \infty)$$
$$\mathbb{D}(\hat{q}, \hat{t})$$
$$\mathbb{D}(q, \hat{t})$$
$$\mathbb{D}(q, t)$$

Fig. 2. Adversaries categorized by computational power and type of oracle access. An arrow represents inclusion, *i.e.*, $A \rightarrow B$ represents $A \subseteq B$.

4 Quantum Key-Recovery Attack

We present a generic attack to recover the key of F_r of Sect. 2.2. The key recovery is performed by translating the problem to a relation$_{p,q,R}$ problem in the terminology of Sect. 2.4, where an evaluation of $F_r(\mathbf{k}, x)$ is used to build the functions f and g and to recover the key $\mathbf{k}$. However, various technicalities occur in this approach, most importantly as there may, for one test value x, be multiple keys $\mathbf{k} \neq \mathbf{k}'$ that fulfill the relation. These technicalities are resolved via the use of a *threshold* τ, which indicates the number of test values to be considered. The threshold τ provides a trade-off between accuracy (of the key guessing) and complexity (of the attack). We first state the definition of colliding key sets for a block cipher in Sect. 4.1. The generic attack is then given in Sect. 4.2.

Without loss of generality, it is fair to consider F_r only for keys $\mathbf{k}$ such that $k_i \neq k_j$ for all $i \neq j$. Indeed, if two keys collide, the corresponding keyed block ciphers cancel each other out and we are effectively considering a scheme based on $r - 2$ permutations which is less secure. Furthermore, note that if $\sigma : \{1, \ldots, r\} \rightarrow \{1, \ldots, r\}$ is a permutation and $\mathbf{k}' = (k_{\sigma(1)}, \ldots, k_{\sigma(r)})$, then

$$F_r(\mathbf{k}, \cdot) = F_r(\mathbf{k}', \cdot).$$

In other words, for any key $\mathbf{k}$, there are $r!$ elements of K^r (including $\mathbf{k}$) giving the exact same function F_r. As such, in our attack we will simply view keys as *unordered sets* from $\binom{K}{r}$ rather than *ordered lists* from K^r, or formally, $F_r : \binom{K}{r} \times X \rightarrow X$.

4.1 Colliding Key Sets

The success of the generic attack depends on the probability that there exist colliding key sets for the block cipher. Although it is written in terminology of F_r of Sect. 2.2, it is merely a standalone combinatorial statement.

Definition 3. *Let $E : K \times X \rightarrow X$ be a block cipher. Let $r \geq 1$ and $\tau \geq 1$ be two positive natural numbers. We define by* $\mathsf{collkeyset}_E(r, \tau)$ *the probability that* there exist two distinct key sets $\mathbf{k}, \mathbf{k}' \in \binom{K}{r}$ such that

$$F_r(\mathbf{k}, 1) \| \cdots \| F_r(\mathbf{k}, \tau) = F_r(\mathbf{k}', 1) \| \cdots \| F_r(\mathbf{k}', \tau),$$

where F_r is defined in Sect. 2.2.

If E is an ideal cipher, i.e., if $E \xleftarrow{\$} \mathsf{Block}(K, X)$, the probability $\mathsf{collkeyset}_E(r, \tau)$ can be straightforwardly computed.

Lemma 1. If $E \xleftarrow{\$} \mathsf{Block}(K, X)$, then

$$\mathsf{collkeyset}_E(r, \tau) \leq \binom{|K|}{r}^2 / |X|^{\tau}. \tag{8}$$

For $\alpha := \lceil \log_{|X|}(|K|) \rceil$, assuming that $(2\alpha)^2 r \leq |X|$,

$$\mathsf{collkeyset}_E(r, 2\alpha r + 1) \leq \frac{4}{|X| - 2\alpha r}. \tag{9}$$

Proof. Pick any two distinct sets $\mathbf{k}, \mathbf{k}' \in \binom{K}{r}$, at most $\binom{|K|}{r}\left(\binom{|K|}{r} - 1\right) \leq \binom{|K|}{r}^2$ choices. As $\mathbf{k}$ and $\mathbf{k}'$ both consist of r distinct elements and are no permutation of each other (by definition of $\binom{K}{r}$), $\mathbf{k}$ contains at least one element that does not occur in the rest of $\mathbf{k}$ or in $\mathbf{k}'$. W.l.o.g., $k_1 \notin \{k_2, \ldots, k_r, k'_1, \ldots, k'_r\}$.

The probability that

$$\forall\, i = 1, \ldots, \tau \ : \ E_{k_1}(i) = \left(E_{k_2}(i) \oplus \cdots \oplus E_{k_r}(i)\right) \oplus \left(E_{k'_1}(i) \oplus \cdots \oplus E_{k'_r}(i)\right) \tag{10}$$

is at most $\frac{(|X| - \tau)!}{|X|!} = 1/|X|^{\tau}$. This completes the proof of (8).

Remains to prove (9). Using that $(m - n + 1)^n \leq m^{\underline{n}} \leq m^n$, we get from (8):

$$\begin{aligned}
\mathsf{collkeyset}_E(r, 2\alpha r + 1) &\leq \binom{|K|}{r}^2 / |X|^{2\alpha r + 1} = \frac{(|K|^{\underline{r}})^2}{(r!)^2 \cdot |X|^{2\alpha r + 1}} \\
&\leq \frac{|K|^{2r}}{(r!)^2 \cdot (|X| - 2\alpha r)^{2\alpha r}} \cdot \frac{1}{|X| - 2\alpha r} \\
&= \frac{|K|^{2r}}{(r!)^2 \cdot |X|^{2\alpha r} \cdot \left(1 - \frac{2\alpha r}{|X|}\right)^{2\alpha r}} \cdot \frac{1}{|X| - 2\alpha r} \\
&\leq \frac{1}{(r!)^2 \cdot \left(1 - \frac{2\alpha r}{|X|}\right)^{2\alpha r}} \cdot \frac{1}{|X| - 2\alpha r}, \tag{11}
\end{aligned}$$

where the last step holds as $\alpha \geq \log_{|X|}(|K|)$.

Note that

$$\left(1 - \frac{2\alpha r}{|X|}\right)^{\alpha} \geq 1 - \frac{2\alpha^2 r}{|X|} \geq \frac{1}{2},$$

where the first step holds as $(1-x)^y \geq 1 - xy$ and the second step by assumption that $(2\alpha)^2 r \leq |X|$. We thus obtain for (11):

$$\mathsf{collkeyset}_E(r, 2\alpha r + 1) \leq \left(\frac{2^r}{r!}\right)^2 \cdot \frac{1}{|X| - 2\alpha r} \leq \frac{4}{|X| - 2\alpha r},$$

which completes the proof of (9). $\qquad\qquad\square$

4.2 Generic Attack

Theorem 1. *Let $E : K \times X \to X$ be a block cipher, and let $r \geq 1$ be a positive natural number. Consider F_r of Sect. 2.2. Let $\tau \geq 1$ be a positive natural number. There exists a distinguisher $\mathcal{D} \in \mathbb{D}(\tau, \hat{t})$ with $t = O\left(\tau \cdot |K|^{r/(r+1)}\right)$ that recovers the key of F_r with success probability at least $1 - \mathsf{collkeyset}_E(r, \tau)$.*

Proof. Let $\mathbf{k} = (k_1, \ldots, k_r) \in \binom{K}{r}$ be the secret key to F_r, i.e.,

$$F_r(\mathbf{k}, x) = E_{k_1}(x) \oplus \cdots \oplus E_{k_r}(x).$$

As a first step, the distinguisher queries $F_r(\mathbf{k}, i) = z_i$ for $i = 1, \ldots, \tau$. Then, define the following two functions:

$$f : K \to X^\tau, \qquad\qquad g : K \to X^\tau,$$
$$f(l) = E_l(1) \| \cdots \| E_l(\tau), \qquad g(m) = \big(E_m(1) \oplus z_1\big) \| \cdots \| \big(E_m(\tau) \oplus z_\tau\big).$$

Next, evaluate the quantum relation-finding algorithm of Sect. 2.4 for parameters $p = r - 1$, $q = 1$, and R as the relation that all elements of the tuple XOR to 0:[6]

$$R = \{(a_1, \ldots, a_r) \mid a_1 \oplus \cdots \oplus a_r = 0\}.$$

The relation-finding algorithm makes

$$O\left(\tau \cdot |K|^{r/(r+1)}\right)$$

evaluations of E (the factor τ corresponds to the number of evaluations of E per evaluation of f and g).

Note that by construction, there is at least one set of candidate keys for the algorithm: $\mathbf{k}$. If this is the only set of candidate keys, then the algorithm will output the correct key and $\mathcal{D}$ succeeds. On the other hand, there exist more than two sets of solutions with probability at most $\mathsf{collkeyset}_E(r, \tau)$. Therefore, the attack succeeds with probability at least $1 - \mathsf{collkeyset}_E(r, \tau)$. $\qquad\square$

From Theorem 1 and Lemma 1 we obtain the following corollary.

---

[6] The attack can be simplified by putting $z_1 \| \cdots \| z_\tau$ inside relation R and considering $p = r$ and $q = 0$. We follow current approach for intuitiveness.

Corollary 1. *Let $E : K \times X \to X$ be an ideal cipher, and let $r \geq 1$ be a positive natural number. Consider F_r of Sect. 2.2. Put $\alpha = \lceil \log_{|X|}(|K|) \rceil$, assume that $(2\alpha)^2 r \leq |X|$, and let $\tau = 2\alpha r + 1$. There exists a distinguisher $\mathcal{D} \in \mathbb{D}(\tau, \hat{t})$ with $t = O\left(\tau \cdot |K|^{r/(r+1)}\right) = O\left(|K|^{r/(r+1)}\right)$ that recovers the key of F_r with success probability at least $1 - \frac{4}{|X| - 2\alpha r}$.*

The estimation of offline complexity presents an asymptotic relation as a function of $|K|$ only. In addition to absorbing τ, the big O notation hides various constant factors that depend on r, deriving from the underlying quantum search algorithm.

5   Quantum Security Analysis

For our quantum security analysis of F_r we recall a classical result on its idealized counterpart F_r^{id} due to Patarin for $r = 2$ [43,44] and its generalization to $r \geq 3$ by Mennink and Preneel [39]:

Lemma 2. *Let $r \geq 2$ be integral. For $q \leq |X|/67$, we have*

$$\mathrm{Adv}_{F_r^{id}}^{\mathrm{prf}}(\mathbb{D}(q, \infty)) = \frac{q}{|X|}.$$

The analysis in [39,43,44] is performed to cover information-theoretic distinguishers. It considers deterministic distinguishers which query their oracle (either F_r^{id} or ρ) q times adaptively, and which are computationally unbounded.

Using Lemma 2, we can derive the following upper bound on the success probability of a quantum distinguisher (from $\mathbb{D}(q, \hat{t})$) in distinguishing F_r for random keys $\mathbf{k} = (k_1, \ldots, k_r) \xleftarrow{\$} K^r$ from a random function ρ.

Theorem 2. *Let $E : K \times X \to X$ be a block cipher, and let $r \geq 2$ be integral. For $q \leq |X|/67$, we have*

$$\mathrm{Adv}_{F_r}^{\mathrm{prf}}(\mathbb{D}(q, \hat{t})) \leq r \cdot \mathrm{Adv}_{E}^{\mathrm{prp}}(\mathbb{D}(q, \hat{t})) + \frac{q}{|X|}.$$

Proof. Let $\mathbf{k} = (k_1, \ldots, k_r) \xleftarrow{\$} K^r$, $\boldsymbol{\pi} = (\pi_1, \ldots, \pi_r) \xleftarrow{\$} \mathrm{Perm}(X)^r$, and $\rho \xleftarrow{\$} \mathrm{Func}(X, X)$. Consider any distinguisher $\mathcal{D} \in \mathbb{D}(q, \hat{t})$. We have

$$\mathrm{Adv}_{F_r}^{\mathrm{prf}}(\mathcal{D}) = \left| \mathbf{P}\left(\mathcal{D}^{F_{r,\mathbf{k}}} = 1 \right) - \mathbf{P}\left(\mathcal{D}^{\rho} = 1 \right) \right|$$

$$\leq \left| \mathbf{P}\left(\mathcal{D}^{F_{r,\mathbf{k}}} = 1 \right) - \mathbf{P}\left(\mathcal{D}^{F_{r,\boldsymbol{\pi}}^{id}} = 1 \right) \right| + \mathrm{Adv}_{F_r^{id}}^{\mathrm{prf}}(\mathcal{D}). \quad (12)$$

The first term of (12) satisfies

$$\left| \mathbf{P}\left(\mathcal{D}^{F_{r,\mathbf{k}}} = 1 \right) - \mathbf{P}\left(\mathcal{D}^{F_{r,\boldsymbol{\pi}}^{id}} = 1 \right) \right| \leq \sum_{i=1}^{r} \left| \mathbf{P}\left(\mathcal{E}^{E_{k_i}} = 1 \right) - \mathbf{P}\left(\mathcal{E}^{\pi_i} = 1 \right) \right| \quad (13)$$

$$\leq r \cdot \mathrm{Adv}_{E}^{\mathrm{prp}}(\mathcal{E}),$$

for some distinguisher $\mathcal{E}$ with online complexity q and offline complexity at most $\hat{t}$. Clearly,

$$\mathsf{Adv}_E^{\mathrm{prp}}(\mathcal{E}) \leq \sup_{\mathcal{E} \in \mathbb{D}(q,\hat{t})} \mathsf{Adv}_E^{\mathrm{prp}}(\mathcal{E}) \leq \mathsf{Adv}_E^{\mathrm{prp}}(\mathbb{D}(q,\hat{t})).$$

Using Lemma 2, the second term of (12) satisfies

$$\mathsf{Adv}_{F_r^{\mathrm{id}}}^{\mathrm{prf}}(\mathcal{D}) \leq \sup_{\mathcal{D} \in \mathbb{D}(q,\hat{t})} \mathsf{Adv}_{F_r^{\mathrm{id}}}^{\mathrm{prf}}(\mathcal{D}) \leq \sup_{\mathcal{D} \in \mathbb{D}(q,\infty)} \mathsf{Adv}_{F_r^{\mathrm{id}}}^{\mathrm{prf}}(\mathcal{D}) = \mathsf{Adv}_{F_r^{\mathrm{id}}}^{\mathrm{prf}}(\mathbb{D}(q,\infty)) \leq \frac{q}{|X|}.$$

We have hence obtained

$$\mathsf{Adv}_{F_r}^{\mathrm{prf}}(\mathcal{D}) \leq r \cdot \mathsf{Adv}_E^{\mathrm{prp}}(\mathbb{D}(q,\hat{t})) + \frac{q}{|X|}.$$

As the derivation holds for any $\mathcal{D} \in \mathbb{D}(q,\hat{t})$, this completes the proof.   □

The step that facilitates the application of Lemma 2 is mainly due to our formalization of distinguishers in Sect. 3. It is interesting to see that the classical world equivalent of Theorem 2 would read

$$\mathsf{Adv}_{F_r}^{\mathrm{prf}}(\mathbb{D}(q,t)) \leq r \cdot \mathsf{Adv}_E^{\mathrm{prp}}(\mathbb{D}(q,t)) + \frac{q}{|X|},$$

and the security analysis is fairly identical. The reduction in the proof of Theorem 2 therewith clearly demonstrates that the analysis directly generalizes to many other proofs in symmetric key cryptography and it is therefore of independent interest. Rather than writing the direct security proof, we could have equally well departed from the techniques of Hallgren et al. [21] and Song [51]. However, as pointed out in Sect. 1, these techniques are stronger and more involved by design, and we believe that for our case a direct proof is easier to grasp.

The question as to what level of PRP security a block cipher E offers is beyond the scope of this work; it strongly depends on the strength of E against cryptanalysis. For example, in the classical setting, assuming that E is a strong enough cipher, we have $\mathsf{Adv}_E^{\mathrm{prp}}(\mathbb{D}(q,t)) \approx \frac{q}{|K|}$. If the distinguisher can make quantum offline evaluations, we know that, due to Grover's algorithm, $\mathsf{Adv}_E^{\mathrm{prp}}(\mathbb{D}(q,\hat{t})) = \Omega\left(\frac{q}{|K|^{1/2}}\right)$. Assuming that E is strong enough and Grover's algorithm describes the best possible attack on E, Theorem 2 gives security of F_r as long as the complexity satisfies $q \ll \min\{|K|^{1/2}/r, |X|\}$. Using a block cipher with a key twice the state size, e.g., AES-256, one obtains optimal security.

6   Discussion

Theorem 2 suggests that F_r achieves security up to $\min\{|K|^{1/2}/r, |X|\}$ queries, provided that Grover's algorithm is the best way of breaking the underlying block cipher. On the other hand, the attack of Sect. 4 only reaches $|K|^{r/(r+1)}$, indicating a gap between the best attack and best security bound. The tightness appears to be lost in Eq. (13) of the proof of Theorem 2, which upper bounds the advantage of guessing a key $\mathbf{k} \in K^r$ by the advantage of guessing one of its elements $k_i \in K$. While this step is a conventional and reasonably harmless proof technique in countless works on non-quantum symmetric key security, for analysis against quantum distinguishers this step entails a significant loss.

Recall that the bound of Lemma 2 holds for any $r \geq 2$. Now, consider F_r, and assume that the adversary is able to recover $r - 2$ keys. This effectively reduces F_r to F_2, which, as suggested by Lemma 2, should not have an influence on the bound. Instead, if one recovers $r - 1$ out of r keys, the lemma cannot be applied, and the problem of breaking F_r reduces to the problem of recovering $r - 1$ keys. In other words, intuition tells that security up to at least $\min\{|K|^{(r-1)/r}, |X|\}$ could be attainable. Well hidden in this intuition are, however, various conceptual difficulties. Most importantly, it requires the formalization of "block ciphers being secure conditioned on the absence of key recovery." Additionally, it requires a mechanism to verify whether a distinguisher has recovered a key of $E_{k_1} \oplus \cdots \oplus E_{k_r}$, without having access to $E_{k_1}, \ldots, E_{k_r}$ separately.

Acknowledgments. This work was supported in part by the Research Council KU Leuven: GOA TENSE (GOA/11/007). In addition, this work was supported by the European Commission through the Horizon 2020 research and innovation programme under grant agreement No H2020-ICT-2014-645622 PQCRYPTO and grant agreement No H2020-MSCA-ITN-2014-643161 ECRYPT-NET. Bart Mennink is supported by a postdoctoral fellowship from the Netherlands Organisation for Scientific Research (NWO) under Veni grant 016.Veni.173.017. Alan Szepieniec is supported by a Ph.D. Fellowship from the Institute for the Promotion of Innovation through Science and Technology in Flanders (VLAIO, formerly IWT). The authors would like to thank Stacey Jeffery and the anonymous reviewers of PQCrypto 2017 for their useful suggestions.

References

1. Abed, F., Forler, C., List, E., Lucks, S., Wenzel, J.: RIV for robust authenticated encryption. In: Peyrin [45], pp. 23–42
2. Anand, M.V., Targhi, E.E., Tabia, G.N., Unruh, D.: Post-quantum security of the CBC, CFB, OFB, CTR, and XTS modes of operation. In: Takagi, T. (ed.) PQCrypto 2016. LNCS, vol. 9606, pp. 44–63. Springer, Cham (2016). doi:10.1007/978-3-319-29360-8_4
3. Andreeva, E., Bilgin, B., Bogdanov, A., Luykx, A., Mennink, B., Mouha, N., Yasuda, K.: APE: authenticated permutation-based encryption for lightweight cryptography. In: Cid and Rechberger [15], pp. 168–186
4. Andreeva, E., Bogdanov, A., Luykx, A., Mennink, B., Tischhauser, E., Yasuda, K.: Parallelizable and authenticated online ciphers. In: Sako, K., Sarkar, P. (eds.) ASIACRYPT 2013. LNCS, vol. 8269, pp. 424–443. Springer, Heidelberg (2013). doi:10.1007/978-3-642-42033-7_22
5. Andreeva, E., Daemen, J., Mennink, B., Van Assche, G.: Security of keyed sponge constructions using a modular proof approach. In: Leander, G. (ed.) FSE 2015. LNCS, vol. 9054, pp. 364–384. Springer, Heidelberg (2015). doi:10.1007/978-3-662-48116-5_18

6. Bellare, M., Impagliazzo, R.: A tool for obtaining tighter security analyses of pseudorandom function based constructions, with applications to PRP to PRF conversion. Cryptology ePrint Archive, Report 1999/024 (1999)
7. Bellare, M., Kilian, J., Rogaway, P.: The security of cipher block chaining. In: Desmedt, Y.G. (ed.) CRYPTO 1994. LNCS, vol. 839, pp. 341–358. Springer, Heidelberg (1994). doi:10.1007/3-540-48658-5_32
8. Bellare, M., Rogaway, P.: The security of triple encryption and a framework for code-based game-playing proofs. In: Vaudenay, S. (ed.) EUROCRYPT 2006. LNCS, vol. 4004, pp. 409–426. Springer, Heidelberg (2006). doi:10.1007/11761679_25
9. Bernstein, D.J., Buchmann, J., Dahmen, E. (eds.): Post-Quantum Cryptography. Springer Science & Business Media, Heidelberg (2009)
10. Bhaumik, R., Nandi, M.: OleF: an inverse-free online cipher. IACR Trans. Symmetric Cryptol. **1**(2), 30–51 (2016)
11. Bogdanov, A., Knudsen, L.R., Leander, G., Standaert, F.-X., Steinberger, J., Tischhauser, E.: Key-alternating ciphers in a provable setting: encryption using a small number of public permutations. In: Pointcheval, D., Johansson, T. (eds.) EUROCRYPT 2012. LNCS, vol. 7237, pp. 45–62. Springer, Heidelberg (2012). doi:10.1007/978-3-642-29011-4_5
12. Brassard, G., Høyer, P., Tapp, A.: Quantum cryptanalysis of hash and claw-free functions. In: Lucchesi, C.L., Moura, A.V. (eds.) LATIN 1998. LNCS, vol. 1380, pp. 163–169. Springer, Heidelberg (1998). doi:10.1007/BFb0054319
13. Buhrman, H., Dürr, C., Heiligman, M., Høyer, P., Magniez, F., Santha, M., de Wolf, R.: Quantum algorithms for element distinctness. SIAM J. Comput. **34**(6), 1324–1330 (2005)
14. Chen, S., Steinberger, J.P.: Tight security bounds for key-alternating ciphers. In: Nguyen and Oswald [42], pp. 327–350
15. Cid, C., Rechberger, C. (eds.): FSE 2014. LNCS, vol. 8540. Springer, Heidelberg (2015)
16. Cogliati, B., Lampe, R., Patarin, J.: The indistinguishability of the XOR of k permutations. In: Cid and Rechberger [15], pp. 285–302
17. Cogliati, B., Lampe, R., Seurin, Y.: Tweaking even-mansour ciphers. In: Gennaro, R., Robshaw, M. (eds.) CRYPTO 2015. LNCS, vol. 9215, pp. 189–208. Springer, Heidelberg (2015). doi:10.1007/978-3-662-47989-6_9
18. Cogliati, B., Seurin, Y.: EWCDM: an efficient, beyond-birthday secure, nonce-misuse resistant MAC. In: Robshaw and Katz [48], pp. 121–149
19. Grover, L.K.: A fast quantum mechanical algorithm for database search. In: Miller, G.L. (ed.) Proceedings of the Twenty-Eighth Annual ACM Symposium on the Theory of Computing, Philadelphia, Pennsylvania, USA, 22–24 May 1996, pp. 212–219. ACM (1996)
20. Hall, C., Wagner, D., Kelsey, J., Schneier, B.: Building PRFs from PRPs. In: Krawczyk, H. (ed.) CRYPTO 1998. LNCS, vol. 1462, pp. 370–389. Springer, Heidelberg (1998). doi:10.1007/BFb0055742
21. Hallgren, S., Smith, A., Song, F.: Classical cryptographic protocols in a quantum world. In: Rogaway, P. (ed.) CRYPTO 2011. LNCS, vol. 6841, pp. 411–428. Springer, Heidelberg (2011). doi:10.1007/978-3-642-22792-9_23
22. Hoang, V.T., Krovetz, T., Rogaway, P.: Robust authenticated-encryption AEZ and the problem that it solves. In: Oswald, E., Fischlin, M. (eds.) EUROCRYPT 2015. LNCS, vol. 9056, pp. 15–44. Springer, Heidelberg (2015). doi:10.1007/978-3-662-46800-5_2

23. Impagliazzo, R., Rudich, S.: Limits on the provable consequences of one-way permutations. In: Goldwasser, S. (ed.) CRYPTO 1988. LNCS, vol. 403, pp. 8–26. Springer, New York (1990). doi:10.1007/0-387-34799-2_2

24. Iwata, T.: New blockcipher modes of operation with beyond the birthday bound security. In: Robshaw, M. (ed.) FSE 2006. LNCS, vol. 4047, pp. 310–327. Springer, Heidelberg (2006). doi:10.1007/11799313_20

25. Iwata, T., Mennink, B., Vizr, D.: CENC is optimally secure. Cryptology ePrint Archive, Report 2016/1087 (2016)

26. Iwata, T., Minematsu, K., Guo, J., Morioka, S.: CLOC: authenticated encryption for short input. In: Cid and Rechberger [15], pp. 149–167

27. Kaplan, M.: Quantum attacks against iterated block ciphers. CoRR abs/1410.1434 (2014)

28. Kaplan, M., Leurent, G., Leverrier, A., Naya-Plasencia, M.: Breaking symmetric cryptosystems using quantum period finding. In: Robshaw, M., Katz, J. (eds.) CRYPTO 2016. LNCS, vol. 9815, pp. 207–237. Springer, Heidelberg (2016). doi:10.1007/978-3-662-53008-5_8

29. Krovetz, T., Rogaway, P.: The software performance of authenticated-encryption modes. In: Joux, A. (ed.) FSE 2011. LNCS, vol. 6733, pp. 306–327. Springer, Heidelberg (2011). doi:10.1007/978-3-642-21702-9_18

30. Kuwakado, H., Morii, M.: Quantum distinguisher between the 3-round Feistel cipher and the random permutation. In: Proceedings of IEEE International Symposium on Information Theory, ISIT 2010, 13–18 June 2010, Austin, Texas, USA, pp. 2682–2685. IEEE (2010)

31. Kuwakado, H., Morii, M.: Security on the quantum-type Even-Mansour cipher. In: Proceedings of the International Symposium on Information Theory and its Applications, ISITA 2012, Honolulu, HI, USA, 28–31 October 2012, pp. 312–316. IEEE (2012)

32. Landecker, W., Shrimpton, T., Terashima, R.S.: Tweakable blockciphers with beyond birthday-bound security. In: Safavi-Naini, R., Canetti, R. (eds.) CRYPTO 2012. LNCS, vol. 7417, pp. 14–30. Springer, Heidelberg (2012). doi:10.1007/978-3-642-32009-5_2

33. Lucks, S.: The sum of PRPs is a secure PRF. In: Preneel, B. (ed.) EUROCRYPT 2000. LNCS, vol. 1807, pp. 470–484. Springer, Heidelberg (2000). doi:10.1007/3-540-45539-6_34

34. Luykx, A., Preneel, B., Tischhauser, E., Yasuda, K.: A MAC mode for lightweight block ciphers. In: Peyrin [45], pp. 43–59

35. Magniez, F., Santha, M., Szegedy, M.: Quantum algorithms for the triangle problem. SIAM J. Comput. **37**(2), 413–424 (2007)

36. Malozemoff, A.J., Katz, J., Green, M.D.: Automated analysis and synthesis of block-cipher modes of operation. In: IEEE 27th Computer Security Foundations Symposium, CSF 2014, Vienna, Austria, 19–22 July 2014, pp. 140–152. IEEE Computer Society (2014)

37. Mandal, A., Patarin, J., Nachef, V.: Indifferentiability beyond the birthday bound for the XOR of two public random permutations. In: Gong, G., Gupta, K.C. (eds.) INDOCRYPT 2010. LNCS, vol. 6498, pp. 69–81. Springer, Heidelberg (2010). doi:10.1007/978-3-642-17401-8_6

38. Mennink, B.: XPX: generalized tweakable even-mansour with improved security guarantees. In: Robshaw and Katz [48], pp. 64–94

39. Mennink, B., Preneel, B.: On the XOR of multiple random permutations. In: Malkin, T., Kolesnikov, V., Lewko, A.B., Polychronakis, M. (eds.) ACNS 2015. LNCS, vol. 9092, pp. 619–634. Springer, Cham (2015). doi:10.1007/978-3-319-28166-7_30

40. Mennink, B., Reyhanitabar, R., Vizár, D.: Security of full-state keyed sponge and duplex: applications to authenticated encryption. In: Iwata, T., Cheon, J.H. (eds.) ASIACRYPT 2015. LNCS, vol. 9453, pp. 465–489. Springer, Heidelberg (2015). doi:10.1007/978-3-662-48800-3_19

41. Minematsu, K.: Parallelizable rate-1 authenticated encryption from pseudorandom functions. In: Nguyen and Oswald [42], pp. 275–292

42. Nguyen, P.Q., Oswald, E. (eds.): EUROCRYPT 2014. LNCS, vol. 8441. Springer, Heidelberg (2014)

43. Patarin, J.: A proof of security in $O(2^n)$ for the XOR of two random permutations. In: Safavi-Naini, R. (ed.) ICITS 2008. LNCS, vol. 5155, pp. 232–248. Springer, Heidelberg (2008). doi:10.1007/978-3-540-85093-9_22

44. Patarin, J.: Introduction to mirror theory: analysis of systems of linear equalities and linear non equalities for cryptography. Cryptology ePrint Archive, Report 2010/287 (2010)

45. Peyrin, T. (ed.): FSE 2016. LNCS, vol. 9783. Springer, Heidelberg (2016)

46. Peyrin, T., Seurin, Y.: Counter-in-tweak: authenticated encryption modes for tweakable block ciphers. In: Robshaw and Katz [48], pp. 33–63

47. Reyhanitabar, R., Vaudenay, S., Vizár, D.: Authenticated encryption with variable stretch. In: Cheon, J.H., Takagi, T. (eds.) ASIACRYPT 2016. LNCS, vol. 10031, pp. 396–425. Springer, Heidelberg (2016). doi:10.1007/978-3-662-53887-6_15

48. Robshaw, M., Katz, J. (eds.): CRYPTO 2016. LNCS, vol. 9814. Springer, Heidelberg (2016)

49. Rogaway, P.: Efficient instantiations of tweakable blockciphers and refinements to modes OCB and PMAC. In: Lee, P.J. (ed.) ASIACRYPT 2004. LNCS, vol. 3329, pp. 16–31. Springer, Heidelberg (2004). doi:10.1007/978-3-540-30539-2_2

50. Shor, P.W.: Algorithms for quantum computation: discrete logarithms and factoring. In: 35th Annual Symposium on Foundations of Computer Science, Santa Fe, New Mexico, USA, 20–22 November 1994, pp. 124–134. IEEE Computer Society (1994)

51. Song, F.: A note on quantum security for post-quantum cryptography. In: Mosca, M. (ed.) PQCrypto 2014. LNCS, vol. 8772, pp. 246–265. Springer, Cham (2014). doi:10.1007/978-3-319-11659-4_15

52. Tani, S.: Claw finding algorithms using quantum walk. Theor. Comput. Sci. **410**(50), 5285–5297 (2009)

53. Zhandry, M.: How to construct quantum random functions. In: 53rd Annual IEEE Symposium on Foundations of Computer Science, FOCS 2012, New Brunswick, NJ, USA, 20–23 October 2012, pp. 679–687. IEEE Computer Society (2012)

54. Zhandry, M.: A note on the quantum collision and set equality problems. Quant. Inf. Comput. **15**(7&8), 557–567 (2015)

55. Zhandry, M.: A note on quantum-secure PRPs. Cryptology ePrint Archive, Report 2016/1076 (2016)

56. Zhang, S.: Promised and distributed quantum search. In: Wang, L. (ed.) COCOON 2005. LNCS, vol. 3595, pp. 430–439. Springer, Heidelberg (2005). doi:10.1007/11533719_44

Transitioning to a Quantum-Resistant Public Key Infrastructure

Nina Bindel[1], Udyani Herath[2], Matthew McKague[2], and Douglas Stebila[3]([⊠])

[1] Technische Universität Darmstadt, Darmstadt, Germany
[2] Queensland University of Technology, Brisbane, Australia
[3] McMaster University, Hamilton, ON, Canada
stebilad@mcmaster.ca

Abstract. To ensure uninterrupted cryptographic security, it is important to begin planning the transition to post-quantum cryptography. In addition to creating post-quantum primitives, we must also plan how to adapt the cryptographic infrastructure for the transition, especially in scenarios such as public key infrastructures (PKIs) with many participants. The use of hybrids—multiple algorithms in parallel—will likely play a role during the transition for two reasons: "hedging our bets" when the security of newer primitives is not yet certain but the security of older primitives is already in question; and to achieve security and functionality both in post-quantum-aware and in a backwards-compatible way with not-yet-upgraded software.

In this paper, we investigate the use of hybrid digital signature schemes. We consider several methods for combining signature schemes, and give conditions on when the resulting hybrid signature scheme is unforgeable. Additionally we address a new notion about the inability of an adversary to separate a hybrid signature into its components. For both unforgeability and non-separability, we give a novel security hierarchy based on how quantum the attack is. We then turn to three real-world standards involving digital signatures and PKI: certificates (X.509), secure channels (TLS), and email (S/MIME). We identify possible approaches to supporting hybrid signatures in these standards while retaining backwards compatibility, which we test in popular cryptographic libraries and implementations, noting especially the inability of some software to handle larger certificates.

1   Introduction

Since the initial advent of modern symmetric and public key cryptography in the 1970s, there have only been a handful of transitions from one widely deployed algorithm to another. These include: from DES and Triple-DES to AES; from MD5 and SHA-1 to the SHA-2 family; from RSA key transport and finite field Diffie–Hellman to elliptic curve Diffie–Hellman key exchange; and from RSA and DSA certificates to ECDSA certificates. Some of these transitions have gone well: AES is nearly ubiquitous today, and modern communication protocols predominantly use ECDH key exchange. Transitions involving public key infrastructure

© Springer International Publishing AG 2017
T. Lange and T. Takagi (Eds.): PQCrypto 2017, LNCS 10346, pp. 384–405, 2017.
DOI: 10.1007/978-3-319-59879-6_22

have a more mixed record: browser vendors and CAs have had a long transition period from SHA-1 to SHA-2 in certificates, with repeated delay of deadlines; the transition to elliptic curve certificates has been even slower, and still today the vast majority of certificates issued for the web use RSA.

In the medium-term, we are likely to see another transition to *post-quantum* public key cryptography. Some aspects of the post-quantum transition will be straightforward: using post-quantum key exchange in protocols that support negotiation such as the Transport Layer has already been demonstrated [9,10], and can be adopted piecewise. Other migrations will be harder, especially when it is difficult for old and new configurations to operate simultaneously. A recent whitepaper [12] discusses some of these issues at a high level.

The transition to post-quantum cryptography is further complicated by the relative immaturity of some of the underlying mathematical assumptions in current candidates: because they have not been studied for very long, there is a higher risk that they might be insecure. This motivates *hybrid* operation, in which both a traditional algorithm and one or more post-quantum algorithms are used in parallel: as long as one of them remains unbroken, confidentiality or authenticity can be ensured. This leads us to three research questions:

1. What are the appropriate security properties for hybrid digital signatures?
2. How should we combine signature schemes to construct hybrid signatures?
3. How can hybrid signatures be realized in popular standards and software, ideally in a backwards-compatible way?

1. Security Notions for Hybrid Digital Signatures. The widely accepted security notion for digital signatures is *unforgeability under chosen message attack* (EUF-CMA): the adversary interacts with a signing oracle to obtain signatures on any desired messages, and then must output a forgery on a new message. Hybrid signatures should retain that property. Boneh and Zhandry [8] first studied security notions for digital signature schemes against quantum adversaries, and gave a quantum analogue of EUF-CMA in which a quantum adversary is able to interact with a quantum signing oracle and thereby obtain signatures on quantum states of its choosing (which may be in superposition).

As we transition to post-quantum digital signatures, Boneh and Zhandry's definition might be overly strong: for example, we might be using a signature scheme for the next five years, and during this period we are confident that no adversary has a quantum computer, and moreover we are definitely not signing anything in superposition; but later, the adversary may eventually be able to use a quantum computer. We describe several security notions depending on how quantum the adversary is. We use the notation X^yZ to denote the adversary's type with respect to three options:

- X: whether the adversary is classical ($X = C$) or quantum ($X = Q$) *during* the period in which it can interact with the signing oracle;
- y: whether the adversary can interact with the signing oracle classically ($y = c$) or quantumly ($y = q$); and

Table 1. Combiners for constructing hybrid signatures using schemes Σ_1 and Σ_2; $\max\{\mathsf{X}^y\mathsf{Z}, \mathsf{U}^v\mathsf{W}\}$ denotes the stronger unforgeability notion with respect to the natural hierarchy of security notions.

Combiner	Combined signature $\sigma = (\sigma_1, \sigma_2)$	Unforgeability	Non-separability
Single-message combiners			
$C_\parallel$	$\sigma_1 \leftarrow_\$ \mathsf{Sign}_1(m); \sigma_2 \leftarrow_\$ \mathsf{Sign}_2(m)$	$\max\{\mathsf{X}^y\mathsf{Z}, \mathsf{U}^v\mathsf{W}\}$	No
$C_{\text{weak-nest}}$	$\sigma_1 \leftarrow_\$ \mathsf{Sign}_1(m); \sigma_2 \leftarrow_\$ \mathsf{Sign}_2(\sigma_1)$	$\mathsf{X}^y\mathsf{Z}$	$\mathsf{U}^c\mathsf{W}$-2
$C_{\text{str-nest}}$	$\sigma_1 \leftarrow_\$ \mathsf{Sign}_1(m); \sigma_2 \leftarrow_\$ \mathsf{Sign}_2((m, \sigma_1))$	$\max\{\mathsf{X}^y\mathsf{Z}, \mathsf{U}^v\mathsf{W}\}$	$\mathsf{U}^c\mathsf{W}$-2
Dual-message combiners			
D_{nest}	$\sigma_1 \leftarrow_\$ \mathsf{Sign}_1(m_1); \sigma_2 \leftarrow_\$ \mathsf{Sign}_2((m_1, \sigma_1, m_2))$	$\mathsf{U}^v\mathsf{W}, \mathsf{X}^y\mathsf{Z}^*$	$\mathsf{U}^c\mathsf{W}$-2

Unforgeability: If Σ_1 is $\mathsf{X}^y\mathsf{Z}$-eufcma and Σ_2 is $\mathsf{U}^v\mathsf{W}$-eufcma, then $C(\Sigma_1, \Sigma_2)$ is ...-eufcma.
Non-separability: If Σ_1 is $\mathsf{X}^y\mathsf{Z}$-eufcma and Σ_2 is $\mathsf{U}^v\mathsf{W}$-eufcma, then $C(\Sigma_1, \Sigma_2)$ is ...-nonsep.
* Unforgeability of $D_{\text{nest}}(\Sigma_1, \Sigma_2)$ under $\mathsf{X}^y\mathsf{Z}$-eufcma-security of Σ_1 in a restricted sense.

– Z: whether the adversary is classical ($\mathsf{Z} = \mathsf{C}$) or quantum ($\mathsf{Z} = \mathsf{Q}$) *after* the period in which it can interact with the signing oracle.

These security notions form a natural hierarchy ($\mathsf{Q}^q\mathsf{Q} \implies \mathsf{Q}^c\mathsf{Q} \implies \mathsf{C}^c\mathsf{Q} \implies \mathsf{C}^c\mathsf{C}$) with separations between each level of the hierarchy.

We describe a second security property specifically related to hybrid signatures, called *non-separability*: for a hybrid signature involving two (or more) signature schemes, is it possible for an adversary to separate the hybrid signature into a valid signature in any of the component signature schemes? This security property is interesting in the context of a transition. Suppose a signer issues hybrid signatures during a transition. Suppose further that there is a verifier who can understand both hybrid signatures and single-scheme signatures, but possibly acts upon them differently. The goal of non-separability is to prevent an attacker from taking a hybrid signature and turning it into something that the verifier accepts as coming from a single-scheme signature—thereby misrepresenting the signer's original intention. Specifically, if $\Sigma' = C(\Sigma_1, \Sigma_2)$ is the hybrid signature scheme from using combiner C to combine signature schemes Σ_1 and Σ_2, then we say Σ' is $\mathsf{X}^y\mathsf{Z}$-τ-nonsep if it is hard for an $\mathsf{X}^y\mathsf{Z}$-adversary to construct a valid Σ_τ signature given access to a signing oracle for Σ'. Our notions are aided by a *recognizer* algorithm, which a verifier can apply to a signature to attempt to help distinguish separated hybrid signatures.

2. Signature Combiners. Having laid out security properties for hybrid signatures, we proceed to investigate how to construct hybrid schemes using *combiners*. Table 1 shows the combiners we consider: concatenation and three forms of nested signatures. These particular combiners are motivated by two factors: that they are fairly natural constructions, and three of them arise in our applications.

3. Hybrid Signatures in Standards and Software. Our goal is to provide a guide for how to transition to hybrid post-quantum digital signatures in various standards and software. We consider three standards: X.509 for certificates [14], the Transport Layer Security (TLS) protocol for secure channels [15], and Cryptographic Message Syntax (CMS) [20] as part of Secure/Multipurpose Internet Mail Extensions (S/MIME) [22] for secure email. For each, we ask:

(3.a) How can hybrid/multiple signature schemes be used in the standard?
(3.b) Is this approach backwards-compatible with old software?
(3.c) Are there potential problems involving large public keys or signatures?

We identify promising techniques for hybrid X.509 certificates, and hybrid S/MIME signed messages; using multiple signature algorithms in TLS does not seem immediately possible, though one mechanism in the current draft of TLS 1.3 seems to allow multiple client authentications and a recent proposal could allow multiple server authentications. The software we tested had no problems with certificates or extensions up to ~10 kB (accommodating ideal lattice schemes), and some software up to ~80 kB (accommodating hash-based schemes), but none could handle the megabyte-plus size public keys of the largest lattice-based scheme; details appear in Sect. 5.

2 Signature Schemes and Unforgeability

Definition 1 (Signature scheme). *A digital signature scheme Σ is a tuple $\Sigma = (\Sigma.\mathsf{KeyGen}, \Sigma.\mathsf{Sign}, \Sigma.\mathsf{Verify})$ of algorithms:*

- *$\Sigma.\mathsf{KeyGen}() \twoheadrightarrow (sk, vk)$: The probabilistic key generation algorithm that returns a secret or signing key sk and public or verification key $vk \in \mathcal{VK}_\Sigma$.*
- *$\Sigma.\mathsf{Sign}(sk, m) \twoheadrightarrow \sigma$: The probabilistic signature generation algorithm which takes as input a signing key sk and a message $m \in \mathcal{M}_\Sigma$, and outputs a signature $\sigma \in \mathcal{S}_\Sigma$. The space of random coins is $\mathcal{R}_\Sigma$.*
- *$\Sigma.\mathsf{Verify}(vk, m, \sigma) \to 0$ or 1: The verification algorithm which takes as input a verification key vk, a message m, and a signature σ, and returns a bit $b \in \{0, 1\}$. If $b = 1$, we say that the algorithm accepts, otherwise we say that it rejects the signature σ for message m.*

If a proof for Σ is being given in the random oracle model, we use $\mathcal{H}_\Sigma$ to denote the space of functions from which the random hash function is randomly sampled. We say that Σ is ϵ-correct if, for every message m in the message space, we have that $\Pr\left[\mathsf{Verify}(vk, m, \sigma) = 1 : (sk, vk) \leftarrow_\$ \mathsf{KeyGen}(), \sigma \leftarrow_\$ \mathsf{Sign}(sk, m)\right] \geq 1 - \epsilon$ where the probability is taken over the randomness of the probabilistic algorithms.

2.1 Unforgeability Security Definitions

The standard definition of security for signature schemes is *existential unforgeability under chosen message attack* (EUF-CMA). In the traditional formulation of unforgeability dating back to Goldwasser et al. [18], the adversary can obtain q_S signatures via signing oracle queries, and must output one valid signature on a message not queried to the oracle. This cannot be directly quantized: if the adversary is allowed to query oracles in superposition, we cannot restrain the adversary's forgery to be on a *new* message since the experiment cannot keep a copy of messages queried to the signing oracle for later checking.

An equivalent formulation in the classical setting demands the adversary output $q_S + 1$ valid signatures on distinct messages. Boneh and Zhandry [8] use this formulation to give a quantum analogue of EUF-CMA.[1] That notion involves a fully quantum adversary throughout so is quite strong. We envision a hierarchy of intermediate notions, distinguishing between whether the honest parties are signing classical or quantum messages (i.e., does the adversary have access to a classical or quantum signing oracle?) and whether the adversary is classical or quantum during the period it has access to the signing oracle (i.e., are we concerned about a quantum adversary only in the future, or also now?).

In our notation X^yZ, X denotes the type of adversary ($X = C$ for classical or Q for quantum) while the adversary is able to interact with the signing oracle; y denotes the type of access the adversary has to the signing oracle; and Z denotes the type of adversary after it no longer has access to its signing oracle. Combinatorially, there are $2^3 = 8$ possibilities, but some do not make sense, such as C^qZ or Q^yC. Figure 1 shows our unified definition for EUF-CMA parameterized for any of the four types of adversaries in the standard model, i.e., without access to a random (or hash) oracle. It follows the EUF-CMA formulation of Boneh and Zhandry [8] but separates out the adversary to be a two-stage adversary $(\mathcal{A}_1, \mathcal{A}_2)$, where $\mathcal{A}_1$ (of type X) interacts with either a signing oracle (of type y) and outputs an intermediate state st (of type X), which $\mathcal{A}_2$ (of type Z) then processes. The input to $\mathcal{A}_1$ and the output of $\mathcal{A}_2$ are always classical.

Figure 2 shows how the experiment is altered in the classical or quantum random oracle model: at the start of the experiment, a random function H is sampled uniformly from the space of all such functions $\mathcal{H}_\Sigma$. (In the classical setting, it is common to formulate the random oracle using lazy sampling, but such a formulation does not work in the quantum setting.) For simplicity, we assume the adversary has quantum random oracle access whenever it is quantum. We define advantage as $\mathrm{Adv}_\Sigma^{X^yZ\text{-eufcma}}(\mathcal{A}) = \Pr\left[\mathrm{Expt}_\Sigma^{X^yZ\text{-eufcma}}(\mathcal{A}) = 1\right]$.

2.2 Separations and Implications

Our family of notions C^cC-, C^cQ-, Q^cQ-, Q^qQ-eufcma form a natural hierarchy. These implication induce an ordering on security notions, so we sometimes write $C^cC \leq C^cQ$ etc. Note, the stronger the security notion the smaller the advantage of an adversary $\mathcal{A}$ breaking a signature scheme of corresponding security. For example, let the signature scheme Σ be C^cQ-secure. C^cQ is stronger than C^cC, i.e., $C^cQ \geq C^cC$. Hence, $\mathrm{Adv}_\Sigma^{C^cQ\text{-eufcma}}(\mathcal{A}) \leq \mathrm{Adv}_\Sigma^{C^cC\text{-eufcma}}(\mathcal{A})$. Similarly we use $\max\{\cdot, \cdot\}$ based on this ordering.

Due to space constraints, we defer details on the results to Appendix B. The implications are straightforward. Each of the separations $A \not\Rightarrow B$ follows from a common technique: from an A-secure scheme Σ, construct a (degenerate) A-secure scheme Σ' that is not B-secure, because the additional powers available

---

[1] A brief overview of notation for quantum computing appears in Appendix A.

$\text{Expt}_{\Sigma}^{\text{X}^{y}\text{Z-eufcma}}(\mathcal{A}_1, \mathcal{A}_2)$:	Classical signing oracle $\mathcal{O}_S(m)$:

1   $q_S \leftarrow 0$

2   $(sk, vk) \leftarrow_\$ \Sigma.\text{KeyGen}()$

3   $st \leftarrow_\$ \mathcal{A}_1^{\mathcal{O}_S(\cdot)}(vk)$

4   $((m_1^*, \sigma_1^*), \ldots, (m_{q_S+1}^*, \sigma_{q_S+1}^*)) \leftarrow_\$ \mathcal{A}_2(st)$

5   If $(\Sigma.\text{Verify}(vk, m_i^*, \sigma_i^*) = 1 \; \forall \, i \in [1, q_S + 1])$
      $\wedge \left(m_i^* \neq m_j^* \; \forall \, i \neq j\right)$:

6   Return 1

7   Else return 0

8   $q_S \leftarrow q_S + 1$

9   $\sigma \leftarrow_\$ \Sigma.\text{Sign}(sk, m)$

10   Return σ to $\mathcal{A}$

Quantum signing oracle $\mathcal{O}_S(\sum_{m,t,z} \psi_{m,t,z} |m, t, z\rangle)$:

11   $q_S \leftarrow q_S + 1$

12   $r \leftarrow_\$ \mathcal{R}_\Sigma$

13   Return state $\sum_{m,t,z} \psi_{m,t,z} |m, t \oplus \Sigma.\text{Sign}(sk, m; r), z\rangle$ to $\mathcal{A}$

Fig. 1. Unified security experiment for $\text{X}^y\text{Z-eufcma}$ in the standard model: existential unforgeability under chosen-message attack of a signature scheme Σ for a two-stage adversary $\mathcal{A}_1$ (of type X), $\mathcal{A}_2$ (of type Z) with signing oracle of type y; if y = c then $\mathcal{A}_1$ has classical access to the signing orcale, otherwise quantum access.

to a B-adversary allow it to recover the secret signing key of Σ that was cleverly embedded somewhere in Σ'.

- $\text{C}^c\text{C-eufcma} \not\Rightarrow \text{C}^c\text{Q-eufcma}$: In the public key for Σ', include a copy of the signing secret key encrypted using an RSA-based public key encryption scheme. Assuming breaking RSA is classically hard, the encrypted signing key is useless to a C^cC-adversary, but a C^cQ-adversary will be able to break the public key encryption, recover the signing key, and forge signatures.
- $\text{C}^c\text{Q-eufcma} \not\Rightarrow \text{Q}^c\text{Q-eufcma}$: In the public key for Σ', include an RSA-encrypted random challenge string, and redefine the $\Sigma'.\text{Sign}$ so that, if the adversary queries the signing oracle on the random challenge string, the signing key is returned. Assuming breaking RSA is hard for a classical algorithm, a C^cQ-adversary will not be able to recover the challenge while it has access to the signing oracle, and thus cannot make use of the degeneracy to recover the signing key; a Q^cQ adversary can.
- $\text{Q}^c\text{Q-eufcma} \not\Rightarrow \text{Q}^q\text{Q-eufcma}$: Here we hide the secret using a query-complexity problem that can be solved with just a few queries by a quantum algorithm making queries in superposition, but takes exponential queries when asking classical queries. The specific problem we use is a variant of the *hidden linear structure* problem [4].

3   Separability of Hybrid Signatures

In Sect. 4, we will investigate combiners for constructing one signature scheme from two. Before looking at specific combiners, an interesting security property arises in general for combined signature schemes: is it possible for a signature in

$\underline{\text{Expt}_{\Sigma}^{\text{X}^{\text{y}}\text{Z-eufcma}}(\mathcal{A}_1, \mathcal{A}_2):}$

0 $H \leftarrow_\$ \mathcal{H}_\Sigma$
1 $q_H \leftarrow 0,\, q_S \leftarrow 0$
2 $(sk, vk) \leftarrow_\$ \Sigma.\text{KeyGen}()$
3 $st \leftarrow_\$ \mathcal{A}_1^{\mathcal{O}_S(\cdot), \mathcal{O}_H(\cdot)}(vk)$
4 $((m_1^*, \sigma_1^*), \ldots, (m_{q_S+1}^*, \sigma_{q_S+1}^*))$
   $\leftarrow_\$ \mathcal{A}_2^{\mathcal{O}_H(\cdot)}(st)$
5 // continues as in Figure 1

$\underline{\text{Classical random oracle } \mathcal{O}_H(x):}$

14 $q_H \leftarrow q_H + 1$
15 Return $H(x)$

Quantum random oracle
$\underline{\mathcal{O}_H(\sum_{x,t,z} \psi_{x,t,z} |x, t, z\rangle):}$

16 $q_H \leftarrow q_H + 1$
17 Return state $\sum_{x,t,z} \psi_{x,t,z} |x, t \oplus H(x), z\rangle$

Fig. 2. $\text{X}^{\text{y}}\text{Z-eufcma}$ experiment in the classical and quantum random oracle models; if $\text{X} = \text{C}$, then $\mathcal{A}_1$ has classical access to the random oracle, otherwise quantum access; similarly for Z and $\mathcal{A}_2$.

$\underline{\text{Expt}_{C, \Sigma_1, \Sigma_2, C(\Sigma_1, \Sigma_2).R}^{\text{X}^{\text{y}}\text{Z-}\tau\text{-nonsep}}(\mathcal{A}_1, \mathcal{A}_2):}$

1 $q_S \leftarrow 0$
2 $(sk', vk') \leftarrow_\$ C(\Sigma_1, \Sigma_2).\text{KeyGen}()$
3 $st \leftarrow_\$ \mathcal{A}_1^{\mathcal{O}_S(\cdot)}(vk')$
4 $(m^*, \sigma^*) \leftarrow_\$ \mathcal{A}_2(st)$
5 If $(\Sigma_\tau.\text{Verify}((vk')_\tau, m^*, \sigma^*) = 1)$
   $\wedge\, (C(\Sigma_1, \Sigma_2).R(m^*) = 0)$
6   Return 1
7 Else return 0

$\underline{\mathcal{O}_S:}$

8 If $y = c$, use classical signing oracle
   $\mathcal{O}_S$ from Figure 1 for $C(\Sigma_1, \Sigma_2)$.
9 If $y = q$, use quantum signing oracle
   $\mathcal{O}_S$ from Figure 1 for $C(\Sigma_1, \Sigma_2)$.

Fig. 3. Unified security experiment for $\text{X}^{\text{y}}\text{Z-}\tau\text{-nonsep}$: τ-non-separability of a combiner C with signature schemes Σ_1, Σ_2 with respect to a recognizer $C(\Sigma_1, \Sigma_2).R$ for a two-stage adversary $\mathcal{A}_1$ (of type X), $\mathcal{A}_2$ (of type Z) with signing oracle of type y. $(vk')_\tau$ denotes the projection (extraction) of the public key associated with scheme Σ_τ from the combined scheme's public key vk', which we assume is possible.

a combined signature scheme to be separated out into valid signatures for either of its individual component schemes?

Let C be a combiner, and let Σ_1, Σ_2 be signature schemes. Let $\Sigma' = C(\Sigma_1, \Sigma_2)$. The initial idea for the security notion for non-separability is based on the standard EUF-CMA experiment: given a signing oracle that produces signatures for the combined scheme Σ', it should be hard for an adversary to produce a valid signature for Σ_1 ("1-non-separability") or Σ_2 ("2-non-separability").

However, this approach needs some refinement. In all of the combiners we consider in Sect. 4, the combined signature contains subcomponents which are valid in the underlying schemes. This makes it impossible to satisfy the naive version of non-separability. For example, suppose we have a signer issuing signatures from a combined signature scheme. Suppose further we have a verifier for one of the underlying signature schemes *who is also aware of the combined signature scheme*. Given signatures from the combined scheme, it should be hard to make a signature that is valid in one of the underlying signature schemes *and which is not recognized as being from the combined signature scheme.* In sum: separability is about downgrading.

Figure 3 shows the τ-non-separability security experiment, X^yZ-τ-nonsep, with $\tau \in \{1,2\}$ for signature scheme Σ_1 or Σ_2. It checks the ability of a two-stage X^yZ-adversary $(\mathcal{A}_1, \mathcal{A}_2)$ to create a valid Σ_τ signature; the adversary's pair has to "fool" the recognizer algorithm $\Sigma.R$ which is supposed to recognize values used in a combined signature scheme Σ.

Formally, a recognizer related to a combined signature scheme $\Sigma = C(\Sigma_1, \Sigma_2)$ is a function $\Sigma.R$ that takes one input and outputs a single bit. For a signature scheme Σ_τ with message space $\mathcal{M}_{\Sigma_\tau}$, it may be that $\Sigma.R$ yields 1 on some elements of $\mathcal{M}_{\Sigma_\tau}$ and 0 on others: the purpose of R is to recognize whether certain inputs are associated with a *second* signature scheme.

Because the X^yZ-τ-nonsep experiment is parameterized by the recognizer algorithm R, each R gives rise to a different security notion. If R is vacuous, it can lead to a useless security notion. We can make statements of the form "If $\langle$*some assumption on Σ_1 and Σ_2*$\rangle$ and R is the algorithm ..., then $C(\Sigma_1, \Sigma_2)$ is X^yZ-1-non-separable with respect to recognizer algorithm R." However, a statement of the form "C is not 1-non-separable" is more difficult: one must quantify over all (or some class of) recognizer algorithms R. We will say informally that "C is not τ-non-separable" if the way that Σ_τ is used in C is to effectively sign the message without any modification, since the only recognizer that would recognize all signatures from C would cover the entire message space of Σ_τ.

One can view a recognizer algorithm as a generalization of the long-standing technique of "domain separation". Starting from scratch, it might be preferable to build combiners that explicitly include domain separation in their construction, thereby eliminating the need for recognizer algorithms. Since our combiners are motivated by existing protocol constraints, we do not have that luxury.

4   Combiners

We now examine several methods of using two signature schemes Σ_1 and Σ_2 to produce hybrid signatures. For all our combiners, the key generation of the combined scheme will simply be the concatenation of the two schemes' keys: $sk' \leftarrow (sk_1, sk_2)$; $vk' \leftarrow (vk_1, vk_2)$. The verification algorithm in each case is defined in the natural way. Proofs/proof sketches appear in Appendix C.

4.1 $C_\|$: Concatenation

This "combiner" is the trivial combiner, which just places independent signatures from the two schemes side-by-side:

- $C_\|(\Sigma_1, \Sigma_2).\mathsf{Sign}(sk', m)$: $\sigma_1 \leftarrow_{\$} \Sigma_1.\mathsf{Sign}(sk_1, m)$, $\sigma_2 \leftarrow_{\$} \Sigma_2.\mathsf{Sign}(sk_2, m)$.
  Return $\sigma' \leftarrow \sigma_1 \| \sigma_2$.

Theorem 1 (Unforgeability of $C_\|$). *If either Σ_1 or Σ_2 is unforgeable in the classical (or quantum) random oracle model, then $\Sigma' = C_\|(\Sigma_1, \Sigma_2)$ is* *unforgeable in the classical (or quantum, respectively) random oracle model. More precisely, if Σ_1 is X^yZ-eufcma-secure or Σ_2 is U^vW-eufcma-secure, then $\Sigma' = C_\|(\Sigma_1, \Sigma_2)$ is $\max\{X^yZ, U^vW\}$-eufcma-secure.*

Clearly, $C_\|$ is neither 1-non-separable nor 2-non-separable: σ_1 is immediately a Σ_1-signature for m, with no way of recognizing this as being different from typical Σ_1 signatures. Similarly for σ_2.

4.2 $C_{\text{str-nest}}$: Strong Nesting

For this combiner, the second signature scheme signs both the message and the signature from the first signature scheme:

– $C_{\text{str-nest}}(\Sigma_1, \Sigma_2).\text{Sign}(sk', m)$: $\sigma_1 \leftarrow_\$ \Sigma_1.\text{Sign}(sk_1, m)$, $\sigma_2 \leftarrow_\$ \Sigma_2.\text{Sign}(sk_2, (m, \sigma_1))$. Return $\sigma' \leftarrow (\sigma_1, \sigma_2)$.

Theorem 2 (Unforgeability of $C_{\text{str-nest}}$). *If either Σ_1 or Σ_2 is unforgeable in the classical (or quantum) random oracle model, then $\Sigma' = C_{\text{str-nest}}(\Sigma_1, \Sigma_2)$ is unforgeable in the classical (or quantum, respectively) random oracle model. More precisely, if Σ_1 is X^yZ-eufcma-secure or Σ_2 is U^vW-eufcma-secure, then $\Sigma' = C_{\text{str-nest}}(\Sigma_1, \Sigma_2)$ is $\max\{X^yZ, U^vW\}$-eufcma-secure.*

$C_{\text{str-nest}}$ is not 1-non-separable: σ_1 is immediately a Σ_1-signature for m, with no way of recognizing this as being different from typical Σ_1 signatures. However, since the inputs to Σ_2 in $C_{\text{str-nest}}$ have a particular form, we can recognize those and achieve 2-non-separability:

Theorem 3 (2-non-separability of $C_{\text{str-nest}}$). *If Σ_2 is X^yZ-eufcma-secure, then $\Sigma' = C_{\text{str-nest}}(\Sigma_1, \Sigma_2)$ is X^cZ-2-nonsep with recognizer $R(m) = (m \in \{0,1\}^* \times \mathcal{S}_{\Sigma_1})$.*

4.3 D_{nest}: Dual Message Combiner Using Nesting

Some of our applications in Sect. 5 require a combiner for two (possibly related) messages signed with two signature schemes. For example, in our X.509 certificates application, we generate one certificate signed with Σ_1, then embed that certificates as an extension inside a second certificate signed with Σ_2.

– $D_{\text{nest}}(\Sigma_1, \Sigma_2).\text{Sign}(sk', (m_1, m_2))$: $\sigma_1 \leftarrow_\$ \Sigma_1.\text{Sign}(sk_1, m_1)$, $\sigma_2 \leftarrow_\$ \Sigma_2.$ $\text{Sign}(sk_2, (m_1, \sigma_1, m_2))$. Return $\sigma' \leftarrow (\sigma_1, \sigma_2)$.

This dual-message combiner is not designed to give unforgeability of *both* messages under *either* signature scheme, though it does preserve unforgeability of each message under its corresponding signature scheme, as well as give unforgeability of both messages under the outer signature scheme Σ_2.

Theorem 4 (Unforgeability of D_{nest}). *If either Σ_1 or Σ_2 is unforgeable in the classical (or quantum) random oracle model, then $D_{\text{nest}}(\Sigma_1, \Sigma_2)$ is unforgeable (in a certain sense) in the classical (or quantum, respectively) random oracle model. More precisely, if Σ_1 is X^yZ-eufcma-secure, then the combined scheme $D_{\text{nest}}(\Sigma_1, \Sigma_2)$ is X^yZ-eufcma-secure with respect to its first message component only. If Σ_2 is U^vW-eufcma-secure, then $D_{\text{nest}}(\Sigma_1, \Sigma_2)$ is U^vW-eufcma-secure.*

D_{nest} is not 1-non-separable: σ_1 is immediately a Σ_1-signature for m, with no way of recognizing this as being different from typical Σ_1 signatures. However, since the inputs to Σ_2 in D_{nest} have a particular form, we can recognize those and achieve 2-non-separability:

Theorem 5 (2-non-separability of D_{nest}). *If Σ_2 is X^yZ-eufcma-secure, then $\Sigma' = D_{\text{nest}}(\Sigma_1, \Sigma_2)$ is X^cZ-2-nonsep with respect to recognizer algorithm $R(m) = (m \in \{0,1\}^* \times \mathcal{S}_{\Sigma_1} \times \{0,1\}^*)$.*

5 Hybrid Signatures in Standards

We now examine three standards which make significant use of digital signatures—X.509 for certificates, TLS for secure channels, and S/MIME for secure email—to identify how hybrid signatures might be used in PKI standards, and evaluate backwards-compatibility of various approaches with existing software. Source code for generating the hybrid certificates and messages we used for testing, as well as scripts for running the tests, are available online at https://www.douglas.stebila.ca/code/pq-pki-tests/.

5.1 X.509v3 Certificates

The X.509 standard version 3 [14] specifies a widely used format for public key certificates, as well as mechanisms for managing and revoking certificates.

The structure of an X.509v3 certificate is as follows. The body of the certificate (called a `tbsCertificate`) contains the name of the certificate authority as well as information about the subject, including the distinguished name of the subject, the subject's public key (including an algorithm identifier), and optionally some extensions, each of which consists of an extension identifier, value, and a flag whether the extension is to be considered critical. (If a critical extension can not be recognized or processed, the system must reject it; a non-critical extension should be processed if it is recognized and may ignored if it is not.) The `tbsCertificate` is followed by CA's signature over the `tbsCertificate` signed using the CA's private key, along with an algorithm identifier.

Our goal will be to construct a hybrid certificate which somehow includes two public keys for the subject (e.g., one traditional and one post-quantum algorithm) and two CA signatures. Notably, the X.509v3 standard says that a certificate can contain exactly one `tbsCertificate`, which can contain exactly one subject public key, and all of this can be signed using exactly one CA signature. This makes creating backwards-compatible hybrid certificates challenging.

Table 2. Compatibility of hybrid X.509v3 certificates containing large extensions.

	Extension size (and corresponding example signature scheme)				
	1.5 KiB (RSA)	3.5 KiB (GLP [19])	9.0 KiB (BLISS [16])	43.0 KiB (SPHINCS [6])	1333.0 KiB (TESLA-416 [2])
GnuTLS 3.5.11	✓	✓	✓	✓	✓
Java SE 1.8.0_131	✓	✓	✓	✓	✓
mbedTLS 2.4.2	✓	✓	✓	✓	✓
NSS 3.29.1	✓	✓	✓	✓	✓
OpenSSL 1.0.2k	✓	✓	✓	✓	✓

Approach 1: Dual Certificates. The simplest approach is of course to create separate certificates: one for the traditional algorithm, and the other for the post-quantum algorithms. (This would be a dual-message analogue of the concatenation combiner $C_\parallel$ from Sect. 4.1.) This approach leaves the task of conveying the "hybrid" certificate (actually, two certificates) to the application, which will suffice in some settings (e.g., in S/MIME and some TLS settings, see the following sections), but is unsatisfactory in others. (This approach and the next both require assigning additional object identifiers (OIDs) for each post-quantum algorithms, but this can be easily done.)

Approach 2: Second Certificate in Extension. Since X.509v3 does not provide any direct way of putting two public keys or two signatures in the same certificate, one option is to use the standard's extension mechanism. Let c_1 be the certificate obtained by the CA signing `tbsCertificate` m_1 (containing subject public key vk_1) using signature scheme Σ_1. Construct certificate c_2 by the CA signing `tbsCertificate` m_2 (containing subject public key vk_2 as well as (an encoding of) c_1 as an extension in m_2) using signature scheme Σ_2. The extension containing c_1 would use a distinct extension identifier saying "this is an additional certificate" and would be marked as non-critical. This is an instantiation of the dual message nested combiner D_{nest} from Sect. 4.3. (Alternatively, the extension could contain a subset of fields, such as just the public key and CA's signature, rather than a whole certificate.)

By marking the "additional certificate" extension as non-critical, existing software (not aware of the hybrid structure) *should* ignore the unrecognized extension and continue validating the certificate and using it in applications without change. Is this really the case—is this approach backwards-compatible with old software, and do large public keys or signatures cause problems?

Experimental Evaluation of Approach 2. We constructed hybrid certificates following approach 2. The "outside" certificate c_2 contains a 2048-bit RSA public key, and is signed by a CA using 2048-bit RSA key. The extension for embedding c_1 in c_2 is identified by a distinct and previously unused algorithm identifier (OID), and is marked as non-critical. Because post-quantum public keys and signatures vary substantially in size, we use a range of extension sizes to simulate the expected size of an embedded certificate for various post-quantum signature algorithms; the extension sizes we use are across the columns of Table 2, derived from public key and signature sizes summarized in Table 5 in the Appendix. For our purposes of evaluating backwards compatibility, it does not matter whether the extension actually *contains* a valid post-quantum certificate, just that it is the *size* of such a certificate. The hybrid certificates were created using a custom-written Java program using the BouncyCastle library.

Table 2 shows the results of using command-line certificate verification programs in various libraries; all libraries we tested were able to parse and verify X.509v3 certificates containing unrecognized extensions of all sizes we tested.

5.2   TLS

TLSv1.2 [15] is the currently standardized version and is widely deployed. Ciphersuites with digital signatures allow servers and (optionally) clients to authenticate each other by presenting their public key and signing certain messages. While the parties can negotiate which signature algorithms to use, which public key formats to use, and which CAs to trust, once having done so they can each use only a single public key and signature algorithm to authenticate.

The current draft of TLSv1.3 [23] does not change how server authentication works. However, it has a "post-handshake authentication" mode for clients [23, Sect. 4.5.2], where clients can be requested to (further) authenticate using a certificate for a given algorithm. This would allow client authentication using two (or more) signature schemes. This is an example of the concatenation combiner $C_{\parallel}$ from Sect. 4.1, since each client signature is over the same handshake context data structure. A proposal for "exported authenticators" [24] is currently before the TLS working group and would allow a similar approach for server authentication, although it envisions that this takes place out-of-band (e.g., at the application layer). Neither would require hybrid certificates as in Sect. 5.1.

TLS data structures allow certificates of size up to 2^{24} bytes $= 16$ MiB, which would accommodate even very large post-quantum algorithms. However, TLS record layer fragments can be at most 16 KiB; TLS messages can be split across multiple fragments, but this increases the risk of incompatibility with poorly implemented software and can be problematic with datagram transport (UDP).

Experimental Evaluation of Hybrid Certificates in TLS. Table 3 shows the results of testing the compatibility of a variety of TLS libraries and web browsers when using the hybrid certificates from Approach 2 of Sect. 5.1.

In the top half of the table, we test whether popular TLS libraries can be used to establish a TLS 1.2 connection using an RSA certificate with an extension of the given size. In each case, the experiment is carried out between that library's own TLS server and TLS client command-line programs (in the case of Java, we wrote a simple HTTPS server and client using built-in libraries). Only Java completes connections with extensions the size of a TESLA-416 [2] certificate (1.3 MiB), and mbedTLS cannot handle certificates with extensions the size of

Table 3. Compatibility of TLS connections using hybrid X.509v3 certificates containing large extensions.

	Extension size in KiB				
	1.5	3.5	9.0	43.0	1333.0
Libraries (library's command-line client talking to library's command-line server)					
GnuTLS 3.5.11	✓	✓	✓	✓	✗
Java SE 1.8.0_131	✓	✓	✓	✓	✓
mbedTLS 2.4.2	✓	✓	✓	✗	✗
NSS 3.29.1	✓	✓	✓	✓	✗
OpenSSL 1.0.2k	✓	✓	✓	✓	✗
Web browsers (talking to OpenSSL's command-line server)					
Apple Safari 10.1 (12603.1.30.0.34)	✓	✓	✓	✓	✓
Google Chrome 58.0.3029.81	✓	✓	✓	✓	✗
Microsoft Edge 38.14393.1066.0	✓	✓	✓	✗	✗
Microsoft IE 11.1066.14393.0	✓	✓	✓	✗	✗
Mozilla Firefox 53.0	✓	✓	✓	✓	✗
Opera 44.0.2510.1218	✓	✓	✓	✓	✗

a SPHINCS [6] certificate (43 KiB). (For GnuTLS and OpenSSL, we found they could handle an 80 KiB extension but not a 90 KiB extension).

In the bottom half of the table, we test whether popular web browsers can be used to establish a TLS 1.2 connection to a TLS server run using the OpenSSL command-line s_server program using an RSA certificate with an extension of the given size. Microsoft browsers on Windows 10 cannot handle SPHINCS-sized extensions, and no browser except Safari could handle TESLA-416-sized extensions (1.3 MiB). (Curiously, Safari was able to handle a 1.3 MiB extension with an OpenSSL command-line server despite OpenSSL's own command-line client not being able to handle it.)

5.3   CMS and S/MIME

Cryptographic Message Syntax (CMS) [20] is the main cryptographic component of S/MIME [22], which enables public key encryption and digital signatures for email. In an S/MIME signed email, a header is used to specify the algorithms used, and then the body of the email is divided into chunks: one chunk is the body to be signed, and the other is a Base-64 encoding of a CMS SignedData object. The SignedData object contains several fields, including a set of certificates and a set of SignerInfo objects. Each SignerInfo object contains a signer identifier, algorithm identifier, signature, and optional signed and unsigned attributes.

Approach 1: Parallel SignerInfos. To construct a standards-compliant hybrid signature in S/MIME, one could put the certificate for each algorithm in

Table 4. Compatibility of hybrid S/MIME approaches.

	Approach								
	0	1	2.a	2.b (attribute size in KiB)					2.c
				1.5	3.5	9.0	43.0	1333.0	
Apple Mail 10.2 (3259)	✓	✓	✓	✓	✓	✓	✓	✓	✓
BouncyCastle 1.56 with Java SE 1.8.0_131	✓	–	✓	✓	✓	✓	✓	✓	✓
Microsoft Outlook 2016 16.0.7870.2031	✓	×	✓	✓	✓	✓	✓	✓	✓
Mozilla Thunderbird 45.7.1	✓	×	✓	✓	✓	✓	✓	×	✓
OpenSSL 1.0.2k	✓	×	✓	✓	✓	✓	✓	✓	✓

Approach 0: both RSA-2048.
Approach 1: one RSA-2048, one with unknown algorithm of similar key and signature size; unable to test Approach 1 on BouncyCastle.
Approach 2.a, 2.c: both RSA-2048.
Approach 2.b: outer RSA-2048, inner random binary extension of given size.

the SignedData object's set of certificates (with no need for hybrid certificates from Sect. 5.1), and then include SignerInfo objects for the signature from each algorithm. This is an example of the concatenation combiner $C_\|$ from Sect. 4.1.

Approach 2: Nested Signature in SignerInfo Attributes. For an alternative and still standards-compliant approach, we could use the optional attributes in the SignerInfo object to embed a second signature. We need to convey the certificate for the second algorithm, as well as the signature (using the second algorithm) for the message. There are several options based on the standards:

(2.a) Put a second certificate in the set of certificates, and put a second SignerInfo in an attribute of the first SignerInfo.
(2.b) Put a hybrid certificate in the set of certificates, and put a second SignerInfo in an attribute of the first SignerInfo.
(2.c) Put a second SignedData in an attribute of the first SignerInfo.

These approaches require defining a new attribute type, but this is easily done. The CMS standard indicates that verifiers can accept signatures with unrecognized attributes, so this approach results in backwards-compatible signatures that should be accepted by existing software.)

If the extra data is put in the *signed* attribute of the first SignerInfo, then we are using the strong nesting combiner $C_{\text{str-nest}}$ from Sect. 4.2; if the extra data is put in the *unsigned* attribute of the first SignerInfo, then we are using the concatenation combiner $C_\|$ from Sect. 4.1.

Experimental Evaluation of CMS and S/MIME Approaches. We tested five S/MIME libraries/applications for acceptance of S/MIME messages from each approach above. The configurations and results appear in Table 4.

Regarding approach 1, the S/MIME and CMS standards appear to be silent on how to validate multiple SignerInfo objects: should a signed message be considered valid if *any* of the `SignerInfo` objects is valid, or only if *all* of them are? Apple Mail accepted in this case, whereas the three others we were able to test rejected, so approach 1 is not fully backwards-compatible. In principle all the tested libraries support approaches 2.a–2.c. We only tested multiple attribute sizes in one of these three approaches (2.b), but the results should generalize to 2.a and 2.c. Only Thunderbird struggled with very large attributes.

5.4 Discussion

Summarizing our experimental observations, backwards compatibility is most easily maintained when post-quantum objects can be placed as non-critical extensions (attributes in the S/MIME case) of pre-quantum objects. These constructions end up leading to one of our nested combiners, either D_{nest} for X.509 certificate extensions or $C_{str-nest}$ for S/MIME and CMS. Both these combiners offer unforgeability under the assumption that either scheme is unforgeable. For non-separability, the pre-quantum algorithm would be the "outside" signature Σ_2 in both D_{nest} and $C_{str-nest}$, and so we get 2-non-separability under unforgeability of the pre-quantum scheme, not the post-quantum scheme. Extensions up to 43.0 KiB were mostly (but not entirely) handled successfully, which covers many but not all post-quantum schemes; the largest schemes such as TESLA-416 would be more problematic to use in hybrid modes with existing software.

Acknowledgements. NB acknowledges support by the German Research Foundation (DFG) as part of project P1 within the CRC 1119 CROSSING. DS acknowledges support from Natural Sciences and Engineering Research Council of Canada (NSERC) Discovery grant RGPIN-2016-05146.

References

1. Akleylek, S., Bindel, N., Buchmann, J., Krämer, J., Marson, G.A.: An efficient lattice-based signature scheme with provably secure instantiation. In: Pointcheval, D., Nitaj, A., Rachidi, T. (eds.) AFRICACRYPT 2016. LNCS, vol. 9646, pp. 44–60. Springer, Cham (2016). doi:10.1007/978-3-319-31517-1_3
2. Alkim, E., Bindel, N., Buchmann, J., Dagdelen, Ö.: TESLA: tightly-secure efficient signatures from standard lattices. Cryptology ePrint Archive, Report 2015/755 (2015)
3. Barreto, P., Longa, P., Naehrig, M., Ricardini, J.E., Zanon, G.: Sharper ring-LWE signatures. Cryptology ePrint Archive, Report 2016/1026 (2016)
4. de Beaudrap, N., Cleve, R., Watrous, J.: Sharp quantum versus classical query complexity separations. Algorithmica **34**(4), 449–461 (2002)
5. Bellare, M., Rogaway, P.: Optimal asymmetric encryption. In: Santis, A. (ed.) EUROCRYPT 1994. LNCS, vol. 950, pp. 92–111. Springer, Heidelberg (1995). doi:10.1007/BFb0053428
6. Bernstein, D.J., et al.: SPHINCS: Practical Stateless Hash-Based Signatures. In: Oswald, E., Fischlin, M. (eds.) EUROCRYPT 2015. LNCS, vol. 9056, pp. 368–397. Springer, Heidelberg (2015). doi:10.1007/978-3-662-46800-5_15

7. Bindel, N., Herath, U., McKague, M., Stebila, D.: Transitioning to a quantum-resistant public key infrastructure (full version). Cryptology ePrint Archive, April 2017

8. Boneh, D., Zhandry, M.: Secure signatures and chosen ciphertext security in a quantum computing world. In: Canetti, R., Garay, J.A. (eds.) CRYPTO 2013. LNCS, vol. 8043, pp. 361–379. Springer, Heidelberg (2013). doi:10.1007/978-3-642-40084-1_21

9. Bos, J.W., Costello, C., Naehrig, M., Stebila, D.: Post-quantum key exchange for the TLS protocol from the ring learning with errors problem. In: 2015 IEEE Symposium on Security and Privacy, pp. 553–570. IEEE Computer Society Press, May 2015

10. Braithwaite, M.: Google Security Blog: Experimenting with post-quantum cryptography, July 2016. https://security.googleblog.com/2016/07/experimenting-with-post-quantum.html

11. Buchmann, J., Dahmen, E., Hülsing, A.: XMSS - a practical forward secure signature scheme based on minimal security assumptions. In: Yang, B.-Y. (ed.) PQCrypto 2011. LNCS, vol. 7071, pp. 117–129. Springer, Heidelberg (2011). doi:10.1007/978-3-642-25405-5_8

12. Campagna, M., et al.: Quantum safe cryptography and security: an introduction, benefits, enablers and challengers. Technical report, ETSI (European Telecommunications Standards Institute) June 2015. http://www.etsi.org/images/files/ETSIWhitePapers/QuantumSafeWhitepaper.pdf

13. Chen, A.I.-T., Chen, M.-S., Chen, T.-R., Cheng, C.-M., Ding, J., Kuo, E.L.-H., Lee, F.Y.-S., Yang, B.-Y.: SSE implementation of multivariate PKCs on modern x86 CPUs. In: Clavier, C., Gaj, K. (eds.) CHES 2009. LNCS, vol. 5747, pp. 33–48. Springer, Heidelberg (2009). doi:10.1007/978-3-642-04138-9_3

14. Cooper, D., Santesson, S., Farrell, S., Boeyen, S., Housley, R., Polk, W.: Internet X.509 Public Key Infrastructure Certificate and Certificate Revocation List (CRL) Profile. RFC 5280, May 2008

15. Dierks, T., Rescorla, E.: The Transport Layer Security (TLS) Protocol Version 1.2. RFC 5246, August 2008

16. Ducas, L., Durmus, A., Lepoint, T., Lyubashevsky, V.: Lattice signatures and bimodal Gaussians. In: Canetti, R., Garay, J.A. (eds.) CRYPTO 2013. LNCS, vol. 8042, pp. 40–56. Springer, Heidelberg (2013). doi:10.1007/978-3-642-40041-4_3

17. Fischlin, R., Schnorr, C.P.: Stronger security proofs for RSA and Rabin bits. J. Cryptol. 13(2), 221–244 (2000)

18. Goldwasser, S., Micali, S., Rivest, R.L.: A digital signature scheme secure against adaptive chosen-message attacks. SIAM J. Comput. 17(2), 281–308 (1988)

19. Güneysu, T., Lyubashevsky, V., Pöppelmann, T.: Practical lattice-based cryptography: a signature scheme for embedded systems. In: Prouff, E., Schaumont, P. (eds.) CHES 2012. LNCS, vol. 7428, pp. 530–547. Springer, Heidelberg (2012). doi:10.1007/978-3-642-33027-8_31

20. Housley, R.: Cryptographic Message Syntax (CMS). RFC 5652, September 2009

21. Nielsen, M.A., Chuang, I.L.: Quantum Computation and Quantum Information. Cambridge University Press, Cambridge (2000)

22. Ramsdell, B., Turner, S.: Secure/Multipurpose Internet Mail Extensions (S/MIME) Version 3.2 Message Specification. RFC 5751, January 2010

23. Rescorla, E.: The Transport Layer Security (TLS) protocol version 1.3, draft 19, March 2017. https://tools.ietf.org/html/draft-ietf-tls-tls13-19

24. Sullivan, N.: Exported authenticators in TLS, draft 01, March 2017. https://tools.ietf.org/html/draft-sullivan-tls-exported-authenticator-01

A   A Brief Review of Quantum Computation

A full explanation of quantum computation is beyond the scope of this paper; see a standard text such as Nielsen and Chuang [21]. We can rely on a subset of quantum computation knowledge.

A quantum system is a complex Hilbert space $\mathcal{H}$ with an inner product. Vectors in $\mathcal{H}$ are typically denoted using "ket" notation, such as $|x\rangle$, and the complex conjugate transpose of $|y\rangle$ is denoted by $\langle y|$, so that their inner product of $|x\rangle$ and $|y\rangle$ is given by $\langle y|x\rangle$. A quantum state is a vector in $\mathcal{H}$ of norm 1. For two quantum systems $\mathcal{H}_1$ and $\mathcal{H}_2$, the joint quantum system is given by the tensor product $\mathcal{H}_1 \otimes \mathcal{H}_2$; for two states $|x_1\rangle \in \mathcal{H}_1$ and $|x_2\rangle \in \mathcal{H}_2$, the joint state is denoted by $|x_1\rangle |x_2\rangle$, or more compactly as $|x_1, x_2\rangle$.

Some quantum states can be represented as superpositions of other quantum states, such as $|x\rangle = \frac{1}{\sqrt{2}} |0\rangle + \frac{1}{\sqrt{2}} |1\rangle$. More generally, if $\{|x\rangle\}_x$ is a basis for $\mathcal{H}$, then we can write any superposition in the form $|y\rangle = \sum_x \psi_x |x\rangle$ where ψ_x are complex numbers such that $|y\rangle$ has norm 1.

Quantum operations on $\mathcal{H}$ can be represented by unitary transformations $\mathbf{U}$. A side effect of the fact that quantum operations are unitary transformations is that quantum computation (prior to measurement) is reversible, imposing some constraints on how we quantize classical computations. In particular, suppose we want to quantize a classical algorithm A which takes an input $x \in \{0,1\}^a$ and gives an output $y \in \{0,1\}^b$. First, we would imagine the classical reversible mapping $\{0,1\}^a \times \{0,1\}^b \rightarrow \{0,1\}^a \times \{0,1\}^b : (x,t) \mapsto (x, t \oplus A(x))$. Then we construct the corresponding unitary transformation $\mathbf{A}$ which acts linearly on superpositions of such states: $\mathbf{A} : \sum_{x,t} \psi_{x,t} |x,t\rangle \mapsto \sum_{x,t} \psi_{x,t} |x, t \oplus A(x)\rangle$. For full generality, we may allow a workspace register alongside the input and output registers, and thus we in fact use $\mathbf{A} : \sum_{x,t,z} \psi_{x,t,z} |x,t,z\rangle \mapsto \sum_{x,t,z} \psi_{x,t,z} |x, t \oplus A(x), z\rangle$.

B   Unforgeability Separations and Implications

Theorem 6 ($Q^qQ \implies Q^cQ \implies C^cQ \implies C^cC$). *If Σ is a Q^qQ-eufcma-secure signature scheme, then Σ is also Q^cQ-eufcma-secure. If Σ is a Q^cQ-eufcma-secure signature scheme, then Σ is also C^cQ-eufcma-secure. If Σ is a C^cQ-eufcma-secure signature scheme, then Σ is also C^cC-eufcma-secure.*

Theorem 7 ($C^cC \nRightarrow C^cQ$). *If the RSA problem is hard for classical computers and there exists a signature scheme Σ that is C^cC-eufcma-secure, then there exists a signature scheme Σ' that is C^cC-eufcma-secure but not C^cQ-eufcma-secure.*

Proof. Let Π be a public key encryption scheme that is IND-CPA-secure against classical adversaries and whose security relies on the hardness of the RSA problem, e.g., [17] or OAEP [5]. However, a quantum adversary could use Shor's algorithm to factor the modulus and decrypt ciphertexts encrypted using Π. We construct a scheme Σ' that is based on Σ, but the public key of Σ' includes a Π-encrypted copy of the Σ secret key:

- Σ'.KeyGen(): $(sk, vk) \leftarrow_s \Sigma$.KeyGen(). $(dk, ek) \leftarrow_s \Pi$.KeyGen(). $c \leftarrow_s \Pi$.
  Enc(ek, sk). $vk' \leftarrow (vk, ek, c)$. Return (sk, vk').
- Σ'.Sign(sk, m): Return Σ.Sign(sk, m).
- Σ'.Verify($vk' = (vk, ek, c), m, \sigma$): Return Σ.Verify(vk, m, σ).

The theorem then follows as a consequence of the following two claims, the proofs of which are immediate.   □

Claim 1.
If Π is IND-CPA-secure against a classical adversary and Σ is C^{c}C-eufcma-secure, then Σ' is C^{c}C-eufcma-secure.

Claim 2. If there exists an efficient quantum adversary $\mathcal{A}$ against the message recovery of Π, then Σ' is not C^{c}Q-eufcma-secure.

Theorem 8 (C^{c}C $\not\Rightarrow$ C^{c}Q). *If the RSA problem is hard for classical computers and there exists a signature scheme Σ that is C^{c}Q-eufcma-secure, then there exists a signature scheme Σ' that is C^{c}Q-eufcma-secure but not Q^{c}Q-eufcma-secure.*

Since the basic idea for the proof of Theorem 8 is similar to that of Theorem 7, and due to space constraints, we leave details to the full version [7]. Briefly, the idea of the construction of the scheme for the separation is as follows. Here, we put an encrypted *random challenge* in the public verification key, and if the adversary asks for that challenge to be signed, we have the signing oracle return the signing key. Intuitively, only an adversary that can break the challenge while it has access to the signing oracle (i.e., a quantum stage-1 adversary) can solve the challenge. The scheme Σ' is shown below.

- Σ'.KeyGen(): $(sk, vk) \leftarrow_s \Sigma$.KeyGen(). $(dk, ek) \leftarrow_s \Pi$.KeyGen(). $s^* \leftarrow_s \{0, 1\}^{256}$.
  $ch \leftarrow \Pi$.Enc(ek, s^*). $vk' \leftarrow (vk, ek, ch)$. $sk' \leftarrow (sk, s^*)$. Return (sk', vk').
- Σ'.Sign($sk' = (sk, s^*), m$): If $m = s^*$, return sk. Else, return Σ.Sign(sk, m).
- Σ'.Verify($vk' = (vk, ek, ch), m, \sigma$): Return Σ.Verify(vk, m, σ).

Theorem 9 (Q^{c}Q $\not\Rightarrow$ Q^{q}Q). *Assuming there exists a quantum-secure pseudorandom family of permutations, and a signature scheme Σ that is Q^{c}Q-eufcma-secure, then there exists a signature scheme Σ' that is Q^{c}Q-eufcma-secure but not Q^{q}Q-eufcma-secure.*

Similar to Theorem 8, we will construct a signature scheme where the secret key is hidden behind a problem which is hard for some adversaries and easy for others. Here the hidden problem will be on oracle problem where a small number of queries suffices to retrieve a secret string when the oracle is queried in superposition, but a large number of queries is required if the oracle is queried classically. We will use the *hidden linear structure* problem [4].

Definition 2 [4]. *The hidden linear structure problem is as follows: given oracle access to $\mathcal{B}_{s,\pi}(x, y) = (x, \pi(y \oplus sx))$, where $x, y, s \in GF(2^n)$ and $\pi \in Perm(\{0, 1\}^n)$ with s and π chosen uniformly at random, determine s. (Here, $Perm(S)$ denotes the set of all permutations on a set S.)*

The hidden linear structure problem requires 2^b classical queries to solve with probability 2^{2b-n+1} (i.e. $O(2^{n/2})$ queries to solve with a constant probability), and one query to solve with quantum queries [4]. Unfortunately, describing π requires an exponential number of bits in n, but we can replace the random permutation π with a family of quantum-safe pseudo random permutation with a short key. This results in an oracle with a short description. Supposing that the PRP is indistinguishable from a random permutation in time $c_\mathcal{P}$ except with advantage $p_\mathcal{P}$, the resulting restricted oracle problem is indistinguishable from the hidden linear structure problem except with advantage $p_\mathcal{P}$. From now on we assume that π is implemented by a PRP.

Our construction starts with a Q^cQ-eufcma-secure signature scheme Σ. For our purposes, we will need $\Sigma.\mathsf{Sign}$ to be deterministic. That is, for a particular message and signing key the signature should always be the same. If this is not the case, then we can use standard techniques to make it so, for example by providing randomness through a quantum-secure PRF applied to the signing key and the message. Let us suppose that it takes at least time c_Σ for an adversary to win the Q^cQ-eufcma security game with probability at least p_Σ.

We will need to address several parts of messages for signing. For a message m we will define $m.x, m.y, m.z$ to be bits 1 to 256, bits 257 to 512, and bits 513 to 768 of m, respectively. In particular, m must be at least 768 bits long. Bits beyond 768 will play no special role in the signing algorithm, but remain part of the message. Also let $\delta_{a,b}$ be the Kronecker delta, which is 1 when $a = b$ and 0 otherwise.

We now define our signature scheme Σ' as follows:

- $\Sigma'.\mathsf{KeyGen}()$: $(sk, vk) \leftarrow_\$ \Sigma.\mathsf{KeyGen}()$. $s \leftarrow_\$ \{0,1\}^{256}$. $t \leftarrow_\$ \{0,1\}^{256}$. $vk' \leftarrow (vk)$. $sk' \leftarrow (sk, s, t)$. Return (sk', vk').
- $\Sigma'.\mathsf{Sign}(sk', m)$: Return $(\Sigma.\mathsf{Sign}(sk, m), \mathcal{B}_{s,t}(m.x, m.y), sk \cdot \delta_{s,m.z})$.
- $\Sigma'.\mathsf{Verify}(vk', m, (\sigma, u, v, w))$: If $\Sigma.\mathsf{Verify}(vk, m, \sigma)$ accepts, $(u, v) = \mathcal{B}_{s,t}(m.x, m.y)$ and $w = sk \cdot \delta_{m.z,s}$ then accept, otherwise reject.

Since we are interested in the case of quantum access, we define the quantum version of the signing oracle by $U_{\Sigma',sk}$, which has the action

$$U_{\Sigma',sk} |m, a, b, c, d\rangle = |m, a \oplus \sigma, b \oplus u, c \oplus v, d \oplus w\rangle$$

where $\sigma = \Sigma.\mathsf{Sign}(sk, m)$, $(u, v) = \mathcal{B}_{s,t}(m.x, m.y)$, and $w = sk \cdot \delta_{s,m.z}$. Note that $U_{\Sigma',sk}$ is its own inverse.

Lemma 1. *Suppose that, with classical queries, at least $c_\mathcal{B}$ queries to $\mathcal{B}_{s,t}$ are required to determine s with probability $p_\mathcal{B}$, and that it takes at least time c_Σ for an adversary to win the Q^cQ-eufcma security game for Σ with probability at least p_Σ. If a (possibly quantum) adversary $\mathcal{A}$ with classical access to a $\Sigma'.\mathsf{Sign}$ oracle and vk runs for time $c < \min\{c_\mathcal{B}, c_\Sigma\}$, then $\mathcal{A}$ wins the Q^cQ-eufcma security game for Σ' with probability at most $p \leq p_\mathcal{B} + p_\Sigma + 2^{-256}c$.*

The lemma can be proven by noting $\mathcal{B}_{s,t}$ and Σ are not related, so we can basically add the probabilities of determining s through $\mathcal{B}_{s,t}$, producing valid signatures without s, and guessing s directly.

Lemma 2. *Suppose Σ.Sign is deterministic. If, given quantum query access to $\mathcal{B}_{s,t}$ it is possible to recover s with 1 query, then 3 quantum queries to $U_{\Sigma',sk}$ suffice to efficiently generate any polynomial number of valid signatures for Σ'.*

The basic mechanism here is to use a standard technique in quantum computing called uncomputing to construct a quantum oracle for $\mathcal{B}_{s,t}(x,y)$ out of two calls to $U_{\Sigma',sk}$. Then it is possible to determine s and recover sk with one more call to $U_{\Sigma',sk}$.

We are now in a position to prove Theorem 9.

Proof (Proof of Theorem 9). We use Σ' as defined earlier, with $\mathcal{B}_{s,t}$ being the oracle for a quantum safe hidden linear structure problem, which exists by the existence of $\mathcal{P}$. By Lemma 2, Σ' is not Q^qQ-eufcma-secure since a quantum adversary allowed quantum oracle access to Σ'.Sign can efficiently generate a polynomial number of signatures using a constant number of oracle queries.

Now suppose we have a quantum adversary $\mathcal{A}$ which has classical oracle access to Σ'.Sign and runs in time $2^b < \max\{2^{n/2-2}, c_\Sigma\}$. $\mathcal{A}$ obtains s through classical oracle access to $\mathcal{B}$ with probability at most $2^{2b-n+1} + p_\mathcal{P}$. Then we can set $p_\mathcal{B} = 2^{2b-n+1} + p_\mathcal{P}$ and apply Lemma 1 to find that $\mathcal{A}$ breaks unforgeability of Σ' with probability at most $p_\Sigma + 2^{2b-n+1} + \delta + 2^{b-256}$. If $\mathcal{A}$ runs in polynomial time, then $b \in O(\log(\text{poly}(n)))$ and hence Σ' is Q^cQ-eufcma-secure. $\square$

C   Proofs for Combiners

C.1 $C_\parallel$: Concatenation

Proof (Proof of Theorem 1 – unforgeability of $C_\parallel$). Suppose $\mathcal{A}$ is an R^sT-adversary that finds a forgery in $\Sigma' = C_\parallel(\Sigma_1, \Sigma_2)$ — in other words, it outputs $q_S + 1$ valid signatures under Σ' on distinct messages. We can construct an R^sT algorithm $\mathcal{B}_1$ that finds a forgery in Σ_1. $\mathcal{B}_1$ interacts with an R^sT challenger for Σ_1 which provides a public key vk_1. $\mathcal{B}_1$ generates a key pair $(sk_2, vk_2) \leftarrow_\$ \Sigma_2.\text{KeyGen}()$ and sets the public key for Σ' to be (vk_1, vk_2). When $\mathcal{A}$ asks for $\sum_{m,t,z} \psi_{m,t,z} |m,t,z\rangle)$ to be signed using Σ', we treat t as consisting of two registers $t_1 \| t_2$, $\mathcal{B}_1$ proceeds by passing the m, t_1, and z registers to its signing oracle for Σ_1, then runs the quantum signing operation from Fig. 1 for Σ_2.Sign on the m, t_2, and z registers. There is a one-to-one correspondence between $\mathcal{A}$'s queries to its signing oracle and $\mathcal{B}_1$'s queries to its signing oracle.

If Σ_1 is proven to be secure in the random oracle (rather than standard) model, then this proof of $C_\parallel(\Sigma_1, \Sigma_2)$ also proceeds in the random oracle model: $\mathcal{B}_1$ relays $\mathcal{A}$'s hash oracle queries directly to its oracle, giving a one-to-one correspondence between $\mathcal{A}$'s queries to its hash oracle and $\mathcal{B}_1$'s queries to its hash oracle. This holds in either the classical or quantum random oracle model.

If $\mathcal{A}$ wins the R^sT-eufcma game, then it has returned $q_S + 1$ valid signatures $\sigma'_i = (\sigma'_{i,1}, \sigma'_{i,2})$ on distinct messages m_i such that $\Sigma_1.\text{Verify}(vk_1, m_i, \sigma'_{i,1}) = 1$ and $\Sigma_2.\text{Verify}(vk_2, m_i, \sigma'_{i,2}) = 1$. $\mathcal{B}_1$ can extract from this $q_S + 1$ valid signatures under Σ_1 on distinct messages. Thus, $\mathrm{Adv}_{\Sigma'}^{\mathsf{R^sT\text{-}eufcma}}(\mathcal{A}) \leq \mathrm{Adv}_{\Sigma_1}^{\mathsf{R^sT\text{-}eufcma}}(\mathcal{B}_1)$. Similarly it holds for Σ_2: $\mathrm{Adv}_{\Sigma'}^{\mathsf{R^sT\text{-}eufcma}}(\mathcal{A}) \leq \mathrm{Adv}_{\Sigma_2}^{\mathsf{R^sT\text{-}eufcma}}(\mathcal{B}_2)$.

It follows that $\mathrm{Adv}_{\Sigma'}^{\mathsf{R^sT\text{-}eufcma}}(\mathcal{A}) \leq \min\{\mathrm{Adv}_{\Sigma_1}^{\mathsf{R^sT\text{-}eufcma}}(\mathcal{B}_1), \mathrm{Adv}_{\Sigma_2}^{\mathsf{R^sT\text{-}eufcma}}(\mathcal{B}_2)\}$. Thus, if either $\mathrm{Adv}_{\Sigma_1}^{\mathsf{R^sT\text{-}eufcma}}(\mathcal{B}_1)$ or $\mathrm{Adv}_{\Sigma_2}^{\mathsf{R^sT\text{-}eufcma}}(\mathcal{B}_2)$ is small, then so too is $\mathrm{Adv}_{\Sigma'}^{\mathsf{R^sT\text{-}eufcma}}(\mathcal{A})$.

C.2 $C_{\text{str-nest}}$: Strong Nesting

Proof (Proof of Theorem 2 – unforgeability of $C_{\text{str-nest}}$). This proof follows the same approach as the proof of unforgeability for $C_{\|}$ (Theorem 1). Details appear in the full version [7]. □

Proof (Proof sketch of Theorem 3 – 2-non-separability of $C_{\text{str-nest}}$). We can construct a reduction $\mathcal{B}_2$ which is an $\mathsf{X^cZ\text{-}eufcma}$ adversary for Σ_2. $\mathcal{B}_2$ generates a keypair (vk_1, sk_1) for Σ_1, and interacts with an $\mathsf{X^cZ\text{-}eufcma}$ challenge for Σ_2. When $\mathcal{A}$ classically queries its signing oracle to obtain a signature under Σ' of m_i, $\mathcal{B}_2$ signs m_i with Σ_1 to obtain $\sigma_{i,1}$. Afterwards, $\mathcal{B}_2$ passes $(m, \sigma_{i,1})$ to its Σ_2 signing oracle and returns the resulting $\sigma_{i,2}$ to $\mathcal{A}$. Eventually, $\mathcal{A}$ returns (μ^*, σ^*) such that $\Sigma_2.\mathsf{Verify}(vk_2, \mu^*, \sigma^*) = 1$ but $\Sigma'.R(\mu^*) = 0$, i.e., $\mu^* \notin \{0, 1\}^* \times \mathcal{S}_{\Sigma_1}$. This means in particular that $\mu^* \neq (m_i, \sigma_{1,i})$ for all i. Moreover, all the $(m_i, \sigma_{1,i})$ are distinct, since all m_i are distinct. This means we have $q_S + 1$ valid message-signature pairs under Σ_2, yielding a successful forgery for the $\mathsf{X^cZ\text{-}eufcma}$ experiment for Σ_2. Thus, $\Pr[S_1] \leq \mathrm{Adv}_{\Sigma_2}^{\mathsf{X^cZ\text{-}eufcma}}(\mathcal{B}_2)$. □

C.3 D_{nest}: Dual Message Combiner Using Nesting

Proof (Proof sketch of Theorem 4 – unforgeability of D_{nest}). This theorem contains two statements. The first statement is: If Σ_1 is $\mathsf{X^yZ\text{-}eufcma}$-secure, then $D_{\text{nest}}(\Sigma_1, \Sigma_2)$ is $\mathsf{X^yZ\text{-}eufcma}$-secure with respect to its first message component only. $D_{\text{nest}}(\Sigma_1, \Sigma_2)$, when restricted to its first message component only, is just Σ_1, so the first statement follows vacuously.

Now consider the second statement: $D_{\text{nest}}(\Sigma_1, \Sigma_2)$ is $\mathsf{U^vW\text{-}eufcma}$-secure if Σ_2 is $\mathsf{U^vW\text{-}eufcma}$-secure. Suppose $\mathcal{A}$ is a $\mathsf{U^vW}$ algorithm that outputs a forgery for $\Sigma' = D_{\text{nest}}(\Sigma_1, \Sigma_2)$ — in other words, it outputs $q_S + 1$ valid signatures under Σ' on distinct messages. We can construct an $\mathsf{U^vW}$ algorithm $\mathcal{B}_2$ that finds a forgery in Σ_2. $\mathcal{B}_2$ interacts with an $\mathsf{U^vW}$ challenger for Σ_2 which provides a public key vk_2. $\mathcal{B}_2$ generates a key pair $(sk_1, vk_1) \leftarrow_s \Sigma_1.\mathsf{KeyGen}()$ and sets the public key for Σ' to be (vk_1, vk_2). When $\mathcal{A}$ asks for $\sum_{m,t,z} \psi_{m,t,z} |m, t, z\rangle)$ to be signed using Σ', we treat t as consisting of two registers $t_1 \| t_2$, $\mathcal{B}_2$ proceeds by passing the m, t_2, and z registers to its signing oracle for Σ_2, then runs the quantum signing operation from Fig. 1 for $\Sigma_1.\mathsf{Sign}$ on the m, t_1, and z registers. There is a one-to-one correspondence between $\mathcal{A}$'s queries to its oracle and $\mathcal{B}_2$'s queries to its oracle. As before in the proof of Theorem 1, if Σ_1 is proven to be secure in the random oracle model, then this proof of $C_{\text{weak-nest}}(\Sigma_1, \Sigma_2)$ also proceeds in the random oracle model: $\mathcal{B}_2$ relays $\mathcal{A}$'s hash oracle queries directly to its hash oracle, giving a one-to-one correspondence between $\mathcal{A}$'s queries to its (classical or quantum) hash oracle and $\mathcal{B}_2$'s queries to its (classical or quantum, respectively) hash oracle.

If $\mathcal{A}$ wins the U$^\vee$W-eufcma game, then it has returned $q_S + 1$ distinct tuples $(m_{1,i}, m_{2,i}, \sigma_{1,i}, \sigma_{2,i})$ such that $\Sigma_1.\mathsf{Verify}(vk_1, m_{1,i}, \sigma_{1,i}) = 1$ and $\Sigma_2.\mathsf{Verify}(vk_2, (m_{1,i}, \sigma_{1,i}, m_{2,i}), \sigma_{2,i}) = 1$.

Hence, $\mathcal{B}_2$ can extract $q_S + 1$ valid signatures under Σ_2 and thus it holds that $\mathsf{Adv}_{\Sigma'}^{\mathsf{R^sT\text{-}eufcma}}(\mathcal{A}) \leq \mathsf{Adv}_{\Sigma_2}^{\mathsf{R^sT\text{-}eufcma}}(\mathcal{B}_2)$. $\qquad\qquad\qquad\square$

Table 5. Post-quantum signature schemes; keys and signature sizes, estimated certificate sizes, and claimed security level

Scheme	Size (bytes)				Security
	Public key	Secret key	Signature	Certificate	(bits)
Lattice-based					
GLP [19]	1 536	256	1 186	3.0 KiB	100
Ring-TESLA-II [1]	3 328	1 920	1 488	5.1 KiB	128
TESLA#-I [3]	3 328	2 112	1 616	5.2 KiB	128
BLISS [16]	7 168	2 048	1 559	9.0 KiB	128
TESLA-416 [2]	1 331 200	1 011 744	1 280	1 332.8 KiB	128
Hash-based					
XMSS [11]	912	19	2 451	3.6 KiB	82
SPHINCS [6]	1,056	1,088	41,000	42.3 KiB	>128
Rainbow [13]	44 160	86 240	37	44.5 KiB	80

ORAMs in a Quantum World

Tommaso Gagliardoni[1], Nikolaos P. Karvelas[2(✉)], and Stefan Katzenbeisser[2]

[1] IBM Zurich Research Labs, Rüschlikon, Switzerland
[2] Technische Universität Darmstadt, Darmstadt, Germany
karvelas@seceng.informatik.tu-darmstadt.de

Abstract. We study the security of *Oblivious Random Access Machines (ORAM)* in the quantum world. First we introduce a new formal treatment of ORAMs, which is at the same time elegant and simpler than the known formalization by Goldreich and Ostrovsky. Then we define a new security model for ORAMs, based on a strong, adaptive, game-based security definition, which we show to be at least as strong as other existing notions in the literature. We extend such security notion to the post-quantum setting in the natural way, i.e., by considering classical ORAMs resistant against quantum adversaries. We show a standard quantum attack against an insecure instantiation of PathORAM, one of the most efficient general ORAM constructions to date, introduced by Stefanov et al. On the other hand, we show that PathORAM is post-quantum secure if instantiated using post-quantum underlying primitives. Furthermore, we initiate the study of *quantum ORAMs (QORAMs)*, that is, ORAM constructions meant to be executed between quantum parties acting on arbitrary quantum data. We address many problems arising when formalizing QORAM security through a novel technique of independent interest (which we call *safe extractor*), modeling a quantum adversary able to extract information from a quantum system in a computationally undetectable way. Finally, we provide a secure QORAM construction (based on PathORAM and a quantum encryption scheme introduced by Alagic et al.) which has the interesting property of making read and write operations *inherently equivalent*.

Keywords: Quantum security · Privacy Enhancing Technologies · Oblivious RAM

1 Introduction

Since the introduction of Shor's quantum algorithm [31] for solving the discrete logarithm and factoring problems it has become clear that, once scalable quantum computers become available, many of today's most widely used cryptographic tools will become obsolete. In response to this threat, new cryptographical constructions have been proposed, that are based on mathematical problems, believed to be quantum-hard [4,6,11,21,24,27].

Although encryption schemes are an important building block for many of the existing cryptographic tools, more complex architectures are built by combining various cryptographic primitives. In such cases, it is natural to wonder if

© Springer International Publishing AG 2017
T. Lange and T. Takagi (Eds.): PQCrypto 2017, LNCS 10346, pp. 406–425, 2017.
DOI: 10.1007/978-3-319-59879-6_23

merely replacing the underlying primitives with their quantum-secure counterparts yields quantum-secure architectures. Various recent works [2,10,39] have found a negative answer to such question: not only this is not the case for many known constructions, but also whole families of security proofs can be identified, which do not hold in a quantum setting.

Under this light, an interesting direction is the problem of building a quantum-secure *Oblivious Random Access Machine (ORAM)*. Oblivious RAM was introduced in the early '90s by Goldreich and Ostrovsky in [19] as a mean of software protection. It has since received an increasing deal of attention from the cryptographic community and has been used as building block for many applications ranging from secure processors [25] to privacy preserving health records [26]. With ongoing constant improvements in the research towards a functional quantum computer, it is therefore reasonable to wonder if and under which conditions such architectures would still remain secure in a quantum world.

A major obstacle to tackle this problem is given by the fact that the ORAM definition given in [19] is rather involved. Although this is usually a good thing given the level of formalism required in modern cryptography, the drawback is an increased difficulty met when analyzing the security of a given construction. In the field of provable security in particular, this has shown to be detrimental for the efforts of the community to analyze even the most basic ORAM constructions. In other words, the complex formalism given in the original formulation makes it very hard to prove a certain ORAM secure; in fact, all the existing proofs we are aware of [29,30,33,34,36,37] are rather 'sketchy', and do not fully respect that formalism anyway. We believe this to be a substantial problem in achieving a useful treatment of the theory for real-world applications. We thus find it legitimate to reach a compromise between excessive and insufficient formalism.

Our Results. In this paper, we provide many contributions to the study of ORAM security, both in the classical and in the quantum world.

First, we develop a new formal model for describing ORAMs, simpler than the one originally proposed by Goldreich and Ostrovsky, yet elegant and elastic enough to cover most of the existing interesting constructions in a rigorous way.

We complete the model with a novel, game-based security definition for ORAMs, which is very flexible and at least as strong as all the other models proposed to date. We start by defining *access patterns*, which are the adversarial views produced during an execution of data requests. Our adaptive indistinguishability notion states that, for any computationally bounded adversary, it should be difficult to distinguish between the execution of different data requests by looking at the resulting access patterns, even by allowing the adaptive execution of polynomially many learning queries. To our knowledge, this is the first time that these notions are defined in a homogeneous framework that allows for a formal treatment of any ORAM construction, without going to formal extremes that make it useless in practice.

Our new model allows us to argue about the extension of ORAM security to the quantum setting in a straightforward manner. To our knowledge, this is the first work where the quantum security of ORAMs is analyzed. In line with most of the existing ORAM security scenarios, we consider honest-but-curious adversaries, which are able to interact classically with the scheme, but can perform local quantum computation. Our model therefore falls in the category of so-called 'post-quantum' security [7]. In particular, as every ORAM scheme uses some sort of encryption in order to protect the privacy of the storage, it is interesting to relate the security of an ORAM construction to the security of the encryption scheme it uses. Because ORAM constructions can rely on many other different primitives in addition to encryption schemes, it is not reasonable to expect that post-quantum security can be achieved by merely switching to underlying post-quantum encryption. As a didactical counterexample, we show that Path-ORAM [34], the most efficient general ORAM construction, can be attacked by a polynomially bounded quantum adversary by exploiting the weakness of a not-carefully-chosen PRNG, even if the underlying encryption primitive is post-quantum secure. However, we show that Path-ORAM, if instantiated using *both* a post-quantum secure encryption scheme *and* a post-quantum secure PRNG, indeed achieves security against quantum adversaries. This result is important from a practical perspective, as it shows an easy way to build efficient post-quantum ORAMs in a completely black-box way.

Furthermore, we go beyond the post-quantum model of security by initiating the study of *Quantum ORAMs (QORAMs)*, that is, ORAM constructions meant to be executed between quantum parties acting on arbitrary quantum data. We motivate this study by noting that, once quantum computers start being available, it would be natural to expect that many parties involved in an ORAM protocol would need to act on quantum data, i.e., *qubits*. This motivation is further strengthened by the practical consideration that the first commercially available quantum computers would be very expensive, and server-client models are likely to appear, where computationally limited quantum clients will interact with more powerful quantum servers.

Finally, in adapting our new classical security model to the QORAM case, we address the difficulty of defining a notion of 'honest-but-curious quantum adversary' in a sound way. This concept, in fact, is not well-defined in a quantum scenario, because there is no notion of 'read-only' for quantum states: an adversary able to read a quantum communication channel will also disturb it with high probability. We solve the problem by defining a *safe extractor*, as an abstract way of modeling a quantum algorithm able to extract information from a quantum system without disturbing it "too much". This is a technique of independent interest, which we believe can be used to model quantum adversaries in many different scenarios.

Related Work. Oblivious RAM was introduced in the '90s by Goldreich and Ostrovsky in their seminal work [19] as a means to protect software from piracy. Since then, ORAM has received a lot of attention from the cryptographic community [16,17,20,29,30,33–36], and the constructions proposed are becoming more and more efficient.

An ORAM can be thought as a client-server model, where the client outsources to a server data blocks of fixed size, and wants to access them afterwards in a way that does not reveal which blocks have been accessed. In [19] Goldreich and Ostrovsky propose a construction, where the client's data is stored in a pyramid-like structure. The heavy communication cost of such a construction left much space for further improvements in the original scheme, which were made by subsequent works like [29,36]. In [23], privacy leakage was identified in most of the solutions proposed so far, and countermeasures were proposed.

The ORAM landscape changed radically after the introduction of tree-based ORAMs, by Shi et al. [33]. In these solutions the client's data blocks are stored in a binary tree and every block is randomly associated with a leaf of the data structure. Perhaps the most intuitive approach in tree-based ORAM contructions was proposed by Stefanov et al. in their Path-ORAM solution [34].

In a concurrent and independent work, Garg et al. [16] proposed an alternative formal model for describing ORAMs, together with a simulation-based security definition. We compare this model to ours, and conclude that they are classically equivalent. However our model has the advantage of being game-based, and can also be adapted to the QORAM case.

2 Preliminaries

In the rest of this paper we will use the term 'classical' for 'non-quantum', $n \in \mathbb{N}$ as the security parameter, and $\perp$ as a special symbol denoting an error or lack of information. PPT stands for 'probabilistic polynomial time', and by 'algorithm' we mean a uniform family of circuits; therefore 'PPT algorithm' stands for 'uniform family of poly-sized Boolean circuits with randomness'. Given a security *game*, or *experiment*, the output 1 denotes success (winning condition), while 0 denotes failure (loss condition). For the definitions of *secret-key encryption scheme* (SKES) $\mathcal{E} = (\mathsf{KeyGen}, \mathsf{Enc}, \mathsf{Dec})$, *classical indistinguishability of ciphertexts game under chosen plaintext attack* $\mathsf{Game}_{\mathcal{A},\mathcal{E}}^{\mathrm{IND\text{-}CPA}}(n)$, and *Discrete Logarithm Problem (DLP)*, we point the reader to [18]. Intuitively, a SKES is IND-CPA secure if no computationally bounded adversary can reliably distinguish between the encryption of two plaintexts of his choice even if allowed to adaptively learn polynomially many other encryptions.

Quantum Security Models. We refer to [28] for commonly used notation and quantum information-theoretic concepts. QPT stands for 'quantum polynomial time'; therefore 'QPT algorithm' stands for 'uniform family of poly-sized quantum circuits'. We will denote by $\mathcal{H}_d$ a Hilbert space of dimension 2^d. We will denote pure states with ket notation, e.g., $|\varphi\rangle$, while mixed states will be denoted by lowercase Greek letters, e.g. ρ. The set of positive, trace-preserving bounded operators on $\mathcal{H}$ (that is, the set of all possible mixed states on $\mathcal{H}$) will be denoted by $\mathfrak{D}(\mathcal{H})$, while $\|.\|_{Tr}$ is the *trace norm*, and $\|.\|_{\diamond}$ is the *diamond norm*. The *computational base* for a Hilbert space $\mathcal{H}_d$ is the set of orthonormal vectors denoted by $\{\,|0\ldots00\rangle, |0\ldots01\rangle, \ldots, |1\ldots11\rangle\,\}$.

Post-quantum Security for Encryption. We first recall the notion of *post-quantum security* [7]. The idea is to define, for a given cryptographic primitive, notions of security which are supposed to remain meaningful even in a world where quantum computers have been introduced and are available to the adversary. The model considered is where an adversary can interact classically with the given primitive, or oracle, but additionally has access to a quantum computing device for performing extra computation not normally available to classical adversaries. In this work, given the security model traditionally used in the study of ORAMs, we will only consider post-quantum security as in the canonical meaning. We recall that for a classic SKES $\mathcal{E} =$ (KeyGen, Enc, Dec) to be post-quantum secure, it has to provide *post-quantum indistinguishable ciphertexts under chosen plaintext attack* (or, be pq-IND-CPA secure), i.e. for any QPT algorithm $\mathcal{A}$ with oracle access to Enc, it must hold that $\left| \Pr \left[\mathsf{Game}_{\mathcal{A}^{\mathsf{Enc}}, \mathcal{E}}^{\mathsf{IND-CPA}}(n) = 1 \right] - \frac{1}{2} \right| \leq \mathrm{negl}(n)$.

Quantum Encryption. In this work we also consider *quantum primitives* [12], that is, cryptographic functionalities meant to be natively realized through a quantum computer, by acting on quantum information (qubits). Here the oracles themselves are usually not classical, but defined as operations $\mathcal{O} : \mathfrak{D}(\mathcal{H}) \to \mathfrak{D}(\mathcal{H})$ acting directly on qubits. For the formal definitions of *symmetric-key quantum encryption scheme*, and security (used henceforth throughout this work), we refer the reader to [1].

Pseudorandom Number Generators. We briefly recall the security notions for *pseudorandom number generators*.

Definition 1 (PRNG, pq-PRNG). *Let ℓ be a polynomial such that $\ell(n) \geq n + 1 \ \forall n \in \mathbb{N}$. A* pseudorandom number generator, *or PRNG (resp.,* post-quantum pseudorandom number generator, *or pq-PRNG) with expansion factor $\ell(.)$ is a deterministic polynomial-time algorithm $\mathcal{G} = \mathcal{G}_\ell$ such that given as input a bitstring s of length n, (the* seed*), outputs a bitstring $\mathcal{G}(s)$ of length $\ell(n)$; and for any PPT (resp., QPT) algorithm $\mathcal{D}$: $|\Pr[\mathcal{D}(r) = 1] - \Pr[\mathcal{D}(\mathcal{G}(s)) = 1]| \leq \mathrm{negl}(n)$, where $r \xleftarrow{\$} \{0,1\}^{\ell(n)}, s \xleftarrow{\$} \{0,1\}^n$, and the probabilities are over the choice of r and s, and the randomness of $\mathcal{D}$.*

In particular, a PRNG which is *predictable* cannot be secure, because it is trivially distinguishable from random (actually the converse also holds, as Yao [38] shows). As an example of separation between classically and post-quantum secure PRNG we consider the Blum-Micali PRNG [22] (which is DLP-based, and vulnerable to a state-recovery quantum attack, see [15] for details).

Lemma 2. *Under the DLP hardness assumption, there exists a PRNG $\mathcal{G}^*$ which is* quantumly predictable. *I.e., there exists a non-negligible function ν and a QPT algorithm $\mathcal{D}$ which, on input any n values output by $\mathcal{G}^*$ on any random seed, predicts the $(n+1)$-th value output by $\mathcal{G}^*$ with probability at least $\nu(n)$.*

3   The New ORAM Model

In this section we recall the concept of classical *Oblivious Random Access Machine (ORAM)*, and we define and analyze security models against classical and quantum adversaries. Defining ORAMs in a fully formal way is a delicate and strenuous task [19]. Therefore, in the following we will introduce a simplified model which covers all existing ORAM constructions without delving too much into the fine print - but still retaining a reasonable level of formalism - and which has the advantage of being much easier to treat. We believe our model will prove to be a valuable tool in the formal analysis of existing ORAM constructions, which is an aspect too often overlooked.

Informally, an ORAM is an interactive protocol between two parties: a *client* C and a *server* S, which we model as two PPT Turing machines (or, in our case, uniform families of circuits) sharing a communication tape (circuit register) Ξ. In this scenario, a computationally limited C wants to outsource a *database (DB)* to the more powerful S. Moreover, C wants to perform *operations* on the DB (by interactively communicating with S) in such a way that S, or any other honest-but-curious adversary A having read-only access to Ξ and S's internal memory, cannot determine the nature of such operations. The security notion of an ORAM protocol is hence a particular notion of *privacy*.

We start by defining *blocks*, the basic storage units used in an ORAM construction. A block is an area of memory (circuit register) storing a B-bit value, for a fixed parameter $B \in \mathbb{N}$ which depends on C's and S's architectures. A *database* (DB) of size $N \in \mathbb{N}$ is an area of S's memory which stores an array $(\mathtt{block}_1, \ldots, \mathtt{block}_N)$ of such blocks. As we assume this database to reside on the server's side, we will denote it as $S.\mathtt{DB}$.

Next we define *data units* as the basic units of data that the client wants to access, read, or write. Formally, a data unit is a D-bit value for a fixed parameter $D \leq B$ which depends on C's and S's architectures. Every block encodes (usually in an encrypted form) a data unit, plus possibly additional auxiliary information such as a block identifier, checksum, or hash value. Since every block can encode a single data unit, at any given time t it is defined a function $\mathtt{Data}_t : S.\mathtt{DB} \to \{0,1\}^D$. With abuse of notation, we will denote by $\mathtt{Data}(\mathtt{block})$ the data unit encoded in the block $\mathtt{block}$ at a certain time. The client C can operate on the database through *data requests*.

Definition 3 (Data Request). *A data request to a database $S.\mathtt{DB}$ of size N is a tuple $dr = (op, i, data)$, where $op \in \{read, write\}$, $i \in \{1, \ldots, N\}$, and $data \in \{0,1\}^D$ is a data unit ($data$ can also be $\perp$ if $op = read$).*

Finally, we define the *communication transcript* $\mathtt{com}_t$ at time t to be the content of the communication channel Ξ at time t of the ORAM protocol's execution. Notice that in this way, we define the communication transcript as a function of time, but since an ORAM is a multi-round interactive protocol we will just consider $\mathtt{com}$ as a discrete function of the round $1, 2, \ldots$ of the protocol. We can now define ORAM, assuming that a server's database is always initialized empty (usually with randomized encryptions of 0 elements as blocks), and the client 'populates' the database with appropriate *write* operations.

Definition 4 (ORAM). *Let $\tilde{N} \in \mathbb{N}, M \geq D$. An ORAM ORAM with parameters $(D, \tilde{N})$ is a pair (ORAM.Init, ORAM.Access) of two-party interactive randomized algorithms, such that:*

1. *ORAM.Init$(n, N) \rightarrow (\mathcal{C}, \mathcal{S})$ takes as input a security parameter n and $N < \tilde{N}$; and outputs client and server tapes $\mathcal{C}$ and $\mathcal{S}$, where $\mathcal{S}$ includes a database $\mathcal{S}.DB = (block_1, \ldots, block_N)$;*
2. *ORAM.Access$(\mathcal{C}, \mathcal{S}, dr) \rightarrow (\mathcal{C}', \mathcal{S}', com)$ takes as input clients and server $\mathcal{C}$ and $\mathcal{S}$, and data request dr issued by $\mathcal{C}$, and produces communication transcript com, and updated client and server $\mathcal{C}'$ and $\mathcal{S}'$.*

An ORAM must satisfy *soundness* and *security*. We define security in Sect. 3.1. The meaning of the soundness property is that the ORAM protocol 'should work', i.e., after any execution of ORAM.Init or ORAM.Access, the two parties $\mathcal{C}$ and $\mathcal{S}$ must be left in such a state that allows them to continue the protocol in the next round. A general definition of soundness (cf. [19]) is rather involved, and goes outside the scope of this work, which is more focused on the security model. In [15], we provide a formal description for the minimal soundness conditions which must hold for *any* ORAM construction. However, providing such description requires referring directly to some of the internal components of the ORAM scheme under exam, and in particular it makes the definition of ORAM dependant *at least* on the underlying encryption scheme[1]. As in this work we focus on the security of ORAMs instead, and in order to lighten notation and increase readability, we omit this dependance here, and we stick to Definition 4.

3.1   Classical and Post-quantum Security

We now look at the security model for ORAMs against classical and quantum adversaries. Traditionally, the threat model in this case is defined by an *honest-but-curious adversary* $\mathcal{A}$. This means that $\mathcal{A}$ is some entity who wants to compromise $\mathcal{C}$'s privacy by having access to the communication channel $\mathcal{Z}$ and $\mathcal{S}$'s internal memory, but who is not allowed to modify the content of the channel against the protocol. In general, one does not lose generality by assuming that $\mathcal{S}$ itself is the adversary: $\mathcal{S}$ must behave 'honestly' (in the sense that he follows the protocol), but at the same time he will use all the information he can get through the interaction with $\mathcal{C}$ in order to compromise $\mathcal{C}$'s privacy.

Formally, this model is defined in terms of *access patterns*, which are the adversarial views during an execution of data requests in ORAM.Access. Security

---

[1] One might wonder why the definition of ORAM should depend on an encryption scheme, and why not on other cryptographic primitives, such as PRNGs or hash functions. The reason is that not all ORAM constructions use such primitives (cf. [19, 29,36]), while the encryption of the database is a minimal requirement for security, and present in all known ORAM constructions to date. Such semantic artifice is therefore not restrictive in practice.

requires that the adversary's view over a certain run of the protocol does not leak any information about the data requests executed by $\mathcal{C}$. This formulation reminds of the definition of *semantic security* for encryption schemes [18]. As in that case, equivalent but easier-to-deal-with formulations can be given in terms of *computational indistinguishability of access patterns*. In this work, we consider an adaptive, game-based indistinguishability notion stating that for any two data requests, no computationally bounded adversary knowing the access pattern of the client having executed one of the two, can distinguish the one executed.

Definition 5 (Access Pattern). *Given ORAM client and server $\mathcal{C}$ and $\mathcal{S}$, and a data request dr, the* access pattern $ap(dr)$ *is the tuple $(\mathcal{S}.DB, com, \mathcal{S}'.DB)$, where $(\mathcal{C}', \mathcal{S}', com) \leftarrow ORAM.Access(\mathcal{C}, \mathcal{S}, dr)$.*

Taking into account only computationally bounded adversaries, we formally define next a *classical* (resp. *quantum*) *ORAM adversary*, and define the security of an ORAM through the indistinguishability game $\text{Game}_{\mathcal{A},\text{ORAM}}^{\text{AP-IND-CQA}}(n)$.

Definition 6 (Classical and Quantum ORAM Adversary). *A classical (resp. quantum) ORAM adversary $\mathcal{A}$ is a PPT (resp. QPT) algorithm which has complete control of $\mathcal{S}$, as long as the ORAM's soundness is preserved.*

Notice that 'complete control' means that we consider adversaries which can be potentially more powerful than mere 'honest-but-curious'. However, as the soundness of the protocol must still be preserved, it is unclear whether this can strengthen the adversary at all in practice. Therefore, we only claim that our security model is *at least as strong* as the one(s) commonly considered in the ORAM literature.

Definition 7 ($\text{Game}_{\mathcal{A},\text{ORAM}}^{\text{AP-IND-CQA}}(n)$). *Let $ORAM = (ORAM.Init, ORAM.Access)$ be an ORAM construction, n a security parameter and $\mathcal{A}$ an ORAM adverary. The computational indistinguishability of access patterns game under adaptive chosen query attack $\text{Game}_{\mathcal{A},\text{ORAM}}^{\text{AP-IND-CQA}}(n)$ proceeds as follows:*

- *$\mathcal{A}$ chooses $N \leq \tilde{N}$;*
- *$(\mathcal{C}, \mathcal{S}) \leftarrow ORAM.Init(n, N)$;*
- *(first CQA learning phase)*
  For $i = 1, \ldots, q_1 \in \mathbb{N}$, $\mathcal{A}$ repeats (adaptively) the following:
  - *$\mathcal{A}$ chooses a data request dr_i;*
  - *$\mathcal{C}$ executes $ORAM.Access$ on dr_i;*
  - *$\mathcal{A}$ receives $ap(dr_i)$;*
- *(challenge phase):*
  - *$\mathcal{A}$ chooses two data request dr^0 and dr^1;*
  - *$\mathcal{C}$ flips a random secret bit $b \xleftarrow{\$} \{0, 1\}$ and executes $ORAM.Access$ on dr^b;*
  - *$\mathcal{A}$ receives $ap(dr^b)$;*
- *(second CQA learning phase)*
  For $j = 1, \ldots, q_2 \in \mathbb{N}$, $\mathcal{A}$ repeats (adaptively) the following:
  - *$\mathcal{A}$ chooses a data request dr_j;*

- $\mathcal{C}$ executes $ORAM.Access$ on dr_j;
- $\mathcal{A}$ receives $ap(dr_j)$;
- $\mathcal{A}$ outputs a bit b' and wins the game iff $b = b'$.

Notice that, since $\mathcal{A}$ is polynomially bounded, q_1 and q_2 are at most polynomials in n. We are now ready to define the classical and post-quantum security notions. From these definitions, it will become clear that if an ORAM is pq-AP-IND-CQA-secure, then it is also AP-IND-CQA-secure, however the converse does not hold (under standard hardness assumptions).

Definition 8 ((Post-quantum) Access Pattern Indistinguishability Under Adaptive Chosen Query Attack). *An ORAM construction* ORAM *has computationally indistinguishable access patterns under adaptive chosen query attack (or, it is AP-IND-CQA-secure) iff for any classical ORAM adversary* $\mathcal{A}$, *it holds that:* $\left| \Pr \left[\mathsf{Game}_{\mathcal{A},ORAM}^{AP\text{-}IND\text{-}CQA}(n) = 1 \right] - \frac{1}{2} \right| \leq negl(n)$. *Furthermore,* ORAM *has post-quantum computationally indistinguishable access patterns under adaptive chosen query attack (or, it is pq-AP-IND-CQA-secure) iff the above also holds for any quantum ORAM adversary.*

3.2   Comparison with [16]

The security definition of Garg et al. [16] states that for any ORAM adversary it must be computationally hard to distinguish between the access pattern distributions produced by a real client and by a simulator producing bogus transcripts, even if the adversary is allowed to choose adaptively the data requests to be executed by the real client. The original definition in [16] does not take into account quantum adversaries, but can be easily extended in that sense. Readapting this definition to our detailed formalism, we obtain the following definition, which we use to show that the two models are actually equivalent.

Definition 9 (Access Pattern Simulability Under Adaptive Chosen Query Attack). *An ORAM construction* ORAM *has simulable access patterns under adaptive chosen query attack (or, it is AP-SIM-CQA-secure) iff for any classical ORAM adversary* $\mathcal{A}$ *the following two distributions are computationally indistinguishable:*

1. $ap(dr \leftarrow \mathcal{A})$;
2. $ap(dr \xleftarrow{\$} \{ 'read', 'write' \} \times \{ 1, \dots, N \} \times \{0,1\}^D)$.

Theorem 10. *An ORAM construction* ORAM *is AP-SIM-CQA secure iff it is AP-IND-CQA secure.*

The idea is to go through a hybrid argument in the same way that shows IND-CPA security for encryption schemes to be equivalent to Real-or-Random security (see for example [5]). Details can be found in the full version [15].

3.3 PathORAM

As a first application of our new formalism (but also because we will make heavy use of it through the rest of the paper), we recall here PathORAM, one of the most efficient ORAM constructions proposed to date, introduced by Stefanov et al. in [34]. We only give a high-level explanation of PathORAM, and for a thorough description of the construction, as well as a detailed proof of its functionality, we refer to [32].

In PathORAM a client stores N blocks of bitsize B on a server, in a binary tree structure of height $T = \lceil log_2 N \rceil$. Each node of the tree can store a constant amount Z of blocks. Every block encodes (in an encrypted form, using an IND-CPA SKES) a data unit of bitsize D. Every block is mapped to a leaf of the tree, and this mapping is recorded in a so-called *position map* by the client[2]. A read (or write) operation for a block $\texttt{block}_i$ is performed by the client, by downloading the path (tree branch, denoted $\texttt{DPath}$) from the root of the tree to the leaf indicated in the client's position map; $\texttt{block}_i$ is then randomly remapped to another leaf in the position map. The client decrypts all the blocks in the downloaded path, and for every valid (non-empty) block $\texttt{block}_j$ found, the client checks its corresponding leaf in the position map, and moves $\texttt{block}_j$ (if there is enough available space) to the node in the path, closest to the leaf level belonging both to the downloaded path and the path to the leaf of $\texttt{block}_j$ given by the position map, thus yielding an updated tree branch. If a block does not fit anywhere in the downloaded path, an extra storage, called *'stash'* is used by the client to store this overflowing block locally. The blocks found in the stash are also examined during every read (or write) operation and checked if they can be evicted from the stash and placed in the tree. In [32] it is showed that the size of the stash is bounded by $O(\log N)$ with high probability. In the following we will ignore the use of the stash for simplicity. Finally, all the blocks in the updated tree branch are re-encrypted (re-randomized) and the new tree branch (denoted $\texttt{UPath}$) is sent to the server.

In [15] we provide a full description of PathORAM (which from now on we denote by $\texttt{PathORAM}$) according to our new formalism. Then, also in [15], we prove the (classical) security of $\texttt{PathORAM}$ by using our new security framework. The idea of the proof is to build a reduction using a black-box adversary against $\texttt{PathORAM}$ to break the IND-CPA security of the SKE used. We stress that this is the first full formal proof of $\texttt{PathORAM}$'s security, and its simplicity is made possible by the new security model we introduced.

Theorem 11. *Let $\mathcal{E} = (\mathsf{KeyGen}, \mathsf{Enc}, \mathsf{Dec})$ be an IND-CPA SKE, and let $\mathcal{G}$ be a PRNG as from Definition 1. Then, $\texttt{PathORAM}$ instantiated using $\mathcal{E}$ and $\mathcal{G}$ is an AP-IND-CPA secure ORAM.*

---

[2] Due to its size, the position map has to be stored recursively to smaller PathORAMs as in [33]. For ease of exposition (and without loss of generality), we will assume here that the position map is stored locally.

3.4 Post-quantum Security of PathORAM

When trying to argue about the post-quantum security of a complex protocol, a starting point (although not always sufficient) is usually to consider what
happens by replacing all the underlying components with post-quantum counterparts. Clearly, in the case of any complex protocol (including ORAMs), it is
not reasonable to expect to achieve post-quantum security if we do not replace
all the underlying components in this way.

A careful examination of PathORAM's construction details reveals that an
important role in the security is played by the pseudorandom number generator
used to map a block to a leaf during every access. Even if we assume that IND-
CPA SKES such as AES [13] are post-quantum secure, a badly chosen PRNG can
make PathORAM vulnerable to quantum adversaries. As a didactical example,
we provide here an explicit quantum attack against such instance of PathORAM.

Theorem 12. *Let $\mathcal{E} = (\mathsf{KeyGen}, \mathsf{Enc}, \mathsf{Dec})$ be a pq-IND-CPA SKE, and let $\mathcal{G}^*$ be
the PRNG from Lemma 2. Let PathORAM* be the ORAM obtained by instantiating
PathORAM using $\mathcal{E}$ and $\mathcal{G}^*$, i.e., PathORAM* $= \mathsf{PathORAM}_{\mathcal{E},\mathcal{G}^*}$. Then, under the
DLP hardness assumption, PathORAM* is AP-IND-CQA secure, but not pq-AP-
IND-CQA secure.*

Proof. To prove the theorem and show the attack, it is sufficient to provide a
QPT algorithm $\mathcal{A}$ and a non-negligible function ν such that $\mathcal{A}$ wins the game
$\mathsf{Game}^{\text{AP-IND-CQA}}_{\mathcal{A},\mathsf{PathORAM}^*}(n)$ with probability at least $\frac{1}{2} + \nu(n)$.

We start by making a key observation concerning the access patterns pro-
duced in PathORAM. Let $\mathsf{dr} = (\mathsf{op}, i, \mathsf{data})$ be a data request sent by $\mathcal{C}$. By only
examining the communication transcript com resulting from the execution of
this data request, one can see which path (branch of the tree) $\mathcal{S}$ sent to $\mathcal{C}$, thus
learning the leaf r_i to which i was mapped to, even without knowing i itself. In
normal circumstances, this is of no use to an adversary, because this value r_i
becomes immediately obsolete, being replaced by a new fresh value output by
the PRNG in the position map. But it is important in our attack as we will see.

Let $\mathcal{D}$ be the QPT algorithm (the 'PRNG predictor') of Lemma 2. We build
the adversary $\mathcal{A}$ with oracle access to $\mathcal{D}$. First of all, $\mathcal{A}$ chooses $n, N \leq \widetilde{N}$
and starts the AP-IND-CQA game by calling PathORAM*.Init(n, N). For his
attack, $\mathcal{A}$ fixes an arbitrary identifier $i \in \{1, \ldots, N\}$, and an arbitrary data
unit $\mathsf{data} \in \{0, 1\}^D$.

During the first CQA learning phase, $\mathcal{A}$ asks $\mathcal{C}$ to execute $k = \mathsf{poly}(n)$ consecutive data requests of the form ('write', i, data). $\mathcal{A}$ records the resulting access
patterns from all these queries, $\mathsf{ap}_1, \ldots, \mathsf{ap}_k$, which include the communication
transcripts $\mathsf{com}_1, \ldots, \mathsf{com}_k$ and then, by the observation made before, a 'history'
$(r_i^{(0)}, \ldots, r_i^{(k-1)})$ of the past mappings of block i at the beginning of the execution of every data request from 1 to k. These mappings, in turn, are k outputs
of $\mathcal{PRG}^*$, and they are given as input to the algorithm $\mathcal{D}$, which then outputs a
candidate prediction r^* for the current secret leaf value $r_i^{(k)}$.

Then $\mathcal{A}$ executes his challenge query by using data requests $(\mathsf{dr}^0, \mathsf{dr}^1)$ with
$\mathsf{dr}^0 = (\text{'write'}, i, \mathsf{data})$, and $\mathsf{dr}^1 = (\text{'write'}, \mathsf{j}, \mathsf{data})$ for $j \neq i$, and records

the resulting access pattern $\mathtt{ap}_{k+1} = \mathtt{ap}(\mathtt{dr}^b)$ (where b is the secret bit to be guessed). At this point, the adversary looks at this last communication transcript $\mathtt{com}_{k+1}$ and, by the observation made at the beginning of the proof, checks the leaf index r related to the tree branch exchanged during the execution of the challenge query. If $r = r^*$, then $\mathcal{A}$ sets $b' = 0$ (where b' is $\mathcal{A}$'s current 'guess' at b), otherwise $\mathcal{A}$ sets $b' = 1$.

However, before outputting his guess b' in order to win the AP-IND-CQA game, $\mathcal{A}$ has to perform an additional check (during the second CQA challenge phase) in order to verify whether $\mathcal{D}$ had correctly guessed the right value $r_i^{(k)}$ or not. The problem here is that, if $\mathcal{D}$ is unsuccessful (which happens with probability as high as $1 - \delta$), we cannot say anything about the predicted value r^*. In fact, in that case $\mathcal{D}$ could potentially act maliciously against $\mathcal{A}$, and output a value r^* which maximizes the probability of b' being wrong in the above strategy: for example, $r^* = r_j^{(0)}$. For this reason $\mathcal{A}$ performs the following 'sanity check' after the challenge query:

- if $b' = 1$, then $\mathcal{A}$ demands the execution of an additional query of the form ('write', i, $\mathtt{data}$), and verifies that the resulting path leads to leaf r^*. This guarantees that r^* was actually correct, and it was not observed during the challenge query just because $\mathtt{dr}^1$ was chosen, as guessed.
- Otherwise, if $b' = 0$, then $\mathcal{A}$ demands the execution of an additional query of the form ('write', j, $\mathtt{data}$), and verifies that the resulting tree branch *does not* lead to leaf r^*. This guarantees with high probability that $\mathcal{D}$ did not maliciously output the secret leaf state for element j instead of i.

It is easy to see that in the case of misbehavior of $\mathcal{D}$, both of the above tests fail with high probability. In fact, in the case $b' = 1$, the current mapping of element i leads to leaf $r_i^{(k)}$, which was *not* correctly predicted by $\mathcal{D}$ by assumption. In the latter case instead, recall that $\mathcal{A}$ had guessed $b' = 0$ because during the execution of the challenge query he observed the leaf r^*; this could only lead to a fail in the case that $r_j^{(0)} = r_i^{(k)}$, which only happens with negligible probability at most ϵ, or if $r_j^{(0)} = r^*$, which is detected by the sanity check.

Finally, if the above sanity check is passed, $\mathcal{A}$ outputs b', otherwise he outputs a random bit.

Notice that (provided $\mathcal{D}$ was successful) this strategy is always correct, *except* in the case that: $\mathtt{dr}_1$ was chosen (probability $\frac{1}{2}$) *and* the initial mapping of $\mathtt{block}_j$ (which is $r_j^{(0)}$), coincides with $r_i^{(k)}$. As already mentioned, the latter event can only happen at most with probability ϵ negligible in the bit size of $\mathcal{PRG}^*$'s output, and hence in the security parameter n (it is easy to see that this is a minimum requirement for any classically secure PRNG, as $\mathcal{PRG}^*$ is). Thus:

$$\Pr\left[\mathsf{Game}_{\mathcal{A},\mathsf{PathORAM}^*}^{\mathtt{AP-IND-CQA}} \to 1 \middle| \mathcal{D} \text{ succeeds}\right] \geq 1 - \frac{\epsilon}{2}. \tag{1}$$

On the other hand, if $\mathcal{D}$ fails (which happens with probability $(1 - \delta)$ at most) and predicts a wrong value $r^* \neq r_i^{(k)}$, the above strategy still succeeds with probability at least $\frac{1}{2} - \frac{\epsilon}{2}$ (again, because of the remote possibility that $r_j^{(0)} = r_i^{(k)}$). Hence:

$$\Pr\left[\mathsf{Game}_{\mathcal{A},\mathtt{PathORAM}^*}^{\texttt{AP-IND-CQA}} \to 0 \,\middle|\, \mathcal{D} \text{ fails}\right] \leq \frac{1}{2}(1 + \epsilon). \tag{2}$$

Thus, combining 1 and 2, the adversary's overall success probability is:

$$\Pr\left[\mathsf{Game}_{\mathcal{A},\mathtt{PathORAM}^*}^{\texttt{AP-IND-CQA}} \to 1\right]$$

$$= \Pr\left[\mathcal{A} \text{ wins}\right] \cdot \Pr\left[\mathcal{D} \text{ succeeds}\right] + (1 - \Pr\left[\mathcal{A} \text{ loses}\right] \cdot \Pr\left[\mathcal{D} \text{ fails}\right])$$

$$\geq \delta\left(1 - \frac{\epsilon}{2}\right) + \left(1 - (1 - \delta)\frac{1}{2}(1 + \epsilon)\right) \geq \frac{1}{2} + \frac{1}{2}\delta - \frac{1}{2}\epsilon,$$

which concludes the proof, because ϵ is negligible, while δ is not. $\qquad\square$

As we have just shown, a PRNG which is not post-quantum secure is enough to break `PathORAM`'s security in a quantum setting. It is natural then to wonder whether the attack on `PathORAM` can be avoided by using a post-quantum secure PRNG, *in addition* to a post-quantum secure encryption scheme, when instantiating `PathORAM`. The next theorem gives a positive answer to this question.

Theorem 13. *Let $\mathcal{E}$ be a pq-IND-CPA SKE, and let $\mathcal{G}$ be a pq-PRNG as from Definition 1. Then, `PathORAM` instantiated using $\mathcal{E}$ and $\mathcal{G}$, is a pq-AP-IND-CPA secure ORAM.*

Proof. The proof follows step-by-step the proof of Theorem 11 given as in [15]. In fact this time, since $\mathcal{G}$ is a pq-PRNG by assumption, the new output values used to update the position map in `PathORAM` are indistinguishable from random (and therefore, in particular, unpredictable) even for QPT adversaries. As $\mathcal{G}$ has an internal state which is completely unrelated to $\mathcal{E}$'s internal randomness, the security arguments at every step in the proof of Theorem 11 remain unchanged. Therefore, any QPT adversary who can distinguish the execution of two data request sequences with probability non-negligibly better than guessing, can be turned into a successful adversary against the pq-IND-CPA security of $\mathcal{E}$, or against the pq-PRNG, against the security assumptions. $\qquad\square$

4   Quantum ORAM

In this section we initiate the study of *quantum ORAMs (QORAM)*, that is, ORAM constructions operating on *quantum data*. We define a quantum block, as a B-qubit quantum state $\psi \in \mathfrak{D}(\mathcal{H}_B)$ for a fixed parameter $B \in \mathbb{N}$ which depends on $\mathcal{C}$'s and $\mathcal{S}$'s architectures. A *quantum database* (QDB) of size $N \in \mathbb{N}$ is then a quantum register of $\mathcal{S}$ which stores N quantum blocks. We do not impose any restriction on the nature of the states stored in the quantum blocks, however in the following, for simplicity, we abuse notation and denote multipartite system with a tuple of quantum blocks $(\psi_1, \ldots, \psi_N)$. Assuming that this quantum register resides on the server's side, we will denote it as $\mathcal{S}.\mathtt{QDB}$. As usual, we will abuse notation and write that $\mathcal{S}.\mathtt{QDB}(i) = \psi$ if ψ is the state obtained by tracing out all but the i-th subsystem of $\mathcal{S}.\mathtt{QDB}$, and that $\psi \in \mathcal{S}.\mathtt{QDB}$ if $\mathcal{S}.\mathtt{QDB}(i) = \psi$ for some $i \in \mathbb{N}$. The client $\mathcal{C}$ operates on the quantum database through *quantum data requests*, which are tuples of the form $\mathtt{qdr} = (\mathtt{op}, i, \varphi)$, where $\mathtt{op} \in \{\mathrm{read}, \mathrm{write}\}, i \in \{1, \ldots, N\}$, and $\varphi \in \mathfrak{D}(\mathcal{H}_D)$ is the quantum equivalent of the classical $\mathtt{data}$, called a quantum data unit, i.e. a quantum state $\varphi \in \mathfrak{D}(\mathcal{H}_D)$ of D qubits, where $D \leq B$ depends on $\mathcal{C}$'s and $\mathcal{S}$'s architecture.

We define the *quantum communication transcript* $\mathtt{qcom}$ at time t during an execution of a QORAM protocol, to be the content of the communication registers (Ξ, Ψ) at time t of the protocol's execution. As in the ORAM case, in the following we will consider $\mathtt{qcom}$ as a discrete function of the round $1, 2, \ldots$ of the protocol. Notice however that since this time $\mathcal{C}$ and $\mathcal{S}$ are also allowed to exchange quantum data through Ψ, it might not be possible for an adversary to obtain a full transcript of $\mathtt{qcom}$ without disturbing the protocol. We address this issue in the security section. Letting B and D be fixed constants (the *quantum block size*, and *quantum data unit size*, resp.) and assuming that a server's QDB is always initialized empty and the client 'populates' the database, we can now define a QORAM as follows.

Definition 14 (QORAM). *Let $\widetilde{N} \in \mathbb{N}, M \geq D$. A QORAM QORAM with parameters $(D, \widetilde{N})$ is a pair (QORAM.Init, QORAM.Access) of two-party interactive quantum algorithms, such that:*

1. *QORAM.Init$(n, N) \to (\mathcal{C}, \mathcal{S})$ takes as input a security parameter n and $N < \widetilde{N}$; and outputs client and server quantum registers $\mathcal{C}$ and $\mathcal{S}$, where $\mathcal{S}$ includes a QDB $\mathcal{S}.\mathtt{QDB} = (\psi_1, \ldots, \psi_N)$;*
2. *QORAM.Access$(\mathcal{C}, \mathcal{S}, \mathtt{qdr}) \to (\mathcal{C}', \mathcal{S}', \mathtt{qcom})$ takes as input clients and server registers $\mathcal{C}$ and $\mathcal{S}$, and quantum data request $\mathtt{qdr}$ issued by $\mathcal{C}$, and produces communication transcript $\mathtt{qcom}$, and updated client and server $\mathcal{C}'$ and $\mathcal{S}'$.*

As in the classical case, we diverge slightly here from the notation used in the full version [15], which explicits the dependance of the QORAM definition from the QSKES used, as we only consider the aspect of security here.

4.1   QORAM Security

As in the classical model, the security will be given in terms of adaptive access pattern indistinguishability. We first define the quantum access pattern and the security game. As it often happens in the quantum world, there is a caveat: it is unclear what a 'honest-but-curious' quantum adversary is. In fact, the problem is even more general: we do not have a notion of 'read-only' for quantum channels, as the mere act of observing the data in transit through Ψ can destroy it. We solve this issue by introducing the notion of *safe extractor*. The intuition behind this novel technique is to allow our adversary to extract any kind of (quantum) information he wants from a certain physical system, *as long as such extraction is hardly noticeable by any other party.* In this case we say that the action of the adversary on the physical system is *computationally undetectable.*

Definition 15 (Safe Extractor). *Let φ_A be the state contained in a quantum register A. A safe extractor for A in the state φ_A is a QPT algorithm χ with additional classical input x of size polynomial in n, acting on A and outputting a quantum state ψ of qubit size polynomial in n, and such that the action of χ on φ_A is computationally undetectable.*

Here, *computationally undetectable* means that no QPT algorithm can reliably distinguish whether a quantum operation takes place or not by just looking at the processed quantum state, even in presence of auxiliary information such as, e.g., additional entangled registers. More formally:

Definition 16 (Computational Undetectability of Quantum Action). *Let L, A, B be quantum registers of size polynomial in n, and φ_A a quantum state on A. A quantum algorithm Λ acting on L and A has computationally undetectable action on φ_A iff for any bipartite quantum state φ_{AB} such that $(\varphi_{AB})_A = \varphi_A$, and for any QPT algorithm $\mathcal{D}$ acting on A and B and outputting 0 or 1:*
$$\left| \Pr\left[\mathcal{D}\left(\varphi_{AB}\right) = 1\right] - \Pr\left[\mathcal{D}\left(\left(\Lambda \otimes \mathbb{I}_B\right)\left(|0\rangle\langle 0|_L \otimes \varphi_{AB}\right)_{AB}\right) = 1\right]\right| \leq negl(n).$$

Notice that Definition 15 depends on the state contained in the quantum register considered. That is, χ might be a safe extractor for a given quantum register if that register is in a certain state, but not in a different one. Of course one could define χ to be a safe extractor for a register *tout court* if it is a safe extractor for *any* state of that register according to Definition 15, but this would considerably reduce the power of the adversary. Instead, this definition allows the adversary to use χ adaptively, only at certain points of his execution, when he is guaranteed that the action of χ on the current state of the QORAM will be computationally undetectable. The additional classic input to χ serves a useful purpose here, as it can be seen as a way for the adversary to communicate instructions to χ about how to perform the extraction in a safe way (for example, $\mathcal{A}$ might encode a certain measurement basis through this classical input.) With abuse of notation, and without loss of generality, we will write $\psi \leftarrow \chi(\text{qcom}, \mathcal{S}.\text{QDB})$ to denote that χ performs the following:

- as a classical input, χ gets the classical part of a quantum communication transcript qcom (that is, the content of the classical channel Ξ) and additional classical information by $\mathcal{A}$;
- χ acts on the quantum registers Ψ and $\mathcal{S}.\text{QDB}$;
- finally, χ produces a quantum output ψ.

More specifically, we define a QORAM adversary as follows.

Definition 17 (QORAM Adversary). *A QORAM adversary is a QPT algorithm $\mathcal{A}^{\chi}$ with quantum oracle access to χ, where: $\mathcal{A}$ has complete control of $\mathcal{S}$, as long as the QORAM's soundness is preserved; and χ is a safe extractor for the joint register $(\mathcal{S}.\text{QDB}, \Psi)$ for any of its states during the execution of $\mathcal{A}$.*

We stress the fact that our safe extractor technique can be generalized to many other scenarios. In fact, it expresses in a general way the intuition behind a plethora of techniques which have been independently used in many other works, see for example [3,8–10,14]. Although specific applications might need a refinement of the definition, we believe this new technique to be a very general tool of independent interest, which can be useful in the study of different quantum security reductions.

Definition 18 (Quantum Access Pattern). *Given a QORAM client and server $\mathcal{C}$ and $\mathcal{S}$, a quantum data request qdr, and a QORAM adversary $\mathcal{A} = A^\chi$, the quantum access pattern observed by $\mathcal{A}$, denoted by $qap_{\mathcal{A}}(qdr)$, is the pair of quantum states (ψ, ψ'), where: $\psi \leftarrow \chi(qcom, \mathcal{S}.QDB)$; $(\mathcal{C}', \mathcal{S}', qcom') \leftarrow QORAM.Access(\mathcal{C}, \mathcal{S}, qdr)$ and $\psi' \leftarrow \chi(qcom', \mathcal{S}'.QDB)$.*

Definition 19 ($\mathsf{Game}_{\mathcal{A},QORAM}^{QAP-IND-CQA}(n)$). *Let $QORAM = (QORAM.Init, QORAM.Access)$ be a QORAM construction, n a security parameter and $\mathcal{A} = A^\chi$ a QORAM adverary. The computational indistinguishability of quantum access patterns game under adaptive chosen query attack $\mathsf{Game}_{\mathcal{A},QORAM}^{QAP-IND-CQA}(n)$ proceeds as follows:*

- *$\mathcal{A}$ chooses $N \leq \widetilde{N}$;*
- *$(\mathcal{C}, \mathcal{S}) \leftarrow QORAM.Init(n, N)$;*
- *(first CQA learning phase)*
  For $i = 1, \ldots, q_1 \in \mathbb{N}$, $\mathcal{A}$ repeats (adaptively) the following:
  - *$\mathcal{A}$ chooses a quantum data request qdr_i;*
  - *$\mathcal{C}$ executes QORAM.Access on qdr_i;*
  - *$\mathcal{A}$ receives $qap_{\mathcal{A}}(qdr_i)$;*
- *(challenge phase):*
  - *$\mathcal{A}$ chooses two quantum data requests qdr^0 and qdr^1;*
  - *$\mathcal{C}$ flips secretly $b \xleftarrow{\$} \{0,1\}$ and executes QORAM.Access on qdr^b;*
  - *$\mathcal{A}$ receives $qap_{\mathcal{A}}(qdr^b)$;*
- *(second CQA learning phase)*
  For $j = 1, \ldots, q_2 \in \mathbb{N}$, $\mathcal{A}$ repeats (adaptively) the following:
  - *$\mathcal{A}$ chooses a quantum data request qdr_j;*
  - *$\mathcal{C}$ executes QORAM.Access on qdr_j;*
  - *$\mathcal{A}$ receives $qap_{\mathcal{A}}(qdr_j)$;*
- *$\mathcal{A}$ outputs a bit b' and wins the game iff $b = b'$*

Definition 20 (Quantum Access Pattern Indistinguishability Under Adaptive Chosen Query Attack). *A QORAM construction QORAM has computationally indistinguishable quantum access patterns under adaptive chosen query attack (or, it is QAP-IND-CQA-secure) iff any QORAM adversary $\mathcal{A}$ wins $\mathsf{Game}_{\mathcal{A},QORAM}^{QAP-IND-CQA}$ only with negligible advantage.*

4.2 PathQORAM

We describe now the construction for a novel QAP-IND-CQA-secure QORAM scheme, which we call *PathQORAM*, and has the interesting property that read and write operations are inherently equivalent. The idea is to modify PathORAM with the quantum symmetric-key encryption scheme proposed in [1], but we need some additional care for ensuring soundness, since each time $\mathcal{C}$ inspects an unknown quantum state on a tree branch DPath, will destroy it with high probability. To solve this issue we let $\mathcal{C}$ store the classical identifier i together with the data unit in the block. This identifier is still classical, of a fixed length K. Once a node in DPath is decrypted, it will be transformed to $|i\rangle \langle i| \otimes \varphi$. The first register can be measured in the computational basis without being disturbed, and without disturbing the state φ (which is not entangled with $|i\rangle$). So the trick for $\mathcal{C}$ is to find out when he is decrypting the right element by *only* measuring the first K qubits of the decrypted block, and only act on the quantum data unit when the right identifier is found. Notice how other different approaches used classically to instantiate PathORAM, such as identifying blocks by storing a local table with the hash values of the data units, might not work so smoothly when translated to the quantum world.

In [15] we provide a full description of PathQORAM, and we show that the following interesting property holds: the operations of 'write' and 'read' have the *same* effect. Since qubits from the server's database cannot be copied, and cannot be removed or added (otherwise this would compromise indistinguishability), the action of a read or write operation is simply to swap a state in the database with a state in $\mathcal{C}$'s memory. In fact, QORAM.Access swaps φ known by $\mathcal{C}$ with σ stored in $\mathcal{S}$. The *quantum stash* works in a similar fashion: every time an element is 'written' in the stash, it is actually 'swapped' with an empty block in the tree.

The security of the construction follows from the Q-IND-CPA security of the quantum encryption scheme $\mathcal{E}_Q$, and from the security of the pqPRNG $\mathcal{G}^3$.

Theorem 21. *Let $\mathcal{E}_Q$ be a Q-IND-CPA SKE and let $\mathcal{G}$ be a pq-PRNG as from Definition 1. Then, PathQORAM instantiated using $\mathcal{E}_Q$ and $\mathcal{G}$ is a QAP-IND-CPA secure QORAM.*

Sketch. The proof basically follows the steps of the proof of Theorem 13 with some important differences, as shown in the full version [15]. In fact, the reduction $\mathcal{D}$ cannot store a local unencrypted copy of the tree, because of the No-Cloning Theorem, but it can store a tree of the (classical) unencrypted identifiers with the same mapping of $\mathcal{S}$.QDB at any time frame. When simulating $\mathcal{C}$ for a given quantum data request, $\mathcal{D}$ can hence identify all the blocks in the downloaded path, but cannot re-randomize them. She will work around this issue by replacing every time the encrypted blocks with 'artificial' blocks obtained by encrypting (through the encryption oracle of $\mathcal{E}_Q$) the 'right' identifier and a

---

[3] Our PathQORAM construction is secure by using a merely post-quantum secure PRNG. However notice that, in a quantum scenario such as the one we consider, quantum mechanics allows to generate truly random numbers.

bogus data unit. The success probability of the adversary $\mathcal{A}$ cannot be affected too much by this substitution, otherwise $\mathcal{D}$ could break the Q-IND-CPA of $\mathcal{E}_Q$.

□

Acknowledgments. We are grateful to the anonymous reviewers for insightful comments, and to Marc Fischlin and Christian Schaffner for many fruitful discussions. This work has been funded by CYSEC, CRISP, and the DFG as part of projects S4 and S5 within the CRC 1119 CROSSING. Tommaso Gagliardoni is supported by the EU ERC PERCY, grant agreement no. 32131.

References

1. Alagic, G., Broadbent, A., Fefferman, B., Gagliardoni, T., Schaffner, C., St. Jules, M.: Computational security of quantum encryption. In: Nascimento, A.C.A., Barreto, P. (eds.) ICITS 2016. LNCS, vol. 10015, pp. 47–71. Springer, Cham (2016). doi:10.1007/978-3-319-49175-2_3
2. Ambainis, A., Rosmanis, A., Unruh, D.: Quantum attacks on classical proof systems: the hardness of quantum rewinding. In: FOCS (2014)
3. Anand, M.V., Targhi, E.E., Tabia, G.N., Unruh, D.: Post-quantum security of the CBC, CFB, OFB, CTR, and XTS modes of operation. In: Takagi, T. (ed.) PQCrypto 2016. LNCS, vol. 9606, pp. 44–63. Springer, Cham (2016). doi:10.1007/978-3-319-29360-8_4
4. Baldi, M., Bianchi, M., Chiaraluce, F., Rosenthal, J., Schipani, D.: Enhanced public key security for the mceliece cryptosystem. J. Cryptol. **29**(1), 1–27 (2016)
5. Bellare, M., Desai, A., Jokipii, E., Rogaway, P.: A concrete security treatment of symmetric encryption. In: 38th Annual Symposium on Foundations of Computer Science, FOCS 1997, Miami Beach, Florida, USA, 19–22 October 1997, pp. 394–403 (1997)
6. Berlekamp, E.R., McEliece, R.J., van Tilborg, H.C.A.: On the inherent intractability of certain coding problems (Corresp.). IEEE Trans. Inf. Theory **24**(3), 384–386 (1978)
7. Bernstein, D.J., Buchmann, J., Dahmen, E.: Post-Quantum Cryptography. Springer, Heidelberg (2009)
8. Boneh, D., Dagdelen, Ö., Fischlin, M., Lehmann, A., Schaffner, C., Zhandry, M.: Random oracles in a quantum world. In: Lee, D.H., Wang, X. (eds.) ASIACRYPT 2011. LNCS, vol. 7073, pp. 41–69. Springer, Heidelberg (2011). doi:10.1007/978-3-642-25385-0_3
9. Boneh, D., Zhandry, M.: Quantum-secure message authentication codes. In: Johansson, T., Nguyen, P.Q. (eds.) EUROCRYPT 2013. LNCS, vol. 7881, pp. 592–608. Springer, Heidelberg (2013). doi:10.1007/978-3-642-38348-9_35
10. Boneh, D., Zhandry, M.: Secure signatures and chosen ciphertext security in a quantum computing world. In: Canetti, R., Garay, J.A. (eds.) CRYPTO 2013. LNCS, vol. 8043, pp. 361–379. Springer, Heidelberg (2013). doi:10.1007/978-3-642-40084-1_21
11. Brakerski, Z., Langlois, A., Peikert, C., Regev, O., Stehlé, D.: Classical hardness of learning with errors. In: STOC (2013)
12. Broadbent, A., Schaner, C.: Quantum cryptography beyond quantum key distribution. Des. Codes Crypt. **78**(1), 351–382 (2016)

13. Daemen, J., Rijmen, V.: The Design of Rijndael: AES — The Advanced Encryption Standard. Information Security and Cryptography. Springer, Heidelberg (2002)
14. Dupuis, F., Nielsen, J.B., Salvail, L.: Secure two-party quantum evaluation of unitaries against specious adversaries. In: Rabin, T. (ed.) CRYPTO 2010. LNCS, vol. 6223, pp. 685–706. Springer, Heidelberg (2010). doi:10.1007/978-3-642-14623-7_37
15. Gagliardoni, T., Karvelas, N.P., Katzenbeisser, S.: ORAMs in a quantum world. IACR Cryptology ePrint Archive (2017)
16. Garg, S., Mohassel, P., Papamanthou, C.: TWORAM: efficient oblivious RAM in two rounds with applications to searchable encryption. In: Robshaw, M., Katz, J. (eds.) CRYPTO 2016. LNCS, vol. 9816, pp. 563–592. Springer, Heidelberg (2016). doi:10.1007/978-3-662-53015-3_20
17. Gentry, C., Halevi, S., Jutla, C., Raykova, M.: Private database access with HE-over-ORAM architecture. IACR ePrint, 2014/345 (2014)
18. Goldreich, O.: The Foundations of Cryptography - Volume 2, Basic Applications. Cambridge University Press, Cambridge (2004)
19. Goldreich, O., Ostrovsky, R.: Software protection and simulation on oblivious RAMs. J. ACM 43(3), 431–473 (1996)
20. Goodrich, M.T., Mitzenmacher, M., Ohrimenko, O., Tamassia, R.: Privacy-preserving group data access via stateless oblivious RAM simulation. In: SODA (2012)
21. Hoffstein, J., Pipher, J., Silverman, J.H.: NTRU: a ring-based public key cryptosystem. In: Buhler, J.P. (ed.) ANTS 1998. LNCS, vol. 1423, pp. 267–288. Springer, Heidelberg (1998). doi:10.1007/BFb0054868
22. Katz, J., Lindell, Y.: Introduction to Modern Cryptography. Chapman and Hall/CRC Press, Boca Raton (2007)
23. Kushilevitz, E., Lu, S., Ostrovsky, R.: On the (in)security of hash-based oblivious RAM and a new balancing scheme. In: SODA (2012)
24. Lyubashevsky, V., Micciancio, D.: On bounded distance decoding, unique shortest vectors, and the minimum distance problem. In: Halevi, S. (ed.) CRYPTO 2009. LNCS, vol. 5677, pp. 577–594. Springer, Heidelberg (2009). doi:10.1007/978-3-642-03356-8_34
25. Maas, M., Love, E., Stefanov, E., Tiwari, M., Shi, E., Asanovic, K., Kubiatowicz, J., Song, D.: PHANTOM: practical oblivious computation in a secure processor. In: CCS (2013)
26. Maffei, M., Malavolta, G., Reinert, M., Schröder, D.: Privacy and access control for outsourced personal records. In: IEEE S&P (2015)
27. Micciancio, D., Peikert, C.: Hardness of SIS and LWE with small parameters. In: Canetti, R., Garay, J.A. (eds.) CRYPTO 2013. LNCS, vol. 8042, pp. 21–39. Springer, Heidelberg (2013). doi:10.1007/978-3-642-40041-4_2
28. Nielsen, M.A., Chuang, I.L.: Quantum Computation and Quantum Information. Cambridge University Press, Cambridge (2000)
29. Pinkas, B., Reinman, T.: Oblivious RAM revisited. In: Rabin, T. (ed.) CRYPTO 2010. LNCS, vol. 6223, pp. 502–519. Springer, Heidelberg (2010). doi:10.1007/978-3-642-14623-7_27
30. Shi, E., Chan, T.-H.H., Stefanov, E., Li, M.: Oblivious RAM with $O((\log N)^3)$ worst-case cost. In: Lee, D.H., Wang, X. (eds.) ASIACRYPT 2011. LNCS, vol. 7073, pp. 197–214. Springer, Heidelberg (2011). doi:10.1007/978-3-642-25385-0_11
31. Shor, P.W.: Algorithms for quantum computation: discrete logarithms and factoring. In: FOCS (1994)
32. Stefanov, E., Shi, E.: Path O-RAM: an extremely simple oblivious RAM protocol. CoRR, abs/1202.5150 (2012)

33. Stefanov, E., Shi, E., Song, D.X.: Towards practical oblivious RAM. In: NDSS (2012)
34. Stefanov, E., van Dijk, M., Shi, E., Fletcher, C.W., Ren, L., Xiangyao, Y., Devadas, S.: Path ORAM: an extremely simple oblivious RAM protocol. In: CCS (2013)
35. Wang, X.S., Huang, Y., Chan, T.H., Shelat, A., Shi, E.: SCORAM: oblivious RAM for secure computation. IACR ePrint, 2014/671 (2014)
36. Williams, P., Sion, R., Carbunar, B.: Building castles out of mud: practical access pattern privacy and correctness on untrusted storage. In: CCS (2008)
37. Williams, P., Sion, R., Tomescu, A.: Privatefs: a parallel oblivious file system. In: CCS 2012 (2012)
38. Yao, A.C.-C.: Theory and applications of trapdoor functions (extended abstract). In: FOCS (1982)
39. Zhandry, M.: How to construct quantum random functions. In: FOCS (2012)

Author Index

Printed in the United States
By Bookmasters